PIMLICO

692

FIERY HEART

Nicholas Roe is Professor of English at St Andrews University. He is the author of *Wordsworth and Coleridge: The Radical Years* (1988), *John Keats and the Culture of Dissent* (1997), and most recently *The Politics of Nature: William Wordsworth and Some Contemporaries* (1992; 2002).

FIERY HEART

The First Life of Leigh Hunt

———

NICHOLAS ROE

PIMLICO

Published by Pimlico 2005

2 4 6 8 10 9 7 5 3

Copyright © Nicholas Roe 2005

Nicholas Roe has asserted his right
under the Copyright, Designs and Patents Act 1988
to be identified as the author of this work

First published in Great Britain by Pimlico in 2005

Pimlico
Random House, 20 Vauxhall Bridge Road,
London SW1V 2SA

Random House Australia (Pty) Limited
20 Alfred Street, Milsons Point, Sydney,
New South Wales 2061, Australia

Random House New Zealand Limited
18 Poland Road, Glenfield,
Auckland 10, New Zealand

Random House South Africa (Pty) Limited
Endulini, 5A Jubilee Road, Parktown 2193, South Africa

Random House UK Limited Reg. No. 954009

A CIP catalogue record for this book
is available from the British Library

ISBN 0-7126-0224-0

Papers used by Random House UK Limited are natural,
recyclable products made from wood grown in sustainable forests.
The manufacturing processes conform to the environmental
regulations of the country of origin

Typeset by Palimpsest Book Production Ltd,
Polmont, Stirlingshire

Printed and bound in Great Britain by
Mackays of Chatham Kent plc

Jane and Matthew, David, Seamus and Nicky

You will see Hunt – one of those happy souls
Which are the salt of the Earth, and without whom
This world would smell like what it is – a tomb;
Who is, what others seem; his room no doubt
Is still adorned with many a cast from Shout,
With graceful flowers tastefully placed about;
And coronals of bay from ribbons hung,
And brighter wreaths in neat disorder flung;
The gifts of the most learn'd among some dozens
Of female friends, sisters-in-law and cousins.

P. B. Shelley, 'Letter to Maria Gisborne'
Leghorn, 1 July 1820

CONTENTS

ILLUSTRATIONS

(between pages 196–197)

Leigh Hunt's father Isaac in middle age
Title page of Isaac Hunt's pamphlet published at Philadelphia in 1775
Eagle Hall, Southgate
The Grammar School at Christ's Hospital
Frontispiece to Elhanan Winchester's poem *The Process and Empire of Christ* (1793)
Charcoal sketch of Marianne Hunt
Leigh Hunt aged twenty-five
An Adonis in loveliness. George, Prince of Wales, in his prime
The face of English justice. Edward Law, 1st Baron Ellenborough
A scene of English justice. The Court of King's Bench, Westminster
The gatehouse at Surrey Gaol
Hunt as he appeared soon after release from prison
Republican integrity: John Hunt
Leigh Hunt's Hampstead
F. J. Sarjent, pencil sketch of the Vale of Health, c. 1804
The silver cup presented to Hunt at Plymouth in 1822

PREFACE

Leigh Hunt's first life ended in August 1822 with Shelley's cremation on the beach at Viareggio, Italy. He missed the essential qualification for Romantic myth, an early death, and lived on to become 'the last survivor of a race of giants'. But suppose for a moment that Hunt had joined his friend Shelley on the fatal voyage, and they had perished together in the Gulf of Spezia. Then they might have come down to us as two exiled Romantic freedom fighters about whom, as Byron said of Shelley, 'the world was ill-naturedly, and ignorantly, and brutally mistaken'.[1]

Sharing Shelley's death would have fulfilled one of Hunt's deepest desires, but his life had a different trajectory. He was only thirty-seven when Shelley drowned, and he lived on for the same number of years. Today he survives as the original of Charles Dickens's feckless Harold Skimpole in *Bleak House*; as the author of once-popular anthology pieces like 'Abou Ben Adhem' and 'Jenny Kissed Me'; as an unwelcome influence on Keats, a persecutor of Lord Byron, a sponger on Shelley. This book is about the first life of Leigh Hunt, and in it we see why those Romantic poets sought Hunt's company, courted his approval, and prized his friendship.

They were not alone in doing so. On 6 May 1822 a group of liberal-minded citizens met in Plymouth to present Hunt with a silver cup. Its inscription reads:

To Leigh Hunt
In admiration of his long
continued and successful exertions in the cause of
FREEDOM, TRUTH and HUMANITY,
his eminent talents and numerous virtues.

In May 1822 Hunt was on the point of quitting England for Italy, and the Plymouth tribute highlights his public reputation during his first life. For years Hunt had been a scourge of the corrupt regency establishment, a dauntless moderniser who called for parliamentary reform, freedom of the press, sexual equality and liberty of conscience. Descended from oppressed races in Barbados and Ireland, Hunt was a passionate advocate for the abolition of slavery, and his campaign for an Irish state free from British chains – which brought him two years in jail – has undiminished force today. His friends at Plymouth were proud to sign themselves 'a few lovers of free discussion on all subjects'. Hunt's first life had secured them that right.

Free discussion was dangerous, and especially so when the subject was poetry. Here, too, Hunt was a modernist energetically 'making new' and experimenting with a poetic language more audaciously colloquial than Wordsworth and Coleridge's *Lyrical Ballads*. When Hunt's masterpiece *The Story of Rimini* was published in 1816, its narrative dash and sexual frankness opened new realms of possibility for young poets like John Keats. Hunt was the first to offer sustained public acclaim for Wordsworth, and with Hunt's encouragement Keats matured fruitfully as a poet. Hunt survived to influence Victorian writers such as the Brownings and Dickens, and he finished his life contemplating poems on steam power and electricity. The twentieth-century modernists Ezra Pound and W. H. Auden were already an idea.

Hunt was always drawn to autobiographical self-examination. His earliest attempts were poems about his schooldays, and at the age of twenty-five he composed a prose memoir for the *Monthly Mirror*. Autobiographical sketches continued to appear in Hunt's articles and essays, and his controversial book *Lord Byron and some of his Contemporaries* (1828) included its 'Recollections of the Author's Life' at length. That narrative cast back to his distant ancestors in Barbados, and finished in 1825 with Hunt's return from Italy to the 'neighbourhood of London'. The *Autobiography* of 1850 added just three further chapters about his later years.

Before Hunt died on 28 August 1859, he had prepared a new edition of his *Autobiography* that incorporated numerous revisions to the narrative. Still, much remained unsaid. The book was seen through the press by his eldest son, Thornton, who contributed a sympathetic introduction alerting readers to his father's silences on some topics, especially his family life. Thornton might have added that Hunt also kept quiet about his parents' adventures in revolutionary Philadelphia and London, and that he said little about his passionate friendships with men and women.

One of my aims in *Fiery Heart* is to offer a full portrait of Hunt's first life, tracing his heroic achievements as a poet and journalist who battled against 'things as they are' while waging a private war on ill health and the invisible demons of depression and anxiety. I have drawn earlier generations of Hunts in Barbados and America into the story, by way of suggesting how his 'tropical' – and colonial – inheritances affected his personality and poetry. Throughout the book I glance forward from Hunt's first life to see afresh his later poems and autobiographical writings. Thornton Hunt noted his father's reticence about his parents and brothers, his wife Marianne and her sister Elizabeth, and I have explored these fraught relationships in some detail. Hunt's complex home life was a brave attempt to live out ideals of free love that Hunt and Shelley both cherished, although the resulting tensions were suppressed in Hunt's autobiographical recollections. In 1817 the Hunts' family home at the Vale of Health in Hampstead attracted Percy and Mary Shelley, Benjamin Haydon, William Hazlitt, Charles and Mary Lamb, John Hamilton Reynolds, and John Keats with his portfolio of youthful poems. This bohemian household has often been seen as a benign seedbed of Romantic genius, but it was also an arena of violent rivalries and quarrels that precipitated at least one suicide attempt. There was much that Hunt had to overlook to ensure that he could remember Shelley, in particular, as an airy spirit. *Fiery Heart* seeks to recover that tempestuous private life, and the anguish that compelled Hunt's idealisation of his friend.

After Hunt's death his library and papers were dispersed, and when Edmund Blunden began his biography of Hunt in the 1920s he regretted that no life had been written 'when some who had known him were alive, and when the documents were mainly assembled'.[2] When I came to be interested in Hunt in the 1970s, it was difficult to make sense of the daunting mass of his publications: the copiousness of his *Examiner* newspaper, the little volumes of poetry, the dozens of Victorian periodicals, and the idiosyncratic collection of correspondence put together by Thornton Hunt. The sources for Hunt's life then were Blunden's *Leigh Hunt: A Biography* and *Leigh Hunt's 'Examiner' Examined, 1808–1825* (a survey of the paper), and Louis Landré's enormous *Leigh Hunt (1784–1859): Contribution à l'histoire du Romantisme Anglais*. Luther Brewer's two books, *My Leigh Hunt Library: The First Editions* and *My Leigh Hunt Library: The Holograph Letters*, charted routes through the private correspondence and published works, and there was Humphrey Milford's *Poetical Works of Leigh Hunt* along with various selections from the political and critical writings. But there was no *Complete Works of Leigh Hunt*, no *Collected Letters of Leigh Hunt*. His manuscripts are still scattered in libraries around the globe.

For most of the later twentieth century, literary critics ignored or patronised Hunt: Harold Bloom's *The Visionary Company* (1961), for instance, saw him as a disreputable minor figure cast aside in Keats's magisterial advance to the 'vision of tragic humanism that ends his career as a poet'. It was difficult to domesticate the sublime 'Visionary Company' in Hunt's library at the Vale of Health, or to find 'Prometheus Rising' on suburban Hampstead Heath. As a poet Hunt did not aim for visionary peaks and unearthly intimations; he found Wordsworth's elemental landscapes thoroughly uncongenial. Hunt's poetry offered instead a humanised Romanticism in touch with people in their communities. His need for those conversations arose from a different tragic humanism: twentieth-century poets such as Blunden, Betjeman and Larkin, who had experienced world wars and the bleakness of post-war Britain, learned much from him.

When I began researching this biography several developments made the kind of book I wanted to write possible. The manuscripts from the Carl H. Pforzheimer Library published in *Shelley and his Circle 1773–1822* included rich seams of material relevant to Hunt. Donald Reiman's volumes of *The Romantics Reviewed* included Hunt reviewing and reviewed by his contemporaries. The life had been revisited briefly by Ann Blainey, and Andrew Motion's biography of Keats had given Hunt fresh attention. Eleanor Gates's *Leigh Hunt: A Life in Letters* supplemented Thornton Hunt's edition, and at the University of Toledo David Cheney had painstakingly assembled the materials for a complete edition of Hunt's letters.

With these resources in place, I set off in Hunt's footsteps through Philadelphia and London, Margate, Oxford, Hampstead and Marlow. I visited Hunt's haunts in Italy, and was fortunate to be shown his apartments on the ground floor of Byron's Casa Lanfranchi at Pisa. My search for Hunt's manuscripts took me to libraries in the United Kingdom, the United States and Italy, and I am grateful to all the librarians and individuals who assisted my work by being as curious about Hunt as he was himself. My full acknowledgements appear elsewhere in the book.

Fiery Heart: The First Life of Leigh Hunt has six sections, beginning with the remarkable generations of transatlantic Hunts who from the 1600s onwards led peripatetic lives in Britain, America and the Caribbean. His parents were the latest of these, and their experiences in Philadelphia and London during the storms of revolution provide the backdrop to Hunt's early years as 'The Young Poet, 1791–1807'. In this second section we follow Hunt through the harsh regime of Christ's Hospital, and see him as a prize-winning poet and the first modern theatre critic. The death of Hunt's mother, his courtship of his wife Marianne, and persistent nervous and depressive illnesses accompany his emergence in Part III of the book as the battling journalist, '*Examiner* Hunt'. As in his schooldays, Hunt was fearless in publicly defending causes and principles, but he could suddenly adopt a defensive *alter ego* and retreat to the sick-room. Part IV, 'Prison Years, 1812–1815', accompanies Hunt into Surrey Gaol where he converted rooms in the prison infirmary to form a fanciful bower. This was a period that mingled intense suffering and creative achievement, and provided the basis for the inclusive 'family of love' he would endeavour to establish with Marianne, her sister Bess, the Shelleys, and a wider circle of men and women. Part V reveals Hunt's domestic life at the Vale of Health, his tangled dealings with publishers and friends like Byron, Haydon and Keats, and the beginnings of his relationship with Shelley. The final section of the book, 'In the Warm South', traces the paths of Hunt and the Shelleys as they move from their idyllic months at Marlow in spring 1817, through London and Hunt's last years as a campaigning journalist, to Italy and the fatal effort to establish a new community at Pisa. *Fiery Heart: the First Life of Leigh Hunt* closes, as Hunt's own first life did, on the beach at Viareggio.

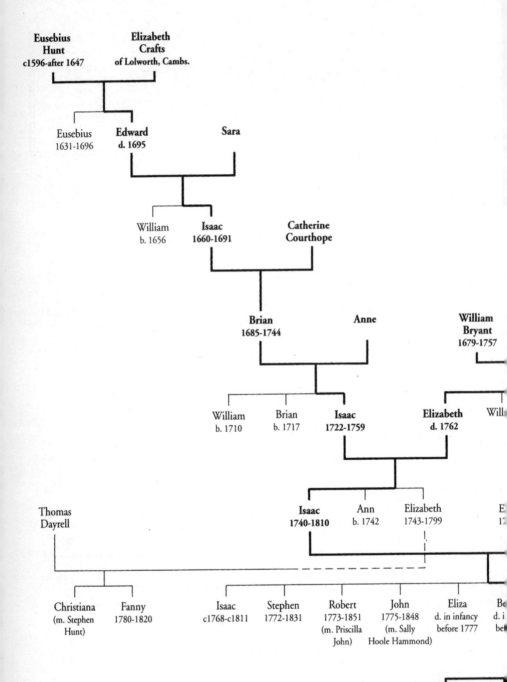

Eusebius Hunt c1596-after 1647 — **Elizabeth Crafts** of Lolworth, Cambs.

Eusebius 1631-1696

Edward d. 1695 — **Sara**

William b. 1656

Isaac 1660-1691 — **Catherine Courthope**

Brian 1685-1744 — **Anne**

William Bryant 1679-1757

William b. 1710

Brian b. 1717

Isaac 1722-1759 — **Elizabeth** d. 1762

Will

Thomas Dayrell

Isaac 1740-1810

Ann b. 1742

Elizabeth 1743-1799

E 1

Christiana (m. Stephen Hunt)

Fanny 1780-1820

Isaac c1768-c1811

Stephen 1772-1831

Robert 1773-1851 (m. Priscilla John)

John 1775-1848 (m. Sally Hoole Hammond)

Eliza d. in infancy before 1777

B d. i be

Thornton 1810-1873

Jo Hor 1812-

The Hunt Family

from the Sixteenth to the Nineteenth Century

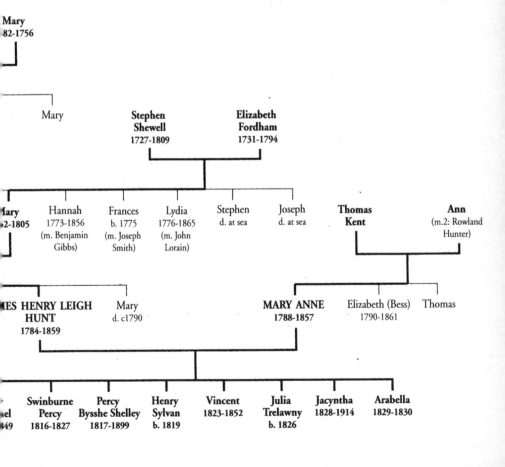

Mary
82-1756

Mary

Stephen Shewell 1727-1809   **Elizabeth Fordham** 1731-1794

| Mary
2-1805 | Hannah
1773-1856
(m. Benjamin Gibbs) | Frances
b. 1775
(m. Joseph Smith) | Lydia
1776-1865
(m. John Lorain) | Stephen
d. at sea | Joseph
d. at sea | Thomas Kent | Ann
(m.2: Rowland Hunter) |

ES HENRY LEIGH HUNT 1784-1859   Mary d. c1790   **MARY ANNE** 1788-1857   Elizabeth (Bess) 1790-1861   Thomas

| el
49 | Swinburne Percy
1816-1827 | Percy Bysshe Shelley
1817-1899 | Henry Sylvan
b. 1819 | Vincent
1823-1852 | Julia Trelawny
b. 1826 | Jacyntha
1828-1914 | Arabella
1829-1830 |

PROLOGUE:

THE WIT IN THE DUNGEON

A May morning in 1813. Lord Byron writes this jaunty verse to his friend Tom Moore, the poet of *Irish Melodies*:

> To-morrow be with me, as soon as you can, sir,
> All ready and dress'd for proceeding to spunge on
> (According to compact) the wit in the dungeon –
> Pray Phoebus at length our political malice
> May not get us lodgings within the same palace![1]

Next day they set out from Byron's lodgings at 4, Bennet Street, St James's. We can follow them along Pall Mall and Whitehall, over Westminster Bridge and into the suburbs on the south bank of the Thames. This murky warren of streets and alleys is Southwark – and it is classic ground, the site of Chaucer's Tabard Inn and Shakespeare's Globe. Here too are Guy's and St Thomas's Hospitals, the Marshalsea Prison, the King's Bench Prison and Surrey Gaol in Horsemonger Lane, where Byron's carriage comes to a halt. Looking up, the two visitors can see on the gatehouse roof the great gallows-beam for public hangings. Here, at a peak of revolutionary panic just ten years earlier Colonel Edward Marcus Despard and six others had been executed for a treasonable conspiracy 'of most alarming magnitude'.[2]

  Like Tom Moore, Despard was an Irishman. He had served with distinction as one of Nelson's fellow-officers in the Caribbean, and he was the King's superintendent of the Honduras. Complaints from local officials had led to Despard's recall, but no charges were brought and he was informed that his post had been abolished. Humiliated and discharged by the authorities he had served, Despard moved into radical politics and was soon active in the London Corresponding Society, the United Englishmen and the United Irishmen. Suspected of sedition, he was imprisoned for two years between 1798 and 1800. On release he set about organising a military coup against the British establishment. Despard's co-conspirators were inhabitants of London's discontented underworld: freethinkers, Jacobins, discharged sailors and soldiers, labourers, drifters. Meeting in taverns like the Tyger, the Flying

Horse and the Bleeding Heart, they devised '*the completest plan in the world*': an insurrection to secure political rights and independence for Ireland. They would seize the Tower of London, sack the Bank of England, and assassinate King George '*with four balls or chain shot*'.[3] Throughout the country others would be awaiting news that the London mail coaches had not arrived. That would be the signal to begin the British Revolution.

But Despard's plot was leaked. The conspirators were arrested, tried for treason before Lord Ellenborough, and condemned to death. On Monday, 21 February 1803 Despard stood before the gallows at Surrey Gaol and addressed the crowd below. He wished his fellow-citizens 'health, happiness, and prosperity' and looked forward to a time 'when the glorious cause of Liberty shall effectually triumph'. Then he was hanged, cut down and beheaded. A surgeon clumsily hacked at his neck until one of the executioners wrenched off the head and held it up to the crowd. The citizens of London later accompanied Despard's coffin to St Paul's Churchyard, where they gave him a hero's burial.[4]

Stepping through the small door in the prison gate, Byron and Moore glance up the staircase Despard had climbed to the scaffold. Ahead of them is a courtyard, and at the far side are the debtors' cells. Moore has visited before, and leads the way. He turns left towards the prison infirmary, a single-storey building separated from the prison yard by a row of palings. They pass through a green gate and into a little garden bordered with heart's-ease, sunflowers and young trees. Runner beans are starting to climb a trellis beside a green door. Moore ushers Lord Byron inside.

Green venetian blinds disguise the iron bars at the windows, and in the shaded interior a piano is positioned so that the player can gaze into the garden. Rose-patterned paper covers the walls and overhead the ceiling is painted as a breezy summer sky – bright azure blue, with white clouds billowing from corner to corner. Letters, manuscripts, pamphlets and newspapers are scattered about. Volumes of Chaucer, Shakespeare and Spenser are crammed on to shelves alongside vases of flowers, sprigs of greenery, and busts of Homer and Apollo. Byron notices the edge of each shelf has been lined with a bright red fringe. Over the fireplace is the portrait of a serious man with a republican look.

Their host steps forward, hand open in welcome. He is tall, dark, and evidently in poor health . . .

Part I: Transatlantic Hunts, 1600–1790

I may call myself, in every sense of the word, etymological not excepted, a son of mirth and melancholy . . .

The Autobiography of Leigh Hunt (1850)

ONE

FIRST LIVES

He was Autumn's child, a creature of mirth and melancholy. Leigh Hunt's father, Isaac, came from tropical Barbados; his mother, Mary, was descended from Quaker stock in Philadelphia. From her he inherited a tendency to sickliness and depression – he claimed never to have seen his mother smile – yet he also enjoyed the sociable, impulsively sensual temperament of his father. His life's work reflected this double inheritance: Hunt always said that the West Indies were the source of his poetic power, while his independent principles and pacifism emanated from Quaker Pennsylvania. One day he could seem 'beaten down' and dying; on the next he appeared invincibly cheerful. In old age he looked back over a long life of illnesses and debility to see himself impetuously following his father into the fray – 'bold as a lion when defending a friend or a principle' and 'prepared . . . to go through all hazards'.[1]

Isaac and Mary's fortunes veered between tranquillity and fearful disturbances, prosperity and the debtors' prison. In their 'care-stricken home' Hunt grew up a nervous little boy, susceptible to bouts of anxiety. He learned how to guard against these attacks, and the need to do so established the pattern of his life: he was calmed by sheltering landscapes in which he said he felt 'wrapped up', happiest of all in the tiny parlour rooms where he set up his study. Given those surroundings, Hunt wrote poetry out of the luxurious sensations he described as 'double pleasures' – cool rain in summer, frost after autumnal warmth, a blazing fire on an icy night. Such moments brought serenity and a sense of life redeemed – 'bringing the most remote things together', Hunt thought, as if all eternity was gathered into 'now'.[2] Companionship and conversation – more doubled pleasures there – also helped him maintain a precarious balance. Of all Hunt's doublings his friendship with Percy Bysshe Shelley – atheist, poet, angel – would be the most exalted and intense, and Shelley would become the idealised figure associated with the aspirations of Hunt's first life.

Lord Byron nicknamed Hunt 'Leontius' – after the dauntless freedom fighter in Samuel Johnson's tragedy *Irene* ('Virtue and Liberty engross his Soul / And leave no Place for Perfidy or Fear'). It was 'Leontius' Hunt who gave

Byron unstinted public support during the scandalous collapse of his marriage, when even His Lordship's staunchest friends 'shook and shuffled'. John Keats's Hunt was 'Libertas' – from the Latin word for freedom. 'Libertas' was the minstrel

> Of laurel chaplets, and Apollo's glories;
> Of troops chivalrous prancing through a city,
> And tearful ladies made for love, and pity . . .[3]

Yet Keats detected behind Hunt's sunny presence an unsuspected narrative of 'wrong'. The painter Benjamin Haydon also intuited a damaged Hunt: 'a painful, hypochondriac Soul that [dwells] on the *reverse* of its own *real* thoughts, perpetually to illumine its natural and forlorn dinginess'.[4] When Haydon made those remarks he had been arguing bitterly with Hunt about religion and, not for the first time, he seized the opportunity to insult his friend's racial origins and appearance.

What did Hunt look like? Family, friends and even Hunt himself found his appearance curiously elusive. Hunt portrayed himself as 'a pale, slim sort of gentleman, with black eyes . . . or hazle at least'. His eldest son Thornton insisted on his father's 'dark but not pale complexion'.[5] Hunt stood five feet ten and a half inches – tall by contemporary standards – and looked 'slenderer than he really was'. With a robust physique, he appeared to be a man cut out for a life of action, as Thornton noted, yet he shrank from physical contests. Haydon's portrait of Hunt in his mid-twenties shows curly black hair, dark eyes under heavy brows, full lips, and the sallow complexion that Hunt and his friends described as a 'West Indian look'. The poet Bryan Waller Procter noted that Hunt's mouth was expressive and that it protruded 'as is sometimes seen in half-caste Americans'.[6] Such terms reflected nineteenth-century prejudices – but it is clear that Procter believed Hunt to be descended from forebears of mixed races. Hunt wrote of his own 'West-Indian mouth'.[7]

Like the West Indian Toussaint L'Ouverture, Hunt was one of the great Romantic freedom fighters – and he dared to extend libertarian principles to poetic language and versification. Hunt smashed the shackles of eighteenth-century heroic couplets to liberate a more flexible form of English verse that could embrace fluttering pulses, leaps of heart, and all the wayward dance of 'natural impulses'. For these freedoms Hunt faced fierce opposition from the literary and political establishments, who branded his writing 'filthy', 'jaundiced', 'impure', 'under-bred', and Hunt himself 'like the ball of Dung in the fable' – that is, literally, 'dingy'. This astonishing tirade was directed at Hunt's poetry, and it stinks with suspicion and prejudice about his racial background. One reviewer informed Hunt that there 'is not a man or a woman around us, who venerates the memory of a respectable ancestry, or the interests of a yet unpolluted progeny, that will not rejoice to see your poison neutralized'.[8] While William Wordsworth was received by critics as the 'purest . . . and . . . the most classical of living English poets', in the agitated abuse that greeted Hunt's poetry we overhear the sexual and racial dread that haunted the 'respectability' of nineteenth-century imperial Britain.[9]

Hunt's West Indian inheritance was intrinsic to his identity as man and as political reformer, and it proved vital to his achievement in creating a modern, hybrid, virtuously 'impure' poetry: 'I have tropical blood in my veins, inherited through many generations,' Hunt announced to readers of his 1832 *Poetical Works*. That might seem an odd way to introduce a book of poems, but Hunt understood how earlier, Barbadian generations of his family had influenced the 'impulse and sincerity' of his poems and his exuberant 'sallies' of vocabulary and phrasing. Hunt identified himself as an English poet with a 'tropical' sensibility; 'that which is indecent in the cold and gross Laureat', he reminded Robert Southey, 'would be another thing in my West-Indian mouth'.[10]

The sensual and 'fervid' John Keats was another thing, a kindred voice among the rising generation of poets. He imitated Hunt's run-on lines, responded to his pleasure in doubled sensations, and dedicated his first book of poems 'To Leigh Hunt, Esq.' As Keats developed he shed some of the most obvious traits of Hunt's poetic personality, although the 'aching Pleasures' of 'Ode on Melancholy' and the doubled cadences of 'To Autumn' – poised between summer and winter, warmth and chill, fruitfulness and decay, life and death – were profoundly influenced by Hunt. By helping Keats get into print Hunt set his imprimatur on poems that we now recognise as quintessentially Romantic and definitively English – even though Hunt was convinced that his own poetic sensibility was 'tropical' and West Indian. Aldous Huxley said long ago that nature in Wordsworth's poetry is 'tamed' and 'enslaved', that Wordsworthian pantheism could never have survived the reality of nature in the tropics.[11] In Hunt we taste the passion, colour and danger of English Romanticism in a West Indian voice.

To understand Hunt's personality, his achievements as a poet and journalist, and his far-reaching influence – in a word, Hunt's presence – we need to cross the Atlantic in the wake of his forebears, 'adventurous people, who left England for the New World'.[12]

According to family tradition the Hunts were descended from 'Tory cavaliers' who fled to the West Indies during the English Revolution of the seventeenth century. Royalists were indeed exiled to the Caribbean and, whether or not the family myth was based upon fact, the island was well known as a 'dunghill' to which 'rogues and whores' were brought as labourers. Early visitors reported that Barbadians were 'debauched' by drinking 'Rumbullion' or 'Kill Divill', a crude and diabolically alcoholic rum, 'a hott hellish and terrible liquor'. By the beginning of the eighteenth century white settlers enjoyed elegant houses, fine clothes and cultivated entertainments, supported by the forced labour of thousands of slaves in the sugar plantations. Barbados was the first landfall for slavers making the lethal middle passage from Africa, and among Hunt's ancestors were slave-owning planters as well as 'native' Barbadians.[13]

The family had early associations with the market town of South Molton, Devon, and later generations had links with Cambridge University. Hunt's great-grandfather Brian Hunt described himself as 'Son of Isaac AM of Sidney Sussex Grandson of Edwd. Hunt DD & great grandson of Eusebius Hunt DD . . . all of Cambridge, & Ministers of ye Church of England'.[14] Careers at Cambridge and in the Church sound thoroughly orthodox, but in 1662 Edward Hunt was suddenly 'ejected' from his living at Dunchideock village near Exeter. As a Presbyterian Edward supported the 'primitive organisation of the church' – no bishops, no ecclesiastical hierarchies. Such levelling views had been widespread during the civil war and interregnum, but at the restoration of Charles II in 1660 the bishops were reinstated. Dismissed from Dunchideock, Edward went to Exeter where he attended 'secret meetings' with dissenters who had 'nothing else to doe but lie gnaweing at the root of Govermnt & religion'.[15] In later life he migrated back to South Molton where he died in 1695.

Here, in one of Hunt's seventeenth-century ancestors, are the tenacity and independence that would shape the family and land three generations of Hunts in prison. Edward and his wife Sara had two sons: William, born in 1656, emigrated and settled as a merchant at Barbados; Isaac, born in 1660, was an undergraduate at Sidney Sussex College, and then Rector of Foots Cray, Kent, until his death aged thirty-one. Isaac had married Catherine Courthope of Wadhurst, Sussex, and their son Brian – Hunt's great-grandfather – was born in 1685. Brian studied at Corpus Christi College, Cambridge, where he inherited a silver dish, five gold guineas and £250 from his grandfather Edward. He married while at college, was ordained, and made a visit to his Uncle William in Barbados.[16]

For some years Brian served as a naval chaplain, and by 1717 he 'had ye good Vicarage of Quadring' on the Lincolnshire fens. But he didn't settle, and in 1722 received a bounty of £20 from the Society for the Propagation of the Gospel before quitting England to become Rector of St John's Parish near Charles Town (Charleston) in South Carolina. The living at St John's brought him £110 a year – hardly a pittance in those days – and he was entitled to the produce of some 360 acres of land. This sounds like a good living, but his letters to the Bishop of London complained that he was about to sink into 'beggary'. His wife Anne was sick and 'swoln to a great degree [with] dropsy', and there were four children to look after. Again and again Brian says that he would leap at any opportunity to go to Philadelphia, New York, or 'those burning islands' of the Caribbean.[17]

Brian's isolation grew more acute when a scandal broke. In May 1727 he officiated at the clandestine marriage of a fifteen-year-old heiress to a young Englishman. Charles Town merchants had been appointed trustees of the girl's fortune and to secure their interests they opposed her marrying without their 'privity & consent'. The lovers dodged this prohibition by moving to St John's where Brian accepted them as parishioners, published the banns, and married the couple in a secret midnight ceremony.[18]

Charles Town was outraged. Brian was accused of 'gross and repeated vices and imoralities of drunkeness, quarrelling, defamation, lying, insolent abusive and scurilous language sowing discord amongst neighbors and such like'. Angry letters were dispatched to London calling for the removal of this 'Scandalous Clergyman'.[19] Family stories about Brian Hunt in South Carolina may have helped his great-grandson towards the sympathetic theme of his finest poem. In The Story of Rimini Hunt adapted the tragic episode of the lovers Paolo and Francesca from Dante's Inferno, to show the danger of 'setting authorized selfishness above the most natural impulses, and making guilt by mistaking innocence'.[20] For daring to question social and religious 'forms' in his poem, Hunt faced accusations identical to the insults hurled at his great-grandfather Brian.

Friends spoke for Brian's good character, but his difficulties were just beginning. His salary was suspended – 'stupendous! afflicting! tormenting!' – and creditors closed in: 'I was poor & ow'd money . . . I was arrested . . . for debt, to my great loss & disgrace, being put in ye common prison of Charles Town'. 'Trod on & vilified & reduced to the lowest ebb of misery', Brian was locked up alone in his cell where he poured out his unhappiness in a fourteen-page letter to the Bishop of London.[21] Fortunately, help proved to be closer at hand when by 'unforseen providence' Brian was released. The newly wedded couple had cleared his debts.

Brian resigned from his parish, and sailed for Barbados. By September 1728 he was in London, busy penning another letter to the Bishop for his 'distressed families sake, still in Carolina consisting of a bed-rid wife . . . & 4 young children unprovided for'. He would risk health and hardship, and once again 'traverse ye rough seas' as chaplain on a ship bound for the West Indies. Having visited Barbados and served in the navy, Brian knew the hazards of life among the 'burning islands' – tropical heat, hurricanes and epidemics of yellow fever, malaria and typhoid. Nevertheless, by 1731 he had settled with his ailing wife and their children as Rector of St Joseph's on the rugged Atlantic coast of Barbados.[22]

The experiences of this transatlantic generation of Hunts have much in common with the troubled seas that would assail Hunt's parents, and aspects of Brian's character – unsettled, bold, controversial, compassionate, selfdramatising – all reappeared in Hunt's personality. One of Brian's sons, Isaac, became a curate at St Michael's, Bridgetown, and was greatly admired by his congregation. He died of a fever on Christmas Day, 1759, and was buried in the chancel of his church.

Isaac had married well. According to Hunt, his wife Elizabeth was 'an O'Brien, or rather Bryan', assiduous in 'attentions to negroes and to the poor' and 'very proud of her descent' from '*Irish* kings' (the O'Briens/Bryans can trace their lineage back to Brian Boru, tenth-century King of Ireland).[23] They had three children: a son, Isaac, born *circa* 1740 (Hunt's father) and two daughters, Ann and Elizabeth.[24] To all three children 'the worthy Rector and his wife were a little too indulgent'.[25] But before we take up the story of Hunt's father, we should pause for a moment with his grandmother Elizabeth.

Elizabeth's parents were the wealthy Barbadian planter William Bryant and his wife Mary. The Bryants' gravestone described Mary as 'a native of this island', indicating either that she was descended from the few Carib Indians who survived European diseases like tuberculosis and smallpox, or that her forebears were slaves transported from Africa.[26] It was from Mary and her daughter Elizabeth that Hunt inherited his 'West-Indian look' and, like them, he traced his fathers and mothers to the oppressed races of Ireland and the Caribbean.

How had the Barbadian climate affected Hunt's ancestors? His ideas about 'tropical blood', 'animal spirits' and impulsive feeling were culled from Griffith Hughes's *Natural History of Barbados*, published at London in 1750. Hunt owned a massive leather-bound copy of this book, and in it he read about the island's extraordinary animal and plant life – Thick Plushy Sea Moss and the Black-Nicker-Tree, the Sea Bat, the Shooting Sea Egg, the Forty Leg Worm, Hen Turds and Fidler Flies, Club Men and She Biters, Whirligigs and Haw Nickers, the Marbled Snail, the Wild Dolly Pea, and the Forbidden-Fruit-Tree temptingly 'delicious [in] Taste and Flavour'.[27] Language flourished as profusely as native Barbadian fauna, and we catch echoes of this in the extravagant verbal mutations of Hunt's poetry: the 'jerked feather' and 'twangling pearl', 'ripe sunshine' and 'purple smearings', 'clump woods' and 'giddy whirls', 'hod-men', 'the squire-carver', a 'handy squirrel', 'dabbled roses' and 'backs of street roads'.

Hughes's *Natural History* also explained how climate could influence character and shape a person's life. According to Hughes, tropical temperatures 'rarefied' the blood, increased circulation, diffused 'Animal Spirits' and produced 'Health and Chearfulness'.[28] Such conditions could encourage liveliness, although more ominously the transition from 'Sprightliness to Irascibility' was said to be both natural and easy. Hughes also explained that colder climates 'interrupted' the blood, producing symptoms of pain and depression that could be alleviated by vigorous exercise or 'strong spiritous liquors' like that hellish dram Rumbullion. Here was a quasi-scientific explanation for the cheerfulness and the fiery temper Hunt inherited from his father, as well as the melancholy he associated with his mother's northern temperament. What Hughes could not tell Hunt was how to set his own course through those stormy latitudes.

In 1757 young Isaac sailed northwards across the Caribbean and up the American coast to another fertile colony, where the air was 'sereen & Sweet from the Cedar, Pine & Sarsefrax, wth a wild Mertile that all send forth a most fragrant smell'.[29] In 1681 Charles II had granted Pennsylvania to William Penn as a colony in which the Quakers could enjoy religious liberty – and many had remarked that the freedoms of the new world seemed to be inhaled with the fragrant air of the forests. Penn's original plans for the settlement instructed that ground should be left open for gardens, orchards and fields, so as to create a 'greene Country Towne'.[30] Memories of the great fire of London were still fresh, and space between buildings ensured that fire would not spread as destructively as in the old city. Settlers came to Pennsylvania from all over Europe and religious groups of all kinds were represented: Quakers, Anglicans, Catholics, Baptists, Presbyterians from Ireland and Scotland, Mennonites and Lutherans from Germany. By the mid-eighteenth century Penn's green town between the Delaware and Schuylkill Rivers was the 'wonder of the world'.[31] This was Philadelphia, City of Brotherly Love.

Philadelphia was soon a flourishing centre for trade: timber from the forests supplied the shipyards, and shipbuilding brought all kinds of industries to the Delaware wharfs – sailmakers, carpenters, founders, joiners, ropemakers, ship's chandlers. The streets were paved and lit at night by whale-oil lamps, and citizens had the security of a night-watch and fire service. Along Chestnut Street, Walnut Street and Spruce Street were the coffee-houses and taverns in which clubs, societies and committees debated, drank and brawled America's future into being.[32]

This was the city that attracted the young printer Benjamin Franklin, founder of the Library Company, the American Philosophical Society, the Pennsylvania Hospital, the Fire Brigade, and a scheme for insuring houses against fire.[33] In 1749 Franklin published an earnest pamphlet of *Proposals Relating to the Education of Youth in Pennsylvania,* and during the same year was among the 'few private gentlemen of Pennsylvania' who met to plan an academy.[34] The Academy opened in 1751 teaching Latin, Mathematics and English, and four years later it became the College and Academy of Philadelphia with William Smith, a graduate of Aberdeen University, as its first Provost.[35] It had three parts: a charity school for boys and girls; the Academy, comprising the English and Mathematical Schools; and the College, with the Schools of Latin, Greek and Philosophy. Students attended from all over the American colonies and the Caribbean, creating a literate community of authors and readers who eagerly joined in the pamphlet wars of the 1760s. Isaac arrived from Barbados in 1757 'ready spoilt', according to Hunt, and with plenty of money 'to spoil him more'. He enrolled and began his studies in this noisy schoolroom of the American Revolution.[36]

As a student Isaac enjoyed his freedom and his new friends, and became 'the scapegrace who smuggled in the wine, and bore the brunt of the tutors'.[37] He progressed rapidly through the curriculum of grammar and pronunciation, and excelled in classes on public speaking and oratory – little suspecting that one day this would save his life. In the Latin, Greek and Philosophy Schools, Isaac studied classical texts and delivered 'English and Latin orations . . . with proper grace both of elocution and gesture'. Having taken a public examination he entered the Philosophy Schools where studies combined Latin and English, logic and metaphysics, arithmetic, algebra, fractions, equations, logarithms and Euclid's *Elements*. Recommended reading for the evenings included the *Spectator* and, 'for the improvement of style and knowledge of life', Samuel Johnson's *Rambler*. In the second year Isaac continued with logic, surveying, navigation, trigonometry and architecture; afternoons were given over to rhetoric, using Longinus's *On the Sublime*, Horace's *Ars Poetica*, and Aristotle's *Rhetoric* and *Poetics* as guides. Isaac's final year was devoted to Moral Philosophy (ethics, natural and civil law, civil history, government, trade and commerce) and Natural Philosophy (mechanics, hydrostatics and pneumatics, light and optics, astronomy, the natural history of vegetables and animals, chemistry, fossils and agriculture). In spring 1763 Isaac's last afternoons in the college were given over to 'compositions and declamations on moral and physical subjects'. If any student had a spare moment, French could be studied 'at leisure'.[38] This was an immensely challenging curriculum, alert to the latest developments in a range of disciplines. At the Universities of Oxford and Cambridge teaching still harked back to the medieval academy of classics, rhetoric and mathematics.

In May 1763, with Benjamin Franklin in the audience, Isaac graduated and delivered his 'farewell oration' with such eloquence that Provost Smith immediately appointed him tutor in the English School.[39] Others in the audience had been impressed too, so much so that 'two young ladies fell in love with him'. Isaac was a handsome young man with prospects, already singled out for success. The first of the two young ladies Isaac courted was Elizabeth Shewell, twenty-one years old, a 'noted beauty' and the sister of a wealthy merchant named Stephen Shewell. Isaac and Elizabeth formed an attachment, although his interest soon turned to Elizabeth's young niece Mary and he threw his artistic energies into winning the younger woman. 'It was in reading . . . the poets and other classics of England, that he completed the conquest of my mother's heart,' Hunt writes: 'He used to spend his evenings in this manner with her and her family, a noble way of courtship; and my grandmother became so hearty in his cause, that she succeeded in carrying it against her husband, who wished his daughter to marry a wealthy neighbour.'[40]

Mary was born in 1752, the second daughter of Stephen Shewell and

Elizabeth Fordham who lived on Front Street facing the Delaware River. Mary had four sisters – Elizabeth, Hannah, Frances and Lydia, and two brothers, Stephen and Joseph. Their parents were from Quaker families who prospered with Philadelphia's rising fortunes.[41] Stephen was in the biscuit and flour trade, with a fleet of ships sailing throughout the West Indies and across the Atlantic. Determined to consolidate his wealth through family connections, Stephen had objected when his sister Elizabeth, the 'noted beauty', was courted by an impoverished young artist called Benjamin West. Undeterred, West had abandoned Philadelphia for Italy where he quickly established a reputation in the academies of Florence, Bologna and Parma. In West's absence Elizabeth had fallen for eloquent Isaac Hunt, only to be spurned in favour of her young niece Mary. By 1763 West's career was flourishing. He settled in London where he found an old friend from Philadelphia, William Smith, the College Provost, willing to help introduce him to London society. Meetings with Edmund Burke, Dr Johnson and Sir Joshua Reynolds followed, and West was soon exhibiting his work and confidently making his way. He hadn't forgotten Elizabeth, and now invited her to come over to London where they were married on 2 September 1765, at St Martin-in-the-Fields.

Two years later, on 18 June 1767, Isaac and Mary were married under the gleaming white spire of Christ Church on Second Street, Philadelphia. The Rector, Jacob Duché officiated. Stephen Shewell had relented so far as to give them a house 'in the front and most Capital Street of the City'. Isaac was now practising as a lawyer and had been called to the bar of most of the courts in New Jersey and Pennsylvania.[42] The future was bright, but for one setback. He had applied for his Master's degree from the college, only to be refused on the grounds that he was 'at present unworthy of any further Honors'.[43] Unworthy? To understand this rebuff, we must enter the tumult of Philadelphia politics in the 1760s, the decade that led up to America's break from Britain.

The American Declaration of Independence, 4 July 1776, listed some twenty-seven 'injuries and usurpations' by Britain. Petitions for redress had brought 'repeated injury', and the United Colonies had determined on their future as 'Free and Independent States'. In London ministers were unaware of the self-reliant mood of the colonies, out of touch with the prosperous, well-educated individuals who protested against British oppression. That vocal opposition had been fostered in large part by the Philadelphia Academy. Faculty and graduates eagerly participated in the scurrilous 'Wordy-War' about government in the colonies. Satires, pamphlets, ballads and broad-sides, mock-debates, plays, caricatures and cartoons poured from the Philadelphia printshops and booksellers. One of the most outspoken authors was 'Jack Retort, Student in Scurrility of Quillsylvania', otherwise known as Isaac Hunt.

The controversy began in summer 1763 when the Quaker-dominated Assembly at Philadelphia refused to send relief to Pennsylvania frontiermen, the 'Paxton Boys', who had massacred a group of Indians at Conestoga. In retaliation the Paxton Boys marched on Philadelphia, threatening to kill the native Americans they suspected were sheltered by Quakers. Volunteers armed to protect the city, with Benjamin Franklin leading preparations, until a parley ended the crisis. The episode was settled peacefully but with elections to the Assembly due in 1764 it excited a furious debate about the government of Pennsylvania and relations with the 'mother country'.[44]

David James Dove, one-time English master at the college, weighed in with his pamphlet *The Quaker Unmask'd*, raging at the 'inexpressible Absurdity' of the Quakers' 'Pity for Indians'.[45] Isaac's response, *A Looking-Glass for Presbyterians*, deflected Dove's assault on 'wise and judicious' Quakers and targeted the suspect motives of Scottish-Irish Presbyterians who, Isaac claimed, were 'undermining' the government of the city. 'The inhabitants of *Pennsylvania* enjoy the most extensive Privileges both civil and religious of any People in the World,' Isaac wrote. 'Let us then, like true *Britons*, warmly oppose any that wou'd presume to deprive us of them.'[46] Isaac had hoisted his colours. Pennsylvanians were *Britons*. With the election looming he contributed to a gathering of satirical ballads, *The Election a Medley*, and denounced anyone suspected of disloyalty to Britain, including 'Bigot Teachers', 'Piss-Brute-tarians', and 'those Dablers in Politics . . . the learned *Owls* of the College'.[47] Transforming College Hall into a satirical 'Scurrility Hall', Isaac parodied his undergraduate declamations in a series of mad-cap dialogues. Many of the jokes are irrecoverable, but at least one was directed against himself as the 'little *Limb of the Law*' courting Mary Shewell: 'We *did for him in Barbados*, 'tis true: But he'll get the pretty *Quaker* Girl in Market-Street yet'.[48] Schoolmaster David Dove received a mock obituary illustrated with a splendid copperplate engraving by Henry Dawkins, showing a caricature of Dove in 'conference' with Satan. This image, along with Dawkins's cartoons of the Paxton crisis and the 1764 Philadelphia election, were the earliest use of cartoons in American political life. The Philadelphia wordy-war and Isaac Hunt's satirical poems had encouraged a truly momentous development in American culture.[49]

Isaac's former patron at the College, William Smith, was a Scottish Presbyterian and by no means impressed by his protégé's 'scurrilous and scandalous pieces . . . reflecting on the Government of this Province, as well as on this College itself where he had received his Education and his former Benefactors in it'.[50] Hence Isaac's unworthiness to receive an MA. There was more to Isaac's pamphlets than personal abuse: he had an instinct for vigorous verse as this passage, apparently directed at David Dove, shows:

O Thou whose *mushroom* Birth in Dirt begins
In *Slush and Slime of stinking* Sooterkins;
Whether you *curse your King*, count o'er your *Pelf*,
Blaspheme your God, or *damn your wretched Self*,
Fling up your Mother's Duds, or beat your Wife,
Or whate'er else employs your wicked Life,
IBIS, thou stinking filthy Bird of *Nile*,
Which slimy Clysters, through thy beak, defile,
O *Ibis*, wherefore would you *thus* engage . . .

Isaac's image of Dove as a grotesque wading bird feeding on filth might be
a snippet from a Philadelphian *Dunciad* modelled after Pope's satirical poem.
Isaac's fondness for wordy-play produced this spirited Rumbullion rap,

Whipper-Snapper, dipper-dapper, Rat-screw,
Prick-ear'd, learn'd, errata-grammar-brat grew

– an exciting whirligig of sounds, as exuberant as Barbadian nature. Isaac's
youngest son would prove a hungry 'grammar-brat' too, and he would learn
to write by copying from his father's pamphlets.

Whipper-snapper wordy-war with David 'Ibis' Dove and the College owls
was not winning Isaac friends. Shortly after his marriage he wrote to Benjamin
Franklin explaining how political embroilments had damaged his legal career.
Franklin replied from London on Christmas Eve 1767, offering friendly
advice:

London Decem 24. 1767

Mr Hunt
Dr Sir

I received yours of Octo. 10 and perceive with concern that you are
still persecuted as a heretic in politics. It is remarkable that the objection to you as a libeller should come from that person who is himself
one huge, living, walking talking libel against all the worthy characters
that come in his way. You ask me my advice on the occasion. The best
I can give you at this distance is to redouble your diligence in the studies
pertaining to your profession till you have acquired such eminence and
excellence in it, that those who now wantonly abuse you, shall when
they have occasion for law be forced to solicit your assistance; and pay
you well for that friendship they now take so much pains to render
themselves unworthy of. Depend upon it great merit in your profession
will force its way. Acquire that and every thing else will follow. Be indefatigably diligent and you will be greater than your adversaries. Be frugal

and you will [be] richer. Be temperate and abstemious and you will live
to walk over their graves. Be virtuous and you will be happy. This I
wish you very sincerely.

> Your affectionate Friend
> and humble Servant

Isaac Hunt Esq
   a Lawyer in Philad[a][51]

Franklin knew all about the 'living, walking talking libel' David Dove, and
was alert to Isaac's talents and weaknesses. With professionalism Isaac could
fulfil the promise he had displayed at the college Commencement; frugality
and temperance would police his sybaritic sensibility. Above all redoubled,
indefatigible *diligence* would enable Isaac to carry the day. Franklin's repeated
emphasis shows that he knew how easily Isaac could be distracted. It was good
advice well given, setting out the terms on which Isaac might overcome his
libellous entanglements, while also making him aware of the potential for
unhappiness.

Over the nine years following, Isaac and Mary had four sons: Isaac, born
around 1768, Stephen in 1772, Robert in 1773, and John, 1775. Two further
children did not survive infancy, Benjamin (named after Franklin) and a
daughter Eliza (named after her great-aunt, Elizabeth Shewell/West). As a
boy Stephen narrowly escaped kidnapping by Indians, who 'saw in his dark
face, and long black hair, a resemblance to themselves'.[52] Hunt mentions this
incident in his *Autobiography*, and reflects how his brother might have been
taken away to be brought up in the Pennsylvania forests as a native American.

Tension between America and the 'mother country' ratcheted up. Imports
from Britain and Ireland were boycotted; the 'Boston Massacre' of March
1770 created martyrs to the American cause, and was answered two years later
by an attack on the *Gaspee*, a schooner used by the British customs service;
the Tea Act of 1773, intended to secure a monopoly for the East India
Company, was resisted by a group of men disguised as Indians dumping a
cargo of tea overboard – the Boston Tea Party. Close co-operation between
the provinces led up to the First Continental Congress held at Carpenters'
Hall, Philadelphia, in September 1774. The prayer in Congress was offered
by Jacob Duché, who took as his text Psalm 35, 'Plead thou my case, O Lord,
with them that strive with me, and fight thou against them that fight against
me.' Following Duché's ten-minute extempore prayer beseeching God's
support for the American cause, Congress resolved to halt trade with Britain
and issued a Statement of Rights and Grievances on matters of government
and taxation. For the moment they stopped short of an outright break with
Britain, but the lines had been drawn.

On 22 February 1775 the *Philadelphia Gazette* advertised a newly published pamphlet: 'THE POLITICAL FAMILY, or A DISCOURSE pointing out the Reciprocal Advantages which flow from an uninterrupted Union between Great-Britain and her American Colonies. By *ISAAC HUNT*, Esq'. The title sets out exactly what is inside: 'Let us . . . consider *Great-Britain* and her American *colonies* as a family, the establishment of which depends upon unity, friendship, and a *continued.* series of mutual good offices'. If Isaac's loyalism was 'political heresy' in Philadelphia, pointing to the *'reciprocal advantages'* of trade and British military protection placed him way beyond the pale. His father-in-law Stephen Shewell applauded, but Isaac knew that to write on this subject was 'delicate and hazardous'. His fortunes would now reach a crisis.[53]

'Committees of Observation' were formed in the colonies to police the boycott of British goods. On 17 August 1775 one George Schlosser, a member of the Philadelphia Committee, detained a pedlar suspected of selling British linen. The pedlar, happily named William Conn, appealed for help to Isaac who issued a writ against Schlosser. When summoned before the Committee of Observation to explain himself, Isaac delayed until the committee declared his behaviour 'by no means satisfactory'.[54] Isaac's was the single instance of open defiance of committee authority in Philadelphia, and public feeling demanded an apology. The date was set for 6 September 1775, when Isaac was collected in the morning and taken to one of the coffee-houses to make his confession. The knockabout days of 'Scurrility Hall' were long gone. Isaac was man-handled into a cart and paraded around the streets accompanied by soldiers playing pipes and drums – a traditional means of ridicule, and ominously like a tumbrel to the gallows. The mob hooted and jeered, and a stone wounded Isaac so severely that his eyesight was permanently damaged. The parade might have ended with a tarring and feathering, or worse, had Isaac not been able to collect his wits and summon his skill as a public speaker. He stood up in the cart and, a witness reported, 'politely acknowledged he had said and acted wrong . . . asked pardon of the public and committed himself under the protection of the associators, to defend him from any gross insults from the populace'.[55] He made the same apology in various places around the city, and was at last returned to a prison in Market Street. Isaac bribed his guard, and that evening he was aboard one of Stephen Shewell's boats as it weighed anchor and slipped down the Delaware into the darkness. After eighteen years in Philadelphia 'Jack Retort' fled to Barbados, and then on to London.

These terrifying experiences scarred Isaac, and Mary never recovered from the shock. Stephen Shewell's fleet of ships was burned to prevent the British seizing them, and he was forced to supply provisions for the rebels.[56] Many years later his youngest daughter Lydia recalled that Stephen had 'lost a fortune' during the revolution, and was 'thrown out of business'.[57] He survived the war, and so did Isaac, Mary and the boys – but only just, and at considerable long-term cost. It would not be until 1808, three years after Mary's death, that Hunt and his brothers started to find out about the property and money their parents left behind when they fled from Philadelphia.

In London Isaac found that his expertise in colonial law was useless in the mother country he had supported at such great personal risk. He thought of going on stage, revealing an attraction to the theatre that would reappear in his youngest son, but after the hazards of recent years he needed steady employment. On 17 January 1777 Isaac, like many of his ancestors, was ordained in the Church of England. He contemplated a return across the Atlantic as a missionary in Newfoundland, then settled for a comfortable position as minister of Bentinck Chapel, Paddington, at the edge of London between Regent's Park and the open fields. Here Isaac's eloquent sermons made the chapel a fashionable attraction, with crowds and carriages at the door. One of the congregation paid to have his portrait engraved.[58]

Across the Atlantic, Mary and her sons were living at Stephen Shewell's house awaiting an opportunity to rejoin Isaac. John's birth in 1775 delayed their journey, and Stephen seems to have cherished a hope that his daughter would remain in Philadelphia (Mary's sister Frances later hinted that their father's 'sympathizing tenderness' depended on a break with Isaac).[59] Some two years after Isaac's 'carting', Mary and the boys boarded an old frigate, the Earl of Effingham, bound for London. The voyage proved uneventful until a terrific storm off the Isles of Scilly. With the ship almost under water, Mary kept up the spirits of her own children and, as the tempest increased, courageously rallied the other passengers as well.[60] The ship was driven at last into Swansea Bay, and safety. The Hunts went on by carriage to London, and sought out their relatives in the city.

Mary had not seen her Aunt Elizabeth, now Elizabeth West, for some twelve years. She was living at 14, Newman Street, and her husband Benjamin West was now the most successful painter in Britain and a confidant of George III. Under their roof the Hunt family was reunited, and for a time it must have seemed that their troubles were over. Isaac, Mary and their family moved to the airy ridge of Hampstead village, the 'Northern Heights' about five miles from London, a haven for refugees and émigrés during the revolutionary era and beyond. St John's church, with its broad nave and steeple surrounded by trees, may have reminded Mary of churches in Philadelphia. From Hampstead Isaac walked through the lanes to preach at Southgate, a village in a landscape of trees, meadows and cottages.[61] Luck appeared to be with him. James Brydges, Duke of Chandos, lived nearby and was so impressed by Isaac that he invited him to become tutor to his young nephew, James Henry Leigh. And so the Hunts uprooted themselves once again, and moved to Eagle Hall, Southgate, a large house close to the Duke's estate.

The Duke of Chandos was a Privy Councillor, Lord Steward of George III's Household, and a person 'for whom the king had a personal regard'.[62] As a tutor to his family, Isaac was perfectly placed to win the goodwill of a powerful, aristocratic patron who might help him make his way in the Church. Isaac was well educated and eloquent. His graceful manners, loyalism and orthodox opinions recommended him. All of this would ensure his elevation, and a bishopric was by no means impossible. To celebrate their arrival in the English establishment Isaac and Mary decided to name their youngest son after the Duke of Chandos's nephew. James Henry Leigh Hunt was born at Eagle Hall on Tuesday, 19 October 1784, a day that was 'hazy and still' midway in a month of warm sun and sharp frosts.

It was an auspicious name. The aristocratic James Henry Leigh was the uncle of a young lady who would become the most celebrated novelist of the age: Jane Austen.[63] Despite Hunt's radical political views and tireless campaigning to eradicate courtly and aristocratic abuses, he never forgot the expectations associated with his naming and always felt a sense of kinship with 'gentry'.[64] The circumstances of his childhood, however, would be very different from those enjoyed by his privileged namesake. Instead of leading onwards and upwards to a mitre and a seat in the House of Lords, Isaac's prospects dwindled into years of poverty and debt.

TWO

THE POLITICAL FAMILY

'The universe itself was nothing but a poor sitting-room in the year '89 or '90, with my mother in it bidding me sing, Miss C. at the pianoforte, harpsichord more likely, and my little sister, Mary, with her round cheeks and blue eyes, wishing me to begin.' They enjoyed sentimental songs like James Hook's 'Alone, by the light of the moon', fashionable lyrics by Thomas Dibdin, Thomas Linley, Stephen Storace, and opera airs from continental composers like Giovanni Paisiello, Nicolò Piccini and Domenico Cimarosa. Family associations made

> Come let us dance and sing,
> While all Barbados bells shall ring

a favourite. 'Dans votre lit' was a 'gallant, but very decorous' song in which Mary imagined she heard her brother's name. So Hunt's lifetime of music and singing began, surrounded by a circle of attentive women.[1]

By 1791 little Mary had died leaving Hunt, nine years younger than his brother John, the baby of the family. As the 'least robust' of the children he was given an 'ultra tender and anxious rearing', and the 'ultra-sympathising' child repaid his mother's doting attention by turning her into a saint. Hunt loved his mother with 'unspeakable' intensity, and agonised over what she had endured at Philadelphia and afterwards. One memory of her acquired special radiance:

> in a severe winter, as she was taking me home, she was petitioned for charity by a woman sick and ill-clothed. It was in Blackfriars' Road, I think about midway. My mother, with the tears in her eyes, turned up a gateway, or some such place, and beckoning the woman to follow, took off her flannel petticoat and gave it her. It is supposed that a cold which ensued, fixed the rheumatism upon her for life. Actions like these have doubtless been often performed, and do not of necessity imply any great virtue in the performer; but they do if they are of a piece with the rest of the character. Saints have been made for charities no greater.[2]

For the rest of his life Hunt remembered this scene of winter charity as a touchstone of human kindness. He would refer to it many times, most poignantly so in relation to Shelley.

His father appeared wholly to blame for the family's misfortunes. Despite his promising situation in the Church, Isaac did not achieve the success he believed he deserved. It's easy to blame Isaac's failures on his fondness for wine and good living, but important as well to remember that at the close of the eighteenth century the economic status of the middle class was insecure. As Isaac's prospects fluctuated, the family could alternately anticipate a bishop's palace or time in the debtors' prison. Earlier generations of the family had experienced similar setbacks, and Hunt's own career would lurch perilously between prosperity and prison.

During the 1780s the family never settled for long in one place. As creditors closed in or better times beckoned, they moved restlessly between Lisson Green and Southgate, Hampstead and Finchley. Disappointments gradually altered Mary's face, and her mouth was 'drawn down with sorrow at the corners'. Underlying her sense of blighted fortune was the damage caused by what she had witnessed at Philadelphia, which had 'agonized her feelings'. Hunt recalls that a boxing match in the street caused her an 'agony of distress', and that she used to take him on long detours to prevent him glimpsing soldiers parading in Regent's Park, determined that he must 'dislike war & bloodshed'. 'I wish with all my heart,' Mary wrote, 'the time would arrive when nations shall learn war no more.'[3]

So Hunt grew up a sickly child, 'very curious to know about soldiers'. It was thought unlikely that he would survive into teenage years. He was afflicted first with 'dropsy in the head', then with smallpox, recovering from one illness only to be 'seized by another'. His sickliness was compounded by night terrors and a highly sensitive imagination. Returning from a visit to Calais for his health, Hunt aged four and his mother passed through Deal where he saw from the beach 'a shoal of porpoises tumbling along in the foam'. These were 'fearful creatures of some sort': the word 'porpoise' seemed to have an 'awful, mouth-filling sound', demanding yet stifling speech.[4] Another awful word was 'Mantichora'. 'It had the head of a man, grinning with rows of teeth, and the body of a wild-beast, brandishing a tail armed with stings . . . I took the word to be a compound of *man* and *tiger*.' His brothers teased him by grinning and whispering in hollow tones, '"The Mantichora's coming! The Mantichora's coming!"' In the twilight terrible creatures – part animal, part human – prowled around the little boy in forms he was as yet unable to bring into words. Many years later Hunt described how the gorgeous woman-snake in Keats's *Lamia* called up 'admiration, pity, and horror . . . excited by humanity in a brute shape'. As with the Mantichora's devouring grin – Hunt says he 'never imagined it seen in profile' – it was the engorging mouth of Keats's 'palpitating snake' that fascinated and disturbed him. When Hunt wrote his brilliant commentary on *Lamia*, he had come to see that 'painful shapes had a soul of humanity' demanding the interest of poets.[5]

Hunt taught himself to write by copying his father's sermons. An example of his handwriting at five years old shows Isaac's loops and flourishes, traits that his writing never lost. He was fond of reading and 'plentifully supplied with children's books'. These included fairy tales such as 'Jack the Giant-Killer'; sentimental fiction and popular romance like Thomas Day's *Sandford and Merton* and *The Seven Champions of Christendom*; and classics including *Paradise Lost*, *Pilgrim's Progress*, *Hamlet*, and poems from *Elegant Extracts*. There was also a 'picture-book' in which lurked a Mantichora. Accompanying this rich mixture were more demanding scenes of instruction, when he had to recite Latin words before meals. 'Panis. Poema. Vinum. Versus. Por ...por ...porculus m ...m ...marinus'. In one sense the method worked: in March 1791 he wrote to his Aunt Lydia in Philadelphia boasting that he could 'perfectly repeat 2063 words'. The association of language and eating – literally, now, 'mouth-filling' words – continued in Hunt's idea of poetry as a 'cornucopia'. He thought of the poet as hungering for language, and introduced Keats in the *Examiner* as 'a striking specimen of the restlessness of the young poetical appetite, obtaining its food by the very desire of it'.[6] Hunt's choice of a title for his high-spirited celebration of English poetry, *The Feast of the Poets*, reflected this lifelong association. When the 'young poets' Keats and Shelley gathered at Hunt's home the fare was always poetry, food and wine – although Hunt's own earnings as poet and journalist were seldom sufficient to pay the bills.

In all of these ways Hunt's early experiences of songs, music, words, writing and reading fostered a unique lyrical sensibility in which the domestic and the social figured importantly. But his parents' well-intentioned concern had less benign effects. Mealtime exercises may have caused Hunt's stutter – his famishing inability to get his tongue around words, owing to fear or his parents' high expectations of him. Certainly, when he arrived at Christ's Hospital in 1791 he found that his stammering got worse because he was frightened of the masters. And the scarcity of food made matters worse, for his words were no longer rewarded with a full bowl.

The contented scene with mother and sister was a rare one in Hunt's early life, as this rueful observation about his parents suggests: 'She stood by him through . . . all; and in everything did more honour to marriage, than marriage did good to either of them: for it brought little happiness to her, and too many children to both.'[7] What lay behind these unhappy reflections? Isaac and Mary had a large family to provide for, and now they were beyond help from Stephen Shewell it was essential that Isaac's career prospered. One of Mary's letters, however, regretted that their friends had 'not obtained for us

what we had expected'.[8] Benjamin West repeatedly mentioned Isaac's difficult circumstances to the King, who 'said he would speak to the bishops' and
that Isaac 'should be provided for'. But nothing was done, and the Duke of
Chandos, once so enthusiastic about Isaac's abilities, no longer seemed willing
to help. Hunt explained cryptically that His Majesty had been 'prepared with
questions, which the duke was not equally prepared to answer'.[9]

Exactly what Hunt meant by this was not disclosed until he revised his
Autobiography in the months before his death, adding numerous manuscript
notes to be incorporated in the new edition. He emphasised Isaac's public roles
in Philadelphia and London as the 'honest loyalist'. The most significant of
Hunt's alterations, however, was the addition of a passage revealing Isaac's
involvement with a suspected American rebel and spy, Colonel John Trumbull.[10]

During the American war John Trumbull had served in the patriot army
against the British, and was aide-de-camp to General Washington before
resigning his commission in 1777. Determined to pursue a career as an artist
– or spy – he travelled to Paris where Benjamin Franklin gave him a letter of
introduction to Benjamin West. Despite whisperings about his American
sympathies, West was already one of the foremost painters in London and
prominent in the Royal Academy. By the end of 1780 Trumbull had also
settled in London as one of West's students, living 'publicly & peacably' until,
on 19 November, he was arrested. Among his papers were letters in which
he recommended a friend as 'essentially serviceable to the cause of America'.[11]
Such pro-American sentiments looked suspicious, and his army record during
the revolution darkened the picture considerably. Trumbull was locked up in
Tothill Fields Prison to await a charge of Treason.

Benjamin West hurried across town to see him, dreading that this association might now be a disadvantage. Charles James Fox made 'kind visits'
encouraging Trumbull to contact Edmund Burke for help. His letters to Burke
survive, along with one to the Treasury Solicitor that mentions he is writing
on 'advice from . . . friends better acquainted with the forms of Law than I
am'.[12] One of those friends was Isaac Hunt, and Trumbull later paid tribute
to 'an effort . . . made through Mr Hunt . . . which does honor to him, and
was pushed so far as almost to endanger his own safety'.[13] Isaac took up
Trumbull's case with all the reckless zeal of his Philadelphia days, urging
other Americans in London to lend support. His eagerness, according to Hunt,
did 'mischief with the King' who 'conceived an impression . . . unfavourable
to the future clergyman'.[14]

Through Burke's intervention Trumbull was released on bail in June 1781,
and promptly fled to Paris and then America. In more peaceful times he would
return to London, beginning his series of historical paintings of the revolution including *The Death of General Warren at the Battle of Bunker's Hill* and,
most famously, *The Declaration of Independence*. Meanwhile, Isaac was left to
face the consequences of involving himself in the case: he had displeased the

King, lost the favour of his patron, and antagonised the civil authorities.

Like Brian Hunt before him, Isaac felt that his loyal exertions had been ignored. In a 'Memorial' document dated May 1787, he applied to the Commission for American Loyalists set up to assist individuals who had supported Britain. He recounted his personal and professional demonstrations of loyalty while in Philadelphia, calculated his losses in property and income at some £3,000, and urged 'reconciliation with our American brethren' while warning against the 'designs of France'. This application succeeded, and brought Isaac a pension of £100 a year. The respite was temporary, for Isaac's debts continued to mount and in due course he would become 'deeply acquainted with prisons' – and so did his family. The effect on Mary is suggested by Hunt's recollection that his father's impracticality, 'always scheming, never performing', had taken 'hope out of the heart that loved him'.[15]

The family moved to Hampstead again. How they coped at this difficult time is revealed by Elizabeth West's 'Household Account Book', a fascinating record of eighteenth-century domestic economy in a prosperous London family. The Wests lived well. An order on 7 April 1787 required '2 Duck, Rabbits, Ham, Fillet of Veal, Broccoli, Sallad, Oranges and Lemons'. In her book Elizabeth West costed medical bills, school fees, a skylight and blinds for her husband's gallery, as well as everyday outgoings such as water taxes, parish rates, and payments for coal, hay and straw, mackerel and lozenges, pencils and paper, candles, teapots and a copy of the new American Constitution. She paid five shillings for 'opening Phillis'.

In January 1785 Elizabeth spent a little over £9 to clear 'Isaacs Bill'. A year later the Account Book records numerous payments to Mary Hunt between January and April 1786. The following list is particularly revealing:

gave Isaac Hunt	2–12–6
grocery	1– 3–6
bottle Gin	0– 2–6
D° Brandy	0– 3–0
2 Cans	0– 1–4
Hamper	0– 1–0
Butter	0– 4–9
2 Cannisters	0– 2–0
	4..10..7
2 p^r Shoes	15
	5 5 7

Just underneath this account is the memo 'Expended for Isaac Hunt 5–5–7', and the next few entries record payments of a further eight guineas to Mary Hunt.[16]

The Wests evidently helped out by supplying provisions: Isaac's two 'cannisters' probably contained tea and coffee, while the gin and brandy and the two cans (probably porter) show how Isaac managed to keep up his spirits. Hunt kept quiet about his father's drinking, but his own abstemious habits were certainly a reaction to it. Joseph Farington, the painter and diarist, remarked that Isaac was

> a clever man but addicted to drinking, and eventually killed Himself by that practise, though he lived to apparently 60 years of age [in fact 69]. He was wholly witht. conduct and took no care to appear decent in His person but often was seen in a dress almost grotesque.[17]

Hunt's older brother John described their father bitterly, as 'a bad friend, a bad member of society, a bad father, and a bad husband' and regretted the 'sad scenes' he had 'witnessed and shared in, owing to [Isaac's] indolence and sensuality and want of self-respect'. Here John reveals the actuality behind Hunt's more guarded references to Isaac as an 'improvident and unhappiness-producing person'.[18]

So family life struggled on 'between quiet and disturbance, between placid readings and frightful knocks at the door, and sickness, and calamity, and hopes, which hardly ever forsook us'.[19] Those 'frightful knocks' were from angry creditors, and John's harsh words don't suggest that Isaac had only an occasional lapse. Hunt was never as extreme as John in condemning their father, but what he didn't admit outright may have been repressed to emerge, later, in distressing physical and nervous ailments. And when that happened, Hunt's instinct would be to retreat into the company of caring women as he had done as a child with his mother, his sister and his Aunt Elizabeth West.

As a boy Hunt wrote a poem, 'Macbeth; or, the Ill Effects of Ambition', and when he wrote in his *Autobiography* about 'frightful knocks at the door' he was well aware that the phrase recalled the famous comic scene in *Macbeth* where the drunken porter is slowly roused by Macduff and Lennox: 'Here's a knocking indeed! . . . Knock, knock, knock! Who's there, i' th' name of Beelzebub?' (II. iii. 1–4). Hunt had read Thomas De Quincey's essay 'On the Knocking at the Gate in Macbeth' in which the 'knocking at the gate' signals the resumption of 'the goings-on of the world' after the murder of Duncan.[20] What Hunt remembers as an adult, however, is the noisy interruption – not the scene of disturbance or trauma.

The hysterical symptoms with which Hunt struggled throughout his life first assailed him after his mother's death, with the guilty realisation that he had been as neglectful as his father. In his *Autobiography* the account of that first nervous attack and convalescence included the painful recollection of seeing a child 'all over sores, and cased in steel, the result of the irregularities

of its father'.[21] This was another sickly, damaged infant, although for Hunt
its significance was symbolic rather than personal. When he was seeking an
explanation for John Bellingham's murder of Prime Minister Spencer
Perceval, he traced the crime back to infancy, to the 'indolent selfishness' and
also the 'mistaken fondness' of parents: 'The infant is the promise and picture
of the man; and many a toy, that has been kicked and destroyed out of the
way in a fit of childish rage, has been the prototype of a human being displaced
in the same manner years afterwards.'[22] Neglect and exceptional fondness
were qualities Hunt associated with his own parents: within three months of
Perceval's murder and those speculations about childhood, Hunt was afflicted
by another upsurge of nervous illness.

Towards the end of his life Hunt was at pains to present Isaac in a positive light. He remembered how his father had some 'great acquaintances',
and had taken him to the House of Commons where they saw Prime Minister
Pitt speaking and MPs 'lounging on the benches'. When he revised his
Autobiography just before his death, he added: 'I bless and am grateful to his
memory'. He thought Isaac's support for Trumbull 'worthy and disinterested',
a noble example of independence that would have been impossible had he
'attained the bishoprick he looked for, and left us ticketed and labelled among
the acquiescent'.[23] Isaac's disinterestedness would be the pattern on which
Hunt shaped his own career as an editor, journalist and critic – although
Hunt's stance of principled independence developed into a strategy to place
himself beyond the obligations, compromises and disappointments that had
broken his father.

From Hampstead Isaac and the family 'crossed the water' to Southwark, and
made their home in a cell in the King's Bench Prison. The old eighteenth-
century debtors' gaol was wrecked during the Gordon Riots of 1780 and a
new prison had been erected on the site, three storeys high and proportioned
like a barrack block. It was routine for whole families to accompany debtors
to prison, and the King's Bench was equipped to cater for eight hundred
inmates. There was a coffee-house, a marketplace, a public kitchen, and two
pubs nicknamed the 'Tap' and the 'Brace' where 'the heavy whet' flowed. But
nothing could diminish the shock and shame of imprisonment. The Hunts
stayed in one of the cells, fifteen feet by ten, containing three beds. Looking
out at the courtyard they could see the prison walls, thirty-five feet high and
surmounted with a row of iron spikes, beyond which were the roofs and chimneys of London's burgeoning suburbs. Hunt was aged a little over two years,
and this harrowing scene remained with him as one of his earliest memories
– 'the first room I have any recollection of is a prison'.[24] Just as Charles
Dickens poured anguished memories of his family in the Marshalsea Prison
into novels like *David Copperfield* and *Little Dorrit*, Hunt's recollections of
the King's Bench resurfaced in later life and writings. That warren of 'confined

and unwholesome abodes' haunted him with spectres of 'aged and unhappy parents . . . lamenting over their offspring – respectable wives watching the sick beds of their husbands – children partaking of the scanty meal of their afflicted parents, – and that meal, perhaps, procured by the sacrifice of some necessary piece of raiment'. 'This is not an imaginary picture,' Hunt continued, 'but a common and every-day scene.'[25] It revived with devastating effects when, in 1813, he was sentenced to two years in Surrey Gaol – a stone's throw away from the King's Bench.

In time Isaac was able to buy his way out of prison, but was obliged to reside within three miles of it until he cleared his debts. A new development of terraced houses at Union Street, Lambeth, became the Hunts' next home, two hundred yards from Hercules Buildings where William and Catherine Blake lived in the 1790s. For centuries this area had been known as Lambeth Marsh, low-lying, foggy, waterlogged, susceptible to floods and outbreaks of typhus and cholera. By the close of the eighteenth century, however, Lambeth was the scene of feverish property development as London pushed further and further south. Hunt and his mother would have been able to wander through what remained of the lanes to market gardens, fields and cattle pens, and a short walk away on the bank of the Thames were Lambeth Palace and St Mary's church.

Isaac's straitened circumstances made it imperative that he settle his boys in work. The eldest son, Isaac, had gone to sea and nothing was heard from him for many years. The others were soon making their way closer to home. Here is Hunt, aged six, describing his older brothers with admiration:

> My brother Stephen is to be a lawyer, Robert is with the Prince of Wales engraver and I heard the old folks say he will very soon make a better picture than his Master. My Brother John is a Typographer.[26]

John's destined line of work was to have far-reaching consequences. On 1 February 1791 Isaac apprenticed him to the printer Henry Reynell of Piccadilly, initiating the training that would equip him to be publisher of the *News* and the *Examiner*.[27] Those papers would have a huge impact on the political and cultural life of Britain, and they owed much to Isaac and Mary Hunt's increasingly radical opinions.

At the beginning of the French Revolution Isaac had published a loyalist pamphlet, *The Rights of Englishmen*, that declared 'perfect satisfaction' with the 'present ministers' and made ominous comparisons between revolutionary agitation in Britain and events in America in 1776. Having met Tom Paine in Philadelphia, he was aware of Paine's 'deep rooted malice' to Britain. Now, Isaac warned, the 'sovereign-deposing, bishop-kicking, title-levelling American' planned to revolutionise 'the government of England on the models of those in France and America'. That meant a 'mob assembly'. The pamphlet is shadowed by memories of Philadelphian 'tyranny' and 'the ignominy of a ride in a cart, or a coat of tar and feathers'.[28]

Isaac's disappointments since coming to Britain ensured that this rekindled loyalism was short lived, and it wasn't long before the Hunts were associating with a vocal minority every bit as controversial as Isaac had been in Philadelphia. After 1791 Hunt's parents responded to 'new opinions' and 'speculations regarding the welfare of human kind'.[29] In other words, they were caught up in the intellectual whirlwind unleashed by the French Revolution. Unadvantaged by loyalism in an earlier revolution, they had no inclination to rally once again to 'Church and King!' Moving sharply away from former allegiances, Isaac and Mary became Unitarians, Universalists and Republicans, backing the cause of the people and humanity against the establishment Isaac had courted in vain.[30]

It was thirsty work. On Sunday, 18 May 1794, Isaac was enjoying an afternoon drink in the Swan Tavern near Westminster Bridge. Six days earlier, Thomas Hardy, John Horne Tooke, 'Citizen' John Thelwall and other leaders of the reform movement had been arrested and imprisoned in Newgate and the Tower. Pitt's Terror was under way. Habeas Corpus had been suspended and London was swarming with spies and informers. A jug of porter and a verse or two about 'rat-faced, prick-nos'd Billy Pitt' would have been sufficient to make Isaac a marked man: 'Jacobin. Thelwallite. Haul him in'. Later that evening there was a knocking at the door. Isaac was ridden into custody for 'seditious expressions', held overnight, and questioned on Monday morning by magistrates. The interview didn't lead to further proceedings, although it may have encouraged the authorities to look back over Isaac's involvement in the murky Trumbull affair.

Isaac's more considered opinions as a dissenter aligned him with the intellectual wing of the reform movement, with men and women like Joseph Priestley, Richard Price, Anna Barbauld and Samuel Taylor Coleridge. All of them were Unitarians who campaigned for liberty of conscience, the separation of church and state, an extension of the suffrage and an end to the French war. The conversations seven-year-old Hunt now overheard at his parents' fireside glowed with arguments for political and religious liberty. When he grew up fireside gatherings would always set the scene for political discussion and poetry, in his domestic life and in his writings. In the dangerous year 1819, he would think of his *Indicator* magazine as a 'private room' for converse, sheltered from the dangers of the public 'tavern rooms' Isaac had frequented.

Isaac and Mary were admirers of Elhanan Winchester, minister of the Universalist chapel in Artillery Lane. Born in 1751 at Brookline,

Massachusetts, Elhanan Winchester preached as a Baptist, then as a Calvinist, before intensive study of the Bible made him 'well persuaded of the truth of the UNIVERSAL RESTORATION'.[31] He was a charismatic public speaker, a formidable controversialist, a prolific author of sermons, discourses, prophecies and poems. Winchester lived for some years at Philadelphia, and in 1787 came to London where he preached the benevolent, inclusive doctrine that all creation would be redeemed and restored to God. In his view there was no scriptural authority for eternal damnation – even Satan had prospects. Winchester's massive epic poem *The Process and Empire of Christ* included this optimistic scene:

> At length [Satan's] rage and blasphemies subside;
> His heart, more hard than nether milstone, seems
> At last to melt, and soften; he begins
> Now to reflect, and wishes to repent . . .[32]

Like Benjamin Franklin and Tom Paine, Winchester viewed the progress of liberty in Europe with eager anticipation. When Isaac and Mary joined his congregation they effectively abandoned their hopes of finding favour with the hard-hearted establishment, and pitched in their lot with the friends of liberty. Isaac's Philadelphia pamphlet, *The Political Family*, had trumpeted a loyal alliance between Britain and the American colonies. Universalist doctrine did away with all such narrow considerations, and gave spiritual sanction for extending 'friendship' and 'unity' to the whole world under a republican, millenarian banner. To further the cause Isaac printed a proposal for an academy to be called the 'Cosmopolitical Seminary'.[33] Perhaps Satan would sign up?

Elhanan Winchester returned to America in 1794, like Joseph Priestley who emigrated to escape the church-and-king mobs that had wrecked his home at Birmingham. Hunt's memories of Winchester harked back to the earlier 1790s, and he identified those years as the period when Universalism started to shape his intellectual and emotional life. 'It was hence that I learned the "impiety" . . . of the doctrine of eternal punishment,' he recalled.[34] We can trace its influence in his attacks on fire-and-damnation Calvinist Methodism, in his response to the carnage of Waterloo, and in his compassionate presentation of Paulo and Francesca in *The Story of Rimini*. Hunt's poem was 'tolerant and reconciling', but Winchester's warning that ideas of 'Universal Restoration' might be held to encourage people in 'evil ways' was prescient. The poem was attacked for 'extreme moral depravity', and behind this hostility to it lurked a horror of speculative thought that dated from the 1790s.

Hunt's conversational style, his fireside evenings of poetry and music, and even his encouragement of 'young poets' may all be traced from the inclusiveness of Universalism. Winchester's successor at Artillery Lane, William

Vidler, recommended 'natural affection' and the 'pleasure of domestic affections' that 'make the mind cheerful, thereby giving it a fitness for the performance of every day'.[35] Fitness for life – physical and spiritual – would become increasingly significant for Hunt as an adult, especially at the many times he was afflicted with depression and anxiety. Hunt's seemingly carefree persona and his philosophy of cheerfulness have often been dismissed as bland sentimentalism, evidence of a superficial attitude to life. This is to miss completely his hard-won strategy for coping with physical and psychological distress, a form of personal therapy that grew out of the Universalist ideas he had absorbed before he was ten years old.

When Hunt was asked what he would like to be when he grew up, his first idea was to follow his father and become a clergyman. But then colourful uniforms and the forbidden world of soldiers crossed his mind. So he thought of being 'clergyman & soldier at once', and 'pinched up my hat with large pins; and putting on one of my father's bands, would mount a chair with a wooden sword in my hand, & preach'.[36] The childish performance foreshadowed Hunt's life as a journalist and poet. His first steps in that direction would take him away from the political family, to a much more worldly school than Isaac's Cosmopolitical Seminary.

Part II: The Young Poet, 1791–1807

New splendour seem'd to flush the glowing sky,
And Nature rise with visage doubly fair . . .

Leigh Hunt, *The Palace of Pleasure*

THREE

AT SCHOOL

What school would six-year-old Hunt go to? Isaac's precarious circumstances meant that the great public schools were not a possibility. Equally, it would be demeaning to send his boy to one of the charity schools for paupers. Fortunately, there was an institution that offered a middle way: Christ's Hospital.

Founded by royal charter in 1562, the school was intended as an institution for 'the fatherless children and other poore men's children that were not able to kepe them . . . where they should have meate drincke and cloths, lodging and learning and officers to attende uppon them'.[1] Located in the heart of the City of London, in Hunt's time the school provided a free education for the sons of poor citizens, preparing them for lives as tradesmen, merchants, naval officers, clergymen and scholars. Although Christ's Hospital was a charitable institution funded by wealthy benefactors, it had achieved a unique status independent of the national charity school system. It was also distinct from the public schools – such as Eton and Harrow – in that some areas of the curriculum had a practical emphasis and its culture was merito-cratic: 'the cleverest boy was the noblest, let his father be who he might'.[2]

On 1 April 1791 Isaac submitted a petition to the Governors of the school, explaining that he had 'a Wife and five Children one of whom is under the Age of Fourteen, & dependant upon the Petitioner for Maintenance & Education'. There was '*no probable Means for the Education of the said Child, unless the said Governors of* CHRIST'S-HOSPITAL *should admit* him'. The document was certified by Jacob Duché, Rector of Christ Church, Philadelphia. Duché's revolutionary ardour had cooled, and when he arrived in England he brought the 'private Register Book' from which he now vouched for Isaac and Mary's lawful marriage 'according to the Form of the Church of England'. The petition was successful, but there was one more formality to be completed. Disenchanted with 'Church and King', Isaac and Mary had not had Hunt baptised. Evidence of baptism was required before he could enter Christ's Hospital and so, on 30 October 1791, the 'said child' was chris-tened at St George the Martyr, Southwark. On 24 November James Henry Leigh Hunt was 'Cloath'd', putting on for the first time the long, buttoned blue coat and distinctive yellow stockings worn by the boys of Christ's Hospital.

For the next eight years the school would be his home. It stood behind the houses on the north side of Newgate Street, one of the oldest thoroughfares in the city and famous for its butchers' shops and slaughterhouses. On the corner of Newgate Street was Newgate Prison, the English Bastille. Daniel Defoe was imprisoned here in 1703, and drew on his experiences when he consigned Moll Flanders to the 'clamour, stench and nastiness' of 'that horrid place'. The prison was rebuilt in 1770, and again after it was burned by the Gordon Rioters. But in popular memory and folklore it remained a place of dread, 'a school and nursery of crime', 'an emblem of hell, and a kind of entrance into it'.[3] Prisoners were hanged on a scaffold erected in the street outside the main gate, and from Christ's Hospital the boys could hear the bell of Holy Sepulchre church tolling the hour for executions. To the north of Christ's Hospital, the prospect was equally grim. St Bartholomew's Hospital was here, adjoining the Smithfield meat market. Terrified animals driven to the market were a familiar sight for the schoolboys, and Smithfield itself was a spectacle of uproar and slaughter. Cattle and sheep were whipped across the cobbles, while stinking carcasses bled and steamed. In *Oliver Twist* Dickens described Smithfield as nearly ankle deep in filth and mire.

Located between a prison, a hospital and a slaughterhouse, Christ's Hospital has attracted an aura of myth as the 'fam'd school' of 'youthful bards'.[4] Here Samuel Taylor Coleridge and Charles Lamb were educated, and their recollections in 'Frost at Midnight', *Biographia Literaria* and 'Christ's Hospital Five and Thirty Years Ago' hark back to scenes in the 'day-spring' of their lives. In the 'cloisters dim' Coleridge, the *'inspired charity-boy'*, discovered Bowles's sonnets and made visitors pause while he recited Homer. As the myth grew over two centuries, the actuality of life in the school was overlooked or given a nostalgic glow.

For Hunt the school was an ancient English institution, with associations going back to 'the famous Whittington' and beyond, 'solid, unpretending, of good character, and free to all'.[5] But for the schoolboys it was also a place of terror, stalked by a supernatural presence called the 'Fazzer' much as Newgate Prison was haunted by the malign spirit of a black dog. The Fazzer was in fact nothing more than one of the boys, but it was also 'audacious, unknown, and frightening', and of 'supernatural fearfulness'.

Christ's Hospital had some six hundred pupils, accommodated in twelve wards or dormitories. These had 'rows of beds on each side, partitioned off, but connected with one another, and each having two boys to sleep in it'. In the middle were bins for bread, and overhead hung a large chandelier.[6] Each ward was in the care of a nurse, who was responsible for the boys' welfare. These nurses were 'almost invariably decent people', Hunt writes, and 'almost' carries some emphasis. He was later in the care of a nurse who 'conducted herself very ill, & kept us very dirty'.[7]

We can picture Hunt on his first day at school, away from home and alone for the first time. He has been examined by an apothecary, questioned about his Latin and reading, and now sits on his bed in the long ward cherishing his favourite book, a little 'History of England'. He is proud of his blue uniform but frightened by the crowds of bigger boys and their strange harsh slang: 'crug', 'crags', 'gags', 'tad', 'brassers' and 'skulking'. Bells keep ringing, and everything smells strange – the wool of his coat, scrubbed wood, and a stink from somewhere. At six o'clock he eats supper with the other boys in the Great Hall, looking up from his coarse bread ('crug') at the high windows and the huge picture of James II and his courtiers. Afterwards he ventures shyly through the cloisters, watching other groups of chattering boys, before being summoned back to the ward for prayers and then bed, still feeling hungry.

So the routine began. He would wake to the 'call of a bell' at six o'clock in summer, seven in winter, wash in cold water and dry himself with a coarse towel. At another bell he would go to breakfast (crug and watery beer), and on to school until eleven o'clock. Then came an hour's play before the bell for lunch. This was the main meal of the day, but week by week it was miserably scanty and unvaried:

Sunday: boiled beef and broth (with throat-stopping 'gags' of beef fat).
Monday: crug, butter, milk and water.
Tuesday: roast mutton – a 'small slice'.
Wednesday: crug and butter with rice milk, 'ludicrously thin' but with
    sugar, ginger or cinnamon to make it palatable.
Thursday: boiled beef and broth, again with gags of fat.
Friday: 'scanty crags' of boiled mutton and broth.
Saturday: crug and butter, and 'pease porritch'.

All the food was portioned so that appetites were dulled, not satisfied, and because there were no vegetables the boys' diet was unhealthily deficient.[8] Afternoon classes ran from one o'clock until four in the winter (five in summer), then there was crug and cheese for supper at six and, in winter, bed straight afterwards.

On Sundays long hours were passed in Christ Church, Newgate Street, where the boys were seated high up in the galleries on either side of the organ. These services were excruciatingly 'somniferous' (Hunt's word), relieved only by fidgeting and mimicking the preacher. Hunt recalls that one was famous for saying 'murracles' instead of 'miracles'. Another had only two audible phrases, with an interval of humming between them, and the boys mimicked his sermons like this: 'the dispensation of Moses, hmmm, or, Mosaic dispensation, hmmmm, was dispensed by Moses, hmmmmmm, as his Mosaic dispensation'.[9] And there was no escape. Hunt was not allowed to stay out of the school overnight except during the three-week summer holiday (this restriction encouraged some boys to go 'skulking' on adventures out of bounds). It was not long before Hunt discovered a retreat inside the school walls. On one occasion he was confined to the sick ward after scalding his legs, and enjoyed weeks of delicious recovery when he could read his books, and play the flute for his nurse and her daughter. Hunt had attracted another nurturing feminine circle, and took up a role he would adopt many times in later years: the sickly invalid, surrounded by attentive women. His frequent retreats to the sick-room also became a strategy to cope with the stresses of his clashes with authority. Repeatedly, in a pattern formed at Christ's Hospital, Hunt's most combative journalistic forays would be succeeded by a period of recuperation enclosed in 'the strong armour of sickness'.[10]

The academic structure of Christ's Hospital was divided into separate schools. The Writing and Reading Schools taught literacy, and the practical skills necessary for trade and commerce; the Mathematical and Drawing Schools trained boys for the navy and East India Company. And the Under and Upper Grammar Schools gave boys the classical education necessary at that time for careers in the law and the Church. The Upper School comprised two classes, called Little and Great Erasmus; over them were more senior scholars, known as Deputy Grecians, and at the pinnacle were the Grecians, who were destined for University.

Because Hunt could read, and already knew some Latin, he was put at first into the Under Grammar School. The master was the genial and languid Mr Field, and under his 'handsomely incompetent' tuition Hunt's 'grammar always seemed to open in the same place'.[11] He proceeded in due course to the Upper School, which was overseen by an accomplished bruiser, James Boyer,

a short stout man, inclining to punchiness, with large face and hands, an aquiline nose, long upper lip, and a sharp mouth. His eye was close and cruel. The spectacles which he wore threw a balm over it. Being a clergyman, he dressed in black, with a powdered wig. His clothes were cut short; his hands hung out of the sleeves, with tight wrist bands, as if ready for execution; and as he generally wore grey worsted stockings, very tight, with a little balustrade leg, his whole appearance presented something formidably succinct, hard, and mechanical.

With Boyer Hunt studied Homer, Cicero, Ovid, Virgil, Terence, Demosthenes and the Greek Testament. He credited Boyer with being 'a good verbal scholar

. . . conscientiously acting up to the letter of time and attention' (compare Coleridge's view that Boyer was a 'zealous and conscientious' teacher). But Hunt also suspected that Boyer was not, at heart, a teacher with a sense of vocation – devoted to the spirit, as well as the letter, of his profession. 'Few of us cared for any of the books that were taught,' Hunt recalled, 'and no pains were taken to make us do so.' He adds that he would have had pity for Boyer 'if he had taught us to do anything but fear'.[12]

In his first days at the school Hunt was timid and confused, and his stutter increased. The boys teased and mimicked his inability to speak, and in 'one fit of impatience' Boyer hit him so violently with a book that it knocked out one of his teeth. Boyer relished 'spiting' pupils, thumping and slapping, kicking and beating them. Even Coleridge, of whom Boyer allegedly thought highly, generally received 'an extra cut' at the end of a flogging because he was 'such an ugly fellow!' Hunt recalls that Boyer had a trick 'of pinching you under the chin, and by the lobes of the ears, till he made the blood come'; 'many times [he] lifted a boy off the ground' by his ears. Hunt comes close to accusing Boyer of murder: 'I have seen him beat a sickly-looking boy about the head and ears, till the poor fellow, hot, dry-eyed, and confused, seemed lost in bewilderment'. Adding that 'not long after' this same boy 'died out of his senses', Hunt remarks: 'there is no saying how far [Boyer's] treatment of the boy might have contributed to prevent a cure'.[13] If we glance back at Hunt's portrait of Boyer's thickset, 'punchy' physique, it seems to be over-laid with the shadow of Newgate Prison. Boyer's grotesquely tight stockings and wrist bands with 'hands hung out' suggest a figure trussed up in a strait-waistcoat and ready to be led to the gallows.

Boyer's viciousness was aped by senior boys. Shortly after Hunt arrived one of them tore his 'History of England' out of his hands, using a hook that he carried around to spike and steal apples, cakes and books. Older boys in the Mathematical School strolled around casually knocking over juniors who got in their way; the calculated insolence, Hunt observed, 'lay in the boy not appearing to know that such inferior creatures existed'.[14]

There were two places Hunt visited with his mother on days away from school. One was a large rambling house at Austin Friars, close to the old London Wall, the home of the wealthy merchant Godfrey Thornton and his family. Here Hunt and his mother enjoyed convivial company, good food and music. By contrast, Benjamin West's house at 14, Newman Street was a haven of calm. The moment the street door closed, the clamour of the city subsided and Hunt and his mother entered a temple of art. Passing through the hall they reached a glass door opening into West's gallery, a long, carpeted aisle lit from skylights and hung with West's sketches. Statues of Venus and Apollo were placed at a corner leading to the painting room, and here Hunt 'gener-ally found the mild and quiet artist at his work' surrounded by his pictures:

Death on the Pale Horse, The Scotch King hunting the Stag, Moses on Mount Sinai, a sketch for *Christ Healing the Sick, Sir Philip Sidney giving up the Water to the Dying Soldier, The Installation of the Knight of the Garter*. Hunt recalled that his mother's favourites were *The Deluge, Ophelia before the King and Queen* and *The Angel slaying the Army of Sennacherib*, and that she used to point out to him paintings relating to 'liberty and patriotism, and the domestic affections'. Elizabeth West would be waiting in the parlour, a small room lined with engravings and coloured prints from Rubens, Raphael and Angelica Kauffman. Hunt listened to his mother and great-aunt discussing old times in Philadelphia – the college, Benjamin Franklin, Isaac's carting, difficult Stephen Shewell, the busy wharves on the Delaware. By now Benjamin West was one of the most securely established men in London; he was settled, prosperous, and his work was sought after. Yet he never lived down the suspicion of pro-American sympathies and did not disguise his admiration for the French. At the Peace of 1802 West travelled to Paris where he met Napoleon and other revolutionaries, and he would continue an admirer long after Napoleon's defeat in 1815.

West's house and garden had been designed to capture the elegance of a Florentine villa. The gallery resembled an arcade, from which an archway between two columns with marble busts opened on to a lawn bordered with flowers. A clipped bay tree and urns holding roses expressed the classical and republican feel of the garden, and it offered a hospitable, domestic charm as well. One image we have of the building shows the West family relaxing on a summer afternoon. Pet dogs play on the lawn, doves cluster above the high windows of his painting room and the house cat keeps an eye on a robin in the bird bath. Combining domestic serenity with ideals of patriotism and freedom, the Wests' house and garden would be an enduring influence on Hunt. He would recreate its cultured ambience when he laid out his rooms and garden in Surrey Gaol and, later, when he made his home at the Vale of Health in Hampstead.[15] In all of Hunt's many homes there would be engravings, busts, books and treasured portfolios of prints – everything, in fact, that he had enjoyed at the Wests' as a boy – except the hush, the sense of seemly order, and the conspicuous wealth.

After three years Hunt rebelled against the system, against bullies (or 'brassers'), tyrannical monitors, and the odious expectation that juniors would 'fag' for seniors. Being a fag meant making an older boy's bed, cleaning his shoes, running for books and so on. Other duties were just as servile, and one of them – standing in front of an open fire to screen the older boy from the heat – amounted to torture. Hunt tells us how fagging involved demeaning entertainments, such as eating cakes adulterated with filth – 'the most disgusting humiliation [of] swallowing compounds that would sicken a ditch-reptile'. Fags at Christ's Hospital also supplied sexual favours and endured 'the most degrading and disgusting labours, the most shameless and immodest insults' and 'unnatural amusements'.[16]

Hunt's opposition to 'wanton school tyranny' caught the revolutionary spirit of the times. Many of these school confrontations were on behalf of 'a friend or a good cause', evidence of his intense, idealistic attitude to friendship as 'the most spiritual of the affections'. 'I had a delight in being attacked,' he recalled.[17] His closest friends were John Wood, a schoolboy poet, and John Rogers Pitman, later a prolific writer and editor. Another friend, Frederick Papendieck, was the son of Christopher Papendieck, a courtier. It was at their home in Spring Garden, off Charing Cross, that Hunt first heard Mozart.[18] Thomas Mitchell, who became a classical scholar, and Thomas Barnes, later editor of *The Times*, would be lifelong friends and collaborators. To them should be added James Scholefield, subsequently Professor of Greek at Cambridge, and Barron Field, son of the apothecary at the school. With Barnes, Mitchell and Pitman he would skulk out of the cloisters to go swimming in the New River or boating on the Thames (where Barnes toppled in while reading Seneca). Perhaps it was on one such escapade that Hunt heard a band playing Mozart's military air 'Non più andrai'.[19]

With these adventures came moments of platonic 'bliss' in company with particular friends: 'I loved my friend for his gentleness . . . I thought him a kind of angel'.[20] This preceded 'any maturer feeling', Hunt cautions us, and certainly there is nothing in his *Autobiography* as rampant as John Betjeman's Marlborough pash:

> Alone beside the fives-courts pacing, pacing,
> Waiting for God knows what. O stars above!
> My clothes clung tight to me, my heart was racing . . .[21]

As Hunt entered his teens his 'delightful affection' for Frederick Papendieck brought a tenderness for his friend's sister, who was in 'delicate health'. She died aged just fifteen, whereupon Hunt – by now a young man of feeling – promptly fell for the next pretty face he saw. And the next. And the next. When he looked back on these schoolboy crushes, Mozart's Cherubino came to mind. 'I was in the situation of the page in Figaro: –

> Ogni donna cangiar di colore;
> Ogni donna mi fa palpitar.'[22]

With his hot blushes and fluttering heart Hunt, too, was a kind of angel, waiting for God knows what.

Isaac's wealthy sister Elizabeth Dayrell came over from Barbados with her two daughters, Christiana and Fanny, and her sister Ann. Their visit transformed

the Hunts. Elizabeth cleared the family's debts. Isaac 'grew young again'.
Mary 'raised her head'. Cousin Christiana 'conceived a regard' for Hunt's
older brother Stephen, and on 23 July 1798 they were married at the Old
Church, St Pancras. This was 'kept secret a little while', and it became a
matter of 'honour' for Hunt to defend it.[23] Possibly Christiana was under age,
but Hunt's word 'conceived' may also explain the mystery.

Aunt Elizabeth settled in a country house south of the Thames at Merton,
and in 1795 Hunt had passed three happy summer weeks in the garden and
orchard. The food was like nothing he had tasted before. Instead of crug
and water, there was coffee, tea, 'noble hot joints, and puddings, and sweets, and
Guava jellies, and other West Indian mysteries of peppers and preserves,
and wine'.[24] Other senses were heightened too. Walking beside the River
Wandle he saw a girl as if in a vision, 'standing in the water with bare legs,
washing some linen. She turned as she was stooping, and showed a blooming
oval face with blue eyes, on either side of which flowed a profusion of flaxen
locks.'[25] He thought the girl was a 'Naiad', a 'poetical vision realized' like his
cousin Fanny who was 'a lass of fifteen, with little laughing eyes, and a mouth
like a plum'. Fanny flirted with her *petit garçon* of thirteen, and 'Cherubino'
wandered in 'a vague dream of beauty, and female cousins, and nymphs, and
green fields' unable to forget 'her plump little mouth'. When he returned to
school, Fanny gave him a locket in the shape of a heart – and then married
the young man of twenty-three to whom she had been engaged all along.
Hunt tells us that he 'wore the heart a long while'.[26]

The Hunts' other visitor from Barbados at this time, Aunt Ann, was less
welcome. Ann Courthope owned slaves on her Barbados estate, and when
she visited England she brought one of them, Samuel, as her servant. Hunt
remembered Aunt Ann as 'an elderly maiden who piqued herself on the delicacy of her hands and ankles, and made you understand how many suitors
she had refused'. Like the indolent Lady Bertram in *Mansfield Park* – who
is married to a West Indian planter – Ann cared for nothing more than 'a
becoming set-out of coffee and buttered toast . . . taken up to her in bed,
with a suitable equipage of silver and other necessaries of life'. This spoiled
woman announced that slavery was 'indispensable' to a 'lady-like establishment', as if human beings were another 'set-out' at her disposal. 'It was
frightful,' Hunt recalls, 'to hear her small mouth and little mincing tones
assert the necessity not only of slaves, but of robust corporeal punishment
to keep them to their duty.' And Samuel? Samuel knew that 'there was no
such thing as a slave in England'. Having left two wives in Barbados, he was
caught by an English maidservant, 'a pretty girl, who had manoeuvred till
she got him stuck in a corner; and he insisted upon telling us all that she
said and did'.[27]

In the earliest issues of the *Examiner* Hunt attacked 'West Indian
Merchants' who continued 'furious against abolition', brilliantly representing

their inhumanity by imagining the kind of man who could have married his aunt:

> a West Indian Planter in all his pride and despotism . . . who sees his children whip their slaves and their rocking-horses with the same emotion, and who tells you . . . when the most piteous cries interrupt the gay luxury of your repast 'It is only a few fellows I have ordered to be punished'.

Hunt's *Examiner* campaign drew on the first-hand knowledge of slavery brought home to him as a child. There was a deeper identification as well, when Hunt encouraged readers to feel that there are 'ties and families as dear in Africa', and hearts 'capable of as tender a feeling', as there are in England.[28]

His parents encouraged him to 'speculate' beyond received ideas and established opinions: he was grateful for visits to a synagogue that helped 'universalize' his spiritual outlook, and was more responsive to 'unbigoted' religion than to the 'doctrine of eternal punishment'.[29] That sounds unremarkable – a bright schoolboy was being encouraged to think. But 'speculate' was also a buzz word of the 1790s: it signalled a willingness to embrace the daring, dangerous, blasphemous ideas that erupted into consciousness during the French Revolution. 'At that early period,' Hunt writes in a draft of his *Autobiography*,

> owing doubtless to what I heard at home, to the contradictions I already began to feel elsewhere, & perhaps in some degree to the tempest of the French Revolution, which was then at its height, & was destined to shake up the whole mind of the world, I unquestionably felt inclined to be an innovator; to redress wrongs; and reconcile discords . . .[30]

Just outside the gates of Christ's Hospital was the bustling centre of the London book trade. A short walk would take Hunt to Paternoster Row – he always called it '*book-street*' – and St Paul's Churchyard where the radical bookseller Joseph Johnson had his premises.[31] The print and bookshops teemed with pamphlets and broadsides about the French Revolution: his father's *Rights of Englishmen*, Paine's *Rights of Man*, Burke's *Reflections on the Revolution*, Wollstonecraft's *Vindication of the Rights of Man* and *Vindication of the Rights of Woman*, and Godwin's *Political Justice* all appeared on bookstalls within yards of the school.

Innovation was the order of the day and Christ's Hospital – orthodox, high Tory – could not remain isolated from the storms raging around its ancient walls. Directly opposite the school on Newgate Street was the Salutation and Cat tavern. Here the old bluecoats Coleridge, Lamb and Dyer whiled away evenings with pipes, tobacco, Egghot, Welsh Rabbits and endless talk of poetry, metaphysics, and plans to found the idealistic community of Pantisocracy in

Pennsylvania. Reports of the mind-shaking scheme swept across Newgate Street into the school: 'Col gave a toast – listen, Hunt, – "America! Health! Republicanism!"' 'Col says he loves his *Friend*, Hunt, and such as *he* is, all mankind are or *might be*!'

Right in front of Hunt, experienced day by day, were the petty tyrannies, slavery and violence of his own microcosm, Christ's Hospital, 'a system of alternate slavery and tyranny, fitted to make alternate slaves and tyrants in the political world'. Hunt came to see how naturally the schoolboy bully grows into the 'flourishing man of the world', while the one-time fag strings along as his political fixer, private secretary and 'spin-doctor':

> instead of carrying his master on his back, and eating cakes steeped in a gutter, he helps him through the dirt of politics, canvasses and votes at his bidding, or at best makes a servile bargain of what talent he may possess, screens every powerful delinquent, persecutes every powerless adversary, makes a private, perhaps a public, jest of enthusiasm, tramples in all that he can upon the community, is flourishing, scornful, hateful, shallow, and unhappy.

Hunt would refer to memories of his schooldays many times in explaining the ills of society at large. Fortunately, his schoolboy reading had alerted him to a very different network of influence: England's poets – Chaucer, Spenser, Shakespeare and Milton – had been nurtured 'under a different system' and had never endured school as a 'tyranny within a tyranny'.[32] English poetry and English liberties were inseparable.

Boyer bored and terrified him, but there remained the thrill of delving into three forbidden books: Lemprière's *Classical Dictionary*, Tooke's *Pantheon* and Spence's *Polymetis*. The *Pantheon* was a special favourite because it contained an engraving of Venus that looked like the nurse's daughter. Hunt spent hours trying to copy it, dreaming of the 'nymph' in the sick ward 'lifting her arms to tie / Her locks into a flowing knot'.[33] Lemprière, Tooke and Spence were banned because they were written in English 'so that nothing . . . might be out of the reach of the young scholar's understanding'.[34] This was scandalous because it meant that young scholars like Hunt and, later, Keats, who also enjoyed these books, could find out about classical literature and myth without the discipline of mastering the original languages (at Shelley's Eton, by contrast, the 'Eton Latin Grammar' was written in Latin). The *Classical Dictionary*, *Pantheon* and *Polymetis* were suspect for making high classical culture available in vernacular English, and giving anyone who could read 'access' to knowledge hitherto the preserve of an élite. And in the panicky 1790s, knowledge of the classics was dangerous: while the 'free doctrines' of classical republicanism resounded in the 'alarming echo of them struck by the French Revolution', in Lemprière Hunt read of the 'celebrated, brave, learned' tyrannicide Caius Cassius.[35] The *Classical Dictionary* was in fact a primer in sedition.

When Hunt tired of his Latin grammar and turned to Lemprière or Tooke, he was claiming the liberty to imagine and enjoy the classics more democratically. In later years he would write poems in that spirit, combining classical subjects with erotic and liberal themes, and in the indignant response of the critics he heard an echo of Boyer's incandescent rage on discovering that he had a copy of the *Pantheon* open under his desk.

Lemprière let Hunt dream of being elsewhere, beyond the schoolrooms and the ward, and the English poets were likewise 'a never-ceasing consolation'. The association of poetry and freedom stayed with him, and in his journalism Hunt would often recruit Chaucer, Spenser, Shakespeare and Milton as liberal heroes, persuaded that their imaginative genius had never been tainted by the 'induced selfishness' of the public school system. The first publication of *Cooke's Pocket Edition of Select Poets* was a red-letter day. This was in 1794, when Hunt was almost ten years old:

> How I loved those little sixpenny numbers containing whole poets! I doated on their size; I doated on their type, on their ornaments, on their wrappers containing lists of other poets, and on the engravings from Kirk. I bought them over and over again, and used to get up select sets, which disappeared like buttered crumpets; for I could resist neither giving them away, nor possessing them. When the master tormented me, when I used to hate and loathe the sight of Homer, and Demosthenes, and Cicero, I would comfort myself with thinking of the sixpence in my pocket, with which I should go out to Paternoster-row, when school was over, and buy another number of an English poet.[36]

The idea of Cooke's sixpenny volumes as comfort food suggests how Hunt's association of language with eating had developed. Out of hours he savoured Spenser, Collins and Gray, and subscribed to the Minerva Library in nearby Leadenhall Street – for he was an insatiable 'glutton of novels'.[37] Now that he was separated from his family, books and poems he could 'doat' on helped compensate for the maternal love formerly lavished upon him. They drew to him the attention and affection his parents had once given him, and were a temptation overcoming all scruples because they were associated with self-nurturing and the desire to please others.

In a draft for his *Autobiography*, Hunt recalls impulsively giving away a book that didn't belong to him: 'I made a present of it,' he writes; 'the wish to give was irresistible; & I gave'. When the rightful owner of the book accused him of theft, Hunt was 'ashamed; very sorry; very full of remorse'. But the schoolfellow's complaints became scornful, bringing other boys who sided 'with the offender', 'roused' his self-respect, and eventually made him feel in the right. Looking back, Hunt saw that this had been 'an ill & dangerous process'. He was beyond reproach: 'I left the school-room that morning with a partic- ular air of self-resumption, putting on my gloves at the door, & cherishing a book under my arm, as if nothing had happened'.[38] Here, in a Christ's Hospital anecdote, was a pattern of behaviour that persisted for the rest of Hunt's life. As an adult he often regarded others' money and property as sustenance for him, rightfully at his disposal, like the buttered crumpets and books he handed round the table for all to enjoy. This attitude, formed early, strained many of his friendships although, more positively, Hunt's extraordinary capacity for 'self-resumption' would enable him to endure and survive illness, prosecu- tions, imprisonment, domestic unhappiness and long years of poverty.

By 1794, aged ten, Hunt was writing his own poetry. His first poem honoured the Duke of York's 'victory' at Dunkirk in July 1794 – and, having written it, he was mortified to discover that the skirmish was in fact one more defeat in a protracted rout of British troops. Undaunted, Hunt embarked on ambitious imitations of admired poets such as Spenser and Thomson, and completed a long poem, 'Thor', in Latin. At twelve years old he wrote 'Macbeth; or, The Ill Effects of Ambition', a melodramatic lyric of 'struggling passions'. Then in September 1798 Coleridge published 'Frost at Midnight' in his *Fears in Solitude* pamphlet. Hunt was among the first to read this when it appeared in Joseph Johnson's bookshop, and years later would recall how Coleridge had been a 'stimulus to the literary ambitions of his school-fellows'.[39]

At the centre of Coleridge's poem were memories of Christ's Hospital. Coleridge's yearning for companionship and home chimed with Hunt's own feelings: the 'stern preceptor's face' brought before him Boyer's cruel eyes, and the lines where Coleridge remembered how he was

> reared
> In the great city, pent 'mid cloisters dim,
> And saw nought lovely but the sky and stars[40]

spoke so powerfully to Hunt that he began to think of a poem of his own that might emulate what Coleridge had done. In 'Remembered Friendship' Hunt wrote of his most deeply felt experiences at the school: his friendships, his delight in classical mythology, and moments that might rival 'Frost at Midnight' such as the prospect from the ward window, when,

> for a while, before the gentle sweets
> Of sleep had clos'd our eyes, how oft we lay
> Admiring thro' the casement open'd wide
> The spangled glories of the sky . . .[41]

One glory was the moon 'bursting forth' from clouds, likened in Hunt's poem to a vision of 'love resistless' and the birth of Venus: 'So Cytherea from the frothy wave / Rose in luxuriant beauty'. In due course Hunt's vision of Venus 'thro' the casement open'd wide' may have helped Keats to the conclusion of his 'Ode to Psyche':

> A bright torch, and a casement ope at night,
> To let the warm Love in![42]

Keats's lines are warm with human intimacy – a reminder, perhaps, of the presence of his beloved Fanny Brawne who was living just next door at Wentworth Place. Hunt's schoolboy lines about Cytherea and the 'frothy wave' may seem remote from this neighbourhood of Hampstead, but Keats's copy of the third edition of Hunt's *Juvenilia*, with 'Remembered Friendship' on page twenty-five, was on his bookshelf.

FOUR

JUVENILIA

For eight years Christ's Hospital was Hunt's home, and then on 20 November 1799 everything changed. Now fifteen, he had to quit the old cloisters, school-rooms and wards and enter the world beyond. His stammer made it impossible for him to become a senior pupil or 'Grecian', and there were pressures from home too. The war with France and poor harvests had pushed up the price of food, making money even tighter in the Hunt family. His mother hoped her 'steady sensible good boy' would quickly settle into a job.[1] But Hunt was reluctant to move on, and missed no opportunity of slipping back to school to visit his friends, his nurse and her daughter. Aunt Elizabeth had died shortly before, so there was no prospect of resuming his idyllic vacation life at Merton.

Hunt's brothers were productively employed. John had been apprenticed to the printer Henry Reynell for seven years, and once stood for so long in a cold printing-house that he made himself ill 'and swelled so much that he could not sit down'.[2] His fellow-apprentice was Henry's son Carew Henry Reynell. Anticipating freedom to set up his own business, John married Sally Hoole Hammond on 17 October 1797 at St Mary's, Lambeth (Carew Reynell had married Sally's sister Anne Hammond on 2 June).[3] Robert Hunt was apprenticed to an engraver of pictures, and Stephen was making his way in the law. As the executor of Aunt Elizabeth's will, Stephen stood to 'have half her property' and was 'awaiting remittances from Barbadoes'.[4] He bought a large house in Great Ormond Street.

It was time for Hunt to earn a living as well, and he tried shadowing each brother in turn. He was almost inclined to 'discuss possibilities' with a master printer, but had been more attracted by the thought of servant girls in the printer's kitchen than the chance of a job. When familiarising himself with engraving he never got as far as holding a burin, and he passed the hours in Stephen's law office scribbling poems on the blotting paper. 'I proclaimed aloud to my family, that I was fit to be nothing but an author.'[5]

At this time Hunt lived with his parents at Prince's Street, off Bedford Row, Holborn, close to Gray's Inn and Lincoln's Inn Fields. A walk along Holborn brought him to his schoolboy haunts, and *'book-street'* where he was already well known. At night he sat up with a candle and a pot of coffee to write poems, and lay in bed until the next afternoon. He would saunter out to the bookstalls until it was time to slip into Christ's Hospital to drink tea, and then back home to his writing-desk and his poems. Isaac and Mary encouraged him, proud at the amount he contrived to read and write during the odd hours. On his excursions in the city, and in his long nights of poetry, Hunt was also experiencing anxieties shared by other adolescents.[6]

In a draft passage for his *Autobiography* Hunt mentions how 'fine forms and enchanting countenances' would kindle 'feelings, which nature prompted'. There were some 50,000 prostitutes in Georgian London, of all ages and from all levels of society. It was inevitable that on his wanderings through London Hunt would encounter them, and his earliest sketches for his *Autobiography* had been surprisingly frank about these sexual experiences. Many prostitutes were children, like the 'youthful harlot' of William Blake's poem 'London' or the orphan teenager Ann with whom the young Thomas De Quincey took shelter when a homeless runaway. As De Quincey's account makes clear, Ann was one of a large community of prostitutes with whom he had 'fallen in' as a walker of the streets himself. Hunt's recollection is not as explicit as De Quincey's although the drafts of his *Autobiography* include a curious memory of walking the city all night, from Knightsbridge village in the west across to the Barbican beyond St Paul's. He traversed Oxford Street, where De Quincey's Ann worked at night, then circled back to Covent Garden, the Drury Lane theatre, and down to one of the bridges where wretchedly poor people huddled together. Here he watched 'the barges coming up with their black bodies & the lights in them, looking like the monsters with fiery eyes'. 'I shall never forget that night,' he mused long afterwards, 'because so many objects were new to me.' Those monsters with fiery eyes resembled a night-stalking Mantichora, looming out of the darkness as he passed furtively from street to square, excited and ashamed and unable to return home.[7]

Hunt called the London prostitutes 'visions from Tooke's Pantheon'. What in his schooldays had been titillating glimpses of a naked Venus now flared into embodiments of desire. Depictions of women as classical 'goddesses' were a popular kind of soft pornography, caricatured by cartoonists like James Gillray and exploited by Nelson's Lady Hamilton in her erotic 'attitudes' from classical myth. Down at street level a French visitor described English prostitutes ecstatically as 'les plus ravissantes créatures du monde', and likened them to classical sculptures by Praxiteles and Phidias.[8] Hunt's awareness that his own sexual urges were also 'felt by millions' stayed with him into adult life, and became a key theme in his journalism about sexual equality. He set about reforming a hypocritical society that condemned sexual energy yet tolerated – and even encouraged – prostitution and the degradation associated with it. Like Blake and D. H.

Lawrence, Hunt had seen and understood 'the strange mass of inconsistency and injustice, of assumed strength & happiness, & real weakness & care' that made up contemporary life.[9]

In 1800 Britain had been at war with France for seven years. Just two years previously, the rebellion of Wolfe Tone's United Irishmen was co-ordinated with help from the French, and only narrowly defeated. The Act of Union was intended to secure the situation by integrating Ireland constitutionally with England. Instead, it initiated two centuries of struggle to recover Irish independence, a struggle in which Hunt – who believed himself descended from the Irish – was to take close interest. Napoleon's run of victories seemed unstoppable, and news was expected at any moment that his army had crossed the Channel and landed on the coast of Kent. James Gillray's cartoon *The Promis'd Horrors of the French Invasion* showed London with guillotines busy and streets flowing with blood. To boost morale, Robert Barker's famous Panorama at Leicester Square depicted 'a correct VIEW of LORD NELSON'S VICTORY at the NILE' from '10 in the Morning till Dusk'. Housed in a rotunda building, the panorama gave an all-embracing 360-degree re-enactment of the naval battle of August 1798, 'lighted only by the fire from the ships, and those blown up and burning, producing an effect seldom seen by the oldest seamen'. In Fleet Street a rival representation of 'the glorious BATTLE of the NILE' promised as a special attraction 'the blowing up of the French Admiral's ship' (the flagship *L'Orient*) and, as a side-show, designed by Mr Turner, 'a truly grand and awful Representation of a STORM AT SEA'.[10] Shows like these, advertised on the front page of *The Times*, were the talk of the town and doubtless they attracted Hunt too. On the bookstalls he turned over new publications such as *The Secret Annals of the Revolution* and William Blair's 'Essay on the Anti-Venereal Effects of Nitrous Oxide'. William Godwin's new historical novel *St. Leon* had just appeared, along with fresh editions of favourite poems like James Beattie's *The Minstrel*, Erasmus Darwin's *Botanic Garden*, and anonymous curiosities such as *Lyrical Ballads, with a few Other Poems* published by Mr Arch in Gracechurch Street. In other ways, too, the horizons of Hunt's cultural life were growing.

Playing to popular interest in Egypt after the Battle of the Nile, on Monday, 11 March 1800 the Theatre Royal in Drury Lane staged Andrew Franklin's Comic Opera *The Egyptian Festival* featuring the comedian Jack Bannister. Under Sheridan's management the Drury Lane theatre had been refurbished, and now boasted a gigantic auditorium that could seat some 3,600. People from all walks of life were eager theatre-goers: princes and nobility, gentry and citizens were accommodated in private boxes, galleries and the pit, so that the theatre contained a cross-section of London society. The house was brightly lit with oil lamps and chandeliers, and with a full audience the heat and uproar were overwhelming. Catcalls and boos, applause and hisses mingled with the orchestra's music and the cries of orange-sellers. As the curtain rose for *The Egyptian Festival*, the fifteen-year-old Hunt, at his first play, saw elaborate scenery depicting the Bay of Alexandria and, in the background, the blazing beacon fire of the Pharos – one of the ancient wonders of the world. The setting and story were timely and patriotic, telling of how a tyrant was stripped of power, lovers were made happy, and the wrongs of the oppressed put right.[11] Next morning the reviews praised the scenery as 'most striking'; the music was 'pathetic, lively, grave, and gay', but the dialogue 'extremely dull and uninteresting'.[12] Hunt, who had never seen anything like *The Egyptian Festival* before, was enchanted by Bannister's comic acting in the character of Longbow. Many years later he recalled 'excellent Jack Bannister' as if he had seen John Bull himself: 'a handsome specimen of the best kind of Englishman, – jovial, manly, good-humoured, unaffected, with a great deal of whim and drollery', who in later life had 'settled down into a good English gout'.[13] In the weeks following his visit to *The Egyptian Festival* Hunt was frequently at performances of comedies by dramatists like Frederic Reynolds and Thomas Dibdin, entertained by the actors' 'grimaces', 'grins' and 'chatterings' but puzzled to find that when he got back home he couldn't recall a single word.[14] These first glimpses of the London stage encouraged Hunt to set about reforming the grotesque gestures and distorted delivery that passed for acting. Over the next few years he would emerge as the most influential theatre critic of the age.

The excitement of playgoing was accompanied by a growing confidence in his poetic talent. Unlike Coleridge, at Christ's Hospital Hunt had not been included in Boyer's 'Liber Aureus' of aspirant poets. But, shortly after leaving the school, his poems started to appear regularly in London journals. In July 1800 the publisher Richard Phillips launched an educational magazine, the *Monthly Preceptor, or Juvenile Library*, which advertised a monthly prize for poems and essays. Hunt was gripped by this opportunity to display his literary talents and, encouraged by Isaac, he submitted an essay on history and biography for the first issue. He made his mark immediately. Eagerly turning over the pages he saw the announcement that 'Master HENRY LEIGH HUNT, aged 15, educated at Christ's Hospital' had gained fourth prize – a copy of '*Dr. Knox's Essays*'.[15] It is worthwhile pausing to investigate this book – Alexander Knox's recently published *Essays on the Political Circumstances of Ireland* – for it set out opinions and arguments that influenced Hunt's view of Irish affairs. Published at 'the Anti-Jacobin Press' Knox's book was, unsurprisingly, a furious denunciation of the United Irishmen, those 'systematic traitors' who had attempted to subvert 'the happy

Constitution': 'Good, easy, undesigning men, sit quietly at their fire-sides,' Knox warned, 'while the guileful anarchists are diffusing their principles, and maturing their schemes, of insurrection and revolution.'[16] But Knox was not just a rabid anti-Jacobin. As an Irishman descended from Scottish planters, he took care to disentangle 'the mischievous designs' of the United Irishmen from the legitimate political claims of the Irish Catholics. If the climate of '*menace*' and '*alarm*' could be removed, he suggested, Catholic emancipation would be achieved through a hands-off process of 'silent, but resistless, energy of good sense and growing benevolence'.[17] And that was the 'Irish problem' sorted. Bizarrely mingling alarm and complacency, Knox came to represent for Hunt a thoroughly wrong-headed approach to Ireland. In later years Hunt would make brilliant use of this prize volume, albeit in a way that the editors of the *Monthly Preceptor* would not have anticipated or approved.

Issues two and three of the *Monthly Preceptor* noticed a 'very excellent and superior translation from Master H. L. Hunt' and a 'commendable essay'. Triumph came in issue five, when Hunt won the first prize of books to the value of three guineas for a translation of Horace's ode on the theme of the virtuous life. Some sense of the value of that prize can be gained from a comparison with prices in Elizabeth West's cash book, which records her cook as receiving five guineas for six months' employment.

Hunt's translation shows that he had mastered the mild surprises of eighteenth-century poetic diction. Mountains have 'proud summits', streams 'glide', the Zephyr is a 'refreshing breeze', the sun has a 'parching ray', and so on. At the age of fifteen, Hunt shows skill rather than the startling originality of a young poet who has found his distinctive voice. There are a few lines that may have arisen from Hunt's recent experiences as he walked around London,

> And free from care, too distant stray'd
> Within its dark embowr'ing shade;
> The prowling wolf, with blood-shot eye,
> Unarm'd beheld me wand'ring nigh;
> And, while I shook in silent dread,
> With howls the rav'ning monster fled!

This passage is conventional enough in many respects, but we can recognise 'the grim terror of the wood' as fitting into a pattern in Hunt where fiery eyes and a predatory monster are associated with anxieties and troubling temptations. The setting for this nightmare confrontation is a 'dark embowr'ing shade' – a scene that will reappear in Hunt's later poems at moments when he tests individual passion and liberty against social and religious constraints.

By this time the *Monthly Preceptor*'s competitions were drawing scores of entries from all over Britain and Ireland. Among the prizewinners were some who later became famous: a 'T. L. Peacock' received an 'Extra Prize' for a poem, and one 'Master Thomas Quincy' (not yet walking the streets of London with Ann) sent in a winning translation from Cicero. Hunt was already in distinguished company, and the judges had indeed noticed something impressive in his translation from Horace. Hunt himself was in no doubt that his poem was out of the common run, and when he entered it for the competition, he enclosed a letter explaining why:

> Gentlemen,
> I herewith transmit you my unassisted translation of the before mentioned passage from Horace, the success of which my warmest wishes must naturally attend. If its freedom and diffuseness are contrary to the design you hold out in proposing a *translation*, I must here beg leave to apologise for it, (the only manner in which I believe it is possible) by referring to the observation which the ingenious Mr. Mickle has made in his preface to his Lusiad, that when we attempt a close and literal translation of the poet, it is impossible to preserve the poetical and harmonious beauties of the original: which brings to my remembrance an assertion of M. de Voltaire, in which he very aptly observes, when speaking of a bad or good translation, 'the letter, it may be truly said, killeth, but the spirit giveth life'.
> I am, Gentlemen,
> Your very obliged humble servant,
> J. H. L. Hunt.

Hunt's display of precociousness carries through into a postscript:

> To the above authorities let me add the still higher one of Horace himself, who says, in his Art of Poetry, 'Nec verbum verbo curabis reddere sibus interpres'.

'The translator should not translate literally, word for word.' At the very start of his writing career Hunt was claiming a creative 'freedom and diffuseness', and in years to come this spirit would prove a controversial characteristic of his original poetry. The young poet was already finding his way.

Hunt's competition successes continued, bringing him in December 1800 a silver medal for an essay 'On Humanity to the Brute Creation as a Moral and Christian Duty'. In this and other pieces written after leaving Christ's Hospital, Hunt gained experience and encouragement that would help his career as a journalist. As significant in the longer term was the *Monthly Preceptor*'s willingness to publish his poems, independent of the competition.

One of these was 'Retirement', a meditative exercise in rhyming couplets, featuring moralised figures like 'Contemplation', 'pois'nous Envy' and 'loud Contention'. Between 1700 and 1800 innumerable poems on contemplative retirement had been published and Hunt's was only the latest variation on a well-tried theme. What impresses about 'Retirement' is Hunt's attempt to emulate William Collins's celebrated 'Ode to Evening', evoking a mood of twilight reverie when 'honied flow'rs . . . scent the floating hours'. Alongside conventional representations of virtues and vices are hints of real life: a dread of Isaac's fondness for claret in 'hot Intemp'rance', mingled with scenes from the debtors' prison in 'Pity [turning] dewy eyes, / Where gasping Penury unfriended lies'.

Hunt's hunger for literary achievement was rivalled only by his father's ambitions. Elated by successes in the *Monthly Preceptor*, Isaac now set about collecting his son's poems with a view to publishing them as a book. Publishers might be reluctant to take a risk on an unknown 'Master H. L. Hunt', but Isaac had already seen how to turn this difficulty to advantage. Publication would depend upon finding subscribers willing to pay in advance for the book, underwriting the production costs in return for grateful acknowledgement in the opening pages. This was a common practice at the time. Charlotte Smith's best-selling *Elegiac Sonnets* had been phenomenally successful in promoting a literary career by appealing to her readers' charity. Her spendthrift husband, Benjamin, had been imprisoned for debt in King's Bench Prison, where Isaac could have met the resourceful Charlotte writing to keep her large family afloat. A gifted child might be a similar icon of needy sensibility. It would take effort and tact, but, presented carefully, the plight of the youthful poet might open the doors of the wealthy and powerful to Isaac once again, so restoring the fortunes and prestige of the family. And his youngest son would be launched into public life.

James Whiting, a printer in Finsbury Place, priced the book at six shillings a copy. Helped by Elizabeth and Benjamin West, Isaac and Mary now set about recruiting subscribers. Mary called on friends and looked up acquaintances. Isaac lost no time in dispatching letters to politicians, public figures and the aristocracy, and then chased contacts among booksellers and in the Church. Elizabeth West trawled the art world, and Benjamin put word around in the Royal Academy. By spring 1800 they had assembled an extraordinary list of over eight hundred subscribers, including painters and publishers, writers and politicians, clergymen and dissenters, scientists, lawyers, bankers and diplomats. The book was published in March 1801 as *Juvenilia; or, a Collection of Poems* and, on opening it, Hunt's first readers would have seen a list of subscribers running over fifteen double-columned pages. For Edmund Blunden the subscription list was fittingly described as Isaac's 'masterpiece', an apotheosis of eighteenth-century networking that draws in individuals – eminent, rich, influential, liberal, or merely generous – from all areas of contemporary life.

The importance of painting and the Royal Academy to Hunt is underlined by some twenty distinguished Academicians who subscribed to his book. Among them are Thomas Banks, sculptor, and James Barry, the quarrelsome Professor of Painting from 1782 until his expulsion in 1799. Graceful notice is given to Sir William Beechey, styled 'Portrait Painter to her Majesty', and listed here too is John Russell, who was portrait painter in crayons to the King and the Prince of Wales. Francesco Bartollozi, who engraved the frontispiece to *Juvenilia*, was a subscriber; so too was the American historical painter John Singleton Copley. A contribution came from Robert Bowyer, 'Miniature Painter to the King', who would engrave Hunt's portrait for the third edition of *Juvenilia*. Also present are Richard Cosway, miniaturist, Swedenborgian and animal magnetist; Thomas Daniell, landscape painter; Henry Fuseli, close friend of William Blake and Mary Wollstonecraft; John Hoppner and his rival Thomas Lawrence, portrait artists; John Landseer, engraver and father of Sir Edwin Landseer the Victorian animal painter; George Stubbs, painter of animals and anatomist; and Thomas Stothard whom Turner called 'the Giotto of England'. Representing another branch of the arts was James Wyatt the architect, who in 1795 had erected William Beckford's gothic Fonthill Abbey near Bath. Benjamin West, the President of the Academy, his wife Elizabeth, and sons Raphael and Benjamin were all donors.

Another name on the list is John Boydell (not an RA) whom Sir Joshua Reynolds once toasted as 'the Commercial Mycaenas of England'. In 1789 Boydell had set up the 'Shakespeare Gallery', to which many RAs contributed, and he also made a best-selling engraving of West's famous historical painting, *The Death of General Wolfe*. West's controversial pupil Colonel John Trumbull, the American patriot, painter and suspected spy, paid his six shillings too.[18]

From the publishing world came well-known booksellers like Thomas Cadell, John Cuthell, John Hatchard, George Kearsley and Charles Rivington III, along with some names that deserve more particular notice: John and Arthur Arch, booksellers in Gracechurch Street, who had recently published Wordsworth and Coleridge's *Lyrical Ballads*; Joseph Johnson, the Unitarian bookseller in St Paul's Churchyard; John Murray II, soon to be the publisher of Lord Byron and of Hunt's *Story of Rimini*; James Perry, founder of the *European Magazine*, and editor and owner of the *Morning Chronicle*; Richard Phillips, publisher of the *Monthly Magazine* and the *Monthly Preceptor*. One subscriber in this group, John Scott, was employed in the War Office, the source of several subscriptions, where Hunt himself would shortly be employed. In later years Scott would attack John Lockhart for his harsh criticism of Hunt in the 'Cockney School' essays, leading to a duel at Chalk Farm in which Scott was mortally wounded. But in 1800 this controversy lay two decades in the future.

Writers, lawyers and politicians listed in the first edition of *Juvenilia* include George Dyer, Christ's Hospital bluecoat, poet and pamphleteer; William Gifford, star satirist of the *Anti-Jacobin*; Sir Philip Francis, reputed author of the 'Junius' letters; Edward Jerningham, poet; John Lamb, brother of Charles; and Henry Pye, the Poet Laureate. The radical William Cobbett subscribed for twelve copies. The culture of dissent is represented by John Disney, Unitarian and friend of Joseph Priestley; Gilbert Wakefield, Unitarian, classicist and reformer; and John Horne Tooke, politician and philologist. Also present are Thomas Erskine, the lawyer who defended the reformists at the treason trials in 1794; Sir Francis Baring, the most successful financier of the day, and Abraham Newland, chief cashier at the Bank of England. Another notable London figure is Patrick Colquhoun, magistrate, whose survey had estimated the number of prostitutes working in the city. Numerous civic and state officers and dignitaries contributed: the Chamberlain and Aldermen of London, and representatives of the British Museum, the City Chamber, the Navy Office, the Pay Office, the Police Office, the Seal Office, the Secretary of State's Office, the Treasury, the Office for Trade and Plantations, and the War Office.

The Hunts' transatlantic links raised funds from New Providence, New York, Rhode Island and Baltimore. Long-lost brother Isaac subscribed from Philadelphia although the Shewell branches of the family, who were aware of Hunt's ambitions as a writer, evidently chose not to contribute. From closer to home subscriptions came from Rufus King, the American Ambassador in London, and Mr Williams the American Consul.

Among the many leading scientists and physicians in the list of subscribers are Robert Batty, obstetrician; Thomas Dale, an authority on erysipelas or 'St Anthony's Fire', from which Hunt suffered; John Mason Good, Unitarian, of Guy's Hospital; John Robert Hooper, medical writer; John Lettsom, founder of the Medical Society; and William Murdock, the inventor of coal-gas lighting and chief engineer at Boulton and Watt's Soho foundry near Birmingham.

Ten subscribers came from Christ's Hospital, including Arthur Trollope, the headmaster. James Boyer did not support his former pupil. Christopher Papendieck of Windsor, father of Hunt's school friend Frederick, signed for six copies; Barron Field, another school friend, took one; James Henry Leigh forwarded six shillings, as did James Whiting the printer. Prominently listed was 'Hunt, Isaac, M. A. of the Universities of Philadelphia and New York'.

These are only some of the many well-known individuals who subscribed to the first edition of *Juvenilia*. Launching the book with such a tremendous fanfare led its author to believe, with understandable pride and pleasure, that he had 'arrived' on the literary scene. In some respects a gathering-in of the great, the subscription list also represented a reservoir of goodwill touching all shores of contemporary political opinion: whichever way events now flowed, Hunt would be able to turn to one patron or another for support. The remarkable subscription list draws together the wide variety of figures who over the years had been involved with the family's wayward fortunes. And the poems themselves reveal Hunt trying to come to terms with those mingled experiences too.

The contents of *Juvenilia* are organised in sections so as to display Hunt's mastery of different poetic forms: sonnets, pastorals, elegies, odes, hymns and Spenserian allegory. There are translations from Anacreon and Horace, including his prize poem. The section called 'Miscellanies' includes 'Retirement', and two poems, 'Remembered Friendship' and 'Christ's Hospital', recalling the school which is now idealised as the 'quiet haunt' of 'youthful bards' (there is no mention of Boyer and his thrashings). Public themes appear in 'The Negro Boy, A Ballad' (an anti-slavery poem) and the 'Epitaph on Robespierre'. Two poems deal with British patriotism and the Napoleonic threat: 'Written at the Time of the War in Switzerland', dating from 1798, and 'Speech of Caractacus to Claudius Caesar', a confrontation depicted in Thomas Banks's first marble sculpture.[19] The 'Progress of Painting', an irregular ode with notes, salutes contemporary academicians James Barry, Henry Fuseli and Benjamin West. Also among the contents are poems imitating or emulating Samuel Johnson, Thomas Gray, the ancient Celtic genius Ossian, Alexander Pope, William Collins, James Thomson and Edmund Spenser.

Juvenilia announced a gifted prodigy who was already matching himself with England's greatest poets. Two of the 'Pastorals' are dedicated to prominent subscribers, the Earl of Guildford and Thomas Erskine. And, probably at Isaac's urging, the book was dedicated 'To the Hon. James Henry Leigh', nephew of the Duke of Chandos and Isaac's former pupil, in gratitude for the Hunt family's 'many obligations'. With that background in place, we can begin to see that *Juvenilia* is more complicated, more disturbing, and much more interesting than a mere youthful *tour de force*.

While *Juvenilia* gives us a sense of Hunt's accomplishment as a writer its dedication was a reminder of his father's many difficulties (including the Trumbull affair, and the Duke of Chandos's faltering support). The frontispiece illustrates the dismal scene from 'Retirement' where 'gasping Penury unfriended lies', and this figure of disappointment looms ominously over the book, which is itself haunted by the fear of dissipated potential and lost promise. Painted by Benjamin West's son Raphael, and engraved by West's fellow-Academician Francesco Bartollozi, the prostrated figure in a rat-infested garret resembles Romantic images of Thomas Chatterton, the archetype of neglected and suicidal genius. Two opening poems in the collection,

'Macbeth; or, the Ill Effects of Ambition' and 'Content', develop the theme of 'struggling passions' and 'fierce desire' and the contrasting attractions of a peaceful, pastoral retreat. Similarly, 'Retirement, or the Golden Mean' associates 'hot Intemp'rance' with 'mad Ambition', and contrasts both with pastoral repose and 'Chearfulness'. Appearing so early in his poetry in relation to intemperance and the perils of ambition, the idea of 'Chearfulness' would acquire a complex force in Hunt's later writings. In *Juvenilia* 'Chearfulness' is associated with everything the Hunt family had not enjoyed: 'sufficiency, content, and health' allied to a 'golden mean' of temperate behaviour, and an idealised, nurturing friendship which forms the subject of four poems in the book. Gathered behind a list of illustrious subscribers, or friends in kind, Hunt's poems reveal him trying to come to terms with his life up to now, and in particular with his extraordinary but volatile father and his West Indian inheritance.

The book concludes with a long ambitious poem, *The Palace of Pleasure*, in which family history looms large. This imitation of Spenser's allegorical romance, *The Faerie Queene*, deliberately adopts Spenser's curious antique language in words such as 'Bale' (misery), 'Imp' (child) and 'Leman' (mistress or concubine) with the aim of appearing 'more like the original' in its 'unstudied harmony and simplicity of nature'. *The Palace of Pleasure* tells how 'a valiant knight', Sir Guyon, is snatched away by 'airy sylphs' to a fabulous palace where 'The Fairy Pleasure' reclines her seductively 'dazzling form'. Sir Guyon is taken directly from the Second Book of Spenser's *Faerie Queene*, where his adventures climax in a testing encounter with the 'faire Enchauntresse' Acrasia in her sensual 'Bowre of blis'. Hunt's Guyon is similarly tempted by various allegorical figures like 'Delicacy soft with languid eye', and 'Young Wantonness', whose 'red and fiery eyne' are like the 'fiery eyes' Hunt had seen burning on the darkened Thames. Soon Pleasure begins to take on a daemonic aspect. Bacchus's 'intoxicating bowl' is revealed as 'poison', and Guyon is precipitated into a desert of repentance where he is assailed by 'imps from hell' and 'righteous Justice'. Rescue comes from the allegorical figure of 'Content' and her followers ('Temp'rance', 'Repentance', 'Grave Wisdom, chearful Health, and Peace'), through whom the knight is returned to a sublime northern scene of 'rocky steeps' where, restored to himself, he pursues his 'advent'rous way' in 'Majesty severe'.

But Spenser is not Hunt's only source. The landscape of 'sinful pleasure' – the 'hot bosom of the Passions' – which ensnares Guyon resembles the sun-beaten island of Barbados:

> There is, ywashed by the murm'ring main,
> A Fairy land, yclept Temptations Isle,
> So fair, it seem'd as Eden there had lain,
> Such sweet Enchantment o'er the coast doth smile!

And ah! poor mortal wight it doth beguile
With waving trees that deck the shores around . . .

The stanza concentrates the Hunt family's long association with the beguiling, seemingly paradisal island of Barbados where

the bright Sun, as though he had stood still,
Sheen'd o'er the beauteous land each rolling day . . .

In Guyon's story the destructive temptations to which 'tropical blood' is susceptible culminate in the 'pois'nous goblet' that invites 'the soul to quaff away its care' while entangling the knight in a 'web of Woe'. For 'Guyon', read 'Isaac'. Through the allegorical world of *The Palace of Pleasure* Hunt could reform his father, although Isaac's presence both behind and within *Juvenilia* explains why he soon came to regret the public notice it had brought him: 'My book was unfortunately successful everywhere.'[20]

Juvenilia brought Hunt public acclaim. The reviews were admiring, and at literary parties he was applauded as a young genius. Between 1801 and 1803 four editions of *Juvenilia* were published, each prefaced with a fresh list of subscribers. Isaac highlighted some individuals with flattering remarks. Among them were the late Duke of Bedford ('The disinterested patriot-promoter of useful science – benefactor of the industrious poor – the friend of man'); the politicians William Pitt and Charles James Fox ('the British Demosthenes'); 'Right Hon. Lord Nelson, Duke of Brontï, &c'; Benjamin Franklin ('Son of the late ingenious Benjamin Franklin, *prime conductor* of the American Revolution, and principal *founder* of the United States of America'); the University of Philadelphia ('the Alma Mater of the author's father') and Revd William Smith, DD ('Provost of the University of Pennsylvania on its first establishment – one of the first who diffused the light of science over the new world'); Revd William Vidler, the Universalist ('the catholic and worthy successor in Artillery-Street Chapel, of the late eminent, eloquent preacher of the love of God to man, Elhanan Winchester – the powerful maintainer of the sovereignty of Jesus Christ over Satan and the kingdom of darkness – the savage Calvinist and hard-hearted Predestinarian'). Edward Jenner, pioneer of vaccination, became a subscriber, and so did William Wilberforce, the abolitionist; Richard Payne Knight, the connoisseur; and Richard Brinsley Sheridan, MP, playwright, and owner of the Drury Lane theatre. The kindly Thornton family contributed, and from Philadelphia Stephen Shewell belatedly forwarded a subscription, with a note to the effect that if Hunt came to Philadelphia he would 'make a man of him'.[21]

* * *

A final glance at Hunt's subscribers in the third edition of *Juvenilia* reveals Sir Simon Le Blanc, 'one of the Judges of the Court of King's Bench'; Lord Eldon, 'lord high chancellor of England'; and Lord Ellenborough, 'chief justice of the court of King's Bench'. A distinguished company. We shall meet all three of them again.

FIVE

NATIVE SCENES

In the first years of the new century Hunt moved between several addresses in London. He stayed with his parents at Bedford Row and later at Evesham Buildings in Somers Town, then in an area of dilapidated houses north of Bloomsbury where the British Library now stands. Robert Hunt lived at Robert Street, Bedford Row and subsequently with his brother John at London Street, Fitzroy Square. Stephen had a legal address at Warwick Court, Holborn. Hunt flitted between them all, and in years to come would seldom be able to settle in one home for more than a few months.

Juvenilia had brought Hunt opportunities, and the many subscribers and readers enlarged his circle of acquaintance. He met Thomas Maurice who was a librarian at the British Museum, a poet, a claret-savouring sentimentalist, and the author of two immense works of oriental scholarship: *The History of Hindostan* and, in seven volumes, *Indian Antiquities*. Herculean effort was involved in creating those books, for Maurice's weak eyes obliged him to squint through a magnifying glass as he wrote. When Hunt visited him in 1801 he was laboriously compiling the Museum's catalogue of holdings. They talked of authors, books, and once, Hunt recalled, of an eccentric gentleman who was convinced that the smell of freshly turned earth was salubrious. Every morning on Primrose Hill he would dig a hole, and inhale deeply.[1]

Maurice gave Hunt a ticket to the Reading Room at the British Museum, and here the sixteen-year-old began to learn Italian. In due course this would enable him to read the poets of the *Parnaso Italiano*, including Ariosto, Tasso and Dante. In the Reading Room he encountered Richard Llwyd, the Welsh bard and author of a topographical poem, *Beaumaris Bay*. Llwyd took Hunt to meet a fellow-Welshman, antiquary and poet, William Owen (later Owen Pughe), who was living at Islington with his books and a bardic harp. Together, Llwyd and Owen put Hunt in touch with contemporary Welsh nationalism, a movement that was part of a wider imaginative quest for the roots of modern culture.

The Welsh cultural renaissance had gathered pace during the eighteenth century, thanks to Evan Evan's *Specimens of the Poetry of the Antient Welsh*

Bards (1764) and the enthusiasm shown by Thomas Gray's poetic evocations of the Welsh. Owen was active in the London Gwyneddigion Society, which revived the eisteddfod, and he had a hand in editing poems by the fourteenth-century bard Dafydd ap Gwilym. Since 1793 he had been compiling a Welsh–English dictionary, inventing words where necessary by way of proving the Welsh language more copious than English. When Hunt met Owen he had just published *The Myvyrian Archaiology of Wales*, a collection of Welsh poetry from the misty druidic times down to the Middle Ages. Having welcomed Hunt into his snug, book-lined parlour, Owen began to recite those ancient poems while playing his harp. The fire flickered. The tea kettle steamed. Out of the clouds of time emerged tales of the heroic Welsh, invested with a powerful aura of national myth: Hu Gadarn, 'progenitor of the Cymry'; Dyfnwal Moelmud, law-giver; Catwg Ddoeth, saint and sage; Geraint Fardd Glas, 'the Blue Poet'; and Llywarch Hen, 'Prince of the Cumbrian Britons'.

Hunt was captivated, and it didn't matter that several of those heroes were the inventions of Edward Williams, a.k.a. Iolo Morganwg. In a letter of 7 April 1802 he anticipated a visit to Owen and mentioned 'venerable Hoel' – that is, Hywel ab Owein, the twelfth-century poet who featured in Owen's researches. Hoel was also known to Hunt from Gray's stirring ode, 'The Bard', which he had read with his mother years before. By now Hunt would have recognised Gray's poem as a highly sophisticated form of 'wordy-war' that voiced the patriotic energies of the ancient Welsh harpers – those 'lost companions' whom Gray believed had been slaughtered by King Edward's invading army. As they drank tea in suburban Islington, Richard Llwyd and William Owen did not look very like Gray's doomed poet with his 'haggard eyes' and 'hoary hair', but they kept alive the spirit of the ancient poet-patriots who had gathered to curse '"Edward's race"'. The most unfortunate of English kings was Edward II, horribly murdered at Berkeley Castle at the behest of his Queen, Isabel. Gray's 'She-Wolf of France, with unrelenting fangs' had been a frightening spectre at Christ's Hospital, lurking in her grave somewhere beneath the flagstones in the cloisters.[2]

Years afterwards Hunt wrote about Owen's Welsh translation of *Paradise Lost*, *Coll Gwynfa*, recalling their meetings and Owen's recovery of the ancient poets who had been persecuted for 'consecrat[ing] their native hills'.[3] Although Hunt did not write poetry in the bardic manner, his journalism showed that the patriotic spirit of Richard Llwyd and William Owen had proved an inspiring example. Hunt's own forebears came from Ireland, another nation whose traditions had been oppressed, and his ceaseless championing of Irish causes showed how closely he identified with the Celtic inhabitants of those 'native hills'.

Two more acquaintances Hunt made after leaving Christ's Hospital were the Robertson brothers. Henry Robertson, who shared Hunt's enthusiasm for music, became opera critic for the *Examiner* and treasurer of Covent Garden Theatre. Hunt dedicated a sonnet to him in his collection *Foliage*. John Robertson was sallow skinned, scarred by smallpox, romantically inclined and irresistibly drawn to disastrous love affairs.[4] One of his friends, Elizabeth Kent, had been impressed by Hunt's *Monthly Preceptor* essay on the humane treatment of animals – she had thought of entering the same competition herself. She was promised that the prize-winning author would visit, although this momentous encounter would be delayed for a few days. John Robertson and Hunt were about to set off on a walking tour from Margate in Kent along the south coast to Brighton.

Their route was sufficiently well-known to be included in the 1792 *Description of Brighthelmstone, and the Adjacent Country*.[5] The cliff-top prospects at Beachy Head and the gentler pastoral scenes of the South Downs appealed to contemporary tastes for the sublime and the picturesque – hence J.M.W. Turner's many studies of this coastline. Bathing at resorts like Margate and Ramsgate attracted the health-conscious; Brighton beckoned to the fashionable. For Hunt and his friend, however, there was an added thrill of anticipation: they would be walking along the front line of Britain's war against the French.

The 'hoys' departing for Margate were moored at the Custom House Quay, between London Bridge and the Tower. Each boat could carry seventy passengers and, depending on the wind and tide, the voyage down the Thames estuary might take anything from eight hours to three days. Standing on the quay that Wednesday morning in September 1801, Hunt noticed that their fellow-passengers were on the whole a respectable crowd. This was noteworthy, for it differed from the popular reputation of the Margate hoy, which famously mingled together citizens from all parts of town – lawyers, dockers, courtiers and costermongers, lamplighters, ladies of fashion and painted beaux – with 'laughing, roaring, dancing, fun and music'.[6] The *Margate Guide* of 1775 mentioned that the 'Hoy, like the Grave, confounds all Distinction; high and low, rich and poor, sick and sound, are indiscriminately blended together'.[7] Margate's sea water and coastal air would cure all kinds of ailments, including cancer, ruptures, asthma, madness, glandular fever, and skin complaints like scrofula and psoriasis. Sailing downstream past Deptford and Greenwich they entered the lower reaches of the Thames, and discovered that the hoy they had boarded was of a disappointingly sober character. The sombre company were Methodists on a chartered Temperance excursion. Their boat was called the 'Methodist Hoy', and it sailed 'by Divine Providence'.

Instead of the dancing, fun and music Hunt had anticipated, entertainment on board was confined to games of riddles and arithmetical puzzles interspersed with psalms and hymn-singing. The boat passed Gravesend at dusk, when Hunt's 'godly friends' went to their narrow berths below. As night fell the wind freshened, and the hoy beat out into open sea and a heavy swell.

Hunt was striding around the deck to keep warm when he stumbled over a woman, curled up asleep in clothes saturated with sea water. Here was a 'good cause' like the ones that roused him at Christ's Hospital. He went below deck seeking shelter for the woman among the righteous: 'Not a soul would stir,' he recalled: 'they left her to the care of the "Providence" under which they sailed.' This was a moment to which Hunt returned many times, pondering the hard-heartedness of those 'saints snoozing away in comfort'.[8]

On Thursday morning they docked at Margate. Hunt and Robertson disembarked, and walked briskly into town. They saw the New Square, with its elegant houses; the Theatre Royal, modelled on Covent Garden; and the New Assembly Room, 'a handsome building of the Ionic order, with Venetian windows, emblemature, and cornice'. The Assembly Room was the centre of social life; its great ballroom was reputedly the largest in Europe, and there were elegant rooms for coffee, tea, cards and billiards. Public breakfasts were held here too, and, since the building fronted the sea, one could view the bathing rooms where visitors drank sea water for its curative powers. From these rooms the more intrepid could step into one of the bathing machines, a horse-drawn contraption with a canvas canopy that was lowered to form a tent over the water, allowing its occupants to bathe in complete privacy and 'without any violation of public decency'.[9] The inventor of the bathing machine was a Margate worthy, Benjamin Beale.

As Hunt and Robertson set off on the Ramsgate road they passed another example of local ingenuity that Turner took care to include in his paintings. This was Hooper's Mill, a curious modification of windmill technology in which 'the sweeps, or fliers, move horizontally, and are inclosed with shutters'.[10] From Ramsgate the travellers headed around Pegwell Bay to Sandwich where the old harbour was 'squalid and clogged up' though formerly famous for oysters. At Deal, Hunt remembered the porpoises that had frightened him as a child.

For the next three days they ate ravenously at inns and farmhouses, and slept wherever they could. There were numerous places to visit. On Friday they scrambled around Dover Castle, where a hopeful prisoner let down a box to collect spare change. They looked over the cliff and thought of Shakespeare's Earl of Gloucester, blinded and left to 'smell / His way to Dover', and then they ventured into the underground barracks where 'soldiers lie in burrows, like rabbits'.[11] Crossing the town, they climbed the Western Heights to the military stronghold. Although intensive fortification of the coast did not begin until after Hunt's tour, at Dover he could see the defences in place to resist a French landing. Exactly a year later, William Wordsworth passed through the town and wrote two sonnets contrasting English liberty with Europe 'yet in Bonds' a few miles across the sea.[12] Hunt did not share Wordsworth's foreboding, but he did experience the wariness of local people. In the remote areas of Romney and

Pevensey Marshes, the two strangers were regarded with suspicion. They might be French spies, or excise men on the trail of smugglers.

After Dover, their route took them through Folkestone, across the marsh to Dymchurch and New Romney, where they lodged for Friday night, then westwards to Rye, Winchelsea, Hastings and the expanse of Pevensey Marsh. They knocked at a lonely house where they could see people seated comfortably round a fire, but were told 'with insolent speeches, to be gone'. There was nothing for it but to press on across the marsh, wary of the drains and sluices. The next day, Sunday, they saw the ruins of Pevensey Castle then set off around the cliffs at Beachy Head, up the valley of the River Ouse to Lewes and so to Brighton and the Old Ship Inn – completing one hundred and twelve miles in four days.

It had been Hunt's first independent venture. Covering some thirty miles a day was a remarkable achievement for a city-dweller unused to long-distance walking on this scale, and Hunt says it 'did us good'. The walk had brought him face to face with people in distress, and with others who couldn't care less: the saints on the Margate hoy, content to leave a woman out in the storm, and the farmers who turned away two travellers at nightfall. He had met innkeepers whose seeming hospitality masked greedy self-interest, and the prisoner at Dover Castle seeking a pittance to augment his allowance of food.

The coach from Brighton to London took just eleven hours: an early start from the Old Ship Inn set them down at Charing Cross at five in the evening. Shortly after their return Robertson fulfilled his promise and took Hunt to meet Elizabeth Kent, who lived with her older sister Mary Anne, brother Thomas, and their mother Ann at 2, Little Titchfield Street, part of the new neighbourhood to the north of Oxford Street. All but one of the original eighteenth-century buildings were demolished in the 1920s, to make way for an extension of the London Polytechnic. The single surviving house indicates that these were terraced brick houses running between Great Portland and Titchfield Streets, unobtrusively set back from grand Cavendish Square. Nelson and Lady Hamilton's illegitimate daughter, Horatia, was nursed at a house in Little Titchfield Street, safely away from the public gaze.

Ann Kent's husband, Thomas, had been a linen-draper at Brighton with a taste for extravagant 'fast' living. Their first child Mary Anne was born in September 1788 and baptised at St Andrew's church, Pershore, on 26 October 1788.[13] When Thomas died his family was left destitute. They moved to London where Ann began to make a living as a seamstress, sewing from morning to night and bringing up the children with a fierce sense of purpose that didn't flinch from beating them. Young Thomas took after his father. He became a medical student but wavered in that profession and eventually found a course of life 'apart', probably emigrating to Australia.[14] Elizabeth, who was born and baptised in March 1790, was an intelligent, highly-strung girl who had inherited her mother's determination to succeed. Just out of dame school, she was ambitious to enter the *Monthly Preceptor*'s competitions and eager to hear Hunt's views about kindness to animals. This gives us a clue to her personality. At the start of the twenty-first century the idea of 'animal rights' is as controversial a topic as it was two hundred years ago, when calls for the humane treatment of animals were linked with radical arguments for natural rights and sexual equality. Supporters of the French Revolution like John Oswald, Thomas Paine and Mary Wollstonecraft considered animals our 'fellow creatures'; Samuel Taylor Coleridge had written a poem 'To a Young Ass', in which he daringly hailed the 'Innocent Foal' as his 'BROTHER'.[15] At eleven years old Bess Kent was already attracted to such unconventional and 'advanced' ideas of fraternity.

At their first meeting Hunt saw in Bess a bright, vivacious girl, who was unfazed by his reputation as the famous author of *Juvenilia*. She was teaching herself languages and history, reading novels and poetry and was determined, she said, to study botany as well. Mary Anne had just turned thirteen, and was occupied in dress-making – a painstaking and weary business but one in which she persevered. Hunt asked Mrs Kent if he might call again. He was assured that he would be welcome, said his farewells, bowed, and left.

Following that first visit Hunt called often at Little Titchfield Street, and on one occasion stayed overnight. He was feeling chilled and feverish. Next morning the symptoms of erysipelas, or St Anthony's fire, had appeared – an angry scarlet rash erupted across his face and body, accompanied by pains in his muscles and joints. This was a violent attack, and he was unable to leave his bed. What had brought it on? Erysipelas is a bacterial infection of the skin, arising from a cut or some other damage, so perhaps Hunt's long walk had left him with sores on his feet. Or possibly the condition flared up as a result of anxiety. Whatever its cause, Hunt's illness gathered nurses around him: the sick-room idyll at Christ's Hospital was revived in Little Titchfield Street, and Ann Kent allowed him to stay as a lodger with two rooms for his own use.[16] As he made a deliciously gradual recovery – it took 'many weeks' – Bess read aloud to him from Pope's translation of Homer, a work that Hunt disliked. Mary Anne sewed. Hunt watched. She was less precocious than her younger sister and, like many girls at this time, had received no formal school education. Although Mary Anne worked all day Hunt could see she had an 'inclination to pleasure' and seemed pleased and interested to meet him. She had dark eyes, glossy black hair, and already showed a 'genial' figure – 'like a little Houri's', he thought, 'with a joyous undulation of back & bosom'. The erotic attraction was powerful, immediate, enduring – although at first Hunt sublimated sexual passion into an idea of 'something better'.[17] He surrounded Mary Anne with a romantic aura like the beautiful Alma, Spenser's 'virgin bright' in *The Faerie Queene*,

faire, as faire mote ever bee,
And in the flowre now of her freshest age;
Yet full of grace and goodly modestee . . .
(II. ix. 18)

In Spenser's poem Alma – meaning 'bountiful' – represents the 'golden mean' of a generous and temperate soul. Now this figure had become part of his life, steadily devoted to the well-being of her widowed mother and family, and to his own comfort and recovery.

On one occasion Bess tired, and asked Mary Anne to read. Laying aside her work, and relieved by the prospect of a moment's respite, Mary Anne took up the translation of Homer and read aloud in a voice that was untrained but full of feeling. Hunt had come to Titchfield Street to meet his young admirer Bess Kent but found himself irresistibly drawn to her sister, who reminded him of how his poor mother had faced difficult times in the past. Mary Anne needed his care: there were signs already of the pallor and sickness he associated with his mother and little sister. Hunt would rescue her and together they would read Spenser, Thomson, Collins and Gray. He would educate her and, eventually, Mary Anne would become his wife. As a first step, she must change her name to Marian. Marian was more appropriate to his romantic idea of her, and a reminder of his mother, who was known as Maria.

Hunt's feelings for Marian developed like one of his idealised friendships at school, utterly out of touch with actuality. She was his 'favourite'. They read to each other, enjoyed private jokes, and were happy in the idea of being happy. He felt he had a sense of direction and purpose in his life, so much so that he got up earlier in the morning, and went eagerly in the evenings to Little Titchfield Street. Hunt was in earnest and the older by four years, yet, having little emotional resilience, his poise could slip to reveal a vulnerable and demanding side to his nature that was prey to 'jealous anxieties'. Given Marian's streak of stubbornness and Hunt's insecurities, it should have been clear from the start that their relationship would be a difficult one.

During 1802 Marian's mother was courted by a twenty-eight-year-old publisher, Rowland Hunter, whom Hunt met many times at Little Titchfield Street and grew to like. He was the grand-nephew of the Unitarian bookseller Joseph Johnson, whose premises at St Paul's Churchyard had been a haven for writers and intellectuals since the 1770s. Hunter had been brought up in the culture of dissent: he attended Anna Barbauld's Unitarian school at Palgrave in Suffolk, and Johnson (who may have been his legal guardian) subsequently trained him to enter the book trade.[18] For Hunt this connection would prove valuable in years to come. More immediately, books were now brought to the Kent household, and with these came doubled pleasures. Hunt would read to Marian, holding his book in one hand while stroking her dark hair with the other.

In a draft for his *Autobiography*, Hunt recalled his early relationship with Marian. The setting is the Kent house in Little Titchfield Street:

> On Sunday evenings, a stranger might have wondered to find a set of such lively persons (for we none of us wanted animation) all collected together in the drawing room, all silent as the grave, & all intent upon books, so that the crackling of the fire was audible, & the snuffing of a candle took a sound of license and authority.[19]

The *Autobiography* is revealing for having almost nothing to say about Hunt's relation to Marian, but unused drafts like this one are less circumspect. Hunt sketches a scene of apparently tranquil intimacy, but now senses that much had been amiss: 'a set of lively persons' were 'silent as the grave', and a claustrophobic atmosphere meant that the snuffing of a candle was a happy distraction. In 1802 he could not have foreseen that he was at the beginning of a long and troubled courtship.

Rowland Hunter and Ann Kent were married early in 1803, and during April the eighteen-year-old Hunt left the pleasures and tensions of Little Titchfield Street for a while. Frederick Papendieck had recently matriculated at Trinity College, Oxford, and was keen to welcome his old school friend. On Wednesday, 20 April Hunt boarded the coach for Oxford. He took one of the seats on top of the coach, wrapped himself up in a cloak, and set off in heavy showers of hail and rain that continued for all of the fifty-five-mile journey. As he entered Oxford from Shotover Hill it was still raining bitterly, and Hunt needed strong tea and toast to recover. He chatted with Papendieck, then dropped exhausted into bed.[20]

Over the next days Hunt and Papendieck explored the colleges, sauntered in Christ Church meadow and gazed at the skyline of spires. They walked to Woodstock and back. Although the late April weather brought squalls and hail they rowed on the Isis and Cherwell and once, at Iffley, got into difficulties and capsized. Hunt wrote lyrically to Marian of the 'swelling lawns', 'venerable shades' and 'silver streams' he had discovered. He thought the colleges could have become his 'natural home', except that the cloisters and quadrangles recalled the monastic institutions and 'monkery' of earlier times. The reality of university life was described by a contemporary as 'gaming, drinking and every kind of licentiousness', while many academics were somnolent or lived elsewhere. At Cambridge Byron and Coleridge took full advantage of the opportunities for debauchery (both left without degrees), while Wordsworth's account of his years at St John's College in *The Prelude* overlooked the day-to-day demands of drinking, brawling and whoring. Keats's visit to Oxford left him with gonorrhoea, most likely from one of the college harlots at Magdalen. Drinking, sex and violence might plausibly be associated with 'monkery', but Hunt was of course presenting a carefully sanitised version of what he was up to, suitable for Marian's eyes – and her mother's. He threw himself into college life with enthusiasm, and described for her an exemplary routine of early rising, music, boating, dinner, more music, and evenings of improbably 'sober conversation' with 'the best fellows in the world'. Papendieck's expenses for the week – 11s. 6d. – were higher than anyone else's in the college.[21]

Like Hunt's walk to Brighton his Oxford excursion shows him striking out into new environments and discovering fresh sources for thought and reflection. The reputation of *Juvenilia* had preceded him – Papendieck's father had subscribed for six copies – but now for the first time his pride in the book received a check. Walking one afternoon in the gardens of Trinity College, Hunt fell into conversation with one of the Fellows, Henry Kett, nicknamed 'Horse' by the undergraduates because of his long, equine profile. Hunt remembered this encounter, and wrote about it as a formative moment in his poetic life. Horse Kett had published his own collection of *Juvenile Poems* ten years previously, so their talk had turned naturally enough to poetry. Hunt mentioned the success of his *Juvenilia* and Kett responded with the hope that Hunt would 'feel inspired "by the muse of Warton"'.[22] Hunt was not yet familiar with this name, and Kett's well-intentioned recommendation of Warton's 'muse' was a double-edged encouragement. Thomas Warton had been a Fellow of Trinity, Professor of Poetry, and Poet Laureate. He was a friend of Samuel Johnson, and he had nurtured the talent of Trinity College undergraduate poets like William Lisle Bowles. Although Warton had died in 1790, he helped to stimulate a vital new English poetry that accompanied the French Revolution: through Bowles his influence extended to Coleridge, Southey and Wordsworth.

Warton's 'Sonnet: To the River Lodon' is a good example of the poetry Kett recommended Hunt to study. It begins by recalling a youth coloured by Spenserian romance – 'Ah! what a weary race my feet have run, / Since first I trod thy banks with alders crown'd, / And thought my way was all through fairy ground . . .' – and closes with a subdued retrospect:

> Sweet native stream! those skies and suns so pure
>   No more return, to chear my evening road!
>   Yet still one joy remains, that not obscure,
> Nor useless, all my vacant days have flow'd,
>   From youth's gay dawn to manhood's prime mature;
>   Nor with the Muse's laurel unbestow'd.

The sonnet is a compact autobiography, in which thoughts and feelings consecrate Warton's native landscape and measure changes in the poet himself. It soon had numerous imitators. In 1789 Bowles published an immensely popular volume, *Fourteen Sonnets*, which responded to Warton's example and impressed young Wordsworth and Coleridge. One of Coleridge's early poems, his 'Sonnet to the River Otter', echoed Warton in its opening lines:

> Dear native Brook! wild Streamlet of the West!
> How many various fated years have past,
> What happy and what mournful hours, since last
> I skimm'd the smooth stone along thy breast . . .

Wordsworth's 'Tintern Abbey' drew upon the structure of Warton's sonnet and his masterpiece, the autobiographical *Prelude*, elaborated at epic length Warton's analogy between the flow of the river and the course of the poet's mind.

Hunt had read Coleridge's and Bowles's sonnets while at Christ's Hospital but, like many others in 1803, he had not yet read Wordsworth and was unaware of wider developments in contemporary poetry. Reading Warton would have introduced him to some of those new directions, but what Hunt remembered more precisely was that Kett had wished for Warton's *muse*. In Warton's *The Pleasures of Melancholy* (1745) that muse is identified as 'Contemplation', who leads the poet to 'twilight cells and bow'rs' where imagination reveals the 'mystic visions' that 'Spenser saw'. Contemplation's retreats represent a darkling, introspective space in which poetry turns to private experiences, and the power of imagination or 'Fancy' to realise a 'visionary' landscape. We have seen already how in *The Palace of Pleasure* Hunt imitated Spenser's *Faerie Queene* to reflect upon unhappiness in his childhood. His *Juvenilia* had been genuinely impressive for the skill with which he had imitated other writers, and it had deservedly drawn admiration. But Warton's example showed that 'Contemplation' – creative thought – could lead 'out of the trammels of the regular imitative poetry [and] versification' to more original sources in 'nature'.[23] In *The Pleasures of Melancholy* Warton traced poetry's spirit to a remote location that Hunt knew well through Richard Llwyd and William Owen: here was 'Contemplation' pictured as a 'smiling babe', 'deeply list'ning to the rapid roar / Of wood-hung Meinai, stream of Druids old' – an inspiration fostered by the ancient Bards of Wales.

Hunt's letters to Marian from Oxford were, he told her, 'moulded by the rich and genuine feelings of the heart' – but in other respects they had not been entirely truthful.[24] He didn't mention anything about capsizing on the river at Iffley. Instead, he invented a heroic account of how he had rowed strenuously upstream at night, thrown off his coat and waistcoat, and so contracted a 'villainous cold' with 'tormenting cramp' and 'hands full of blisters': 'I have been lying on three soft chairs very restless and in great pain'. While assuring

Marian of his recovery he postponed his return to London until the end of April for fear of alarming his mother, who was 'apt to be affected on very slight causes'.[25] 'I *am* in love', he reminded Marian (and himself), adding a 'word or two' of regret about her childish handwriting. And then he found space to finish: 'remember me affectionately [to] my sister Betsy, whom I always wish to have in my heart'.[26]

SIX

THEATRES OF WAR

Following the Union between Britain and Ireland in 1800, Prime Minister Pitt believed that civil rights for Irish Catholics would follow, preventing the possibility of further unrest. George III didn't see things this way, and dismissed the idea as a 'Jacobinical' measure that only a 'personal enemy' would propose.[1] Pitt resigned and the Speaker in the House of Commons, Henry Addington, became Prime Minister. The war had dragged on for seven years and now seemed to be at stalemate. A negotiated peace would be prudent. Following protracted discussions, during which it was agreed that Britain would withdraw from Malta, the Peace of Amiens was proclaimed on 29 April 1802. For a time, hostilities between Britain and France ceased.

Thousands of British tourists hurried over to Paris to gaze at the new buildings and fashions and, if possible, glimpse Napoleon himself. Among them were the Whig leader Charles James Fox and the lawyer Thomas Erskine; the poets Samuel Rogers and Thomas Moore went too, as did young William Hazlitt and the painters Joseph Farington and Henry Fuseli. The one-time Jacobin William Wordsworth wrote a sonnet mocking these 'Men of prostrate mind' paying court to Napoleon, and then made a sentimental journey to Calais where he met his former lover, Annette Vallon.

A popular haunt of visitors at Paris was the Louvre, where the spoils of the French campaigns were exhibited. Benjamin West and his son Raphael visited in September 1802, taking *Death on the Pale Horse* to exhibit. West caused a sensation when he was seen chatting to Napoleon, who expressed approval of his painting. While in Paris, West also hosted a public breakfast at which radicals, poets and painters gathered around his table. Among the guests were Arthur O'Connor, leader of the United Irishmen, accompanying Lady Oxford; Joel Barlow, American revolutionary and poet; John Hurford Stone, an English Jacobin who had long been resident at Paris; Helen Maria Williams, poet, novelist and a supporter of France since 1790; Thomas Erskine, and John Kemble the actor-manager of Covent Garden Theatre.

Reports quickly reached London, and the tranquil façade of West's home in Newman Street was shattered. Having seen West at Paris, Joseph Farington decided that the 'Historical Painter to the King' and President of the Royal Academy did not have an '*English mind*'. His 'partiality to Buonaparte' was an 'excessive indiscretion'. Soon after West's return from Paris to London another menace was uncovered when Colonel Edward Despard and his accomplices were arrested for plotting a violent coup against George III and the government.[2]

Hunt would have heard at first hand about West's visit to Paris, and he could not have missed the sensational news of Despard's conspiracy and brutal execution at Surrey Gaol. From the windows of Whitehall, Addington and his ministers surveyed a deteriorating domestic situation and, on the international scene, gathering tension with France over Britain's continued occupation of Malta. Militia Acts in 1802 and March 1803 raised men for the army, and over the summer the Military Service Bill set out plans for recruiting volunteer regiments throughout the country. By October 1803 this 'insurrection of loyalty' amounted to some 300,000 volunteers.

Hunt's visit to Oxford in April 1803 had been a holiday, although the storms of this bleak, unseasonable spring were in keeping with the unsettled mood of the country. Seen against that background, his excursion appears as a timely retreat from a city ill at ease; in which the state's barbaric punishments had been witnessed by a sullen populace and where the authorities were once again preparing for war. Given the history of his family and their kinship with the Wests, it would not be surprising to find that Hunt, like his granduncle, was not entirely of an '*English mind*' regarding recent events. On the other hand, the strong establishment presence among subscribers to *Juvenilia* could be used to show that Hunt was 'one of us' – an implication he would soon come to regret.

Britain's war with France resumed on 18 May 1803 – the 'Peace' had been a temporary break in hostilities that would continue for twelve more years. James Gillray marked the occasion with *Maniac-Ravings – or – Little Boney in a Strong Fit*, a cartoon of Napoleon hopping with rage at British duplicity and threatening 'Invasion! Invasion! Four hundred and eighty thousand Frenchmen! British slavery & everlasting Chains!'[3] *The Times* responded to the renewed threat in a patriotic 'War Ode', urging readers to 'grasp the spear' and 'meet th'insulting foe':

> The slaves may threat, – the British heart
> Disdains to feel alarms;
> Inspir'd by Freedom's sacred flame,
> We dare defend the British name
> Against a world in arms.[4]

Hunt's mother wrote to her sister in Philadelphia, reporting that the King had been 'deranged in his mind' and that the Duke of York's infatuation with Maria Fitzherbert had revived. These were the 'sett of men' whose misrule had brought the country to 'confusion and misery'. 'We hear a great deal about Bonaparte and his preparations for invading this Country,' she went on. 'I wish he would be content with the power he has already attained, and leave Old England in quiet.' At the same time, she confessed to thinking Bonaparte 'a wonderful man' for furthering God's 'great purpose'. The Corsican might yet prove to be Britain's salvation, and even 'the means of harmonizing the world'.[5]

When Hunt wrote about the invasion scare in his *Autobiography*, he deliberately recalled the bailiffs who had disturbed the tranquillity of his childhood home. 'A knock at the doors of all England awoke us up from our dreams. It was Bonaparte, threatening to come among us.'[6] Hunt had not the 'slightest belief' that Napoleon would invade, but nevertheless seized the chance to live out his childhood fascination with the military: he joined the St James's Volunteers, one of the new regiments Addington optimistically hoped would form the front line against invasion.

The regiment was 'embodied' in March 1803 and quickly signed up hundreds of volunteers who all swore 'the oath of allegiance and fidelity to his Majesty'. According to *The Times*, this proved 'the high estimation in which that corps is held, and . . . the eagerness and alacrity with which people come forth in the hour of danger to serve their King and Country'.[7] But for any eighteen-year-old an added attraction was the garish red uniform. Hunt long remembered how this unlikely regiment had 'mustered a thousand strong', with 'grenadiers, light infantry, a capital band, and to crown all, a Major who was an undertaker in Piccadilly . . . a very fat man with a jovial, youthful face'.[8]

On 30 September, the Volunteers 'fired with ball at Chalk Farm'. Their target was 'an exact resemblance of BONAPARTE', *The Times* reported, noting the 'whimsical effect' of the shooting.[9] The next week, Thursday, 6 October, they divided into two companies representing the French and English armies, and staged a 'mock fight' along the banks of the new Paddington Canal. Spectators were 'astonished' at a surprise attack on the English, but the French were forced back and the bugle horn sounded a retreat. Battle was joined on the bridges and banks along the length of the canal as far as Wormwood Scrubs, where the day was decided:

> they attacked each other, front to front, for nearly half an hour, sometimes firing by divisions, at other times by vollies, and the ammunition being a third time expended, the business ended with the surrender of the French troops to the English, who immediately marched across the bridge, and took possession of the field of victory.[10]

'Never did so young a corps behave so well,' trumpeted *The Times*. After three cheers from the crowd the Volunteers marched back to town, Hunt remembered, 'in right warlike style'.[11]

Hunt took a short vacation in mid-October at Enfield, visiting a young lawyer called John Marriott and his wife Anne, 'a pretty lively woman'. He read Rousseau, and admired his 'deep knowledge of the heart'.[12]

During the autumn and winter Hunt's red-coated Volunteers were regularly on stage. On 26 October – 'a glorious day for Old England', *The Times* called it – they joined the parade of 15,000 soldiers in Hyde Park, 'strong, hardy, active young men, full of ardour, full of British courage; disciplined beyond all expectation'. This was a 'superb and encouraging spectacle' and beyond 'adequate description', declared *The Times* in a column packed with loyal references to 'the first city of the universe', a 'beloved and venerable sovereign', and 'the first naval power of the universe'.[13] Another memorable moment came on 16 February 1804 when the St James's Volunteers mustered 'at Burlington House, at nine o'clock, to be inspected'. This was to be an occasion of 'skill, grace, vigour, address, example, ascendancy, mastery, victory'. Hunt stood to attention, and watched as their Commander-in-Chief, Colonel, Lord Amherst, 'a gallant figure on a charger', cantered into the parade ground only to be pitched unceremoniously over his horse's head on to the ground.[14]

There was a strong element of public performance in all of this, indeed Hunt's *Autobiography* presents the St James's Volunteers as a comic preface to his recollections of the theatre. Three of his fellow-Volunteers, Charles Farley, John Emery and Michael Kelly, were professional actors, and Hunt recognised they were all part of a long-running show in which 'war is clothed and recommended'.[15] At the time, though, the volunteer regiments represented a patriotic mobilisation to meet a national emergency – and the author of *Juvenilia* was willing to play his part. Hunt's experience of life in the ranks gave authority to his later *Examiner* attacks on military corruption and incompetence, and he drew on these scenes for his popular protest ballad *Captain Sword and Captain Pen* which moved from a pageant of 'military gaiety' in the street ('Stepping in music and thunder sweet') to the horrifying butchery on the battlefield:

> Down go bodies, snap burst eyes;
> Trod on the ground are tender cries;
> Brains are dash'd against plashing ears . . .

Like Wilfred Owen in the next century, Hunt sets out to expose 'the old lie' that 'made the thing they go through / Shocking to read of, but noble to do'. In his poem 'the bullet-like sense' of warmongers is finally overthrown by the 'line of Captain Pen', that is, the peace-loving writers among whom Hunt counted himself.[16]

Captain Sword and Captain Pen is one of the great English protest poems, even though Hunt had never witnessed battle at first hand (his description of soldiers' boots 'treading red mud' embellishes the harmless 'Battle of Paddington Canal').[17] Edmund Blunden, who served in the trenches throughout the First World War, described Hunt's poem as true to 'what *can* happen to flesh and blood in war', and viscerally alert to the 'maimed and blood-saddened men . . . still suffering in hospitals and private houses'. Unlike Captain Sword, the Volunteers embodied a disinterested patriotism (without 'mercenary motive') that appealed to Hunt's idealism. The sense of disciplined endeavour 'for Old England' stayed with him throughout his life, and was later directed into his campaign for the traditional liberties of the nation. As Hunt paraded in his red uniform, the nature of the wordy-war that he would fight as a stalwart recruit of 'Captain Pen' was becoming clearer.[18]

An indication of Hunt's developing views came in a letter of 11 February 1804 to Marian's mother. His reason for writing was to enclose a letter for Marian, patching up a quarrel and restoring 'our former love', and he took the opportunity to mention that John's plan to publish a newspaper had run into trouble:

I am afraid all is over with our paper: one of the proprietors has withdrawn his assistance at the very moment when every thing was ripe for publication: this was highly inconsiderate, and very much chagrines my brother John. I am sorry for him, because printing a newspaper is much more lucrative than book-printing, and he had set his heart on this mode of entering into business, which for years has been a favourite project.[19]

This letter announces the collaborative scheme ('our paper') that would eventually change Hunt's life and make his name as a journalist. The mention of a respectable and lucrative venture was for Mrs Hunter's eyes, and Hunt took care to imply his own prudence in worldly matters:

he will suffer for it, as he will have to pay all the expenses incurred, which are very heavy. It was but a little time after this defection, this very morning, a footman came from Buckingham House to desire the Editor would send the paper to Her Majesty: no design ever had better prospects. This is not the first time I have felt the blessing of independence: some time ago the loss of a lucrative literary employment would have fallen heavily upon me . . .

Personal fortitude in the face of 'defection' and expense; the prospect of royal favour at his fingertips: all are trailed by way of enabling Hunt to assume an air of worldly 'independence'. As Hunt wrote his letter he recalled how the 'young poet' of *Juvenilia* had depended on subscriptions, much as John had relied on a 'proprietor' who had let him down. The two brothers were learning fast. 'Independence' would be the watchword of the *News* and the *Examiner*, and the papers would keep their distance from fickle patrons and self-interested advertisers. For the moment, though, he was aiming for steady employment: 'I have only to increase my comings in with a little less pleasant labour, and thank God that I am out of the reach of disappointment.'[20]

The 'less pleasant labour' was a clerkship in the War Office. Isaac had negotiated this post for his son through the same channels from which subscriptions to *Juvenilia* had flowed. Opening the alphabetical index of new subscribers for the third edition had been the Earl of Aylesbury, the Bishop of St Asaph, and Lord Amherst (last seen head over heels in the parade ground), followed by the Prime Minister, 'Rt. hon. Henry Addington, First Lord Commissioner of the Treasury, and Chancellor of the Exchequer'.[21] Addington's brief term as Prime Minister had kept him in the shadow of Pitt, who returned to head the government in May 1804. He was steady and cautious, lacking Pitt's flair and charisma; in other words, he was exactly the man to broker the 1802 peace with France. And Addington was kindly, described by a contemporary as 'cheerful and conversible, and very civil, which always makes good company'. He was among the 'great acquaintances' Isaac had made since arriving in London and, as we have seen, *Juvenilia* had drawn subscribers from various government offices.[22]

There were opportunities here. Hunt takes up the story of his first job in his *Autobiography*: 'The situation was given me by Mr. Addington, then Prime Minister, afterwards Lord Sidmouth, who knew my father.' So it was that, early in 1805, aged twenty, Hunt went to work at Whitehall in 'an humble situation in a government office' with the forty other clerks who were supervised by the 'Examiner of Army-Accompts'.[23] At some time in the next two years, Hunt may have met a certain John Dickens, Charles's father, fulfilling a similar role as a clerk for the navy.

Hunt looked back on his War Office work as a comic aberration like his spell in the militia: he struggled with his 'sorry stock of arithmetic', and wasted time in 'perpetual jesting'.[24] But he would spend the next three years as a government employee, dividing time between his duties as a clerk and his rapidly widening literary commitments. That Hunt said little about his War Office career does not mean that it left no impression.[25] No doubt he found the office routine dreary, hence the relief of 'jesting'. Yet he was also gaining an insight into the bureaucratic machine behind the pomp and circumstance of military life. What started to form at this time was Hunt's sense of how government was manipulated by aristocratic officers, so that an apparently civil administration was in reality 'military at heart', 'nothing but a servant

of the aristocracy, and (more or less openly) of a barrack-master'.[26]
Government in Britain, he began to see, was the puppet of a military establishment dedicated to war between states and a repressive 'threatening of
force' on the domestic front.

   In summer 1806, Hunt called on Addington at his home at White Lodge,
Richmond Park, 'to thank him for the clerkship', and he was impressed when
the minister quoted from Pope's 'Epistle to Dr Arbuthnot',

> – not in fancy's maze he wander'd long,
> But stoop'd to truth, and moraliz'd his song . . .

The couplet brought into focus some of the choices Hunt himself was facing.
After this interview, overwhelmed, he retreated to the park where he 'sat on
the grass . . . in a dream' wondering how he could reconcile 'verse-making'
with office book-keeping.[27] Confronting him for the first time was a dilemma
that would persist throughout his life. It can be formulated in various ways
– how to reconcile reality and reverie, actuality and imagination, or, as Hunt
preferred to express it, politics and poetics.

Hunt's poems were continuing to reach the public in the *Cambridge
Intelligencer*, the *Morning Chronicle*, the *European Magazine* and the *Monthly
Magazine*, and he contributed short articles to an evening broadsheet, the
Traveller. A note in the *Poetical Register* for 1801 announced that 'Mr J. H.
L. Hunt is engaged in the composition of a tragedy called "The Earl of
Surrey"', and over the next three years he also completed a comedy, and a
farce.[28] His anti-slavery ballad, 'The Negro Boy', was republished as a
pamphlet and set to music. The *Monthly Mirror* for May 1804 included Hunt's
'Ode to the Memory of Robert Burns', celebrating Scottish patriotism in the
'blythsome strain' of Burns's six-line 'Standard Habbie' stanza:

> While as thy songs o' freedom sound,
> The mighty spirits pour around,
> Of Scots wha hae on patriot ground,
>   Wi' Wallace bled;
> The groves wi' aweful grandeur crown'd
>   Bow to the dead![29]

Burns's 'songs o' freedom' placed him alongside the English Jacobin poets
Blake, Wordsworth and Coleridge during the revolutionary 1790s, and Hunt's
poem – written some eight years after Burns's death – shows that his voice
continued to inspire. As an old man Hunt read in his copy of *The Life and
Works of Robert Burns* that Henry Addington had been the poet's 'warm
admirer', and was moved to write affectionately in the margin: 'I salute thy

gentle ghost, my second patron.'³⁰ This was a 'bow to the dead', and a triumph
for Burns's liberal spirit – the intervening years had seen Hunt quarrel with
Addington who, as Lord Sidmouth, had presided over the brutal violence of
the Peterloo Massacre.

Hunt followed Burns in another sense too: he started writing songs. One
of his earliest memories was of his mother singing to him (he thought her
songs were authentic English melodies only to find, years later, that they were
mostly 'borrowed' from Italian composers).³¹ At Christ's Hospital he discovered Mozart, and learned the flute to impress his nurse's daughter; later,
while visiting Trinity College he had played harpsichord and flute with
Frederick Papendieck. Through Papendieck's family he had been introduced
to Michael Kelly, actor, singer and St James's Volunteer, with a view to getting
his farce staged at a London theatre. Kelly was a splendidly rakish character,
a wine merchant turned songwriter skilled in adapting melodies and blending
vintages. He was so notorious for improving his own songs with 'borrowings'
that Sheridan labelled him an 'importer of music and composer of wines'.³²

Hunt did not see the script of his play again, but Kelly was nevertheless
important for making him aware of the London musical scene. Hunt would
become a well-informed and influential critic of concerts and opera, able to
capture the uniqueness of a singer and a performance in brisk verbal sketches
that recall Isaac's skill at caricature. He wrote of Angelina Catalani's 'ante-
lope face' and 'amazingly powerful voice . . . trying its strength with choruses
and orchestras'. Reputations meant nothing to Hunt. The great Elizabeth
Billington seemed to him a catch-penny pretender, 'a fat beauty, with regular
features' who specialised in *coloratura* trills; the celebrated tenor, John Braham,
affected the piano-forte style, that is, 'very soft on the words *love, peace,* &c.,
and then bursting into roars of triumph on the words *hate, war,* and *glory*'.
Serenading together, Braham and Billington could persuade an audience 'to
fancy that they enjoyed the highest style of the art'. Giudetta Pasta, by
contrast, was for Hunt the real thing: a tragic actress whose singing was equal
to the 'force, tenderness, and expression' of her acting: 'All noble passions
belonged to her.'³³

Hunt's musical ear would prove vital for his literary criticism. When he
wrote about poetry he attuned himself to the 'musical secret' of versification
rather than to technical or formal matters. Like Braham and Billington, who
could dazzle with what Hunt called the 'execution' of a performance, a poet
might write verse that was technically accomplished but without the passionate
music of genuine poetry. For Hunt a poet's musicality was the true measure;
when he came to review John Keats's first collection, he noted various 'faults'
before welcoming the promise of the young man's 'fine ear' and 'the harmony
of his verses'.³⁴

Hunt's musical tastes were shared by his friend John Robertson, an 'agreeable bass singer', and his brother Henry who was said to be 'one of the very

best amateur singers . . . an almost faultless "reader at sight", always in tune, invariably in good temper'.[35] Through these acquaintances Hunt's circle of musical friends would expand to include the composer Vincent Novello and his family. Rowland Hunter had given Hunt an introduction to the music publisher, J. S. Button, and in August 1803 he took Bess to a musical evening 'at Mr Button's' where they heard the famous violinist François Barthélémon perform. They did not get home until two the following morning.[36] Button published three of Hunt's poems set to music by John Whitaker: 'Silent Kisses', 'Love and the Aeolian Harp' and 'Mary, dear Mary, List, Awake'. All three were popular successes, and 'Mary, dear Mary' was included in song collections until 1860.

In May 1805 his brother John launched a weekly paper, the *News*, and Hunt 'went to live with him in Brydges-street, and write the theatricals in it'.[37] Their friend John Marriott was drawn in as a contributor too. Published on Sundays, the *News* consisted of eight pages featuring a lead political essay, items on domestic and international issues, provincial and London reports, financial business, and theatricals. Over the next two and a half years Hunt would write, 'with six or eight exceptions', every theatrical article and review in the paper, an astonishing output for someone who was also holding down a daytime clerical job – even if he did turn up late in the mornings. During 1807 he was writing theatricals for *The Times* as well.[38]

The *News* coincided with a period of international commotion. Napoleon became Emperor of France in 1804 and, the following year, King of Italy. Until mid-1805 his armies stood poised to cross the Channel and invade Britain, but when Austria joined the Anglo-Russian alliance against France they withdrew and marched east to confront the Austrians on the Danube. Nelson's victory at Trafalgar, on 21 October 1805, also brought the stunning news of his death, a blow compounded on 2 December by the rout of the Austrians and Russians at Austerlitz. These punishing events may have hastened Pitt's decline and his death, aged just forty-six, on 23 January 1806.

The so-called 'Ministry of All the Talents' followed. This was a more liberally inclined coalition intended to secure political stability, formed around William Wyndham, Lord Grenville. It comprised the Whig allies of Charles James Fox, with Addington (now Lord Sidmouth) and his friend Edward Law, Lord Ellenborough, as Chief Justice. Fox became Secretary of State for Foreign Affairs and, although peace with France was not an option, for a time it seemed that parliamentary reform would once again be on the agenda. But Fox's health collapsed over the summer and on 13 September he, too, was dead. When Grenville was returned as Prime Minister in an October general election, the impetus for reform had lost momentum.[39]

Two causes close to the Foxite party, however, remained alive, and both were taken up by the *News*. The paper's campaign against the slave trade continued on 22 February 1807 with an account of 'an *English* plantation in Demerara', accompanied by demands for the ending of this 'detestable enormity'. When abolition came the following month, the *News* welcomed 'a measure so essential to sound policy as well as to justice and humanity'. The campaign for Catholic emancipation fared less well: in April 1807 its opponents exploited anti-papist feeling to bring down the 'Ministry of All the Talents' in favour of a reactionary administration under the ageing Duke of Portland.[40] 'No Popery' had won the day, and Catholic emancipation was postponed for two decades. Today, long after John Hunt was writing in the *News*, we can appreciate the courage and foresight of his argument that Ireland required the '[r]edress of grievances, on the broad scale of general impartiality, [and] the enjoyment of civil rights equally imparted to Catholics and Protestants'. Drawing on Hunt family history, John added: 'When shall we be wise, if experience itself is incompetent to teach us? surely the example of America should have taught us that a high spirited and determined people are not to be opprest.'[41]

Around this time John wrote to Hunt, 'I hear of the increased interest you take in public matters with much satisfaction.'[42] Hunt's quickening interest appears most clearly in relation to his old friends, the Papendiecks. In July 1806 he visited the family at their fashionable home on the Thames at Barnes Terrace (perhaps it was on this occasion that he made the short walk to Richmond Park to see Addington). The theatres were closed over the summer, and Hunt needed a break. His visit gave him that, but not in the way he expected. He found his friends obsessed with courtly tittle-tattle. Mrs Papendieck's mother, 'a good-natured fine old lady', was all in a flutter about the Prince of Wales: 'she described his entrance into a room, and gingerly putting forward her right foot, cried out "Oh such a leg! It was enchanting!"' This was what Hunt called 'the vortex of a court', a miasma of hypocrisy in which rank, wealth, self-interest, 'enchanting' legs and 'pleasing the great' took precedence over honesty and self-respect. He listened aghast as her daughter described the Prince of Wales as 'the finest gentleman she knows', while admitting she knew that he could behave like a '*perfect blackguard*': 'one Court day, after he had been charming every body with the elegance of his manners, she heard him address his groom in a style of the most disgusting vulgarity and in words which she should blush to repeat'. 'So much for the Heir Apparent,' Hunt observed.[43]

There was reason for this court mania. Frederick's father, Christopher Papendieck, was a member of the Queen's Household, mingling with the ushers, grooms, and quarterly waiters as one of the 'Pages of the Back Stair' (for which he received £80 a year).[44] And now Hunt's school friend Frederick was being lured into the courtly labyrinth, 'to wait on such and such a person' and 'to behave with deference'. Thomas Mitchell had warned Hunt of this change, and now he saw for himself that Papendieck had 'no opinion of his

own before the rich and the great'. A rift was inevitable, and Hunt wrote to
Marian that his friend had become so 'vain and selfish' that their former affection had cooled to 'common acquaintance'.[45]

Hunt's awareness of court politics reinforced his belief that principled independence was a 'blessing', and his views started to influence the *News*. On
domestic issues the *News* was pursuing a campaign against corruption. The
paper exposed bribery in the army – 'it is not merit, but money, that makes
a soldier' – and mismanagement at Christ's Hospital, where the Vicar of
Edmonton, whose living was known to be worth £1,200, had fraudulently
enrolled a son 'on the Charity'.[46] As an employee in the 'Army-Accompts'
office and one-time pupil at the school, Hunt was the source of both stories.

In February 1806 John moved into a new market with an evening paper,
the *Statesman*. Maintaining the successful innovations of the *News*, the
Statesman announced 'strong features of impartiality' both in recording
'actions of Ministry' and in its '*unbiassed* and liberal Theatrical Criticism'.[47]
Launching another paper alongside the flourishing *News* shows John's tremendous ambition and energy as a businessman and, behind that, a sharpening
political commitment. Hunt voiced his hopes for 'a large circulation in the
Ministerial circles', and asked Marian to forward copies to the courtly vortex
at Barnes Terrace.

In other respects publishing was 'much depressed'.[48] A new initiative was
needed, and on 1 December 1806 John branched into literature by issuing
monthly selections from prose writers of the previous century, entitled *Classic
Tales, Serious and Lively*. Each issue cost 2s.6d. and the completed series was
bound into five volumes. The contents were calculated to appeal to a broad
market, and included Henry Mackenzie, Oliver Goldsmith, Henry Brooke,
Voltaire and Samuel Johnson. Illustrations were supplied by Robert Hunt,
and introductions to some of the selections were written by Hunt who took
the opportunity to put forward his own literary ideas. The eighteenth-century
horizons of Hunt's reading apparent in *Juvenilia* had been swept away. Now
William Cowper and Robert Southey were hailed as the 'most original poets
of our time' (with reservations about the 'affected homeliness' of some of
Southey's ballads). Hunt praised Charlotte Smith's sonnets, and gave polite
attention to Maria Edgeworth, Anna Laetitia Barbauld and John Horne Tooke.
Henry Mackenzie's 'liberal spirit' and 'liberality of sentiment' were recommended, and here Hunt announced a theme that would persist throughout
his own writings: art's demand for 'liberty of thought and speech'. The liberal
tone continues in his comments on prose style, notably in his observation that
'the most perfect style seems to be that which avoids the negligence while it
preserves the spirit of conversation'.[49] Mentioned as an aside, this provides
a keynote for the prose style Hunt perfected for himself. Without reading
Wordsworth, Hunt had arrived at a stylistic ideal resembling the *Lyrical*

Ballads manifesto for poetry that would adapt 'the language of conversation . . . to the purposes of poetic pleasure'.

Hunt's remark that 'imagination is the soul of poetry' flowed with the new currents of contemporary thinking, and would have been perfectly intelligible to Thomas Warton and Coleridge. Distinctively Hunt's, though, was his attack on religions that 'paralyse the lips from smiling and the heart from bounding with affection'. His essay on Johnson revealed the emergence of his own identity and philosophy as a writer: 'if the end of instruction be the happiness of the community, I would rather gather my conclusions from a writer, who leaves me in a better humour with the world and therefore in a better condition to exert myself for its welfare'.[50]

Exertion on behalf of 'the community' appeared early in Hunt's theatrical reviews for the *News*. The 'decline' of the English theatre evident on stage each evening could, he thought, be traced to the 'depravation of public taste [and] public virtue'. At Drury Lane a riot in the audience was 'as much to be expected as the rising of the curtain'.[51] From the outset Hunt's criticism of literature, theatre and other arts dovetailed with his social and political campaigns: corruption had infiltrated the military, Christ's Hospital and, he now discovered, the management of theatres and the reviewing of plays. The problem was 'the system of puffing' and the 'green room' conspiracy. Managers laid on free tickets and lobster suppers with lashings of wine, by way of encouraging reviewers to cry up dreadful plays and deplorable acting. As in politics, the 'great *existing* reason' for the decline was 'mere want of critical opposition'. Hunt and the *News* would fill that gap: 'independence in theatrical criticism would be a great novelty'.[52]

What was contemporary theatre reviewing like? Here is a typical review in the *Traveller*, puffing a Covent Garden production by George Colman and that 'importer of songs' Michael Kelly:

> A New Musical Farce, entitled *We fly by Night*, was brought out last night, and received with the warmest approbation. – Indeed it is irresistibly laughable. It has all the good properties of a Farce – broad humour – comic incident – probable equivoque – and ludicrous character. It is a trifle which Mr. Colman hastily wrote, and Mr. Kelly set to music for the Little Theatre, and which, we understand, was kept back on account of the death of the Duke of Gloucester. It has some good puns, and many that are wretchedly bad; but it is upon the whole so whimsical, and is so laughably supported by Mr. Munden, Mr. Fawcett, Mr. Liston, Mr. Farley, and Mr. Blanchard, that he must be fastidious indeed who does not enjoy its merriment.[53]

This fly-by-night reviewer contrived to magnify a 'trifle' that was 'hastily written' and, frankly, 'wretchedly bad' into a comic masterpiece that would pack the house. Hunt enjoyed puns and whimsy, and he had written a farce that Mr. Kelly had mislaid. But he also saw the need for a more discriminating criticism, unswayed by green room blandishments and courtly deference ('kept back on account of the death of the Duke of Gloucester'). Accordingly, he refused free tickets and dinner invitations, broke with the convention of 'puffing', and offered instead a combative critical judgement from which the leading tragic and comic actors of the day would not be exempt.

The London stage was disgraced by 'wretched dramas which are called new without the least pretension of originality', and by actors whose 'histrionic genius' exaggerated the 'surfaces and externals' of character.[54] They hammed up 'unmeaning dialogue' with 'the most powerful expression', much as Braham and Billington roared *hate*, *war* and *glory*.[55] We've already encountered the leading tragic actor of the day, John Kemble, at Benjamin West's breakfast in Paris. On stage, Kemble excelled at soliloquy and roles that demanded a powerful, imperious presence. Hamlet, Macbeth and, especially, Coriolanus suited his talents best, although Hunt noted that his studied manner meant that 'he never pulls out his handkerchief without a design on the audience'.[56] Kemble's pronunciation was contrived too. Instead of 'innocent', Kemble said 'innocint'. On Kemble's lips 'conscience' sharpened into 'conshince'; 'virtue' smiled into 'varchue'; 'odious' puckered down to 'ojus'; and 'hideous' was swallowed into a hiccup: 'hijjus'.[57] Kemble's 'methodical expression', as Hunt called it, was restricted to 'external habits': he seemed unable to comprehend inner, 'mental character'. Kemble's sister Sarah Siddons, by contrast, Hunt found 'always natural, because on occasions of great feeling . . . the passions should influence the actions'. Her passionately 'natural carelessness' disclosed the heart and 'the action of the mind'. As Lady Macbeth, Siddons's face was 'a volume of terrible meaning'.[58]

On 13 December 1806, the *News* announced the publication of Hunt's *Critical Essays on the Performers of the London Theatres*. Gathering his reviews from the previous two years, *Critical Essays* established Hunt as the first modern theatre critic. The book did much to open the way for the more celebrated Shakespeare criticism of Coleridge, Lamb and Hazlitt, all of whom, like Hunt, were concerned with 'action of the mind'.[59] The responses to Hunt's book were enthusiastic: 'the public are indebted, deeply indebted, to Mr. Hunt, as being the first popular writer who has diffused rational sentiments respecting the performers'; 'we cannot but recommend this judicious critic as a guide to dramatic judgment'; a third praised the 'discernment which we very seldom discover in the remarks of newspaper-writers on the passing events of the stage'.[60] Only the *Satirist* came out against him, indeed, against all four Hunts involved in the book. It suggests their public profile as a family enterprise:

In short, this wonderful work, this literary sun is to throw a radiance over the whole house of HUNT. Mr. Leigh Hunt writes, Mr. R. Hunt designs the vignette, Mr. *Maecenas* John Hunt prints and publishes, and the *reverend* father of these Hunts subscribes it round to the trade.[61]

Hunt's 'theatricals' brought important new acquaintances. The young painters Benjamin Haydon and David Wilkie were so impressed by the 'remarkably clever theatrical critiques in the "News"' that they decided to arrange a meeting with the critic.

Just three years earlier Haydon had arrived in London, an ambitious eighteen-year-old crackling with energy and enthusiasm. As a boy in Plymouth, Devon, he had decided that he was destined to revive the tradition of English historical painting. From then on he pursued his life's work on an epic scale and with unwavering self-confidence. His vision of art's role in shaping national identity was Napoleonic in grandeur, and in some ways foreshadowed Victorian schemes for civic culture. In London the fulfilment of his ambitions appeared to come quickly. The teenager met fellow-painters Fuseli and Wilkie, enrolled at the Royal Academy, and was adopted by society patrons such as Lord Mulgrave and Sir George and Lady Beaumont. Convinced of his own genius and the high calling of his art, Haydon had an impressive, overwhelming presence. He saw in Hunt a like-minded young man – fearless, independent, witty, gossiping and sociable, 'one of the most delightful beings': 'Hunt and I liked each other so much we soon became intimate.'[62]

When the 'Prospectus' for another new paper to be published by John Hunt appeared in October 1807, it capitalised on the success of Hunt's theatricals by announcing that 'IMPARTIALITY' would be extended to the reporting of 'POLITICS' and 'FINE ARTS'. The 'Prospectus' mentioned Benjamin West and David Wilkie with respect, but it would be the rising young historical painter, Haydon, who would be championed in the 'Fine Arts' columns of the *Examiner*.

SEVEN

HEART AND HYPOCHONDRIA

While Hunt was cultivating an unassailable independence in the *News*, in private life he was engulfed by mental and physical anguish. His *Autobiography* devotes a whole chapter to 'Suffering and Reflection', but is less than forthcoming about why he had so suddenly been afflicted. Nineteenth-century readers would have expected Hunt's *Autobiography* to foreground his public roles rather than scenes from private, family life – scenes which, if noticed at all, would conventionally have been limited to an acknowledgement of marital bliss. When Thornton Hunt observed that his father's narrative was 'characteristically pronounced in its silence' about 'obvious family incidents', he drew attention to something typical of the author yet remarkable even in those reticent times.[1]

One 'incident' on which Hunt remained more or less silent was his relationship with Marian: in the first edition of his *Autobiography*, which runs to 968 pages in three volumes, she is mentioned just once. She was the 'good daughter' to whom Hunt 'ultimately became wedded for life'.[2] Thornton believed Marian's younger sister Bess – by implication, the 'bad daughter' – would have proved the better companion for his father. He described her as intelligent, literary, 'ardent' in feeling (which also meant bad tempered), and resolved in her opinions.[3] A perfect match for Hunt, one might think, except that when they first met she had come too close to competing with him. Hunt's ideal wife was modelled on his mother's passivity and melancholy, and he passed over Bess for Marian's 'cherishable' form and her 'mouth made for kisses'.[4]

Hunt's earliest surviving letter to Marian addressed her as a comforting, maternal presence: 'one whose image is always with me, whose idea soothes my slumber at night and wakes with me in the morning'.[5] Absorbed by his rhapsodic 'image' and 'idea' of Marian, he was scarcely ready for any kind of relationship, and soon revealed the vulnerable, demanding side of his nature which required Marian to admire and attend. He would be her guide and tutor, Marian the compliant pupil. When he was sickly, Marian must be a prompt and sympathetic nurse – and she should be aware that 'even a tune on the flute . . . may enliven the hour of sickness'.[6] If the nineteenth-century wife was expected to be an 'angel in the house', Hunt intended a more specialised role for Marian: the angel in the sick-room. She would fulfil that wish, although not in the way that he expected. Their strange relationship resembles the Pygmalion story in Ovid's *Metamorphoses* (Pygmalion, King of Cyprus, makes a statue of a perfect woman and loves it so intensely that Aphrodite brings it to life). Hunt, the devoted idealist sought to transform Marian – young, un-educated and, he assumed, malleable – into a perfect embodiment of feminine mildness. Early in 1803 they were engaged to be married.

Miffing and tiffing – mostly by Hunt – characterised their relationship from the start. When Marian was preoccupied with packing for a visit to Brighton, Hunt flounced: 'you might have come down before a *quarter to nine*, considering I was not to see you for a week'.[7] That was in summer 1803. Early next year, when the engagement was temporarily 'off', there was a row with Marian's mother that rendered Hunt tragically unfit 'to come to tea'. By now he was adept at using his sickliness, which was real enough, to manip-ulate others. There is also evidence that John, with whom Hunt was living at this time, disapproved of Marian. But within days Hunt was writing 'with a beating heart' imploring the return of 'our former love', urging Marian not to keep him 'long in suspense'.[8]

At a first glance these ups and downs seem typical of any brittle, adolescent passion; when they first met, Marian was thirteen, and Hunt approaching his seventeenth birthday. For him, though, the idea of a 'beating heart' meant much more than the pulse of passion. His susceptibility to palpitations and irregular heartbeats meant that excitement or nervousness frequently produced the sensation of something physically moving his heart. His stressful relationship with Marian, combined with long hours and overwork, provoked physical symptoms that could be alarming but which also helped him discover his own identity as a writer.

From 1804 onwards the engagement settled down for a time, with Hunt encouraging Marian to 'improve' and 'excel': 'I myself am an example,' he airily informed her. And Marian, determined not to be patronised, resisted by giving him a nickname: 'Dr Henry'.[9] On the back of one of Hunt's letters she scribbled, 'Dr Henry to gratify you is certainly is one of my first studies' (*sic*).[10] Marian could be snippy too, but her letters from these early years have been lost so that she is glimpsed only through Hunt's reproaches and exhor-tations: 'read oftener than you do'; 'your way of expressing yourself . . . is sometimes violent and generally coldly rough'; '*prefer scratching out to hasty blots and rescriptions*'; 'I wished you to write me careful, neat, unblotted letters'; 'I flatter myself that your love for me has arisen out of a respect for my mind'.[11] And so on. Hunt had resisted the physical thuggery of Christ's Hospital, but in these letters he hadn't outgrown the condescension of a senior schoolboy to a junior. Telling Marian he 'flattered himself' that she loved him for his mind betrayed his lack of self-knowledge and a complete failure, so far, to comprehend her individuality. Ironically, had he said the same of Marian's sister Bess, the grotesque sentiment would have had a kernel of truth. There are more appealing aspects of Hunt's correspondence with Marian, but in most of them she is represented as negligent, inattentive, incapable. To see Marian clearly, we too must resist 'Dr Henry'.

Marian's difficulties with spelling, grammar and writing reflected her lack of formal education. That said, one of Marian's letters that has come down to us is written in ink with a neat, steady copperplate hand. And the spelling is perfect.[12] As we've already seen, she was an accomplished seamstress who would later turn her skilful co-ordination of eyes and hands to the delicate art of cutting silhouettes. A figure or head cut out of dark card, and mounted against a white background, created a one-dimensional precursor of black and white photography. She also excelled as a sculptor – her bust of Shelley remains one of the most striking likenesses of him – and in correspondence she could hold her own in exchanges with both Percy and Mary Shelley. All of this should alert us to be wary of Thornton's claim that his mother could not give 'stedfast attention' to his father's literary conversation, and that she had been responsible, ultimately, for an unsatisfactory marriage.[13] Edmund Blunden took the different view that, by passing over Bess for Marian, Hunt was 'the loser by the decision through half a century of an unequal compact'.[14] There is nothing to indicate that Hunt ever felt himself 'the loser': however unsatisfactory the relationship appeared to others, it lasted, apparently with undiminished affection, for more than half a century. And marrying Marian meant that Bess would not have to be passed over at all. Far from it.

The only surviving portrait of Marian is a charcoal sketch depicting a world-weary woman. Her features and skin are smooth and there's a hint of the adolescent openness of countenance that first attracted Hunt. Marian's eyes are dark and quite wide apart; her nose is delicate, her neck plump, and her hair is parted smoothly in the middle and swept up (this style dates from the 1830s). The dark glossy hair forms a graceful outline to the face, and another striking detail in the profile is the firm jawline. Marian's chin is a strong one, indicating the determination she inherited from her mother. She seems to have a mobile, expressive mouth, too, the downturn in the portrait suggesting passivity and sadness but the potential to laugh and argue as well.

Although the portrait dates from Marian's middle age, it retains the animated spirit and expressive manner that Hunt had termed 'rough'.[15] These resolute qualities determined her to hold out against Dr Henry's efforts to subdue and mould her to what he assumed was 'the natural tenderness of her sex'.[16] By August 1806 the relationship was again in trouble, with Hunt admitting he no longer felt 'uniformly warm' towards her. Five days later he wrote again: 'Beware, my dearest, dearest Marian, how you slide into that negligent state of affection, which thinks it has nothing more to do to preserve the love of another than to profess every now and then an unaltering affection, without taking care to *alter* what might be *altered* or to pay attention.'[17]

In March 1807, Marian was at Brighton to recover after the long London winter, and to escape Hunt's demands and reproaches. It is also possible that her mother was contriving to separate them: she disapproved of his political and religious opinions, and was suspicious of his attentions to Bess. But in Marian's absence Hunt rallied, made amends for his '*seeming* forgetfulness' of her, and forwarded a box of oranges and some novels 'to contribute to the health of my darling girl'.[18]

Marian's illness was related to the tensions of her relationship with Hunt and the difficulties of her home life. One of her symptoms was 'a great deal of pain' – so much, in fact, that her back needed support.[19] Another was alarming attacks of spitting and vomiting blood, treated by applying leeches to draw off more blood and by the standard remedy of bleeding. It is difficult today to ascertain the physical cause of Marian's blood-spitting: the same trouble would recur fifteen years later, at another distressing time when it may have been related to incipient consumption. In spring 1807 her illness was probably caused by a gastro-intestinal condition – most likely an ulcer that would flare up from time to time throughout her life.

Assisting Marian's recovery meant that Hunt was able to make amends for ignoring his mother on her deathbed. He had not found time to visit the 'little miniature house' at Somers Town where she was languishing, 'tormented with rheumatism' – and then, suddenly, it was too late. On 5 November 1805 word came that Godfrey Thornton had died: his hospitable home at Austin Friars had welcomed Hunt from Christ's Hospital.[20] Worse news was to follow. Within days Hunt heard of his mother's lonely death, and on 11 November 'Maria Hunt' was buried in the churchyard at Hampstead.[21]

His life collapsed. In the months following his mother's death the twenty-one-year-old Hunt endured 'a nervous condition, amounting to hypochondria', a term that by the early nineteenth century had acquired the sense in which it is used today. Hunt's symptoms were a 'melancholy state of mind', 'palpitations of the heart', fears of 'sudden death' and a morbid introspective spiral around which he would chase 'a cause of causes for anxiety'.[22] He was all too aware that these terrors had 'no cause whatsoever'; nevertheless, he seemed to be haunted by something he could not see or place. It was as if the night terrors of his childhood – the ravenous, grinning Mantichora – now stalked him in forms he 'never saw, or could even imagine'.[23]

A contemporary handbook of *Domestic Medicine* noted that nervous disorders, including Hunt's erysipelas, 'often proceed from affections of the mind, as grief, disappointments, anxiety, intense study, &c.' and listed typical symptoms as 'straitness of the breast, with difficulty of breathing; violent palpitations of the heart; sudden flushings of heat . . . the pulse very variable, sometimes uncommonly slow, and at other times very quick'.[24] All of these resemble what Hunt suffered, and his attempts at a cure followed the recommended treatments of the day. By adopting a 'spare' diet and plenty of exercise he could alleviate the physical manifestations of sickness – although trying to 'outstarve' his illness in the approved manner made him so 'weak and giddy' he was incapable of walking. Horse-riding and fresh air he found more effective therapies, however, easing his palpitations and reviving his vigour. In February 1806 – some three months after his mother's death – Hunt left London to visit the market town of Gainsborough, Lincolnshire, where he stayed with Charles Robertson, the artist brother of John Robertson who had brought Hunt and Marian together. Soon Hunt was reporting that daily rides, on one occasion as far as Doncaster, had cured his heart of its 'vagaries': 'the brisk air playing on my face seems to fill my veins with a new spirit of health'.[25] But this was a temporary respite from the symptoms rather than the causes of his malaise.

Hunt's illness would probably be classified now as a hysterical condition brought on by stress and an inability to resolve feelings of grief and guilt about his mother. Hunt accounted for his symptoms in terms of 'bodily ailments', and perceptively ascribed his recovery from a later attack to the 'unconscious' removal of an 'internal obstruction'. Hunt thought that his illness was 'owing to living too well' – culpably so, while his mother lay dying – and prescribed for himself a spartan regime of vegetarian food and exercise.[26] This was a telling self-diagnosis, startlingly modern in its effort to probe the emotional and psychological causes of his own disorder. It was during this first attack of 'hypochondria' that Hunt encountered the child 'all over sores, and cased in steel', and reflected on paternal 'irregularities'. This happened on one of his excursions from Gainsborough and, years afterwards, he described how that scene continued to affect him: 'I confess that I would rather have seen the heart of the very father of that child,' Hunt wrote,

> than I would the child himself. I am sure it must have bled at the sight. I am sure there would have been a feeling of some sort to vindicate nature, granting that up to that moment the man had been a fool or even a scoundrel. Sullenness itself would have been some amends; some sort of confession and regret.[27]

Unable to contemplate the child's suffering, Hunt clings to the hope that natural feeling of some sort survived in the father. By this time he was writing as a father himself, although in 1806 the scene of familial 'irregularities' had been a horrifying reminder of his own irresponsibilities and of the need for remorse.

Amends. Confession. Regret. While Hunt's regime of 'super-abstinence' was recommended by contemporary medical authorities, its harshness was also an attempt to purge his identification with Isaac. This was a penance Hunt eagerly embraced: through self-denial, he would attain the temperate life he had celebrated in *The Palace of Pleasure* (not recognising that this regime implies 'moderation in self denial' too).[28]

Looking back over this first period of 'hypochondria', it appeared as a necessary rite of passage. In retrospect Hunt could see how the 'gay and confident spirit' of the prodigy-about-town had been curbed, shaping a more humane cast of mind that was patient and content with 'little pleasures'. Benjamin Haydon, the painter, was a volatile friend, but he understood the unhappy depths of Hunt's personality, his 'morbid sensibility of temperament' and the 'painful, hypochondriac Soul' beneath his outward gaiety.[29] By deliberately cultivating cheerful habits Hunt retained an 'air of cheerfulness', and he attributed this resilience to the 'cheerful opinions' of Universalism: enduring hypochondria, an illness 'neither visible nor even existing', gave him reason to doubt whether 'evil, considered in itself, existed'.[30] But Haydon noted that Hunt's hatred of orthodox Christianity and 'the gloomy prospects of damnation' betrayed his lingering dread at the possibility of being devoured in hell 'where there shall be weeping & wailing & knashing of teeth'.[31] 'Hence,' Haydon concluded, 'hence his horror of being left alone *even for an hour!*'[32] Hunt's philosophy of 'cheerfulness' was hard-won, and we can now appreciate how much personal torment was masked by the breezy, irresponsible manner Dickens caricatured in Harold Skimpole in *Bleak House*. Behind a blithe exterior, Hunt battled with a monstrous affliction that devoured from within – and was all the more frightening for having 'no cause whatsoever'.[33]

One of his strategies for coping was to celebrate the heart as the centre of human well-being – physical, emotional, spiritual. In this he was indebted to Rousseau, whom he thought displayed 'a deep knowledge of the heart', although Hunt's knowledge also had a personal, physiological basis.[34] Suffering from palpitations had made him acutely sensitive to heart movements, so that when he wrote to Marian of the 'vagaries' in his pulse, or of his heart 'beating' with anticipation, his remarks reflected an unusually intense heart-consciousness. 'When the heart is not in action,' he told Marian in a letter of July 1806, 'happiness is not in being.'[35] Hunt's phrase unfolds to reveal the heart's action as a super-sensitive indicator of individual and social welfare. As Hunt knew, the American Declaration of Independence had declared that 'all men are created equal, that they are endowed by their Creator with certain unalienable Rights, that among these are Life, Liberty and the pursuit of Happiness'. Violation of those rights would be a heartfelt insult to individuals and, by the same token, the heart in action could, literally, betoken the well-being or otherwise of the body politic. When in another

letter of August 1806 Hunt suggested to Marian that wisdom came from 'a
knowledge of the human heart', the cliché was refreshed by this heightened
awareness of what the organ's various actions might signify.[36] A wise 'heart
knowledge' gave insight into human nature like Rousseau's, and, less conventionally, was attuned to super-subtle emotional and spiritual influences.

Hunt's understanding of 'heart knowledge' would be central to *The Story
of Rimini*, and a core of strength for him in the aftermath of Shelley's death.
It would grow into the mystical 'sense of religion at heart' that Hunt described
in *Christianism* (1832) and *The Religion of the Heart* (1853), becoming a creed
of 'cheerfulness' that kept 'the body in health, and the mind in good temper',
ensured 'the advancement of the common good', and responded to 'the vital
spirit of the universe, the great cause of cheerfulness as well as life'.[37]

In July 1807 he left London for a vacation. In the company of an office
acquaintance, John Stuart, and his family, Hunt took a hoy down the Thames
to revisit Margate. He bathed, walked over the cliffs with Miss Stuart, and
wrote to London teasing 'Betsey' that, despite these exertions, he still had
'strength enough to write her something like a letter'.[38] Another letter followed,
this time to Marian who had remained at Brighton: they had not seen each
other for some five months. He was 'stout and hearty', flirting with Miss
Stuart and seeing 'romance spreading in her mind'; 'she is as fond of the
moon as you are,' he let Marian know, 'and the other day began talking to
me about the setting sun looking like a promised land.'

'You need not be jealous,' Dr Henry reassured Marian, 'while you try to
improve yourself, and fix in your mind those complacencies of thinking and
of wishing, which produce a mild demeanour . . . I wish you to improve yourself in reading, to preserve my respect and esteem: I wish you to be mild, to
preserve my love. Your absence from home is the best opportunity you can
have for these improvements.'[39] He signed off, 'I know you will write a long
letter to your affectionate HENRY.'

Another lecture. He was still trying to sculpt Marian into a mild *mater
dolorosa*. Marian, however, was becoming cannily aware of how Hunt's mother-
fixation might be turned to her advantage. But she was content, for now, to
bide her time.

Part III: 'Examiner' Hunt, 1807–1812

I cannot but greatly applaud the boldness as well as the ability of your attacks upon the ruinous and unworthy conduct of our present rulers – and I am persuaded that the Press alone can now be looked to as the saviour of our country.

Henry Brougham to Leigh Hunt, 1812

EIGHT

THE *EXAMINER*

The 'Prospectus of the *Examiner*', 'A New Sunday Paper Upon Politics, Domestic Economy, and Theatricals', announced that

> *The Gentleman who has hitherto conducted, and is at present conducting, the* THEATRICAL DEPARTMENTS *in the* NEWS, will criticise the Theatre in the *EXAMINER*, and as the public have allowed the possibility of IMPARTIALITY in that department, we do not see why the same possibility may not be obtained in POLITICS.[1]

Behind this public-spirited statement by John Hunt lurked private worries. Isaac's partisan role in the American Revolution had brought misery to his family. As they embarked on their new publishing venture, his sons were determined not to make the same mistake.

In 1808 readers could choose between established monthly journals like the *Gentleman's Magazine* and the *Edinburgh Review*; weeklies like *Bell's Weekly Messenger* (independent) and Cobbett's *Political Register* (allied to the reformer Francis Burdett); and daily newspapers like the *Morning Chronicle* (Whig), *The Times*, the *Morning Post* and the *Courier*. The *Post* and *Courier* were mouthpieces of the government and court, in the pay of ministers and the Prince of Wales. Stationed securely above the swirl of events and shifting allegiances, the *Examiner* would offer weekly reports and editorial commentary from an independent perspective. Reference to 'THEATRICAL DEPARTMENTS *in the* NEWS' assumed an educated and literate readership, setting the *Examiner* apart from overtly populist journals such as William Cobbett's *Political Register*. In the *Examiner*, readers would find politics alongside material of cultural interest. Robert Hunt, who had ambitions as a painter, would contribute on the Fine Arts. There would be no tittle-tattle about adultery, seductions, horse-racing, prize-fighting and cock-fighting. Whereas other newspapers of the day such as *The Times* were packed with advertising, the Prospectus promised 'NO ADVERTISEMENTS WILL BE ADMITTED in the *EXAMINER*'. Quack doctors peddling 'promises of instant restoration' would not disgrace its pages.[2]

Preparations for publication continued through the winter, and the first number appeared early on Sunday, 3 January 1808. The *Examiner*'s quarto format was more compact than the usual broadsheet, but by printing with minute type in double columns the sixteen pages of a single issue contained an extraordinary amount. The price was 8½d. of which almost half was 'stamp duty', a government tax imposed to raise revenue, squeeze profits, and curb the influence of the press. That the *Examiner* succeeded 'gloriously', as Hunt said, was evidence of the nation's hunger for news that had not been manipulated or 'spun'.[3]

On the front page of 'No. 1' was Hunt's editorial leader, 'The Political Examiner', entitled 'On the Separation of Russia from the British Interest'. In January 1808 this story wasn't fresh news, although readers would have recognised that Hunt was tackling the most decisive recent event of the war. Napoleon had defeated the Russian Emperor Alexander, hitherto Britain's ally, back in June 1807; they made peace at the Treaty of Tilsit, and agreed to force Denmark, Sweden and, in the south, Portugal, into their sphere of influence. By winter 1807–8 Britain was isolated.

Hunt's angle on this notorious piece of treaty-mongering was a hard-hitting polemic on the follies of national leaders. Monarchs and emperors are 'mere men walking . . . in a kind of sunny mist, that renders the appearance gigantic', he writes, adapting a proverbial image to the contemporary scene and describing Alexander's volte-face with witty contempt: Alexander 'was the ally of England because he thought her alliance was to his interest, he meets the French in battle, is beaten, drinks a bottle of wine with that "*upstart*" and "*usurper*" his enemy [Napoleon], and separates from his English ally because he thinks the French one more to his interest'. 'If we must wonder at the Emperor of Russia,' Hunt concludes, 'let us wonder at him just as we wonder *what it is o'clock*, or *whether it will rain*, or at any other wonderful thing not at all wonderful.'[4] Hunt's reviewing for the *News* had exposed the flummery of the theatre; the *Examiner* would set about incompetent players on the world stage. Hunt signed off with his personal emblem, the image of a hand with a pointing index finger ☞. From now on, this 'Indicator hand' would identify all of his contributions.

The first *Examiner* reprinted the 'Prospectus', again giving upper-case emphasis to 'IMPARTIALITY' in 'POLITICS'. 'Foreign Intelligence' from France, Germany, Spain, and reports 'From the American Papers' of November 1807 were indeed treated impartially, without editorial comment. On other pages, however, a more distinctive vision started to emerge. French and British decrees and counter-decrees about shipping were given a satirical slant. So was the Prince Regent of Portugal, who had fled to Brazil leaving instructions that his countrymen were to display '*good harmony . . . to the armies of nations with whom they find themselves united on the Continent*'. 'Find themselves!' was Hunt's astonished response at the Prince abandoning his country to the French:

'Find themselves!'[5] Resistance to the abolition of slavery in Jamaica, and rumours of an approaching American war received close consideration.

An editorial column headed 'The Examiner' presented Hunt's views on double-dealing princes and emperors, on the derangement 'of royal intellect', on 'the execrable traffic in mankind' and 'guilty men' in Jamaica. He also voiced his hopes that Britain and America will 'shake hands and be wise'.[6] Coverage of the arts included news of an exhibition at the Pennsylvania Academy of Fine Arts, Philadelphia, mentioning that Benjamin West's paintings of *Lear* and *Ophelia* will be shown. Hunt's 'Theatrical Examiner' devoted four columns to *Much Ado about Nothing* at Drury Lane Theatre, a play as 'natural as it is lively' and performed with 'much animation' except for 'an astonishing disregard of chronological propriety' in the costumes. Under 'Law' were details of court actions for adultery and 'seduction'. On the back page, well away from the rigorous announcements of the 'Prospectus', the *Examiner* reported a scuffle in a box at Drury Lane ('a pugilistic contest' over a 'STRUMPET' by two 'BOX-LOUNGING BLACKGUARDS') and the imprisonment of a 'detestable old monster . . . on the serious charge of infamously assaulting an infant child, his scholar, under the age of ten years'. Notices of marriages and deaths followed, and, at the bottom of the page: 'Printed and published by JOHN HUNT, at the Office of THE EXAMINER, 15, Beaufort Buildings, Strand.'

Hunt now divided his time between his weekday job in the War Office, writing for the *Examiner*, and theatre reviewing late into the night. In the first year of the paper he contributed thirty-six theatrical reviews, including an account of the revival of *King Lear* at Covent Garden. The play was Nahum Tate's 'improved' version performed throughout the eighteenth century in which Cordelia survives and marries Edgar in the last scene. Hunt's review was a penetrating discussion of Shakespeare's tragedy, showing why the fatal catastrophe was 'natural and unavoidable'. Not surprisingly he was 'disappointed in the performance': Kemble as Lear 'damped the glowing business of the action'.[7] There was, however, nothing that could dampen the glow on the night of Tuesday, 19 September, when the theatre was gutted by fire. Five months later, on 24 February 1809, its rival in Drury Lane also succumbed, leaving nothing but 'an immense heap of ruins'.[8] Both theatres were quickly rebuilt, but when theatre managers attempted to pass the costs on to London's theatre-going citizens, they kindled another conflagration, the 'OP Riots', in which Hunt would take a leading role in securing a return to the old prices for tickets.

Beginning with the third *Examiner* Hunt's friend Henry Robertson contributed a regular column devoted to Italian Opera. Unlike the theatre, Italian Opera was the specialised interest of 'higher classes'. It received 'miserable treatment' in the press, while the 'unmusical and illiberal' exclaimed against any encouragement given to foreign composers. Jealousy and bad taste had long consigned Mozart to obscurity (like Shakespeare's catastrophe in *Lear*, Mozart's 'improbable' plots were a problem).[9] As with Hunt's theatrical criticism, the *Examiner* would redress such hostility: Robertson's campaign to break with prejudice and advance Italian music and opera was integral to the wider aims of the *Examiner* announced in the Prospectus. His 'Opera Letters' continued up to 1812, and included reviews of *Così fan Tutte* ('electrical effect'), *The Magic Flute* (marred by a company 'deficient in number as well as excellence'), and *The Marriage of Figaro* ('inexhaustible freshness, vigour, and originality').[10] The same period saw the rise and reign of the prima donna Angelina Catalani. Gifted with a 'wonderful voice', Catalani was always 'ambitious to outshine others' and, in performance, 'resolved to prevent the other performers from being heard'. Hunt remembered that 'the louder they became, the higher and more victorious she ascended'.[11]

From now on, Saturdays were hectic with the rush to get copy to the press; Sunday saw the *Examiner* published and distributed; and then the routine began again for another week. Hunt's energy and determination were immense. In addition to his weekly 'Political Examiner', 'Examiner' and 'Theatrical Examiner' columns, he revisited the Vicar of Edmonton's fraudulent attempt to enrol his son at Christ's Hospital and speculated on the governors' reluctance to hold an inquiry.[12] This local instance of a cover-up by powers-that-be would soon be repeated on a national scale, confirming Hunt's growing sense of widespread malaise. Looming large among his worries was the burgeoning popularity of Methodism, an irrational enthusiastic sect alien to the impartial, unprejudiced spirit of the *Examiner*.

On 8 May Hunt published the first of seven 'Essays on Methodism' attacking 'the Calvinist Methodist [who] breathes out fire and slaughter against all who differ with his opinions'.[13] Hunt's quarrel with the Methodists focused on their mistaking bodily symptoms as evidences of spiritual rapture or divine intervention. Hunt knew all about palpitations and leapings of the heart. For him those physical manifestations were associated with his mother's death; with fears of his own sudden extinction; and with anxiety, debility and depression. He had already attempted to rationalise and then to cure his affliction through exercise and a strictly regulated diet. In comparison, the Methodists were 'religious debauchees', mired in the 'extreme selfishness' of the sensual body, and they had 'nothing to do with those qualities for which we love our fellow-creatures, such as benevolence, good-temper, and *universal philanthropy*'. His memories of the Margate hoy were still fresh.

Religion emerged elsewhere in the *Examiner* during 1808, in the long-running campaign to win civil rights for Irish Catholics. When the most recent petition was rejected Hunt warned shrewdly that 'if ACHILLES in the midst of battle had bared his heel . . . he would hardly have done a more foolish thing than we are at present doing in our treatment of the Irish'.[14] The *Examiner* would take up their cause again.

On the international scene in 1808, the 'awful crisis' of Spanish and Portuguese capitulation to Napoleon emerged as the major story: 'The whole Continent . . . has kissed his foot'. Hunt attributed Napoleon's successes to 'silent and scientific' military prowess, and pointed to opportunities afforded by the incompetence of his enemies, most recently Spain and Portugal and, as events were shortly to reveal, Britain: 'We hesitate, our enemies determine; we delay and make flourishes about the edges, they dash to the heart of things.'[15] Faced by the *'corrupt politics* of his enemies', Napoleon presented himself as a liberator; he carried 'conquest in one hand and improvement in the other', and 'the nations he overthrows are usually in want of such a conqueror'. Meanwhile, the Prince of Wales enjoyed a characteristically ostentatious and expensive birthday celebration at Brighton, including a breakfast banquet at the Pavilion and a grand military parade on Newmarket Hill. Defended by an army of dandies in 'laced jackets and long pigtails rather than active and hopeful soldiers', Britain was ripe for Napoleon to take.[16]

In March the court martial of Lieutenant-General John Whitelocke, for a military débâcle in South America, reached the verdict that he was 'TOTALLY UNFIT AND UNWORTHY TO SERVE HIS MAJESTY IN ANY MILITARY CAPACITY WHATEVER'.[17] Two weeks later, Hunt launched a campaign against 'military purchase' – that is, promotion to senior ranks for cash payment, or through sexual intrigue, or both. In joining the St James's Volunteers, Hunt had been one of thousands who responded to a national emergency. Now events were uncovering the worthlessness of the country's military leaders: Hunt's memory of 'a gallant figure on a charger' pitched into the parade-ground dust no longer seemed an unfortunate accident. It was typical of the 'military aristocracy'.

The fifteenth 'Political Examiner' ('On the Necessity of a Military Reform') marked Hunt's arrival as a journalist to be reckoned with. Surveying the deplorable state of the armed forces, he darted from high-spirited, satirical wit to sardonic reflection:

> A young gentleman wishes to be a soldier – I beg pardon, an officer – and if he is asked what talents he possesses for command, the answer is quite ready, 'Sir, I have some hundred pounds in my pocket'. It is this system which together with the dilatory privileges of seniority and the gross favouritism of the higher powers, has rendered the finest soldiers as useless as straws and shed the blood of hundreds of my gallant countrymen.[18]

Most culpable of those 'higher powers' was the Commander-in-Chief who 'maintains his mistresses upon the sale of commissions'[19] – in other words,

the Duke of York, the same Duke whose 'victory' at Dunkirk Hunt had celebrated with a poem, only to discover the reality of an English defeat. Summer
1808 brought more evidence of rot in the system. On 1 August Sir Arthur
Wellesley's expeditionary force landed in Portugal, and secured a much-needed
victory at the Battle of Vimieiro. That was on 21 August. Next day, Wellesley
was succeeded in command by Sir Harry Burrard, who was superseded immediately by Sir Hew Dalrymple. This was an unseemly scramble for credit and,
not surprisingly, the gains at Vimieiro were squandered. Negotiations between
the British and French were formalised at the Convention of Cintra on 30
August, and the French army withdrew with its equipment intact.

News of the treaty broke in Britain on 16 September, whereupon elation
at Wellesley's victory swiftly turned to outrage. Robert Southey denounced
Cintra as a 'grievous national disgrace'. William Wordsworth remarked that
there was not 'a street, not a public room, not a fire-side in the island which
was not disturbed as by a local or private trouble'. The long shadow of Cintra
fell over *Childe Harold*, in which Byron imagines posterity sneering at 'these
champions cheated of their fame, / By foes in fight o'erthrown'; 'Britannia
sickens, Cintra! at thy name' (I. 24–26). Up to the minute with breaking news,
the *Examiner* reported on Cintra from 17 September onwards. By early
October, it had become 'the Universal Subject', enabling Hunt to draw
together the various themes of his journalism that year. Here was another
consequence of the 'lazy and disgusting corruption' of 'military purchases'.
Yet, throughout, the government had maintained a *'SUSPICIOUS
SILENCE'*. No one had been recalled from Portugal. No explanations had
been sought.[20]

On 23 October Hunt's 'Political Examiner' on 'Military Depravity' brought
forward the case of Major Hogan, an 'experienced and useful officer' repeatedly *'noted for promotion'* and as often passed over for younger men who had
'seen no service'. In a pamphlet, 'Appeal to the Public and a Farewell Address
to the Army', Hogan set out his applications for promotion and described the
personal remonstrance to the Duke of York in which he alluded to *'low intrigue
or PETTICOAT INFLUENCE'*. His determination to make his story public
brought a cash bribe of £400 with an anonymous letter promising 'much
benefit' if he kept silent.

Hogan published. In 'Military Depravity', Hunt drew on the pamphlet to
attack the 'military system',

> a dastardly carcass of corruption, full of sottishness and selfishness, preying
> upon the hard labour of honest men, and never to be moved but by its lust
> for women or its lust for money: and the time has at length arrived, when
> either the vices of one man must be sacrificed to the military honour of
> the country, or the military honour of the country must be sacrificed to the
> vices of one man, – an alternative truly monstrous and detestable.

The newspapers, political reviews, indeed 'the whole public voice of the country' have 'called upon his Royal Highness the DUKE OF YORK as the promoter and foster-father, if not the begetter, of these corruptions'.[21] The following week Hunt's 'Political Examiner' concluded with a wider rallying call: 'A reform in military matters will do away but one corruption; A REFORM IN PARLIA-MENT WILL PURIFY THE WHOLE CONSTITUTION.'[22]

'Military Depravity' hit its mark. Two months later, on Christmas Day 1808, the *Examiner* announced that 'HIS ROYAL HIGHNESS THE DUKE OF YORK having ORDERED A PROSECUTION to be commenced against the *EXAMINER* for its Strictures on Major HOGAN'S Pamphlet, an ADDRESS TO THE PUBLIC on the subject will appear on Sunday next'.[23] This libel charge made it unthinkable for Hunt to continue in government employment. Next morning he resigned from the War Office. His letter to Viscount Castlereagh, Secretary at War, explained that his post was incompatible with the 'sound freedom of thinking and speaking' and 'public duty' of the *Examiner*. This was a principled gesture, much in the spirit of Isaac's views on American independence, placing the 'purity and public ends' of his motives above 'every petty consideration'.[24] On New Year's Day 1809, the *Examiner* congratulated readers that 'enquiry' into corruption 'has been roused'. The paper's proprietors faced their impending prosecution as 'brothers by birth', proud to be 'brothers in suffering, if they can do one atom of service to the Constitution and help to awaken the eyes, the hands, and the hearts of Englishmen to the only effectual means of resistance against the common enemy'.[25]

The first weeks of 1809 brought news that the 'feeble, inconsistent, inconsequent, and useless' Board of Enquiry on Cintra had concluded that 'no further military proceeding is necessary on the subject'.[26] Then that story was sidelined by further scandalous allegations, combining sex, bribery and military corruption, brought against the Duke of York and his mistress Mrs Mary Anne Clarke. 'The sensation in London . . . is marvellous,' Lamb reported, as the gutter press overflowed with 'ballads, caricatures, lives of Mrs Clarke, in every blind alley'. 'Always of a gay turn, and very expensive habits', Mrs Clarke was rumoured to take money for persuading the Duke to make promotions. The matter was brought before the House of Commons by Gwyllym Wardle, MP for Okehampton, and for two months in February and March 1809 the case was debated. Hunt dined with Wardle on 1 March, and the *Examiner* followed his campaign closely. No one was surprised when the Duke was cleared, although his resignation as Commander-in-Chief followed and the prosecution for 'Military Depravity' was withdrawn. The *Examiner* was left to count the legal costs – £99 13s. 4d. had been spent in preparing a defence.[27]

Hunt's début as a journalist had been upbeat, assured and independent of party affiliations although, as Hunt's dinner with Wardle suggests, in other respects it was not exactly 'IMPARTIAL'. The *Examiner* had begun in 1808 by 'being of no party', Hunt would recall, 'but Reform soon gave it one'.[28] From now on Hunt's remarks on the Duke of York – 'a spendthrift, a debauchee, an adulterer'[29] – showed how easily his prized 'freedom of thinking and speaking' could slide into recklessness and 'scurrility'. The *Examiner* had escaped its first encounter with the law, but the potential for further confrontation was apparent.

Hunt's family history and his life at Christ's Hospital provided rich sources of material for the *Examiner*. In the second number of the paper he elaborated his attack on the planters of Jamaica by asking readers to imagine themselves as slaves:

> Let us suppose for an instant that a powerful black nation, possessed of resources to which our wealth is but poverty, and of sciences to which our knowledge is but ignorance, should invade our own country, carry off thousands of white men, husbands divided from their wives, and daughters rent from their parents, and make them toil in a distant country to render a species of liquor pleasant to the palate.

Others had urged readers to respond to the claims of common humanity, for example Hannah More in *Slavery: A Poem*,

> Revere affections mingled with our frame,
> In every nature, every clime the same;
> In all, these feelings equal sway maintain . . .
>   117–19[30]

Such humanitarian arguments echoed the Universalists' 'natural affection' for humankind, and in the *Examiner* Hunt's Barbadian origins brought a sense of more intimate kinship:

> are there not ties and families as dear in Africa, are there not bosoms capable of as tender a feeling, of as manly an indignation? How miserably ridiculous then is it to see the inhabitants of a little island setting up their petty interests against the happiness of a great continent. What would the Jamaica Planters have? Do they seriously request us to continue the Slave Trade for their sakes?

Hunt's editorial commitments brought problems. In April 1808 an 'obstinate cold' flared into serious illness, rendering him unable to contribute to the *Examiner* for a month. June brought a holiday in Nottingham, at the invitation of a former schoolfellow Samuel Payne. Hunt vividly described his journey 'jammed up in a hot coach with a silent farmer, a sleepy, lisping young man, and a revered wigsby of the usual dimensions, who railed against the Unitarians, and, what was worse, gave me no room for my legs'. Once there, Hunt did not relax. He rode in Sherwood Forest, where 'the inhabitants still talk of Robin Hood to strangers', toured factories, and on one evening went to the theatre where he learned with pleasure that the actress, Miss Woodfall, was 'marvellously frightened at the idea of my being in the boxes tonight'. An 'intelligent young physician', Dr James Clarke, took him to see 'the baleful effects of opium' which local women were 'constantly taking'. Clarke was interested in the latest advances in medicine. He explained the benefits of smallpox vaccination, a controversial treatment that Hunt observed had become 'a political question'. Back in his laboratory, Clarke wired Hunt to a galvanic machine and administered a jolt of electricity. He said he felt as if he had been 'shot through the head'.[31]

In autumn 1808 Marian once again fell ill with 'nerves', perhaps owing to the difficult domestic situation at Little Titchfield Street. Her mother now had a son, Rowland, and a daughter, Nancy, by Rowland Hunter. With Bess and Thomas Kent also living at home, strains were inevitable. Hunt believed Marian's illnesses had been treated with 'wavering and irresolution', and advised her mother that she would 'feel more comfortable elsewhere'. John Hunt's offer to lodge her with his family was rebuffed by Mrs Hunter but Marian did escape to find a cure at Ramsgate.[32]

Preoccupied with his responsibilities in London, Hunt forgot Marian's address. His letters, 'scribbled in a hurry' and 'directed at random', went astray. Marian wrote home complaining she had 'heard from nobody', thereby giving her mother opportunity to needle Hunt. He apologised to Marian for 'foolish neglects', and to make amends sent her a song he had recently composed, 'Love and the Aeolian Harp', informing her that it would shortly be published. But two weeks later Hunt still remained 'very uncertain' where Marian was living.[33]

Their relationship had reached a crisis. He could hardly find time to write letters and, when he did so, Marian was expected to take comfort from his own sense of pleasure and well-being: 'I believe there is nothing that pleases me in yourself half so much as your patience & cheerfulness in the midst of suffering . . . it is really a great satisfaction to me'.[34] Thanks, Dr Henry – but this was in fact a give-away. By declaring himself satisfied at her resemblance to his saintly, sickly mother, Hunt's letter shifted their strange, unstable relationship in Marian's favour.

Marian wrote asking Hunt to send a reminder of his mother. This did the trick, and Hunt replied by return of post to the correct address. 'I have not sent you immediately what you wished; but I will do it, my dear, dear girl . . . There is nothing which my mother has left behind her, to which you are not the proper heiress in the truest sense of the word.' In his next he enclosed two letters 'written with failing eyes, a trembling hand, and an aching heart by my mother, who is now an angel in heaven'. These were the 'melancholy', 'sacred', 'strengthening' tokens of his heart. This exchange clinched his iden-tification of Marian with his mother: he had found his angel in the sick-room. 'We shall be happy, very happy, I trust, my dear Marian,' he wrote, 'for I have nothing more to desire either in this world or the next, but to make you happy in the one, and to meet, in your company, my mother in the next.'[35]

Far from seeing that his seven-year relationship with Marian had been difficult, if not a disaster, Hunt was looking forward to marriage. Money had been a problem,

> I have seen so much of the irritabilities, or rather the miseries arising from want of a *suitable* income, and the best woman of her time was so wearied and finally worn out with the early negligence of others in this respect, that if ever I was determined on anything, it is to be perfectly clear of the world and ready to meet the exigencies of a married life.[36]

Hunt's new-found confidence about money reflected a recent development that promised financial security beyond anything he had known. Better times lay ahead.

Hunt's solicitor brother Stephen had been corresponding with John Lorain, an attorney at Philadelphia, seeking information about the property Isaac and Mary had abandoned at the time of the American Revolution. As the husband of Mary Hunt's sister Lydia Shewell, Lorain was related to the Hunt brothers and might be expected to act in their interests. On 11 November Lorain forwarded a will drawn up in 1772 for Mary Bickley Tonge (Mary Hunt's aunt) bequeathing £30, a silver case and, most tantalising, 'my Lot of land situate in the City of Philadelphia . . . near the centre . . . to my said niece Mary Hunt wife of Isaac Hunt . . . her heirs and assigns for ever'.[37] Lorain described this, somewhat evasively, as a plot in Market Street 'in possession of some person who has no right to it'. The land was likely to sell for $10,000, if the Hunts would authorise Lorain to act on their behalf. 'No time should be lost,' Lorain added: 'You had better give this subject some thought.'[38] The power of attorney authorising Lorain to act for the Hunts was duly forwarded.

Good news came from another direction too. The *Examiner* was 'getting on gloriously'. Its reputation was growing week by week, and each Monday after-noon a second edition 'designed for Country Readers' was printed in time to catch the mail coaches. By the end of 1808 weekly sales were well over 2,000 and rising, not far behind the *Morning Chronicle* (around 3,000 copies) and *Post* (about 4,500). Back copies of the *Examiner* were changing hands for four and five shillings each. John had agreed that Hunt should receive a regular salary. And in January 1809 James Whiting, publisher of Hunt's *Juvenilia*, paid the enormous sum of £800 to join the brothers as a partner.[39]

These were heady days. Flattering acknowledgements from readers included correspondence from Francis Wrangham, an English Jacobin of the 1790s, expressing delight at the *Examiner*'s 'spirit and elegance'. At Enfield School the paper was read by the teachers and pupils, among them John Keats. In the remote village of Ecclefechan in the Scottish border country, the *Examiner*'s 'weekly coming was looked for . . . The place of its delivery was besieged by an eager crowd, and its columns furnished the town talk till the next number came.' The painter David Wilkie, at home in Cults in north-east Fife, anxiously scanned the paper when it arrived. A letter came for 'Lee Hunt Esq' from John Murray, publisher of the Tory *Quarterly Review*, soliciting an essay on 'the state of the Drama'. Hunt would have been 'most willing' to contribute, but declined because the *Quarterly*'s politics were 'in direct opposition to his own'.[40] Believing himself clear of worldly worries, he was ready for married life.

But was Marian? Letters from spring 1809 suggest she had yet to decide. Bess was becoming more demonstrative about her feelings for Hunt, and the row between John and Mrs Hunter showed no sign of abating. John was a deist, and Hunt was emerging in the *Examiner* as an outspoken critic of the government. Mrs Hunter viewed both brothers with disapproval, but with a new family of her own, and Hunt's fortunes apparently improving, she was also keen to see Marian settled.

Marian, now aged twenty, was out of town at High Wycombe. She was there to improve her health, enjoying a lively social life and dancing with the 'red coats'. In May she confided to Bess that, with marriage drawing close, her '"gay days were all over"', though not, she trusted, '"*all* her happiness"'. She inserted the word '*all*' as an afterthought, as if to say, '"*most* of my happy days are gone as well as all my gay ones"'.[41] Bess had watched her sister's relationship, and didn't have to read between the lines to understand what was at stake for all three of them. It was Bess who had admired Hunt first. Far from keeping her feelings for Hunt secret, as Edmund Blunden believed, a mutual affection had grown. Adopting one of her mother's stratagems, she showed Hunt the letter from Marian. Even at this late stage the marriage might be called off.

Bess's warnings were ignored. Hunt's response to Marian, dated Monday, 30 May, reveals how completely he was absorbed by the idea of their happiness:

I must insist, Miss Kent, that you will retract, renounce, disavow, and utterly disclaim all such meanings as may be naturally put upon such words; for if I did not think, that you would be happier than ever you have been, when you are my wife, I would not marry you, whatever struggle it might cost me: but no: – is not your happiness wrapped up in mine? Will not you be a thousand times happier when you are mine, when we are always with each other, able to look upon each other, to speak to each other, to perform a thousand offices for each other, to be one. Ah, I am sure you did not mean what you said, did you?

Bess had immediately seen that Marian's letter should have turned Hunt against the marriage, but he had long made up his mind that Marian was not capable of saying or writing what she meant. To seal his vision of married bliss he contrasted their future happiness with what may be a reference to Dante's two lovers, Paolo and Francesca, who 'delight to be perpetually united'.[42] He did not add that their perpetual union was protracted in hell.

Within days of writing his letter to Marian, Robert Hunt reviewed A. J. Oliver's painting of *Paulo and Francesca* at the Royal Academy Exhibition:

This piece has a forcible effect, and the lovers are of those graceful forms which plant 'sweet love in gentle hearts'. They have just fatally finished reading a luxuriant account [of] how 'Launcelot was thrall'd in love'. The incident is taken from the 5th Canto of Dante's Inferno, shewing the dreadful effect of licentious books.[43]

The two 'graceful forms' belong to Francesca and her lover Paulo, brother of her husband Giovanni. Whether or not Hunt went to see this painting, the 'forcible effect' of Dante's incident stayed with him, and in years to come he would see how Dante's tragic love triangle could be mapped on to his own life.

As if sensing that Marian's head had been turned by one of the soldiers at High Wycombe, Hunt now acted swiftly. Another letter to Marian was dispatched on Wednesday, 7 June, sealed in an extra envelope and endorsed 'In closure, because the paper is so easily seen through'. When she unfolded the paper, Marian read that the arrangements for her marriage were under way, and she need only name the day of her return:

as you 'seriously' assure me that you are much better, I have only to say, that if you do not think coming to town will hurt you, *every thing is ready for you in this house*: – the *day after* your arrival, with God's blessing, I hope you will accompany me to the altar, and become mine by every tie of reason, of religion, & sound affection. This is the sum total of the *plan* of which I was to write next week, and I shall settle it all with Mrs. Hunter, as you have allowed me, my dearest love, before you return: – I have only to add, that as I shall get a license, the day depends upon yourself, and I am sure, from what I have known so long of your heart & your head, that nothing will prevent you from making your Henry as happy as you can. So pray weigh all this well, and write me an answer, directly from your heart.[44]

Having spent years instructing Marian to write in a formal, considered manner, Hunt's new heart-consciousness demanded from her a spontaneous expression 'direct from the heart'. The house ready to receive Marian was John's home at Beaufort Buildings in the Strand, where Hunt was also living. Mrs Hunter had already rejected a proposal that Marian should live there, hence Hunt's care to mention that he would 'settle it all'. He was also eager to reassure Marian that John was now well disposed: 'My brother John . . . *says* that he shall be truly happy to see you in the family . . . and he seems as anxious as myself that an event, so suitable & I am sure so necessary to my happiness should take place'. The emphasis on '*says*' reminded Marian that John was a man of his word, although 'seems as anxious as myself' might indicate that he was not convinced the marriage 'should take place'. Countering Marian's fondness for 'gaieties' was necessary: 'we have and must still decline them, that is, *fine* visitings, & *fine* parties'. She was offered more sober routines such as Sunday visits to 'pay our respects to Mrs. Hunter' and to meet Benjamin Haydon. It was hardly a prospect of passionate, newly wedded life, although Hunt signed off by promising her – albeit in terms of his 'rights' as a husband – that once married he would be 'more your lover afterwards'.[45]

So why did they go through with it? Ill health meant Marian had become more like the suffering woman adored by Hunt – although she was showing an unwelcome liking for dances – and he genuinely believed that the happiness of each was 'wrapped up' in the other. From the first he had been passionately attracted to her, and when they were together Hunt was so physically demonstrative that Barron Field reproached him for 'broad attentions' and 'vulgarity'.[46] As a young girl Marian had been drawn by Hunt's intensity and chivalrous attention, and there was the added inducement of rivalry with her sister. Above all, and despite the little they had in common, there was a bond of feeling between them that would survive numerous misunderstandings, struggles and setbacks.

Marian's reply to Hunt's letter of 7 June was gratifyingly prompt and affectionate. In London there had been negotiations about the day for the wedding. Hunt suggested Monday, 19 June. Mrs Hunter proposed the Sunday – Thornton said 'for some special reasons of the greater privacy' – and this was readily agreed.[47] The need for 'privacy' echoed Hunt's own letter to Marian of Monday, 12 June, setting out what had been arranged: 'you & I can then dress just as we please, and dine in Titchfield St without any body knowing any thing of the matter, & walk home quietly to Beaufort Build^{gs} in the afternoon'.[48] Rowland Hunter would apply for a licence, and the marriage would take place at St Clement Danes in the Strand with Rector William Gurney officiating. He was a 'sensible man' and certainly not 'drunken' – Marian had expected that Isaac would officiate.

* * *

Perhaps it was during these hectic days of early June that Hunt decided to cool himself with a dip in the Thames. As he dried and dressed he noticed a 'respectable-looking manly person' whom he recognised as 'Gentleman' Jackson, the prize-fighter, waiting for another bather. He overheard the name 'Byron'. Hunt had read the poet's first collection, *Hours of Idleness*. For a while he watched His Lordship's head bob up and down in the water, then came away.[49]

Everything seemed set, but the wedding would not take place just yet. Thornton claimed that the delay arose because Marian was not yet twenty-one, hence the need for 'privacy' – although Marian had been born in September 1788, so that delaying the wedding until 3 July would not have solved the problem.[50] The difficulty lay elsewhere. John was by no means reconciled to seeing Marian in the family: he could foresee extra expenditure and disruption to domestic routines, both of which would jeopardise production of the *Examiner* from Beaufort Buildings. He had recently received a letter from Marian to his brother, 'put it in his desk' and omitted to pass it on. Hunt, meanwhile, was planning to start married life in John's house – although it emerged in his letter of 12 June that John had not in fact been informed of the wedding plans: 'As to my brother,' Hunt wrote, 'I feel so uneasy under deception of any kind, especially towards him, that I think it better, & so does your mother & Mr Hunter, to tell him the whole affair at once'. Bess was apparently also trying to stall the marriage, giving further cause for 'agitated' feelings.[51] 'I seem as if I were going to be very happy,' Hunt informed Marian: his curiously detached manner in this letter helped ensure that uneasy feelings did not bring on a nervous attack.

On Monday, 3 July they were married at St Clement Danes. Rector William Gurney signed the register; then Hunt, who gave his full name and crossed the 't' of Hunt with a flourish extending down the page. Marian, signing as Mary Anne Kent, emulated her husband's flourish on the 't', though less extravagantly. Present as witnesses were Rowland Hunter, Ann Hunter and Elizabeth Kent. Bess signed her name directly beneath her sister's, as if the marriage had three parties.[52]

NINE

PLUTO'S DOG

There was no honeymoon. Hunt and Marian lived at Beaufort Buildings with John, Sally and their son Henry, and on Sunday, 9 July Hunt's *Examiner* articles appeared, as usual, over his 'Indicator' signature. Week by week in summer 1809 he urged 'the necessity of Constitutional Reform' to regenerate the parliamentary system. He also sniped at rival newspapers for their 'mercantile' money-getting principles.[1]

In Europe events were moving fast. After Cintra the French quickly regained control of Spain, and took Madrid on 5 November 1808. A small contingent of British troops led by Sir John Moore harassed the French army, then retreated west into Portugal reaching Corunna in January. Here, Hunt reported, 'the whole remains of this fatiguing and futile expedition, were embarked'. Moore was killed in this final retreat, and immortalised in Charles Wolfe's 'The Burial of Sir John Moore at Corunna':

> Not a drum was heard, not a funeral note,
>   As his corse to the rampart we hurried;
> Not a soldier discharged his farewell shot
>   O'er the grave where our hero we buried.

Napoleon's triumph was complete. 'Spain, to all appearances, is irrecoverably gone; and if Spain is gone,' Hunt judged, 'Portugal will go too. Remember that.'[2]

In an attempt to recover the situation, Sir Arthur Wellesley returned to Portugal with an army of 30,000 men. On 12 May they sprang a surprise attack, routing the French and driving them back into Spain and defeat at Talavera. Hunt was willing to 'give Sir ARTHUR his due', but sceptical about what had been gained. He recalled how the Duke of York's defeat in Holland had been presented to the public as a resounding triumph: 'the enemy was never handled so severely'. The recollection was timely, for the same issue of the *Examiner* noted a new military expedition to the River Scheldt, and army dispatches claiming the '*SURRENDER OF FLUSHING*'. Was this reliable intelligence, or merely 'an ardent anticipation of the surrender'?[3]

* * *

There was no doubt about tensions on the domestic front. Life in the apartment at Beaufort Buildings was difficult, and for Hunt there was no respite
from the pressures and demands of the *Examiner* office. A month after the
wedding, he fell ill. Elizabeth West wrote to advise about medicines and
encourage Marian in her new role:

> Mrs Wests affec^c regards attend Mr Leigh Hunt & is sorry to find that
> he is confined to his Chamber, wrapped up she hopes in *Flannel* & that
> He will gargle his throat with Port Wine, or Brandy & water, or camphor-
> ated spirit and water and rub the outside of the Throat with the camphor-
> ated spirit. I always do so when a sore throat is coming and find the
> greatest benefit from this practice; I have seen your Brother John this
> morn^g, – hope that M^{rs} L Hunt is well & that she will prove to be a
> good Nurse, that you may be well is the wish of your affec^c Eliza West

> Newman   Mr West writes in best wishes for the
> 20th Augt return of your health & spirits.
>   adieu[4]

Port, brandy and camphorated spirit did the trick: Hunt did not miss a week
from the *Examiner*. Soon afterwards, the Hunts moved out of Beaufort
Buildings to Gowland Cottage in Beckenham, a village about eight miles to
the south of London. The rural air would be good for their health, although
Gowland Cottage was damp, unfurnished and, as they quickly discovered, 'no
more fit to stand rain and wind than a box of paper'.[5]

Throughout the autumn of 1809 London was shaken by the 'Old Price'
riots at the rebuilt Covent Garden. When the theatre reopened on Monday,
18 September, it was gorgeously adorned with marble, bronze Grecian
lamps, Ionic pillars, a statue of Shakespeare, and casts from antique sculptures of Minerva, Venus, Bacchus and Apollo. But ticket prices had been
increased, and expensive private boxes installed. Covent Garden had gone
up market, violating the 'ancient and indisputable rights of the Pit'. On the
first night *Macbeth* was greeted with uproar as the audience demanded a
return to the old ticket prices. The kilted Kemble, 'plaintively bowing' and
'tenderly disconsolate', could not make himself heard and the performance
was abandoned. Confident that right was on their side, the audience refused
to disperse until two o'clock the next morning. There ensued three months
of tumult, confusion and noise, with Hunt and the *Examiner* encouraging
the protesters to 'reinvigorate their efforts' to disrupt performances and
force a return to the old prices. By December the managers of Covent
Garden capitulated.[6]

*   *   *

Because Beckenham was 'out of the road of coaches', Marian was left alone awaiting Hunt's arrival or, more often, one of his notes: 'I return home in the morning at the usual time'; 'I am sure you will not see me until Sunday'; 'theatre and a late supper last night have made me very late this morning . . . I do not return to dinner, but I hope I shall be with you before dark'; 'I shall be at home as early as possible tomorrow'. Their relationship had grown steadier in marriage – more stable, caring and openly passionate. 'But one more day, my dearest love, and I shall be in your arms again.'⁷ By January 1810 Marian was pregnant, and walks in the lanes and fields did her 'an incalculable deal of good'.⁸

Relations with the Hunters improved: Hunt sometimes stayed with them when unable to get back to Beckenham. Joseph Johnson died on 20 December, leaving his nephew Rowland Hunter £1,500 and a share in the bookselling business at St Paul's Churchyard.⁹ Isaac Hunt's health also deteriorated during this winter. Unable to bear the thought that his wife was dead, he had taken to consoling himself with saying '"She is not dead but sleeps"'; 'I verily believe the image became almost a literal thing with him,' Hunt recalled.¹⁰ Isaac passed his last months with his pipe and claret, reading sermons and the Bible, and reminiscing about his political acquaintances.

Isaac's memoirs, had he written them, would be a colourful source of anecdotes about the revolutions in America and France – but the past was a country to which he was reluctant to return. In December 1809 Hunt took a message from Isaac to Elizabeth West, 'requesting to see her before he died'. Elizabeth had coped with Isaac's waywardness and debts, helped Mary out of difficulties, and supported their children. All this for the man who had jilted her in Philadelphia. Years afterwards, Hunt recalled her response to Isaac's request: 'She grasped my hand, looked at me as steadily in the face as her shaking head would allow, and said, while her eyes filled at once with tears & resentment, "Never".'¹¹

Two years had passed since Mary Hunt's brother-in-law, John Lorain, had requested the power of attorney that would enable him to sell her property in Philadelphia. Given the Hunts' straitened circumstances, it is curious that they had not been more active in pursuing this matter, and now another letter arrived from Lorain requesting a 'proper' power of attorney. The Hunts gathered and drew up a detailed response, authorising Lorain to take possession of the property, superintend it, and remit any profits 'until the property *is sold*, which we wish to be done when a proper price, the value of our Interests in it, can be obtained'. The letter was signed by Isaac, his sons and their wives. After a short delay, on 18 January 1810 they all put their names to a second power of attorney, the 'proper' legal document that would secure their American inheritance.¹²

Isaac died the next day. At his funeral the pall bearers quarrelled across his coffin for the remnants of the candles, 'which put me upon a great many reflections', Hunt remembered, 'both on him and on the world'.[13] Isaac was buried in the churchyard of St Botolph, Bishopsgate, on 25 January. He was sixty-nine. In Philadelphia the Shewell family had also gathered for a funeral. Old Stephen Shewell, Mary Hunt's father, had died in December 1809 leaving $60,000 in his will and numerous properties in and around Philadelphia.[14] Some months would pass before the Hunts heard this news.

Letters to the *Examiner* showed that Hunt's articles on Methodism had stirred controversy. Sensing sales, he collected them into a pamphlet, *An Attempt to Shew the Folly and Danger of Methodism*, published by John Hunt late in 1809. The *Critical Review* welcomed Hunt's arguments for 'more liberal sentiments' against 'narrow principles . . . exclusion and intolerance'; the *Monthly Mirror* praised Hunt's 'threefold character' of politician, 'theological polemic' and dramatic critic, caricaturing him as 'a human *Cerberus*'.[15] It was a good cartoon, instantly recognisable: in his public roles Hunt was vigilant as Pluto's three-headed dog at the gate of the under world, while his pamphlet had warned against the infernal doctrine of Calvinist-Methodism. But the *Monthly Mirror*'s jest would soon be turned against him by a furious adversary – one who delighted to walk among the fires of Hell.

In September 1809 the *Examiner* published a review of William Blake's exhibition at Broad Street, in which Robert Hunt described Blake as 'an unfortunate lunatic, whose personal inoffensiveness secures him from confinement'.[16] Much the same was said of many homespun visionaries of the time, men and women like Richard Brothers, a naval officer turned millenarian prophet, and Joanna Southcott, mother of the seraph man, Shiloh. According to Robert, Blake's 'bodily personifications of the soul' were 'distorted' representations of the spirit.[17] To the visionary poet of *Songs of Innocence and of Experience*, however, such comments revealed a benighted determination to divide physical 'reality' from the radiant spiritual universe; the review, and by extension the *Examiner*, its editor and publisher, represented the oppressive 'mind forg'd manacles' shackling London and England. Blake retaliated in his prophetic poem *Jerusalem*, transforming the editor of the *Examiner* and Hunt's 'Indicator' colophon into the villain 'Hand'. Perhaps Blake knew that the *Monthly Mirror* had likened Hunt to the three-headed dog, Cerberus, for in *Jerusalem* 'Hand' appears in the 'mighty threatening form' of a triple-headed monster,

> three strong sinewy necks & three awful & terrible heads,
> Three brains in contradictory council brooding incessantly

Triple forms or trinities are found elsewhere in Blake's works, usually representing humanity's fall into division, spiritual darkness and intellectual strife. Ironically, the *Examiner*'s tolerant, inclusive attitude to religion proved too orthodox to accommodate Blake the Romantic visionary.[18] He had his revenge, although decades would pass before the Pre-Raphaelite poets, whose careers had been forwarded by Hunt, would discover Blake's genius.

While Blake raged at the calumnies 'in a Sunday paper cald the examiner Publishd in Beaufort Buildings',[19] Hunt was preoccupied with the government's disastrous foreign policy. By autumn 1809 the campaign to open a new front in Holland had failed. Most of the army withdrew, leaving a garrison on the marshy island Walcheren – 'a deadly place', Hunt called it, plagued with 'malignant fever'. When the army was evacuated in December most of the soldiers were sick with malaria, or already dead.[20] To Hunt this débâcle was 'the climax of absurd expeditions', an 'epitome of our vile foreign policies'.[21] It marked a turning point in public affairs, and prompted his first poem of anti-war protest, 'Walcheren Expedition; or, the Englishman's lament for the Loss of his Countrymen':

> No ship came o'er to bring relief
>   No orders came to save;
> But DEATH stood there and never stirr'd,
>   Still counting for the grave.
> They lay down, and they linger'd,
>   And died with feelings sore,
>   And the waves
>   Pierc'd their graves
> Thro' the dark and swampy shore.[22]

Hunt's poem dramatises its quarrel with ministerial policy by combining the rhythms of Thomas Campbell's loyal ode, 'Ye Mariners of England', with echoes of a protest poem from the 1790s, Coleridge's 'Fears in Solitude'. Writing in 1798, Coleridge had viewed the prospect of a French invasion as divine retribution for national corruption. Britain was a 'swamp of pestilence', he had warned: 'We have offended, O my countrymen!' Hunt's poem adapted Coleridge's vision, attributing the army's 'swampy' destruction to the 'Councils obstinate / Of mercenary men'. With such men in power, England 'ne'er shall thrive again'.

Following Walcheren, public anger at the conduct of the war intensified, and Hunt seized the opportunity to sharpen his attacks on 'our corruption at home and our wretched attempts abroad'. The Duke of Portland's government was in terminal disarray, and by the end of October 1809 Portland himself was dead.[23] Rivalry between Canning, the Foreign Secretary, and Castlereagh, Hunt's former superior at the War Office, broke into open conflict. Following a duel, which they survived, both men resigned. Ten days later, Hunt published a 'Political Examiner' observing that the 'mutilated

ministry' was held in 'universal contempt' and could not survive. He looked
to the Foxite Whigs to assert the rights of 'free and popular government'
(Charles James Fox's words) and take 'conciliatory views with regard to
Ireland'. George III's well-known opposition to any such conciliation made
Hunt's next speculation risky:

> The subject of Ireland . . . is no doubt the great trouble in the election of
> his majesty's Servants; and it is this, most probably, which has given rise
> to the talk of a Regency, a measure to which the Court would never resort
> while it felt a possibility of acting upon its old principles. What a crowd of
> blessings rush upon one's mind, that might be bestowed upon the country
> in the event of such a change! – Of all monarchs indeed since the Revolution,
> the successor of GEORGE the Third will have the finest opportunity of
> becoming nobly popular.[24]

The *Morning Chronicle* was sympathetic to Hunt's views and reprinted this
paragraph, whereupon the *Morning Post* took up the cudgels:

> Never, surely, was any thing more calculated to insult the good sense, or
> *horrify* the *PURE* and amiable nature of his ROYAL HIGHNESS; nor was
> ever any thing more calculated to call forth the *indignation* and *execration*
> of a *loyal* and *admiring* People, upon the *WRETCH* who is capable of
> broaching an idea at once so repugnant to the feelings of the illustrious
> HEIR APPARENT, and to the ardent wishes of every good and (also)
> virtuous subject. To the *indignation* and *execration* of the British *nation* do
> we, therefore, consign this *damning* specimen of the *abominable* and *infam-*
> *ous* sentiments by which the *base Faction* are impelled in their most *unprin-*
> *cipled* and *diabolical* pursuit.[25]

On the following Sunday, 8 October, Hunt shrugged off the *Morning Post*'s
attack as a *'jeu d'esprit'* – but he had already withdrawn to his favourite stronghold, and was writing 'in a sick room'.[26] He stayed there for three weeks,
during which he contributed nothing to the *Examiner* (foreign news appeared
on the front pages instead). Meanwhile, Hunt's 'crowd of blessings' in the
Examiner had caught the eye of the Attorney-General, Sir Vicary Gibbs: to
him the 'plain, direct, and libellous meaning' of Hunt's paragraph was that
the 'aera' of anticipated joy would be 'the death of his present Majesty'.[27] A
libel charge was issued to James Perry, proprietor of the *Morning Chronicle*,
and the publisher John Lambert; *The King* v. *the Hunts* would follow. 'Be it
so,' Hunt responded with laconic bravado: 'the EXAMINER prospers.'[28] He
was well aware that prosecution brought publicity, boosted sales, and enhanced
his reputation.

On Saturday, 24 February 1810, Perry and Lambert were brought to trial before Lord Ellenborough (a subscriber to Hunt's *Juvenilia*) and a jury comprising eight 'special' and four ordinary jurors. 'Special' jurors were freeholders from the property-owning classes whose political views had been scrutinised by Crown officers to ensure the required verdict.[29] As Hunt recalled, 'the framers of the indictment' against Perry and Lambert had 'calculated on the usual identification of a special with a Tory jury'.[30] Perry spoke in his own defence, and summed up by reminding the jury that 'the cause of the Liberty of the Press in England . . . is in your hands this day'. They withdrew, consulted for two minutes, returned, and gave 'NOT GUILTY'. When the *Examiner* reported the case on 4 March, the verdict was followed by a short article:

THE KING *v.* HUNTS

A similar information, which had been filed against the Proprietors of the *Examiner* for a paragraph containing the original paragraph copied by the *Morning Chronicle*, was then announced in its course for trial; but the Attorney General immediately rose and said, 'My Lord, I withdraw that'.[31]

Even the most carefully packed jury might discover a mind of its own.

Hunt speculated that the government prosecuted Perry because they expected him to 'cut a very ridiculous figure, which should at once damn that gentleman's cause and our own'. Now the 'hatchet of vengeance' had been deflected. Legal fees had cost the *Examiner* nearly £100, but the liberty of the press was 'no longer a mere name – a toleration – a sufferance from the existing government':

The right of criticising the plans, elucidating the measures, and denouncing the faults of the King's Ministers, is recognized on every hand to its fullest extent. We are no longer to be called wretches, at least by law, for objecting to the most odious measures; we are no longer to be called interested villains for exclaiming against the waste of treasure, or traitorous villains for wishing a total change of system . . . wretches and villains will be no other than they always were, – the servile, the corrupt, the grasping, the wasters of human and national life.[32]

Bounding out of the sick-room, Hunt resumed his stance of principled authority with even greater assurance: Perry's was a 'signal victory' that would resound across Europe, giving Napoleon himself pause in his 'meditations upon invading this country'.[33] Closer to home, Hunt felt sufficiently confident to respond to the *Edinburgh Review*'s allegations that the country was splitting into factions of 'courtiers' ('for arbitrary power'), democrats ('*for revolution and republicanism*'), and the dwindling '*old constitutional Whigs* of England'.[34] According to the *Edinburgh*, 'Weekly Papers' like the *Examiner* were fomenting revolution, and civil war loomed. In three issues of the *Examiner* Hunt refuted the *Edinburgh*'s misrepresentations, and restated the reformists' arguments for restoring the Constitution.[35] His articles were republished by John Hunt as a pamphlet.

From the wreckage of Portland's ministry Spencer Perceval emerged, ambitious to construct a broadly based administration but frustrated by the Whigs' refusal to join. At the War Office, Lord Liverpool was upbeat about Wellesley's endeavours in Spain and Portugal, although after Talavera the strategic situation had once again turned against the British. The soldiers were hungry and demoralised: 'I have been sixteen months without a bed and most of the time in the open fields lying in my clothes,' one of them complained in November: 'I was eight days without provisions being served out to me, only what I could forage for myself.'[36] By autumn 1809, Wellesley's soldiers had withdrawn to Portugal. The ranks seethed with rumours that their commander was enjoying a life of leisure, hunting deer on the Duke of Braganza's estate, and planning to return home. One disaffected senior officer reported 'Lord Wellington is unpopular with his army, equally in all ranks, in the greatest degree possible'.[37] Ahead of them lay a gruelling campaign that would last through the summer of 1810, as they held out against the massive army Napoleon had ordered to drive the British from Portugal.

Resigned to yet another year of equivocally 'brilliant occurrences', Hunt was astonished by the Poet Laureate's panegyric to the new year:

> Raptur'd I pour the verse again,
> To hail the *British* Monarch's lengthen'd reign,
> To celebrate the rising Year . . .

With these lines Henry James Pye welcomed 1810, the fiftieth anniversary of George III's accession. The *Examiner* published Pye's 'Ode for the New Year' in full, recognising that the poem was 'a matter of office' but in other respects unaccountable in the light of recent events:

the Laureat thinks himself warranted to cry out,

> Raptured I pour the verse again.

Raptured he pours! A man in his senses pouring an Ode with rapture for the year 1810! If Mr. PYE had applied this to his tea or his wine after finishing the verse, every transport might have been allowed him; but when all the well-known blessings of the present Reign are considered, such as the loss of America, the Suspension of the Habeas Corpus, the Introduction of Foreign Troops into England, the Oppression of Ireland, the war with France, the Alliances, the taxes, the Paper-inundation, the enormous Debt, the contemptible Court-quarrels, the Defalcations and Corruptions of Office, the Omnipotence of wretched Ministries, up to the late deadly Expedition, what sort of inspiration must influence that verse-maker, who for one or two hundred per annum, can sit down and be in raptures 'To celebrate the rising year?'

Habeas Corpus was an Act that dated from Charles II's reign, ensuring that there would be no imprisonment without trial. It was repeatedly suspended during the revolutionary panic of the 1790s and the Napoleonic wars, when German troops were garrisoned in Britain to suppress insurrection. The 'Paper-inundation' was the controversial introduction of paper currency, widely viewed as a symptom of national decline. When read alongside Hunt's catalogue of delinquency and decline, Pye's 'rapturous Ode' was a 'libel on the good sense of the nation', 'a complete specimen . . . of the true Laureat flattery and fiction', 'poetry . . . at the height of its prostitution'.[38]

Pye was a ludicrous figure and, like all poets laureate, easy to mock. But in writing at length about the 'Ode' and the Laureate, Hunt had a serious purpose. He was reflecting on how poets, including himself, ought to respond to a time of national alarm and despondency. The role of 'stipendiary poet' was evidently ridiculous: it degraded poetry, poets and the nation. So were poetics and politics incompatible? Hunt had already published his protest ballad 'Walcheren Expedition', and he noted grimly that Pye's ode 'utters no patriotic sigh for the dead'. Later in 1810 he would project a visionary romance, 'The Planet of the Poets', in which poets of 'good moral tendency' were rewarded and those who 'prostituted their genius', as Pye had done, were punished. It was clear that Pye's 'poetry and politics' were 'of one fond, believing pitch', but what would be a poetry of 'good tendency' for the difficult times ahead?

TEN

GATHERING FAME, LOSING FORTUNE

When Rowland Hunter took over Joseph Johnson's bookshop, he continued the weekly dinners Johnson had held in 'a little quaintly shaped upstairs room, with walls not at right angles'.[1] Those alignments might have been forcibly skewed by the intellectual rumpus at Johnson's table. For four decades his guests had comprised a roll-call of radicals and dissenters, poets, philosophers, politicians, travellers and scientists: Benjamin Franklin and Tom Paine; William Godwin, philosopher author of *Political Justice*; the feminist Mary Wollstonecraft; the poets Anna Laetitia Barbauld, William Cowper and William Wordsworth; William Frend, Coleridge's Unitarian tutor at Cambridge; the mathematicians John Bonnycastle and Thomas Malthus; Maria Edgeworth, the novelist; and the playwright Thomas Holcroft. Other guests came from Johnson's Unitarian world: Richard Price and Joseph Priestley; John Aikin (Anna Barbauld's brother), editor of the *Monthly Magazine* and the *Athenaeum*; George Dyer, Christ's Hospital bluecoat, reformer and poet; and the classical scholar and controversialist Gilbert Wakefield. The list could go on. In short, Johnson's salon was the intellectual powerhouse of London radicalism.

At one of Rowland Hunter's dinners, on 23 February 1810, Hunt met two survivors from Johnson's circle: William Godwin and John Bonnycastle whose *Introduction to Astronomy* was presented to John Keats as a school prize.[2] On this occasion Hunt also re-encountered the painter Henry Fuseli, 'a small man, with energetic features, and a white head of hair'. Fuseli was well known as the illustrator of Shakespeare and Milton, and he also explored the psychology of dreams in paintings like *The Nightmare*.[3] Hunt may also have encountered George Dyer and John Aikin, both of whom would contribute to his magazine the *Reflector*.

A few weeks after Hunt dined with Godwin, London seemed to be on the verge of a mass insurrection. John Gale Jones – one of the popular orators of the 1790s, now a member of parliament – had been committed to Newgate for publishing a 'scandalous and libellous hand bill' about the House of Commons. When Cobbett's *Political Register* published a defence of Jones

by Sir Francis Burdett, the member for Westminster, Burdett was deemed
to have breached parliamentary privilege and condemned to imprisonment
in the Tower. The mob surged on to the streets. Ministers' houses were
attacked; the militia and the volunteers were called out; the Tower guns were
loaded, and there was talk of 'revolutions'. Hunt stayed at his editor's desk
in Beaufort Buildings to bring the latest news to *Examiner* readers, stopping
the press at 1 a.m. on Sunday, 8 April to include a letter from Burdett defying
the authorities and resisting 'unlawful' arrest. Burdett eventually went
quietly, and was released after a few weeks. But the precedent was alarming,
as Hunt explained: 'our liberties can look for no quarter whenever it shall
please the House to decree their annihilation'. Cobbett, to his shame, had
tried unsuccessfully to 'compromise with Administration' by dropping his
political writing. When the deal failed, he was convicted of seditious libel
and imprisoned. This was a warning, Hunt noted, to those who were too
readily 'cowed down by attack'.[4]

Hunt and John found some respite amid the convivial company at Thomas
Hill's house in Sydenham, a few miles south of London. Hill was the proprietor of the *Monthly Mirror*, 'a jovial bachelor, plump and rosy as an abbot'.
After their Saturday scrambles to publish the *Examiner*, the Hunts could relax
at Hill's table – and the 'wine flowed merrily and long'.[5] They met Edward
Du Bois, the *Monthly Mirror*'s editor and an 'excellent scholar' whose 'quips
and cranks were infinite'. The Scottish poet Thomas Campbell, whose
Pleasures of Hope and *Gertrude of Wyoming* Hunt admired, was always 'over-
flowing with humour and anecdote'. Also present were the brothers James
and Horace Smith, whose parodies of Wordsworth, Coleridge, Byron and
Scott in *Rejected Addresses* would be a bestseller of 1812. Perhaps some of the
Rejected Addresses were rehearsed at Sydenham, for the festive group included
Theodore Hook, 'merry *jongleur*' and 'extempore poet', whose teasing so
pleased Campbell that he tore off his wig and flung it at Hook exclaiming
'"You dog! I'll throw my laurels at you"'. Hunt also met the famous comic
actor Charles Mathews (brother of William Wordsworth's Jacobin associate,
William Mathews) and was delighted by his impersonation of Kemble
'objecting to stiffness' in another actor. 'Next morning,' Hunt recalled, 'in
returning to town, we felt ourselves very thirsty. A pump by the road-side,
with a plash around it, was a bewitching sight.'[6]

Following the riots in London, one of Hill's festive Sundays was prolonged
over two days. At eleven o'clock on the morning of Monday, 23 April 1810,
Hunt wrote to Marian,

My dear, dear girl,
    In order to quiet your fancy for this evening (for I know you would
be thinking all sorts of horrors about me) I write to tell you that I sleep

at Sydenham tonight, and shall return home in the morning at the usual time: therefore your imagination will go quietly to bed, and not throw me off a stage-coach, tumble me in a ditch, or have me knocked down by robbers. The country is delicious, but two days away from you will be quite enough for me, especially as I cannot look upon a green field or a cottage without growing impatient. Pray take care of yourself, my love, for your own sake, for the sake of ours, and for the sake of your affectionate HENRY.

A postscript mentions 'Mr. Du Bois says everything that is kind and gallant', and adds that Hunt's old friend Barron Field has 'just got up' and sends '4,0000000000000 comps'.[7] Perhaps this occasion saw Hunt and John projecting their new magazine on politics and fine art, the *Reflector*: its prospectus was dated 'April 1810', although it would be another eight months before publication of the first issue.[8] Their idea for a title was a nod towards the *Monthly Mirror* which that month carried a favourable review of Hunt's pamphlet on Methodism, and a 'MEMOIR OF MR JAMES HENRY LEIGH HUNT. WRITTEN BY HIMSELF' with an engraved portrait. Hunt was clearly in reflective mood.

The 'Memoir' is dated '*Examiner Office, April* 20, 1810', that is, the Friday before the festivities at Thomas Hill's house. This was Hunt's first attempt at autobiographical writing and, although just six pages in extent, it represented the beginning of the *Autobiography* he would publish forty years later. Hunt begins by confessing to a low opinion of 'biography of living persons', but is nevertheless ready to disclose such 'important secrets' as a 'dark complexion' and a 'very happy' marriage:

Well: – I was born at Southgate, in October, 1784. My parents were the late Rev. I. HUNT, at that time tutor in the Duke of CHANDOS'S family, and MARY, daughter of STEPHEN SHEWELL, merchant of Philadelphia, whose sister is the lady of Mr President WEST.[9]

Those advantageous social connections had not helped Hunt's mother:

She was indeed a mother in every exalted sense of the word, in piety, in sound teaching, in patient care, in spotless example. Married at an early age, and commencing from that time a life of sorrow, the world afflicted, but it could not change her: no rigid œconomy could hide the native generosity of her heart, no sophistical and skulking example injure her fine sense or her contempt of worldly-mindedness, no unmerited sorrow convert her resignation into bitterness . . . At the time when she died, the recollection of her sufferings and virtues tended to embitter the loss; but knowing what she was, and believing where she is, I now feel her memory as a serene

and inspiring influence, that comes over my social moments, only to temper
cheerfulness, and over my reflecting ones, to animate me in the love of
truth.

Rising above her afflictions, Mary presides benignly over her son's progress
from 'embittered' loss to restored cheer. The trauma Hunt had experienced
after her death does not disturb this myth, although it registers in the serene
maternal influence 'that comes over my social moments, only to temper cheerfulness'. Shadowing the narrative are 'social moments' of a *dis*tempered
quality, like the ones that had distracted him from his mother's deathbed.
Here, for the first time, Hunt employed the technique of oblique revelation
that he would perfect in his 'Recollections of the Author's Life' in *Lord Byron
and some of his Contemporaries* and in the *Autobiography*.

Hunt goes on to survey his schooldays at Christ's Hospital; the '*imitative
enthusiasm*' of *Juvenilia*; the dark period of 'alternate study and morbid idleness' before his emergence as a theatre critic; and his resignation from a
'government office' because of hints from 'higher orders, who could not
contemplate with pleasure a new paper called the *Examiner*'. His present role
as editor is mentioned, and so is the promise of his ongoing 'literary studies'.
The 'Memoir' closes by recalling his talent for 'self-resumption' in the face
of criticism. Hunt's claim to have been 'abused and vilified by every publication' overlooked the positive reception his work had enjoyed, but it helped
sharpen his image as the champion of public good who had selflessly preserved
'singleness of conduct', 'first principles' and 'truth'. Such was the resolute
private character behind Hunt's steady gaze in the portrait by John Jackson
(reproduced in the illustrations between pp. 196 and 197).

The 'Memoir' signalled the twenty-five-year-old Hunt's arrival as a public
figure. *Juvenilia* had been placed firmly in the past, and the *Examiner* established as his platform before the public. October 1810 brought further recognition. A letter arrived informing Hunt of his election to the Philosophical
Society that met in Hatton Garden, not far from Christ's Hospital.[10] At some
time this year Hunt made an acquaintance who would become a lifelong
friend. Charles Ollier, a banker at Coutts, called at the *Examiner* office with
a piece of theatrical criticism. The two men stayed in touch, sharing their
delight in flute music and Shakespeare.[11] There were momentous events in
Hunt's family life too. On 10 September Marian gave birth to their son,
Thornton, named after the old family friend Godfrey Thornton. Hunt's school
friend Thomas Mitchell wrote with congratulations, and so did Benjamin
Haydon:

> I congratulate you with all my soul on the safety of an amiable wife and
> the birth of a son. It is a grand thing to have occasioned the existence of

a thinking being, one, who *may* be famous in this World, and immortal in
the next – I feel my heart expand at the fancy . . .'[12]

This spectacular surmise was typical of Haydon, who perceived everything
– life, friendships, artistic ambition – in a frame of sublime significance. When
the *Examiner* described Haydon's painting *The Assassination of Dentatus* as 'a
treat served up by the hand of genius', he was convinced that he would soon
be dining with the immortals.[13]

From their first meeting in 1807 Hunt had warmed to Haydon's tempestuous passion for art, nicknaming him 'Pictor Tonans', the 'Thunderous
Painter'. Tragically, though, Haydon's extraordinary presence was combined
with an unstable personality: quick to take offence, unforgiving, resentful.
When *Dentatus* was moved from the Great Room to a less prominent location in the Royal Academy, Haydon detected President West's 'rascality'.[14]
The quarrel deepened beyond recovery in 1812, when Haydon published
three letters in the *Examiner* arguing that the Academy had 'completely failed'
to nurture British art and the 'grand style' of painting, while jealously
concealing 'every Picture of real merit'.[15] Haydon had reason to feel ill-treated
by the Academy, and there was some truth in what he said. But to go public
with his criticisms in a newspaper alienated potential patrons at the very
moment when he most needed their support: Wilkie had already warned
Haydon that while 'Hunt gets his living by such things, you will lose all chance
of it'.[16] Haydon survived as a painter, but, years later, when his paranoia finally
had turned to self-loathing, he committed suicide.

During autumn 1810 Hunt kept up with his demanding editorial routines in
the *Examiner* office, and was busy gathering copy for the first number of the
Reflector. Each day he wrote home to his 'beloved wife and her darling little
boy', and worried about them in damp Gowland Cottage. When he went
home, he immediately contracted colds and rheumatism; when he returned
to the *Examiner* office, sickness made him feel 'the dreariness of a London
morning' all the more acutely. By October Hunt was so ill that he was unable
to provide copy for the *Examiner*.[17]

Back at Gowland Cottage, with little Thornton wailing in his cradle, Hunt
sketched out the plan of a poem in three cantos, 'The Planet of the Poets'.
A poet walks out 'on an autumnal night to meditate', and is immediately
'wafted' by his Muse from Beckenham to Venus. The planet proves to be 'the
residence of departed poets', and here he converses with 'great poets, chiefly
English' on 'the present state of things on earth'. The poet then takes his
return flight to Beckenham, encountering *en route* 'the rising spirit of a young
poet, who died prematurely'.[18]

The next decade would see Hunt shaping the careers of two young poets,
both of whom died young and whose spirits would alter the course of his own

life, and haunt modern Romantic myth. But when Hunt was sketching his plan for a poem he was preoccupied with his own situation: Gowland Cottage was cramped, and the strains of being a father for the first time were beginning to tell. 'The Planet of the Poets' amounted to an escapist fantasy in which the dead young poet would encounter among 'a troop of blessed spirits' his own 'sainted mother'. Hunt dated the manuscript of his projected poem 'Beckenham, 22^d October, 1810', some five years after his mother's death.

As autumn turned to winter it looked as if Hunt's career as a poet might be grounded by circumstances, and he was increasingly aware that his political and poetic ambitions were pulling him in different directions. Pressures were mounting in other ways too. The *Examiner* reprinted an article from the *Stamford News* entitled '*One Thousand Lashes!!*', in which John Scott described in excruciating detail '*an English Military Flogging*' with the 'lacerating cat o' nine-tails'. The article was brought to the attention of the Attorney-General, who found nothing objectionable in the account of an English soldier

> stripped naked, – his limbs tied with ropes to a triangular machine, – his back torn to the bone by the merciless cutting whipcord, applied by persons who relieve each other at short intervals, that they may bring the full unexhausted strength of a man to the work of scourging.

But when the article claimed that 'in no country in Europe . . . is the military character so degraded', it was libellous; and when it alleged that 'Bonaparte does *not* treat his refractory troops in this manner', its seditious tendency came to the surface.[19]

By 11 November Hunt felt well enough to resume work, and he informed readers that the King's recent relapse into madness showed 'no promise of returning health' and that a Regency was in prospect.[20] He added that the *Examiner* had received another indictment for seditious libel, noting wryly that 'the punishment for being *found innocent* on these occasions, is to pay a large sum for law expences; and of this our magnanimous Ministers are well aware'. As the year drew to a close the *Examiner* once again faced an expensive confrontation with the government, and Hunt cheered readers and himself 'with the old English word of battle – The Truth and the Constitution!' But the future looked bleak.[21]

Bess had joined Marian to help with three-month-old Thornton, although it was soon obvious that leaky Gowland Cottage was not habitable for another winter, and they all returned to London to live in Rowland Hunter's house at Carburton Street.[22] Benjamin Haydon joined them for Christmas dinner. This cannot have been an easy time for Marian: she now had the support of her mother while nursing Thornton, but with the whole family living under one roof old tensions revived. At some point in this winter Marian's name was changed again, and she became Marianne.

Gowland Cottage was so uncomfortable that Hunt could not 'reconcile it to his conscience' to hand it over to another tenant; with his family now living in London, he kept on the empty cottage 'at the expense of his purse'.[23] Perhaps he anticipated that funds would soon arrive from Philadelphia. The power of attorney forwarded to John Lorain after Isaac's death had produced a swift response – on 17 June 1810 Lorain had written as administrator of Stephen Shewell's estate, mentioning that none of Shewell's property had been sold except a 'small barren spot'.[24] This letter marks the beginning of a complicated saga that would entangle the Hunts and Stephen Shewell's American descendants for over half a century. From the surviving letters and legal papers, it appears that the Hunts were cheated of a fortune by their American relatives.

An inventory of 'The Property of Stephen Shewel Esqre', undated but presumably from around 1810, lists his extensive properties at Philadelphia:

Three houses taken by Mr. Gibbs at valuation.
Two houses belonging to Miss E. Shewells estate.
One house in Pewter Platter Alley.
Ground Rent sold.
Ground Rent in Pewter Platter Alley.
Joseph Bond's mortgage.
Various Bonds unsettled about—
Bank Stock sold.

Two turnpike shares not sold.
Half of Port Royal on Susquehannah value not ascertained.
Half of an old steel furnace at Fenton not valued.
About 500 acres of land in South Carolina thought to be very valuable.
Furniture &c. of little value, beside various uncertain property in land.

Stephen Shewell had lost heavily at the Revolution of 1776, but evidently his heirs in Philadelphia and London could still expect much from his estate. All depended on the executors John Lorain and Joseph Smith (the husband of another of Mary Hunt's sisters, Frances Shewell).

'Your Grandfather was one of the most careless men as to his Estate that I ever knew,' Lorain informed Robert Hunt, omitting to mention that carelessness in such matters might leave his executors some administrative leeway. Lorain now moved quickly to dispose of assets including Mary Hunt's property in Philadelphia – that is, those 'Three houses taken by Mr. Gibbs at valuation'. On 7 July Lorain wrote again, this time to Stephen Hunt, enclosing £464 14s. 'from the Shewell Estate'. Scrawled on the paper is a calculation showing that after deducting costs Hunt and his three brothers would each receive £115 5s. 6d. Lorain explained further:

> Besides this, I hold a mortgage of Benj Gibbs on account of the heirs of Mary Hunt on three houses namely the Mansion house, the house next to it and the house on West side of Front Street, amount of mortgage Seven thousand eight hundred Dollars. Benjamin Gibbs taking advantage of the law in the case of intestates took those three houses at valuation of the Jury appointed.

Having been granted the power of attorney, Lorain sold Mary Hunt's houses 'at valuation' and had no objection to the purchaser 'taking advantage of the law'. There had been no further correspondence with Mary's heirs and, so far, no money had been forwarded to them from the sale. It would be another ten months before Lorain remitted £2,000, 'for sale of property in Philadelphia'. What the Hunts did not know was that, having bought their mother's houses 'at valuation', Benjamin Gibbs had quickly sold them on – presumably at a profit. Who was this sharp businessman? As it turns out, Gibbs was yet another of the Hunts' relatives in Philadelphia: he was the husband of Mary Hunt's sister, Hannah Shewell, and therefore a brother-in-law of the executors John Lorain and Joseph Smith.

Other hopeful relatives emerged. Hearing news of the Shewell estate, Hunt's long-lost eldest brother Isaac surfaced in Quebec. Isaac junior had crossed to England with his mother and brothers in 1777, then returned to Philadelphia 'in the bloom of manhood, a fine looking youth' only to be 'thrown upon a world of temptation & sin'. He joined the American army, deserted, and fled to Canada. Now he was in a deplorable state, distressed, sickly, and unable to come to Philadelphia to claim his inheritance. Lorain suggested Benjamin West might help out, and 'get him to London'.

Relations between the Hunt and Shewell families had been under stress since Isaac and Mary's marriage back in 1767. In June 1811 one of Mary's younger sisters, Frances, contacted Robert Hunt in a letter about the family rift. The source of the problem seems to have been old Stephen Shewell's refusal to assist Mary or her sons while they were linked with Isaac. 'There has been an unfortunate misunderstanding some how, which I am totally unable to illusidate,' Frances began:

> but of this I can assure you – no effort on my part has been wanting to excite the tenderest sympathy – and had I possessed one half the influence enjoyed elsewhere actions, more than words, would have excited my feelings.
> But ah! Robert – had your beloved Mother been here she would have more acutely felt the deprivation – she would then brobably have found a Father willing to relieve her every want, and with sympathizing tenderness

come forward with the necessary aid – but fearful of discord – and cruel dissentions – would have been under the painful necessity, of suffering in silence, and refusing from his hand the proferr'd boon – I speak this from conviction – the bare suspicion of my being necessiated caused animosity. Heaven forgive me for this reflection, and sacred be the relics of the dead.

From Frances's letter it appears that Mary Hunt, 'fearful of discord', was caught between the demands of a tyrannical father and her loyalty to her husband Isaac. Frances indicates that had Mary not followed Isaac to London in 1777 and stayed 'here', in Philadelphia, her father would have assisted 'with sympathizing tenderness'. When Mary continued loyal to Isaac, Stephen Shewell disclaimed his paternal care. Frances had also faced their father's anger, when he suspected her of 'being necessiated' – poor and in need, like Mary. Frances's letter helps explain Hunt's belief, right to the end of his life, that Stephen Shewell had behaved meanly to his mother, and that the Shewell sisters had deprived the Hunts of their inheritance:

They and their husbands, agreeably to the American law of equal division, were in receipt of a pretty property in lands and houses; our due share of which, some inadvertence on our parts appears to have forfeited. I confess I have often wished, at the close of a day's work, that people were not so excessively delicate on legal points, and so afraid of hurting the feelings of others, by supposing it possible for them to want a little of their grand-father's money.[25]

A painful letter of February 1812 shows Hunt in severe financial straits, trying to clear a debt of £340 and anticipating a third 'remittance' from John Lorain.[26] It never arrived. The intrigue about the Shewell property dragged on, and in 1856, six years after the publication of Hunt's *Autobiography* and three before his death, the rights to the land at 'Port Royal on Susquehannah' had still not been clarified. By this time, however, Hunt's fame was such that his cousin Elizabeth, the daughter of Lydia and John Lorain, wrote ingratiat-ingly, 'When I was a girl the thought of you was like a happy dream.'[27] Evidently her parents had thought so too.

ELEVEN

POLITICS AND POETICS

On 3 January 1811 Hunt left Marianne, five-month-old Thornton and Bess for a break in Cambridge. He was acting on medical advice, but in piercingly cold weather the journey did him little good. He gazed out of the coach on a dismal landscape of ditches and stumpy willows, 'like the worst pictures of Holland', and tried to ignore the squalling of a 'miserable, indulged infant' in the seat opposite. He arrived 'with feet as cold as ice', and passed the evening in the warmth of James Scholefield's rooms at Trinity College.[1]

Next morning Hunt was up early to write a 'theatrical' on *Lost and Found*, a new comedy he had enjoyed at the Lyceum the previous Wednesday. Having mailed his review to the *Examiner* office, he explored the college and was impressed by libraries 'as big as palaces', the statue of Isaac Newton 'full of thought and dignity', and Benjamin West's painting of St Michael trampling Satan. This made Hunt feel as if he 'belonged'. The college treasures on display included a pair of Queen Elizabeth's shoes ('formidable feet'), and tiny Chinese shoes with a picture of a woman's bound foot, 'a hoof of flesh terminated by a claw'. He ventured into the town and was greeted 'with respect and hospitality'. He dined with another school friend, John Wood, now a Fellow of Pembroke Hall, and thought how he would have enjoyed college rooms and 'a regular stipend'. But he reflected that, had he pursued a university career, he would not have been 'so soon out into the world', and, anyway, had not Oliver Goldsmith said that the City of London was the 'first of universities'?[2] Hunt returned there on Saturday, 12 January, to check on the progress of his latest publishing venture.

While Hunt was in Cambridge his new magazine the *Reflector* had appeared in London. Its purpose was to display the '*mind*' of the age, and its opinions were 'exactly those of the *Examiner*, speaking freely of all parties [and] most anxious for Reform'.[3] The first issue contained twenty-four articles, some of them by Hunt's Christ's Hospital friends Barron Field, Thomas Barnes and James Scholefield. George Dyer contributed 'On Defects and Abuses in Public Institutions', 'On the English Constitution' and 'On the Catholic Claims'; John Aikin submitted 'Modes of Living and Thinking' and 'On War'. Most

of the first issue, however, was supplied by Hunt himself: two of his contributions, 'The English as a Thinking People' and 'On the Spirit Proper for a
Young Artist', encapsulated the *Reflector*'s preoccupation with politics and
the liberal arts. Hunt also published his translation of Catullus's poem, 'Atys
the Enthusiast', a portrait of a self-mutilating religious fanatic. Finally, he
authored three essays focusing the journal's concern with '*mind*'. The first,
'Remarks on the Past and Present State of the Arts in England', noticed
Benjamin West at 'the head of his profession', the 'daring imagination' of
Fuseli, and 'our first landscape-painter . . . Mr Turner'. The rising star
Benjamin Haydon was introduced: 'a fine eye for correctness and colour, with
an ambitious vehemence of style that promises grandeur of character but not
refinement'.[4] In his 'Retrospect of the Theatre' and 'Retrospect of Public
Affairs' Hunt was on territory familiar to *Examiner* readers: he found 'little
consolation for the present, or hope for the future'.[5]

New recruits joined the *Reflector* in subsequent issues, including Thomas
Mitchell, John Aikin's daughter Lucy, and Charles Lamb. Hunt had heard of
Lamb at Christ's Hospital and from mutual friends, and Lamb's brother John
had subscribed to *Juvenilia*. The first issue of the *Reflector* had attracted
Lamb's attention, and he sent three contributions in the manner of his later
'Elia' persona: 'On the Inconveniences Resulting from Being Hanged', 'On
the Dangers of Confounding Moral with Personal Deformity', and 'On the
Probable Effects of the Gunpowder Treason in this Country if the
Conspirators had Accomplished their Object' – a piece of speculative sedition in which Lamb conjectured how a 'tremendous explosion . . . in our
days' would produce a 'mighty benefit'.[6] Lamb's essays in the *Reflector*
signalled the emergence of a major new writer, the first of Hunt's many literary
discoveries and protégés.

While welcoming Lamb into the fold, Hunt barred the gate to others. His
Feast of the Poets in the *Reflector* updated the satirical 'Sessions of the Poets'
tradition of the seventeenth century and applied it to contemporary writers.
The plot of the poem was simple: 'Apollo gives the poets a dinner; and many
verse-makers, who have no claim to the title, present themselves, and are
rejected.' Hunt admitted to 'thinking of nothing but showing [his] wit', and
he succeeded in alienating 'almost every living poet': Wordsworth is presented
as a poet in 'second childhood'; Coleridge 'muddles' in prose; and Campbell
is lectured about 'invention'. The Tory critic William Gifford, formerly a
leading satirist of the *Anti-Jacobin*, is introduced as 'a sour little gentleman'.
There are moments of dramatic intelligence and shrewd observation, as in
the line capturing Gifford's frosty presence: 'He bowed, looked about him,
seemed cold, and sat down.' Hunt's peculiar turns of phrase also inject a
quirky vitality: 'the godhead went pop in'; 'lumb'ring just like a bear up'; and
'claps each a long stilt on', to rhyme with 'Milton'. When 'time and reflection' had 'moderated judgment', Hunt revised the *Feast* in ways that made it

genuinely influential, and posterity has endorsed his more considered estim-
ates of his contemporaries. At one point in the *Feast* Hunt alluded to 'a poem
I've by me', meaning a poem he had in prospect: Edmund Blunden noted
that this was Hunt's earliest mention of *The Story of Rimini*.[7]

In the *Examiner*, meanwhile, Hunt's poetry was developing in conversation
with his political writing – for example in 'Catullus's Return Home to his
Estate at Sirmio, Imitated':

> O best of all the scatter'd lands, that break
> From spreading sea or hill retiring lake,
> How happy do I drop within thy breast!
> With what a sigh of full contented rest!
> Scarce trusting, that my vagrant toil is o'er,
> And that these eyes behold thee safe once more!
> Is aught so blest as such a loose from care,
> When the soul's load rests with us in the chair;
> When we return from pilgrimage, and spread
> The loosen'd limbs o'er all the well-known bed!
> This of itself repays the grinding toil,
> And gives to failing knees the fresh'ning oil.
> Hail, lovely Sirmio; meet thy master's smiles;
> And laugh, thou sparkling lake, thro' all thine isles!
> Laugh, ev'ry social spot; your master's come!
> Laugh, ev'ry dimple on the cheek of home![8]

Most of *Juvenilia* had been 'imitations', but this attempt to capture the essence
of a Latin lyric marked a fresh direction. 'Catullus's Return Home' is a poem
of domestic and social 'content', evoking familiar scenes in Hunt's uniquely
odd cadences: 'hill retiring lake', 'such a loose from care', and 'the soul's load
rests'. As in the *Feast*, Hunt deliberately unsettles received ideas of elegant
poetic diction to create a modish, colloquial classic.

When it appeared in the *Examiner*, 'Catullus's Return Home' made a
striking contrast to other material published on the same page. It was followed
by a '*COURT AND FASHIONABLES*' column on the Prince of Wales's
birthday celebrations at Brighton. While British soldiers, including the
Prince's own regiment, were embarking for the war in Portugal, His Royal
Highness was partying in an 'uncommonly splendid uniform':

> His *jacket* and *pantaloons*, of Austrian costume, were of *scarlet*, elegantly
> embroidered . . . The *cap* and *blue pelisse*, lined with *white ermine*, were
> correspondingly beautiful, and vied in splendour with the *Sabre attaché*,
> whose workmanship and embroidery seemed excellence itself.[9]

'Seemed excellence itself' said it all. In the same issue of the *Examiner*, Hunt pointed out that the Prince's celebrations would have been 'splendid' indeed, 'had every body reason to be satisfied with the gorgeousness of this appearance!' As a young man the Prince had been witty, musical, an 'accomplished mimic', and he was interested in painting and architecture, but these admirable qualities were spoiled by vanity, self-indulgence and an irritable, spiteful nature.[10] The Prince squandered vast amounts of money on palaces, paintings, fashionable clothes, an endless succession of mistresses, military pageants, fêtes, feasting, drink and drugs. He had married his second wife, Caroline of Brunswick, for money – and immediately separated from her. Regrettably, there was no more to the Prince than embroidery and ermine: a glance behind the gorgeous costume revealed the Prince as he really was – a bloated, laudanum-sodden, middle-aged playboy. With the Prince of Wales, 'a good leg and a gracious smile must suffice instead of a good life and commanding virtue'.[11] The scene of honourable happiness, content and sociability in 'Catullus's Return Home' represented all that the Prince lacked.

With George III continuing insane, the 'good leg' was proclaimed Prince Regent on 5 February 1811. The Regency Act set limits to his power. No irrevocable measures could be taken, lest the King should recover, but everyone expected that the Prince would keep his word and forward the plans of his Whig friends: he would support parliamentary reform and Catholic emancipation; clamp down on expensive military adventures; and curb the profligacy and corruption of court and government. Hunt hoped for the best. The Regent might even mend his ways and 'act with the real dignity of patriotism' – there were indeed 'glorious opportunities of reconcilement and reform'. Would the Regent seize this opportunity, and brighten into power?[12]

The trial for alleged seditious libel in the article '*One Thousand Lashes!!*' was drawing closer. In 'Politics and Poetics, or, the Desperate Situation of a Journalist Unhappily Smitten with the Love of Rhyme', Hunt depicts himself as a poet-journalist who evades lawyers and printer's devils by retreating to a 'poetic nook', where his spirits lift 'on winged ecstasies'. This 'waking dream' is all too fitful, and soon the Muse's 'foes return':

> Freedom and Fiction's self no more avail,
> And lo! my Bower of Bliss is turned into a jail!

The editor of the *Examiner* is forced to confront the ironies of freedom and responsibility:

> The enduring soul, that, to keep others free,
> Dares to give up its darling liberty,
> Lives whereso'er its countrymen applaud,
> And in their great enlargement walks abroad . . .
> . . . I yield, I yield. – Once more I turn to you,
> Harsh politics!

Fascinated by the 'ghastly rites' of journalism and as readily enchanted by the 'haunted glades' of poetic reverie, for Hunt politics and poetics were fruitfully entangled rather than mutually exclusive. Romantic poetry has often been said to 'escape' the realities of the world; from now on Hunt's poems would reveal a fertile interaction with their contexts.

Spotting the brilliance of Charles Lamb's début in the *Reflector*, Hunt was quick to respond creatively. The third *Reflector* had included Hunt's suggestive scene of transition, 'at that still and delightful hour, when it is just too dark to read but too light to have candles'.[13] This prelude to reverie helped him towards the essay 'A Day by the Fire', in which he traces the contemplations of a 'Firesider' – Hunt's invented word – on 'a day's enjoyments by the fireside'.[14] A confidential manner is established at the outset:

> I am one of those that delight in a fireside, and can enjoy it without even the help of a cat or a tea-kettle. To cats indeed I have an aversion, as animals that only affect a sociality without caring a jot for any thing but their own luxury; and my tea-kettle, – I frankly confess, – has long been displaced, or rather dismissed, by a bronze-coloured and graceful urn . . .[15]

The essay follows the Firesider's thoughts as they range over a 'small set of visitors', Chaucer, the word '*snug*', climate and language, *Paradise Lost*, Shakespeare, the weather in ancient Greece and Rome – until evening brings the 'still and delightful hour' evoked in what has become a prose-poem:

> Twilight comes; and the hour of the fireside, for the perfection of the moment, is now alone. He was reading a minute or two ago, and for some time was unconscious of the approaching dusk, till on looking up, he perceived the objects out of doors deepening into massy outline, while the sides of his fireplace began to reflect the light of the flames, and the shadow of himself and his chair fidgeted with huge obscurity on the wall. Still wishing to read, he pushed himself nearer and nearer to the window, and continued fixed on his book, till he happened to take another glance out of doors, and on returning to it, could make out nothing. He therefore lays it aside, and restoring his chair to the fireplace, seats himself right before it in a reclining posture, his feet apart upon the fender, his eyes bent down towards the grate, his arms on the chair's elbows, one hand hanging down,

and the palm of the other turned up and presented to the fire, – not to keep it from him, for there is no glare or scorch about it, – but to intercept and have a more kindly feel of its genial warmth . . . The evening is beginning to gather in. The window, which presents a large face of watery grey intersected by strong lines, is imperceptibly becoming darker; and as that becomes darker, the fire assumes a more glowing presence. The contemplatist keeps his easy posture, absorbed in his fancies; and every thing around him is still and serene. The stillness would even ferment in his ear, and whisper, as it were, of what the air contained; but a minute coil, just sufficient to hinder that busier silence, clicks in the baking coal, while every now and then the light ashes shed themselves below, or a stronger but still a gentle flame flutters up with a gleam over the chimney. At length, the darker objects in the room become mingled; the gleam of the fire streaks with a restless light the edges of the furniture, and reflects itself in the blackening window; while his feet take a gentle move on the fender, and then settle again, and his face comes out of the general darkness, earnest even in indolence, and pale in the very ruddiness of what it looks upon. – This is the only time perhaps at which sheer idleness is salutary and refreshing. How observed with the smallest effort is every trick and aspect of the fire! A coal falling in, – a fluttering fume, – a miniature mockery of a flash of lightning, – nothing escapes the eye and the imagination. Sometimes a little flame appears at the corner of the grate like a quivering spangle; sometimes it swells out at the top into a restless and brief lambency; anon it is seen only by a light beneath the grate, or it curls around one of the bars like a tongue, or darts out with a spiral thinness and a sulphureous and continued puffing as from a reed. The glowing coals meantime exhibit the shifting forms of hills, and vales, and gulfs, – of fiery Alps, whose heat is uninhabitable even by spirit, or of black precipices, from which swart fairies seem about to spring away on sable wings; – then heat and fire are forgotten, and walled towns appear, and figures of unknown animals, and far-distant countries scarcely to be reached by human journey, – then coaches, and camels, and barking dogs as large as either, and forms that combine every shape and suggest every fancy; – till at last, the ragged coals tumbling together, reduce the vision to chaos, and the huge profile of a gaunt and grinning face seems to make a jest of all that has passed.——[16]

Hunt's vision of domestic life shows a remarkable lyrical sensitivity, the visual imagination of a painter and, perhaps, an intelligence that anticipates the techniques of cinematic art. As evening gathers, objects and outlines mingle in the light of the fire, a 'glowing presence' that coils, clicks, flutters, quivers, curls and darts its restless accompaniment to the Firesider's thoughts (like the companionable form of the 'thin blue flame' in Coleridge's 'Frost at Midnight'). Gradually absorbed by the heart of the fire, the Firesider imagines a world of walled towns, unknown animals and far-distant countries – until the coals tumble, and the vision consumes itself to reveal a 'gaunt and grinning' death's-head, or leering Mantichora.

Hunt's prose is full of the quick of experience, drawing a world of 'the most remote things' into the 'perfection of the moment'. This manner continues in his later writings, most notably perhaps in his *Indicator* piece, 'A Now, Descriptive of a Hot Day', and it was a model for many later writers, including Charles Dickens and Robert Browning who adapted Hunt's extempore voice to their own art. The relish for 'the worth of little pleasures', which Hunt linked with hypochondria, would be a keynote in later essays like 'Strawberries', 'Breakfast in Summer' and 'Autumnal Commencement of Fires'.[17] Were the little pleasures in these essays a welcome distraction from politics? Or did they help forward *Examiner* Hunt's campaign for reform?

'A Day by the Fire' celebrates domesticity and draws attention to Hunt's philosophy of 'cheer' evident in the 'social voice' of visitors, their 'mutual sense', 'joyous faces', and 'hours peculiarly congenial' passed amid the 'kindly feel of . . . genial warmth'.[18] Fireside conviviality nurtures in a broader sense: Hunt would later call this quality 'sociality', a genial heart(h)-felt power to set against malignity and encroaching chaos. Elsewhere in the *Reflector*, his essay 'On the Present and Future Character of the Prince Regent' explains why some individuals are willing to sacrifice the 'genial warmth' of home and hearth for the greater public good:

> The predominant spirit, all over the world, in every class of society, is a love of comfort; and what with this natural desire to be happy, the ties of domestic life, the daily routine of society . . . it may safely be asserted not only that a democratic spirit, taken in the full extent of the epithet now used, is not natural to a people in the present condition of society, but that whenever it does appear, it arises entirely from the faults, and the gross faults too, of the court or government.[19]

The 'democratic spirit' arises in response to the 'gross faults' in public life that violate domestic and social life: oppression, violence, injustice. Although Hunt does not say so explicitly, the scene of domestic cheer in 'A Day by the Fire' actively impels an 'anxiety for Reform', as Hunt pointed out to the Prince of Wales: 'The best praise [the people] can hereafter give you is to be chearful subjects; and all that they desire on your part is to leave them no excuse for being otherwise.'[20]

'Catullus's Return Home' made poignant contrast to reports about the Prince of Wales, and the poem acquired fresh point when it was republished in the *Examiner* in 1812 with a short introductory essay. Prominent in this little essay was Hunt's belief that 'poetry may really do something . . . even in a day of disaster'.[21] In making this claim Hunt anticipated the twentieth-century debate thrashed out by Auden and his contemporaries as to whether poetry makes things 'happen'. For Hunt, poetry's engagement with its readers would be a crucial way of gathering support for the reform campaign – and his poetry appeared with increasing frequency in the *Examiner* from 1811 onwards. He was still modernising classical poems: Catullus's 'Acme and Septimius', 'Catullus to Cornificius', and Horace's odes 'To Pyrrha' and 'To Mæcenas'.[22] Each was prefaced with a discussion of earlier translations, to draw out the qualities Hunt especially prized: 'delicacy of sentiment' expressed in a style of 'elegant terseness', 'well tempered' passion written with a style of 'passionate abruptness', 'a plain and natural longing after *the society and conversation of a friend*', and 'natural touches of feeling and *human* manner, as opposed to every other species of mannerism, which are the same in all ages'. Taken together, these statements amounted to a manifesto for poetry that was natural, humane, sympathetic and sociable – poetry that might 'really do something . . . even in a day of disaster'.

TWELVE

THE FEARLESS ENLIGHTENER

The trial for seditious libel in '*One Thousand Lashes!!*' was due at the Court of King's Bench, 'the *third* attack . . . upon the Proprietors of the *Examiner*'.[1] In the run-up Hunt redoubled his efforts, taunting the government for its failure to silence him:

> Certainly, the more the present state of things is considered, the more we look about us and see who and what are the prominent persons and actions in the upper part of our sphere, – so much the more must we admire the glorious opportunities of reconcilement and reform, which will be enjoyed by the successor of GEORGE the Third.[2]

This was defiant. The attempt to prosecute an identical passage from the *Examiner* had collapsed just months earlier. With a third libel charge imminent, Hunt was raising the stakes and daring the Attorney-General to issue yet another *ex officio* information (legal charge) for seditious libel.

The same issue of the *Examiner* drew attention to the judicial hounding of Peter Finnerty, an Irish journalist and a champion of freedom of the press and civil rights. In 1797, when Castlereagh was Chief Secretary to the Dublin administration, Finnerty was pilloried, jailed and fined for exposing the rigged trial and execution of a United Irishman, William Orr. Twelve years later Finnerty had accompanied and reported on the disastrous Walcheren expedition, only to be ordered home by Castlereagh in a determined effort to persecute his former adversary. Finnerty responded with an article in the *Morning Chronicle*, which attracted a libel charge. The *Examiner* carried a transcript of Finnerty's trial, with an account of the evidence Finnerty sought to make public and how the court authorities attempted to silence him – as they had tried to silence the Hunts. Finnerty cited three instances of Castlereagh's reign of terror in Ireland: 'an affidavit of *a father and son tortured side by side*'; 'another from Mr. Hughes, whom Lord Castlereagh saw after the torture had been inflicted; his back was raw from the scourge, and his shirt one mass of blood flung loosely around him'; and a third from a 'yeoman' who in 1798 had seen 'three peasants whipped and tortured *without trial*'. The transcript continued:

The COURT. – What does this prove?

Mr. FINNERTY. – It goes on to state, that these cruelties were committed with Castlereagh's sanction and privity.

The COURT. – You have been often told that these things were irrelevant. Do not compel us to send you back to prison till next Term, in order that you may come here to receive our judgment in a becoming manner.[3]

Finnerty's willingness to publicise such 'horrid testimonies' was seized upon by Castlereagh as a pretext to stop him reporting Walcheren. This was exactly the kind of ministerial censorship that Hunt, as the editor of a 'free Journal', could never accept. On Friday, 5 February Finnerty was found guilty of a 'cool, deliberate' libel on Castlereagh, and sentenced to eighteen months in Lincoln Prison.

Next day the Prince of Wales was installed as Regent, and by the end of the week it was already clear to Hunt that the Whigs, who had expected 'to rush at once to the head of affairs', had been 'carelessly dropped from the PRINCE'S hand'.[4] The Regent had deserted his friends; Spencer Perceval and the Tories would continue in office. There would be no change of Ministry, no revival of the Foxite Whigs, no 'glorious opportunities of reconcilement and reform'. Hunt took stock of the moment, and observed: 'If ever there was a time, when it became public writers among us to be bold – I may say adventurous – in advocating the cause of individual freedom, that obligation is now in full force.'[5] This call to action appeared in the *Examiner* on Sunday, 17 February: within five days he would be standing in the Court of King's Bench where Peter Finnerty had been sentenced.

The jury comprised ten 'common' and only two hand-picked 'special' jurors. The 'common' jurors were working men: two victuallers, a cutler, a cook, a cabinet-maker, a baker and a grocer, an oilman, a stationer and a 'porkman'; the two 'special' jurors were gentlemen. Lord Ellenborough presided, and the defence was conducted by the brilliant young Scottish lawyer Henry Brougham, who had been a founding contributor to the *Edinburgh Review*. Brougham was a vigorous presence in London Whig circles, an MP, a prominent abolitionist, and an opponent of the 'abuse of flogging in the army and navy'.[6] To focus readers' attention on the trial, the *Examiner* reported the fate of a marine sentenced to three hundred lashes for 'mutinous expressions', '200 of which only were inflicted, *he being unable to sustain the whole of the sentence*'.[7] In other words, he was dead.

The Attorney-General detailed the tendency of the alleged libel, to create disaffection in the minds of the soldiers of this country; to repre-sent to them, that they are treated with improper and excessive severity, and (what is still more mischievous), that the treatment of the French soldiers, under Buonaparte, and the means used to oblige them to under-take the military service in France, are preferable to those which are made use of in Great Britain, towards the soldiers of our army. The effect of this is obvious: it tends to raise a discontent and disaffection in the minds of the soldiers themselves; it tends to disincline others from entering the service. If that effect was to be produced, how fatal to the very existence of the country the consequences must be, it is unnecessary for me to state.[8]

Brougham had been instructed to make 'as full and unshrinking a defence of the article in question, as his talent and spirit should direct'.[9] After a skirmish on technicalities Brougham set out the defence from a broad base, reminding the jury that 'the intention of the defendants was good' and that fundamental liberties were at stake: 'You are now to determine, whether an Englishman still enjoys the privilege of freely discussing public measures.'[10] Naming two 'gallant officers' opposed to flogging, Sir Robert Wilson and Brigadier-General Stuart, Brougham doubted whether an 'evil intention' could be imputed to his clients for expressing similar opinions:

Is there any safe subject for discussion, if we are to be told that our argu-ments tend to excite revolt? . . . is there no danger of mutiny to be appre-hended from the infliction of these military floggings, in the sight and hearing of thousands of soldiers and peasantry, although the danger which the mere narrative of them is to produce be so great? Is this fund of peas-antry, out of which your future soldiers are to be drawn, to hear with their own ears, and see with their own eyes, the horrors of a military flogging without thinking twice before they enter the army? All this is a chimerical fear; let their eyes feast on the sight, let their ears be glutted with the sound; all is safe, there is no fear of their being moved: but have a care how you describe or comment upon all this . . . for a single word of argument will occasion those troops to revolt, and that peasantry to turn their attention to some other way of life, who saw and heard a military flogging with the coolest satisfaction![11]

Was the article 'an inflammatory libel'? Or did Hunt 'still [have] the privi-lege of expressing himself as his feelings and his opinions dictate?'[12] The jury withdrew. After an hour, they requested a copy of the *Examiner* containing the alleged libel, retired again for forty-five minutes, and then returned to the court with their verdict.[13] The *Examiner* had won for a third time.

   The Hunts' acquittal brought congratulations from the 'liberal of all parties' and, in the ministerial papers, 'sullen silence', 'peevish surprise' and 'undisguised rage'. The *Courier* lashed itself into paroxysms of 'absurdity', and Hunt imagined his opponents wailing 'over the shocking increase of humanity and public spirit, so fatal to selfishness and public corruption'.[14]

In Henry Brougham, Hunt had secured an influential ally and friend. Two weeks after the acquittal, news came of a success in the campaign against military flogging: from now on, courts martial had the option of sentencing to imprisonment instead of corporal punishment – a significant step, in Hunt's view, 'towards the abolition of that degrading torture'. Ironically, however, the same *Examiner* reported that the proprietor of the *Stamford News*, John Drakard, had been tried for seditious libel in the original '*One Thousand Lashes!!*' article. Brougham was once again counsel for the defence but, this time, half of the jury had been drawn from the 'special' list. On 29 May Drakard stood in the Court of King's Bench, where the Hunts had been acquitted, and was sentenced to eighteen months in prison and a £200 fine. A subscription was launched, and by the end of July some £426 had been raised. Ten guineas came from Drakard's supporters at the *Examiner* office.[15]

The two libel trials for '*One Thousand Lashes!!*' proved what many had long suspected: the barrage of informations for libel amounted to a concerted effort 'to reduce the liberty of the press to nihility'.[16] Even establishment opinion was outraged. Commenting on the case against the Hunts, *The Times* judged that the charge

> cannot be called a libel against any body. It is therefore, or was supposed to be, a libel against nobody, but yet tending to excite mutiny in the army: for this Messrs. HUNTS were prosecuted by the ATTORNEY GENERAL, and have been acquitted. If any thing could carry conviction to the minds that some change ought to take place in the law of libels or in the administration of it, it would be, that no one can in this, or a variety of other cases, give a precise description of the person or thing affected by such libels . . .

The Whigs fastened on this issue, and *The Times* noted that the Attorney-General 'has to see LORD HOLLAND provided with a list of the criminal informations he has already prosecuted'.[17]

Henry Fox, Lord Holland, was the nephew and protégé of Charles James Fox, the charismatic gambler, bon viveur and parliamentarian. By 1811 he had emerged as leader of the Foxite Whigs, the faction that had continued to call for parliamentary reform. On 4 March Holland tabled a motion in the Lords, proposing an inquiry into the Attorney-General's '*discretionary*' powers in framing indictments for libel.[18] The evidence was overwhelming: in the thirty years to 1791 there were seventy *ex officio* informations; between

1800 and 1805, fourteen; and between 1807 and 1810 *forty-two* such prosecutions.[19] Just a few months previously John Gale Jones and Sir Francis Burdett had been jailed without trial, igniting four days of riots in London. The trials of Peter Finnerty, John Drakard and the Hunts had all involved 'special juries' and other interference with the legal system. The outcome of Lord Holland's motion was eagerly awaited.

The latest prosecution had thrust Hunt to the forefront of the reform movement. The trial was discussed in parliament and reported throughout the country: instead of silencing the *Examiner*, it had made its editor a prominent national figure, discussed in taverns and coaches, coffee-houses, clubs and colleges. Hunt was now a marked man, sought out by like-minded reformists while his enemies waited for another opportunity to destroy him.

Two episodes illustrate Hunt's new-found fame. Shortly after the trial he was invited to dine at Holland House, the political and cultural home of the Foxite Whigs.[20] This was the most fashionable political and literary salon in town, the resort of politicians, poets, radicals and revolutionaries, ambassadors, and members of the Royal Academy and Royal Society.[21] Lord Holland had been among the subscribers to the first edition of Hunt's *Juvenilia* and, following the libel trial, the two men had a mutual friend in Henry Brougham. Hunt's father would immediately have sensed opportunities – a connection with the political establishment, helpful introductions, perhaps even a parliamentary career. But his son had learned to be more circumspect. Reflecting that a dinner at Holland House might compromise his independence, Hunt stayed away.[22]

A different invitation came in a letter from an undergraduate at University College, Oxford; it was dated Saturday, 2 March:

> Sir,
>   Permit me, although a stranger, to offer my sincerest congratulations on the occasion of that triumph so highly to be prized by men of liberality; permit me also to submit to your consideration, as to one of the most fearless enlighteners of the public mind at the present time, a scheme of mutual safety and mutual indemnification for men of public spirit and principle, which if carried into effect would evidently be productive of incalculable advantages; of the scheme the enclosed is an address to the public, the proposal for a meeting, and shall be modified according to your judgment, if you will do me the honour to consider the point.
>   The ultimate intention of my aim is to induce a *meeting* of such enlightened unprejudiced members of the community, whose independent principles expose them to evils which might thus become alleviated, and to form a methodical society which should be organized

so as to resist the coalition of the enemies of liberty which at present renders any expression of opinion on matters of policy dangerous to individuals. It has been for want of societies of this nature that corruption has attained the height at which we now behold it, nor can any of us bear in mind the very great influence, which some years since was gained by *Illuminism* without considering that a society of equal extent might establish *rational liberty* on as firm a basis as that which would have supported the visionary schemes of a completely-equalized community.

Although perfectly unacquainted privately with you, I address you as a common friend of *Liberty*, thinking that in cases of this urgency and importance, that etiquette ought not to stand in the way of usefulness.

My father is in parliament, and on attaining 21 I shall, in all probability, fill his vacant seat. On account of the responsibility to which my residence at this University subjects me, I of course, dare not publicly to avow all that I think, but the time will come when I hope that my every endeavour, insufficient as this may be, will be directed to the advancement of liberty.

> I remain sir,
> Your most obedient servant,
> P. B. Shelley.[23]

The bold, idealistic nature of his unknown correspondent was striking. Hunt could see that the enclosed 'address' – like scores of other manuscripts that arrived in the *Examiner* office – came with an implicit request to publish. But this letter was out of the usual run. Congratulating Hunt on his recent acquittal and introducing himself as a man of 'liberality', P. B. Shelley claims kin as 'a common friend of *Liberty*'. He packs his letter with ideas, plans and prospects: 'a scheme of mutual safety', 'an address to the public', 'the proposal for a meeting', and 'a methodical society' that 'might establish *rational liberty*'. While likening his proposed society to the Illuminati – the European network of freethinkers, republicans, and deists – P. B. Shelley also appeals to the '*rational liberty*' of William Godwin's *Political Justice*. He concludes his letter by anticipating a safe family seat in the unreformed House of Commons (Hunt later observed, '[h]e had only to become a yea and nay man in the House of Commons, to be one of the richest men in Sussex').[24]

P. B. Shelley was evidently the son of Timothy Shelley, the indolent member for New Shoreham who never said a word in the House. Was this just an undergraduate hothead going through a rebellious phase? How could the threat to 'independent principles' be countered by joining a society? John Thelwall's London Corresponding Society had tried that in the 1790s, only to be crushed by the 'enemies of liberty'. Still, it was intriguing that the young man had read Godwin's book. Published eighteen years previously, *Political Justice* had not aged well. In the 1790s it had seemed to contain the 'oracles of thought', and Godwin was talked of, looked up to, and sought after.[25] But no one bothered with those two unwieldy volumes in 1811.

As Hunt mused over P. B. Shelley's letter, news came that Lord Holland's motion had been defeated. Only thirty-six peers had voted on this crucial question. Why was the government so terrified of questions and accountability? Hunt needed a term for the 'sore disease' that afflicted 'people in power', and settled on 'Exetasophobia, or Horror of Inquiry'. His nonce word derived from the Greek *exetasis* – close examination or scrutiny – and was intended to suggest the government's paranoia about public investigation.[26] The letter was put to one side while Hunt dealt with the more urgent matter of his editorial on the 'Failure of Lord Holland's Motion' and the causes and consequences of 'Exetasophobia'.

Percy Bysshe Shelley was disappointed that the 'fearless enlightener' had not replied. Except for one close friend, Shelley was isolated at Oxford: to have someone of Hunt's stature take his schemes seriously would have guaranteed his belief that liberty was a common cause, and that equality would attend 'a more advanced & ameliorated state of society'.[27] The editor of the *Examiner* might have helped him find publishing opportunities and, what Shelley craved most, an audience.

Shelley was born on 4 August 1792 into a wealthy Whig landowning family in Sussex, the son of Timothy Shelley and his wife Elizabeth. The family home, Field Place, was comfortable, although Shelley's parents were distant and more or less indifferent about his education and future. As a schoolboy at Syon House and Eton College, Shelley cultivated intense, idealistic friendships much as Hunt had done at Christ's Hospital. Like Hunt, too, he relished victimisation and martyrdom at the hands of bullies and 'school-tyrants'.[28] At Eton Shelley developed a passion for experimenting with chemistry, astronomy and electricity, and was fascinated by how 'mainstream' science – or 'natural philosophy' – overlapped with his occult pursuits in alchemy, necromancy and psychic phenomena. He was also aware that science had advanced in step with the revolutions in America and France: Benjamin Franklin had drawn down lightning with kites, and Shelley had repeated this experiment at Field Place.

When Shelley went up to University College in October 1810 he continued to live at the same iconoclastic intensity, consumed by his arcane interests and reading. He made contact with a like-minded undergraduate, Thomas Jefferson Hogg, who later wrote this account of Shelley's college rooms:

books, boots, papers, shoes, philosophical instruments, clothes, pistols, linen, crockery, ammunition, and phials innumerable, with money, stockings, prints, crucibles, bags, and boxes, were scattered on the floor and in every place; as if the young chemist, in order to analyse the mystery of creation, had endeavoured first to re-construct the primeval chaos . . . An electrical machine, an air-pump, the galvanic trough, a solar microscope, and large glass jars and receivers, were conspicuous amidst the mass of matter. Upon the table by his side were some books lying open, several letters, a bundle of new pens, and a bottle of japan ink, that served as an inkstand; a piece of deal, lately part of the lid of a box, with many chips, and a handsome razor that had been used as a knife.[29]

Hogg frequently embellished his recollections of Shelley, but this one rings true: chipped deal and a razor-turned-knife have the presence of things seen. These were the rooms of a student obsessed by cutting-edge science, by the quest for the origin of the universe and a 'first cause' (Hogg's reference to Shelley analysing 'the mystery of creation' is faithful to their correspondence in winter 1810–11).[30] Scientific progress would bring social and political liberty: 'Truth whatever it may be has never been known to be prejudic[i]al to the best interests of mankind,' Shelley informed his father: '"Religion fetters a reasoning mind with the very bonds which restrain the unthinking one from mischief" – this is my great objection to it.'[31] William Blake would have embraced Shelley as a kindred spirit; Timothy Shelley shuddered at his son's impiety. Together, Shelley and Hogg determined to publish their views as republicans and atheists convinced of the irresistible triumph of rational truth.

Pamphlets would bring this truth to the people. Shelley had already planned to publish 'A Poetical Essay on the Existing State of Things' and donate the proceeds to Peter Finnerty.[32] The Necessity of Atheism was published on 14 February 1811 as a rationalist interrogation of religion that concluded: 'no degree of criminality can be attached to disbelief' because 'there is no proof of the existence of a Deity'.[33] Copies were sent to the Vice-Chancellor and heads of colleges, and Shelley reported that 'the Bishops have the Atheism'.[34] The Oxford booksellers, Slatter and Munday, had displayed the pamphlet for just twenty minutes before it was spotted by a Fellow of New College, who was horrified that such impious material was on sale. He ordered it to be burned and the authors sought out.

Shelley's letter to Hunt was written in the midst of the ensuing crisis. Hunt had faced repeated prosecutions from the government, and now young Shelley was confronted by the University and Church. They were both beleaguered 'Friends of Liberty'. On Monday, 25 March the Masters and Fellows of University College summoned Shelley to account for The Necessity of Atheism, and minuted his 'contumacious' attitude. When he refused 'to disavow the publication', he was expelled.[35] Next morning he took the coach to London.

On Sunday, 24 March, the *Examiner* published Hunt's article on how 'court-influence' and the Church stifled intellectual freedom in the universities. When Shelley read this, skulking in London at 15, Poland Street and crackling with hatred of the University's 'tyrranical violent proceedings', it must have seemed that Hunt had come through for him. Hunt's first paragraph alluded to 'the "necessity" of some vile subserviency to the times'. Was this a sly reference to *The Necessity of Atheism* for *Examiner* readers who knew about goings-on at University College? The article was unquestionably an informed assault on the 'bigotry', 'ignorance' and 'contempt for learning' Shelley had endured at Oxford.[36]

Reinvigorated by the language of the *Examiner*, on Friday, 29 March Shelley wrote a belated letter of explanation to his father. Two sceptical yet open-minded students had been anxious 'to obtain a satisfactory, or an unsatisfactory answer from men who had made Divinity the study of their lives'. What had ensued was an attempt by the authorities to enforce 'subserviency':

> – How then were we treated? not as our fair, open, candid conduct might demand, no argument was publickly brought forward to disprove our reasoning, & it at once demonstrated the weakness of their cause, & their inveteracy on discovering it, when they publickly expelled myself & my friend.[37]

Shelley had been 'candid' in publishing his opinions; the authorities responded with resentment of open, 'publick' discussion. Their 'cause' was not 'argument', or 'reasoning', or 'study', but, as Hunt had explained, 'inveteracy' – the maintenance of power. And this required that Shelley should be 'publickly expelled'.

In succeeding weeks Shelley's negotiations with his father quickly broke down. He was short of money, and in April he contacted Rowland Hunter with a proposal for publishing a poem. Perhaps this was the 'Poetical Essay on the Existing State of Things'. Possibly it was *The Wandering Jew* – the long, sensational poem Shelley had written at school now had fresh point for its exiled author. It was dedicated to Sir Francis Burdett in recognition of his 'active virtues', so that an approach to Hunter was in many ways an obvious move: Joseph Johnson had published radical authors, and his successor might be expected to have maintained that tradition. In the event Hunter declined to publish, but directed Shelley to a source of sympathetic advice. Thornton Hunt recalled:

Shelley had brought a manuscript poem which proved by no means suited
to the publishing house in St. Paul's Churchyard. But Mr. Hunter sent the
young reformer to seek the counsel of Leigh Hunt.[38]

With an introduction from Hunter, Shelley made his second approach to the
'fearless enlightener'. This time he received a 'polite note' from Hunt inviting
him to breakfast on Sunday, 5 May.

Looking back over many years to this first meeting with Shelley, Hunt
recalled 'a youth, not come to his full growth; very gentlemanly, earnestly
gazing at every object that interested him, and quoting the Greek dramatists'.[39]
In May 1811 Hunt was twenty-six, Shelley a gangling eighteen-year-old with
long hair and expensive 'rumpled' clothes.[40] Shelley reported their meeting
just three days after it took place. 'I dined with him on Sunday [5 May],'
Shelley wrote to Hogg:

> – he is a Deist despising J[esus] C [hrist] &c & yet having a high venera-
> tion for the Deity, the consequence of our acquaintance was a long argu-
> ment, but he certainly means the same as an Atheist, they differ but in
> name. He will not allow this; with him God is neither omnipotent,
> omnipresent, nor identical, he destroys too all those predicates *in non*, against
> which we entered our protest, he says that God *is* comprehensible, not
> doubting but an adequate exertion of reason (which, he says, is by no means
> to be despaired of) would lead us from a contemplation of his works to a
> definite knowledge of his attributes, which are by no means limited. Now
> here is a new God for you – In practise such a Deist is this is [*sic*] an
> Atheist, as he believes that this Creator is by no means perfect, but composed
> of good & evil like man, produces that mixture of these principles which
> is evident – Hunt is a man of cultivated mind, & certainly exalted notions;
> – I do not entirely despair of rescuing him out of this damnable heresy
> from Reason – Mrs. Hunt is a most sensible woman, she is by no means a
> Xtian, & rather atheistically given . . .[41]

Weary after a long night seeing the *Examiner* through the press, Hunt probably expected that Shelley would want to talk politics and poetry. That
morning's *Examiner* carried Hunt's leader on the campaign in Portugal, a
piece that cut through military propaganda to war 'as it really is'. What Hunt
encountered in his 'long argument' with Shelley, however, was a restatement
of *The Necessity of Atheism* – the 'protest' to which Shelley refers in his letter
to Hogg. That Shelley was eager to hear Hunt's views on religion might
indicate that he had noticed the reference to 'necessity' in Hunt's university
article, and understood it to refer to him. Shelley's account of their discussion is consistent with his pamphlet, and with what we know of Hunt's religious beliefs. Compared with the rigour of *The Necessity of Atheism*, Hunt's

views were more akin to the undogmatic inclusiveness of Universalism. Shelley's assessment of Hunt's 'exalted notions' suggests polite puzzlement, and their breakfast 'produced no intimacy'.[42]

In August Shelley eloped to Scotland with the sixteen-year-old Harriet Westbrook, beginning a restless career that would take them around Britain, to Ireland and the continent. Five years would pass before Hunt met Shelley again.

THIRTEEN

EIGHTEEN HUNDRED AND ELEVEN

Following Hunt's acquittal at the '*One Thousand Lashes!!*' trial his acquaintance with Henry Brougham grew into close friendship, warmed by shared political views and a mutual interest in poetry. In May 1811 Brougham protested at William Cobbett's 'wilful misrepresentation' of the Drakard case, and advised that it would be 'worthwhile to contradict this'. Hunt promptly obliged with two 'Political Examiner' articles reproving Cobbett's 'shuffling', 'malevolent' behaviour.[1] Brougham reciprocated by reading Hunt's poems in manuscript, forwarding suggestions and lending books.

The Hunts moved to 37, Portland Street, a few yards from Marianne's childhood home at Little Titchfield Street. During the summer Hunt and Haydon saw a good deal of each other: they made an excursion to rural Primrose Hill, and on 28 July breakfasted and passed the day together. That evening they dined with David Wilkie, who had nearly finished his picture *The Village Festival*. Haydon was full of praise for this scene of rustic merriment, although aware as always of professional rivalry (*The Village Festival* eventually brought Wilkie £800). Two years ago he had described Wilkie as 'a cold, calculating, cautious, clear-headed Scotchman'; now his journal recorded the wish that they would 'go down to Posterity in an united blaze'. By adopting a 'spare' diet on Hunt's recommendation, Haydon had found himself 'adequate to study after dinner' and redoubled efforts on his own painting. One study he completed this year was his portrait of Hunt as a dark sensualist who was disconcertingly in touch with Haydon's own repressed desires (see the cover of this book).[2]

Hunt had been corresponding on friendly terms with Thomas Moore, and was impressed by the plaintive music of his *Irish Melodies* (1808):

> No more to chiefs and ladies bright
>   The harp of Tara swells:
> The chord alone, that breaks at night,
>   Its tale of ruin tells.
> Thus Freedom now so seldom wakes,
>   The only throb she gives

Is when some heart indignant breaks,
To show that she still lives.[3]

One of the *Irish Melodies* held a personal appeal: according to family tradition Brian Boru, celebrated in Moore's poem 'Remember the Glories of Brien
the Brave', was one of Hunt's ancestors.[4] *The Feast of the Poets* had praised
Moore as a 'poet, so gifted and rare', but Moore's letter to Hunt of 11
September 1811 presumed too far. His comic opera *M.P., or the Blue-Stocking*
had opened at the Lyceum the previous Monday, 9 September. This was a
concoction of routine jokes at the expense of intellectual women, politicians
and the French, interspersed with sentimental songs – in other words, a sure
crowd-pleaser. It had already been reviewed in *The Times*. 'The only misrepresentation I can accuse them of (& *that* I feel very sensibly),' Moore told
Hunt,

> is the charge of Royalism and Courtier-ship which they have founded upon
> my foolish clap-trap with respect to the Regent – this has astonished me
> . . . & it is merely lest *you* should be led into a similar mistake . . . that I
> trouble you with this note.
>   If the child's plea 'I'll never do so again' could soften criticism, I may
> be depended upon, from this moment, for a most hearty abjuration of the
> Stage . . .[5]

Moore had mistaken his man: his letter reeked of the old 'system of puffing'
and review-mongering. When Hunt's 'Theatrical Examiner' appeared on the
Sunday following it proved to be one of his longest, extending over three
pages. Despite or because of Moore's attempt to disarm criticism, Hunt was
on his most combative form. Instead of 'an opera worthy of its poet' – who
was unquestionably 'one of the most accomplished men of his time' – Moore
had produced 'a farce in three acts of the old complexion! A string of common-
places, the more unsightly from the few pearls mingled with them!' The 'few
pearls' were the songs – these displayed Moore's true lyrical genius; the
remainder was an 'unambitious, undignified, and most unworthy compilation
of pun, equivoque, and clap-trap!' In a calculated response to Moore's letter,
Hunt drew attention to the incident Moore claimed most to regret: 'a horse-
race is supposed to take place behind the scenes, and a spectator rushing
forward, announces that the horse *Regent* is about to start, and "promises a
glorious race"'. Hot tip or easy laugh? Either way, in Hunt's view it was 'a
common stage trick, quite unworthy indeed of Mr. MOORE'.[6]
    By stressing that his disappointment was proportionate to his esteem for
Moore, Hunt managed to preserve their mutual regard. Moore's next letter
thanked Hunt for his 'Poem in the Reflector', *The Feast of the Poets*, adding
'if my praises could be thought *disinterested* enough to please you'. This slightly

bristly acknowledgement and Moore's recognition of Hunt's 'good opinion of me in general' showed that equanimity had been restored – though there remained the potential for further upsets, especially where Moore's links with the establishment were concerned.[7]

Summer 1811 brought 'refreshing' news of a French retreat in Portugal, tempered immediately by the rumour, soon substantiated, that the Regent had restored his brother the Duke of York – a man utterly compromised in public and private life – as Commander-in-Chief of the army. This was a scandalous development, a matter for public 'regret, indignation, and contempt'.[8] It compounded the Regent's misjudgement in having abandoned his Whig supporters, and obliterated any lingering hope that he would make good.

Hunt recalled this period with some particularity in his *Autobiography*. Whereas the Prince of Wales was formerly understood 'to be the jovial advocate of liberality in all things, and a sponsor in particular for concession of the Catholic claims',

> the Prince of Wales, now become Prince Regent, had retained the Tory ministers of his father; he had broken life-long engagements; had violated his promises, particular as well as general, those to the Catholics among them; and led *in toto* a different political life from what had been expected. The name, therefore, which used to be hailed with rapture, was now . . . received with hisses.[9]

Political allegiances were shifting, with many Whigs withdrawing their support for the Prince, now a figure of 'universal distrust'.[10] Even the Regent's long-time friend and apologist Richard Brinsley Sheridan found his loyalty strained. He owed his seat in the Commons to the Prince's patronage, but increasingly resented attempts to influence his voting on Irish matters. In February 1812 Lord Moira's motion calling for civil rights for Irish Catholics came before parliament, the fifth such motion since 1805. Byron supported it in the House of Lords; in the Commons, Sheridan came under pressure not to vote. Technically Sheridan was a member of the Prince's household, but had decided that while the Prince and his ministers continued 'array'd against the Catholic claims they cannot have a vote in their support from me and therefore I ought not to continue to owe my seat to their Master'. In the event Sheridan voted in favour of the motion, but like earlier attempts to grant Irish Catholics civil and religious liberty it was heavily defeated.[11]

From now on Hunt took every opportunity to attack the Regent. The appointment of a Private Secretary to an obscure sinecure, 'the *Paymastership of Widows' Pensions*', showed that 'the time is passed . . . for any further dependence on [the Prince's] natural or acquired sagacity':

the PRINCE is really a very weak man, – a truth, of which the nation has put off its conviction from year to year, from month to month, and from day to day, till the humiliating and afflicting secret is to be kept no longer.[12]

'Newspaper Flummery' from the Regent's lackeys at the *Courier*, *Morning Herald* and *Morning Post* was held up for ridicule, and Hunt turned his 'Theatrical Examiner' reviews to the same task. A flattering portrait of Charles II in the play *Royal Oak* provided an opportunity to expand upon 'the real historical *Charles*'. 'Of all the princes of England', Hunt writes, Charles was 'the very last perhaps that has any claim upon the indulgence of her posterity, having been as slavish to her enemies as he was tyrannical to herself'.[13] Hunt's 'perhaps' offered readers pause for reflection – surely the Regent was likely to have as little 'claim upon the indulgence of posterity'? John Keats responded in a little poem 'Written on 29 May, the Anniversary of Charles's Restoration, on Hearing the Bells Ringing':

> Infatuate Britons, will you still proclaim
> His memory, your direst, foulest shame?
> Nor patriots revere?

Remarking 'each traitorous lying bell' that tolled in memory of Charles was a way of damning those who now proclaimed the Regent's virtues. Turning from Hunt on the 'historical *Charles*', *Examiner* readers had only to cast their eyes across to the next page to find a report of the extravagant fête held at the Prince's residence, Carlton House, to celebrate his Regency:

It would be a difficult task to describe, in terms adequate, the effect produced by the profusion of magnificent objects, which, at every glance, conveyed an exalted idea of princely taste, national grandeur, and the fine arts, cherished in a state of perfection. The apartments were decorated with splendour perfectly new. The Palace was a scene of enchantment . . .

The interior struck the beholder with astonishment. The grand table extended the whole length of the Conservatory, and across Carlton House, in the length of two hundred feet. Two feet of space was allotted each guest in the original calculation. Along the centre of the table, about six inches above the surface, a canal of pure water continued flowing from a silver fountain, beautifully constructed at the head of the table. Its faintly waving, artificial banks, were covered with green moss and aquatic flowers; gold and silver coloured fish were, by a mechanical invention, made to swim and sport through the bubbling current, which produced a pleasing murmur where it fell, and formed a cascade at the outlet. At the head of the table, above the fountain, sat his Royal Highness the Prince Regent on a throne of crimson velvet, trimmed with gold . . .

... Along those tables, the Royal family of England, and that of the Bourbons, and the Noblesse, were seated conformably to their respective ranks. On the *right hand* of the Prince Regent was placed *the Duchess d'Angouleme* – on his left, the Duchess of York. From the Library, and room beyond, branched out two great lines of tables under canvas far into the gardens, each in the shape of a cross, all richly served with silver plate, and covered with every delicacy that the season could possibly afford. When the whole company was seated, there was a line of female beauty more richly adorned, and a blaze of jewellery more brilliant, than England probably ever displayed before.

The Prince Regent sustained the Royal Host throughout with all the dignified and unabating courtesy that so arduous a character requires.[14]

This fantastic 'Palace of Pleasure' was contrived to display the Regent's solidarity with European royalty and the Duke and Duchess of York. It could be argued that entertainment on this scale kept London's merchants employed, and helped boost popular morale. Visitors to the 'gaudy scene' were admitted for two weeks after the fête, and the pressure was 'almost intolerable'.[15] But grotesque comparisons were inevitable, and when viewed against the contemporary scene in England, the fête appeared outrageously wasteful. *Examiner*s for June 1811 listed damaging floods in Shropshire and Worcestershire; the defeat of yet another motion for relief of Irish Catholics; some 118 bankrupt traders; and the suicide of Ann Handley, 'a young woman scarcely 17 years of age, who died in consequence of having taken 30 grains of opium'. The enlistment of her brother as a soldier was felt to be insufficient reason for her repeated complaint of being 'very unhappy'.

The *Examiner*'s comment on the Carlton House fête appeared on 30 June:

The amount of property advertised as having been lost by different persons at the PRINCE REGENT'S Fête . . . exceeds 2000£. . . . No estimate has yet been published of the cost of the Carlton-house Gala. When it is known, it would be curious to learn how many unfortunate debtors the money would have returned to their afflicted families and to society.[16]

In November the *Examiner* reprinted panegyrics from the *Morning Herald*, describing how visitors to Brighton had relished 'the *exhilarating hope* of beholding the Prince', only to endure '*heartfelt disappointment*' when he failed to appear. The *Herald* also pointed to the 'dignified appearance' of the Duke of Cumberland '*on the saddle*', adding tactfully, 'indeed, *excepting the Prince* we never observed his superior for that particular; BUT THE PRINCE IS HAPPILY BORN TO EXCEL IN EVERY ACCOMPLISHMENT' (the italics and caps here are from the *Examiner*).[17] To call 'a lusty gentleman just fifty, "'beauteous'" was a ludicrous 'excess of admiration' – and it was dangerous too. Elaborately spun 'panegyric and pathos' about the Regent and his entourage might be accepted at face value, with grave consequences for the nation:

> if we are to trust their way of talking . . . we must acknowledge that both they and the nation are contented to see his Royal Highness conducting himself as he does; – that his taste, his habits, and his connexions are all worthy of the age in which he lives; – that they behold in him nothing but what is likely to make his reign respectable and happy; – in short, that his subjection of great matters to little is a proof of his good policy, and that his dresses covered with gold are a sort of prophetic announcement that he is henceforward to be covered with glory.[18]

The reports of Carlton House and Brighton show the *Examiner*'s quarrel with the Regent building towards a clash with 'Ministerial Editors' and the Tory press. As the year drew to a close, Hunt's sense of a mission – of 'something at stake' – was gathering momentum:

> while there is a chance that the *Examiner* may catch [the Regent's] eye even in a wrapper that brings him some new trinket or piece of furniture, I shall not cease to speak of him and to him as becomes an Englishman . . .[19]

The echo of William Blake's vision of national regeneration –

> I will not cease from mental fight,
> Nor shall my sword sleep in my hand,
> Till we have built Jerusalem,
> In England's green and pleasant land[20]

– was a coincidence: Hunt had certainly not read a word of Blake's *Milton*, to which that famous lyric is a preface. Nevertheless, Hunt was now embarked on a 'mental fight' as strenuous as William Blake's against the 'Satanic mills' of materialism. And he was determined that his campaign should not be confused with the activities of disreputable rivals.

The fifth of November was of momentous significance in the radical calendar, a date that marked the acquittals of Thomas Hardy, Horne Tooke and John Thelwall in the treason trials of 1794. Celebrations were held in the Crown and Anchor tavern, at which orator Henry Hunt addressed the company in 'a long and coarse abuse' which Hunt discovered to his disgust had been attributed to him. 'I have been drinking at a dinner I never saw, speaking of my enemy in a way I should despise, and uttering sentiments which in common with every sound Englishman I should abominate'. Hunt dismissed his namesake as a rabble-rouser 'imitating the revolutionary language of a French mob'. He attempted to distance himself, claiming to be comparatively 'obscure' and 'little known'; the *Examiner*, unlike the 'vulgar and turbulent' Henry Hunt, was 'decent in conduct, and unequivocal in principle'. Hunt signed this article with his customary 'Indicator' colophon and, unusually, added his own name in capitals – to emphasise which Hunt was the 'person connected with the *Examiner*'.[21]

Despite efforts to ensure that the public identified Leigh Hunt as *Examiner* Hunt, he would be confused with Henry Hunt 'of notorious character' again. The *Examiner* was integral to his public presence, one of the rallying points that gave him 'a sense of support'. His tendency to adopt an editorial manner even when arguing with his friends could lead to other kinds of complication. In November, possibly Monday, 25 November, Hunt met up with his old friends Thomas Mitchell, Thomas Barnes and Barron Field. What should have been a happy reunion turned sour: Mitchell took offence when one of Barnes's jokes 'placed him in a foolish light before the other sex' (Marianne and Bess were present too). The company broke up in bad humour. Allowing a day for tempers to cool, Hunt wrote soothingly to Mitchell, reminding him: 'we all have our weaknesses & self-loves, & we should all bear with them'.[22] Mitchell, still feeling bruised, found Hunt's superior tone 'a little ex cathedra Examinantis', but was willing to be conciliated and another gathering was arranged.

Most striking about this episode is not the quarrel, but how Hunt's behaviour in private life was now being seen in terms of his '*Examiner*' persona. What appeared to Shelley as Hunt's editorial high-mindedness often came over to others as conceit: that 'we all have our weaknesses & self-loves' was hardly a discovery, yet Hunt assumes that his observation will come as a revelation to Mitchell. It was Hunt's strength and his misfortune that in speaking 'ex cathedra Examinantis' he affronted Lord Byron, who thought Hunt had 'conceited himself into a martyr', and alienated a poet with allegedly little sense of self, John Keats, who came to resent Hunt's seeming unwillingness 'to give other minds credit for the same degree of perception as he himself possesses'. This was not outright arrogance, however. Hunt's '*Examiner*' persona was invented – or conceited – as a response to politics and theatricals in the contemporary press. It was also related to his need to maintain intellectual and emotional equilibrium amid the stresses of his personal life. His apparent 'self-sufficiency' could seem patronising and aloof, but, like his philosophy of cheer, it was a studied manner overlaying anxieties that he struggled, day by day, to keep in check. 'Conceiting himself into a martyr' as editor of the *Examiner* was a survival strategy in sometimes desperate circumstances; equally, Hunt could appear to Keats as 'vain' and 'egotistical' in a sentence that begins by observing that he is 'a pleasant fellow in the main when you are with him'.[23]

*   *   *

Hunt's sense that the Regency was a 'prophetic announcement' of national doom was corroborated elsewhere, in Anna Barbauld's disturbing poem *Eighteen Hundred and Eleven*. Barbauld begins with the 'deeds of blood' engulfing Europe: 'Still the loud death drum, thundering from afar, / O'er the vext nations pours the storm of war'. And then she turns to the fate of Britain:

> And think'st thou, Britain, still to sit at ease,
> An island Queen amid thy subject seas,
> While the vext billows, in their distant roar,
> But soothe thy slumbers, and but kiss thy shore?
> To sport in wars, while dangers keep aloof,
> Thy grassy turf unbruised by hostile hoof?
> So sing thy flatterers; but, Britain, know,
> Thou who hast shared the guilt must share the woe.
> Nor distant is the hour; low murmurs spread,
> And whispered fears, creating what they dread . . .
>
> (39–48)[24]

Barbauld's poem captures the restive mood of the country at this moment, described by Henry Brougham as 'most dangerous & unfortunate'.[25] Her evocation of 'low murmurs' and 'whispered fears' tapped into anxieties lying deeper than present discontents, stirring uneasiness about the nation's future. To understand why *Eighteen Hundred and Eleven* should have been so unsettling to its first readers, beyond its treatment of present crisis, we need to glance back at England's dissenting culture in the eighteenth century.

Anna Lætitia Aikin was born in 1743 into a Unitarian family, and from 1758 her father was tutor in languages and literature at the Dissenting Academy in Warrington, where the Unitarian scientist Joseph Priestley also taught. In the late eighteenth century such academies were the engine rooms driving political, social, scientific and industrial change – much as Isaac Hunt's Philadelphia Academy helped form ideas that impelled the American Revolution. While Oxford and Cambridge Universities clung to the old classical curriculum and the established Church, dissenting academies and the dynamic minds they fostered were receptive to new currents of thought. Priestley was the most radiant example of dissenting intellect, moving restlessly between chemical experiments and political reform, linguistic and grammatical theory, and investigations into light and electricity. All areas of his activities supplied Priestley with evidence of progressive improvement.

Warrington Academy and Joseph Priestley provided Anna Lætitia Aikin with a uniquely stimulating intellectual environment. In 1772 she sent her first collection, *Poems*, to Joseph Johnson. He published it the following year, and in twelve months it had run to four editions. Hunt knew this book well, and recommended 'A Summer Evening's Meditation' for its Miltonic grandeur and daring imaginative voyage across the universe, 'the trackless deeps of space, / Where, burning round, ten thousand suns appear'.[26] Anna married Rochemont Barbauld, a dissenting minister, in 1774 and moved with him to Palgrave in Suffolk where they ran a school for boys. Rowland Hunter was one of their pupils. By 1787 the Barbaulds had settled in Hampstead, welcoming the French Revolution as 'the model of the world' and supporting the campaign for democratic reform and a 'regenerate land'.[27] Joseph Johnson continued to publish her pamphlets: *An Address to the Opposers of the Repeal of the Corporation and Test Acts* (1790), which advocated civil rights for dissenters, *An Epistle to William Wilberforce* (1791), on the abolition of the slave trade, and *Sins of Government* (1793). Her two children's books, *Hymns in Prose* and *Lessons for Children*, both published by Johnson, were popular. To Unitarians like Barbauld, Priestley and Coleridge, God's purposes were being fulfilled through advances in human knowledge, and the glorious dawn, the millennium, was in prospect. Coleridge struck this note of jubilant optimism in his poem of 1796, 'Religious Musings', in which his 'young anticipating heart' welcomed a 'blest future' and 'promis'd years' of unimaginable glory.

But the millennium had not arrived on cue and, as years passed and the century turned, it became more and more difficult to proclaim the imminence of paradise regained. By 1811, Anna Barbauld's mood had darkened, as her poem *Eighteen Hundred and Eleven* reveals. War, the collapse of commerce, bankruptcies, the gluttonous 'Luxury' of a few and 'ghastly Want' of the many, all signalled the country's imminent downfall. The theme of Barbauld's poem is the passing of Empire: as earlier empires had risen, flourished and eventually faded, so now in Britain, 'enfeebled despots sway' and 'evil days portend'. The changeful 'Genius' of national prosperity had abandoned the once 'favoured shore' to decline and disaster.

Barbauld's willingness to contemplate 'London's faded glories' alongside its newly powerful successor, America, brought bitter criticism from the Tory press, which she might have expected, but also from fellow-liberals and reformists at the *Eclectic Review* who found the poem 'in a most extraordinary degree unkindly and unpatriotic'.[28] This hostility is one measure of the nervous national mood in February 1812, when Rowland Hunter published the poem over the imprint 'J. Johnson and Co'. Hunt's gathering sense of foreboding during this winter resembles Barbauld's. Looking back over 1811, he saw the country suspended in 'a kind of lazy hopelessness'. The French war, now in its seventeenth year, was deadlocked. Bread was scarce. Sanctions against America depressed trade, and each week the *Examiner* carried long lists of bankruptcies. In Nottingham workmen smashed the new mechanical looms that threatened to put them out of work. The appearance of a comet in the sky over London contributed to Hunt's sense that 1811 had been 'a strange, unsettled, and perplexing year'.[29] As he took stock of the nation in his end of year survey, he would have recalled a distasteful exchange in the *Examiner* that had seemed to encapsulate that mood.

The arrival of the brig *Traveller* at Liverpool, owned, commanded and crewed by blacks from Sierra Leone, had caused a considerable stir and prompted Hunt's powerful leader on 'Negro Civilization'. This wasn't just another rehearsal of abolitionist arguments for equality of rights for black people. Hunt's target was the insidious development of racial science among contemporaries, notably the Dutch anatomist Pieter Camper whose theory of 'facial angle' displayed the physical gradation from a man to a monkey. The facial features and physiognomy of black people were presented by Camper as akin to the 'animal character', while Europeans conformed to the ideal profile of classical Greek statues. Hunt dismisses the pseudo-aesthetic bases of Camper's theory, pointing out that physiological features such as his own sallow skin are the result of environment, climate and 'artificial' cultural practices – 'regularity and colour [are] not a necessary announcement of mind'.[30]

A tumultuous correspondence ensued. Four letters to the *Examiner* came from Benjamin Haydon, who expressed 'astonishment' that Hunt would not admit the 'continued brutality' and 'total incapacity' of blacks. He signed himself, as usual, 'AN ENGLISH STUDENT'. Hunt replied on 8 September with a measured editorial statement, discounting Haydon's fulminations about the physical 'deformities' of blacks, and pointing out that such arguments had been 'repeated and answered a hundred times [and were] no longer any thing to do with the subject'.[31] Haydon wrote again to point out that Pieter Camper's and Johann Blumenbach's theories were borne out by his own anatomical studies as an artist.[32] He was skilfully answered by Hunt, whose outlook was of course reinforced by personal and ancestral factors. Hunt recommends Haydon to read 'the most well-known publications that treat of this subject', among them Thomas Clarkson's *History of the Abolition of the Slave-Trade* and Bryan Edwards's *History of the West Indies*. These books gave accounts of acute, intrepid, and high-minded black people such as the hero of St Domingo's rebellion, Toussaint L'Ouverture, 'an illustrious character, who deserves the admiration of everybody for his genius and the veneration for his great virtues'.[33] In a private letter to Haydon, Hunt said he regarded him as a 'strange machine'. The remark sounds innocuous, but it cannily turned Haydon's argument against him by pointing out that in physiological terms Haydon's own bodily 'machine' – receding hair, beaky bespectacled nose, and immense mouth – looked sufficiently bizarre.[34]

The eruption of this quarrel in the *Examiner* is a reminder of the fragility

of Hunt and Haydon's friendship, and of how readily hatreds and prejudices could revive even though abolitionist arguments had carried the day.
As significant, perhaps, is the immediacy with which the argument about
'Negro Civilization' carried over into a debate which has become a *cause
célèbre* of English Romanticism – the controversy surrounding Lord Elgin's
acquisition of the Parthenon sculptures. Was Elgin a saviour or destroyer
of ancient Greek art? Were the sculptures genuinely ancient? The argument
was covered by the *Examiner* on several occasions and 'English Student'
Haydon – to whom the sculptures were a blazing revelation of 'divine truth'
– contributed prominently.

Back in 1809 'English Student' sent to the *Examiner* 'a simple narrative
of facts' about Lord Elgin's rescue of 'what remained of ancient Athens'.
'Posterity will do LORD ELGIN ample justice,' Haydon affirmed. Robert
Hunt likewise hailed the arrival of the sculptures as 'an era in the history of
the Arts in England': their 'perfect proportion' combined with 'inimitable
grace, beauty, and dignity' made them the supreme example of how the arts
'enrich, inform, and exalt a nation'.[35] Influential figures like Richard Payne
Knight of the Society of Dilettanti doubted that the marbles were Greek,
and, with the government proving reluctant to purchase them for the nation,
in July 1811 they were stored in a shed at Burlington House. Although inac-
cessible to the public, the 'Elgin Marbles' were by now the focus of political
controversy: while penny-pinching ministers 'felt no generous glow of regard
for the liberal Arts and Sciences', to admire the sculptures or write poems
about them, as John Keats would soon do, was to display 'exalted' taste and
public-spirited opinions.[36]

Haydon's ideas about the Marbles came from long hours spent sketching
and studying them. He was also influenced by the aesthetic theories of Johann
Winckelmann for whom the sculptures were the 'purest springs of art', 'standards of real beauty, grace and elegance, in the human form' to which all
civilisations aspired.[37] Anatomical details were of obvious significance for an
artist, and so was colour. Winckelmann had thought, wrongly, that the sculptures were originally white: 'As white is the colour which reflects the greatest
number of rays of light, and consequently is the most sensitive, a beautiful
body will, accordingly, be the more beautiful the whiter it is.'[38] Combining
Winckelmann's aesthetics with the racial science of Camper and Blumenbach,
Haydon concluded that the sculptures demonstrated the racial superiority of
Europeans:

In referring to the divine works of the Greeks . . . their standard of high
form for an intellectual being was totally the reverse of all these brutal characteristics: – their feet were arched (and it can be mathematically proved
that an arched foot is best adapted for supporting erectly), the *inner* ankle
higher than the outer, the pelvis wide, the calf low, full and vigorous; all

the muscles that enable an intellectual being to keep himself erectly, distinctly and visibly marked; all the muscles of the shoulder-blade, shoulder and back, finely divided, according to their principal offices of action; the ball of the thumb, which enables an intellectual being to grasp by squeezing it against his fingers, enormous, his hand arched, and his thumb long; his capacity for intellect immense, in comparison with his capacity for sense; and large lobes to his ears. – These are the characteristics in form of an intellectual European. In examining negroes, I soon perceived them to sink from these characteristics of intellect in form, and approach those of the brute.[39]

Like the science of Camper and Blumenbach, Haydon's characteristics of 'intellectual' and 'brute' humanity were entirely a matter of aesthetic preference: his idea of the body of 'an intellectual European' reflected a Platonic ideal of human form and 'facial angle' that he saw in the Greek statues. Haydon lived long enough to 'thank God' he had changed his mind about 'brain and bodily deficiencies'.[40] But his racial aesthetics did have an influence on his young poet friend, John Keats.

The year 1816 saw the Marbles purchased for the nation, and transferred for exhibition at the British Museum. Haydon had recently proclaimed their 'union of Nature with ideal beauty' in an essay published in the *Examiner*.[41] Keats read this, and wrote two sonnets praising Haydon as a 'stout unbending champion' of beauty, one of the 'great spirits' like his political hero 'Libertas'. Early in March 1817, having accompanied Haydon to view the Marbles, he wrote two more sonnets. Hunt published both in the *Examiner*, placing them prominently between his own editorial column and Robert Hunt's 'Fine Arts' review. Overawed by the sculptures and Haydon's 'definitive' commentary on them, Keats expresses a troubled response. Here is the first:

To Haydon.
With a Sonnet Written on Seeing the Elgin Marbles

HAYDON! forgive me that I cannot speak
   Definitively on these mighty things;
   Forgive me that I have not an Eagle's wings –
That what I want I know not where to seek:
And think that I would not be overmeek
   In rolling out upfollow'd thunderings,
   Even to the steep of Heliconian springs,
Were I of ample strength for such a freak –
Think too, that all those numbers should be thine;
   Whose else? In this who touch thy vesture's hem?
For when men star'd at what was most divine

> With browless idiotism – o'erwise phlegm –
> Thou hadst beheld the Hesperean shine
> Of their star in the East, and gone to worship them.[42]

Confronted with 'what was most divine', Keats's reactions are perplexity, inadequacy, even distress. This is a painful poem, not least so in that reference to 'browless idiotism': Keats means to damn Haydon's opponents, who are intellectually incapable of appreciating great art. To do so he alludes to the racial science underpinning Haydon's appreciation of the sculptures: by implication, Haydon's 'browless' assailants had limited intellectual capacity and were on a level with 'brute' humanity.

From Hunt and Haydon's *Examiner* exchange about 'Negro Civilization' to Keats's sublime vision 'That mingles Grecian grandeur with the rude / Wasting of old time',[43] the reception of the Elgin Marbles was entangled with arguments about politics and racial superiority. Keats's sense of an 'indescribable feud' and 'dizzy pain' conveyed his own feelings of unsettlement and disorientation. And perhaps we also catch in these poems a distant, lyrical echo of the strange year, Eighteen Hundred and Eleven, when questions about Britain's destiny, the Regent, and bodily beauty formed powerful, turbulent currents in the *Examiner*.

At the end of October, Hunt, Marianne and little Thornton visited Hastings for a holiday and were 'very happy', so much so that Hunt searched through his books to find 'some melancholy theme of verse' to 'steady felicity'. He lighted upon the episode of Paolo and Francesca in Canto V of *The Inferno*, a tragic story of love's resilience that was already fortuitously associated with his own courtship and marriage. Hunt resolved to begin the poem that would become *The Story of Rimini*, and what he wrote suggests that politics were another necessary ballast for domestic bliss.[44] He drafted some opening lines set in 'days when Italy with prowess rung', and was drawn by the possibilities of contrasting 'fair Ravenna' with the 'dotage of a realm's despair' as England awaited the succession of a 'pamper'd prodigal, unasham'd in waste'. This first draft did not proceed very far, however. Hunt's repeated attempts to capture satirically the England of 1811 –

> Sure signs of an expiring royalty
> The driv'lling mirth of dying royalty
> The sapless shoots of fading royalty
> The dancing death of smitten royalty
> The fond neglect of sinking royalty[45]

– were all struck through in turn. In contrast, this melodious couplet recalling the romance of the London sky –

So comes the moon, silv'ring the sullen black
Of a slow-moving cloud, & clears the rack!

– indicates the direction in which his new poem would grow.

FOURTEEN

LEVIATHAN

Marianne's fainting and exhaustion indicated that she was pregnant again. At Beckenham the country air had done her good, Hunt thought, but with this pregnancy in the city she was taken ill after walking scarcely a hundred yards.[1] While Marianne was confined in the house at Portland Street, Hunt was out and about meeting friends. Wherever he went he detected an oppressive atmosphere which he thought 'impossible to clear up altogether':

> We seem to be moving about in a sort of twilight, ignorant whether it is the twilight of morn or evening, – whether we shall have day or night after it, – fair weather or storm, – a clearance or a visitation; but nobody, I believe, is unprepared for the worst; and when the heart is sick, and the hope tired out, this is at least something for resolute honesty to grasp.[2]

The national mood was edgy, uneasy – and at least one social gathering Hunt attended turned stormy: at ten o'clock on the evening of Friday, 17 January 1812 Henry Crabb Robinson called on Barron Field at Hare Court in the Temple, where he found Hunt arguing with Charles Lamb about Coleridge. Robinson, who had been foreign correspondent for *The Times* in Spain and was training as a lawyer, was one of the great English diarists. He knew all the literary figures of the day, and for over half a century from 1811 to 1867 kept a vivid record of their meetings, dinners, conversations and quarrels. Robinson knew and admired Coleridge's poems; he was attending Coleridge's lectures on Shakespeare and Milton, and the day before had heard Coleridge address Milton's politics, poems and blank verse. He had arrived at Hare Court direct from an 'exceedingly agreeable' dinner with the speaker. So Robinson was primed for the fray, and attempted to stoke argument by praising Hazlitt's first lecture on English Philosophy delivered earlier in that week at the Russell Institution. Lamb, by now 'getting very drunk', would not agree and abused anyone, Hunt included, who seemed reluctant to acknowledge Coleridge's 'transcendent merits'. Hunt was patient, and took all 'in good part'. When Robinson left at midnight the party looked set to continue into the small hours.[3]

They all met up again on 16 March, this time at Lamb's house in Inner Temple Lane. Poetry is likely to have dominated the conversation, for the preceding week had seen the publication of Lord Byron's *Childe Harold's Pilgrimage*. John Murray had a sharp eye for the literary marketplace, and he had spotted the poem's potential to rival Goethe's pan-European sensation *The Sorrows of Young Werther*. *Childe Harold* seduced its readers by embodying the heartsick mood of contemporary England in the figure of a jaded Regency roué whom most readers identified with Byron himself. By combining Romantic intrigue, exotic travelogue and contemporary satire, Byron swiftly dislodged Walter Scott as the most famous poet of the day.

Crabb Robinson noted that on this occasion Lamb was 'very good-humoured, but at the same time solid' – in other words, still on his feet. His poem 'The Triumph of the Whale' had appeared the day before in the *Examiner* and Robinson thought it 'capital' and also, given the times, 'daring':

> Not a mightier Whale than this
> In the vast Atlantic is;
> Not a fatter fish than he
> Flounders round the polar sea.
> See his blubber – at his gills
> What a world of drink he swills,
> From his trunk as from a spout
> Which next moment he pours out . . .
> Crooked Dolphins they surround him;
> Dog-like Seals they fawn around him, . . .
> Hapless mariners are they,
> Who beguil'd (as seamen say)
> Deeming him some rock or island,
> Footing sure, safe spot, and dry land,
> Anchor in his scaly rind;
> Soon the difference they find;
> Sudden plumb he sinks beneath them:
> Does to ruthless waves bequeath them.
> Name or title, what has he?
> Is he Regent of the Sea? . . .
> By his bulk and by his size,
> By his oily qualities,
> This (or else my eyesight fails),
> This should be the Prince of Whales.[4]

The slimy companions of the 'finny people's King' conjured up memories of the Carlton House gala, at which the Prince of Wales presided over the artificial canal filled with gold and silver fishes. Blubber, swilling and spouting, and the fawning seals all contributed to the fun of Lamb's satire and, as Robinson noted, it had a 'daring' edge too. The 'hapless mariners' tricked into dropping anchor on the 'scaly rind' of the Prince of Whales would remind most readers of Milton's *Paradise Lost*, where Satan 'stretched out huge' on the fiery lake of hell is likened to

> that sea-beast
> Leviathan, which God of all his works
> Created hugest that swim the ocean stream:
> Him haply slumbering on the Norway foam
> The pilot of some small night-foundered skiff,
> Deeming some island, oft, as seamen tell,
> With fixed anchor in his scaly rind
> Moors by his side . . .
>
> I. 200–207[5]

For *Examiner* readers those mariners consigned to 'ruthless waves' were the Whigs, abandoned by the Regent. But to liken the Regent to Milton's 'arch-fiend' Satan, who maliciously 'sought / Evil to others', risked an information for libel from the Attorney-General. The conversation at Lamb's evidently turned on that possibility, with Hunt informing the company that 'Everything is a libel, as the law is now declared, and our security lies only in their shame'. Hunt, Robinson noted, seemed 'prepared for the worst'.[6]

The Regent's political apostasy was a scandal, but, as the Carlton House fête revealed, in the eyes of many he was still the ravishing prince who had gambled and dined and charmed the Foxite Whigs. Twenty years of high living had nevertheless taken a toll. Even the most flattering portraits of the Regent wearing

> a Field-marshal's uniform, with his hair in a long queue, the cordon blue, and a superb brilliant star, a large diamond loop and button in his hat and feather, wearing a sabre, the handle and scabbard of which were most richly studded with jewellery[7]

could not conceal a considerable accumulation of blubber. The Regent was rich meat for satirical cartoonists, and also for Shelley in his ballad 'The Devil's Walk':

> For he is fat, – his waistcoat gay,
> When strained upon a levee day,
>   Scarce meets across his princely paunch;
> And pantaloons are like half-moons
>   Upon each brawny haunch.

With his popping buttons and bursting seams, the Regent was close to physical and mental collapse – in Shelley's words, 'tired', 'maudlin', 'addled'.
Nothing showed this more clearly than his behaviour when the restrictions
on the Regency were lifted on 18 February.

The Regent chose this moment to declare complete satisfaction with the
'present system', and his wish that the Whigs would join the Tories in a new
coalition. To the Whig Lords Grey and Grenville a 'united Administration'
was an 'impossibility'. The *Examiner* commented:

> Surely it is impossible that the Prince of WALES, the friend of Ireland,
> can set at nought the important question of Catholic Emancipation, upon
> which he has so often professed his anxiety: – surely it is too gross to
> suppose, that the Prince of WALES, the friend of FOX, can have been
> affecting habits of thinking, and indulging habits of intimacy, which he is
> to give up at a moment's notice for nobody knows what: – surely it cannot
> be, that the PRINCE REGENT, the Whig PRINCE, the friend of Ireland
> – the friend of FOX, – the liberal, tolerant, experienced, large-minded
> HEIR APPARENT, can retain in power the very Men, against whose opin-
> ions he has repeatedly declared himself, and whose retention in power hith-
> erto he has explicitly stated to be owning solely to a feeling of delicacy with
> respect to his Father![8]

The rhythms, repetitions and upper-case lettering all emphasised Hunt's accu-
mulating outrage at the Regent's volte-face. What rankled most was his deser-
tion of Ireland:

> So much for the Catholic Question, and all that the PRINCE has to do
> with it. What the *Irish* will think of this death to their hopes, it would be
> difficult, perhaps dangerous, to describe.[9]

Bold as a lion when defending a friend or a principle, Hunt went ahead and
did so.

The occasion was an annual dinner to celebrate St Patrick's Day. On Tuesday,
17 March the Benevolent Society of St Patrick gathered, as they had done
for over thirty years, at the Freemasons' Tavern. Lord Lansdowne was in the
chair, supported by the Earl of Moira, Richard Brinsley Sheridan, the Lord
Mayor and other worthies. Hunt was intrigued by the occasion for what it
revealed about attitudes to the Regent among 'the fondest and most trusting
of his subjects', and he reported it in a four-page 'Political Examiner' entitled 'The Prince on St Patrick's Day'.[10]

The Health of the King was toasted with enthusiastic applause and a
rousing 'God Save the King'. The Health of the Regent, however, drew

'partial' applause mingled with '*loud and reiterated hisses*'. Lord Moira, one
of the Prince's old companions, rose to speak, but '*not a word was uttered of
the Regent*': 'even he has nothing to say in favour of his old acquaintance',
Hunt remarked, 'not a word – not a syllable!' Eventually Sheridan rose, a
little unsteadily, to address the company:

> in a low tone of voice [he] returned his thanks for the honourable notice
> by which so large a meeting of his countrymen thought proper to distin-
> guish him. (*Applauses*.) He had ever been proud of Ireland, and hoped that
> his country might never have cause to be ashamed of him (*Applauses*.)
> Ireland never forgot those who did all they could do, however little that
> might be, in behalf of her best interests. All allusion to politics had been
> industriously deprecated by their Noble Chairman. – He was aware that
> charity was the immediate object of their meeting; but standing as he did
> before an assembly of his countrymen, he could not affect to disguise his
> conviction that at the present crisis Ireland involved in itself every consid-
> eration dear to the best interests of the empire. (*Hear, hear!*) It was, there-
> fore, that he was most anxious that nothing should transpire in that meeting
> calculated to injure those great objects, or to visit with undeserved censure
> the conduct of persons whose love to Ireland was as cordial and zealous as
> it had ever been. He confessed frankly that knowing as he did the unal-
> tered and unalterable sentiments of an ILLUSTRIOUS PERSONAGE
> towards Ireland, he could not conceal from the meeting that he had felt
> considerably shocked at the *sulky coldness and surly discontent* with which
> they had on that evening drank the health of the PRINCE REGENT. (Here
> we are sorry to observe that Mr. S. was interrupted by *no very equivocal*
> symptoms of disapprobation) – When silence was somewhat restored, Mr.
> SHERIDAN said, that he *knew the Prince Regent well – (hisses)* – he knew
> his *principles – (hisses,)* – they would at least, he hoped, give him credit for
> believing that he knew them, when he said he did. – (*Applause*.) – He
> repeated, that he knew well the principles of the PRINCE REGENT, and
> that so well satisfied was he that they were all that Ireland could wish, that
> he (Mr. Sheridan) hoped, that as he had lived up to them, so he might die
> in the principles of the PRINCE REGENT – *(hisses and applauses.)* – He
> should be sorry personally to have merited their disapprobation (*general
> applause*, with cries of 'Change the subject and speak out'.) – He could only
> assure them, that the PRINCE REGENT remained unchangeably true to
> those principles. *(Here the clamours became so loud and general that we could
> collect nothing more)*.[11]

Hunt notes that it might have been courteous, 'had it been possible', to distin-
guish between the Prince of Wales as a subscriber to the Benevolent Society
and the Prince Regent as 'a clencher of Irish chains'. But urgent political

considerations made that impossible. At the Freemasons' Tavern public opinion had been heard 'loud and unequivocal in rebuke of the Prince Regent'. How, then, to account for the *Morning Post*'s report of the dinner?

Admittedly, the *Post* was the 'saddest of Ministerial papers', Hunt observed, but its allusions to 'the ungenerous, unmanly conduct displayed at a late public meeting', and to 'a set of worthless beings, whose imbecile efforts are best treated with sovereign contempt' had plumbed new depths of nonsense. Worthless beings? That a paper 'notorious above all others, in the annals of perfidy, scandal, imbecility, and indecency' should slander a society of 'the most respectable Irishmen in London' left Hunt, for once, lost for words:

> – Help us, benevolent Compositors, to some mark or other, – some significant and comprehensive index, – that shall denote a laugh of an hour's duration! –

Hunt's private letters are full of all kinds of inventive marks – crosses, lines, ovals, spheres – but on this occasion he could find no printed symbol adequate to express his disdain. Instead, Hunt lets the *Morning Post*'s execrable 'notions of praise and political justice' speak for themselves:

> The same page, which contained the specimen of contempt above-mentioned, contained also a set of wretched common-place lines in French, Italian, Spanish and English, *literally* addressing the PRINCE REGENT in the following terms, among others: – 'You are the *glory of the People* – You are the *Protector of the Arts* – You are the *Mæcenas of the Age* – Wherever you appear, you *conquer all hearts*, wipe away all tears, excite *desire and love*, and win *beauty* towards you – You breathe *eloquence* – You inspire the Graces – You are an *Adonis in loveliness!*' . . . What person, unacquainted with the true state of the case, would imagine, in reading these astounding eulogies, that this *Glory of the People* was the subject of millions of shrugs and reproaches! That this *Protector of the Arts* had named a wretched Foreigner his Historical Painter in disparagement or in ignorance of the merits of his own countrymen! That this *Maecenas of the Age* patronized not a single deserving writer! That this *Breather of Eloquence* could not say a few decent, extempore words, – if we are to judge at least from what he said to his regiment on its embarkation for Portugal! That this *Conqueror of Hearts* was the disappointer of hopes! That this *Exciter of Desire* (bravo, Messieurs of the *Post*!!) this *Adonis in Loveliness*, was a corpulent gentleman of fifty! In short, that this *delightful, blissful, wise, pleasurable, honourable, virtuous, true,* and *immortal* PRINCE, was a violator of his word, a libertine over head and ears in debt and disgrace, a despiser of domestic ties, the companion of gamblers and demireps, a man who has just closed half a century without one single claim on the gratitude of his country or the respect of posterity![12]

Hunt's clarification of the 'true state of the case' brings ministerial flattery into collision with gross actuality: as an object of shrugs, reproaches and contempt, the '*immortal* PRINCE' rivals Charles II. 'These are hard truths,' Hunt remarked, 'but are they *not* truths?' Begging the question underlined the thoroughness with which the *Examiner* had made its case.

As everyone expected, 'the attorney-general's eye was swiftly on the article', and on Monday, 20 April a fourth indictment for libel was issued against the *Examiner*. Hunt's response was to reprint his 'refutation' of the *Morning Post*'s 'fine epithets' about the Regent – the passage which had drawn the charge.[13] He also looked back over the *Examiner*'s earlier encounters with the law:

> The readers of this Paper may recollect, that one of the three informations which have been filed against it for libel, was founded on a passage in which it was observed, that 'of all Monarchs since the Revolution the Successor of GEORGE the Third would have the finest opportunity of becoming nobly popular'; – so obnoxious a thing was it considered a short time since to suppose that the Prince of WALES might even have a chance of making a fine Sovereign. His ROYAL HIGHNESS has since come to the Throne; and the very men who assaulted us for suggesting that he might become nobly popular, have now resolved upon attacking us for shewing that his conduct is neither noble nor popular.

He would 'neither spare pains . . . *to vindicate the Truth and Necessity of what we have said* . . . nor, in the event of losing our liberties, shall we sit down with a pulse altered for one second, or a disposition to leave unenjoyed one comfort within our reach'.[14] The bravado with which Hunt finished this 'Political Examiner' was typical; equally characteristic were those reflections on his steady heart. The trial was set for 27 June.

The death of the radical John Horne Tooke, the Catholic claims and Luddite riots all attracted the *Examiner*'s attention during spring 1812. A revival of *Julius Caesar* at Covent Garden – 'excellently *got up*' and 'excellently performed' – was packing the house.[15] Roman integrity made a refreshing contrast to the murkiness of present-day politics – until 11 May, when John Bellingham assassinated the Prime Minister, Spencer Perceval, in the lobby of the Commons. This was a matter of 'wonder and abhorrence', 'outcries and horror'. Coleridge immediately blamed political fanatics, and warned Southey of Jacobins among the readers of the *Statesman* and *Examiner*. When those readers turned to the *Examiner*, however, they found Hunt preoccupied with the psychology of the murder, speculating on how madness and violence in adult life may be traced back to parental neglect or misdirected fondness. Hunt knew that his own father's 'irregularities' and his mother's ultra-tenderness had affected his susceptibility to nervous attacks and anxiety.

He could readily conjecture a much more damaging childhood for a Bellingham or a Macbeth.[16]

On the international stage another Caesar was bleeding. Addressing the Commons, Samuel Whitbread had warned that Britain's military efforts in Portugal and Spain 'were beyond our strength'. As the year unfolded, however, events on the Iberian Peninsula and elsewhere in Europe turned against Napoleon: Wellington launched a vigorous spring offensive, and his victory at Salamanca on 22 July was decisive in opening the road to Madrid. Although he would fall back to his Portuguese base over the winter of 1812–13, Salamanca would later be seen as the beginning of the end of French power in Spain. Logistical problems hampered the French throughout, and by early 1812 Napoleon had turned his troops east, to Russia. They took Moscow on 14 September, although the Russians refused either to capitulate or be drawn into battle. As winter set in Napoleon's armies were forced into a catastrophic retreat, leaving 400,000 soldiers dead and wounded, and 100,000 prisoners of war. By mid-December Napoleon was back in Paris, the myth of his invincibility shattered. Amid public astonishment at the turn of events, the *Examiner* counselled that now was the moment to secure peace.[17]

During this stressful year Hunt was grateful for any opportunity to quit the city and wander out through the lanes and fields to 'the gentle eminence of Hampstead, with the sloping sunshine of its fields, its grovy fullness at top, and the church-steeple looking out over the trees'. Under those trees was his mother's grave, an association that made Hampstead the comforting retreat described in his article 'The Regent's Park and Barracks':

> here – said I, – one may yet leave the world behind, with all its noise, its politics, and its nonsense; – here is silence and a sense of complacency; here are spots even which the rural voluptuousness of a SPENSER or MILTON might not have disdained, – shady banks, lawns, fallows, and meads, upland and dell, a far-reaching prospect or a field shut in.

The pressures of family life and the *Examiner* office made him skilful at snatching such moments in favourite rural 'spots'. He could seldom afford to be far from his work, but he perfected his own mode of pastoral content in local, suburban surroundings like Primrose Hill and Hampstead 'with the metropolis completely shut out'.[18] The city's proximity and encroachments of houses and the 'barrack-plague' gave special relish to the sensation of 'entire solitude'. Unlike Wordsworth's solitary communings with nature, Hunt's suburban landscapes are always populated; along Hunt's footpaths there is always the possibility of meeting a friend.

Set high on its ridge, Hampstead had long been a rural community of farms, windmills, and smallholders who grazed sheep and cattle on the common land of the Heath. Because of its height, some 440 feet above sea level, the village was famous for the clarity of its air and during the eighteenth century a fashionable spa tapped the pure water that gushed from springs and wells. Numerous literary and political figures were attracted by this healthy retreat from the city. Joseph Addison, Richard Steele and other members of the Kit-Cat Club met here in the summer. John Gay took a cottage where he wrote *The Beggar's Opera*. Alexander Pope, James Thomson, Mark Akenside, Fanny Burney, Joanna Baillie, the Samuels Johnson and Richardson, Oliver Goldsmith and Anna Barbauld all found Hampstead an inspiring location. The place had an atmosphere of political freedom too. Protestant dissenters preached here, outside the five-mile limit that excluded them from London. Henry Vane, zealous Commonwealth man and a close friend of Oliver Cromwell, lived at Rosslyn House where he was reputedly visited by John Milton and Andrew Marvell. In Hunt's lifetime the village was home to Thomas Erskine.[19] Hampstead's literary-libertarian traditions have continued into the twenty-first century, attracting writers, artists, broadcasters, and the great Labour politician and champion of William Hazlitt, Michael Foot.

For Hunt, Hampstead was a place where his political ideals could be refreshed, revived and redirected through poetry. His verbal sketch of Hampstead suggests a painterly approach that achieves some striking effects: 'sloping sunshine' depicts a warm slant of light; 'grovy fullness' suggests a mass of trees. These verbal traits were to become distinctive features of Hunt's voice in his 'Hampstead Sonnets' and in *The Story of Rimini*. In this free-flowing, impressionistic verse we can recognise a stylistic equivalent of his liberal politics, a lyrical rejoinder to the 'rage for barracks', the threat of land enclosure, and 'a field shut in'.

'The Regent's Park and Barracks' marks the beginning of Hunt's invention of Hampstead as his emotional and spiritual home, a psychic resource as powerful as William Wordsworth's Grasmere, Emily Brontë's Haworth Moor, Thomas Hardy's Wessex and Seamus Heaney's Mossbawn. In the difficult months ahead, he would be drawn there with increasing frequency.

With the libel trial set for 27 June, Hunt prepared himself by drafting an article to appear in the *Examiner* on the Sunday morning after sentence had been passed. He already assumed the worst, warned that public resentment of the Regent would continue unabated, and anticipated the pleasures of martyrdom 'elevating us both in our good opinion and in that of the public'.

'We had just written thus far,' Hunt interjects, 'when news was brought us that the Prosecution was put off for the present on account of the non-appearance of a sufficient number of special Jurymen.' Had the special jurors proved unsuitable? Was the prosecution afraid of the *Examiner*'s counsel, Henry

Brougham? Was this a deliberate pretext for dropping the prosecution? Whatever the motives for putting off the trial, it was clear that a long delay over the summer could now be expected.[20]

Having readied himself for the trial and a guilty verdict, Hunt was left in suspense, suddenly vulnerable to the nervous energy that had sustained him over recent months. The likelihood of a fine had made him uncomfortably aware of the family's debts. Editing the *Examiner* brought him over £500 a year – an extremely good salary – and £300 had recently been received from America.[21] But where did it all go? Hunt had no grasp of mathematics and was 'dismayed' by 'the difference between the sums total which tens, fifteens, & twenties make in the mind, & what they produce upon paper'.[22] Marianne's accounts were 'swelling'. By 14 July 1812 their debts had reached £550, and John, who was astute with money, could see a familiar pattern emerging. Hunt had begun borrowing against his future income from friends like Thomas Mitchell and from professional associates like his physician Dr William Knighton.[23] He breezily assured John that he was '*living quite within my income if I enjoyed it to the full*', and was genuinely surprised and disappointed that he was unable to '*enjoy it to the full*' because 'expenses of the former year' had yet to be settled. But there was more to these problems than financial incompetence. Hunt was unfailingly generous to others, and unable to resist spending on books and paintings when he should have been clearing debts: £50 for a portrait of Milton was, he told John, 'the climax of my improvidence . . . madness, I allow, – poetically speaking'.[24]

Hunt could beguile many people – his charm was a sly means of self-resumption – but John could not be taken in. Ever since the episode at Christ's Hospital when Hunt gave away a friend's book, he had been adept at outfacing obligations with an irreproachable sense of right – '*living quite within my income*'. This capacity for airy insouciance would infuriate brothers, friends and creditors for decades to come. Only gradually did it dawn upon him that 'intellectual independence is comparatively nothing, while thoughtless habits keep one in a kind of wilful dependence'.[25] In summer 1812, though, within days of that awkward letter about money, Marianne gave birth to their second child. The baby was named John after his thrifty uncle.

Early in August Hunt mentioned 'an unexpected attack of an old nervous disorder, which I thought had left me'. It was not as bad as the illness after his mother's death, but severe enough to interrupt his *Examiner* articles and prevent him accepting an invitation from Jeremy Bentham, the philosopher of Utilitarianism.[26] Barron Field, Thomas Mitchell and Tom Moore all wrote sympathetically; Brougham warned that in summer 'hot theatres' were a risk to health; Peter Martin, an *Examiner* reader and 'medical man', cautioned him against 'intense application to literary engagements' and invited him to leave 'the great Oven' for the 'cooler freer air' of Sussex.[27] The suggestion appealed, but Somerset rather than Sussex would be Hunt's destination.

Early on Saturday, 22 August Hunt boarded the coach to Bath. He break-fasted in Slough at an inn 'adorned with geraniums', lunched in Newbury, and reached his destination at half-past ten in the evening. That night he stayed at the Lamb Inn, Bath, where he met his old friend John Marriott who had travelled from Taunton to meet him. On Sunday they looked around the town, dined at three, and then took 'an easy stage' to the village of Old Down where they stayed at 'a large and excellent inn, that has a pretty garden with grotto seats'. In the morning they rose early for the coach to Wells, where they visited the cathedral, and then continued to Glastonbury, 'said to be the burial place of King Arthur'. From Glastonbury they proceeded across the Somerset levels – Hunt thought of King Alfred's exile on the Isle of Athelney – and arrived at Taunton in mid-afternoon. Hunt had tea and strolled around the town enjoying the balmy air, the trees, cottages, brooks, and views of the Blackdown and Quantock Hills. That evening he heard an owl for the first time.[28]

Why did Hunt make this excursion? There were family links with the West Country – Edward Hunt had been dissenting Rector of Dunchideock; more distant forebears came from South Molton – but Hunt was not on the trail of ancestors. A break from London would help speed his recovery, and there was also the prospect of a loan to mend his finances.

Marriott had withdrawn from the law and moved to Taunton where, in 1808, he founded the *Taunton Courier*. He modelled his paper on the *Examiner*, 'above the considerations of party', 'out of sight of petty and grovelling factions – neither royal, nor ministerial, nor oppositional'.[29] Messengers between London and Taunton hastened the transmission of news, and Marriott's network of distributors in the West Country ensured that the paper reached its readers swiftly. On the first page of the first issue the *Taunton Courier* had announced the publication of Hunt's song 'Silent Kisses', along with John Thelwall's forthcoming lecture on 'Bonaparte and the Spanish Patriots' to be delivered at the Angel Inn, Tiverton.

Thelwall was stirring again, and this hero of 1790s radicalism was no stranger to the West Country. Back in 1797 he had visited Nether Stowey, over the Quantock Hills from Taunton, to meet two young English Jacobins, Samuel Taylor Coleridge and William Wordsworth. At that time 'Citizen' Thelwall was the courageous leader of the 'friends of liberty' in the London Corresponding Society, a charismatic orator and aspiring poet. He was at the top of the government's list of mischief-makers when, in May 1794, he was arrested, imprisoned for six months in the Tower and Newgate, and tried for High Treason. Thelwall was acquitted, but this narrow escape from a capital charge made him more circumspect. William Pitt's repressive 'Gagging Acts' of 1795 were contrived to silence him, and by mid-1797, when he arrived at Nether Stowey, Thelwall like Coleridge and Wordsworth was exploring poetry as an alternative channel for revolutionary energies. For Coleridge and Wordsworth, the poems of *Lyrical Ballads* lay a few months in the future; Thelwall's route would take him from Stowey to temporary exile in Wales, and from there to a new career lecturing on elocution, poetry and, eventually, back to politics.

The Quantock Hills and English Romantic poetry are inseparable: here Wordsworth wrote lyrical ballads like 'Simon Lee', 'The Last of the Flock' and 'The Thorn', and Coleridge composed 'Frost at Midnight' and *The Ancient Mariner*. Coleridge had links with Taunton as well. He preached at the Unitarian Chapel in Mary Street, a few minutes' walk from Marriott's home in East Street – the *Taunton Courier* office where Hunt was lodging. Hunt's stay in Taunton in August 1812 signalled a revival there of the radical inspiration of the 1790s: like Thelwall, Hunt had been prosecuted for his political opinions and was now exploring lyrical combinations of politics and poetics that recalled and updated Coleridge and Wordsworth's revolutionary *Lyrical Ballads*.

At Taunton Hunt continued to write his 'politics' for the *Examiner*, and he was also pushing ahead with his new poem *The Story of Rimini*.[30] The opening description of Ravenna seems more like the Vale of Taunton than Italy's Adriatic coast:

> a warm eve, and gentle rains at night,
> Have left a sparkling welcome for the light,
> And there's a crystal clearness all about;
> The leaves are sharp, the distant hills look out;
> A balmy briskness comes upon the breeze;
> The smoke goes dancing from the cottage trees;
> And when you listen, you hear many a coil
> Of bubbling springs about the grassy soil . . .[31]

This evokes the freshness of a summer morning in Somerset – cottages, trees, streams, the distant Blackdown and Quantock Hills. It also signals a vital new poetic voice. 'Ravenna' has the immediacy of things seen at the moment of writing. Spontaneous and familiar, the poem welcomes the reader with a succession of sights, sensations, and an invitation to 'listen' and 'hear'. Hunt's 'hypochondriac' anxiety for company and community may have been a personal factor in the emergence of this voice, but he was also alert to opportunities for addressing wider concerns. Unusual perspectives like 'the distant hills look out', 'a coil / Of bubbling springs' deliberately unsettle readers' expectations about poetic diction, reflecting the poem's broader challenge to social, sexual and religious prejudices. Poetic play and enjoyment could be a way of articulating and sharing social and political ideas – 'a sparkling welcome for the light' – particularly after 1814, when the end of the French wars caused the *Examiner*'s readership to dwindle.

Shortly after his arrival in Taunton, Hunt fell ill and suffered a 'violent palpitation'. He blamed too much exercise and the strain of writing a long political article for the next Sunday's *Examiner*, but he was also anxious about his debts. To comfort himself he bought a pair of lamb's-wool inner soles, and sat in Marriott's parlour singing Allan Ramsay's 'Farewell to Lochaber',

> Farewell to Lochaber, farewell to my Jean,
> Where heartsome wi' her I ha'e mony day been,
> For Lochaber no more, Lochaber no more,
> We'll maybe return to Lochaber no more.

'I could scarcely get through it for the emotions that rose in my throat,' he told Marianne. He was missing her, and worried about money and feelings of nervousness.

On Friday, 28 August Hunt and Marriott set off in a gig over the Blackdown Hills to Upottery, where they met a banker from whom Hunt expected to receive £300. Unfortunately this money matter wasn't resolved, and Hunt was soon feeling feverish. By Wednesday, 2 September he was overcome with 'a dreadful depression of spirits', and hastened back to London. During his absence the *Examiner* office had moved from Beaufort Buildings to 21, Maiden Lane, Covent Garden, an address with pleasing associations: Andrew Marvell lived at Maiden Lane in 1677; Voltaire lodged there on a visit in 1727; and Turner had been born there in 1775. For the moment nothing would lighten Hunt's mood, and he was *'obliged to excuse himself to his Readers for once more leaving the Examiner without the usual articles'*.[32]

Throughout the year Hunt had kept in touch with Henry Brougham. Politics, the dangerous state of the country and 'Luddite mania' concerned them both, although their exchanges of letters in the autumn turned as often to poetry. Hunt forwarded his classical translations and draft sections of *The Story of Rimini*. Brougham responded with praise and advice, enclosing notes, 'out-of-the-way books on Italy', and 'packets about Ravenna' (probably the journal Brougham had kept during a tour of Italy back in 1804).[33] Their liaison was so close as to make the composition of *Rimini* a collaboration between Hunt and his lawyer, two leaders of the liberal cause within and outside the establishment.

Following Hunt's return from Taunton, the *Examiner* became noticeably more literary, a move that suggests a change in Hunt himself. His translations 'Acme and Septimius', 'Catullus's Return to Sirmio', Horace's 'Ode to Pyrrha' and 'Catullus to Cornificius' appeared in successive weeks through September, alongside reports of the Battle of Salamanca and Napoleon's faltering Russian campaign. Hunt's poems this autumn all show a concern for 'domestic enjoyment' and 'comfort'; a 'natural longing for society and conversation'; and language that is 'elegant' and 'passionately abrupt'. The libel trial was pending. Hunt was recovering from 'a severe threat of illness', and poetry, like his flute playing in the Christ's Hospital sick-room, helped lighten his mood.[34] It would be tempting to see this as simple escapism at a time of personal and public crisis, but there was more at stake in his recourse to poetry. In the October general election Brougham contested Liverpool for the Whigs, losing narrowly to George Canning, a liberal Tory and former contributor to the satirical *Anti-Jacobin*. Now was the time for Hunt to announce in the *Examiner* that poetry 'may really do something' even amid 'disaster'. But 'do' what? Poetry of domesticity, society and conversation expressed values essential to the political campaigns of the *Examiner* and Henry Brougham. More than this, the juxtapositions possible in the *Examiner* between reports of dreadful battles and lyrical celebrations of life, between courtly corruption and 'natural touches of feeling', presented a 'powerful contrast' between two kinds of society.[35]

Hunt's Taunton excursion had done him little good – from now on he would refer to illness as 'a Taunton day' – but by the end of the year his campaigns as a journalist and a poet were succeeding on two fronts. It was time for a fresh start.

Part IV: Prison Years, 1812–1815

Is this the Muses' haunt? Is this the bower
  Where Poetry delights to dwell and weave
  Her fairy fictions?

  Henry Robertson, 'Sonnet on the Poet's
Residence in the Surrey Jail, 5 October 1813'

FIFTEEN

IN THE HEART OF THE PLACE

Hunt's decision to move four miles out of London to 'the gentle eminence of Hampstead' was in line with the new direction in his political-poetic thinking. In a letter to Thomas Moore, on 13 September 1812, he mentions intensive work on *The Story of Rimini*, and adds that he is now 'on the look-out . . . in the neighbourhood of Hampstead, – a spot of which I am particularly fond'.[1] Within two weeks he had found 'a cottage at West-end, Hampstead', and moved there on 1 October.

West End was on the winding lane between Kilburn Abbey and Hampstead, a tranquil hamlet of forty houses clustered under a canopy of elms. One of the farms was home to the Brawne family and here Fanny Brawne, John Keats's love, was born on 9 August 1800. Hunt's cottage was close by the Brawnes' house, 'in the heart of the place insulated by a little garden'. Inside were 'humble ceilings and unsophisticated staircases; but there is green about it, and a little garden with laurel'.[2] Having moved 'into the country, though scarcely out of town', Hunt could now walk or take a coach to the *Examiner* office and return home to his laurel garden, his 'little library of poets', and a glass of wine to toast Milton's portrait. His health and appetite rallied, so much so that after 'years' of constipation he became 'regular' and his jaundice began to clear. Marianne was busy sculpting, and Haydon was asked to supply a bust of Apollo for her to copy.[3]

After Beckenham and Portland Street this was an idyll – but even in rural Hampstead Hunt could not escape entirely. A mile away, up on One Tree Hill, the navy had erected a telegraph station as part of a chain linking London with Great Yarmouth. The mysterious movements of the semaphore disks were the nerve system linking the Admiralty with the battlefront – or perhaps warning that a French invasion was imminent.

The King v. *John and Leigh Hunt* would be tried on Wednesday, 9 December at the Court of King's Bench, Westminster Hall, before Lord Ellenborough – by now a name to strike dread. Earlier that year Ellenborough had sentenced the elderly Daniel Isaac Eaton to eighteen months in Newgate Prison and one hour standing in the pillory for publishing Tom Paine's deist pamphlet

The Age of Reason. Shelley saw immediately that this 'outrage . . . to humanity and justice' was yet another attack on intellectual and religious liberty: Ellenborough had 'condemned an innocent man' for publishing ideas.[4] London's citizens cheered Eaton in the pillory, but within months of leaving prison he was dead.

What hope did the Hunts have of a fair hearing? Two weeks before the trial Brougham reported at least two attempts to 'buy off' his clients. Prison would be 'prevented' and a fine waived, on the understanding that they made no further comment about the Regent. 'I need not add,' Hunt recollected, 'that we declined.'[5] Hunt was rallying for the confrontation and his 'Political Examiner' on 6 December – the Sunday before the trial – was a clever manoeuvre designed to unsettle the court before proceedings began. In measured tones of remonstrance, Hunt argued that Ellenborough's situation as a 'Royal Councillor' to the Regent compromised his judicial independence and rendered him unfit to hear the case. His careful manner, 'neither angry, nor uneasy', intimated a touch of ennui at having to go through all this again – and in front of a judge best known for furious outbursts of temper.

In London the trial excited a terrific bustle of interest. Crowds gathered outside Westminster Hall at first light, so many that the public was barred from the courtroom. The defendants arrived smartly dressed and determined to display their 'best countenance'.[6] Hunt was clutching a copy of Milton's masque, *Comus*, as a talisman of invincible virtue. At nine o'clock the courtroom doors closed, conversation subsided, and Lord Ellenborough entered – a jowly block of a man, not unlike James Boyer. The court was brought to order and proceedings began. The charge was that John and Leigh Hunt had published 'with intention to traduce and vilify his Royal Highness the Prince of Wales, Regent of the United Kingdom, and to bring his Royal Highness into hatred, contempt, and disgrace'.[7] The defendants then lodged their statements, affirmed that they were actuated by 'no personal malice', and drew the court's attention to their heavy expenses in previous prosecutions.[8] They pleaded 'not guilty'. Apart from that statement, the Hunts placed their defence entirely in the hands of Henry Brougham.

Brougham's strategy was to present Hunt as unworldly and idealistic, 'a person living in retirement':

He is a young man who lives not in the neighbourhood or within the view of a Court – who has no political connexions – who scarcely knows any public man personally, except, if I may so speak, the man who is his Counsel – who does not know the face of any one man connected with the public affairs of this country. – He is a rigidly studious man; – a man not advanced in life – being, I believe, considerably under thirty, – but always surrounded by books rather than by men. – His delight is to pursue his studies, which he does, incessantly, from Sunday to Sunday, in his retirement – while he also prepares his weekly journal, the topics in which are various, as those of a public journal ought to be, including the History of the Events of the Times in which we live, and among them, Observations on general Politics. – He is devoted to no Political Party; – he knows of none; – of which we have a striking instance, by way of illustration, in the Motto he has adopted for his Paper, which is a quotation from Dean Swift – 'Party is the madness of the many for the gain of a few', and this you must have found, if you know anything of this journal which he conducts. – Among the political topics which occupy his attention, – there are some general ones, in which we are all interested, and in which he has been extremely vigilant. – I mean the system of Military Punishment in this Country – the Criminal Justice of it, and its Administration – the Liberty of the Press, and Fair Discussion – the Purity of the Principles of our free Constitution – the abolition of the Slave Trade – the Amelioration of the present Condition of the Poor – the general Happiness of the Community, promoted, as it would be, by due attention to the lower Classes of it – the general Policy adopted by this Country with respect to our Army Abroad – topics equally interesting to all parties; – and also the leading affairs of our Sister Kingdom. These are three general subjects, the discussion of which runs through his Journal; and in this impartial and general mode of arranging the topics of his discussion, he is led to consider that which I have last stated for your attention, – I mean the System of Government pursued in Ireland . . .[9]

Hunt's impartiality in the *News* and the *Examiner* was in fact essential to his engagement with 'public affairs', but now Brougham presented that editorial stance from a different angle as evidence of Hunt's studious, unthreatening retirement. This was a plausible image of Hunt under humble ceilings at West End but, as Brougham knew, it didn't reflect the reality of his journalism since 1805 or the calculated understatement of his most recent attack on Ellenborough. If Brougham could persuade the jury that Hunt was young, bookish and without 'political connexions', it would help make his case that 'The Prince on St. Patrick's Day' was an inoffensive 'commentary' on the *Morning Post* with no intent to vilify the Regent. That said, there were sections that Brougham frankly admitted he 'trembled' to pass over (when Shelley read a transcript of the trial he noted that Brougham had seemed 'to hesitate').[10] Proceeding gingerly, Brougham suggested the allegation that the Prince was a 'violator of his word' arose from 'just indignation': it was a reminder of the 'most bitter disappointment' experienced by the Prince's supporters when he became Regent. Hunt's reference to 'debt and disgrace' was a knowing allusion to the Prince's financial embarrassments and the 'melancholy fact' that he 'cannot, shall not, pay' because the civil list was insufficient to cover his expenses. The phrase 'despiser of domestic ties' referred 'to things which were matters of public discussion' and of legitimate concern to taxpayers who had to fund separate royal households. That the Prince was said to be 'the Companion of Gamblers and Demireps' was an acknowledged fact of public life 'to be found on the file of the Official Gazette of the English Government; and therefore can be no more the subject of delicacy than of concealment'.[11] Brougham concluded by resting his case on the freedom of the press: 'Let me only know the time when it was first determined in England, that an honest, manly, ardent, hazardous, even an incautious, exposure of NOTORIOUS VICES IN PUBLIC MEN – of OSTENTATIOUS IMMORALITY IN THE HIGHEST STATIONS is a *crime*, and not a *duty*, in those who instruct the People!' (the *Examiner* added the capitals).[12] In response, the Solicitor-General reiterated the prosecution's case that the article was 'a gross, atrocious, wicked and diabolical libel'.

Ellenborough had already made up his mind. Glaring over his wire-rimmed spectacles, he lectured the court about how Brougham had '*imbibed in its fullest extent the spirit of his client*' and was '*inoculated with all the poison of his publication, and the principles from which it proceeded*'. Recovering himself, he instructed the special jurors that the issue to be tried was 'whether we are to live under the dominion of libellers, or under the controul of government and the law'. To Ellenborough's incredulity they withdrew to consider their verdict.[13]

Henry Brougham was summoned out of court to consult on another case. At four o'clock he seized an opportunity to scribble an up-to-the-minute account of the trial for his Whig friend Earl Grey, mentioning the '*full* special jury procured with infinite pains', Ellenborough's 'personal bitterness' and his 'gross and unjustifiable' attack. Brougham expected a guilty verdict: that the jury had retired at all was 'of itself a victory in the circumstances'. At five o'clock news came. Brougham added to his letter, 'P.S. – Accounts just received that in twenty or twenty-five minutes (passed by the court in great agitation) they found us *guilty*.'[14] The Hunts were bailed to appear for sentencing in the next legal term; their security was two old friends, the printers James Whiting and Carew Reynell.

Back at West End, Hunt was soon calm enough to set down his thoughts. 'Our prosecutors will expect us to be exceedingly downcast at the event,' he reflected, 'but we cannot oblige them by saying we are; indeed, after a sickness which luckily attacked us when we had no idea of going to prison, we have latterly been getting much better both in health and spirits, and are doing so at this moment.' He was glowing 'healthfully and afresh' and ready to encounter his sentence.[15] Brougham's defence had been admirable for skill, steadiness, plain speech, and for placing the argument on 'high and broad grounds'. It was momentous in another way, too. Brougham had presented Hunt, and the public, with a different image of the editor of the *Examiner*:

a person living in retirement, secluded from the world, distant from the court, and very unknowing in its ways. – He passes his days certainly not among the profligate part of mankind; – he has acquired, in his solitude, a considerable number of public virtues, and one private moral one, which they who lightly treat on such topics, class either under the head of fanaticism or enthusiasm. – Some there are who look upon him as a well-meaning, innocent young man, ignorant of the world, or retired from it and taking as grievous calamities those vices which men of the world view but lightly.[16]

The *Monthly Mirror*'s pugnacious champion of public good had become the hermit of Hampstead, secluded, private, almost 'Wordsworthian'. The 'fearless enlightener' who would dare anything had been displaced by his *alter ego* – self-protective, studiously aloof, and inclined to withdraw from the world. Like the schoolboy in the sick ward, Hunt, now aged twenty-eight, had retired to the green lanes of West End where, he told Haydon, he was 'getting a good deal better'.[17] The trial had been a climactic moment in Hunt's career as a journalist; now Brougham had set the course of his literary career for the coming years.

With the trial over and his health recovering, Hunt was in carefree mood. Haydon visited at West End and found him cheerfully 'certain of going to Newgate', so close to Christ's Hospital 'he should be in the midst of all his Friends'.[18] The first *Examiner* of 1813 began with his playful fable of the 'beautiful island of Hing', destroyed by the dissolute, extravagant Prince CHIN-HUM (who held a festival 'at which his dinner-table [had] a stream full of gold-fishes down the middle of it'). 'As in those times, so in the present, some persons had got a notion that to speak the truth, and warn the Prince against his follies, was a scandalous thing, not to be endured.'[19] More serious matter came the following week in a long essay signalling that although Hunt sat by his fireside at West End, he was not among those content to be 'habitual slaves of every species of despotism'. Identifying himself with those 'enthusiasts' who 'breathe the free air of opinion', Hunt celebrated John Hampden, the parliamentarian who had opposed Charles I's imposition of 'ship money' and 'saved us from the tyranny of arbitrary taxation'; Andrew Marvell, poet and scourge of tyranny; and King Alfred, father of English liberties and 'most romantic of Kings'. Hunt's exemplary figures were well chosen. Like Milton, Marvell was a republican who shunned courtly corruption. Living in poverty at his Maiden Lane lodgings, Marvell was said to have been dining on a mutton bone when a bribe came from the King. He refused it, Hunt reminded his readers, 'romantically preferring his good conscience and his shoulder of mutton to self-contempt and a pension'. Alfred was famous for his exile at the Isle of Athelney, where he resisted the Danes and, according to legend, burnt the cakes. The founder of English liberties had been a fireside dreamer. Inspired by these examples of the 'eloquent or out-speaking voice of domestic

patriotism', Hunt spoke out on behalf of 'an intelligent, and a free people':
'*the country ought to lift up its voice against the Vices of the sovereign*'.[20]

And then this summons arrived:

In the Kings Bench

                       Middlesex   The King
                                                                  against
      John Hunt and
      Leigh Hunt.

    Take notice that His Majesty's Court of Kings Bench at Westminster
will be moved on Wednesday the third day of February next or so soon
after as Counsel can be heard for the Judgment of the said Court against
the above named Defendants for certain Misdemeanors whereof they are
impeached and by a Jury of the Country convicted and in case the said
Defendants do not then appear the said Court will be moved that their
default may be recorded and the several Recognizances entered into in this
Prosecution estreated into the Exchequer.

                      Dated this 28th day of January 1813.
                               Yours &c.
                         Litchfield & Hobhouse
                        Sol[rs] for the Prosecution

To John Hunt and Leigh Hunt the
above named Defendants . . .
        and also to
James Whiting of Finsbury Place
Finsbury Square in the County of
Middlesex Printer and Carew
Reynell of N° 6 Oxendon Street in the
Haymarket in the same County Printer their Bail . . .[21]

On Wednesday, 3 February 1813 Hunt and his brother attended for sentence.
Just before they entered court James Perry, proprietor of the *Morning
Chronicle*, took them aside and mentioned that ways could be found to
announce a 'manuscript for publication, connected with some important state
and court secrets, and well known and dreaded by the Regent'. This was *The
Book*, dreaded by the Regent because it documented the 'Delicate
Investigation' of 1806 into allegations that his wife Caroline, Princess of Wales,
had given birth to an illegitimate son. Caroline was exonerated, but the public
sniffed royal scandal. Extraordinary measures had been taken by Carlton
House to impound copies, and a single advertisement of *The Book*'s imminent publication could well have overturned the Hunts' sentence. 'We heartily
thanked the kind man,' Hunt recalls, 'and declined the favour.'[22]

In court they were confronted by Mr Justice Le Blanc, another subscriber to Hunt's *Juvenilia*. The twelve-year-old who had imagined Macbeth's struggling conscience,

> 'Who gave the thought, who urg'd the deed;
> Who bade his royal bosom bleed?'

had grown up a 'potent warrior' who was unlike Macbeth in that his attempt on the 'royal bosom' was unacquainted with ambition or malice.[23] Le Blanc told the Hunts that they had been 'tried and convicted of printing and publishing a scandalous and defamatory libel on the Prince Regent'. Their 'mischievous and daring attack' had held up the Regent as an object of 'detestation and abhorrence', and had brought the government into 'disgrace and contempt'. They must now answer for what they had done:

> In order . . . to deter others from committing a like offence, by the example of the present punishment, the Court sentenced the defendants to be each imprisoned for the space of TWO YEARS, – the defendant John Hunt in Coldbath-fields prison, and the defendant Leigh Hunt in his Majesty's Gaol for the County of Surrey, situate in Horsemonger Lane, Southwark; and that at the end of such imprisonment, they should each pay a fine to the King of FIVE HUNDRED POUNDS, and find security for their good behaviour for Five Years, themselves in Five Hundred Pounds, and two sureties for each in Two Hundred and Fifty Pounds each; – and that they should be further imprisoned till those fines were paid, and those securities found.[24]

As the sentence of two years in separate jails fell, the brothers shuddered and 'instinctively pressed each other's arm'. Hunt remembered this moment of fraternal tenderness, and the silent reassurance of touch, to the end of his life. It was a moment of intimacy in the midst of a daunting public occasion, recreated in *The Story of Rimini* when Francesca 'with an impulse and affection free . . . lays her hand upon her father's knee' before she is sent to a marriage that proves to be both exile and imprisonment.[25] As well as the support each brother drew from the other, Hunt realised that they had been strengthened in the knowledge 'that we stood together in the hearts of the people'. He was able to see the Hunts entering his own pantheon of English heroes and martyrs for liberty, exactly as his editorials had intimated.[26] Compared with prison the fine seemed almost a kindness – Hunt was soon reflecting that it 'might have been severer'.[27] Five hundred pounds – Hunt's income for a whole year – was nevertheless a considerable sum to find. Paying the fine would mire him in debt for years to come and the struggle to raise the money initiated a pattern of haphazard borrowing from which he never extricated himself.

Reporting on the sentence in the *Taunton Courier*, John Marriott observed: 'Such is the termination, so far as relates to the mere exercise of power, of a contest between the vindictiveness of a remorseless Court, and the inflexible firmness of an independent Press'. As a lawyer Marriott could see that the trial had not been a straightforward contest about the right to publish – what might now be called 'the freedom of the press'. He summarised the 'sacred right' at issue with bracing clarity: 'It is not the question, Whether the Press shall be licentious with impunity – no such thing – it is the question, Whether the Press ought to be considered licentious in uttering truths of great public concern, – because such truths are disagreeable to those who have rendered their promulgation *necessary*'. The question was in fact 'exceedingly narrow'. It amounted to a struggle for constitutional liberty against a tyranny every bit as oppressive as 'the Government of Bonaparte'. The Hunts' sentence showed that a 'glorious bulwark of freedom has been mined, with a view to its virtual subversion'. The fate of the *Examiner* foretold the destruction of English liberty.[28]

Immediately after sentencing, the Hunts were taken in hackney coaches to their respective prisons. John was dispatched to the north of London, through Clerkenwell to the 'House of Correction' at Coldbath Fields – reputedly the severest prison in Britain. Hunt was sent across Westminster Bridge to Surrey Gaol, accompanied by two court officers and his friend Barron Field. As they clattered past William Blake's Hercules Buildings and along the Borough Road, the officers prepared Hunt to meet his jailer. Mr Ives would call him 'Mister'. Ives called everybody '*Mister*'. Ives was ill. Ives was obstinate. '"In short",' one of the officers confided, Ives was '"one as may be led, but he'll never be *druv*".'[29] Alighted at the prison gate, Hunt could see how in a few more yards Horsemonger Lane continued into a tenter ground and beyond to an expanse of meadows. He looked up at the high wall and formidable gatehouse. He had come here with a clear conscience. He pressed Field's hand, turned, and disappeared through the gate.

Across the prison yard he could see scenes that reminded him of his father in the King's Bench. Forlorn family groups shambled around the prison blocks or leant against the walls, shoulders hunched against the cold. A damp, smoky miasma hung in the air, and the sound of harsh, hacking coughs was everywhere. Hunt waited for what seemed like hours before he was ushered into the presence of the governor. Mr Ives was draining a bowl of broth, but pushed it aside and slowly rose to his feet. He was wearing a white nightcap, and his big red face looked as if it was about to burst with blood.[30] '"Mister, I'd ha' given a matter of a hundred pounds, that you had not come to this place – a hundred pounds!"' Ives spoke in a croaking whisper, but managed an ominous emphasis on the word 'hundred'. This was a prison for the poorest sort – felons, debtors and the like – it wasn't fit for a gentleman. 'Mister, they knows it' – Ives was nodding in agreement with himself – 'I'd ha' given a hundred pounds.' Hunt sensed that a hundred pounds might ease his way to a more gentlemanly institution, and made a vague response about equal justice for all which Mr Ives didn't hear. His faced blazed across the table: 'Mister – they knows it.' There seemed little use in arguing the point. Ives might have a seizure. And Hunt didn't have a hundred pounds.

He would be given a room that resembled Despard's cell – 'a capital apartment', Ives called it, 'no glass, Mister: but excellent shutters'. They agreed that the windows would be glazed, not open to the elements – as was usual – and Hunt could send for his own bed from home. For two nights Hunt occupied a garret in Ives's house, and then moved to his new quarters. The floor and walls were bare stone, the high grated windows impossible to see out of. The noise of chains, ruffian voices, coughing, raucous singing and 'horrible laughter' quickly brought on palpitations and attacks of nerves. He paced restlessly up and down the cell for three hours in an attempt to alleviate the symptoms, but it was already clear that he couldn't cope and that his health would soon deteriorate. John observed that his brother could bear imprisonment were it not for the 'double evil' of the illnesses he had to endure.[31]

Shelley was at Tremadoc in North Wales, 'boiling with indignation' at the 'horrible injustice & tyranny' inflicted on 'a brave, a good, & an enlightened man'.[32] Haydon wrote urging Hunt not to succumb to his 'hypocondrian tendency', and promptly gave way to feverish tendencies of his own:

> After my day's study I generally lay my head on my hand, draw near the fire, and muse upon you till midnight, till I am completely wrapped in the delusion of my fancy. I see you, as it were, in a misty vision. I imagine myself quietly going to you in the solemnity of evening; I think I perceive your massy prison, erect, solitary, nearly lost in deep-toned obscurity, pressing the earth with supernatural weight, encircled with an atmosphere of enchanted silence, into which no being can enter without a shudder. As I advance with whispering steps I imagine, with an acuteness that amounts to reality, I hear oozing on the evening wind, as it sweeps along with moaning stillness, the strains of your captive flute . . .[33]

Haydon meant well, imagining himself on a mission to save Hunt much in the way the angel had freed Peter from King Herod's prison.[34] But that Gothic image of Hunt's flute playing ghostly music in a 'massy prison' was unlikely to dispel gloom. More 'cordial graspings of the hand' came in the post from strangers. Gifts were delivered: books, a box of pears, a hare and black puddings.[35] Shelley proposed a subscription to pay the Hunts' £1,000 fine, and although 'rather poor at present' donated £20. He later made Hunt a 'princely offer' of more money.[36]

The authorities may have assumed that, with the Hunts locked up in separate prisons, the *Examiner* would swiftly cease publication and disappear. Public opinion decided otherwise. The *Taunton Courier* reported admiration and praise for the Hunts 'every where bursting from the lips of a large circle of private Friends and of an admiring Public'.[37] Marie Thérèse Kemble (wife of the actor Charles Kemble) wrote to assure Hunt that of all the London papers, the *Examiner* was unquestionably 'the most read and best credited'.[38] The paper was now selling 7–8,000 copies each week, and immediately after the trial demand far exceeded the print run. A pamphlet account of the trial was quickly published.[39] Thomas Barnes was brought in to supply the *Examiner*'s theatricals. One of his first assignments was Coleridge's *Remorse* at Drury Lane: he praised a plot that 'never languishes' and characters combining 'force of thinking and a power of poetry'.[40] Charles Lamb contributed miscellaneous items to a new column of 'Table Talk'. In prison Hunt responded to the challenge of editing and managing the paper from his cell, and dispatched copy across town to John and to the *Examiner* office. Through February and March his 'Political Examiner' column kept readers up to date with conditions in Horsemonger Lane and Coldbath Fields.

In the midst of this public acclaim, Hunt was alone. A sonnet addressed to Thomas Barnes, written at West End just three weeks earlier, evoked a domestic scene poignantly distant from his solitary 'present residence':

> Nought heard through all our little, lull'd abode
> Save the crisp fire, or leaf of book turn'd o'er,
>   Or watch-dog, or the ring of frosty road.
> Wants there no other sound then? – Yes, one more, –
>   The voice of friendly visiting, long owed.[41]

The sonnet marks Hunt's reassessment of the ideal of the reclusive poet as he looks forward to friendly visitors rather than wintry isolation. Writing to Ives on Friday, 5 February, Hunt expressed as 'his first and greatest wish . . . to be allowed to have his wife and children living with him in the prison' and friends 'allowed . . . during the daytime'.[42] His request was the more urgent, he told Ives, in that the shouting, slamming and 'dinning' of chains had brought on 'palpitations of the heart & other nervous affections, which render a companion not only much wanted, but sometimes hardly to be dispensed with'.[43] Permission was given for Marianne and six-month-old John to be with him during the day, while Thornton was cared for by the Hunters. Barron Field recruited the physician Dr Gooch to help get Hunt moved 'from the dreariness and painful contiguities of his present cell'.[44]

One distressing contiguity was the recollection of Despard. Hunt was oppressed by the thought that he too might not leave the prison alive, and determined to write a journal of 'Recollections & Memorandums' addressed to his sons. Almost immediately his plan expanded to include his present situation and a narrative of his past life: 'I shall say more of myself than of any body, & shall indeed say as little as possible of others where [they were] not in some measure connected with the formation of my character.'[45] Hunt was soon projecting a full-scale 'biography' to be published 'at some distant day'. Emerging forcibly amid illness and distress, the wish 'to say more of myself' was another remarkable example of Hunt's instinct for survival and 'self-resumption'. It would be sustained to the last days of his life, and enabled him to live for posterity in the pages of his *Autobiography*.

William Wordsworth had written his verse autobiography, *The Prelude*, in the unsettled period around the turn of the century, 1798–1805. In Britain these were years when the threats of arrest, imprisonment and execution for polit-. ical opinion were ever-present. The 'blissful dawn' of the French Revolution had been succeeded by sullenness, dereliction and dismay. Sharply in contrast with that prevailing mood, *The Prelude* opens with a joyful greeting to nature as an inspiring alternative to the prison-like city:

> Oh there is blessing in this gentle breeze
> That blows from the green fields and from the clouds
> And from the sky: it beats against my cheek,
> And seems half-conscious of the joy it gives.
> O welcome Messenger! O welcome friend!
> A captive greets thee, coming from a house
> Of bondage, from yon City's walls set free,
> A prison where he hath been long immured.
>
> I. 1–8.

Over many thousands of lines *The Prelude* traces Wordsworth's life to the point at which nature is recognised as a counterpoise to personal despondency and national crisis. Wordsworth – and behind him, Rousseau – has been principally responsible for the idea of Romanticism as a cult of nature. It is important to remember, however, that in *The Prelude* the sublime 'prophet of nature' represents only one version of Romanticism – solitary, egotistical, exclusive. Hunt's prison 'Recollections' comprised his first sustained attempt at self-exploration, and, like Wordsworth's *Prelude*, his *Autobiography* originated at a moment of personal trauma and public discontent. Importantly, however, Hunt offers an alternative image of the *sociable* Romantic. The 'house of bondage' with which Hunt begins his narrative was no mere figure of speech:

> I commence this account on a Sunday evening, in one of the corner top rooms of the Surrey prison, looking out, or rather from which you may look out if you climb high enough, into the inner courts where the felons

walk. It is the highest and furthest room to the right hand, with the two
semicircular windows, as you face the western side of the quadrangle, &
bordering the debtors' or front side. Your mother is busy in preparing
supper; you, John, are fast asleep on our bed, & you, Thornton, are with
your mother's family, away from us at present, on account of your health,
which would not permit your being with us here till we get into better
apartments; but we see you sometimes to dinner & during your absence
talk of you continually, & relate to each other fifty sayings & tricks of yours,
which are the more delightful to recount because we generally keep them,
in this manner, for our own private comfort, & do not help to spoil you &
to tire our friends by babbling them abroad. – But your mother insists I
shall not spoil my gruel either, – so I must drop my pen for this evening,
with a blessing on you both.[46]

Wordsworth's sense of 'blessing' characteristically emerged in a solitary
encounter with nature; no less typically, Hunt's blessing completes a scene of
family intimacy. After a short account of the circumstances leading up to his
imprisonment, Hunt reflects on his poor health and the salutary effects of
the landscape around West End:

> my body might almost as well have been still, as moving along with a luxur-
> ious leisureliness that shook not a particle in it; – besides, I never stepped
> out of doors without a book in my hand, mostly a volume of Spenser or
> Milton, and whenever I came to a stile, there I sat for a quarter of an hour,
> with my back dropped round and my legs dangling, in order to enjoy the
> complicated luxury of resting limbs, a cooling air, a fanciful passage, & the
> sense of being wrapped up in a rural landscape. I think I can now feel
> myself in my favourite spot at the foot of the hill, with the metropolis
> completely shut out from behind, & the church looking over its gentle
> eminence of green trees. On the right is the path leaving to West End, –
> all around me nothing but leaves, & silence, & a pretty undulation of meadow
> ground, – while the grave of my mother which has long ceased to have
> painful associations, seems to breathe over the scene an additional placidity,
> & I feel a grateful sense of present existence & an earnest of a still better
> one hereafter. But I look off my paper, & the charm vanishes.[47]

This was a landscape Hunt had already made his own, in which readers
encounter him as a companionable presence draped over a stile – the genius
of the suburbs. Undulating meadows criss-crossed by lanes make up a semi-
rural scene utterly different from Wordsworth's remote, elemental terrain.
For Hunt, as for Wordsworth, nature was 'wrapped up' with bodily feeling:
Hunt's pleasure is akin to Wordsworth's in 'Tintern Abbey' and leads on to
an intimation of immortality – but without forsaking the present in order to

'see into the life of things'. For Hunt, the highest 'sense of being' arises from the complicated luxury of doubled sensations: 'resting limbs, a cooling air, a fanciful passage', 'leaves, & silence, & a pretty undulation of meadow'. If Wordsworth was drawn to the borders of vision separating this world and beyond, Hunt's ideal situation was a crossing-place on the path connecting two communities.

John's accommodation at Coldbath Fields restricted him to solitary confinement in a cell sixteen feet by nine, 'looking over some natty places towards Hampstead and Highgate'. He was refused books, pens, ink, paper, and was locked up alone from four-thirty each afternoon. John could seem cold and severe, but his formidable powers of survival enabled him to 'bear this disagreeable business with tolerable ease': 'I am hardened into composure,' he told Hunt. Within days the prison governors relented, and his treatment was 'much mended'. Two rooms were painted for him. He was permitted visitors, books, writing materials, and allowed to exercise in the governor's garden.[48]

By the end of February a committee had determined that Hunt should be moved from his cell to some unused rooms in the prison infirmary. His family were to be with him 'night and day'. In place of his former 'lull'd abode' at West End, he could look forward to the seclusion of another of his favourite haunts: the sick-room.[49]

Hunt's new quarters in the infirmary turned out to be two old washrooms. They immediately set about making the larger of the rooms habitable – and for Hunt that did not just mean a fresh coat of paint:

> I papered the walls with a trellis of roses; I had the ceiling coloured with clouds and sky; the barred windows I screened with Venetian blinds; and when my bookcases were set up with their busts, and flowers and a pianoforte made their appearance, perhaps there was not a handsomer room on that side of the water.

Charles Lamb went further, and declared that 'there was no other such room, except in a fairy tale'. Unlike John's bleak cell, these new quarters were 'a bower for a poet'. Hunt had created a 'lull'd abode' in the heart of the prison, 'insulated by a little garden' like his cottage at West End:

> There was a little yard outside the room, railed off from another belonging to the neighbouring ward. This yard I shut in with green palings, adorned it with a trellis, bordered it with a thick bed of earth from a nursery, and even contrived to have a grass-plot. The earth I filled with flowers and young trees.[50]

Bowers came at a price, and bills from the painter and paper-hanger arrived promptly. As always, Hunt was chronically short of money and had to issue 'promissory notes' or IOUs.

It would be tempting to see Hunt's rooms and trellised plot as a retreat, screening off the dreadful prison surroundings much as the trellised wall-paper covered bare stone walls. But romantic, rose-tinted ideas of Hunt's imprisonment have overlaid the distressing actuality of his circumstances and the resourcefulness with which he coped. The gallows was prepared just outside his windows, and then hauled up to the roof of the gatehouse where executions took place. To the journalist Cyrus Redding, Hunt's 'bower' appeared 'cheerful for such a place' although, like most of Southwark, the prison was dangerously 'unwholesome' and 'insalubrious' for one whose health 'seemed by no means strong'.[51] We can gather some idea of conditions for the majority of inmates from a letter on 'Prison Sufferings' submitted to the *Examiner*:

> King's Bench – No medical aid; no allowance of food – every prisoner who is without resource must take his turn in holding the begging box; and many, rather than submit to that degradation, have shut themselves up in their rooms and have become so emaciated from want, as to produce disorders that terminated their miserable existence – no bedding provided, and though the prison cannot with ease contain above 220, there are on average nearly 600 persons confined within the walls. Fleet Prison – No medical aid; no allowance of food, but what is obtained by charity at the grate. Clerkenwell – No bedding, not even straw, and the boards are in a most dirty condition: only one pound of bread a day. Borough Compter, Southwark – No medical aid – no coals – no mops, brooms, or pails. A man, for a debt of one guinea, may remain in this wretched place forty days, lying on the bare boards: the allowance, a two-penny loaf a day, which is not sufficient to support nature. The situation of the debtors in the Old Bailey is miserable in the extreme (the women in particular), crowded together, and many sleeping on the bare boards with little clothing, and during the winter their sufferings from cold were dreadful.[52]

Although Hunt didn't have to endure privations like these, other prisoners at Horsemonger Lane certainly did and their plight could not be overlooked or entirely shut out with wallpaper and green palings. In the prison infirmary Hunt had created an imaginative stronghold within the walls of tyranny, and for many contemporaries that scene came to represent an inspired, lyrical resistance to oppression.

On Tuesday, 16 March Hunt noted in his 'Recollections': 'Today we have moved down into our new lodgings.' 'We' didn't refer to Marianne. One month into Hunt's sentence she had departed for Brighton to look after Thornton, who was 'dreadfully weak' and in need of sea air and salt water bathing. Hunt settled into his new lodgings with Bess, who had come to live in his poet's bower in place of her sister.

SIXTEEN

THE PLACE OF THE HEART

Hunt and Marianne corresponded frequently, in letters that were often passionately sexual. Hunt recalls Marianne with 'a mouth made for kisses'; he reminds her of his 'fond impatient arms': 'I think as you do,' he whispers, 'that when we do meet, we shall mingle into one.' And Marianne: 'fancy where you would like to have me most, and you will know what I dreamt about, &c. &c. &c. !!!'; 'and, and, you know what I mean . . . I must not think about it, if I do I shall grow outrageous'.[1]

Marianne had her dreams – but the rest of her life was taken up by sickly children. Thornton had chicken-pox. Baby John was teething. In demand day and night, Marianne was feeling 'dull', 'unwell', 'melancholy', 'languid, and *very* low spirited'. Her back pain was a constant torment, and although John hadn't yet been weaned she thought she might be pregnant again. 'I cannot describe what I feel now', she told Hunt, 'every thing seems blakk.' 'Oh what miserable nights have I passed!' She worried about Hunt. A thunderstorm terrified her with thoughts that lightning might strike the bars at his windows. These were grim, desolating days for Marianne – and when Thornton didn't rally, weeks turned to months: '*do* send me some wine, for my spirits get so *very* bad I must try to have something to rouse me'. Hunt obliged, and Marianne reported it 'very good'.[2] Turning to alcohol at an unhappy time was an early symptom of Marianne's later dependency.

Hunt, meanwhile, was the centre of an admiring social circle, enjoying Bess's company and evenings of 'bustling talk and merriment after dinner'. There was a lute – essential in any bower – and a piano to accompany Mozart's songs. Under a bust of Homer was Hunt's library of Chaucer, Spenser, Milton, Dryden, and the fifty-six volumes of Italian poetry in the *Parnaso Italiano* – 'a lump of sunshine on my shelves'. On the wall was a portrait of his brother John – possibly the sketch by John Jackson (see illustrations). Everything looked 'neat & compact' and the blinds put up over the windows calmed the interior with a 'green twilight'. By May Hunt's garden was sparkling with flowers – Hampstead had been transplanted to Horsemonger Lane.[3]

One of his first visitors was Sir John Swinburne, grandfather of the poet, 'a pleasant, conversible man, who has seen a good deal of the world'. In his footsteps followed friends like Barnes, Mitchell, Henry Robertson, Charles Ollier, the Gattie brothers, Thomas Hill of Sydenham and Henry Brougham (Ives insisted: 'Mister, *I* calls him *Bruffam*'). Charles Lamb and his sister Mary visited in all weathers, even during the harsh winter of 1813–14. The Hunters came. So did Robert Hunt. John's wife Sally brought news from Coldbath Fields, and their little boys Henry and Marriott played vigorous games of battledore in Hunt's garden. Thomas Alsager, scholar, musician and financial editor of *The Times* lived close to the prison and often called in. He loaned Hunt his copy of George Chapman's Homer. Haydon brought David Wilkie, and supplied portfolios of prints. Other visitors included the philosophers James Mill and Jeremy Bentham, the novelist Maria Edgeworth, and Cyrus Redding.

The 'cutter-up of Tory dukes and kings' called in too. This was William Hazlitt, writer, painter, philosopher, parliamentary reporter and theatre critic for James Perry's *Morning Chronicle*. Born in 1778 Hazlitt, like Hunt, was raised in the culture of dissent. His father, William senior, was a Unitarian minister and for three years, 1783–86, the family had accompanied him to America in quest of a living. William preached widely up and down the East Coast and lectured at Philadelphia Academy where, ten years earlier, Isaac Hunt had also taught. When Hunt first met Hazlitt at the Lambs' in spring 1812, they had known each other by repute for some time. Their American backgrounds would have eased the introduction, and may have been one of the 'pleasant associations' Hazlitt recalled about Hunt. One of Hazlitt's fellow-reporters at the *Morning Chronicle* was the hard-drinking, rumbustious Peter Finnerty, just released from jail. Back in London he was dividing time between the tedium of the reporters' gallery and his favourite boozer at the Cider Cellars, 20, Maiden Lane, where Hazlitt joined him for binges. The Cider Cellars were right next door to the *Examiner* office, and Hunt and Hazlitt could hardly have been unaware of each other's presence. When Hazlitt called on Hunt in prison they both stood shyly 'interchanging amenities at the threshold' – the tentative beginning to a great literary friendship. Hazlitt would soon abandon the *Morning Chronicle* to become a star contributor to the *Examiner*, consolidating its reputation as the pre-eminent political and cultural journal of the day. He also contributed theatricals and fine arts to the *Champion*, having met the editor, John Scott, formerly of Drakard's *Stamford News*, in Hunt's prison rooms.[4]

A roar of laughter like 'ten rusty iron gates scraping along gravel' announced the arrival of Charles Cowden Clarke. CCC had met Hunt at a musical party shortly before his imprisonment, found him fascinating, animated, cordial, winning – and 'fell pronely in love with him'. He was the son of John Clarke, the 'independent-minded' headmaster of Enfield School who was a longstanding reader of the *Examiner*. Brought up in the school,

CCC was a dandyish young man, a good friend but also at times prickly and insecure; instead of bringing acquaintances together, he preferred to keep them in separate compartments – especially if this would preserve feelings of 'friendly debt' for his kindnesses (Keats's words). Now CCC came to the prison bearing baskets of vegetables from the garden at Enfield. By July he was regarded as an 'old acquaintance', and he would be a lifelong friend.[5] CCC was soon proudly relaying his conversations with Hunt to a former Enfield pupil, the medical student and aspiring poet John Keats. Hunt was a charismatic figure for them both. They called him 'Libertas': the name captured the aura of idealism and romance surrounding Hunt in prison, and the decorated cell in which he outfaced tyranny would be woven into Keats's ideas of the imaginative life:

> A rosy Sanctuary will I dress
> With the wreath'd trellis of a working brain;
> With buds, and bells, and stars without a mane;
> With all the gardener, fancy e'er could frame,
> Who breeding flowers will never breed the same –

The exotic 'untrodden region' of 'Ode to Psyche' resembled another hallowed setting with roses, trellis and flowers in which Keats had never set foot: Hunt's rooms in Horsemonger Lane. Keats's misspelling 'mane' for 'name' in one manuscript of the poem suggests that association, and so do the thoughts of 'soft delight' and eager welcome for 'warm Love' with which the poem concludes.[6]

'I continue to mend still, & think I should do so surprisingly if you were all well & at home again,' Hunt wrote to Marianne at the end of April 1813.[7] They had been apart for almost two months. His life had settled into a routine of reading, writing, walking in his garden and receiving visitors. Prison had become home. He felt secure, enclosed, 'wrapped up' – exactly as he felt in Marianne's arms, and he told her so: 'our arms would make us a prison if we had not one already'.[8] He meant this to express their passionate 'mingling into one', although the idea of an imprisoning embrace was disquieting. The moment passed – 'enough of myself' – but it points to another thread in Hunt's letters to Marianne in this spring. For all his expressions of love and tenderness, there is at times a tone of impatience, even of exasperation, that recalls the strained correspondence of their courtship. Why was this?

On 14 May 1813 he wrote to her:

With regard to that letter, I could wish much – very much – that you had not written it; you will be sorry for it when you return. I thought that I had been doing my best to write to you as often and as cheerfully as I could, considering the new task which I have (and which occupies me more than you seem to imagine) and the weight of care and anxiety that pulls at my heartstrings; but if I cannot even contrive to render those who are dearest to me a little happy, I struggle with sorrow to little purpose, for to myself happiness has been a stranger now for these nine months. I must tell you, however, for the sake of your own comfort, and as something like a better excuse than I thought it necessary to give you, that for these three days past I have had a smart fever upon me, accompanied with what I conceive to be a species of influenza in my throat, which makes me eat with great difficulty. This creates a languor and heaviness upon me which united with no very good spirits, and more to do than I have been accustomed, renders me, I fear, a dull companion as well as a bad correspondent; but I do my best to rouse myself, and smile, as I have long been used to smile, with bitterness at my heart.[9]

Hunt steadies himself: 'I love you most heartily, and there is an end of it.'[10] Up to now he had seemed prepared to put up with their separation, cope with his variable health, occupy his mind, and see out his sentence as best he could. He knew Marianne was unwell, that her spirits were as low as his, and perhaps on this occasion he just snapped. That would be understandable. Or was there another cause for his 'bitterness at heart'?

'Bess is all attention to me,' he assured Marianne, 'Bess . . . you do not seem aware, is with me always.' Bess prepares his food. She acts as his secretary. She fetches his books. Bess ensures that Hunt keeps to a strict schedule for writing, sometimes forcing him to break off letters to Marianne ('Betsy tells me my time is almost out'). Bess helps entertain visitors:

We had nobody here on Tuesday, but yesterday Mitchell & Alsager dined with us, & while we were chatting over our wine, Brougham called in, & we had a delightful conversation on *various* things till 6.

We. Us. It was difficult for him to recreate their conversations for Marianne; suffice to say, they 'talked on all sorts of subjects, politics, historians, poets, orators, languages, music, paintings, &c. &c.'. Bess could converse on such topics, but Hunt assumed Marianne would not find them 'altogether amusing'.[11]

By the beginning of May Hunt reported an 'unpleasant encounter' between Bess and her mother, 'of the ancient and unnecessary description'.[12] Mother and daughter were both quick-tempered, and arguments had been frequent. This one was different, however, in that Mrs Hunter was demanding a share of Bess's 'cheering society', the implication being that she objected to the growing intimacy of her daughter's relationship with Hunt. Several years later

Haydon, who was smarting at a quarrel about religion, erupted in a furious attack on Hunt's 'smuggering fondness' for Bess, detailing how he liked to 'dawdle over her bosom, to inhale her breath, to lean against her thigh & play with her petticoats'. Hunt was 'kept tingling by imagining the rest'.[13] So, evidently, was Haydon, whose erotic insinuations echo Iago's: 'They met so near with their lips that their breaths embrac'd' (II. i. 252). Whether heightened by frustration or jealousy, Haydon's was no malign fantasy. He had witnessed the scene he described between Hunt and Bess, and their letters to each other reveal their mutual attraction.

Here is Bess writing in 1823, at a time when they were apart:

Your affectionate kind delightful letter went to my heart's core – what power over me has every word you say – a letter like this before me intoxicates me with delight – it raises my spirits for days to come – for it is happiness inexpressible to feel that I am still dear to you, that you would *wish* to make me happy – even though the distance between us will not allow me to see that wish expressed – in those eyes that speak all their wishes so impressively.

And again, in the same letter:

I know how long and how sensibly, grasps may be felt; and that I too have the sense of such very frequently, that were given months and years since . . . I long most ardently, again to return grasp for grasp, to see that dearest of dear faces . . .[14]

Next, Hunt, writing to Bess in summer 1823:

As to your eyes, madam, you must know, that when they are moved with tenderness, they have a certain overwhelmingness, & tremble & turn like a couple of slippery balls with passionate feeling.[15]

Two years later, Hunt draws a long oval shape – a slippery ball – in a letter to Bess, and writes:

Here is a kiss for you, as long as I can make it. Does it do you good, or harm? Tell me truly.

And two weeks after that:

it would very much inconvenience me not to give you a kiss for your kindness; so here is a long one————————————————————[16]

A long kiss. His letter concludes, 'Embrace with all your heart Your ever affectionate friend LH'. A year later he reflected, 'we wish there were no such distinction in our language between a friend and a mistress'.[17]

By the mid-1820s Hunt and Bess had known each other for twenty-five years. Bess's childish curiosity about the prizewinner had grown into the great passion of her life, and Hunt's letters reveal that he responded with equal warmth. Their adult intimacy dated from their months together in the heart of the prison, a time when Hunt also became 'more of a lover' for Marianne – his most passionate letters to his wife were written while he was living with her sister. If imprisonment brought home to him the depth of his love for Marianne, it also opened the possibility of drawing others into their embrace too. Bess was the first, and there would be many more women and men whom Hunt saw as proxy partners in an extended family of love: Marianne's cousin Virtue Kent, Mary and Percy Shelley, Mary and Charles Cowden Clarke, Mary and Charles Lamb, Mary and Victor Novello, Jane Carlyle. Since Hunt's early childhood attentive communities of women had shaped this urgently inclusive idea of relationships – Hunt needed to be surrounded and 'wrapped up' with love. Memories of Coleridge's Pantisocracy probably contributed an intellectual utopian aspect, and Universalism added a charitable spiritual dimension. Hunt's attempt at sexual openness would greatly impress Shelley, who acted on his ideas, and its possibilities and frustrations shadowed *The Story of Rimini*. In years to come Thornton Hunt's 'Phalanstery' experiment in communal living, which so scandalised Victorian England, owed much to his father's and Shelley's ideas – and Hunt and Bess would both be present there too.

But all of this lay far in the future. In spring 1813 Marianne's despondency, her miserable nights and her longing to be back in London arose from anxieties that she was being supplanted by her sister. And Bess? In 1813 she was twenty-three and intent upon leaving the Hunter household 'to depend upon her own exertions': Hunt could help her break away from her mother and stepfather, and realise her plan of becoming a tutor to young children.[18] When Bess explained these plans to Marianne she had been living with Hunt for nearly three months, and her sister's return to London was still not expected. What had begun as a temporary arrangement had grown into an unconventional ménage with her brother-in-law. And Hunt was introducing her to some of the most famous writers of the day. One of them was expected in the poet's bower on the afternoon of Thursday, 20 May – 'a young man (24) evidently full, by his writings, of good natural feelings & a fine improvable sensibility, but led away . . . by a town life'.[19]

At four o'clock Tom Moore ushered Lord Byron into the green shaded interior – he had arranged the meeting, knowing that Byron admired Hunt's politics and had been entertained by *The Feast of the Poets*. The *Examiner* had

just published Moore's 'Twopenny Post Bag' ridiculing the Regent's glee at
'*my* brilliant triumph and H——t's condemnation'.[20] So an amicable occasion
was assured.

Hunt moved forward, hand open in welcome, delighted to meet the man
he had glimpsed swimming in the Thames. Since then, *Childe Harold* had
made the poet famous. Byron had been gratified by Hunt's recent remarks
in the *Examiner*,

> We like the independence of his opinions, – we like the sturdy good sense
> . . . there are certain passages of his more heart-felt effusions, which have
> even touched our sympathies to the core.[21]

– and now he repaid the compliment by recalling how the sight of Hunt's
Juvenilia at Harrow School had inspired his own first poems. He could even
remember some lines that Hunt would rather have forgotten. A pleasant afternoon ensued. They enjoyed 'plenty of fish and vegetables' and passed a
leisurely evening talking of poetry, politics, books and schooldays, until they
were disturbed by other visitors. Back home again at Bennet Street, the weight-
conscious Byron reported to Lady Melbourne that he had 'dined for the week'
in Surrey Gaol.[22]

Three days later he was back:

> He came on Sunday by himself, in a very frank, unceremonious manner,
> & knowing what I wanted for my poem, brought me the last new travels
> in Italy in 2 quarto volumes, of which he requested my acceptance with
> the air of one who did not seem to think himself conferring the least
> obligation.

'This will please you,' Hunt told Marianne. Hunt had been beguiled himself.
'It strikes me that he & I shall become *friends*,' Hunt determined:

> – literally and cordially speaking; there is something in the texture of his
> mind & feelings, that seems to resemble mine, to a thread; I think we are
> cut out of the same piece, only a different wear may have altered our respec-
> tive naps a little. Thomas Moore & he dine with me again in a few days,
> & if you do not see the former when you return, perhaps you may his
> Lordship, who will be pleased, I am sure, to know you & become
> acquainted.[23]

Like his father Hunt felt more respect for rank than he admitted, although
the slightest sense that he was being patronised by a social superior awakened
unhappy memories of Isaac's career and the subscription list in *Juvenilia*.
Byron's open manner apparently dispensed with formalities, and created an

atmosphere of ease that could be mistaken for intimacy. Byron seemed prouder of being a friend and man of letters, than a lord.[24]

Or so Hunt wanted to believe. What he thought he encountered in Byron was an aristocratic version of himself: independent-minded; personally and politically liberal; open, informal, unprejudiced about social class. Byron and he were of 'the same piece' – an appropriately homely, unpretentious image. Influencing Hunt's response to Byron, probably not at the level of conscious thought, were the family stories of an aristocratic pedigree heard years ago as a child. The Hunts were descended from cavaliers and Irish kings. Hunts had been among the gentry. He was fascinated by resemblances among his ancestors, and to think that Byron and he were cut from the same cloth came near to claiming kinship. To be Lord Byron's friend would offset the disappointments generations of Hunts had endured from patrons and princes. In short, Byron appealed to Hunt's sense of himself as a public figure, and to more elusive insecurities and ambitions inherited from his parents. They were peer-poets. Theirs was a true meeting of minds.

Byron was clear-sighted about Hunt. He could see that the man had courted martyrdom and that his opinionated views, pronounced 'ex cathedra Examinantis', made him 'the bigot of virtue'. But Hunt was 'an extraordinary character', 'a man worth knowing' – he was 'opinionated', certainly, although 'less vain than success might excuse'. Byron admired his talent and integrity, and likened his spirit of independence to 'the Pym and Hampden times'. Foreseeing a glorious future, he resolved to 'go and see him again'.[25]

Byron mentioned to Hunt that a 'rapid succession of adventure' had followed their first meetings in Surrey Gaol. We can't know, but Byron may have been intrigued by, and drawn to, Hunt's unconventional liaison with his sister-in-law. The summer of 1813 was when Byron went to live with his half-sister Augusta, and when their dangerous attraction to each other almost certainly evolved into a sexual relationship. Did Byron find the impetus for this from what he had seen of Hunt and Bess in prison? This has to be speculation, but it is clear that Byron was impressed by Hunt's example as a man unfettered by political bonds – and may also have seen him as a pioneer of sexual freedom.

Hunt and Marianne were reunited on Saturday, 12 June, by which time the birth of their third child was imminent. 'My eldest girl . . . was born in prison,' Hunt writes: 'I was obliged to play the physician myself, the hour having taken us by surprise. But her mother found many unexpected comforts, and during the whole time of her confinement, which happened to be in very fine weather, the garden door was set open, and she looked upon trees and flowers.' They called her Mary, after Hunt's mother; her second name, Florimel, was suggested by the season, the garden, and thoughts of Spenser and *The Winter's Tale*: it meant 'Honey of Flowers'.

Perhaps it was now that Marianne, accompanied by Bess and Thornton, went into London for provisions. They returned by coach,

> and when it stopped at the prison gates, the driver opened the coach-door, and, apologizing for the liberty he was taking, said that, as it seemed unlikely the ladies should be visiting any one *else* in the prison, he presumed we came to see Mr. Leigh Hunt. When answered that he spoke to Mrs. Hunt, he became agitated, asked her if that was her child, and, learning that it was, he caught the child up in his arms and kissed it passionately. He explained his agitation by saying, that what Mr. Leigh Hunt had said about military flogging, had been the means of saving his son from the infliction; and that he should forever bless his name.[26]

That was gratifying. It made even prison worthwhile. Hunt redoubled his efforts in the *Examiner*, keeping up to and sometimes ahead of deadlines for copy.

Publication of extracts from *The Book* had renewed interest in the Regent's treatment of his wife and their daughter Princess Charlotte. While acknowledging public calls for the separation to be resolved, Hunt's proposals were cautious. No one wished to interfere with private 'domestic intercourse'; 'one fair movement of conciliation' from the Regent would calm public anxieties. Another clash with the Regent would be unwise, given that Hunt's own domestic arrangements might receive unwelcome attention: 'He has nothing to do but . . . stretch out his hand to his wife; and every body has mistaken her disposition if she does not meet it like a generous woman and the mother of his child'.[27] The Regent and Caroline? Or Hunt and Marianne?

With Napoleon's retreat from Moscow, France had 'lost something of her character of success' and the advantage in Europe passed to Britain and her new allies Russia, Prussia and Austria.[28] Wellington's success at the Battle of Vittoria on 21 June further loosened the French grip on Spain, and by the end of 1813 they had been pushed north beyond the Pyrenees. In central Europe the Battle of Leipzig in October was followed by a French retreat westward to the Rhine. By November there was talk of a peace treaty, and Wordsworth, who had followed the Spanish campaign closely, chose this moment to signal his allegiance to George III:

> Now that all hearts are glad, all faces bright,
> Our aged Sovereign sits; – to the ebb and flow
> Of states and kingdoms, to their joy or woe
> Insensible; – he sits deprived of sight,
> And lamentably wrapped in twofold night . . .
> Dread King of Kings, vouchsafe a ray divine

> To his forlorn condition! let thy grace
> Upon his inner soul in mercy shine;
> Permit his heart to kindle, and embrace,
> (Though were it only for a moment's space)
> The triumphs of this hour; for they are THINE![29]

Hunt, however, considered it premature to boast of 'triumphs' and of 'putting an end' to Napoleon – he might yet further the 'progress of human improvement'.[30] No good could be expected from the restoration of 'weak despots' in Europe, as events beyond the Atlantic were showing. Renewed hostilities between Britain and America marked the futile efforts of a 'small tyranny' – Britain – to coerce the young, vigorous nation. To Hunt, it was 'out of the nature of things' that Britain should triumph.[31]

Reform and renewal must begin at home. When the Poet Laureate Henry Pye died in August 1813, Hunt proposed that the court-laurel – 'that sapless and shapeless nonentity' – should be abolished.[32] The post was absurd: 'if a good poet accepts it, the office disgraces him; if a bad one, he disgraces the office'. Hunt's three essays on poets laureate in the *Examiner* interweave his ideal of political independence with the Italian and English poetic traditions. He sets out a modern line of 'independent' poets, beginning with Dante, Petrarch and Ariosto, and passing to Chaucer ('among the reformers of his age'), Shakespeare ('nothing stands against him on the score of servility'), Milton, Thomson, Gray and Cowper. Among contemporary poets he considered that Scott, Campbell, Byron, Coleridge and (for the moment) Wordsworth would have too much self-respect to become Laureate. Only the name Robert Southey induced a 'slight sort of chill'.[33]

Southey was duly appointed, abandoning 'what is exemplary and free' for the '*pleasant path of preferment*'. A few days afterwards, Hunt mapped the 'before and after' trajectory along which 'high-minded' English Jacobins of an earlier generation had plunged into compromise. Wordsworth's recent appointment as Distributor of Stamps for Westmorland supplied the pattern. On 25 April the *Examiner* had reprinted these verses (probably by Tom Moore) from the *Morning Chronicle*:

> When Favour's golden hook is baited,
> How swiftly patriot-zeal relaxes;
> In *silent* state see WORDSWORTH seated,
> Commissioner of Stamps and Taxes.[34]

Now Southey was tending after Wordsworth. Recalling the excited gossip at Christ's Hospital about Coleridge, Southey and Pantisocracy, Hunt compared the new Poet Laureate with them:

To see the changes in this mortal life! Formerly Mr. SOUTHEY was all
ardent aspiration after principle and public virtue; now he is content to fall
in with expedience . . . formerly he was for founding romantic colonies in
America, where all should be equal and happy, and the very sound of a
corrupt world be kept at a distance; – now he has plunged into the very
thick of the corruption . . . our primitive, high-minded, and pure-minded
colonist is to go to Court in a sword and bag-wig, and to kiss with a smirking
gratitude the hand of the Prince of Wales![35]

Throughout his life Wordsworth remained silent as a stone about his involve-
ments in revolutionary France, his French lover Annette Vallon and their
daughter Caroline. But Southey was outed as a Jacobin. Four years after
becoming Laureate he was mortified by the publication of his play *Wat Tyler*,
written in the heat of his radical enthusiasm. The revelation that the Laureate
had been an ultra-jacobin produced a sensation. William Hazlitt contributed
a withering review, comparing the Southey who 'admired the preaching of
John Ball' with the Laureate who recommended 'the putting down of the
Examiner'. In the House of Commons Southey was denounced as a 'rene-
gado'.[36]

Expedience would, however, exert an irresistible pressure on Hunt's own
life. When Southey's laureate successor Wordsworth died in 1850, Hunt would
not be slow to signal his availability for a post he had come to consider as 'no
unworthy or useless addition to the links of attachment between prince and
people'.[37] Servitude to Victoria was less culpable than to her immediate predecessors, especially for a poet who had seen life's changes, loved his Queen,
and wished that her family 'may govern us in peace and security till the end
of time'.[38]

The *Examiner* containing Hunt's attack on Southey also published his 'Sonnet
to Hampstead' dated 'Surry Jail, Aug. 27, 1813':

> Sweet upland, to whose walks with fond repair
>   Out of thy western slope I took my rise
>   Day after day, and on these feverish eyes
> Met the moist fingers of the bathing air, –
> If health, unearn'd of thee, I may not share,
>   Keep it, I pray thee, where my memory lies,
>   In thy green lanes, brown dells, and breezy skies,
> Till I return and find thee doubly fair.
>
> Wait then my coming, on that lightsome land,
>   Health, and the Joy that out of nature springs,
>   And freedom's air-blown locks: but stay with me,

Friendship, frank entering with the cordial hand,
And Honour, and the Muse with growing wings,
And Love Domestic, smiling equably.[39]

'The parted bosom clings to wonted home, / If aught that's kindred cheer the welcome hearth', Byron had written in *Childe Harold* (II. 92). Hampstead's long associations of health and political liberty all play into Hunt's memory of a landscape 'doubly fair', the wonted home he could no longer share. But he was not parted entirely from its joys, for 'kindred cheer' had joined him in prison. While Horsemonger Lane was hardly a 'lightsome land of social mirth' – Byron's words again – Hunt, for the moment, had made his home there.

Bess had liked Byron. Marianne, who did not meet him, had doubts about his 'early vagaries' and high living. Byron's visits ceased after Marianne's return from Brighton, although he wrote to Hunt in December to wish that their 'friendship may be permanent' and enclosed copies of his new poems *The Giaour* and *The Bride of Abydos*.[40] They corresponded, exchanged books, and Byron sent Hunt some game. But they would not meet again until summer 1815, after Hunt's release.

The number of Hunt's visitors decreased during the autumn, although Alsager, Barnes, Barron Field and the Hunters continued to call. In October and November Marianne was at Sydenham convalescing, possibly as the result of a miscarriage. Hunt was unwell again too. Earlier in the year the publisher James Cawthorn had expressed interest in a book-length edition of *The Feast of the Poets* with introduction and notes, and had advanced '£50 or 60 at a time'.[41] By November Hunt was 'mending', and busy preparing the *Feast* for publication early in 1814.

The popular poets of the day Scott, Moore, Campbell and Southey, each have a place at Apollo's table, in a celebration that resembles the Regent's feasts at Carlton House, 'rich as an epicure's dreams'. Hunt excuses himself from attendance – 'I haven't the brains, and besides, was not there'[42] – by way of putting comic distance between Apollo's judgements and his own views. These emerged in the hundred pages of critical notes that now accompanied the poem, in which Hunt tackles the hard task of identifying which contemporary poets would survive the test of time.

Byron – not mentioned in the poem – is introduced in the commentary as 'a young nobleman . . . lately rising into celebrity, and who, as far as the world is concerned, is now moving in the very thick of the lustre'. Byron's 'years of fame' were just getting under way. *Childe Harold* was a phenomenon – the first edition had sold out in three days, and by the end of 1812 there had been four more. Hunt doesn't echo the fashionable acclaim, but offers instead a measured characterisation of its 'general vein of melancholy,

– a fondness for pithy, suggesting, and passionate modes of speech, – and an intensity of feeling, which appears to seek relief in its own violence'. Hunt reserves fullest praise for the 'little effusions' published with *Childe Harold*, admiring Byron's 'natural words and native impressions' ('native' indicates the 'impressions' are Byron's own). Byron has already 'taken his place, beyond a doubt, in the list of English Poets'; now his political responsibilities and poetical promise required him to master his destiny.[43]

Natural words and native impressions had been the essence of *Lyrical Ballads*, published some fifteen years earlier. Like Wordsworth, Hunt aims for a more vital, natural poetry to challenge 'pre-established' ideas of what poetry is. In particular he seeks to overturn the prescriptive neoclassical rules associated with 'the cold, critical French school that established itself on the neck of our better literature' ('French school' denoted eighteenth-century critics like Nicholas Boileau).[44] Turning to Wordsworth, he mingles admiration for 'a great living poet' with perceptive criticism of his work. The reviews of Wordsworth's *Poems, in Two Volumes* (1807) had been devastating: although admired by family, friends and a few early Wordsworthians like Thomas De Quincey, the poet's public reputation was low. In *The Feast of the Poets* Hunt breaks with the prevailing view of Wordsworth to become one of his most discerning critics, setting out arguments about Wordsworth's poetry that were subsequently taken up by better-known commentators like Coleridge and Hazlitt. Hunt's overall judgement is unequivocal: Wordsworth is already 'at the head of a new and great age of poetry'. Hunt's *Critical Essays on the Performers in the London Theatres* of 1807 had shown how to reinvigorate the contemporary stage; now his criticism of Wordsworth was forming the taste for a new age of poetry – praising 'instances [where Wordsworth] has set the example', and carefully explaining the 'defects of a great poet'.[45]

Having noted the poems that set Wordsworth alongside Spenser and Milton, Hunt identified a tendency to 'morbidity' in his treatment of madness and heightened emotions, and an 'over-contemplative' abstraction which 'turns our thoughts away from society and men altogether'.[46] Rather than redirecting 'our thirst for extraordinary intelligence to more genial sources of interest', Wordsworth 'substitute[s] one set of diseased perceptions for another'. For Hunt, 'diseased perceptions' evoked the hypochondria against which he was struggling to repair his own 'healthy and natural perceptions' (as in the sonnet on Hampstead). We can see Hunt reflecting on his own aspirations as a poet, when he writes of Wordsworth:

> he says to us, 'Your complexion is diseased; your blood fevered; you endeavour to keep up your pleasureable sensations by stimulants too violent to last, and which must be succeeded by others of still greater violence: – this will not do: your mind wants air and exercise, – fresh thoughts and natural excitements: – up, my friend; come out with me among the beauties of nature and

the simplicities of life, and feel the breath of heaven about you'. – No advice can be better: we feel the call instinctively; we get up, accompany the poet into his walks, and acknowledge them to be the best and the most beautiful; but what do we meet there? Idiot Boys, Mad Mothers, Wandering Jews . . .[47]

Such encounters are not objectionable in themselves, but are 'carried to an excess' that defeats the poet's intention. Hunt accurately summarises Wordsworth's 'worthy purpose' in recommending nature as a teacher, although the phrase 'air and exercise' also recalls Hunt's own attempts to purge his hypochondria. Instead of 'interesting us in the individuals of our species', Wordsworth foregrounds himself and 'makes a business out of reverie': this is a 'dangerous art', Hunt argues, 'giving importance to actions and situations by our feelings' rather than 'adapting our feelings' to the intrinsic significance of those events.[48]

Underlying Hunt's critique of Wordsworth's poetry was a deep identification with it ('we feel the call'). Poetry for both men was a form of therapy: Wordsworth set supreme value on the exaltations of solitary experience, believing that others might share those too. For Hunt, though, 'morbid' and 'over-contemplative' states of mind in Wordsworth were a reminder of his own susceptibility to an inward abyss of depression and anxiety. Hunt had experienced those terrors most recently while in solitary confinement in Surrey Gaol, when he had yearned for the calming influence of familiar landscapes and human company. In gratitude for the 'voice of friendly visiting', he dedicated the *Feast* to Thomas Mitchell, and concluded it with a sonnet to another friend, Thomas Barnes. Brought up in the city, Hunt was 'instinctively' attuned to Wordsworthian nature although he emphasised community and advised that Wordsworth should abandon his solitude for a closer acquaintance with society and 'organized bodies' of humanity.[49] It's significant that when Hunt wrote of the curative effects of 'bathing air' in his Hampstead sonnet, he harked back to the village's eighteenth-century popularity as a spa, or health resort, where people gathered to enjoy both the rural environment and the sociable Assembly Room in Well Walk.

When the *Feast* was published in January 1814, Hunt's friends were delighted. Mitchell thanked Hunt for the dedication – it was 'all that [he] could wish'. Barnes sent congratulations, and set about writing an article on Wordsworth's poetic greatness, defects and 'morbidity' that draws on Hunt's ideas (it was published in the *Champion* in May). Moore wrote warmly, and Byron acknowledged the 'good Sense & friendly admonition' of a 'fellow bard'.[50] Reviews divided according to 'the *political* bearing of Mr. Hunt's mind'. The *British Critic, New Monthly Magazine* and the *Satirist* joined in hostility to a poet who was successful in 'the *sedition line*'. Writing in the *Champion* (a successor

to Drakard's *Stamford News*) John Scott was pleased that a political writer
should have 'come forward' as a poet. Praise came as well from the *Eclectic*
and *Monthly* reviews, while the *Critical* suggested that Hunt's remarks on
Wordsworth could have been more emphatic: 'general society is essential to
the poetical character'. The *Feast*'s style was perceived as a social and political signature: its 'unusual manner', 'pure feeling', 'elegant and conversational
flow', 'easy elegance', 'playful imagination' and 'freedom and spirit' amounted
to a lyrical flight from confinement: 'though his body is in limbo, (for he
dates from the Surrey Jail,) his mind expatiates with the most unbounded
freedom'.[51]

From now on, Hunt's poetry was often read as a coded expression of the
Examiner's social and political ideals. To some eyes, his 'unbounded freedom'
of imagination was equivalent to Despard's conspiracy, his doubled pleasures
as dangerous as *'four balls or chain shot'*.

Leigh Hunt's father Isaac in middle age, 'willing to hear all sides of the question'.
By courtesy of the Luther Brewer Leigh Hunt Collection.

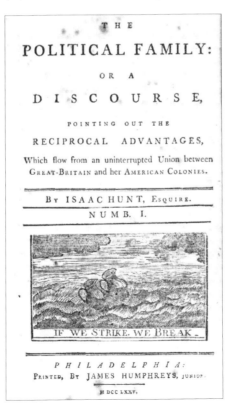

THE

POLITICAL FAMILY:

OR A

D I S C O U R S E,

POINTING OUT THE

RECIPROCAL ADVANTAGES,

Which flow from an uninterrupted Union between
GREAT-BRITAIN and her AMERICAN COLONIES.

BY ISAAC HUNT, ESQUIRE.

NUMB. I.

IF WE STRIKE, WE BREAK.

PHILADELPHIA:
PRINTED, BY JAMES HUMPHREYS, JUNIOR.

M DCC LXXV.

loyalist speaks out. Title page of Isaac Hunt's pamphlet published at Philadelphia in 1775.

Eagle Hall, Southgate.
Hunt was born here
on 19 October 1784.
By courtesy of the
Luther Brewer Leigh
Hunt Collection.

The Grammar School at Christ's Hospital. Hunt recalled that his book 'always seemed to op
in the same place'. R. Ackermann, *History of the Colleges of Winchester, Eton, and Westminster..*
and the Free-School of Christ's Hospital (1816). By courtesy of St Andrews University Library

Frontispiece to Elhanan Winchester's poem *The Process and Empire of Christ* (1793). Winchester's doctrine of universal restoration was a lifelong influence on Hunt. By courtesy of St Andrews University Library.

REV.ᴰ ELHANAN WINCHESTER ,

Preacher of the   Doctrine of

UNIVERSAL   RESTORATION

London Publish'd May 1ˢᵗ 1792 by J. Parsons, Bookseller, Paternoster Row

Charcoal sketch of Marianne Hunt. By courtesy of the Luther Brewer Leigh Hunt Collection.

Leigh Hunt aged twenty-five, 'a pale, slim sort of gentleman, with black eyes... or hazle at least'. Painted by John Jackson and engraved to illustrate Hunt's autobiographical memc in the *Monthly Mirror* (April 1810). By courtesy of St Andrews University Library.

(*Above left*) An Adonis in loveliness. George, Prince of Wales, in his prime.
bove right) The face of English justice. Edward Law, 1st Baron Ellenborough. He subscribed
Hunt's *Juvenilia* in 1801, and eleven years later presided at Hunt's trial for a 'diabolical libel'
on the Prince Regent. Henry W. and Albert A. Berg Collection of English and American
Literature, The New York Public Library, Astor, Lenox and Tilden Foundations.

A scene of English justice. The Court of King's Bench, Westminster, where the Hunt
brothers were tried in December 1812. From *Modern London: being the History & Present
State of the British Metropolis* (1804). By courtesy of St Andrews University Library.

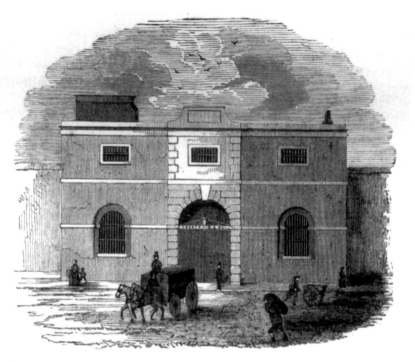

The gatehouse at Surrey Gaol. From Henry Mayhew, *The Criminal Prisons of London and Sc* *of Prison Life* (1862). By courtesy of St Andrews University Library.

(*Above left*) Hunt as he appeared soon after release from prison, in a pencil sketch by
Thomas Charles Wageman, 1815. By courtesy of the National Portrait Gallery, London.
(*Above right*) Republican integrity: John Hunt in a pencil sketch by John Jackson.
By courtesy of the Luther Brewer Leigh Hunt Collection.

Leigh Hunt's Hampstead, published with J. J. Park's *Topography of Hampstead* (1814). ...unt made his home at the Vale of Health in 1815-17 and again in 1821. At centre left West ...nd Lane leads to the hamlet where Hunt lived in 1812-13. Central London lay about four miles to the south, beyond Belsize.

F. J. Sarjent, pencil sketch of the Vale of Health, c. 1804. In 1815–17 Hunt lived at the house on the right end of the terrace, 'the first one that fronts the valley' when viewed (as here) from Caen Wood.

The silver cup presented to Hunt at Plymouth in 1822, to mark his exertions for 'FREEDOM, TRUTH and HUMANITY'. By courtesy of Richard Russell.

SEVENTEEN

ICE AND FIRE

Hunt's first year in prison had been 'a long pull up-hill', and the anniversary of his imprisonment, 3 February 1814, coincided with the harshest winter in living memory.[1] From 26 January until mid-March the country was in the grip of intense cold, snow, frosts and fog. Mail coaches couldn't leave London. The price of bread and coal soared. Reports came of a farmer frozen to death on horseback, of soldiers found in icy rigor mortis at a roadside. Byron was snow bound at Newstead. Further north, the Solway Firth looked 'like a large plain, covered with hillocks of snow'. The Thames iced over, making it possible to walk between Blackfriars and London Bridges. A great 'frost fair' soon got under way. Drinking-tents and brothels such as 'The City of Moscow' and 'The Free and Easy on the Ice' opened for business. Fires were lit, and sheep roasted: 'Lapland Mutton' cost a shilling to taste, and sixpence just to view and warm yourself by the fire. Printers dragged heavy presses on to the ice, risking livelihoods to cash in on a demand for souvenir cards: anything labelled 'bought on the Thames' fetched a good price. Bands performed. Dancing, skittle alleys, puppet-shows, merry-go-rounds and fairground swings completed the scene.[2]

'[N]ever was sick prisoner more heartily tired of a winter than I have been,' Hunt told Thomas Moore on 4 March. There were few visitors. The Lambs braved the big freeze and trudged across town and Thames to comfort him. Mitchell and Barnes, who used to visit frequently, had been away all winter.

Hunt would have heard and read reports of the 'frost fair', but his journalist's eye was drawn by news from the continent. Napoleon was being 'hunted into his last corner'. The Allies – Russia, Prussia, Austria – had crossed the Rhine and were 'on the high road from Basle to Paris'. Wellington advanced into south-west France, taking Bordeaux on 12 March, and just one month later the *Examiner* reported that Paris had been entered by the Allies, 'one of the most striking and important events in the great drama that has been exhibiting during our times'.[3] Spring had returned with what Hunt called 'double luxury' after a winter of 'unexampled severity'. The glint of frost thawed into the glow of illuminations celebrating victory and peace. Napoleon had abdicated.

London was ablaze with patriotism. On Carlton House festoons of lanterns depicted the Allies, Louis XVIII, and the Crown of France, while government buildings proclaimed 'Europe saved by the example of England', 'The Triumph of Legitimate Sovereigns' and 'Europe Delivered!' The Spanish Embassy glittered with 'large ranges of lamps' and the motto 'Good Old Times'. At East India House, where the pillars were hung with lights, the words 'Wellington', 'Allies', 'Peace' and 'Commerce' glowed in deep yellow. King's Oyster Shop lit a fiery squib:

> The King of Rome is not at home,
> Say Paris lads so civil,
> Th'Austerlitz sun, with Boney's done,
> Let's march him to the———

In Southgate the villagers made an effigy of Bonaparte in full military uniform with imperial insignia, and burned it on a bonfire while enjoying a feast of beef and ale.[4] This was only the beginning. Summer 1814 was to see a Great Fair in Hyde Park with two miles of booths and alehouses, arcades, kiosks, apple stalls, roundabouts and swings, military bands, fat ladies, sword-swallowers and fire-eaters. The Battle of Trafalgar was re-enacted on the Serpentine, and overhead rockets sparkled like young stars in the making. After the revels there was not a vestige of grass to be seen.[5]

One of the few who did not share the euphoria was William Hazlitt, for whom Napoleon remained heroically true to the ideals of the French Revolution. He quarrelled with Lamb, spitefully informing him that his 'infinite littleness' made him incapable of appreciating a giant like Bonaparte (he meant small-minded, although Lamb was also physically tiny). Lamb reported to Crabb Robinson that Bonaparte's demise had so confounded Hazlitt he was 'ashamed to show his face'. And in his diary Robinson put down Hazlitt as a 'malcontent'.[6]

Unlike Hazlitt, Hunt was no Bonapartist and although the *Examiner* always spoke of Napoleon as a great man it was careful to 'hold him up as a betrayer of freedom'. Yet the Emperor's downfall – 'but yesterday a King!' – brought mixed feelings. Napoleon had been a legitimate monarch 'chosen by the people'; he had plans for 'society at large', and a philosophical cast of mind. Hunt joined Byron in regretting what Napoleon *might* have been: 'never had man such opportunities of real glory, or so wantonly threw them away'.[7] That said, Hunt shared the general astonishment at 'the first breathless, pouring forth of news':

The Imperial Dictator of a Continent suddenly displaced from his throne, – another revolution effected in France, and in favour of real freedom, – a king restored to his crown, whose succession had been given up for years as a thing of hopeless remembrance, – other monarchs, and even despotic ones, looking on in the mean time with faces of popular feeling, – people in their turn looking at *them* with surprise and regard, – peace, in short, after an interval of twenty years . . .[8]

The provisional French government determined that Napoleon should be exiled to Elba, 'his new and dwindled span of dominion'. The Bourbon dynasty would be restored with Louis XVIII on the throne of France, and the nation's pre-war borders re-established on 'highly favourable' terms.[9] The 'good old times' were indeed back.

Balancing alternatives, Hunt thought the idea of replacing Napoleon with the Bourbons merely a 'choice between two *despotisms*'. What mattered was 'the establishment of real freedom' in France, 'under whatsoever person and whatsoever form of government'.[10] The breathtaking days of early 1814 wakened hopes of improvement and happiness that had lain dormant for more than twenty years. Hunt responded eagerly, sensing that the moment had come to move his political campaign on to a new front.

This year the literary interests of the *Examiner* had once again increased markedly. From now on, quotations from Petrarch, Chaucer, Milton, Shakespeare, Dryden, Southey, Byron and Hunt were woven into articles that viewed national and international developments 'poetically'. Hunt's 'Ode for the Spring of 1814', published in the *Examiner* on 17 April, caught the mood of revival after the long winter of 'tyranny':

> The very captive's wall,
> If wrongly round him, like a curtain flies;
> The green and laughing world he sees . . .[11]

From his infirmary rooms Hunt imagined celebrations of the peace 'exhibiting a kind of perpetual fair', and wrote one of his most imaginative 'Political Examiner' essays, 'The Joy of the Public'. What might have been an escapist fantasy proved to be a canny manoeuvre in which Hunt proposed a truce with his political enemies, while also announcing his unfettered freedom to imagine:

luckily we can easily form a picture of it in our minds; for Attorney-Generals cannot commit one's fancy to custody, and as our imagination never sinned against the happiness of the community by flattering the *** but a truce in these times with reflections that can do Princes no honour and give their people no pleasure. We mingle with the busy pleasure of the streets; we see the joyous faces on all sides; we are carried along hither and thither through lane, square, and country road; here the little boys, looking another way, tumble against us and are off again; there the tradesman and his wife, in order to be in time, toil along under the burden of infants and bundles; here comes a country-grandmother with a huge nosegay for the little ones; there the gallant apprentices push by, with their sweet-hearts under their arm, the latter in their best bonnets and their triangular pinned kerchiefs, the former looking up every now and then at the April clouds, conscious of the new hat and the glossy second-cloth . . . every body's object seems to please and to be pleased; the very dogs seem to think that they know as much of the business as most people; and life appears to be nothing but one long scene of walking, riding, and smiling, thronged windows, dresses, handkerchiefs, green leaves, white ribbons, and flowers.[12]

Hunt's prose is a companionable mingling of circumstance, noting figures, buttoning characters, sketching scenes, gathering momentary encounters into a joyful pageant of life. Carried along pleasurably by the crowd, Hunt finds in passing sights and shows all kinds of human stories – a scene of universal holiday. Writing in prison, he adapts the technique of genre painters like David Wilkie whose *Village Festival* assembles a community from the various narratives of individual villagers. If Hunt's painterly representation of London's festivities in the *Examiner* was a breakthrough for his journalism, it also opened new possibilities for his poetry – as in the opening canto of *The Story of Rimini:*

> Already in the streets the stir grows loud
> Of expectation and the bustling crowd.
> With feet and voice the gathering hum contends,
> The deep talk heaves, the ready laugh ascends;
> Callings, and clapping doors, and curs unite,
> And shouts from mere exuberance of delight,
> And armed bands, making important way,
> Gallant and grave, the lords of holiday,
> And nodding neighbours, greeting as they run,
> And pilgrims, chanting in the morning sun.
> With heaved-out tapestry the windows glow,
> By lovely faces brought, that come and go;
> Till, the work smoothed, and all the street attired,
> They take their seats, with upward gaze admired;
> Some looking down, some forwards or aside,
> As suits the conscious charm in which they pride;
> Some turning a trim waist, or o'er the flow
> Of crimson cloths hanging a hand of snow;
> But all with smiles prepared, and garlands green,
> And all in fluttering talk, impatient for the scene.[13]

Gradually gathering sounds introduce the scene – 'bustling', 'deep talk', 'the ready laugh', 'clapping', 'callings' and 'shouts' – until suddenly we are pitched into the midst of a crowd of soldiers, neighbours and pilgrims. In the London theatre Hunt had glanced up at the boxes, noting the 'conscious' behaviour of those wishing to be seen to advantage, how smiles could be 'prepared', that 'fluttering talk' betrays impatience. Throughout *The Story of Rimini* Hunt reveals a keen observation of gestures, manners and motives: he could readily turn such details to satirical effect, as in his *Critical Essays on the Performers of the London Theatres*, but in his poem satirical disruption is smoothed into an attractively 'fluttering impatience' for what will follow. Even the dogs sense an event.

Hunt's mastery of townscape is highlighted by Wordsworth's repulsion from crowds: where Hunt's urban scene is bursting with narrative possibilities, in *The Prelude* Wordsworth is baffled by the 'thickening hubbub':

> How often in those overflowing streets
> Have I gone forward with the crowd, and said
> Unto myself, 'The face of every one
> That passes by me is a mystery.'
> Thus have I looked, nor ceased to look, oppressed
> By thoughts of what, and whither, when and how,
> Until the shapes before my eyes became
> A second-sight procession . . .
>   VII. 595–602

The Wordsworthian tendency to 'over-contemplation', remarked by Hunt, gradually detaches the poet until human beings seem like phantoms (here, not unlike the crowds that flow over London Bridge in *The Waste Land*). In Wordsworthian mythology the city is a hellish environment beyond the influence of nature, a view that has subsequently been taken to be typical of Romantic attitudes to city life. Hunt offers another perspective, reminding us of an alternative Romantic temperament drawn to human community and domestic gatherings – scenes of life from which Wordsworth had cut himself off, much as Napoleon would now be exiled to Elba. Like Wordsworth, Napoleon had come to represent the misfortune, or folly, of excessive egotism. Formerly 'used to dictate to every body', Napoleon had been banished to 'solitude', 'shut up in a nook', mortified by a 'sense of the friendliness which he had formerly doubted and disregarded'.[14] Extending his sway over an empire of the mind, Wordsworth risks finding himself, like Napoleon, master of a barren, solitary patch while life continues elsewhere.

The winter freeze coincided with Edmund Kean's fiery début at the restored Drury Lane Theatre, where 'immense crowds' queued to see the new theatrical sensation. Jane Austen struggled through snowstorms and a smart frost to travel up to Town, only to find 'the rage for Kean' so great that 'only a 3^d & 4th row could be got'. On 13 February Thomas Barnes reviewed Kean's Shylock for the *Examiner*, noting the actor's diminutive stature, his vehement manner, and voice 'thick and coarse, somewhat between an apoplexy and a cold'. Kean did in fact have a cold that day, as Barnes later acknowledged, but the 'animating soul' of his performance was undimmed.[15] A few days later Barnes saw him as Richard III, and witnessed the theatrical world turned upside-down.

Unlike the patrician Kemble with his high prices and private boxes, Kean was the wild, prowling embodiment of Romantic revolution and specialised in creating 'overpowering sensations' – not least for the women who waited back-stage to be 'stroked' by him between scenes.[16] He performed with the explo-sive energy of the 'illegitimate' theatres – that is, the unlicensed theatres that were not allowed to perform 'legitimate' spoken drama, but made up for this with spectacular action. Kean's Richard was 'perfectly natural', 'humble yet over-awing', and capable of daring 'the simplicities and familiarities of the commonest every-day life'. Here was an actor of and for the people. Crabb Robinson identified Kean's greatest strength when he reported his 'most flagrant defect' as 'want of dignity . . . He gratified my eye more than my ear.'[17]

Later in the year William Hazlitt turned to Kean's performance of Iago and produced a masterpiece of character criticism. From this moment, Kean's fame was entwined with Hazlitt's rise to critical prominence in the *Examiner*. Illegitimate genius was in the ascendant.

Hazlitt had been educated at Hackney Academy where he absorbed the enlightened, rational mindset of dissent and its long-running battle with the political and religious establishments. As a contributor to the *Examiner*, he channelled these energies into combative criticism. Barnes had observed in Kean's performances 'the most complete absorption of the man in the char-acter', and Hazlitt developed this glimpse of Kean into an ideal of imagina-tive intensity, or *gusto*.[18] Kean's performances were usually crackling with gusto, although Hazlitt was surprised to find that his Iago was 'not grave enough'. In Hazlitt's eyes Iago was the prototype of the ambitious, self-driven modern man, distinguished by a 'diseased mental activity' and 'total want of moral principle'. Iago was in deadly earnest, a restless 'adventurer in mischief'. Kean seemed on this occasion unable to absorb the character, and presented Iago's 'indifference to moral good or evil' as a 'laboured levity'.[19] Gusto and Iago could not coexist.

When Hazlitt writes about Desdemona, he takes his cue from Iago's sardonic insinuation that love is merely 'a lust of the blood, and a permission of the will'. He gives Desdemona 'infinite credit for purity and delicacy of sentiment', but points out:

The idea that love has its source in moral or intellectual excellence, in good nature or good sense or has any connection with sentiment or refinement of any kind, is one of those preposterous and wilful errors, which ought to be extirpated for the sake of those few persons who alone are likely to suffer by it, whose romantic generosity and delicacy ought not to be sacrificed to the baseness of their nature, but who treading secure the flowery path marked out for them by poets and moralists, the licensed artificers of fraud and lies, are dashed to pieces down the precipice and perish without help.[20]

Forget what poets and moralists want you to believe about Desdemona's purity and principles. Love is just a four-letter word. The apparent 'impropriety' of her relationship with Othello – 'differences in age, features, colour, constitution' – was spice and fire to Desdemona's lust. Regard for Othello's more noble and 'amiable qualities' came later.

When Hunt read Hazlitt's essay, perhaps he thought back to his own 'rapturous' courtship of Marianne. Had it been lust all along? He couldn't let Hazlitt go unanswered. In the next week's *Examiner* Hunt acknowledged Desdemona's 'superabundance of temperament', but was unwilling to accept that 'love has *no* connection with sentiment or refinement of *any* kind':

while [Hazlitt] applies the term *love* to that animal passion which nobody denies to exist in the most refined attachment, we apply it to the mixture of animal passion with mental or moral regard, – that he is talking of a simple note, and we of a concord, – that he is describing the ground of a picture, and we the drawing and the colouring, and all that gives its finished beauty.[21]

Hunt concludes by quoting in full Shakespeare's sonnet 116, 'Let me not to the marriage of true minds', and it would be tempting to see this reply to Hazlitt as a defence of poetry and nothing more. However Hunt's stress on 'accompaniment', 'mixture' and 'concord' alerts us to his continuing need to reconcile the contradictory temperaments he associated with his father and mother. To the extent that Hunt himself embodied both, his argument with Hazlitt was also directed at himself.

While Hunt and Hazlitt sparred in the *Examiner* about love, lust, 'intellectual excellence' and 'animal passion', Percy Shelley abandoned his first wife, Harriet Westbrook, for Mary Wollstonecraft Godwin (the daughter of philosopher William Godwin and the feminist Mary Wollstonecraft). On 14 July Shelley had written to Harriet in terms eerily resembling Hunt's and Hazlitt's argument:

my attachment to you is unimpaired: I conceive that it has acquired even a deeper & more lasting character, that it is now less exposed than ever to

the fluctuations of phantasy or caprice. Our connection was not one of
passion & impulse. Friendship was its basis, & on this basis it has enlarged
& strengthened. It is no reproach to me that you have never filled my heart
with an all-sufficing passion – perhaps, you are even yourself a stranger to
these impulses . . .[22]

This was Shelley at his most unsympathetic: cold, intellectual, inhuman. If
there was nothing that Hunt would describe as the 'concord' of passion and
friendship in Shelley's letter to Harriet, there was even less self-knowledge.
In little over a year the 'all-sufficing passion' that had consumed Shelley and
divided him from Harriet would result in a tragedy into which Hunt would
be drawn.

Barnes and Hazlitt continued exchanges on Kean's Iago, although their interests soon turned to Wordsworth's new poem, *The Excursion*, published at the
end of August. In his essay 'On Posthumous Fame' Hazlitt had argued that
love of fame springs from an egotistical spirit of 'emulation', and that
Shakespeare was exceptional because he 'scarcely seemed to have an individual existence of his own, but to borrow that of others at will'.[23] Reviewing
The Excursion, Hazlitt presents Wordsworth as the un-Shakespearean, egotistical type. Developing what Hunt had said in *The Feast of the Poets* about
Wordsworth's 'over-contemplative' poetry, Hazlitt finds that Wordsworth
'lives in the busy solitude of his own heart; in the deep silence of thought';
in *The Excursion*, 'an intense intellectual egotism swallows up everything'. 'It
is as if there were nothing but himself and the universe.'[24]
    When John Keats differentiated the 'wordsworthian or egotistical sublime'
from the 'poetical Character' that 'has no self', he was thinking of Hazlitt's
remarks although, in this instance, the idea of Wordsworth's all-consuming
egotism came to him from a seed sown by Hunt.[25] Hazlitt follows Hunt in
'taking leave of [Wordsworth] when he makes pedlars and ploughmen his
heroes', and his *Excursion* review concludes by mocking the poet's claims for
the life of philosophic isolation: 'All country people hate each other.' Hazlitt
had lived in the remote village of Winterslow on the edge of Salisbury Plain,
and knew what it really meant to live 'out of the world':

You cannot do a single thing you like; you cannot walk out or sit at home,
or write or read, or think or look as if you did, without being subject to
impertinent curiosity . . . There is a perpetual round of mischief-making
and backbiting for want of any better amusement. There are no shops, no
taverns, no theatres, no opera, no concerts, no pictures, no public-buildings,
no crowded streets, no noise of coaches, or of courts of law . . . the mind
becomes stagnant, the affections callous, and the eye dull.

Wordsworth had 'described the love of nature better than any other poet', Hazlitt agreed, but it was impossible to admire the inhabitants of his 'boasted mountain districts'.[26]

Hazlitt's *Excursion* review is a masterpiece that develops ideas from Hunt's revaluation of Wordsworth in *The Feast of the Poets*. Other critics followed their lines of argument. Chapter 22 of Coleridge's *Biographia Literaria* (1817) takes one of its themes from Hunt's notes to the *Feast* in elucidating the '*characteristic defects of Wordsworth's poetry*'. Among the 'defects' listed by Coleridge are several Hunt had already explained: Hunt wrote of the 'morbid' subjects of Wordsworth's poems, Coleridge of the 'wilful selections from human nature . . . under the least attractive associations'; Hunt noted in Wordsworth an excess of 'abstraction', Coleridge saw an 'eddying instead of progression of thought', 'an intensity of feeling disproportionate to *such* knowledge and value of the objects described . . . a disproportion of thought to the circumstance and the occasion'.[27] Hazlitt's and Coleridge's criticisms have long been recognised as among the earliest and most perceptive Wordsworth received, but it was Hunt who initiated the critical reassessment that established Wordsworth's reputation.

On 10 April the *Examiner* published Hunt's 'Ode for the Spring of 1814' and his article on the 'poetical picture' of Napoleon's downfall. Later that same day, Byron composed his 'Ode on Napoleon Bonaparte':

> 'Tis done – but yesterday a King!
>   And arm'd with Kings to strive –
> And now thou art a nameless thing
>   So abject – yet alive!

At Enfield Charles Cowden Clarke wrote a 'Sonnet to Liberty' on the 'hard-gain'd trophies of the brave'. John Keats, now an apprentice apothecary, was following events week by week in the *Examiner*, and one of his first poems – a sonnet 'On Peace' – also dates from April 1814:

> Oh Europe, let not sceptered tyrants see
>   That thou must shelter in thy former state;
> Keep thy chains burst, and boldly say thou art free;
>   Give thy kings law – leave not uncurbed the great;
>   So with the horrors past thou'lt win thy happier fate.

The lines echo Hunt's arguments in the *Examiner* on the need to 'curb' Bourbon ambitions: 'That he [Louis XVIII] will not have the power to play the tyrant like some of his predecessors, his subjects will take care, if they remain true to their new charter.' CCC recalled that the *Examiner* 'laid the foundation of [Keats's] love of civil and religious liberty', and it is evident that as the paper became more literary in emphasis from 1814 onwards, aspiring young poets like Keats were eagerly following Hunt's lead.[28]

One who visited Hunt was the nineteen-year-old John Hamilton Reynolds, an insurance clerk who had founded a literary magazine, the *Inquirer*, modelled on Hunt's *Reflector*. He had also published *Safie, an Eastern Tale* in imitation of Byron's *Giaour*. By dedicating *Safie* to Byron, Reynolds ensured that he would be noticed by the most popular poet of the day, and it may have been Byron who gave Reynolds an introduction to Hunt. When they met, Reynolds was about to publish *The Eden of the Imagination*, a fanciful landscape poem influenced by Hunt's 'fine estimate' of Wordsworth's genius in *The Feast of the Poets*.[29] Hunt praised the *Inquirer*, showed Reynolds the manuscript of 'a Mask', discussed Italian poetry, mentioned his own 'Poem of some Magnitude' (*The Story of Rimini*), and was soon lending the young man books and dispensing literary advice. Reynolds was delighted by the 'brilliant Italian Fancy' of his 'excellent Friend', and proud that Hunt had so quickly taken him into his confidence.[30]

What did Hunt see in Reynolds? He could recall himself at nineteen, buoyed up by reviews of *Juvenilia* and his prize-winning poems for the literary magazines. Instead of seeking powerful patrons (Isaac's scheme for *Juvenilia*), Reynolds had followed Hunt's independent course. He had set up his own magazine, and promoted his work with publishers and established writers. Reynolds's alertness to Hunt's poetry and critical ideas was proof of a kindred mind and a new poetic movement: 'It were to be wished that Mr. Hunt would come before the world oftener in his poetical character,' Reynolds noted in *The Eden of the Imagination*, 'for he is really in the possession of a most brilliant fancy'.[31] Reynolds was one to watch.

CCC continued to supply Hunt with vegetables, eggs and books. Barnes brought a copy of *The Excursion*. Determined not to be outdone, Haydon arranged for the gigantic canvas of his *Judgement of Solomon* to be carted over the Thames to Horsemonger Lane for Hunt's approval. Robert Hunt had written rapturously of this 'invention of our young Painter, – young in years, but old in genius and study'.[32] Haydon's painting shows Solomon as a sublime figure to rival Ingres's portrayal of Bonaparte, an association that guaranteed controversy and a good price. When the *Judgement of Solomon* sold for 700 guineas Hunt rejoiced at 'a truly English victory', invited Haydon to 'jubilize' in prison, and unwisely placed himself as the very last of Haydon's many creditors who could now expect repayment.[33]

From May to July Haydon and Wilkie were at Paris, taking the first opportunity to visit the city in eleven years. Haydon sent Hunt a series of sprightly letters full of colourful musings on 'emblems of the furious revolution', on the 'mighty palaces and mighty temples begun by Bonaparte, and left unfinished', and 'Napoleon's private secret closet' at Rambouillet. The letters appeared in the *Examiner* over the initials 'E. S.' – Haydon's usual pen name, 'English Student'.[34]

While Haydon was away Hunt distracted 'the hours of imprisonment and ill health' by writing 'a Mask in allusion to the late events', *The Descent of Liberty*, 'a dramatic compound of poetry, music and scenery' patterned on the 'old and regal entertainments'.[35] This was finished by July, but not published until February 1815 when it appeared with a preface on the 'Origin and Nature of Masks'. Hunt traces the history of the masque from its Florentine origins to its peak of sophistication, celebrating the form as 'the exuberance of an age of real poets'. Seventeenth-century Puritans, he notes, 'put an end' to the tradition, at the very moment when masques would have 'given lustre to the rise of freedom'.

In *The Descent of Liberty* Hunt once again takes a poetic form 'unknown among us for a long time' and makes it new.[36] That masques had been suppressed, and then forgotten, reflected the depressed state of English liberty – summer 1814 was the best possible moment for Hunt to revive this excitingly licentious compound of songs, music, poetry, prose and pageant. For obvious reasons, he chose to play up the carnivalesque 'sports and extravagancies' rather than the courtly side of the masque tradition. Long associated with imaginative freedom and 'natural language', the masque had additional appeal in that it didn't conform to prescriptive neoclassical rules about literary decorum. There was no such thing as a 'correct' masque, as his copy of Milton's *Comus* demonstrated. The more outlandish the poet's imagination, the better. *The Descent of Liberty* moves skilfully between prose, octosyllabics and blank verse, and includes a chorus of cherubs and figures of 'Exercise' and 'Dancing' – Hunt even thought of inviting Wilkie's friend Mr Turner to contribute the scenery. From Horsemonger Lane Prison, he was plotting an assault on the literary establishment and its 'authorized' ideas of what constituted 'literature'.

The Descent of Liberty is set in

> a suffering land,
> Whom the curst Enchanter's hand
> Vex'd with bonds and worse disdain . . .

But 'blessed change' is imminent, and the Shepherds hear an inspiring 'sound in the air' (cue: 'flourish of a small pipe'). They sense 'a new freshness'. In a clash of clouds 'darting out fire', the Enchanter is overthrown and 'falls headlong'.[37] Liberty and Peace emerge with a triumphal pageant that includes the 'Genii of the Kingdoms' representing the Allied nations, the spirits of Spring, Painting and Poetry, and symbolic figures of 'Experience' and 'Education'. Although the masque was traditionally an 'aristocratic' entertainment, Hunt was at pains to emphasise that it was his shepherds, reapers, vine gatherers and rustic figures who represented the triumph of the 'popular Spirit' in England, not Wellington and the despicable Duke of York. 'Change, wondrous change' was now working to improve 'the social atmosphere of the world'.[38] 'Spring' appears, breathing 'Warmth to set the prisoners free', and the 'weary land' is released into bloom:

> Daisies with their pinky lashes,
> And the marigold's broad flashes,
> Hyacinth with sapphire bell
> Curling backward, and the swell
> Of the rose, full-lipp'd and warm,
> Round about whose riper form
> Her slender virgin-train are seen
> In their close-fit caps of green:
> Lilacs then, and daffadillies;
> And the nice-leav'd lesser lillies,
> Shading, like detected light,
> Their little green-tipt lamps of white . . .[39]

Hunt's list of flowers harked back to Perdita's 'flow'rs o' th' spring' in *The Winter's Tale*; the octosyllabic lines recalled Milton's mirthful poem 'L'Allegro'; and 'daffadillies' came from Spenserian pastoral. But the 'pinky lashes' are entirely Hunt's own: as an image of a daisy it is sensually accurate, yet also artfully naïve – almost a form of baby-talk.

After the 'long pull up-hill' of Hunt's first year in prison, in the second he scored off the days to his release.[40] The arrival of a daughter had cheered him, until Marianne and the children were obliged to return to Brighton for their health. Hunt, of course, could not go with them and went through an 'agony of impatience'. The summer heat meant that the marshland around Surrey Gaol became a breeding ground for diseases such as cholera and typhoid. For Hunt, trapped in this pestilent suburb, the conventional association of fresh air and liberty held a special relish. In *The Descent of Liberty* freedom brings a 'lighter', 'fresher, 'vital air' – even 'imprison'd airs . . . freshen once again'.[41]

Reports arrived of messages shuttling to and from Elba, prompting Hunt to warn readers that 'all ground of alarm is not gone by with respect to BONAPARTE':

He is in the vigour of life, with an iron constitution, a professed lover of activity, and with feelings likely to be roused at every glimpse of events, which would open to him the prospect of revenge. Such a man, in the present unsettled state of things, must of necessity be a dangerous one; and the only question is, how to be secure against what he might attempt.[42]

When the Congress of Vienna opened in October, ostensibly to settle the peace and establish a new European order, Hunt predicted that concessions would be required from all parties. Poland's independence from Russia must be assured; Swedish hegemony in Norway should cease. Prussian claims on Saxony and Austrian ambitions in Italy would have to be curbed. Unless '*all* parties' acted to 'renounce what is wrong, the great good that has been held out to the expectation of Europe, will certainly not be obtained'.[43] Weeks passed. Months went by. Business was 'going on' in Vienna. Then news came that Saxony and Prussia would be united. Emperor Alexander determined that Poland must be under Russian control. By late 1814 hopes for a fresh start and a new Europe were unravelling; the 'weakness of *weak* men' was feeding Bonaparte's 'feelings of hope and exultation'.[44]

Throughout the autumn of 1814 Hunt's bulletins in the *Examiner* described how the editor's 'hand is at this minute trembling, as he writes, with the feebleness of thwarted recovery'. He had been ill when he received his sentence, and now feared that prison had irreversibly damaged his health. Readers were informed that he was 'more unwell than usual'; that he had undergone 'a severer attack than almost any he has experienced since his illness'.[45] The shock of assisting at his daughter's birth may have been a contributing factor, and months of sleepless nights with the new baby would not have eased his nerves. If we look back to events following the birth of his second son, John, in summer 1812, we see a similar pattern of events: a birth, followed by a period of separation from Marianne, and then a plunge into illness. Hunt's only relief was his usual cure of vigorous exercise, pacing for hours up and down the infirmary room or around the garden outside.

Late September 1814 brought letters that should have lifted Hunt's spirits. One of the jurors at Hunt's trial, a 'very honest and amiable man', wished to make amends by paying off his fine. Although Brougham recommended him to accept, Hunt himself decided otherwise. Byron wrote, concerned by what he had read in the *Examiner* about Hunt's health, and sent a hare, a pheasant and two brace of partridges.[46] Haydon had strained his eyes and was in Hastings to convalesce, but he risked blindness to forward the 'glorious news' that his native Plymouth had voted him the Freedom of the Borough, 'as a mark of respect for the powers displayed in the "Judgment of Solomon"'.[47] December brought another excited letter. On the first page Haydon had sketched a profile of Shakespeare:

What dye think of this. My dear Hunt, I actually have been in a fever ever since I saw it – Shakespeare! – a bust that bears such individual marks of truth, that I would swear it is not ideal – what a mouth! – if fun & Falstaff be not there – they were never in Nature – would any Artist think of making it open in that way if it had not been his habit – This is a slight sketch from recollection, dont let it be copied, as Bullock would not like it at present – Mr Bullock of the Mona Marble Works has molded it, casted it, and it is now in Town – I saw it yesterday – and have been seeing it ever since Shining to my mind's eye, with an intensity, like as if some spirit invisibly held a looking glass without my consciousness, before my eyes, and catching the Sun on its surface, sent its reflection into the very marrow of my brain with that aching heaviness that twitches every nerve – Do not think I forget you because I have not had time to see you – believe me I look forward to your liberation, with delight, when we shall again stroll round the groves, and quote the dear Shakespeare & talk of Raphael. God bless you my dear fellow & believe

> me yours affectionately
> ever B R Haydon

I hope your Mask will soon be out, I am longing to see it –[48]

George Bullock, cabinet-maker and sculptor, had moulded a Shakespeare bust from the original in Holy Trinity church Stratford, and he was now back in London making reproductions of it. Following Kean's performances, purchasers were more eager than ever to acquire images of the bard, and in Bullock's opinion the Stratford bust bore '*evident signs of its being taken from a cast*' – in other words, from a life mask of the genius himself.[49] Haydon was convinced, and the popularity of the Shakespeare bust in Hunt's circle of friends is suggested by its appearance as an engraving – mouth 'open in that way' – on the title-page of John Keats's first collection of poems.

CCC continued his visits. He had developed a passion for Mozart and sought Hunt's recommendation of his 'most beautiful songs'.[50] Hunt's reply mentions a musical friend who might offer further help: this was Vincent Novello, musician, composer and organist at the Portuguese Chapel, Grosvenor Square, where he introduced the masses of Mozart and Haydn. Novello was an early subscriber to the *Examiner* and he shared Hunt's liberal politics. Cosmopolitan and sociable Novello, his wife Mary Sabilla and their family would be in Hunt's closest circle after his release, along with other musical friends like Henry Robertson, Charles Ollier and his wife Maria, and her brothers Frederick, William, Henry and John Gattie. Hunt wrote two songs for Novello to set to music ('When lovely sounds about my ears' and 'His Departed Love to Prince Leopold') and in 1821 they projected 'Musical Evenings', an anthology of poetry set to music. Vincent Novello's far-reaching influence on music in England was already apparent when, in 1828, he founded the famous musical publishing house with his son Alfred.[51]

In November *The Descent of Liberty* was in the press and by mid-December it was ready. Copies were forwarded to Barnes, Byron, Brougham and CCC.[52] That was cause for cheer, but Hunt's second winter in prison was extremely tough. Early in December he was unable to write, possibly because he had heard that Elizabeth West was ill and not expected to survive.[53] Elizabeth had helped the Hunts when they arrived from America, supported them through difficult times, and she had welcomed him as a schoolboy when he escaped the clutches of Boyer for an hour or two. She died on Tuesday, 13 December.

The end of the year saw a 'New Prospectus' for the *Examiner*. Hunt looked forward to resuming theatre reviews and announced a series of forthcoming articles of 'Miscellaneous Interest, Literature, Manners, &c'. The eighth volume of the *Examiner* would, he said, commence with 'a NEW TYPE', fresh and vigorous in purpose. It would continue to add 'to the character of the English Press, and to the security of that vital and glorious flame of liberty, which is only to be kept alive, from time to time, at the risk of some sort of personal hazard'. In 'general spirit', Hunt assured readers, the *Examiner* 'shall not alter a jot'.[54]

EIGHTEEN

LIFE MASKS

During the two long years in prison Hunt continued his 'Political Examiner' articles, and devoted much time to thinking about and writing poetry. He published *The Feast of the Poets*, wrote his mask *The Descent of Liberty*, and made progress with *The Story of Rimini*, completing the second canto and part of the third 'to cheer [his] long / And caged hours'. In sonnets to Hampstead and to friends like Barnes and Alsager he discovered a language and landscape of the heart, imagining a scene of 'rural feeling' and sociability. Isaac had been premature in pushing forward 'J.H.L. Hunt' as the prodigy of *Juvenilia*. Hunt's response was his principled independence as editor of the *Examiner*, a role that had made him a martyr for English liberty. Now, aged thirty and coming to the end of his prison sentence, he was relaunching himself as a poet on his own terms with substantial work recently published, in the press, and nearing completion.

The constraints of prison life encouraged Hunt to reach out to readers with the companionable voice we heard in his essay 'The Joy of the Public'. That voice is heard again in one of his first articles of 1815, on the prospect of 'Resuming Theatrical Criticism'. Imagining himself taking a hackney coach to the theatre, he releases himself once again into the public world:

> the coach tumbles away, through narrow street and through broad, with the lamps every now and then illustrating our faces – another turn down a street, – a noise and a throng, – the coach heaves with a swing and stops, – the theatre! After descending safely from the insidious steps that seem as if they would run under the coach with you, and from watermen, linkboys, and all the rest of the affectionate bye-standers, who shew such a passion for being 'remembered' by you, – how pleasant to let go the first self-shutting door, and feel the lightsome warmth of the staircase hall, with its lamps and marble steps: then to ascend the said steps, – to enter other doors and to cross other lightsome halls silent as yet, to pass by the statue of Shakespeare (not very fine perhaps, but still Shakespeare), to enter at last the final lobby, to communicate with that ready and civil personage, sometimes expostulatory but always

disinterested, the box-keeper, to hear the dashing key turn about in the twinkling of an eye, to see the theatre open upon, to take your seat! What an idea of space all over the house! Darkness and vacuity seem lingering in it in spight of the light, and the spectators; – the pit seems below the light, and the gallery, in their proper celestial character, speak out from a lofty obscurity. But now the musicians come in lingeringly, one by one, with looks of indifference at the audience, and an utter contempt of the galleries; they commence those horrid scratchings and tweakings of the fiddle-strings, which seem to make the very instruments complain: the stage-lights arise 'like an exhalation', and throw brilliance upon many a young and answering eye before them; the music stops, up rolls the curtain, the play has begun, enter – whom shall we say? – Miss O'Neil: – we feel our prison walls again, and have done.[1]

Every detail is drawn from life as Hunt retraces a familiar route. He savours the imagined pleasures of free movement – 'to let go . . . to ascend . . . to enter . . . to pass by . . . to communicate'. As the 'noise and throng' of the street recede, Hunt encounters the 'box-keeper' with his keys at the threshold of another universe. Hints of Dante's cosmology add a supernatural dimension to the 'pit below the light' and the 'celestial' gallery. Throughout, there is the thrill of the city at night: the coach tumbling along shadowy streets, the 'insidious steps' descending, and the affectionate denizens of London's underworld who remember him. With the sudden expanse of space come horrid scratchings and tweakings, and the stage lights rise to brightening eyes, much as in *Paradise Lost* the 'fabric huge' of Satan's palace, Pandemonium, ascended 'like an exhalation'. The glamorous, disreputable *demi-monde* of the theatre now possessed the stage in the demonic figure Edmund Kean (whom Hunt was impatient to see). Outside in the press of 'affectionate bye-standers' were the whores and other fallen angels from the fringes of the theatrical world.

Hunt writes as if free to 'let go . . . and feel'. In the same issue of the *Examiner* he introduces the 'Round Table' essays as a 'stream of conversation', and in the following week announces more fully that the 'Round Table' will be 'casual', 'unrestrained', 'unshackled', 'extemporaneous' and 'at liberty'. The Arthurian association was important to Hunt, who fancied that his efforts as a poet and moral reformer revived 'the spirit of that great British Monarch'. Hunt knew that King Arthur had never existed outside 'the brain of a poet', but that was exactly the point: like other quasi-mythical figures such as Charlemagne and Robin Hood, the idea of Arthur had the gift to attract and impel 'persons of greater prowess than himself' – as Hunt was now doing in the *Examiner*.[2]

Unshackled and improvisatory traits were widely noted in *The Descent of Liberty*, also published in January 1815. John Hamilton Reynolds sat up half the night 'enraptured' by the 'fresh', 'growing', 'brilliant' effects of Hunt's fancy.[3] All of the reviews related the masque to politics. The *Augustan* remarked on its tokens of a mind 'risen above the pressure of sickness and imprisonment, to the height of Poetry and Philosophy'. The *Critical* welcomed this 'politically poetical poem . . . liberally pouring forth the effusions of patriotic zeal'. John Scott, who visited Hunt in prison, depicted him in the *Champion* as the 'poetical prisoner, seated on a wooden bench, within hearing of the clank of fetters, and with a bare and monotonous brick wall before his sight'. This portrait didn't locate Hunt in his bower or garden or seated at his round table, but followed his self-presentations of 'personal hazard' with the aim of appealing to public sympathy. Emphasising the bleakness of the prison was a way of marking Hunt's courage in adversity. Written in those grim, insalubrious surroundings, Hunt's masque was miraculously 'full of healthful English feeling' and '*prima facie* evidence in favor of the kind and pure character of his mind'.[4]

One thread linking these reviews associates the effusive outpouring of Hunt's writing with his 'patriotic' resistance to oppression. Scott made this explicit: 'Mr Hunt's greatest praise as a poet is intimately connected with what does him most honour as a man. He observes, honestly, and independently, and thinks and feels virtuously.' His only fault, Scott thought, was 'a too licentious indulgence of the shadowy gleamings of his fancy, by permitting them to escape him in a language like themselves, half-formed, new coined, and unsanctioned'.[5]

Scott wrote as a friend. He understood that Hunt's 'licentious' style was in some ways equivalent to his more reckless journalism, and that his fanciful poetic language had been won against constrained surroundings. His remarks also alert us to Hunt's genius in finding an appropriately elusive language to convey rapid impressions. Examples from *The Descent of Liberty* included 'distanced eyes', 'panting leaves' and 'unfinal eyes' (to which Scott 'decidedly' objected). Each is a verbal sketch – fleeting rather than precisely delineated – allowing us to glimpse an abstracted gaze in 'distanced eyes'; the sound and movement of a hot day in 'panting leaves'; and, exactly to the point in this context, the limits of eyesight: 'our present-timed, unfinal eyes, / Knowing but what they see, – and not even that'.[6] Hunt is fascinated by the possibilities and limitations of human perception, seeking to evoke the quick of what is seen: unfinal-eyed, 'unfinalised' and 'present-timed', his writing attunes itself to the process of life in a language that is virtuously 'unsanctioned' by literary authorities.

Still, Scott urged the need for selection, definition and refinement, aware that Hunt's innovations were a gift to his enemies. Hitherto, Hunt had only faced legal sanctions, but to write in an unapproved style was to risk tarring and feathering in the reviews. A hostile notice of *The Descent of Liberty* in the Tory *British Critic* interpreted Hunt's style as the 'pert and vulgar insolence of a Sunday demagogue, dictating on matters of taste to town apprentices, and of politics to their conceited masters'.[7] Hunt's poetry could be read either as a daring experiment, or as a 'seditious', 'vulgar', 'insolent' trespass into cultural matters strictly off limits to Hunt's audience of dangerously literate commoners.

Hunt had entered Surrey Gaol as a hero of English liberty; he would leave it as the most controversial poet of the day. January passed. In his theatricals Hunt listed the actors and actresses he looked forward to encountering with a 'fresher sense on . . . return to liberty'; friends wrote with congratulations on *The Descent of Liberty*, and looked to 'the *happy event*' of his freedom.[8] The *Examiner* announced Byron's marriage to Annabella Milbanke – 'a poet's honeymoon is something worth mentioning' (Byron called it his 'treacle moon', and the marriage would be on the rocks within a year). Charles Lamb, the most frequent visitor to Hunt's fairy-tale room, marked his imminent release with a poem full of sympathetic vigilance. Addressed to four-year-old Thornton, 'To T.L.H. A Child' finds in the little boy's innocence a picture of his father,

> Guileless traitor, rebel mild,
> Convict unconscious, culprit-child,
> Gates that close with iron roar
> Have been to thee thy nursery door;
> Chains that clink in chearless cells
> Have been thy rattles and thy bells;
> Walls contrived for giant sin
> Have hemmed thy faultless weakness in . . .
> Sights, by thee not understood –
> Sights of fear, and of distress,
> That pass a harmless infant's guess!

Lamb looks forward to the 'rescuing hour' that will return son and father to nature, and the 'loved hill' of Hampstead.

Thornton's younger brother John, now aged two, would receive his own poem from his father – 'little ranting Johnny, / For ever blithe and bonny'.[9] The poem pictures the child's 'feints and frolic', and foreshadows his instability as an adult. Bright, volatile, dishonest, and occasionally violent, 'ranting Johnny' would cause Hunt 'perpetual grief and alarm' before his death in 1846 aged just thirty-four.[10] Looking back over his son's unhappy existence, perhaps Hunt traced his difficulties to sights of fear and distress in Surrey Gaol – scenes which, although far from 'understood', had damaged the little boy.

On Thursday, 2 February 1815, the 'rescuing hour' arrived. The busts and the portrait were taken down. Hunt's library came off the bookcases and was packed away. Heaps of manuscripts, papers and back issues of the *Examiner* were gathered together. A carrier collected the piano. Everyone who had followed Hunt's bulletins and poems in the *Examiner* expected him to spring out of prison and 'feel no end in the delight of ranging'.

But this wasn't to be. When Hunt left his rose-trellised walls and summer-sky ceiling he was also abandoning a sanctuary. Delighted as he was to be free, he didn't rush back to Hampstead's lanes and dells as he had many times longed to do. Nor did he go to the *Examiner* office for a reunion with John. He stepped just a few yards along Horsemonger Lane, and stayed with his friend Thomas Alsager – still in sight of the prison that had caged him for two years.

Hunt's sentence had started out as a torment, depriving him of his cottage under West End's clustering elms and thrusting him back into scenes of childhood distress. Once he had established himself in his infirmary rooms, prison quickly became a reassuring enclosure in which he could enjoy his fame while conscious of being 'wrapped up', sought after, cosseted through illnesses, and free to read and write. Marianne had been busy with the children, either with him in prison or away at Brighton. In her absence, Hunt's months with Bess had warmed their affection into love.

But on 2 February he was expelled from this poet's paradise, and he found the transition neither easy nor enjoyable. Writing his 'Political Examiner' immediately after his release, Hunt confessed to a sense of estrangement:

> The world, in short, is new to us, and not altogether comfortably so . . .
> there is no soil, however foreign to one's native feelings, but in the course
> of time will find fibres to grapple with it; and the sudden departure to
> another, even though it be an old and congenial one, is in some measure
> like being torn up by the roots.[11]

Over the two years prison had come to feel like home, and now he was forcibly uprooted and transplanted into a world radically different from the one he had left. England was at peace, and the Allies were dividing up Europe in their own interests. His political opponents were firmly in power. As a celebrated victim of oppression he had been able to use his imprisonment as a platform for his journalism. But what role would the *Examiner* have now?

When the excitement of release subsided, Hunt quickly became disoriented. Having been confined for so long, he found himself unable to shake off a 'morbid wish to return', and he had thoughts of suddenly dying in the streets.[12] Hunt attributed these feelings to a resurgence of his hypochondria: he told Brougham that it was 'a strange companion', 'when I was in prison, it longed for liberty; & now I am at liberty, it has almost renewed my prison'.[13] The 'strange companion' was in fact Hunt himself. Late nineteenth-century psychology would define his condition as agoraphobia, a terror of streets, squares and open spaces. However, it wasn't the *empty* vistas of London that Hunt found alarming, but the prospect of resuming contact with crowds. In his *Autobiography* he recalls, 'I had not the courage to continue looking at the shoals of people passing to and fro.' Like 'the shoal of porpoises tumbling along in the foam' that had frightened him as a boy, the surging crowds seemed 'fearful creatures of some sort'.[14] As his coach drove up the Strand, the people he had imagined so vividly from inside prison now looked purposeless, as if life itself was no more than a 'hideous impertinence'. He made light of these depressive feelings to Byron, describing them as a fit of the 'Azure Fiends', but this was a daunting crisis that revealed how deeply prison had taken hold of his 'native feelings'. Ironically, seclusion in prison had shown him how Wordsworth viewed the city.

From now on Hunt would try to recover the shelter and security that prison had given him. For the rest of his life, friends and acquaintances would be amazed at his spartan way of life, how he would sit wrapped in a dressing gown in a tiny study lined with books. It looked eccentric, unworldly, but what Hunt was forever trying to recreate was the infirmary in Surrey Gaol – a scene where he had been at the height of his public fame, and most fully at liberty in the imagined worlds of his poetry. In years to come, living amid beautiful Italian landscapes at Pisa, Genoa and Florence, he was still in doubt 'whether I would not rather have been in jail'.[15]

Just after Hunt's release CCC set off from Enfield to call on him. CCC's route led across the fields towards Edmonton, and before long he saw a short, sturdy figure walking briskly towards him. He remembered this encounter to the end of his life:

> Keats met me; and, turning, accompanied me back part of the way. At the last field-gate, when taking leave, he gave me the sonnet entitled, 'Written on the day that Mr. Leigh Hunt left Prison'. This I feel to be the first proof that he had committed himself in verse; and how clearly do I recall the conscious look and hesitation with which he offered it![16]

The poem that Keats passed to CCC was this:

> What though, for showing truth to flatter'd state,
>   Kind Hunt was shut in prison, yet has he,
>   In his immortal spirit, been as free
> As the sky-searching lark, and as elate.
> Minion of grandeur! think you he did wait?
>   Think you he nought but prison walls did see,
>   Till, so unwilling, thou unturn'dst the key?

Ah, no! far happier, nobler was his fate!
In Spenser's halls he strayed, and bowers fair,
  Culling enchanted flowers; and he flew
With daring Milton through the fields of air:
  To regions of his own his genius true
Took happy flights. Who shall his fame impair
When thou art dead, and all thy wretched crew?[17]

Did CCC's meeting with Keats happen fortuitously or by design? He was the older by eight years, and he attributed Keats's self-consciousness to their teacher–pupil relationship: Keats's sonnet was the first indication that he was writing poetry, and he was understandably bashful at showing it to his more experienced friend. This was a poignant memory for CCC, and he failed – or refused – to acknowledge that Keats must have intended him to pass the sonnet to Hunt himself. Keats had turned and accompanied CCC part of the way into town, hoping perhaps that he would be asked along to greet Hunt. If that was indeed Keats's wish the invitation wasn't extended. So he handed the sonnet over for CCC to deliver and parted from him, little suspecting that his friend would keep the poem to himself.

The reality of Hunt's situation on leaving prison was, of course, nothing like Keats's idea of him. But the sonnet tells us much about public perceptions of Hunt, and a great deal about John Keats. Born on 31 October 1795 to ambitious middle-class parents, Keats was sent as a boy to Enfield School where CCC's father, John Clarke, was headmaster. The school had long-standing links with Unitarian and Baptist dissent, and a liberal intellectual culture. There was a well-stocked library, and the innovative, enlightened curriculum encouraged intellectual adventure and independence. Hunt's favourite forbidden books at Christ's Hospital – Lemprière's *Classical Dictionary*, Tooke's *Pantheon* and Spence's *Polymetis* – were recommended reading at Enfield, and Keats devoured all three. When Keats was orphaned in 1810 he was well equipped to begin as an apprentice to Thomas Hammond, a surgeon at Edmonton, to prepare for a medical career. By 1815 he had heard a good deal from CCC about Hunt's imprisonment; he had read *The Feast of the Poets* and *Descent of Liberty*, and had started writing his own poems.

Keats was a child of the 1790s, whose boyhood, schooldays and medical training extended from the French Revolution, through the Napoleonic era, to the unsettled post-war years. His immediate environment – the dissenting culture of Enfield School – was receptive to the speculative opinions that had attracted Hunt's parents (unlike Christ's Hospital) and John Clarke was 'independent-minded far in advance of his time'. No wonder, then, that the school took the *Examiner*, 'week after week revelling in the liberty-loving, liberty-advocating, liberty-eloquent articles of the young editor', and that Keats should have been among its avid readers.[18] Enfield School ensured that Keats was introduced to

Hunt's ideas and writings, and we catch something of the school's confident, independent outlook in Keats's 'elate' figure of Hunt.

'Written on the day that Mr. Leigh Hunt left Prison' imagines a 'poetical prisoner' who roams the imaginative worlds of Spenser and Milton. Though 'shut in prison' he discovers poetic 'regions of his own', resurrecting himself to enjoy immortality among the English poets (unlike the 'wretched crew' of the last line). This sonnet was one of Keats's earliest, and it shows him attracted to the idea that gaining poetic fame will involve self-martyrdom, a trial in a vale of soul-making, a dying into poetic life. In February 1815 *Hyperion* and *The Fall of Hyperion* lay years away in the future, but Keats had already sketched out his myth of poetic identity as a response to Hunt's creative survival in prison.

At the moment of 'committing himself' as a poet, Keats had fixed his eyes on Hunt as the embodiment of all that he might achieve himself. But it would be some time before they met. It's difficult for us today to imagine Keats, nervous and shy, fingering a sonnet he had carefully written out, desperate to meet his hero. It proved impossible for CCC as well, for he too had ambitions to become a poet and, as we've seen, he had long cultivated Hunt's interest and support. Keeping Keats away from Hunt secured CCC's position with both – but what might have ensued had Hunt met the nineteen-year-old Keats immediately after leaving prison? The sonnet would have pleased Hunt, and he would have responded generously. But the difficulties of adjusting to freedom quickly overwhelmed him, and it is unlikely that he would have been able to offer Keats the encouragement he had already given Reynolds. Not meeting Hunt in 1815 ensured that Keats went on to his medical training at Guy's Hospital, where he continued to write poetry (often during his surgical lectures). It would be nearly two years before CCC felt sufficiently secure about his own standing with Hunt to introduce his protégé.[19] By then Keats had advanced as a poet, and Hunt had recovered sufficiently to make a decisive impact on his further development.

Hunt emerged from prison as the figurehead for a new generation of young, liberal-minded writers and artists including Benjamin Haydon, Percy Bysshe Shelley, James and Horace Smith, Charles Lamb, Lord Byron, Thomas Moore, CCC, William Hazlitt, John Hamilton Reynolds and, in prospect, John Keats. Vincent Novello, another of this company, marked Hunt's release by commissioning the artist Thomas Wageman to sketch his portrait (see illustrations). Hunt sits at an angle, wearing a dark jacket of heavy material. His black hair is parted in the centre and brushed down to meet his high-collared shirt. The steady gaze is still there although the eyes, which Hunt turns directly on us, appear wary and haunted.

From Alsager's house Hunt and his family moved to 4, Maida Vale, a new development at the outer reaches of the Edgware Road and close to John's home. When the brothers met, they rushed into each other's arms and 'shed tears of manhood'. Hunt fixed up a little apartment as a study, decorating it in white and green so that it resembled a 'box of lilies'. Safely enclosed, he could look out over fields to the trees of Westbourne.[20] Here he set about writing a sprightly 'Round Table' essay in praise of women (who included his mother), to redress Hazlitt's caustic observations the preceding week on women's inability to rise to classical education. The effort of writing told on Hunt, who was still 're-gathering his strength', and this proved to be one of the rare occasions when he failed to produce copy on time.[21]

Still fearful of London's crowds, Hunt forced himself to leave Maida Vale on Monday, 20 February to see Edmund Kean's *Richard III* at Drury Lane. It was the first production he had seen since his release, and he had been led to expect an actor whose stage presence was startlingly natural. What he saw was a diminutive figure under 'a large hat and feather', one leg padded with a bolster to make him limp, declaiming in the voice of 'a hackney-coachman at one o'clock in the morning'. Like the 'artificial' Kemble, Kean was disappointingly *'stagy'*. But as Hunt wrote his review, he recalled Kean's fitful starts of 'truth and originality'. The performance grew on him. The actor's genius appeared in 'occasional bursts, and touches of nature', and in these Kean went far beyond the best actors of the day 'to unite common life with tragedy' as Mrs Siddons had done.[22]

By the end of the review Hunt was looking forward to Kean's next performance, although he attended just one more theatrical production this year – Jack Bannister's farewell on 1 June. Bannister had been the lead in Hunt's first play, *The Egyptian Festival*, and to watch him leave the stage for ever was like parting from an old friend.[23] Hunt wrote no more theatricals this year, resigning them to Hazlitt, who continued to champion Kean while Hunt concentrated on the 'Political Examiner', his contributions to the 'Round Table', and *The Story of Rimini*. Back in 1811 Hunt had chosen the poem's theme to help 'steady [his] felicity'; four years on, the task of completing it helped ease his melancholy.[24]

Hunt continued house-bound except for occasional forays to Hampstead, and a musical evening at Charles Ollier's in May with Henry Robertson, John Gattie and Vincent Novello. Like everyone else, he was amazed by the news that broke on Friday, 10 March: Bonaparte had left Elba and landed in France. 'We want nothing now, to finish the romantic history of the present times,' Hunt wrote, 'but a visit from the Man in the Moon.' His warnings about lack of progress at Vienna were vindicated: Napoleon had seized his opportunity, and 'prepared once more to be lord of the ascendant'.[25] A new revolution was in prospect. When Haydon called, Hunt assured him that Napoleon would 'soon give an account of Master Wellington'. 'Will he?' Haydon replied, unwilling to contemplate Napoleon's return to his 'secret closet' at

Rambouillet: 'I'll bet this will all be a working up for Wellington's glory.'
Hunt dismissed the wager with contempt.[26]

By 19 March the *Examiner* was reporting Napoleon at Lyons, *en route* to
Paris. The headline 'BONAPARTE RE-INSTATED' followed just seven days
later, over this account of his 'extraordinary journey':

> here is an abdicated Sovereign, who, 'exiled', as he describes it, 'to a rock
> in the sea', and living almost excommunicated, under the combined guard
> of a set of Monarchs, to whom he had lost the fortunes of the world,
> suddenly slips forth with a handful of men, lands in the country which he
> formerly governed, and which was then under the rule of its native Princes,
> rides up it in his carriage as if he were on a party of pleasure, presents
> himself to the grand army drawn up in array to oppose him, as if he were
> coming to an every-day review, is received with shouts of transport, dashes
> on a little way further, – stops, – gets out amidst new acclamations, and
> quietly resettling himself in his former palace, calls for his boot-jack, we
> suppose, and asks what there is new tonight at the Opera![27]

Napoleon's restoration galvanised Hunt's circle of acquaintances. Hazlitt was
over the moon, and Moore declared himself 'decidedly *glad of it*'. Byron sick-
ened at the 'barking of the wardogs'.[28] Haydon and Crabb Robinson predicted
dreadful times ahead. Hunt had followed international affairs for years, and
took a steady measure of events: war of some kind was, he thought, 'exceedingly probable'.[29] Within days the Allies published a declaration '*that Napoleon
Bonaparte has placed himself without the pale of civil and social relations; and
that, as an enemy and disturber of the tranquillity of the world, he has rendered
himself liable to public vengeance*'. In Hunt's view this proclamation from 'the
old Court leaven' at Vienna was an 'exquisitely absurd document', a 'flash-
in-the-pan thunderbolt' that deplorably and dangerously urged 'a war of exter-
mination' to assassinate Napoleon.[30] What if Napoleon responded with equal
savagery? Through May and June the *Examiner* followed the '*hue and cry of
Europe against Napoleon's life*', as Wellington and Blücher massed armies on
France's northern frontier (reported 30 April) and Napoleon marched to Lille
to confront them (7 May).[31]

By spring 1815 Hunt had sufficiently mastered his terror of open spaces to
walk from Maida Vale through the lanes to Hampstead. This was an occasion
he had long anticipated and he marked it with a sonnet:

> The baffled spell, that bound me, is undone;
>   And I have breath'd once more beneath thy sky,
> Lovely-brow'd Hampstead; and my looks have run
>   O'er and about thee; and had scarce drew nigh,

When I beheld, in momentary sun,
    One of thy hills gleam bright and bosomy, –
Just like that orb of orbs, a human one,
    Let forth by chance upon a lover's eye.

Forgive me then, that not till now I spoke;
    For all the comforts, miss'd in close distress,
        With airy nod came up from every part,
O'er-smiling speech; and so I gaz'd, and took
    A long, deep draught of silent freshfulness,
        Ample, and gushing round my fever'd heart.[32]

'Mother Nature' was a nurturing presence for Hunt's contemporaries, especially Wordsworth, but Hunt's readiness to compare a Hampstead hillock with a woman's breast would have surprised even the readers of the *Examiner*. This 'Sonnet to Hampstead', Hunt's sixth, is a good example of his supposed vulgarity as a writer – 'orb of orbs', indeed – and phrases like 'looks have run', 'airy nod' and 'o'er-smiling speech' seem quaint, half-realised, possibly meaningless. However, there was more to this poem than smuggering and dawdling.

What looks like adolescent gaucheness should be seen in relation to aesthetic theories of the time: Edmund Burke had defined beauty in terms of 'smooth slopes of earth' and 'the smoothness; the softness; the easy and insensible swell' of a woman's breasts.[33] Following Burke's influential formulation, Hunt's 'bosomy' association of the slopes of Hampstead was intellectually sound, while the diaphanous muslin dresses fashionable during the Regency may indeed have 'let forth by chance' – and not just to the eyes of a lover. But why write the poem, anyway, and what does it tell us about Hunt?

Contrasting with the sense of release, of letting forth, are memories of being 'baffled', 'bound', 'in close distress' – here less the physical fetters of prison than the mental anguish Hunt had endured since his release. A landscape lit up 'in momentary sun' was exactly the kind of fleeting experience that impelled his imagination, and perhaps the most revealing aspect of the poem is its spring to an erotic scene between a woman and her lover. Flickering across the landscape is the urgent, elusive narrative of a 'fever'd heart' – 'the comforts, miss'd in close distress', a figure glimpsed with 'airy nod' – now loosed into language of pleasurable impressions that eventually 'o'er-smile' the poem into silence. What 'comforts' had Hunt missed in his 'close distress' at Maida Vale? Marianne and the children were living there too – so was it simply his beloved Hampstead? Or could it have been Bess, who was also living in their cramped lodgings? Their camaraderie in prison was now less often shared, but there were moments when intimacy gleamed into life again. Could Hunt continue married life with Marianne and the children, all of whom he deeply loved, and also bring Bess fully into the circle of his passionate life?

April 1815 brought an unexpected parcel: a presentation copy of the new two-volume edition of *Poems by William Wordsworth* arrived with the author's compliments. Brougham had met Wordsworth the previous year and had mentioned how highly Hunt valued his poetry. Hunt acknowledged the gift, describing himself as one of Wordsworth's most ardent admirers and enclosing a copy of the *Descent of Liberty*.[34] Although Hunt's reservations about Wordsworth's politics and poetical theories continued, this first exchange between them was mutually respectful and opened the possibility of a meeting.

Lord and Lady Byron were back in London, settled in a large house at 13, Piccadilly Terrace rented from the Duchess of Devonshire. Byron was soon active on the Management Committee of Drury Lane, and in May he wrote offering Hunt his private box 'for Kean's nights – friday – & saturday next – in case you should like to see him quietly – it is close to the stage – the entrance by the private box door – & you can go without the bore of crowding – jostling – or dressing'.[35] Hunt would have accepted but for another relapse that obliged him to rest and 'not do as much as he could wish'.[36] Byron also enclosed for the *Examiner* a clutch of letters from his friend John Cam Hobhouse, who had dashed over to Paris to observe Napoleon's triumphant return (they appeared in the paper on 4, 11 and 18 June). He invited Hunt to meet the new 'Lady B' at Piccadilly Terrace, and thanked him 'for ye. Mask'.[37]

Hunt was too ill to make visits, so Byron came out to Maida Vale to chat with him in his study. He was 'fatter than before his marriage', Hunt recollected, but not fat enough to prevent him riding Thornton's 'magnificent rocking-horse . . . with a childish glee becoming a poet'.[38] The sight of Lord Byron – or any poet – on a rocking-horse was an irresistible anecdote, and it quickly got about. It lurks behind Hazlitt's 'Round Table' essay on 'Milton's Versification' – 'Dr Johnson and Pope would have converted his vaulting Pegasus into a rocking-horse' – from where Keats took it to describe the rhyming couplets of neoclassical poets like Pope: 'They sway'd about upon a rocking horse, / And thought it Pegasus'.[39] Byron bridled at this attack on Pope, who was a poet he greatly admired. He predicted that the next generation of poets would 'tumble and break their necks off our Pegasus . . . we keep the *saddle*, because we broke the rascal and can ride'.[40]

Another poet was in town this spring. Wordsworth had recently been introduced to Haydon by a mutual friend, Sir George Beaumont, and the two men quickly became friends. They shared a high sense of their own artistic calling, and Wordsworth had no difficulty in being persuaded that his likeness should be preserved for generations to come (Haydon also planned to include

Wordsworth in his painting *Christ's Entry into Jerusalem*). Sunday, 11 June was set aside as the day for securing immortality.

Wordsworth arrived in Haydon's Great Marlborough Street lodgings at an early hour, ready for the making of his life mask. This was the closest likeness of a person available before photographs, and it involved excruciating discomfort. Wordsworth sat motionless, breathing through straws pushed up his nose, while Haydon smeared his face with grease before covering it with plaster. Wordsworth then waited, 'hands folded, sedate, steady & solemn . . . unable to see or speak', while the plaster slowly dried and hardened, unaware that John Scott had called and was peeping in at the door. When it was ready the cast was carefully removed, forming a mould from which the life mask of the forty-five-year-old poet would be reproduced.

Breakfast followed, and afterwards Haydon accompanied Wordsworth to Maida Vale where Hunt was delighted to welcome the man he had tipped as 'the greatest poet of the present'. Following Haydon's remark that 'Hunt was ill or it would have been his place to call on Wordsworth', the encounter has usually been interpreted as a magnanimous gesture on Wordsworth's part. But Haydon's talk of Hunt's 'place' tells us more about his awe at Wordsworth than what happened on this day. A different reading of the occasion might be that, having secured his identity for posterity's eyes, Wordsworth felt sufficiently steadied to meet a contemporary whose public standing surpassed his own. Hunt, unlike Haydon, had already done much to forward Wordsworth's reputation and was perceptive about his strengths and limitations as a poet and a man. According to Haydon, Hunt paid Wordsworth 'the highest compliments'. Bidding Hunt farewell, Haydon 'sauntered along to Hampstead' with his new friend, rapt by his 'purity of heart, his kind affections, his soundness of principle, his information, his knowledge, his genius, & the intense & eager feelings with which he pours forth all he knows affect, enchant, interest & delight one'.[41] Hunt watched them go. He also knew about Haydon's stormy enthusiasms.

Haydon thought the meeting with Wordsworth 'interesting', but omitted to mention the controversy that caught Henry Crabb Robinson's attention when he met Wordsworth four days later. 'We talked about Hazlitt,' Robinson says, 'in consequence of a malignant attack on Wordsworth by him in Sunday's *Examiner*.' Wordsworth told Robinson about his visit to Hunt, who 'in a manly way' had asked 'whether he had seen the paper of the morning; saying, if he had, he should consider the call as a higher honour'.[42]

Wordsworth did not admit to having read the paper, but he must have been apprised of its contents then or shortly afterwards. A malignant attack? Hazlitt had in fact written a review of Milton's masque, *Comus*, which concluded with some remarks on Milton's politics: 'Whether he was a *true* patriot, we shall not inquire; he was at least a *consistent* one. He did not retract his defence of the people of England; he did not say that his sonnets to VANE or

CROMWELL were meant ironically; he was not appointed Poet Laureate to a Court which he had reviled and insulted; he accepted neither place nor pension; nor did he write paltry sonnets upon the "Royal fortitude" of the House of STUART, by which, however, they really lost something.' Hazlitt is echoing Hunt's remarks on Southey's apostasy, and cannot resist singling out Wordsworth's sonnet 'Now that all hearts are glad' for particular notice: 'In the last edition of the Works of a modern Poet there is a Sonnet to the King complimenting him on his "royal fortitude" and (somewhat prematurely) on the triumphs resulting from it. The story of the *Female Vagrant*, which very beautifully and affectingly describes the miseries brought on the lower classes by war, in bearing which the said "royal fortitude" is so nobly exercised, is very properly left out of the collection.'[43]

Hazlitt had known Wordsworth since 1798. He had been among the first to praise *Lyrical Ballads*, and he admired 'The Female Vagrant' as a protest against the war. Oddly, though, he seems to have overlooked the fact that some verses from this poem were included in *Poems by William Wordsworth*. He preferred instead to dwell on Wordsworth's sonnet saluting Wellington, the last of the 'Sonnets Dedicated to Liberty'. That sequence of poems begins by invoking the English republicans of the seventeenth century – Sydney, Marvell, Harrington, Vane and Milton. To find the poet, just a few pages later, flattering the 'regal fortitude' of the 'aged Sovereign' who had waged 'perilous war' against liberty was more than Hazlitt could bear. But by May 1815 the tables had turned once more. Napoleon was back in power.

While in London Wordsworth was deliberately avoiding Hazlitt, citing his sexual escapades at Keswick back in 1803 as the reason: the poet told Crabb Robinson a lurid tale of Hazlitt's 'gross attacks on women' and his 'narrow escape' – assisted by Wordsworth himself – from an 'incensed populace'.[44] A more plausible source of ill-feeling, however, was Hazlitt's recent *Examiner* review of *The Excursion*. Uneasy at this notice by a notorious Bonapartist, Wordsworth hadn't acknowledged the review. Hazlitt had reason to feel irked, and his remarks about political consistency had been carefully calculated. In the 'Preface' to *The Excursion*, Wordsworth had announced his grandiose bid to rival *Paradise Lost* and establish himself as the pre-eminent poet in the English tradition. Hazlitt focuses attention on the most recent achievement of this would-be Milton: sonnets friendly to royalty.

Underlying these tense relationships was the awareness that events in Europe were gathering to a crisis. As summer approached news of the 'commencement of hostilities' was expected at any moment. Hunt foresaw that 'the struggle must be dreadful', and hoped that it would 'terminate in the establishment of liberty and truth!'[45] The fateful news of 'desperate action' and 'immense' losses came in a dispatch from Wellington, dated 19 June, reporting the victory at Waterloo. Three days later the *Morning Post* broke the 'Great and Glorious News'. In the next issue of the *Examiner*, Hunt expressed 'afflic-tion and disgust' at 'the sight of so many lives destroyed, so many public burdens increased, and so much misery of all sorts occasioned to families'. Still, the battle's ferocity might have exhausted appetites for war: it had been a narrow victory, by no means certain, gained by the 'inflexible steadiness' of 'inferior officers and common soldiers'.[46]

Haydon's days were passed in tears of joy at 'this glorious conflict'; at night he dreamed about fighting at Waterloo: 'In the history of the world never was there such a period as this of 1815!'[47] Wellington was a 'Great & Glorious Man', and Haydon's 'noble Art' was now poised to make Britain 'the grandest Nation in the World'. Hunt and Haydon argued fiercely about Waterloo when they met, with Hunt believing that Napoleon might survive to 'work an improvement in others' because 'not so powerful as he was formerly'.[48] This sounds whimsical, but after the astonishments of recent months no prospect seemed too outlandish to contemplate: Hunt was regarding events with 'present-timed, unfinal eyes', aware that history had not come to an end.

For many, Waterloo was the conclusion of a forty-year cycle of revolu-tionary history that began in Isaac Hunt's Philadelphia. Shelley traced Napoleon's defeat to his betrayal of the French Revolution, and was outraged by the Allies' revival of 'old Custom, legal Crime, / And bloody Faith'.[49] While Shelley sought to understand events in a long historical perspective, others moved quickly to cash in on 'Waterloo Mania'.

Eyewitness accounts of the battle crammed the bookstalls alongside thanks-giving sermons and prayers, and hundreds of patriotic songs, ballads and odes of which the best known are Scott's 'Field of Waterloo', Southey's 'Poet's Pilgrimage to Waterloo', Wordsworth's 'Thanksgiving Ode' (which famously identified 'Carnage' as God's 'daughter'), and the third canto of Byron's *Childe Harold*. A subscription was launched for the wounded and bereaved, funded through private donations, collections gathered at 'Waterloo Sermons', and royalties from the 'Field of Waterloo'. 'The Waterloo Museum' opened in St James's Street, presenting an 'extraordinary EXHIBITION of the WRECK of the FRENCH ARMY and the magnificent wardrobe of Buonaparte'. Napoleon's carriage was put on display, 'OPENED for public INSPECTION', and a new coach for the London–Leeds route was named 'The Waterloo'. Souvenir hunters scoured the battlefield and returned to advertise their booty: 'Waterloo Armour. – To be Sold'.[50] Wellington coats, hats, trousers and boots came into fashion. John Rennie's new Strand Bridge became Waterloo Bridge, and John Nash's Regent Street would terminate in Waterloo Place.

William Hazlitt succumbed to a different malaise. For weeks after Waterloo he shambled about unwashed, unshaved and drunk, with a black band around his arm, inconsolable at the downfall of his hero.[51]

Part V: At the Vale of Health, 1816–1817

> let the tyrants keep
> Their chains, and bars; let them weep
> With rage to see thee freshly risen
> Like strength from slumber . . .
>
> P. B. Shelley, 'Lines to Leigh Hunt'

NINETEEN

ELABORATE SNARES

While the *Courier* and *The Times* huzza'd Wellington's victory, Hunt counted the war's human cost. His reflections welled up from deep personal sources: memories of the American war and his parents, of his mother's horror of violence and the military, of his post in the War Office and parades with the Volunteers. He had been part of the war machine too. In his *Examiner* article, 'Victory of Waterloo', Hunt attempts to come to terms with the carnage of modern warfare:

> We think first of the countrymen, and then of the fellow beings in general, whom this mysterious evil, war, has been hacking and sweeping away. Right and wrong, friend and enemy, every thing which concerns our immediate habits, and depends upon a chain of circumstances, the blameableness of which is lost in the obscurity of first causes of evil, fades away before feelings like these. – What to us are questions of policy, the satisfactions of revenge, or even the consolations of an admiring tenderness, when we think of all the human creatures that have suffered in this dreadful business? – creatures, the very worst of whom, to speak the language which society must use, have had their excuses of time, place, and education, while the rest were but the other day in the bosoms of their friends or families. What are to us the common feelings of hostility or of triumph, when we think of all those old men cut down with irreverent violence, – of those in vigorous manhood suddenly dashed into all the impotent postures of lifelessness, – of the fine youths in all the variety of talent or good-temper, some of whom but a week or two back were sitting on quiet evenings among their mothers and sisters; others enjoying all the cordiality and expecting enthusiasm of early friendship; and others, perhaps the most painful to remember of all, since they have nothing about them, as it were, to warrant the seriousness of death, or to fit them with an answer to its sudden changes, – walking about in all the lighter susceptibilities of happiness, in vacant airiness, in the harmless rivalry of good looks, – in all which if satire may call it trifling, the retrospective philosophy of moments like these will call the buoyancy of youth and the first wish to be thought well of?[1]

Weighing human suffering against 'policy', Hunt recalls Shakespeare's Henry V before Agincourt: 'if the cause be not good the King himself hath a heavy reckoning to make . . . there are few die well that die in a battle' (IV. i. 132, 141). Confronted with 'mysterious evil' and 'obscure causes', Hunt questions war's human situation and its 'irreverent' destruction of old, young, and those 'most painful to remember'. Here he glanced back at his fellow-Volunteers, young men without a thought of death 'walking about in all the lighter susceptibilities of happiness'. Some had gone into the army and perished. Hunt had not volunteered that far and wrote now as a memorialist impelled, and almost overcome, by thoughts of ingenuous youth on the march to annihilation. In the long embrace of Hunt's final question, colloquial asides such as 'but the other day' and 'as it were' link the imponderables of death and destruction with the contingencies of everyday life – habits, circumstances, times and places, friendship, quiet evenings with the family. These juxtapositions of the cosmic and the homely were a technique that Hunt probably learned from Shakespeare's mingling of unbearable tragedy with the familiar, as when King Lear, on the brink of death, makes his final request: 'Pray you undo this button' (V, iii. 309).

Hunt found a different interweaving of tragedy and homely detail in *The Excursion*, particularly the story of Margaret and her husband Robert in the first book. Wordsworth's subject is the hardship of war for the poor. Famine, sickness and unemployment force Robert to enlist, and Wordsworth's 'tale of silent suffering' records how Margaret and her child languished while awaiting his return. For Wordsworth, who wrote this part of *The Excursion* in 1797, Margaret's experience was 'a common tale'. Hunt most likely follows Wordsworth when he goes on, in 'Victory of Waterloo', to contemplate those who survived:

– What is the happiness that is struck dead, to the misery that is left alive? – What is it all to the fatherless, the childless, the husbandless? – to the mind's eye haunted with faces it shall never see again, – to voices missed in the circle, – to vacant seats at table, – to widowed wakings in the morning, with the loved one never more to be in that bed? – But, – no further.
     We check ourselves here, for our own sakes, and for the sake of others.

In protest literature passages like this are directed against complacent generals and their political masters: Hunt's own *Captain Sword and Captain Pen* is a fine example. While *The Excursion* places Margaret's tragedy in a frame of Christian consolation, 'with soul / Fixed on the Cross', Hunt turns in the *Examiner* to a different providential design:

We bow before the PROVIDENCE, which, if it seems to have resolved that a portion of evil in this world should be unavoidable, perhaps for ever, has filled us with patiences and with hopes, for which our sense of its wisdom and our consciousness that the world is upon the whole much happier than otherwise, are our securities. In the speculations that seem most to baffle us regarding good and evil, and the origin of human actions, there is one thing infinitely consoling, which is sure to grow brighter as our sorrow in other respects grows dark, – and that is, a charity towards *all* our fellow creatures, not one excepted. We even begin to think at last, that we are all included in some grand scheme of happiness, which the experience of sorrow in one world is necessary to make us enjoy to the full in another . . .[2]

There were Christian overtones to this, although Hunt's beliefs were far from orthodox. Those references to 'the PROVIDENCE' and 'some grand scheme of happiness' have a deist ring, while the brightening effects of 'human actions' and 'charity towards *all*' show that Hunt continued to draw on Elhanan Winchester's Universalism. Waterloo was one reason for Hunt's need to balance 'evil in this world', another was his own recent crisis about life's purpose. Patience and hope growing from 'unavoidable evil' were signs of the universal 'Beneficence' Hunt later described in *Christianism* and *The Religion of the Heart*.

For the former student of Enfield School, John Keats, Hunt's *Examiner* articles on Waterloo were essential reading – and may have seeded some of Keats's later conjectures about life as 'the vale of Soul-making'. Hunt's claims that 'sorrow in one world is necessary' and that human understanding 'grow[s] brighter as our sorrow . . . grows dark' resemble Keats's idea of life as a 'gradually darken'd' process of 'sharpening one's vision into the heart and nature of Man – of convincing ones nerves that the World is full of Misery and Heartbreak, Pain, Sickness and oppression'.[3] Keats shares Hunt's emphasis on suffering and the growth of consciousness, and he echoes Hunt in speculating that pain is a necessary part of a 'grander system of salvation than the chrystain religion'. 'Do you not see how necessary a World of Pains and troubles is to school an Intelligence and make it a soul,' Keats writes in April 1819.[4] These words have often been regarded as uniquely Keats's vision of life, but it seems likely that they represent just one of many instances when Hunt's thoughts were absorbed and elaborated – consciously or otherwise – by younger writers. Hunt had already invented Wordsworth as the leading poet of the age. In 1815 he was starting to shape the next generation.

July saw the English man–of–war *Bellerophon*, with Napoleon on board, put into Plymouth Sound. People from all over the country dashed to Plymouth where hundreds of little boats, crowded to the gunnels, put out in hope of ahoying Boney. And there he was! strolling on deck with hands folded behind him, thickset, bronzed and glossy in complexion, attired in a plain green coat with a red collar, white waistcoat and pantaloons, high boots, gold epaulettes, a silver star on his chest. He took out a small eyeglass and surveyed the coast-line and the house and gardens at Mount Edgcumbe.[5] So this was Bonaparte, 'five feet four inches high, well made, stout withal, and a little round shoul-dered'? Well, not entirely. For Byron, Bonaparte was the heroic survivor, 'last single Captive to millions in war'. He would return when Liberty revived in France, and in the interim Byron would play 'The grand Napoleon of the realms of rhyme'.[6] Napoleon had so 'imposed' on the nation's imagination that he remained an awesome presence much as, in Hazlitt's view, the gods of clas-sical mythology continued to exist for poets 'as if they had really been'. Appearing in the *Examiner* a few pages after the sightings of Napoleon, Hazlitt's essay on Milton's *Lycidas* evoked an elegiac music of 'passion', 'tender gloom' and 'serious reflections' appropriate to the Emperor's forlorn grandeur. That Napoleon could retain his former stature, at least in imagination, was suggested by Hazlitt's vision of the Titans in their unfallen glory: 'as we shape towers and men and armed steeds out of the broken clouds that glitter in the distant horizon, so throned above the ruins of the ancient world Jupiter still nods sublime on the top of blue Olympus, Hercules leans upon his club, Apollo has not laid aside his bow, nor Neptune his trident'.[7] Perhaps this haunting passage helped shape Keats's *Hyperion* poems, in which the wars of the Titans and Olympians foreshadow the rise and fall of earthly empires.

Less momentous departures in summer 1815 emphasised the passing of gener-ations. Samuel Whitbread's suicide on 6 July removed one of the most vocal friends of liberty in the House of Commons. Whitbread had been among Fox's allies in the 1790s, and a reformer, abolitionist and opponent of the war ever since. Joshua Toulmin, the Unitarian contemporary of Joseph Priestley and Richard Price, died aged seventy-four on 23 July. For nearly forty years Toulmin was minister at Mary Street Unitarian chapel, Taunton, where young Coleridge had preached in 1797. His passing was noticed by the *Examiner* in an obituary reprinted from John Marriott's *Taunton Courier*. Maurice Margarot was among the Friends of Liberty transported to Botany Bay after the Scottish treason trials of 1794, and the only one to return. He died on 11 November 1815, leaving a widow for whom the *Examiner* helped organise a subscription.[8] Another shock would follow within a year. Hunt marked the death of Sheridan on 7 July 1816 with an obituary recalling his heyday in the world of Burke, Fox and Pitt, Goldsmith, Johnson and Reynolds: 'he was a man of wit, a lively and elegant dramatist, a winning and powerful orator, a sound politician, a lover of real freedom, a careless liver; an Irishman, in short'.[9] Poor Sherry. Careless liver said it all.

Waterloo. Napoleon exiled. Eminent contemporaries dead. Following these transitions the tendency of events became more difficult to ascertain. During autumn 1815 Hunt's articles on the 'Gloomy State of France' provided a holdall for news and rumours on 'the mutability of the present state of things'. The second Peace of Paris on 20 November was a landmark in a period of 'mysterious and angry cast' but otherwise 'barren of news'. As Hunt surveyed the European scene he sensed Napoleon's continuing presence – 'the age, in some way or other, still feels that he lives' – and predicted that his influence would act and react on European politics for years to come. Reports that an insurrection on Barbados had been viciously suppressed came as a reminder that the end of the slave trade in 1807 had not put an end to slavery in the British colonies.[10]

Hunt's need to see life in terms of an inclusive 'scheme of happiness' reflected on his own situation in 1815. Release from prison had proved unexpectedly troubling, and paying the £500 fine snared him in chaotic business arrangements with publishers. In 1814 he had published *The Feast of the Poets* with James Cawthorn, raising at least £50. Then, wanting the remaining money for the fine, he agreed a £450 package with Gale, Curtis and Fenner to publish *The Story of Rimini*, with *The Descent of Liberty* and a new edition of *The Feast* thrown in to sweeten the deal.[11] So far, so good – he had raised the fine by his own efforts, and had no need to rely on subscriptions or donations. But, as usual, there were complications. Hunt seems to have forgotten that in May 1813 he had already agreed with Cawthorn for 'a work in hand', *The Story of Rimini*. And progress on the poem had not been as anticipated. By December 1815 Gale, Curtis and Fenner closed their option on *Rimini*; delivery was three months overdue, and what they had seen of the poem was 'not nearly so long as what was engaged for'.[12] While retaining *The Descent of Liberty* and *The Feast* they demanded the return of their advance, leaving Hunt with no publisher for *Rimini* and owing £450.

This was a 'dog's trick' – and it came on top of other embarrassments. Hunt already owed Sir John Swinburne £100 and a lesser sum to Haydon who had himself recently borrowed from a money-lender. In September, unable to cover family expenses and make a first repayment to Gale and Fenner, Hunt requested £200 from Henry Brougham – or any 'rich person' Brougham might know – in a 'talking & rambling' account of his circumstances. Having rejected Brougham's helpful suggestion concerning the juror who had offered to pay the fine, this was an extremely difficult letter to write. Hunt refers ruefully to his 'lofty' refusal of the money, but admits that his situation is now 'very different'. He might be 'not very thoughtful on money matters', but he has sensed that Byron's seemingly 'fine indifference' to giving and lending might not extend to money (Hunt was right in this, as time would tell). Perhaps Brougham could persuade Lord Essex to help bail him out?[13]

Essex was a young Whig, a friend of Byron's on the Drury Lane Theatre committee. Such a man might be expected to be sympathetic, but the request nevertheless represents a dramatic, though not altogether surprising lapse in Hunt's principles. Hunt suspects that, in money matters, he has been 'playing a sort of vain part to my own mind' and failing to subdue his 'distaste to business' (those are John Hunt's words).[14] The glimmer of understanding is brief. With an 'enough of this', Hunt turns to his 'poem in hand – the Story of Rimini' – and winds up his letter with a P.S. notifying Brougham of his address: '*Mr Hunter's, Vale of Health, Hampstead*'.

Financial insecurity was forcing Hunt into the role of dependant, with all the burdens that had weighed upon his parents thirty years before. This was one family likeness he had long sought to avoid, and from now on his business negotiations over loans and debts would become increasingly tortuous. These labyrinthine trails arose from inept accounting and thoughtlessness with money, but they were also Hunt's way of concealing his compromised independence from himself. Haplessness became a defence strategy; 'playing a vain part to my own mind' was a way of not admitting he had been brought to the same desperate circumstances as his father.

Brougham replied that it was 'out of his power' to lend money – 'every one connected with *land* is at present more or less embarrassed'. Byron he thought 'in very great difficulties' – his marriage was in crisis, and he was seriously in debt – but Lord Essex was 'an exception'. Hunt should write to him, explain his needs, and mention Brougham's name as a personal reference.[15] We don't know if Hunt followed up this suggestion, but Gale and Fenner had by now issued writs against Hunt and his brother John, who had stood as security on the bill. With considerable trouble the money was 'scraped together' and £200 returned to the publisher. Although they were satisfied for the moment, Hunt was of course still in debt. Fortunately a relative stepped in to help, and in October the Hunts moved once more to Hampstead, settling at a cottage in the Vale of Health leased to them by Rowland Hunter.

To the north of Hampstead hill is a valley or hollow on the edge of the Heath – exactly the kind of enclosing landscape Hunt enjoyed feeling 'wrapped up' in. Originally called 'Gangmoor' or 'Hatchett's Bottom', this area was a swampy, malarial wasteland until 1777 when it was drained. A reservoir was constructed, parish almshouses were built, and paupers, laundry-women, squatters and the local sweep moved in. At some time there were tanning pits and a varnish factory here – probably because the stink from both of those enterprises was intolerable closer to Hampstead village.[16] By 1802 the area had been optimistically renamed the Vale of Health, and when Hunt arrived there late in 1815 there was a small cluster of buildings. Development would continue through the nineteenth century, and the Vale became a fashionable suburban enclave that over the years has attracted writers such as D. H. Lawrence, Rabindranath Tagore, Edgar Wallace, John Middleton Murry, Stella

Gibbons and Sir Compton Mackenzie, the painter Muirhead Bone and pianist Alfred Brendel. The bohemian associations began with Hunt but, with several cottages claimed as his, locating exactly where he lived is now difficult. I walked through the Vale on a hot day in May. It was just past noon, silent, and deserted except for an elderly woman sitting in a dark doorway, patiently tearing up old newspapers and so covered with ink she seemed like a goddess of newsprint. She pointed my way around a corner, along a pathway full of foxgloves and elderflower blossom, to where a later building hung with wistaria stands on the site.

Hunt's home was one of the little weatherboarded cottages built at the Vale for summer living, 'the first one that fronts the valley' when viewed from Caen Wood (see illustrations).[17] Its modest rooms would have to accommodate Hunt, Marianne, Bess, three children and their toys, servants, visitors, books, busts, the portraits of Milton and John Hunt, the flute, the lute, sheet music, sewing materials and sculpting tools, back copies of the *Examiner*, an old sofa and chairs, beds and linen, portfolios of engravings, manuscripts, and the magnificent rocking-horse. Hunt established his library and study in a small parlour with just room enough for two people, a piano, some pictures and books. Surrounding the cottage were the washing lines and bleaching lawns used by the laundry-women.

Poetry was now uppermost in his mind, particularly the need to finish and publish *Rimini* – if a publisher could be found. During the summer Byron had praised some draft passages, and in October Hunt sent him the manuscript of the third canto. Byron read it closely, pencilling detailed comments and suggestions alongside Hunt's text. He praised the conception and originality of the writing, and its 'frequent & great happiness of expression'.[18] The opening lines, dating from Hunt's 'caged hours' in prison, he thought 'Very Very good'; Paulo's reveries about Francesca –

> Silence her gentleness before him brought,
> Society her sense, reading her books,
> Music her voice, every sweet thing her looks

– were 'Beautiful', and Francesca's passionate countenance –

> And then she only spoke more sweetly to him,
> And found her failing eyes gave looks that melted through him.

– was 'Superlative'.[19] Byron admired passages where Hunt was 'true to Nature', and found fault with 'occasional quaintness – & obscurity – & a kind of harsh & yet colloquial compounding of epithets'.[20] Among the instances Byron identified were 'The worst of Giovanni', to which he commented:

'Colloquial – say "sin" of –'. The hints of likeness between Giovanni and Paulo '– an air / At times, a cheek, a colour of the hair' were undeniably quaint, and Byron suggested '"a colour of the cheek or hair –" or in lieu of "cheek" "a smile"'. Contrasting the brothers, Hunt had written 'the one / Was somewhat stouter, 't'other finelier spun', cluttering the line with t's and suggesting that Giovanni's physique was 'stouter spun' than his brother. Byron corrected this to 'the one / Was more robust, the other finelier spun'. Hunt's first thought that Paulo should have 'a nose of taste' met with a firm rebuff: 'Say Grecian – Roman – what you will – but not "of taste".'[21] Returning the manuscript, Byron predicted the poem would bring Hunt 'a very high station – but where is the Conclusion? – don't let it cool in the composition?'[22]

Byron's suggestions formed part of an ongoing creative exchange that fed into Byron's work on his own poem, *Parisina*, which shared Hunt's theme of incestuous love. Hunt believed *The Story of Rimini* supplied the sleep-talking 'incident' in *Parisina*; Byron's characters Azo (Parisina's husband) and his bastard son Hugo (Parisina's incestuous lover) appear in Hunt's poem among 'the finest warriors of the court' at Ravenna.[23] The two poems about forbidden love grew towards publication together, although Byron's remarks had gone to the heart of Hunt's stylistic experiments. He accepted just two of Byron's suggestions – 'more robust, the other finelier' went in, and Paulo acquired a 'graceful nose' – and then turned aside from work on the fourth canto to write Byron 'hearty thanks' and defend his 'attempt to bring back an idiomatic spirit in verse'.

Hunt argues that 'modern poetry' is marred by adopting 'sophisticated phrases of *written* language' instead of 'the *spoken* language' of 'real feeling'. He commends the 'nativeness of feeling' and 'nativeness of language' in Ariosto's poetry and *King Lear* – a claim which might appear 'presumptuously spoken', he tells Byron, had it not been 'spoken with far-off reverence'.[24] Had Byron come across 'far-off reverence' in the *Rimini* manuscript he would most likely have scored it through as an unfortunate 'colloquial compounding'. In the intimate space of Hunt's letter, however, it demonstrates how the 'spoken' language of feeling necessarily embraces such irregularities. *The Story of Rimini* embarks on the daring strategy of bringing that language to poetry.

Hunt's idea of an 'idiomatic' poetic voice resembled Wordsworth's *Lyrical Ballads*, and in a longer view represented a Romantic revaluation of the natural over eighteenth-century neoclassical aesthetics. Writing in the *Spectator* in 1712, Joseph Addison had declared that phrases used in conversation 'contract a kind of Meanness by passing through the Mouths of the Vulgar', and poets should 'guard against Idiomatick ways of Speaking'. Samuel Johnson originated the word 'colloquial' in the *Rambler* (1751/2), associating it with 'barbarisms' that must be purified out of the language. An elevated poetic language formed a cultural stronghold against 'the Vulgar' – that is, common people and vernacular speech.

By Johnson's time the language of feeling was one of the most thrilling developments of the literature of sensibility, and Thomas Warton was opening the way for a new poetry of 'native' experiences. Just two decades after Johnson confounded the colloquial with the barbaric, Robert Burns made an over-whelmingly successful bid for acclaim by flaunting those qualities. Burns's *Poems, Written Chiefly in the Scottish Dialect* announced an 'obscure, name-less Bard', 'unacquainted' with what was required 'for commencing Poet by rule' and unashamed to 'sing the sentiments and manners, he felt and saw in himself and his rustic compeers around him, in his and their native language'.[25] Having set the terms on which he should be read, Burns must have been gratified by the reviews: 'native genius bursting through the obscurity of poverty'; 'artless and unadorned . . . flowing . . . from the native feelings of the heart'; 'the force of native humour'; 'native brilliancy'; 'true effusions of genius . . . a power which nothing can bestow, save native soundness'.[26]

When Hunt wrote to Byron thirty years later recommending 'nativeness of feeling' and 'nativeness of language' he encapsulated the spontaneity and naturalism that had gathered into a Romantic revolution in poetry. Instead of looking north to Burns's Scotland and Wordsworth's Lake District, Hunt turned south to invoke the lyrical charm of the Italians. With Shakespeare and Ariosto as allies, Hunt felt bolstered against Byron's criticisms – all of which he took in good part. Byron warmed to the 'originality – & Italianism' of *Rimini*, but remained wary of the 'compounding' of language in Burns and in Hunt.[27] The ideal of natural poetry was an issue on which Hunt and Byron would never see eye to eye.

October passed and Hunt was still without a prospect of seeing *The Story of Rimini* in print. He closed his letter to Byron by asking, in 'reverential style', if he would mention the poem now 'drawing to a close' to John Murray.[28] Paradoxically the fine for his independent journalism in the *Examiner* was now obliging him to seek an establishment publisher. It was seven years since Hunt had declined to contribute to Murray's *Quarterly Review*, and this was an approach that needed a powerful intermediary. Who better than the most famous poet of the day? Byron was already helping Coleridge negotiate with Murray to publish 'Christabel,' and he acted on Hunt's request immediately.

Publishing was in John Murray's blood. He was a highly experienced busi-nessman, and an expert in gauging public taste. In politics he was a staunch conservative, but he had long admired Hunt's theatricals, and Byron's recom-mendation helped. By 4 November Murray had indicated his 'willingness to treat'. Byron let Hunt know, and hastened to reinforce his position by praising *Rimini* to Murray as 'a very wonderful & beautiful performance', 'the *safest* thing you ever engaged in' – Byron knew the man he was dealing with.[29] Hunt forwarded the manuscript complete with Byron's annotations, and Murray read it 'with particular attention'. He could see that *Rimini* was 'peculiar' and unlike anything he had published before. It might take with the public, but there were risks. He proceeded cautiously, aware that Hunt and Byron were concerting this approach – offending Hunt might alienate Byron, with incalculable losses to the house. Then, on 18 December, Hunt wrote to Murray proposing an advance of £450–£500 for the poem, adding breezily that this was 'a sum I happen to want just now'. Unfortunately for Hunt, 'happening to want' exerted no leverage with so shrewd a publisher – on those terms *Rimini* would be an 'extensive speculation', presupposing Byronic sales. But Murray understood exactly how to proceed, and on 27 December Hunt received a reply. The publisher was 'fearful' of venturing the sum he so desperately needed, and invited him to approach other publishers. Then, drastically whittling down Hunt's expectations, Murray went on to suggest a 'trial' edition of 500–750 copies, with the profits split between them and the copyright to return to Hunt after the first edition. This meant that Hunt stood to gain from any second and subsequent editions 'in case the work turn out a prize, as it may do'. Murray copied this letter to Byron, assuring him of his 'anxious desire to serve Mr. Hunt', trusting to His Lordship's 'usual kindness', and regretting that 'as a mere matter of business' he was unable to accept Hunt's 'offer' of *Rimini* for £450. Hunt replied to Murray immediately, agreeing his proposals as 'not at all wanting in liberality, especially under the impression you have of it, as being an experiment'.[30] By playing on Hunt's financial insecurity and his poetic ambitions, Murray had secured *Rimini* on realistic and not ungenerous terms, while dangling the possibility that it had the makings of a bestseller. The poem would appear in an edition of 750 copies, and in the same octavo format as Byron's poems.

By 1 February *The Story of Rimini* was in proofs, and Hunt expected the book itself in a few days.[31] Based on fifty lines in Canto V of *The Inferno*, Hunt's poem tells the human story behind Francesca's revelation to Dante that her love for Paolo survives even in Hell.

Canto I opens on a bright, breezy May morning in Ravenna. Crowds gather in the streets and squares, until with a 'start of trumpets' Guido, Duke of Ravenna, enters with his daughter awaiting the arrival of Duke Giovanni of Rimini, her 'husband yet to see'. She is to be his bride in a political marriage of convenience. 'And hard it is, she thinks, to have no will' as she submits to her father's designs and the pomp and pageantry of the occasion. After a colourful procession a 'glorious figure springs into the square' – amid the shouting and reeling air he displays 'cool mastery' of his 'haughty steed'. All that she sees of this Prince 'is sufficient for the destined bride'.[32] The canto is full of movement, sound, light and colour, human figures and animals – all arranged in suggestive contrasts between liberty and constraint. In this way Hunt cleverly interweaves passages of lively description with the psychological and emotional states of his protagonists.

The first canto ends on a bright note, with the Princess and Prince exchanging looks of 'sweet gravity' and 'touched respect'. When we turn the page to Canto II, however, something is 'amiss'. There is no 'bridal feast'. Hunt's purpose now is a brisk revelation of what has really gone on:

> The truth was this: – The bridegroom had not come,
> But sent his brother, proxy in his room.[33]

The Princess's father has made this arrangement to clinch the match with 'proud' Giovanni, but he was unprepared for his daughter falling in love with the proxy bridegroom. Paulo

>   was a creature
> Formed in the very poetry of nature,
> The effect was perfect, and the future wife
> Caught in the elaborate snare, perhaps for life.[34]

Hunt's concern is what Guido's and Giovanni's plot represents: political and patriarchal coercion, from which there is 'no appeal'. His first sketch of the poem in 1811 had opened on a note of overt protest about courtly corruption and 'smitten royalty'; now Hunt's message is more subtly conveyed through the interaction of individuals, their looks and gestures, and the destructive consequences of the 'elaborate snare'.

The marriage rites are quickly over. Money is 'scattered' to the 'mob'. This mockery of 'largess' is in keeping with what we now know is a 'show' marriage, and contrasts with the first canto's profusion of 'scattery light' and colour. So far, the second canto has noticed only one such detail – it occurs just after the marriage, when

> The proxy, turning midst the general hush,
> Kissed her meek lips, betwixt a rosy blush.[35]

As evening draws in, the Princess leaves the 'dear scenery' of Ravenna to journey through 'piny labyrinths' to Rimini:

>   – a fall of chains, –
> The bride has entered, – not a voice remains; –
> Night, and a maiden silence, wrap the plains.[36]

All of this second canto was written in Surrey Gaol. As he begins the third, Hunt explains that he writes to 'cheer' his 'caged hours' with thoughts of 'things far hence', and that in doing so he has discovered

– more than what it first designed, –
How little upon earth our home we find,
Or close the intended course of erring human kind.[37]

Writing the poem has revealed how much of life is an 'elaborate snare', that
'a fall of chains' encumbers apparently free choices and decisions. In this way
Hunt empathises in a peculiarly intimate way with the Princess's isolation.
Bitter disappointment follows her discovery of her true situation:

The shock, that told this lovely, trusting heart,
That she had given, beyond all power to part,
Her hope, belief, love, passion, to one brother,
Possession (oh, the misery!) to another![38]

While locked in loveless marriage with her 'possessor' Giovanni, she whiles
away hours in Paulo's company. Only now, as intimacy grows between them,
do we learn that the Princess is called Francesca. They eventually meet at her
pavilion in the 'green garden' surrounding the palace, and Hunt's narrative
quickens in tracing the lovers' passionate 'action of mind':

There's apt to be, at conscious times like these,
An affectation of a bright-eyed ease,
An air of something quite serene and sure,
As if to seem so, was to be, secure:
With this the lovers met, with this they spoke . . .[39]

Hunt's light touch creates complex effects. 'There's apt to be', for example,
chattily hesitating between 'likely to be' and a more knowing 'all too likely to
be', hints at the fluttering pulses behind Paulo and Francesca's 'bright-eyed
ease'. The lovers, meanwhile, concentrate on the appearance of calm, 'As if
to seem so, was to be, secure'. Reading 'Launcelot of the Lake, a bright
romance', they set eyes on a situation that mirrors their own:

As thus they sat, and felt with leaps of heart
Their colour change, they came upon the part
Where fond Geneura, with her flame long nurst,
Smiled upon Launcelot when he kissed her first: –
That touch, at last, through every fibre slid;
And Paulo turned, scarce knowing what he did,
Only he felt he could no more dissemble,
And kissed her, mouth to mouth, all in a tremble.
Sad were those hearts, and sweet was that long kiss:
Sacred be love from sight, whate'er it is.

> The world was all forgot, the struggle o'er,
> Desperate the joy. – That day they read no more.[40]

This is the end of Canto III. Hunt echoes the moment in *Paradise Lost* when Adam and Eve are cast out into wilderness: 'The world was all before them' (XII. 646), Milton had written, and it is a world well forgotten, Hunt suggests, as Paulo and Francesca discover paradise in each other's arms. The rest is left to the reader's imagination – and it is part of Hunt's design that at the fatal climax of the poem we should identify with the lovers. Canto IV traces their outward calm and inner pangs, until Francesca's sleep-talking alerts Giovanni. In the ensuing duel Paulo impales himself on his brother's sword, and Francesca dies broken-hearted. At the close of autumn they are returned in death to Ravenna, and

> buried in one grave, under a tree.
> There side by side, and hand in hand, they lay
> In the green ground: – and on fine nights in May
> Young hearts betrothed used to go there to pray.

'What will survive of us is love'. The final line of Philip Larkin's 'An Arundel Tomb' is anticipated by the closing triplet of *The Story of Rimini*, in which Paulo and Francesca's tragedy is gathered into continuing renewals of love and life.[41]

The Story of Rimini is structurally satisfying as a narrative, opening with the springtime pageant of Paulo's arrival at Ravenna and closing with a funeral cortège and an autumnal landscape. Hunt looked back on the poem as 'a true picture, painted after a certain mode', and we can see his dramatic sense and the painterly influence of West, Haydon and Wilkie in his mastery of verbal scenes. He writes with flair and enjoyment in describing the crowd, Paulo's arrival, Francesca's journey to Rimini, and their passionate meeting in the green garden. These brisk, colourful passages are balanced by the emotional and imaginative insight with which Hunt portrays the lovers.

The Story of Rimini is an artful poem about artful behaviour, in which the malign intrigue of the two dukes is doubled and answered by the gentler dissimulation of the lovers – simultaneously transgressive and a discovery of truth. Throughout the poem Hunt's 'free and idiomatic cast of language' responds to inflections of speech under 'natural impulses' of feeling, and attunes the poem to 'real life'.[42] Hunt loosens the rhyming couplets to enable a 'freer spirit of versification' and brings his poem closer to the rhythms and music of spoken English – although it has to be said that the dialogue often falls short of this ideal. So, where Pope's couplets are frequently end-stopped and enclosed, Hunt's sentences flow through successive couplets; whereas Pope usually places the caesura, or pause, in the middle of the line, Hunt's practice is more varied. These linguistic and formal innovations overlap with the poem's wider questioning of authority: recommending a more universal understanding than Dante's 'melancholy theology', Hunt affirms human feelings – we might now say human rights – against institutions of 'authorized selfishness', whether social, political, sexual or religious. The spirit of the poem, in Hunt's view, is 'tolerant and reconciling', looking to the *first* causes of misfortune' by way of seeing 'the danger of confounding forms with justice . . . and making guilt by mistaking innocence'.[43] This, of course, is no help to Paulo and Francesca: ensnared by Guido, Giovanni, and things as they are, their tragedy is unavoidable. But what alternative world did Hunt seek to bring about? Presumably one in which human lives are no longer coerced and mutilated by codes of 'authorized' behaviour and threats of damnation. We can see how this coincides with Hunt's public stance as a journalist and with his Universalist outlook, but we need also to understand how the poem might be related to his personal circumstances and misfortunes. What compelled him to keep writing the poem over four years, two of them spent in prison?

For Hunt, composing *The Story of Rimini* was a 'comfort' – but how exactly did the story of Francesca and Paulo help him address his own situation?[44] He began the poem at Hastings to 'steady' a mood of extreme happiness, and four years later it may have helped him contain the feelings of distress that followed his release from prison. Throughout, its composition reflected on his personal life – most obviously in the way the triangle linking Francesca with the brothers Giovanni and Paulo mirrored his relationship with two sisters, Marianne and Bess. One relationship in each triangle is authorised by marriage, the other deemed illicit. In his poem Hunt tries to resolve the tension between intractable institutions and the claims of human feeling, risking what he recognised as 'the danger of *progressiveness* in love-matters'. In this Hunt joins other sexual revolutionaries of the Romantic era like William Blake, William Godwin, Mary Wollstonecraft, Lord Byron and Percy Shelley in advocating more flexible, open relationships.[45] Less extreme than Blake, less dogmatic than Godwin and Shelley, less strident than Mary Wollstonecraft, less callous than Byron, Hunt reverts to the middle ground of humanity – the crowd – whose marriages survive through patience, persistence and, sometimes, by accommodating 'unauthorized' arrangements between 'family-partners'. When Edmund Blunden surveyed Hunt's determination to marry Marianne instead of her sister Bess, he suggested Hunt was 'the loser by the decision through half a century of an unequal compact'.[46] Blunden's grim surmise overlooks how Hunt and Marianne's long marriage coexisted with the relationship between Hunt and Bess. This isn't to deny that there were difficulties and emotional storms, or to overlook that in 1816 Bess attempted to commit suicide and in the 1830s threatened to do so again.[47] What we can say is that their lives represent one of many brave, often overlooked efforts to realise a more humane and inclusive survival of love.

The Story of Rimini was soon in circulation. On 14 February 1816 Murray sent a dozen copies to Hunt and one each to Byron, Barron Field and Walter Scott. Field responded immediately, praising the 'poetical philosophy' that 'found out the soul of goodness in things evil' and predicting 'a higher seat in the heaven of poetry than Lord Byron'. Thomas Mitchell abandoned his classical studies to applaud the 'powerful effect' of colloquial language; Charles Lamb pronounced the third canto his 'particular favorite'. Byron continued active on Hunt's behalf, declaring the poem 'a devilish good one' and urging Moore to 'set it up before the public eye where it ought to be'. As usual, Haydon surpassed them all: 'my soul is cut in two – and every nerve about me pierced with trembling needles . . . it will establish your genius'.[48]

Reviews praised Hunt's originality. The *Dublin Examiner*, the *Monthly* and the *Eclectic* continued favourably disposed: while doubting the poem's morality they judged it successful in giving passionate language 'a human tone' with 'refreshing vigour'. The *Eclectic* commended 'the easy graceful style of familiar narrative'. Others hesitated over anything that might be construed as 'vulgar', showing that Addison's strictures continued to have currency; the *Monthly*, for example, regretted that '"*A pin-drop silence*" is a milliner's phrase.' In their laboriously sarcastic review for the *Quarterly* – a Tory journal published by Murray – John Wilson Croker and William Gifford exaggerated the traits of Hunt's style to find '*mere vulgarisms* and *fugitive phrases*' and 'an unauthorised, chaotic jargon' in 'every page'.[49] Hunt, who had chastised the 'peevish' Gifford in *The Feast of the Poets*, dismissed the remarks as 'mere foaming at the mouth', but he would not forget them and remained convinced that the poem would have encountered no hostility 'if politics had not judged it'.[50] CCC went into print in a 'fisty-cuffish' pamphlet that rebutted the Croker/Gifford review as 'a tissue of falsehood . . . full as malicious as inconsequent'.[51] But worse was to follow when the 'Cockney School' essays in *Blackwood's Magazine* described Hunt as 'the secret and invidious foe of virtue'. The idea that Hunt was a Satanic infiltrator was linked to his racial 'otherness': the colourful textures of his writing masked an 'unhealthy' and 'jaundiced' conspiracy to 'pollute' the nation. Hunt and *Rimini* were like a tropical plague infecting Englishness and – worse still – the poem's dedication had transgressed 'over the bounds of birth and education' to be 'familiar with a LORD'.[52]

Byron had been among Hunt's first visitors in prison. He had provided books about Italy, read and commented on drafts of *The Story of Rimini*, and helped place it with John Murray. When Byron returned a final extract on 29 January 1816, Hunt responded immediately with a fulsome dedication:

TO
THE RIGHT HONOURABLE
LORD BYRON.

MY DEAR BYRON,

    You see what you have brought yourself to by liking my verses. It is taking you unawares, I allow; but you yourself have set example now-a-days of poet's dedicating to poet; and it is under that nobler title, as well as the still nobler one of friend, that I now address you.

    I shall be thought indeed by some to write a very singular dedication, when I say that I should not have written it you at all, had I not thought the poem capable of standing on its own ground. I am far from insensible of your approbation of it, as you well know, and as your readers will easily imagine; but I have an ambition, at the same time, to have credit given me for a proper spirit; and in fact, as I should be dissatisfied with my poetry without the one, I should never have thought my friendship worth your acceptance without the other.

    Having thus, – with sufficient care, I am afraid, – vindicated my fellow-dignity, and put on my laurel in meeting you publicly, I take it off again with a still greater regard for those unceremonious and unpretending humanities of private intercourse, of which you know so handsomely how to set the example; and professing to be nothing more, in that sphere, than a hearty admirer of what is generous, and enjoyer of what is frank and social, am, with great truth,

My dear BYRON,

affectionately yours,

LEIGH HUNT.

Hampstead,
January 29, 1816.

Hostile critics read this letter as a shocking breach of social etiquette, although its personal terms were identical to those in Wordsworth's recent dedication of his *Poems* to Sir George Beaumont. No one had censured Wordsworth's attempt to be 'familiar with a BARONET', and the political motives for attacking Hunt were obvious. In fact, Hunt's wish to be credited with a 'proper spirit' was an attempt to *resist* familiarity and obligation in order to establish his 'own ground' as a poet, much as he had done as a reviewer and editor. In this 'singular dedication' Hunt pays tribute to his friend's example and achievement, while offering himself as a poet of 'fellow-dignity' whose work is 'capable of standing'.

When Byron received his copy of the poem, he read and accepted the dedication 'as a public compliment & a private kindness', adding:

I am only sorry that it may perhaps operate against you – as an inducement & with some a pretext – for attack – on the part of the political and personal enemies of both: – not that this can be of much consequence – for in the end the work must be judged by it's merits – & in that respect you are well armed. – Murray tells me it is going on well – [53]

By now the collapse of Byron's marriage was public knowledge, and he had reason to be grateful for Hunt's admiration and friendship. On 15 January Annabella had left Piccadilly Terrace with their one-month-old daughter Ada. It soon became clear that they would not return. Within days rumours were circulating about the treatment of Lady Byron, along with allegations of incest and homosexuality. Byron's friend Hobhouse was aware that such charges 'struck at the very existence of Lord Byron as a member of society'; Tom Moore's friend Mary Godfrey wrote: 'The world are loud against him, and vote him a worthless profligate . . . He is completely lost in the opinion of the world.'[54] Byron summed up his situation in a letter to his wife: 'my name has been as completely blasted as if it were branded on my forehead: – this may appear to you exaggeration – it is not so – there are reports which once circulated not even falsehood – or their most admitted & acknowledged false-hood – can neutralize – which no contradiction can obliterate – nor conduct cancel'.[55] Alert to the vagaries of public reputation, Murray was anxious that he had printed too many copies of *The Siege of Corinth* and *Parasina*, and that, as Byron had guessed, Hunt's poem would be tainted by association. But Murray nevertheless agreed at Byron's request to print for private circu-lation fifty copies of two poems on the separation: the heart-seared lyric 'Fare Thee Well!' addressed to Annabella –

> Fare thee well! and if for ever –
> Still for ever, fare *thee* well—
> Even though unforgiving, never
> 'Gainst thee shall my heart rebel . . .

– and 'A Sketch from Private Life', bitterly attacking Annabella's maid, Mary Jane Clermont who Byron believed had been scheming against him.

Amid this destructive public quarrel Hunt and Byron maintained close, cordial relations, and it is clear that Hunt was sticking by his friend as Byron had supported him in prison. In the *Examiner* Hunt placed Byron first in a list of 'Men of Talent in Parliament', distinguished for his 'acknowledged genius, and . . . keen insight into human nature'. He looked to Byron to 'speak oftener' in the House of Lords, and to Henry Brougham in the Commons 'to play a prominent part in the management of his country' (ironically, these two allies of Hunt's would soon be bitter opponents, with Brougham supporting Lady Byron over the separation).[56] Hunt made several visits to

Byron, encountering Hobhouse, Scrope Davies and Campbell, and on one
occasion overheard Coleridge reciting 'Kubla Khan' to the demon lover of
Piccadilly Terrace.[57] Byron reciprocated by sending Hunt tickets for Drury
Lane – 'they are for best place in the house' – and invited Hunt to 'stay here
for a day or two . . . I can give you here bachelor's fare – & room – &
welcome.'[58]

Hunt's 'very candid' assessment of the separation in *Lord Byron and some of
his Contemporaries*, published in 1828, would be maligned in the reviews for
'going public' about a former friendship. But its recollection that Byron had
been 'disconcerted' by the separation and 'felt [it] severely' was true to Hunt's
perception of him early in 1816. Similarly, Hunt's suggestion that the Byrons
had been capable of living on 'good terms' – although utterly unsuited to
each other – presented a fair account of the situation.[59] While Hunt's opinion
of Byron had changed by the mid-1820s, he held tenaciously to his original
impressions of him.

Byron's separation from his wife was agreed and signed on 21 April, a Sunday.
On that day the *Examiner* published 'Distressing Circumstance in Private
Life', Hunt's forthright defence of Byron against 'monstrous' accusations:

> We have the honour of knowing the Noble Poet, and as friendship is the
> first of principles in our theory, involving as it does the final purposes of
> all virtue itself, we do not scruple to confess, that whatever silence we may
> have thought ourselves bound to keep with regard to qualities which he
> could not have possessed, had he been such as the scandal-mongers repre-
> sented him, we should nevertheless . . . have stood by him and his misfor-
> tunes to the last. But knowing him as we do, one fact at least we are
> acquainted with; and that is, that these reckless calumniators know nothing
> about the matter.[60]

Beneath Hunt's article the *Examiner* reprinted 'Fare thee well' and an
innocuous extract from 'A Sketch'. Two days later Byron left London for
the last time and took his new Napoleonic carriage to Dover. He crossed to
Ostend on a journey that would take him to Brussels, the field of Waterloo,
Cologne, then south along the Rhine to the Alps – where the wheels kept
falling off the splendid chariot – and, finally, to Geneva. Here on 27 May
he encountered three fellow-outcasts from English society: the lovers Percy
Shelley and Mary Wollstonecraft Godwin, and Mary's stepsister Claire
Clairmont with whom, in the midst of the separation turmoil, Byron had
already begun an affair. The summer of *Childe Harold III*, 'The Prisoner of
Chillon', 'Hymn to Intellectual Beauty', 'Mont Blanc' and *Frankenstein* was
under way.

It would be six years before Byron and Hunt met again, but they had parted on terms of warm friendship in the face of public hostility. Shelley would inform Hunt: 'I saw Lord Byron at Geneva, who expressed . . . the high esteem he felt for your character & worth'.[61]

TWENTY

SEAS OF TROUBLE

'His Lordship left town for the Continent on Monday,' the *Examiner* announced on 28 April. Immediately below appeared a poem Hunt had completed that week, 'To the Right Honourable Lord Byron, on his Departure for Italy and Greece'. Hunt writes his *bon voyage* in the flowing couplets of *Rimini*, following the 'swift ship' bound for 'classic seas' and watching 'with fancy's eyesight' as Byron, 'half eagerness, half ease', rides 'o'er the dancing freshness'. The wonders of 'Enchantress Italy' are listed, including

> music's whole soul harmonious;
> Poets, that knew how Nature should be wooed,
> With frank address, and terms heart-understood;
> And painters, worthy to be friends of theirs, –
> Hands that could catch the very finest airs
> Of natural minds, and all that soul express
> Of ready concord, which was made to bless,
> And forms the secret of true amorousness.

After the separation scandal this might seem a little too frank, and Hunt's caution – 'my Lord, in Italy take care' – was not calculated to make Byron pause:

> in Italy take care,
> You that are a poet, and have pains to bear,
> Of lovely girls, that step across the sight,
> Like Houris in a heaven of warmth and light,
> With rosy-cushioned mouths in dimples set,
> And ripe dark tresses, and glib eyes of jet . . .

Byron had in fact been tempted as soon as he stepped into the Cour Impériale hotel at Ostend, where he 'fell like a thunderbolt upon the chamber maid'.[1] The epistle concludes with Hunt in his best conversational manner:

And so adieu, dear BYRON, – dear to me
For many a cause, disinterestedly; –
First, for unconscious sympathy, when boys,
In friendship, and the Muse's trying joys; –
Next for that frank surprise, when MOORE and you
Came to my cage, like warblers kind and true,
And told me, with your arts of cordial lying,
How well I looked, when you both thought me dying; –
Next for a rank worn simply, and the scorn
Of those who trifle with an age free-born . . .
Lastly, for older friends, – fine hearts, held fast
Through every dash of chance, from first to last; –
For taking spirit as it means to be, –
For a stretched hand, ever the same to me, –
And total, glorious want of vile hypocrisy.[2]

This echoes several of Hunt's earlier comments about Byron in private letters; it recalls their first meeting in Horsemonger Lane and reaches back to boyhood days, and their 'unconscious' fellowship when Byron read Hunt's *Juvenilia* at Harrow school.

Hunt's cheerfully uneven poem draws together various strands of his thought and writing in recent months, and deliberately disregards Byron's damaged reputation. The poem's style of 'dancing freshness' catches the momentary prompts of 'heart understanding' and the 'dash of chance', while the image of the 'stretched hand' is a reminder of Hunt's open-handed 'Indicator' signature and the 'cordial hands' that had greeted him in prison. Drawing all together is the idea of Italy. No longer associated with Dante's melancholy theology and the tragedy of Paolo and Francesca, Italy is now a 'heaven of warmth and light', the home of 'true amorousness'. Crucially, Hunt's Italy is a 'Copier of Greece' and *pagan* in inspiration. Byron was heading in the right direction, and Lady Byron's 'anxious angel face, pretending ire' – glimpsed in the poem – was unlikely to draw him back.

Early in 1816 the *Examiner* opened its pages to Wordsworth, and two of his sonnets, 'How clear, how keen, how marvellously bright' and 'While not a leaf seems faded', appeared in January and February (Haydon supplied them, with Wordsworth's permission). After Hazlitt's 'malignant attack' this was a gesture of support for Wordsworth, but by no means a signal of approval. Shortly afterwards, Hunt's article 'Heaven made a Party to Earthly Disputes' objected to the way Wordsworth's sonnets on Waterloo had enlisted the 'blest angels' in the Allied cause and claimed a unique understanding of 'this victory sublime'. Wordsworth was 'a true poet', but his assurance 'that Heaven thinks precisely as he does' was like the 'thump of a doubtful fist on a pulpit cushion'.[3]

That Hunt's remarks about Wordsworth had aesthetic as well as political implications became clear when a third Wordsworth sonnet was printed in the *Examiner* on 31 March:

To B. R. Haydon, Painter

High is our calling, Friend! – Creative Art,
(Whether the instrument of words she use,
Or pencil pregnant with etherial hues)
Demands the service of a Mind and Heart
Though sensitive, yet in their weakest part
Heroically fashion'd, to infuse
Faith in the whispers of the lonely Muse . . .

Haydon was ecstatic about the sonnet. Wordsworth's claims for the artist's 'etherial', 'heroic', 'lonely' service expressed Haydon's own feelings of sublime inspiration as he painted *Christ's Entry into Jerusalem* (a recent diary entry noted 'Got the head of Christ in'). But Hunt disagreed: 'High is our calling' was 'not in the very best style of compliment', he informed Haydon, '*when I write you a sonnet, it shall be a better one*'. Hunt's own ideas of 'the proper object of pursuit in art' emerged when his sonnet 'To Benjamin Robert Haydon' turned from 'etherial hues' to commend the painter's appeal to 'human eyes'. Hunt invited Haydon to 'push out' to the Vale of Health 'some sunny Sunday morning', but his critique of Wordsworth's sonnet rankled with Haydon, and it would contribute to the breakdown of their friendship.[4]

Hunt had similar doubts about *The Excursion*. Like Shelley, he deplored its conservatism and was unpersuaded by its narrative in which the Solitary, a man who has passed from revolutionary ardour through disappointment to despondency and 'loss of confidence in social man', is cured by joining the Church of England. Shelley's answer to Wordsworth, *Alastor; or the Spirit of Solitude*, depicted a 'self-centred' poet-figure in the Wordsworthian mould who is destroyed in his quest for fleeting visions of ideal beauty: 'He lived, he died, he sung, in solitude'.[5] *Alastor* was published in February 1816, within days of *The Story of Rimini*, and its message of sympathy and love for 'fellow-beings' chimed with Hunt's.

Ironically, however, Hunt's ideas had been stimulated by *The Excursion*, in which the myths of 'pagan Greece' are said to have enshrined an 'all-pervading Spirit'.[6] Wordsworth shows how modern poetry might revive the imagination of the ancients although, as an orthodox Anglican, he was bound to dismiss the Greeks as 'unenlightened Swains', 'bewildered Pagans of old time'.[7]

Tooke's *Pantheon* had fostered no such prejudices, and Hunt embraced Greek paganism as a humane alternative to the political and religious establishment Wordsworth supported. Haydon reported in his diary: 'Hunt says he prefers infinitely the beauties of pagan Mythology to the gloomy repentance of the Christian'.[8]

Although Wordsworth's poetry set Hunt at odds with Haydon, it drew Hunt and Shelley together when they met later in the year: significantly, one of Shelley's first tokens of friendship was a copy of *Alastor*. Meanwhile, in the same issue of the *Examiner* that marked Byron's departure, Hunt announced: 'J.K. and other Communications, next week'.

In October 1815 John Keats had registered as a student at Guy's Hospital. Since then he had been living south of the Thames at Southwark – 'a beastly place in dirt, turnings and windings' – attending Astley Cooper's surgical lectures, and writing poetry at every opportunity.[9] He had chosen a medical career that might in due course bring financial security and social respectability, but for the moment he was a homeless twenty-year-old trying to find a direction in life through medicine. He had written some light, senti-mental verses during summer 1815, and a verse epistle to his friend George Felton Mathew. His sonnet 'O Solitude' dated from November when the dull evenings made Southwark even more dreary, and at some time in the next months he would compose another, 'How many bards gild the lapses of time', handling the Petrarchan form confidently and welcoming a 'throng' of old poets – 'no confusion, no disturbance rude / Do they occasion'.[10]

The Story of Rimini disturbed Keats into more adventurous writing: here was a dazzling production from an admired contemporary – smart, colourful, controversial. Quickly Keats set down two attempts to 'tell a tale of chivalry' of his own. 'Specimen of an Induction to a Poem' and 'Calidore' both imitated Hunt's loose couplets and unconventional phrasing – 'far clearness', 'easy float', 'bowery shore' – although Keats was unable to sustain *Rimini*'s narra-tive dash and trailed off into description. These poems wouldn't do, but his sonnet on solitude might pass muster: he initialled it 'J.K.' and sent it to Hunt. The poem appeared in the *Examiner* on 5 May:

To Solitude

O SOLITUDE! if I must with thee dwell,
   Let it not be among the jumbled heap
   Of murky buildings; – climb with me the steep,
Nature's Observatory – whence the dell,
Its flowery slopes – its rivers crystal swell,
   May seem a span: let me thy vigils keep
   'Mongst boughs pavilioned; where the Deer's swift leap

Startles the wild Bee from the Fox-glove bell.
Ah! fain would I frequent such scenes with thee;
  But the sweet converse of an innocent mind,
  Whose words are images of thoughts refin'd,
Is my soul's pleasure; and it sure must be
Almost the highest bliss of human kind,
When to thy haunts two kindred spirits flee.[11]

This was Keats's first published poem, and in Hunt's eyes it was a promising début – even though sonnets, odes, hymns and invocations to solitude were commonplace. Unlike Hunt, Keats was a true cockney born in earshot of Bow Bells, but in an important sense he was also a south bank poet. His sonnet had been written amid the murky buildings over the river, and it reached out for suburban pathways and fields as idyllic pastoral alternatives. What did Hunt see in the poem that persuaded him Keats was a rising star? The Petrarchan form and its Italian associations were pleasing, and he would have been glad to see that Keats's solitude was not an isolated Wordsworthian vigil but a populated scene of meetings and conversations: Keats recommended the doubled pleasure of 'two kindred spirits' enjoying 'sweet converse'. In other words, 'To Solitude' was a poem after Hunt's own heart.

Hunt did not yet know who 'J. K.' was, but publication was a greeting in kind – and he could see exactly where the poem would appear to best effect in the *Examiner*. Readers encountered 'To Solitude' between a harrowing description of a soldier's death, and another article on the 'extreme distress' of farmers and country people. The message was clear. At a time of widespread suffering the 'narrow room' of Wordsworthian solitude was not an option, whereas the 'kindred spirit' of Keats's poem might help repair social feeling. By attending to Keats's poem as it appeared in the *Examiner*, we can see how Hunt was continuing to bring poetry into dialogue with urgent public issues.

During this year Hunt published more of his own poems in the *Examiner* than ever before. Among them were his translations from Anacreon and Homer; an extract from *Rimini* and the epistle to Byron; two tender lyrics to his children, 'To T.L.H. Six Years Old, During a Late Sickness' and 'To J.H. Four Years Old'; and a sprightly new poem 'On Hearing a Little Musical Box':

Hallo! – what? – where? – what can it be
That strikes up so deliciously?
I never in my life – what? no!
That little tin-box playing so?
It really seemed as if a sprite
Had struck among us, swift and light . . .

The poem quickly forms a circle of community with its reader, then 'runs along' with 'light leaps of sound'. Hunt's use of poetry to create sociable gatherings was developed in seven verse epistles he published in the *Examiner* between 30 June and 25 August. He adopts the name 'Harry Brown', and addresses four of the poems to his cousin Tom Brown (i.e. Thomas Moore, whose 'Twopenny Post Bag' verses were an influence), and the other three to his friends Hazlitt, Field and Lamb.

Edmund Blunden referred to the verse epistles as Hunt's 'lower style' – and it's worth emphasising that Hunt was making a deliberate stylistic choice.[12] He understood and admired 'high art'. He had an unrivalled knowledge of Chaucer, Shakespeare, Spenser and Milton, and of the Italian tradition including Tasso, Ariosto and Dante. Since his boyhood visits to West's gallery he had studied British and Italian painters, and he enjoyed Italian opera and Mozart. In aiming for a 'lower style' the verbal and metrical requirements of Hunt's writing differed from the discipline of high or 'classical' art, but were no less demanding. The verse letters developed a distinctive lyrical person-ality – an off-the-cuff immediacy, in touch with 'these times and this weather', that came over to readers as personal, unhurried, chattily expansive. This was a breakthrough, and Hunt's mood anticipated Philip Larkin's 'relief' at discov-ering he did not have to 'jack himself up to a concept of poetry', but could 'relapse back into [his] own life and write from it'.[13]

The keynote is pleasure, as in this sketch of a scene at Hampstead:

> But at present, for reasons I'll give when we meet,
> I shall spare you the trouble, – I mean to say, treat; –
> Yet how can I touch, and not linger a while,
> On the spot that has haunted my youth like a smile?
> On its fine breathing prospects, its clump-wooded glades,
> Dark pines, and white houses, and long-allied shades,
> With fields going down, where the bard lies and sees
> The hills up above him with roofs in the trees?
> Now too, while the season – half summer, half spring, –
> Brown elms and green oaks, – makes one loiter and sing;
> And the bee's weighty murmur comes by us at noon,
> And the cuckoo repeats his short indolent tune,
> And little white clouds lie about in the sun,
> And the wind's in the west, and hay-making begun?

There are no jacked-up claims for visionary insight here, no attempt to make the landscape answer to the poet's thoughts and feelings. Instead, Hunt lingers on the 'breathing' scene and his questions invite the reader to 'loiter' for a moment too, creating an effect of 'double pleasure' and participation that is enhanced by the merging of seasons, 'half summer, half spring'. In the

following week's *Examiner*, other sights are encountered on a journey from
Hampstead back into town:

> . . . an air in your face, ever fanning, and sweet,
> And the birds in your ears, and a turf for your feet, –
> And then, after all, to encounter a throng of
> Canal-men, and hod-men, unfit to make song of,
> Midst alehouses, puddles, and backs of street-roads,
> And all sorts of rubbish, and crashing cart-loads;
> And so on, eye-smarting, and ready to choke,
> Till you end in hot narrowness, clatter, and smoke![14]

In terms of classical decorum these details might be 'unfit to make song of',
but Hunt notices them and draws them in. 'All sorts of rubbish' excluded by
earlier writers – even by the poets of *Lyrical Ballads*, who had made great
parade of an unadorned style – are mingled in the democratic flow of Hunt's
poetry. What separates him from Wordsworth in particular is his refusal to
elevate rural remoteness over the populated city. Moving from bright fields
and gardens to the stifling inner city, this passage reverses the trajectory of
Keats's 'To Solitude': Hunt identifies himself as a suburban poet, whose poetry
flows from experiencing city and country life in close proximity:

> In the town, of the town, – in the fields, of the fields;
> In the one, for example, to feel as we go on,
> That streets are about us, arts, people, and so on;
> In t'other to value the stillness, the breeze,
> And love to see farms, and get among trees.[15]

Here at last is the true voice of Hunt's post-prison experience, at liberty to
participate in a world of social converse in which fields, streets, books, calls,
ladies, reading, rhyming, music and song make up an empathetic world of
kindred spirits and 'sociality'.

During the summer of 1816 Hunt appeared more settled and happy than at
any time since his prison sentence. In August Marianne gave birth to their
fourth child, Swinburne, named after Sir John Swinburne who had given
them so much support. There were musical evenings at the Novellos' home
in Oxford Street, with bread and cheese, celery and mugs of beer; picnics in
the quiet meadows of Belsize and by the watercress streams of Gospel Oak;
and gleeful gatherings at the Vale of Health, like the one on Sunday, 22
September with the Novellos, Haydon, and Hunt's old friends John Gattie
and Henry Robertson. In such company Hunt was on his best form, and the
time passed quickly with songs and poems, puns and jokes. Haydon would

have been in good spirits too, for Hunt had fulfilled his promise to write a sonnet that named him 'in succession due' with Michelangelo and 'sweet-souled Raphael'. For the moment Hunt was riding high in Haydon's esteem:

He is like one of those instruments with three legs, which, throw it up how you will, always pitches on two and has a spike sticking for ever up & ever ready for you. He sets at a subject with a scent like a pointer. He is a remark-able man, and created a sensation by his independence, his courage, his disinterestedness in public matters; by the very truth, acuteness, & taste of his dramatic criticisms he raised the rank of newspapers, and gave by his example a literary feeling to the weekly ones more especially. As a poet, I think him full of the genuine feeling and that his third canto in Rimini is equal to any thing in any language of that sweet sort. Perhaps in his wishing to avoid the monotony of the Pope School, he may have shot into the other extreme, and his invention of obscure words to express obscure feelings borders sometimes on affectation, but these are trifles compared with the beauty of the Poem, the intense painting of the scenery, and the deep burning in of the passion which trembles in every line. Thus far as a critic, an editor, & a poet; as a man, I know none with such an affectionate heart, if never opposed in his opinions – his person, his property, his talents are then at your service – with defects of course . . .

This was generous, although Haydon's favour was always a precarious blessing. The curious three-legged jack with its third spike 'ever ready' was a phallic allusion, and when Haydon turned to Hunt's 'defects' –

getting inferior people about him to listen, too fond of shining at any expense in society, too apt when another is beginning to divide attention by exhibiting more knowledge to stop it by a joke

– sexual flirtation rounded up the catalogue: 'a love of approbation from the darling sex bordering on weakness'.[16]

Haydon had glimpsed a vulnerable side of Hunt's personality, and he was beginning to sense that behind the gaiety there was a troubled personality. Still, for a few short weeks in autumn 1816 Hunt basked in Haydon's appro-bation, although he continued to face intractable problems of debt, and his publishing arrangements were becoming more and more complicated.

On 28 March Hunt had written to Murray asking for £50 against the sales of Rimini. Murray responded promptly, informing him that he had 304 copies on hand and that, supposing every copy sold, the total profit would be £91 5s. 0d. of which Hunt stood to receive his half-share of £45 12s. 6d. After £3 2s. 6d. had been deducted for Hunt's own copies, £42 10s. was due to

him which Murray 'very willingly' made up to £50 '& thus we will clear the
account'. On 9 April Hunt tried again to 'bargain' over the copyright of *Rimini*,
his aim being to secure an advance of £450 on 'hopes of the work' and 'reliance
on myself personally'. Murray demurred. Hunt hastened to clarify that what
he sought was in no way to be considered as 'an application for assistance' –
the taint of 'charity' was mortifying.[17] Then came the *Quarterly*'s abusive
notice of *Rimini*, deepening his suspicion that Murray had connived with his
enemies. He was caught up in 'unexpected and unpleasant business', assailed
by 'meannesses & treacheries'.[18] The sum of £250 was still owed to Gale and
Fenner, and they were calling on him for the money. Charles Ollier tried to
raise funds from his employer, Coutts Bank, and helped Hunt with personal
loans in July. Hazlitt's and Jeffrey's praise for *Rimini* in the *Edinburgh* encouraged Hunt to write a rambling ten-page letter to its publisher, Archibald
Constable, detailing the ups and downs of his financial dealings and enquiring,
finally, on page ten, whether Constable would purchase the copyright of
Rimini. The offer was politely declined. Constable had 'numerous engagements' on hand, and directed Hunt back to Gale and Fenner.[19] Francis Jeffrey
invited an article on Henry Howard and Sir Thomas Wyatt for the *Edinburgh*,
but for the moment Hunt's situation was extremely bleak: 'times are bad;
people have little money, & those who have more do not chuse to speculate'.[20]

Hunt explained his 'pretty "sea of troubles"' in long letters to Tom Moore
on 21 May and 3 July. His use of that phrase from Hamlet's soliloquy suggests
it was at this time that John wrote a stern warning about Hunt's inattention
to money matters:

> I certainly shall do every thing in my power to meet the difficulties you
> have so unhappily created. It is quite true, as you know, that I had enough
> of my own just now to struggle with; but in my present troubles I have the
> satisfaction of knowing, that they are solely caused by my endeavours to
> assist others. I heartily wish that your embarrassments arose from the same
> causes, and not from negligence and an inability to resist immediate temp-
> tation, as I believe they do in the main . . . Unless however you *now* make
> a firm stand, the evils you will entail upon yourself must be overwhelming
> – your happiness will be wrecked on that 'sea of troubles' into which you
> have a second time unnecessarily ventured.

For the Hunts the idea of a 'sea of troubles' was more than a dramatic allusion. It conjured up memories of unhappy transatlantic voyages by various
ancestors, and their mother's stormy escape from Philadelphia with her children. It also recalled Isaac's luckless career, a fate John had long determined
he would avoid at all costs. He had already loaned £100 to John Scott, editor
of the *Champion*, and his efforts to extricate Hunt from debt brought him to
the brink of bankruptcy. His brother's laxity with money was alarming, and

his distance from London and apparent neglect of the *Examiner* were not helpful. The paper's circulation had declined after Waterloo, and John was determined that Hunt should get his act together:

> What I would advise you is this – to rouse yourself, and overcome that distaste to business, which has induced you to leave your labours undone till the last moment, and too often to neglect them entirely. To give up, in fact, your entire mornings to the paper – to resume at once the theatricals above all things – to commence the Notices of Books, in which Mr. Hazlitt can aid you – which would I am certain get up the paper, or at least prevent its decrease, which we are now suffering.[21]

We have heard this before, in the letter Benjamin Franklin sent to Isaac nearly fifty years earlier: 'Be indefatigably diligent and you will be greater than your adversaries. Be frugal and you will [be] richer. Be temperate and abstemious.' Hunt should give less time to poetry and more to the *Examiner*. John forwarded two pounds, and promised another eleven 'for the butcher'. Hunt thought vaguely of moving to cheaper accommodation. Buckinghamshire seemed a possibility, he told Moore, 'out of the vortex of London dearness, & yet . . . in reach of one day's post for the Examiner's sake. What say you to joining us *there*? The theatricals my powerful friend Hazlitt will go on with, & I shall take up the Literary Notices.'[22]

Despite his precarious circumstances Hunt was now striking out as a poet with greater confidence. Rather than coming closer into town to be present in the *Examiner* office and the theatres, he contemplated a move further afield where, he told Moore, he could 'rhyme away'. He was soon projecting a book-length volume of 'Letters of Harry Brown', and versions of 'Hero and Leander' and 'Bacchus and Ariadne' told in his 'own fashion'. The publishers Taylor and Hessey declined the verse letters – they had appeared already in the *Examiner* and *Taunton Courier* – although this project continued to have a ghostly existence and *An Epistle to Lord Byron and other Poems* was advertised in John Taylor's *The Identity of Junius* (1816–17). It never appeared. Taylor did, however, warm to Hunt's draft lines for 'Hero and Leander', and forwarded twenty guineas as a part payment for the new poems.[23]

Although John had complained about Hunt's inattention to editorial duties, a glance through the *Examiner* for this year shows that his 'Political Examiner' and 'Examiner' articles appeared regularly (Hunt admitted to being late with copy in the week of Byron's departure, and he missed one week, 18 August, due to baby Swinburne's arrival). He opposed income tax and the 'military encroachment' of a standing army, and reiterated the need for fundamental changes: 'The people of England want peace, economy, a restoration of their very breath and household existence; and to secure these, they must have *Constitutional Reform*.'[24] Hazlitt was writing the theatricals and 'Round Table' essays, and in June his review of the 'Christabel' volume caught for all time the Hamletish Coleridge 'who from an excess of capacity . . . does little or nothing'.[25] Haydon had been monitoring the Select Committee of the House of Commons on the Elgin Marbles, and expected to be called. When the committee rose without inviting his opinion, Haydon rushed into print with a letter to the *Examiner* 'On the Judgment of Connoisseurs', bullishly asserting his professional integrity against the establishment connoisseur Richard Payne Knight's 'complete want of judgment in refined Art':

> No man will trust his limb to a connoisseur in surgery. No minister would ask a connoisseur in war how a campaign is to be conducted . . . why should a connoisseur of an Art, more exclusively than any other without the reach of common acquirement, be preferred to the professional man? What reason can be given, why the Painter, the Sculptor, and the Architect, should not be exclusively believed most adequate to decide on what they best understand, as well as the Surgeon, the Lawyer, and the General?[26]

Haydon was convinced that this intervention swung the argument in favour of purchasing the Marbles for the nation.

Leading public opinion and setting the political and cultural agendas of the day, the *Examiner* was in robust shape and Hunt was moving into what would prove to be one of the most creative periods of his first life. Still, John feared the signs of 'negligence' and 'neglect' that had ruined their father. The brothers were now set on diverging paths.

TWENTY-ONE

YOUNG POETS

'J.K.' was eager to meet Hunt. Cowden Clarke was the obvious intermediary, although his reluctance to arrange an introduction meant that Keats had to proceed carefully. His verse letter 'To Charles Cowden Clarke', written in September 1816, was modelled on Hunt's 'Harry Brown' poems and acknowledged the inspiring example of

> The wrong'd Libertas, – who has told you stories
> Of laurel chaplets, and Apollo's glories;
> Of troops chivalrous prancing through a city,
> And tearful ladies made for love, and pity:
> With many else which I have never known.[1]

Keats hinted that, while they both admired Hunt, he had yet to make his acquaintance and, anyway, his 'dull, unlearned' verses were 'little fit to please a classic ear', and hardly worth notice. This dig did the trick. CCC would show Hunt 'two or three' of Keats's poems.

October was a busy time at the Vale of Health. Hunt's essay for the *Edinburgh* was due, and he was projecting a 'Round Table' article on the domestic life of the 'Maid-Servant'. His sketch of humble life revisits one of the great set pieces of eighteenth-century satire, *The Rape of the Lock*, in which Pope itemised the 'glittering spoil' of trinkets on Belinda's dressing table as tokens of her confused outlook on life. Hunt follows Pope's example when he surveys the maidservant's aspirations to fashion and culture,

> a good looking-glass on the table; and in the window a Bible, a comb, and a piece of soap. Here stands also, under stout lock and key, the mighty mystery, – the box, – containing among other things her clothes, two or three song-books, consisting of nineteen for the penny; sundry Tragedies at a halfpenny the sheet; the Whole Nature of Dreams laid open, together with the Fortune Teller and the Account of the Ghost of Mrs. Veal.[2]

There are the delusions of vanity and dreams here, as there had been in *The Rape of the Lock*, but the maidservant's world has all the warmth that Belinda's lacked.

Marianne was stronger now and Swinburne was adding to the racket of Thornton (6 years old), John (4), and Mary Florimel (3). Unlike the maidservant's room with its seemly trim and secret box, in the Hunts' home the clutter of life and art produced mighty mysteries of a different order. Books and manuscripts were everywhere, some nowhere to be found: a poem Hunt had wanted to publish, 'The Hymn to Intellectual Beauty', sent by one 'ELFIN-KNIGHT', was unaccountably missing. CCC brought several poems by a young man named John Keats, and mentioned that he was the 'J.K.' of 'To Solitude'. Hunt read quickly through the longer of the poems – the epistle 'To Charles Cowden Clarke' – and was immediately impressed by the way Keats's frankly unclassical voice floated references to Tasso, Spenser, Milton, King Alfred and Mozart. If Keats had already known Hunt personally, he could not have written a poem more likely to appeal to him.

Forty-five years later, CCC recalled Hunt's

> unhesitating and prompt admiration which broke forth before he had read twenty lines of the first poem. Horace Smith . . . was not less demonstrative in his appreciation of their merits. The piece which he read out was the sonnet, 'How many bards gild the Lapses of Time!' marking with particular emphasis and approval the last six lines:
>
> > So the unnumber'd sounds that evening store,
> > The songs of birds, the whisp'ring of the leaves,
> > The voice of waters, the great bell that heaves
> > With solemn sound, and thousand others more,
> > *That distance of recognizance bereaves,*
> > Make pleasing music, and not wild uproar.
>
> Smith repeated with applause the line in italics, saying, 'What a well-condensed expression for a youth so young!' After making numerous and eager inquiries about him personally, and with reference to any peculiarities of mind and manner, the visit ended in my being requested to bring him over to the Vale of Health.[3]

CCC had passed his own 'copy books' to Hunt and invited him to look over his poems. He was eager to know whether his 'Sonnet to Liberty' would be acceptable for the *Examiner*, and was piqued when he didn't receive an immediate response.

*   *   *

The first week of October passed, and lapses of time grew to be a problem for Hunt. He had urged CCC to bring Keats to the Vale – any time after Saturday, 12 October was convenient: by then he would have dispatched his article for the *Edinburgh*, and seen the week's *Examiner* into the press. CCC had told Keats of Hunt's interest, and once the term at Guy's was under way Keats sent an excited reply. His letter was dated Wednesday, 9 October: 'The busy time has just gone by, and I can now devote any time you may mention to the pleasure of seeing Mr Hunt – 't will be an Era in my existence.'⁴ CCC would have received Keats's letter on the Wednesday evening or Thursday morning. But then he hesitated. Hunt expected to see them on the Sunday, then on Monday, then Tuesday, and when Wednesday came and there was still no sign of them, he turned to the next Sunday's *Examiner*. That evening a package arrived at the Vale from CCC, containing a copy of a new edition of Samuel Johnson – would Hunt notice it in the *Examiner*? – and a stilted letter asking if he had offended Hunt in any way. Why hadn't Hunt written? Had he read his copy books? And what about the 'Sonnet on Liberty'? CCC's worries had brought on a 'nervous attack'.

Hunt rose to the moment and responded reassuringly about the copy books, offered a criticism of the Johnson 'in a week or two', sympathised with CCC's nerves – and almost forgot about the sonnet: 'When did it come, or by what, or whom?' There was no possibility of placing it in Sunday's *Examiner*, for Hunt's own sonnet to Haydon was scheduled to appear then. Hunt sealed the letter, then thought again. CCC had a good heart. He scribbled on the wrapper: 'Will you come & take your chop with us next Saturday – my birthday? Mr. Haydon I expect will be our guest.'⁵

Haydon was staying nearby at 7, Pond Street, Hampstead, to rest his eyes after making a strenuous 'attack' on *Christ's Entry into Jerusalem*. Hunt had seen a good deal of him, and CCC would have an enjoyable walk out of London from his lodgings in Clerkenwell. Saturday came – 19 October, Hunt's thirty-second birthday. Haydon charged in, and then a ten-gate laugh announced CCC with another guest, Mr John Keats – or so it seems reasonable to conjecture, for the date of Hunt's first meeting with Keats has proved notoriously difficult to ascertain.

Hunt was immediately struck by Keats's compact stature, and strong, lively features quivering with energy and sensibility. Keats's eyes glowed. Everything about him had a fine, fervid presence that reinforced the impression of his poetry. Keats was young. His twenty-first birthday would be on the last day of October, and Hunt was strongly reminded of his own youth as 'a lad, hanging loosely on society, without a prospect and almost without a hope, except that of leaving behind me the promise of something poetical'.⁶ They both admired the rich mines of classical mythology in Lemprière, Tooke and Spence – and Keats's first poem had been an imitation of Spenser. Hunt remembered how he had sat up all night reading and writing – and now here was Keats telling him of nights passed in the same way, and of mornings wearily walking the wards at St Thomas's. 'We became intimate on the spot,' Hunt recalled.[7] CCC would have been looking on as his former pupil over-took him in Hunt's estimation and received an open invitation to visit. John Keats became 'Junkets', a freeman of the Vale.

Haydon immediately 'formed a very high idea of [Keats's] genius', and resolved to keep him away from Hunt.[8] Within days Haydon invited another poet, John Hamilton Reynolds,

> Next Sunday to Hampstead Town
> To meet John Keats, who soon will shine
> The greatest, of this Splendid time
> That e'er has woo'ed the Muses nine

– and he added a spiky aside, 'Now Reynolds it'll, be just as well / If that, you don't to others tell!'[9] Hunt, the 'other' referred to here, was to be kept away, so that for this day at least Haydon would be patron to these exciting new poets. They met at Haydon's temporary abode in Pond Street on Sunday, 27 October, shortly before the painter returned to his London studio and his vast canvas.

On his birthday Keats received via CCC another invitation from Haydon, this time to breakfast at his studio on Sunday, 3 November. Addressing CCC as 'My daintie Davie' – not 'My dear Sir', as hitherto – Keats said he was eager to meet 'this glorious Haydon and all his Creation'. In the meantime, though, he had 'an engagement on Saturday; to which [he had] looked forward all the Week'.[10] It seems likely that he was heading to the Vale to meet Hunt: when the *Examiner* appeared on the following morning, it announced 'The SONNET on CHAPMAN'S HOMER by J.K.' and a selection from Reynolds's new poem the *Naiad*, at 'the earliest opportunity'.[11] There was still no sign of CCC's sonnet to liberty.

Keats had written 'On First Looking into Chapman's Homer' after an evening in company with CCC reading the big folio volume of George Chapman's translation. This was a book that had been doing the rounds. Hunt had borrowed it from Thomas Alsager, and noticed it in the *Examiner* in a manner calculated to whet Keats's appetite: 'CHAPMAN, whose *Homer*'s a fine rough old wine'.[12] To Keats's youthful palate Chapman's poetry was 'loud and bold', its Homeric bouquet a 'pure serene': in just two years' time, those doubled pleasures of wine and poetry would be joined in the Bacchanalian luxuries of Keats's 'Ode to a Nightingale':

> O for a beaker full of the warm South,
>   Full of the true, the blushful Hippocrene . . .[13]

Exchanges of social feeling at the Vale were continued by further conversations in verse. Hunt began a series of sonnets – 'To Mrs. L.H. On her Modelling a Bust of the Author', 'To Miss K.', 'To Henry Robertson, John Gattie, and Vincent Novello', 'To Horatio Smith', 'To John Hamilton Reynolds'. These are light-hearted, occasional poems touching on family, friendships, music, nature, trees, 'suburb gardens' and concern for 'all men's welfare'. Hunt was also contemplating a long poem that in the months ahead would become 'The Nymphs'.

Keats marked his meetings with Hunt in sonnets such as 'Keen, fitful gusts' and 'On leaving some friends', and in 'Sleep and Poetry'. This long meditative poem reflects on Keats's ambitions as a poet, and it concludes with a vivid description of Hunt's library at the Vale. After a long evening of poetry and wine, conversation and laughter, good-nights were exchanged and Keats retired to the temporary bed that had been made up for him:

> and thus, the chimes
> Of friendly voices had just given place
> To as sweet a silence, when I 'gan retrace
> The pleasant day, upon a couch at ease.
> It was a poet's house who keeps the keys
> Of pleasure's temple. Round about were hung
> The glorious features of the bards who sung
> In other ages – cold and sacred busts
> Smiled at each other. Happy he who trusts
> To clear futurity his darling fame!
> Then there were fauns and satyrs taking aim
> At swelling apples with a frisky leap
> And reaching fingers, 'mid a luscious heap
> Of vine leaves. Then there rose to view a fane
> Of liny marble, and thereto a train of nymphs
> Approaching fairly o'er the sward:
> One, loveliest, holding her white hand toward
> The dazzling sun-rise: two sisters sweet
> Bending their graceful figures till they meet
> Over the trippings of a little child:
> And some are hearing, eagerly, the wild
> Thrilling liquidity of dewy piping.
> See, in another picture, nymphs are wiping
> Cherishingly Diana's timorous limbs; –
> A fold of lawny mantle dabbling swims
> At the bath's edge, and keeps a gentle motion
> With the subsiding crystal: as when ocean
> Heaves calmly its broad swelling smoothness o'er

Its rocky marge, and balances once more
The patient weeds; that now unshent by foam
Feel all about their undulating home.

Sappho's meek head was there half smiling down
At nothing; just as though the earnest frown
Of over thinking had that moment gone
From off her brow, and left her all alone.

Great Alfred's too, with anxious, pitying eyes,
As if he always listened to the sighs
Of the goaded world; and Kosciusko's worn
By horrid suffrance – mightily forlorn.

Petrarch, outstepping from the shady green,
Starts at the sight of Laura; nor can wean
His eyes from her sweet face. Most happy they!
For over them was seen a free display
Of out-spread wings, and from between them shone
The face of Poesy: from off her throne
She overlook'd things that I scarce could tell.
The very sense of where I was might well
Keep Sleep aloof: but more than that there came
Thought after thought to nourish up the flame
Within my breast; so that the morning light
Surprised me even from a sleepless night;
And up I rose refresh'd, and glad, and gay,
Resolving to begin that very day
These lines . . .[14]

Benjamin West's gallery had proved formative for Hunt. Now his own home, modelled after West's with engravings, busts and books, was nourishing another poet. Keats follows Hunt's example in 'reading' the prints on the walls, and it's possible to identify what he was looking at: the nymphs approaching a temple could be an engraving from one of Claude Lorrain's 'Bacchanals', or perhaps Poussin's *Triumph of Flora*; the figure of Diana is almost certainly from Titian's *Diana and Actaeon*.[15] Busts of the patriots Alfred and Kosciusko look on, and a print of Petrarch and Laura, neatly bringing together painting and poetry, enables Keats to turn his poem towards the moment of its composition. In a few lines he captures the enthralling experience of being 'at ease' in Hunt's house – a poet who had revealed hitherto unimagined vistas of cultural life. It wasn't an accident that in responding to one of the prints, Keats was drawn to an oceanic image of boundless power and repose.

As October and November brought the end of the year closer, poetry bound
Hunt and Keats together through sonnets addressed to each other or written
in amicable competition. On 30 December, a chilly day, the warmth of the
hearth stirred a cricket into unseasonable chirping that prompted two sonnets.
They set themselves a deadline of fifteen minutes to complete their poems.
Here is Hunt's:

> ### To the Grasshopper and the Cricket.
>
> Green little vaulter in the sunny grass
> Catching your heart up at the feel of June,
> Sole voice that's heard amidst the lazy noon,
> When ev'n the bees lag at the summoning brass;
> And you, warm little housekeeper, who class
> With those who think the candles come too soon,
> Loving the fire, and with your tricksome tune
> Nick the glad silent moments as they pass;
> Oh sweet and tiny cousins, that belong,
> One to the fields, the other to the hearth,
> Both have your sunshine; both though small are strong
> At your clear hearts; and both were sent on earth
> To sing in thoughtful ears this natural song, –
> In doors and out, summer and winter, Mirth.

And here, Keats's:

> ### On the Grasshopper and the Cricket.
>
> The poetry of earth is never dead:
>   When all the birds are faint with the hot sun,
>   And hide in cooling trees, a voice will run
> From hedge to hedge about the new-mown mead;
> That is the Grasshopper's – he takes the lead
>   In summer luxury, – he has never done
>   With his delights; for when tired out with fun
> He rests at ease beneath some pleasant weed.
> The poetry of earth is ceasing never:
>   On a lone winter evening, when the frost
>   Has wrought a silence, from the stove there shrills
> The Cricket's song, in warmth increasing ever,
>   And seems to one in drowsiness half lost,
>   The Grasshopper's among some grassy hills.[16]

Written as an evening entertainment, the two sonnets illustrate how poetry belonged to the routines of life at the Vale of Health. The subject and occasion embodied for Hunt a cluster of double pleasures – 'summer and winter', 'the feel of June' on a candlelit evening, fields and the hearth, indoors and out, and the mirth arising from friendly converse. Hunt's poem is drawn to ideas of happy relationship whereas Keats's is attuned to the song of the earth, the pagan *anima* of poetry, and intuits what Hunt's poem also understands: the desire for continuity. Keats's poem sounds more portentous, possibly more 'philosophical' than Hunt's. But Hunt's lightsome voice is entirely appropriate to his vision of kindred relationship and community.

CCC was right to recall Keats's introduction to Hunt as a '"red-letter day" in the young poet's life', but it was not an untroubled episode.[17] The sudden leap in Keats's confidence is apparent in the letter that addresses his former schoolmaster as 'daintie Davie'. This was a cocky allusion to Burns's 'To Davie Second Epistle',

> Haud to the Muse, my daintie Davie:
> The warl' may play you monie a shavie,
> But for the Muse, she'll never leave ye,
> Tho' e'er sae puir . . .

Keats now had the upper hand: the Scots word 'daintie' means smart, precious, dandified, and describes CCC and his poetry with wounding accuracy. CCC had been reluctant to let Hunt know Keats, and other tensions were apparent in Haydon's wish to see Keats and Reynolds without Hunt present. While they were all excited and inspired by these encounters in late 1816, rivalries were not far below the surface. CCC had been vying with Keats for Hunt's attention; Hunt was the centre of admiring circles, and Haydon longed to attract his own coterie and 'found a School' of followers (deist Hunt would be excluded).[18] By December Keats and Reynolds had written sonnets dedicated to Haydon, with Keats flagging up Wordsworth, Hunt and Haydon as 'Great Spirits' of the present,

> These, these will give the world another heart
> And other Pulses . . .[19]

Reynolds chipped in with his breathless salute, 'Haydon! – Thou'rt born to Immortality!' Stealing a march on Haydon, Hunt would soon enrol Keats, with Reynolds and Shelley, in 'a new school of poetry' announced in the *Examiner*.

Relations with Haydon were, as always, friendly but fractious: 'The greater part of my time has been spent in Leigh Hunt's society,' Haydon confided to his diary, certainly one of the most delightful companions on Earth – full of Poetry & wit & amiable humour. We argue always with full hearts on every thing but Religion & Buonaparte, and we resolved after a little never to talk of them, as I have been examining Voltaire's opinions concerning Xianity & turmoiling my head to ascertain fully my right to put him in.[20]

Haydon had resolved to include Voltaire's head in *Christ's Entry into Jerusalem*, and to Hunt this looked like a deliberate sneer at religious sceptics and, by implication, at his own deism (in his anthology *Classic Tales, Serious and Lively* he had introduced Voltaire as humane, original and wise). Haydon would not back down, and his mention of private 'turmoiling' represented a brief lull in a row that would in a little while erupt again, with damaging consequences for the circle of friends who had only recently come together for the first time.[21]

Why did ideas of nurturing community, of 'sociality', become particularly significant after Waterloo? Twenty years earlier, in the aftermath of the French Terror and British repression of 1793–96, friends of liberty like Coleridge, Wordsworth and Thelwall had retreated to small survival groups in Dorset, Somerset and the Welsh border country. In those fastnesses revolutionary ideals were reinvented as the natural, unprejudiced poetry of *Lyrical Ballads* – a volume Hazlitt always cited as evidence of Wordsworth and Coleridge's levelling affiliations. Hunt's house at the Vale offered a similar kind of haven, drawing in a brilliant group of poets, artists, musicians and radicals that included Keats, Haydon, Hazlitt, Reynolds, CCC, the Novellos, the Olliers, John Gattie, Henry Robertson, the Lambs, Godwin, Horace Smith and, soon, Percy and Mary Shelley. From them sprang the 'new school' of poetry that would update the ideals of *Lyrical Ballads* for the post-revolutionary, post-Napoleonic period.

To hostile eyes, however, Hunt's community at the Vale looked like a dangerously resurgent sect of malcontents. They were prominently associated with the *Examiner*, and had other routes into print through John Hunt and a new publisher, Charles Ollier. During 1815–16 the forces of reaction united by the Holy Alliance were gaining throughout Europe, and Britain was entering a new period of unrest and repression. It would not be long before Hunt was once more under attack.

Waterloo had given Lord Liverpool's administration a temporary boost, but economic depression quickly followed. In March 1815 parliament had imposed Corn Laws to regulate imports of grain, and maintain prices and profits on the home market. This protected landowners – many MPs were drawn from the landed classes – but it pushed up the cost of living for everyone else. Hunt supported the protests to parliament, but understood that measures must be taken to balance the demands of rural producers and urban consumers.[22] From now on the *Examiner*'s burgeoning lists of bankrupts documented the country's distresses, and Hunt devoted eight 'Political Examiners' to the crisis. There were riots, machine-breakings, seizures, executions and imprisonments reported from the industrial cities; from the countryside came stories of farmers reduced to parish paupers, arrears of rent, tithes and poor-rates unpaid, agricultural improvements discontinued, livestock dwindling, tradesmen's bills unpaid, and roaming gangs of poachers and vagrants.[23]

Demands for reform grew louder. In London, mass meetings attracted tens of thousands to Spa Fields, Clerkenwell, where a bullish man in a white top hat stood on the tribune bellowing at the crowd. This was Henry 'Orator' Hunt again, a West Country farmer who was a moving spirit of the post-war reform movement. Like 'Citizen' John Thelwall in the 1790s, Henry Hunt's popularity lay in his ability to give mass unease a potent shape and language. Addressing the people, he worked on their discontent at wartime levels of taxation and high prices:

> Was not their loaf taxed – was not their beer taxed – were not their coats taxed – were not their shirts taxed – was not every thing they ate, drank, wore, and even said, taxed? (*A Laugh.*) What impudence, what insolence was it then in the corrupt and profligate minions of Government to say that the people suffered nothing by taxation.

He pointed over their heads to the walls of 'the British Bastille' – John Hunt's prison at Coldbath Fields – 'where so much tyranny had formerly been exercised'. 'What had become of all the great city patriots,' Henry Hunt enquired, 'that the distressed population of the metropolis had been obliged to send 100 miles for him to preside at their deliberations?'[24] A petition was drawn up calling for an extension of the suffrage, annual general elections and the right to a secret ballot.

Leigh Hunt agreed about taxes and peaceful petitioning, but that reference to 'city patriots' was an affront. From now on the *Examiner* dubbed Henry Hunt 'Mr. Hunt of Bristol' or 'Bristol Hunt' – 'no relation of ours'.[25] The emergence of 'Bristol Hunt', and the fact that he quickly became a figurehead for the revived reform movement, was an indicator of changing times to which the *Examiner* would have to respond. On Monday, 2 December a second Spa Fields meeting led to riots in Smithfield, Skinner Street, Newgate Street and the City. Above the crowd was a tri-coloured flag inscribed with the slogans

Nature – Feed the Hungry –
Truth – Protect the Distressed –
Justice – Punish Crime –

Rumours of 'a Plot somewhere' surged through the alleys and pot-houses of London, 'a Plot somewhere, – in some tap-room or other, like the plot of Despard'.[26]

The *Examiner* noticed the Spa Fields disturbances on its inside pages, but Hunt had decided that the last numbers for 1816 should feature on the front page Hazlitt's essays about 'Modern Apostates' instead of the usual 'Political Examiner'. Appearing at the troubled close of 1816, these articles emphasised how the *Examiner* was now directing its political energies on literary and poetic fronts. Critical chain-shot whirled across Hazlitt's pages. It was aimed broadside at all renegades from liberty, Southey and Coleridge included, and thoroughly eviscerated Wordsworth by revealing the vainglorious plot of his poetry and politics. These angry, brawling paragraphs were later reused by Hazlitt in the more measured pages of his *Lectures on the English Poets* and *Spirit of the Age*. For the moment, however, Hazlitt recommended that poets like Wordsworth 'cannot be too much despised and shunned'.[27] They were 'a nuisance which ought to be abated', like the *Times* newspaper's endorsement of the Bourbon monarchy. Hazlitt was especially infuriated that the Bourbons had revived the idea that they ruled France by divine right. He saw it as

> this detestable doctrine, which would of right, and with all the sanctions of religion and morality, sacrifice the welfare of the universe to the least of its caprices; which would make the rights, the happiness, the liberty of nations, from the beginning to the end of time, dependant on the pampered will of some of the lowest and vilest of the species . . . now that they have restored this monstrous fiction (after twenty years of baffled, malignant opposition to human nature, long glorious and triumphant, and still to be so) you see them with their swords and pens still propping up its lethargic, ricketty form . . .

Hazlitt looks beneath the fine robes of Hunt's corpulent Adonis, and discovers the loathsome creature '*Legitimacy*' squatting on welfare, rights, happiness, liberty, the will of the people, nature and human nature, mind, heart and understanding. This Fuselian spectre is no more than the 'monstrous fiction' of 'perpetual slavery by the grace of God' – a fiction that 'in England first tottered and fell headless to the ground with the martyred Charles'. 'Fine word "legitimate"!' But what would exterminate the monster in France?[28]

Hunt had the answer. Immediately following Hazlitt on bogus 'legitimacy', a column with the headline 'Young Poets' announced 'a new school of poetry rising of late'.[29] Originating in *Lyrical Ballads*, about which there was 'something excessive, like most revolutions', the 'new school' had settled into a steady 'aspiration after real nature and original fancy' that would supplant French neoclassicism and, by extension, other forms of tyranny. Hunt singles out 'three young writers': Percy Bysshe Shelley, also known as 'Elfin-Knight' (whose manuscript Hunt had 'unfortunately mislaid'); John Hamilton Reynolds, known to Hunt since his prison days; and, 'youngest of them all, and just of age', John Keats. Why this emphasis on youthfulness? Hunt was only thirty-two, but meeting Keats around the time of their birthdays had concentrated his attention on a rising generation younger than himself (Shelley was 24, Reynolds 22, and Keats just 21).

Times were changing. Popular protest was active again in England, and 'Young Poets' presented complementary evidence of 'other pulses' in contemporary poetry. While Hazlitt raged against ghosts of the old order, Hunt brought forward three young poets of substance who think, feel, promise, aspire and energetically 'grapple with Nature'. Their poetry gazes into the world to come, Hunt argues,

> . . . like stout CORTEZ, when with eagle eyes
> He stared at the Pacific, – and all his men
> Looked at each other with a wild surmise, –
> Silent, upon a peak in Darien.[30]

Hunt places his quotation of Keats's 'Chapman's Homer' sonnet strategically, so that the close of his 'Young Poets' article stands on the threshold of another of Keats's boundless oceanic prospects. And Shelley's mislaid manuscript, temporarily withheld from readers, promised a future revelation of wonders.

Even the wildest surmise would fall short of the events that unfolded over the next few days.

TWENTY-TWO

ET IN ARCADIA

Sunday, 1 December 1816. At 5, Abbey Churchyard in Bath, Percy Shelley and Mary Godwin received a letter from Hunt that mentioned the 'Young Poets' article, the 'Elfin-Knight' manuscript, and his various money problems. Shelley saw that Hunt had given his poetry its first favourable public notice, and immediately forwarded £50 with a letter explaining some of his own difficulties. A few days later, Shelley was at Marlow on the River Thames in Buckinghamshire, staying with Thomas Love Peacock and his mother at their home in West Street and looking for a house to lease. In two further letters Hunt gave 'sympathy & kindness', offered a copy of the *Examiner* containing 'Young Poets', and asked if Shelley wished his name to appear with the 'Hymn'. He also enclosed £5 as an earnest of the interest he would pay on the money Shelley had advanced.

Shelley's first approach to Hunt in 1810 had adopted the formality of a stranger. This time he was determined to secure the friendship of the man who had proved a staunch ally to that noble pariah, Byron. The surest way to do so was to fall in with Hunt's sympathetic manner, and Shelley responded immediately in a letter as if to 'an old friend'. Yes, he would accept the *Examiner*. The 'Hymn' might fare better if not associated with its 'stigmatised & unpopular' author. 'I am an outcast from human society,' Shelley went on, but 'an object of compassion to a few more benevolent than the rest' among whom Hunt was already pre-eminent: 'With you, & perhaps some others (tho in a less degree, I fear) my gentleness & sincerity find favour, because they are themselves gentle & sincere; they believe in self-devotion & generosity because they are themselves generous and self-devoted.' Shelley mentions his supportive 'domestic circle' – always likely to appeal to Hunt – and adds that these are subjects for private 'conversation'. He is 'exceedingly delighted' by *Rimini*; anticipates welcoming Hunt among Marlow's 'sweet green fields', and is 'strongly tempted' to come to London 'to spend one evening with you, & if I can I will'.[1] He returns the £5, encourages Hunt to spend it on 'some little literary luxury' he has denied himself, and closes: 'Most affectionately yours P. B. Shelley'. A tactful PS adds: 'I will send you an Alastor.'

Everything in Shelley's letter would have impressed Hunt. Shelley had responded generously to his financial plight, with no sense that he was conferring an obligation. In this he resembled Byron – there was no hint of 'charity'. Keats had come to Hunt's notice as an admiring junior, eager to publish his first poem. Shelley was closer in age to Hunt, an active reformer, and a dazzlingly accomplished poet who needed Hunt's encouragement. So far he had failed to identify and connect with an audience for his political pamphlets and poems; *An Address to the Irish People, A Letter to Lord Ellenborough, A Declaration of Rights, Queen Mab* and *Alastor* had all met with 'neglect' and 'oblivion'.[2] When staying at Lynmouth, Devon, in 1812 Shelley had distributed copies in hot-air balloons and bottles cast into the sea, 'vessels of heavenly medicine' that nature's forces would waft to receptive readers.[3] In Hunt Shelley saw the man who had succeeded in uniting politics and poetry and who was read, week after week, by liberals, dissenters and intellectuals throughout the country. Now Hunt had promised publication of the 'Hymn' in the *Examiner*. This was a long-awaited breakthrough, guaranteeing Shelley the readership he craved.

Shelley did go to London. He was at the Vale of Health on Wednesday, 11 December, welcomed into a domestic circle that resembled his own strange ménage at Bath. Mary's stepsister Claire Clairmont, now eight months pregnant with Byron's child, had been living with Mary and Shelley all year – and Mary's most recent letter had warned Shelley, 'give me a garden & *absentia Clariæ*'.[4] The 'poet's house' at the Vale had its strains too, although Shelley was received into cheerfully disordered rooms full of amiable talk – the centre of London's literary and radical life. Hunt had invited the 'young poet' Keats and the witty poet-banker Horace Smith to meet him. Smith wandered down the path from Hampstead to find Keats already there, and then Shelley strode in – 'a fair, freckled, blue-eyed, light-haired, delicate-looking person'. Shelley was tall, fashionably dressed, a *gentleman* – all qualities that appealed to Hunt who noted, however, that Keats did not take kindly to his new friend. On 13 December Mary jotted in her journal: 'Letter from S. – he is pleased with Hunt', and the next day an exuberant Shelley arrived back at Bath.[5]

None of them yet knew the significance of an announcement that had appeared in *The Times* on 12 December:

On Tuesday a respectable female, far advanced in pregnancy, was taken out of the Serpentine River, and brought home to her residence in Queen-street, Brompton, having been missed for nearly six weeks. She had a valuable ring on her finger. A want of honour in her own conduct is supposed to have led to this fatal catastrophe, her husband being abroad.[6]

The respectable female was in fact Harriet Westbrook, Shelley's estranged wife and the mother of his two children Eliza Ianthe and Charles. How and why had she come to this dreadful end?

Shelley and Harriet had parted in June 1814, and since April 1815 Shelley had apparently not seen Harriet at all. Little is known of her whereabouts in the months leading up to her death, though it is possible that in the spring and summer of 1816 she had an affair with an army officer called Maxwell, by whom she was pregnant at her death. This lover, if he existed, left her when the signs of her pregnancy became obvious. Like Claire Clairmont at Bath, Harriet moved into lodgings and took an assumed name to avoid disgracing her family. Alone and depressed, she wrote a farewell letter addressed to her sister Eliza, Shelley and her parents, in which she described how she was 'embittered by past recollections & not one ray of hope to rest on for the future'. Then she committed suicide, probably on Saturday, 7 December.[7]

It all sounds tragically possible – but an alternative narrative also leads to the same 'fatal catastrophe'. In this account Shelley had fathered Harriet's third child while at London in spring 1816, and then abandoned her once again. Basil Montagu, Shelley's legal counsel in his attempts to secure custody of the children, thought it probable that Shelley was the father of Harriet's unborn child. And Shelley had asked the publisher Thomas Hookham to try to locate Harriet in the month before her death.[8]

What mattered for Hunt was Shelley's response to the letter he received from Hookham on 15 December – the day after he had returned from the Vale:

My dear Sir:

It is nearly a month since I had the pleasure of receiving a letter from you, and you have no doubt felt surprised that I did not reply to it sooner. It was my intention to do so; but, on inquiry, I found the utmost difficulty in obtaining the information you desired relative to M$^{rs.}$ Shelley and your children.

While I was yet endeavoring to discover M$^{rs.}$ Shelley's address, information was brought me that she was dead – that she had destroyed herself. You will believe that I did not credit the report. I called at the house of a friend of M$^{r.}$ Westbrook. My doubt led to conviction. I was informed that she was taken from the Serpentine river on Tuesday last, apparently in an advanced state of pregnancy. Little or no information was laid before the jury which sat on the body. She was called Harriet Smith, and the verdict was – *found drowned.*

Your children are well, and are both, I believe, in London.

This shocking communication must stand single and alone in the letter which I now address to you: I have no inclination to fill it with

subjects comparatively trifling: you will judge of my feelings and excuse
the brevity of this communication.

Yours very truly,
   T. Hookham Jr.

Old Bond Street
   December 13th 1816⁹

Overwhelmed by guilt and grief, Shelley turned to the one person who could
be relied upon for support: Hunt. He took an afternoon coach from Bath and
dashed through gales and rain to London. Just three days after his first appearance at the Vale of Health as a 'young poet', Shelley rematerialised as a bedrag-
gled figure almost incoherent with anguish. Hunt took him in and Shelley
recounted the few details he had gathered from Hookham's letter. Hunt immediately dropped his weekly routine and devoted himself entirely to Shelley.
They set about tracing little Eliza Ianthe and Charles, and tried to discover
what had happened to Harriet. Above all Shelley needed to ensure that he
was awarded custody of the children, not the Westbrooks and at all costs not
Harriet's older sister Eliza whom he loathed.

On Monday, 16 December Hunt was with Shelley all day and accompanied him to his solicitor, Longdill, who advised 'caution and resoluteness'.
Shelley's assurances that he would marry Mary removed one pretence for
detaining the children, and Hunt immediately saw that this double prospect
was exactly the news to brighten Mary at Bath. Later that day Shelley wrote
to her explaining what they had learned about Harriet, in a letter that pays
tribute to Hunt's 'delicate & tender attentions' and 'kind speeches of you'.
Shelley's furious attack on the Westbrooks has led to dispute about this letter's
authenticity, although Richard Holmes finds it perfectly in character.¹⁰ From
it we can gather what Hunt and Shelley believed about Harriet's last hours.
They had spent the day contemplating the 'vice & folly & hard heartedness
exceeding all conception' that brought about Harriet's suicide, 'horrors of
unutterable villainy that led to this dark dreadful death'. Shelley shows more
compassion for Harriet than at any point during the past two years:

> It seems that this poor woman – the most innocent of her abhorred & unnat-
> ural family – was driven from her father's house, & descended the steps of
> prostitution until she lived with a groom of the name of Smith, who deserting
> her, she killed herself – There can be no question that the beastly viper her
> sister, unable to gain profit from her connexion with me – has secured to
> herself the fortune of the old man – who is now dying – by the murder of
> this poor creature. Everything tends to prove, however, that beyond the mere
> shock of so hideous a catastrophe having fallen on a human being once so
> nearly connected with me, there would, in any case have been little to regret.

Hookham, Longdill – every one does *me* full justice; – bears testimony to the uprightness & liberality of my conduct to her: – There is but one voice in condemnation of the detestable Westbrooks. If they should dare to bring it before Chancery – a scene of such fearful horror would be unfolded as would cover them with scorn & shame.[11]

Shelley emphasised how Hunt's 'affectionate attentions' had been 'sustainers & restoratives' throughout this awful day, and before sealing his letter enclosed a miniature silhouette of himself that Marianne had cut. It was a token of their belonging to a secure circle of friends while all else was engulfed by trauma, guilt and recrimination.

Shelley desperately needed to shift his sense of responsibility for Harriet's death – to Eliza, to the Westbrooks, to the feckless groom Smith with whom she was alleged to have been living. Most important for his own psychological survival was the idea that 'poor', 'innocent' Harriet had been cast out by her family to become a prostitute. There is no evidence that she had literally taken to the streets, but the idea of her degradation enabled Shelley to transform her death into a scene of persecution that represented the ills of contemporary society. She had suffered so much from 'vice' and 'villainy' and the 'hard heartedness' of an 'unnatural family' that there was 'little to regret' in her death.[12] Harriet had succumbed to the tyranny Shelley had been fighting all his life, and now he would redouble his efforts to overthrow the oppressors.

Wednesday, 18 December brought Keats to the Vale, where he may have heard that Hunt had agreed to take charge of Harriet's children and prepare them for residence with their father. Since first meeting Hunt, Keats like Haydon had been eclipsed by Shelley: he was unable to compete with this tall, gentlemanly, university-educated poet and radical, whose personal tragedy and extreme opinions now absorbed Hunt. Haydon scribbled in his diary how repulsive he found Shelley, physically and intellectually, but Keats tried to echo his atheistical, anti-clerical opinions. In his sonnet 'Written in Disgust of Vulgar Superstition', we can overhear talk at the Vale during these December days: how religion is a 'black spell' enthralling the human mind, an 'outburnt lamp' destined to 'go / Into oblivion'.[13] It would be some time before Keats reclaimed Hunt's attention, but he had enough to occupy him: Haydon had taken his life mask, and he was gathering his poems for a first book.

Shelley's talk now was of his 'agonising & impatient sense of duty'. He had apparently subdued his grief, and resolved to act decisively to obtain custody of the children. He bore no malice, he said, and expected 'immediate compliance'. 'All parties I imagine suffer too deeply to find any consolation in the

unnecessary display of their sensations.'[14] But Shelley did display his sensations within hours of writing his letter to Eliza, as Hunt was to witness.

Hunt had seen Shelley through the shock of Harriet's death, and by Thursday,
19 December was able to resume preparation of the next Sunday's *Examiner*.
That evening he attended Drury Lane to review a revival of James Cobb's
popular comic opera *Ramah Droog*.[15] While he watched the performance, the
first snow of winter was falling over London and, by the time he got back to
Hampstead, the Heath was white over. As Hunt descended the Vale, he could
see dozens of tiny points of light – elfin lanterns – where labourers employed
to landscape and 'improve' the Heath had made their camps. The sight was
enchanting; the reality was a parish scheme to relieve poor people thrown out
of work with the coming of peace.[16] When he approached the door of his
house he 'heard strange and alarming shrieks, mixed with the voice of a man'.
Inside Hunt found a woman having a seizure, with Marianne, Bess and two
young men trying to calm her. One of the young men was Shelley. Next day
the gossips of the Vale were reporting that 'Mr. Shelley, no Christian . . . had
brought some "very strange female" into the house, no better of course than
she ought to be'. The incident had the makings of a scandal. And to think
he brought her into Mr Hunt's house.

　　The woman was certainly in trouble and Shelley, deep in crisis over Harriet,
was ready to believe she was another unfortunate who had 'descended the
steps of prostitution'. As Hunt retells the story, it becomes a scene of resti-
tution in which Shelley makes amends for deserting Harriet and discloses his
true, saintly nature:

> Mr. Shelley, in coming to our house that night, had found a woman lying
> near the top of the hill, in fits. It was a fierce winter night, with snow upon
> the ground; and winter loses nothing of its fierceness at Hampstead. My
> friend, always the promptest as well as most pitying on these occasions,
> knocked at the first houses he could reach, in order to have the woman
> taken in. The invariable answer was, that they could not do it. He asked for
> an outhouse to put her in, while he went for a doctor. Impossible! In vain
> he assured them she was no impostor. They would not dispute the point
> with him; but doors were closed, and windows were shut down.[17]

Hunt is writing with twelve years' hindsight, and six years after Shelley's
death. His story is told in melodramatic terms, although with sufficient detail
to make it verifiable: during the whole of this winter, the only evening on
which Shelley's presence at the Vale could have coincided with Hunt's return
from the opera and snowy weather was Thursday, 19 December.[18] Hunt elab-
orates the incident with details of a wealthy neighbour who rejected Shelley's
call for help, so that finally the woman was

brought to our house, which was at some distance, and down a bleak path; and Mr. S. and her son were obliged to hold her, till the doctor could arrive. It appeared that she had been attending this son in London, on a criminal charge made against him, the agitation of which had thrown her into the fits on her return. The doctor said that she would inevitably have perished, had she lain there a short time longer.[19]

Thornton, who was six years old when the incident happened, matched his father's account and added that Shelley had carried the woman off the Heath on his back.[20]

This was one of Shelley's 'most ordinary actions', Hunt reminded his readers, an action juxtaposed to the inhumanity of the so-called Christians who turned him away. Hunt's priority was to present Shelley as the Good Samaritan, although his account also helps to explain the winter setting of one of Shelley's poems long suspected to be about Harriet's death:

I

The cold earth slept below,
     Above the cold sky shone;
And all around, with a chilling sound,
     From caves of ice and fields of snow,
     The wind of night like death did flow
          Under the sinking moon.

II

The wintry hedge was black,
     The brown grass was not seen,
The birds did rest in the dark thorn's breast,
     Whose roots, beside the pathway track,
Bound hard the soil and many a crack
          The black frost made between.

III

Thine eyes glowed in the gleam
     Of the departing light;
As a starry beam on a deep dark stream
     Shines dimly, so the moon shone there,
     And it shone through the strings of thy tangled hair,
          Which shook in the blast of night.

IV

The moon made thy lips pale, beloved –
     The wind made thy bosom chill –

The air did shed on thy dear head
Its frozen dew, and thou didst lie
Where the bitter breath of the naked sky
Might visit thee at will.[21]

Although Shelley's poem says nothing overtly about Harriet, its imagery seems
to hold eerie echoes of her death – 'below', 'flow', 'sinking', 'stream', and
'tangled hair'. The winter landscape where a woman has frozen to death is
certainly not Hyde Park, where Harriet drowned, but it does resemble the
encounter on Hampstead Heath on the night of 19 December. Shelley
returned to that scene in a short sequel poem that faces death more directly:

That time is dead forever, child,
Drowned, frozen, dead forever!
    We look on the past,
    And stare aghast
At the spectres wailing, pale, and wild,
Of hopes which thou and I beguiled
    To death on life's dark river.[22]

A dark dreadful death. Shelley's friend Thomas Love Peacock observed
that Harriet's 'untimely fate' brought Shelley 'deep agony of mind, which
he felt the more because for a long time he kept the feeling to himself'.[23]
These two melancholy lyrics represent occasions on which that suppressed
agony apparently found a voice: by rescuing the 'strange woman' from her
fate on Hampstead Heath, Shelley was able to make a belated intervention
to prevent a lonely death, although there was no sense of atonement for
hope beguiled.

That December night on the Heath, Shelley had revived an episode of momentous significance for Hunt when his mother helped a sick woman in Blackfriars
Road.[24] Shelley's winter charity was 'of a piece with the rest of [his] character', exactly as Hunt's mother's had been. The week that had started with
Hunt supporting Shelley ended with Shelley taking on the role of Hunt's
mother, and standing in her place as a rescuer for Hunt himself. Anything
associated with Shelley was now sacred.

The Vale soon had another guest. Mary travelled up from Bath to join Shelley,
and they stayed with the Hunts until Sunday, 29 December. Next day, Shelley
and Mary were married at St Mildred's Church, Bread Street – 'magical
effects,' Shelley noted drily – and on New Year's Day 1817 they set off across
country to Bath and Claire. Once the Shelleys had left, Keats came over to
the Vale to pass the evening, and we can sense the gradual relaxation of pres-

sure as they settled down by the fire to write their sonnets about grasshoppers, crickets, sunshine, summer luxuries, and grassy hills.

In December 1816 a combination of poetry, politics, financial straits and bereavement had thrown Hunt and Shelley together, and temporarily eclipsed Keats. What was the personal chemistry that lit up their relationship, making it the most important of Hunt's life? Following traditions of classical Greece and the more recent cult of sensibility, both Hunt and Shelley saw male friendship as an exalted attachment. Hunt had experienced a blissful 'disembodied transport' in the company of school friends, and Shelley had formed a comparably intense regard for his undergraduate friend Thomas Jefferson Hogg, a relationship that certainly had a homosocial aspect: on leaving Oxford, Hogg repeatedly attempted to have affairs with Shelley's girl-friends, partners and wives. Whereas Shelley's relationships with men and women were always volatile and liable to disruption, Hunt needed and carefully nurtured lasting relationships with Marianne, Bess and a large circle of friends. This stability could be disturbed, as Bess's response to the Hunt–Shelley friendship would soon reveal, but the success with which he maintained steady attachments with both men and women was a remarkable gift as well as a necessity. Alongside Hunt's sociability and powerful attraction to women, however, there was a homoerotic aspect to his emotional life – indeed perhaps we can see this as another manifestation of Hunt's feeling for 'double pleasures'. Edmund Blunden did not tackle Hunt's sexuality directly in his biography, but he did admit to finding him not merely 'unconventional' in his relationship with Shelley but distinctly 'abnormal'.[25] Blunden did not explain further, but when he was writing in the 1920s that reference would have been well understood.

Hunt's poem 'The Choice', written shortly after Shelley was drowned, concluded with two places he would wish to be buried. One of them, 'in a gentle village, my old home', was the graveyard of St John's, Hampstead, where his mother lay. 'The other, by the softened walls of Rome' was the resting place of Shelley. Keats too lay under those ancient walls of Rome, as Hunt knew but chose not to mention.

The remaining £250 owed to Gale, Curtis and Fenner became due and, with John's help, it was cleared. But Hunt was now reduced to 'the greatest straits' in meeting domestic expenses.[26] Shelley forwarded money and issued a cheque for £50. Charles Ollier continued to help with small sums, and a letter came from Horace Smith 'making it a matter of grace to accept a bank-note of 100*l*. which he enclosed'.[27] Hunt was negotiating a second edition of *Rimini* with Taylor and Hessey, and poetry was 'a solid good in the way of comfort' as it had always been. He had also found time to enjoy a pantomime, relieved that on stage 'the trips up and thumps are not real'.[28]

*   *   *

Shelley was back at the Vale on Monday, 6 January, pursuing his campaign to secure the children. On the next Friday, Harriet's father initiated Chancery proceedings to appoint guardians for her children, citing Shelley's atheism and his 'blasphemous' poem *Queen Mab* as reasons for refusing custody. 'How much depends on this!' Shelley wrote to Mary, enquiring after Claire (who had just given birth to Byron's daughter, Alba), and adding 'The Hunts send their love.'[29] Hunt stood by Shelley throughout these 'tremendous circumstances', accompanied him to lawyers' offices, offered advice, introduced him to friends, and kept an eye on his health. Shelley told Mary he had not felt any 'perturbations which vitally affect the heart'. Like Hunt, he was a hypochondriac and susceptible to palpitations and other nervous ailments brought on by stress. Thornton recalled one day at the Vale when Shelley collapsed and 'poured forth shrieks, loud and continuous, stamping his feet madly on the ground'. At other times, in light-hearted mood, he joined in the children's playing, rambled on the Heath, and terrified Thornton by appearing as a 'frightful creature' with rampant paws and a great horn of twisted hair. Shelley and Thornton floated paper boats on the Vale of Health pond, and Shelley announced that shipwreck was a death he should like better than any other.[30]

That Shelley was able to maintain any buoyancy of spirit through this first month of 1817 was entirely owing to Hunt and the many social gatherings he arranged during breaks in the legal proceedings. Sunday, 19 January saw Shelley's 'Hymn to Intellectual Beauty' published in the *Examiner*. Hunt had carefully placed the 'Hymn' immediately before a report of a reformist meeting, so that Shelley's celebration of universal beauty –

> never joy illumed my brow
> Unlinked with hope that thou wouldst free
> This world from its dark slavery,
> That thou – O awful LOVELINESS,
> Wouldst give whate'er these words cannot express

– announced a potent response to the reformists' rallying cry:

> Where is the voice, human or divine, which can preach to the exasperation which famine and oppression produces in the minds of men – (*Applause*) – and I will even add in English minds?[31]

Shelley's 'Hymn' was not a respite or escape from the distresses of the nation, the Spa Fields riots, the fat Regent and mad old King. When read in the *Examiner* alongside articles about the awfulness of 'things as they are', it constituted a glorious lyrical force urging each heart and mind to 'love all human kind'.

*   *   *

Next day, Hunt, Marianne, Bess, Shelley, Haydon and Keats gathered for dinner at Horace Smith's home in Knightsbridge Terrace to the west of London. Knightsbridge was still a rural hamlet, but only just: Smith's house looked on to the main road to Bath and Bristol, crowded with traffic all day and into the small hours of the morning. While they talked they could hear the rumble of carriages, wagons with jingling bells, post-chaises, and the clatter of horse guards from the nearby barracks. As Hunt and Shelley knew by now, just yards away from Smith's house was Harriet's last address, Elizabeth Street off Hans Place, and a little further away in the opposite direction lay Hyde Park and the dark stream of the Serpentine. Perhaps those associations contributed to what seems to have been an especially bad tempered occasion – in Haydon's account, at least.

Christianity was the issue, as usual, and Shelley's bold speculations and atheism seem to have made Hunt unusually truculent. It was probably on this occasion that the vegetarian Shelley glanced up from his cabbage and green tea to remark, 'as to that detestable religion, the Christian', and Haydon 'became excessively irritable at Hunt's unfeeling, heartless, and brutal ridicule of Christ and his divine doctrine'. Hunt needled Haydon for putting Voltaire's head in his painting as one of the scoffers – 'now Haydon, there is no disgrace in acknowledging an error. Therefore candidly say you are wrong, & put out his head!' Haydon had always been resentful of Hunt's circle of women, and his flirtation with Bess. Now, according to Haydon, Shelley's talk of free love had made Hunt more daring: 'all women should submit to the infidelities of their husbands without feeling insulted'. There were more brutal jokes about religion, and then Shelley set off on a different tack: 'Shakespeare was not a Christian'. He quoted the Gaoler's words from *Cymbeline*: 'For look you, Sir, you know not which way you shall go' (V. iv. 175). Haydon flung back Hamlet's lines about the 'hallowed and gracious time' of 'our Saviour's birth' and Horatio's response that he did 'in part believe' (I. i. 157–65). Then Hunt questioned Haydon's ambitions as a painter:

Hunt – Haydon you will never be as great a painter as Raphael if you believe in Christianity.

Haydon – But unfortunately for you Raphael was a Christian.

Hunt – Not a jot of it.

Haydon – But I tell you he was. He left a sum for masses to be said for his Soul, & he painted sacred subjects by which he hoped to influence the minds as much as if he had written.

Hunt – Ah, but he did not believe in them.

Haydon – What argument is this? I tell you two facts, and you deny the consequence to be fairly deduced, not by two opposite facts, but by 'not a jot of it' & 'he did not believe it'.

*　　*　　*

Hunt had long regarded Voltaire in *Christ's Entry into Jerusalem* as a personal attack, and he responded in kind. His sonnet to Haydon had made a flattering comparison with Raphael. Now, in company, and in front of the women, he revoked it – '& then every body smiled, and thought that what Hunt said was very conclusive'. '"The question is", Hunt said, "who are the wicked? it is difficult to tell, I believe".' At this point they all moved through to the next room where Marianne and Bess were waiting to go. Hunt looked at them and turned to Haydon: 'Are these creatures to be damned?'[32]

Keats had hung back, and said little. Hunt's affection for Shelley made him uneasy, and he may well have been envious that while he had only published sonnets in the *Examiner*, Shelley's début had been a sophisticated lyric of eighty-four lines. On Christianity, Keats was with Hunt and Shelley. But he also admired Haydon, one of his 'great spirits'. Keats would stick by him, and wait for Hunt to tire of Shelley. His own book of poems would soon be in the press, although Shelley had advised him not to publish.

Haydon believed his paintings were a divine gift, and Hunt's and Shelley's scepticism struck at the foundation of his identity as an artist. For some time now he had allowed irritations and arguments to grow into an overwhelming sense of being slighted – the source, very likely, of Keats's feeling that Hunt and Shelley had 'undervalued' him too (although Hunt did not learn this until years later).[33] After the dinner at Smith's, Haydon would avoid Hunt for two months. Back at his studio in Great Marlborough Street he unleashed a torrent of resentment in his diary. Anger at Hunt's 'artful' arguments surged into fury at his 'vanity', carelessness with 'money matters', his 'smuggering fondness' for Bess, and 'personal cowardice'. All of this flowed from what Haydon recognised was a passion 'that in its heat pours forth truths which have for a long time been collected'.[34]

Haydon's problem with Hunt was jealousy of his fame, of his success, his ability to attract friends, above all his tantalising intimacy with women. Haydon would not marry until 1821, and was tormented by 'dreadful lascivious scenes that haunt one's imagination'. He recognised that his religious mania was a release for 'the fiery urgings of [his] own fiery nature'; irreligious, immoral, and heartless men – Hunt and Shelley, in Haydon's view – had been swallowed up by 'dreadful appetite'.[35] There was considerable self-understanding in Haydon's rage, and his dissection of Hunt's 'morbidity' was also perceptive:

Hunt's imagination is naturally and inherently gloomy, and all his leafy bowers & clipsome waists & balmy bosoms proceed not from a lovely fancy shooting out without effort the beauties of its own superabundant brightness, but are the product of a painful, hypochondriac Soul that struggles by dwelling on the *reverse* of its own *real* thoughts, perpetually to illumine its natural and forlorn dinginess; hence his painful wit, his struggling jokes, his hopeless puns; hence his wish to be surrounded by inferior intellects and being delighted to suck in their honey praise; hence his unwillingness to leave company or be left by them; hence his gloated trifling with Women . . . & hence his seeing only the gloomy prospects of damnation in believing Christianity, and hence his horror of being left alone *even for an hour!*[36]

Haydon had seen into the reality of Hunt's struggle with anxiety and depression, and accurately judged his personality as a needy, pain-full brightness. Hunt's parental inheritance of gloom and hypochondria coupled with shoots of 'lovely fancy' is summarised as a 'natural and forlorn dinginess' – a deliberately insulting reference to Hunt's West Indian appearance. And it was to Hunt's 'dinginess' that Haydon finally attributed his notions about free love or 'infidelities', and his 'gloated trifling' with Bess.

The Chancery case came before Lord Eldon on Friday, 24 January. Guardianship of Shelley's children depended on whether the 'principles of Deism' in *Queen Mab* were construed as dangerous or 'a mere effusion of the imagination'. So pressing were the questions of civil liberty and freedom of conscience, that Hunt, possibly with Shelley's agreement, risked contempt of court and drew attention to the case in the *Examiner*.[37] Hunt, like Shelley, saw despotism poised to invade and disrupt private domestic life. Eldon paused and deferred judgment until March, when he decided against Shelley. The case would not be resolved until July 1818.

On 26 January Mary Shelley returned to London, and a month of intensive social activity began, with Hunt leading musical evenings at the Vale, walks on the Heath, dinners at Godwin's and Horace Smith's, play and opera-going, and a visit to Robert Shout's sculpture shop in Holborn where Shelley ordered busts of Apollo and Venus. CCC, Charles Ollier, John Keats and his brother George, Hazlitt, Basil Montagu, John Hamilton Reynolds and his sisters, the Lambs and Walter Coulson (editor of the *Globe* newspaper) joined the company. Hunt and Hazlitt's essays from the *Examiner* had been gathered into a *Round Table* volume, and early copies of the book were already circulating. By mid-February Claire Clairmont had arrived from Bath with the newly-born Alba and the Shelleys' Swiss *gouvernante* Élise. The baby and Élise were taken in by the Hunts, while Claire lodged nearby to disguise the fact that she was a 'single mother'.

Mary Shelley's journal entry for 9 February gives us the flavour of this month:

Sunday 9th Walk with S. & Hunt to Brougham's in the morning – after dinner Read the arcadia. Several of Hunt's acquaintances come in the evening – Music – after Supper a discussion untill 3 in the morning with Hazlitt concerning monarchy & republicanism.[38]

Mary's notes record weeks of convivial activities. Only occasionally does she allow glimpses of other, more disturbing, goings-on in the Hunt household.

Except for some unsteady months after Hunt's release from prison, the triangular relation between Hunt, Marianne and Bess had been more or less harmonious. However, Haydon made a point of noting Hunt's 'waning' affection for Marianne, and how he would praise Bess 'for qualities which his wife has not, and which he knew she had not when he married her'.[39] Shelley's arrival unsettled them further, so much so – according to Haydon – that Bess attempted suicide. Haydon tried to belittle 'the lady of the "Hampstead Ponds", who, in trying to be pathetic, and hoping she might *not* be drowned, threw herself off a wooden footpath into a Hampstead puddle where it was six inches deep, and was pulled out black with mud and dripping with water, sufficiently disfigured to excite sympathy, yet quite secure (as she wished)'.[40] This was written in 1827 as part of another attack on Hunt, and Haydon's scorn deliberately misrepresents what had happened ten years before, very likely because Haydon had once been convinced that Bess was attracted to him.

The date of Bess Kent's suicide attempt was Saturday, 15 February, when Mary Shelley's journal noted: 'Finish the Arcadia – Shelley goes to town. Mr. Keats calls. Walk out.' Next day, in different ink, Mary added: '– Miss K. is ill.'[41] Was the episode just an attention-seeking flounce? Other circumstances, including Harriet Shelley's recent death, suggest not. The Hampstead Ponds were a system of reservoirs supplying water to London, not six-inch puddles. On 15 February, after two days of rain and a night of storms, they would have been full. In later life Bess certainly did threaten suicide over a 'break' with Hunt, and her stepsister Nancy Hunter said she was 'quite capable of it'. She had always been impetuous and, according to some, extremely bad-tempered. Keats was not the only person to feel slighted by Hunt's preoccupation with Shelley: Bess had long been Hunt's confidante, but now she had been cast aside and made to feel something of what her sister Marianne had long experienced.[42]

One week after Bess's attempt, there was another scare. Mary Shelley's journal gives the bare details: 'Read the Round Table – Go to Clare – Read after dinner – Mr^s Hunt frightens us by staying out late –.'[43] The poet's house at the Vale of Health now housed an intense, volatile community: Hunt, Marianne and their four children, Bess, Percy and Mary Shelley, with (from mid-February) their little boy William, baby Alba, and Élise. Claire was lodging nearby in the village. And there were seemingly endless streams of visitors and meals, with readings, music, drinking and late night discussions. Hunt was struggling to meet *Examiner* deadlines, and Shelley was engrossed with the Chancery case.

No wonder Marianne slipped out for a walk on the Heath. The Hunt circle at the Vale has often been seen as a warm, unconventional community of cheerful solidarity, but what stands out in these anxious winter months is the way Hunt's family and friends were also riven with jealousies, competing loves, rival ambitions and fears of rejection. That Mary Shelley worried about these tensions is evident from her letters wishing Hunt to be 'at peace', bidding 'Miss K. . . . to be good', and advising Marianne to 'cultivate [Hunt's] affection & cherish & *enjoy* his society & I am sure my dear Mary Anne will find her prospects clear very sensibly'.[44]

On Saturday, 22 February Hunt received a reminder from Taylor and Hessey about the promised volume containing 'Hero and Leander', for which they had advanced twenty guineas.[45] Shelley negotiated on Hunt's behalf, but the volume was not ready: Hunt had more than enough to preoccupy him, and once again he was storing up trouble for the future. On Wednesday the 26th Hunt sought Vincent Novello's advice about acquiring a small upright piano to be sent 'into the country'.[46] Next day the Shelleys quitted Hampstead for their new home at Albion House, Marlow. The Hunts had been invited to join them there. They all needed a change of scene.

Outside the Vale unrest had been stirring. For some weeks the *Examiner* had been reporting London on the threshold of revolution, and at the end of January the tension exploded. The Regent was hissed and jeered as he returned from opening parliament, and his carriage was pelted with stones, gravel and rubbish from the street. Then one of the carriage windows shattered. Was this a gunshot from an assassin? Soldiers were called out to patrol the streets. Magistrates around the country were put on alert. Now Hunt went on the offensive in the *Examiner*, exasperated by the 'mighty tenderness' expressed for the Prince: 'the idea of ten poor wretches huddling together in ragged starvation on a bridge at night is at least as much calculated to make us grave and shuddering, as that of a single high-living PRINCE who has his coach-window cracked'.[47]

Poor naked wretches. The talk was of revolutionary conspiracies, and Hunt was inclined to believe 'some sort of conspiracy has existed . . . some actual revolutionary design'.[48] A 'Secret Committee' recommended suspension of Habeas Corpus, and Hunt reminded readers of Despard's dreadful fate on the gallows at Horsemonger Lane: 'Let us not forget the former times of terrors and suspensions, and the fate of poor frenzied DESPARD; who was a conspirator no doubt, but a conspirator rendered mad by that very abuse of power, which we have been threatened to be called upon to submit to for the prevention of treason.'[49] Repression loomed. Hunt countered with a series of letters 'To the English People', warning of an unconstitutional attempt to 'suspend our liberties' and rallying King Alfred, Chaucer, Shakespeare, Hampden and Milton to the struggle:

Come forward then, Fellow-countrymen, every one of you who, to say nothing of sympathy with suffering, has the least respect for common sense and understanding . . . There is not a youth who walks out of doors with a book, not a single scholar who has got beyond his syntax, not a reader of newspapers or reviews, not an individual, young or old, who loves to go to the theatre and hear SHAKESPEARE . . . that ought not to blush at seeing a nation, renowned for every species of literature and greatness, governed against its will by a junto who neither feel what is English, nor can even talk it. – Reform, Reform, Reform: – Petition, *Petition*.[50]

This was not only a grave political crisis, it was a violation of Englishness. The *Examiner* enlisted poetry in the front line of opposition, and Keats contributed a sonnet that saw hope reviving with the return of spring,

> AFTER dark vapors have oppress'd our plains
> For a long dreary season, comes a day
> Born of the gentle SOUTH, and clears away
> From the sick heavens all unseemly stains,
> The anxious Month, relieving of its pains,
> Takes as a long lost right the feel of MAY . . .[51]

Long lost rights preoccupied 'The Hermit of Marlow', Shelley, who rushed out his pamphlet *Proposal for Putting Reform to the Vote*. Hunt quoted it in the *Examiner* on 2 March, praising Shelley's willingness to fund a nation-wide referendum in 'our green and glorious country'.[52] By early spring of 1817 the political-poetical salon at the Vale of Health was leading a coherent campaign, championing Magna Carta and England's traditional liberties against the 'courtiers and official automatons', who on 4 March did indeed suspend Habeas Corpus. From that moment Hunt and his fellow-countrymen risked arrest and imprisonment without trial.

At this critical period, Charles Ollier published *Poems, by John Keats*. By now Keats had abandoned his medical studies, and was able to walk over to give Hunt a presentation copy. They met in Millfield Lane on Hampstead Heath. Opening the book, Hunt found this:

DEDICATION.
———

TO LEIGH HUNT, ESQ.

> GLORY and loveliness have passed away;
> For if we wander out in early morn,
> No wreathed incense do we see upborne

Into the east, to meet the smiling day:
No crowd of nymphs soft voic'd and young, and gay,
 In woven baskets bringing ears of corn,
 Roses, and pinks, and violets, to adorn
The shrine of Flora in her early May.
But there are left delights as high as these,
 And I shall ever bless my destiny,
That in a time, when under pleasant trees
 Pan is no longer sought, I feel a free
A leafy luxury, seeing I could please
With these poor offerings, a man like thee.[53]

While Hunt was warning in the *Examiner* of the destruction of English freedom, in *Poems, by John Keats* he was invoked as 'Libertas', celebrated in the sonnet 'Written on the day that Mr. Leigh Hunt left Prison', praised as the sociable genius of 'Sleep and Poetry'. Keats's 'Dedication' sonnet adapts Hunt's stylistic innovations, and follows Hunt by interweaving English pastoral ('Roses, and pinks, and violets') with figures from classical myth (nymphs, Flora). Amid a scene of loss – 'a time, when . . . Pan is no longer sought' – the 'leafy luxury' of imaginative liberty still survives, and from the 'poor offerings' in Keats's book new pleasures and freedoms may be destined to grow.

The Shelleys were away in Marlow, and Keats had recaptured Hunt's attention. They walked back to the Vale to celebrate, and perhaps it was now that Hunt crowned Keats with laurels, and Keats circled Hunt's head with ivy – an occasion they marked by writing sonnets. Keats was soon embarrassed by this episode – 'I put on no Laurels till I shall have finished Endymion, and I hope Apollo is not angered at my having made a Mockery at him at Hunt's' – but at the time it had not seemed like that.[54] His change of heart marks this occasion as the last on which Hunt and Keats agreed about poetry.

From now on Keats held more aloof. He persevered with *Endymion* on the Isle of Wight and at Margate, where a letter arrived from Haydon warning as a 'brother' of Hunt's 'delusions & sophistications'.[55] Keats promptly wrote to Hunt, chatting about a recent *Examiner*, Hunt's new poem 'The Nymphs', poetic fame, and what a dauntingly 'great thing' it was to be a poet. 'Remember me to them all – to Miss Kent and the little ones all – Your sincere friend John Keats alias Junkets.'[56] Next day, a letter also went off to Haydon. Keats wasn't 'in humor' with Hunt's poetry or his own. Haydon was right: Hunt was a 'self-deluder' who had flattered himself into 'an idea of being a great Poet'. How fortunate that 'brother' Haydon understood the turmoil, the anxiety and the sacrifice art demanded, 'the readiness . . . to die in 6 hours could plans be brought to conclusions'. 'I pray God that our brazen tombs be nigh neighbors'.[57]

In June and July the *Examiner* carried Hunt's long review of Keats's *Poems* praising the book's 'natural tendency', 'sensitiveness', 'fancy', 'imagination', 'simplicity' and 'strong evidences of warm and social feelings'. The 'faults' Hunt noted were an 'over-zealous' application of his own principles: the 'roughnesses and discords' of Keats's versification took his own colloquial experiments to a tendentious extreme.[58] Hunt's reservations weighed more with Keats than his fulsome praise, and they would not meet again until October. The most perceptive idea of Keats during this year, or at any time, was Hunt's: 'all we can hope at present is, that a youth of his ardour may not bring too much upon him too soon'.[59]

Part VI: In the Warm South, 1817–1822

As you perceive, my brother L. has not been able
to contribute to the paper for some months, on
account of health. He is now on his way to Pisa,
to join Mr Shelley and Lord Byron and in
conjunction with the latter will produce
some literary work.

Letter of John Hunt, 'Monday C.B.F. Prison',
(1821)

TWENTY-THREE

MARLOW AND LONDON

'We set off at eleven tomorrow morning,' Hunt told Novello, '& are in all the chaos of packed trunks, lumber, litter, dust, dirty dry fingers, &c.' On Thursday, 10 April they clambered on to the coach, and set off for Marlow. Marianne and Bess rode inside with Johnny, Mary, and the babies Swinburne and Alba, while Thornton and Hunt travelled on outside seats in sunny spring weather. Mary Shelley noted 'a little turmoil in the evening' accompanying the Hunts' arrival. Marianne was 'very unwell' – like Mary, she was pregnant.[1]

At the Vale, Hunt had felt enclosed by the surrounding Heath, and the rooms inside the poet's house had been tiny. For the next few months life in Marlow would be on a much grander scale: Albion House was a long building with a flat stone façade and narrow, pointed windows in Gothic style. Behind a balustrade little latticed windows were set into the tiled roof, and overhead were massive brick chimneys. The house stood on the edge of Marlow and immediately outside the front door was West Street, the busy coach route to Henley. Across the road were fields and the water meadows of the River Thames, Bisham village with its old abbey manor house and, further off, the dark bank of Bisham Wood.

The rooms in Albion House were large, but to Hunt they felt damp and there wasn't much light. Shelley had already fitted out the largest room as a library and set up the busts of Apollo and Venus they had bought from Robert Shout. Domestic arrangements were handled by the Shelleys' four servants and a full-time cook. Behind the house was a lawn and garden, and a turfed mound with a rustic seat, surrounded with trees through which could be seen fields with sheep grazing. That seat had the makings of a bower. Thornton remembered that behind the mound was a small vegetable garden, a deep lane, and nothing beyond but the country.[2] Albion House would be Hunt's home for the next two and a half months, but the piano had still not arrived. His first letter from Marlow was a reminder.

Life soon fell into the leisurely routine Hunt called 'country hours'. He woke late in the mornings and eventually wandered downstairs to find Mary revising the manuscript of her novel *Frankenstein*. Shelley had long since

disappeared to Bisham Wood to work on his poem *Laon and Cythna*. Marianne
was in fragile health, and Bess and Élise were busy looking after the six children – Thornton, John, Mary Florimel, Swinburne, and William and Alba.
The Shelleys' dog had already bitten William. Hunt was composing a new
poem, 'The Nymphs', and retreated to the rustic seat in the garden whenever he had the chance. Afternoons were passed walking to Little Marlow
and Bisham, or along the banks of the Thames to watch fishermen setting
nets. Bess gathered wild flowers to study. Sometimes they all took Shelley's
boat, the *Vaga*, on the river, and for Hunt Mary became a spirit of the water.
He called her 'Marina'. Hunt was nicknamed 'La Caccia' ('The Hunt'),
Marianne became 'Molbincha', Shelley was the 'Hermit', and Albion House
'The Hermitage'. Until the piano arrived at the end of April, evening readings took the place of music with Shelley reciting from Wordsworth and
Spenser. Marianne spent two evenings cutting a silhouette of Mary. After the
others had gone to bed Hunt stayed up long into the night to write for the
Examiner. Sending copy by the post or by carrier meant that he had to be
well beforehand.

Spring advanced, and Hunt took pleasure in the scenery of the Thames
valley with its meadows and woods and water. There were steeples 'issuing
out of clumps of trees', luxuriant hedges with wild flowers, cornfields, brooks,
nooks, and 'pretty looks' from the Marlow lace-makers. Their excursions took
them further afield to the ruins of Medmenham Abbey where, fifty years
earlier, Sir Francis Dashwood's secretive 'Hell-Fire Club' had gathered for
'profane ceremonies' of art, drink, and sex with local girls. Hunt thought the
lurid stories of the club were probably 'much exaggerated'; the people of
Medmenham did not 'think so ill of the club as others', but then '*family* feelings' were probably concerned.[3] Hunt most likely ventured northwards to
High Wycombe and on into the Chiltern Hills to visit Great Hampden, the
home of one of his patriotic heroes, John Hampden. Downstream the Thames
took their boat to Cookham Village and the woods at Cliveden, from where
they could walk to the green glades of Burnham Beeches.

All the time Hunt was garnering images for his new poem, a joyful exorcism
of the 'Hell-Fire Club' and all that it represented about the *ancien régime*.
The poem would feature a pagan landscape haunted by 'Nymphs of all names,
and woodland Geniuses':

> Those are the Naiads, who keep neat
> The banks from sedge, and from the dull-dropp'd feet
> Of cattle that break down the fibrous mould.
> They snap the selfish nets, that, overbold,
> Cross the whole river, and might trip the keels
> Of summer boats.[4]

Banks, sedge, the hoofs of cattle, mud, fishermen's nets, summer boats, a mother blackbird, a hedgehog, 'little corner bowers / Of hedge-row fields', 'forests old', and 'grass-edged lanes / With little ponds that hold the rains' – this is the Thames valley, not Thessaly. Hunt gives us a quintessentially English landscape, animated with presences from pagan mythology – Nymphs, Dryads and Oreads – and some that are all his own – Ephydriads, Limniads and Napeads. These are all creatures associated with the cult of Pan, the benevolent, natural religion of the ancient world that Hunt and Shelley associated with liberty and community, erotic energy and free love. One passage transforms the garden of Albion House into a scene from a print by Claude or Poussin:

> Some sat in shade beneath a curving jut,
> As at a small hill's foot;
> And some behind upon a sunny mound
> With twinkling eyes. Another only shewed
> On the far side a foot and leg, that glowed
> Under the cloud; a sweeping back another,
> Turning her from us like a suckling mother;
> She next, a side, lifting her arms to tie
> Her locks into a flowing knot; and she
> That followed her, a smooth down-arching thigh
> Tapering with tremulous mass internally.[5]

While Hunt was surrounding himself with a bevy of nymphs, Shelley was setting up an altar to Pan in Bisham Woods.

A sunny mound. Down-arching thighs. What had 'The Nymphs' to do with England in 1817? At Marlow Hunt was thirty-five miles away from the *Examiner* office. Had he decided to throw over his journalistic commitments? 'The Nymphs' begins by contrasting a 'healthy' vision with 'the motes of Bigotry's sick eye, / Or the blind feel of *false* Philosophy'. Bigotry and false philosophy encapsulated the ills of contemporary society Hunt had been fighting since his early days with the *News*, whereas his new poem presented the clear-sighted 'feel' of a renovated world in touch with erotic pleasure and 'social glee'. 'The Nymphs' draws to a close with this message:

> Go tell our song
> To such as hang their pale home-withered heads
> For winter-time, and do our kindness wrong:
> And say, that they might bear,
> The more they know us, the moist weight of air . . .

We are back in the clammy Thames valley, where the unemployed poor were encouraged to put up with the weather by Shelley's weekly handouts of money.

That was 'practical charity', Hunt thought. No less practical, however, was Hunt's lyrical insistence that a recovery of pleasure would enhance communal 'kindness'. Such was the significance of the cult of Pan in early summer 1817 – a time when, as Keats had said, Pan was 'no longer sought' in England.

Within days of Hunt's arrival at Marlow news came of bigotry in Liverpool: John Wright, a Unitarian, had been accused of giving blasphemous lectures on religion. Hunt responded immediately with leading articles on the right to freedom of conscience, a journalistic intervention that paralleled the pagan liberties of 'The Nymphs': the present 'alliance of intolerance with exclusive faiths' in the Church of England was manifestly 'inferior . . . to the Pagans'. Hunt and Shelley's cult of Pan was no escapist fantasy: it was an urgent condemnation of the benighted rulers of England, those 'Saints of the Establishment'.[6]

'Albion' was the old name for England, and Albion House inspired its occu-pants with dreams of a rejuvenated nation. Soon Hunt and Shelley were tapping into the green energies of the spring. Bess recalled Shelley rambling out into the fields and woods to read and write and 'speculate on his favourite theme – the advancement of human happiness'. The figure she associated with those memories was not Shelley with a book, quill and manuscript, but an emanation of England, 'his hat wreathed with briony, or wild convolvulus; his hand filled with bunches of wild flowers plucked from the hedges as he passed, and his eyes, indeed every feature, beaming with the benevolence of his heart'.[7] This is Shelley as a green man, the guardian of the English land-scape celebrated in folk tales, in stories of Robin Hood, and in Edward Thomas's poem, 'Lob':

> Jack-in-the-hedge, or Robin-run-by-the-wall,
> Robin Hood, Ragged Robin, lazy Bob,
> One of the lords of No Man's land, good Lob,—[8]

Shelley's likeness to this ancient figure, associated over the centuries with rebels and outlaws, suggests a resurgent sense of English identity in a year of national crisis. The paganism of Marlow was less a return to the classical world than a reinvention of Robin Hood's England – the 'Merry Old England' of practical charity and social justice, ancient forests and grass-edged lanes.

Early summer brought news of sporadic riots and arrests in Taunton, Yorkshire and Nottingham. Then, in June, at the Derbyshire village of Pentrich, came the first signs of co-ordinated insurrection. The Pentrich rising was in fact encouraged and then betrayed by the infamous government *agent provocateur* and spy, 'Oliver'. It was vigorously suppressed by military force, and the leaders imprisoned.[9] Thomas Wooler was arrested for seditious libel in his journal the *Black Dwarf*, and journalist William Hone was interned for 'Blasphemous Parodies' of the Prayer Book – a time-honoured English satirical tradition, about which the authorities had suddenly become supersqueamish. John Hunt immediately called on Hone's wife to enquire about him.[10]

State trials of the Spa Fields rioters were continuing in London. Informers were everywhere – Hunt said that they were the 'jackals of despotism'. Throughout the country were 'miserable and squalid faces in districts of the greatest beauty and fertility', scenes of 'poverty and pale raggedness' in a landscape that 'with a decent impulse of justice' would become 'a paradise of healthy industry'. No wonder, Hunt wrote, that some were forced into 'a desperation of self-remedy which assumes even an aspect of violence'.[11] At the end of June the suspension of Habeas Corpus was continued. Hunt heard a deep and awful groan, resounding throughout the country.[12]

What would resolve this crisis? As Hunt saw it, the confrontation between the reformers and the government was 'now evidently a drawn battle'.[13] He continued to urge the need to petition for peaceful reform, but the threat of a violent revolution was gathering. Could England be put back in touch with its deep traditions of liberty and justice? At Marlow Hunt started to reflect on the politics of nature – not abstract rights and charters, but the physical environment of England: landscapes, rivers, villages and towns, England's folk traditions, English weather. Wasn't the dreadful climate an unsuspected security against oppression? In the warm south, the Mediterranean sunshine, clear air and cloudless skies helped make poverty and oppression more bearable. Albion's clouds, rainy days, chill habits, sluggish blood, and dreary Sundays 'which we try to think good' required a 'set-off' – something that would make life worth enduring. 'This something,' Hunt informed *Examiner* readers, 'is *freedom*.'[14] The way events were tending, England would have nothing but its weather.

In June the proofs for the second edition of *The Story of Rimini* arrived, and Hunt announced that the book would be published in a few days. He was still projecting for the next winter a collection with 'Hero and Leander' plus 'four or five other little stories', and again put off repaying the twenty guineas to John Taylor. Marianne had 'scraped' Shelley's statues of Apollo and Venus to put them in 'proper condition' for his library (this meant that they appeared white, as Winckelmann's idealist view of Greek art required).

The second half of June was glorious summer weather, but the date for the Hunts' return to London had long been fixed. On Wednesday the 25th Hunt, Marianne, Thornton and Shelley set off for town. Bess and the other children would remain at Marlow. Because it was mid-week Hunt could write his 'politics' once they were settled in their new home at 13, Lisson Grove

North, a recent terraced development to the west of Regent's Park. Marianne thought the house small but comfortable 'till better times'.[15] The good news was that they would be close to the Novellos and to John Hunt's home at Maida Hill. It was less of a comfort to think that 22, Lisson Grove North, a few doors away, would soon be Haydon's home.

Letters went to and fro between Lisson Grove and Marlow. Marianne had forgotten to arrange the present for Shelley's twenty-fifth birthday (probably a brooch containing a lock of hair). She had no money to buy the flannel and lawn Mary had asked for. Marianne would lend the caps Mary needed for her new baby. The Hunts had left behind a large tablecloth, and one of Mrs John Hunt's sheets. Would Mary send them? Cold baths were good for Hunt's health, Mary knew, and she found them a benefit too: could he spare the metal tub he had abandoned at Albion House? He had left behind a packet of prints too. The Hunts' soap dish would have to wait: it could be sent up to town with the cutting of yellow stonecrop. Bess called stonecrop 'vegetable sunshine'.[16]

Hunt set about contacting friends and acquaintants. Hazlitt was among the first callers to Lisson Grove; CCC was invited to a poetry 'festivity'; no one knew where Keats was. By the end of June Shelley was back at Marlow, and twelve days later Bess and the children set off for Lisson Grove.[17] In August the *Morning Chronicle* attempted to spread tittle-tattle that linked Shelley's Chancery case, *Queen Mab*, and 'the Lady with whom he lives'. Hunt alerted Shelley, and promptly set the record straight in the *Examiner*. The legal case was remarkable and important. Shelley's book was full of talent and principle, 'and the Lady *is* his wife'.[18]

Mary gave birth to a daughter, Clara Everina, on 2 September. Then, in mid-September, Hunt was called unexpectedly to Marlow – Shelley needed to consult him about a letter on the Chancery case.[19] That done, Shelley set off for London leaving Hunt and Marianne to enjoy a few days' holiday in fine autumn weather. They kept 'country hours', rose late, and walked all morning. Mary said she saw little of them. Back at Lisson Grove on the 25th, the Hunts were joined by Shelley, 'much teazed' by the law, pale, languid and ill. Consumption was suspected, and Italy had been recommended as a 'certain remedy'. Through October Shelley would spend more time at Lisson Grove than Marlow: 'I nurse myself,' he told Mary, '& these kind people nurse me with great care.'[20]

Soon the old quarrels of the Vale of Health flared up again. Keats arrived at Hunt's on 6 October to find Shelley there too: Hunt was evidently still 'infatuated', and everybody seemed 'at Loggerheads'. Hunt was critical of Haydon's painting, and told Reynolds he had doubts about Keats's new poem *Endymion*. Reynolds passed that on. Haydon took Keats aside and warned him not to show *Endymion* to Hunt. Keats agonised over being thought 'Hunt's elevé'.[21] This was all as it had always been, although Hunt's sense that the long, diffuse narrative of *Endymion* was not entirely successful has stood the test of time. Hunt was the first critic to grasp Keats's genius for lyrical compression.

In the midst of these spats Hunt faced more pressing matters: Marianne's pregnancy, money, the Chancery case, Shelley's health, the state of the country. The *Examiner* office had moved from Maiden Lane to 19, Catherine Street, Strand, opposite Somerset House and a short walk from Drury Lane. In early October London enjoyed days of autumnal warmth, but the nights were cold, and just a few streets away from the *Examiner* office a young discharged sailor named Robert Johnson had died of exposure after three nights in the open, starving and scarcely able to speak. Nothing had been done to help him. Here was yet another instance of 'habitual hard-heartedness' in a 'money-getting country'. The death was afflicting, but what could one make of the thousands of people who had passed by? Hunt responded to the tragedy with some of his finest prose. Under the headline 'Fellow-Creatures Suffered to Die in the Streets', he imagined 'the inclemency of dews, and cold, and the cutting east wind . . . what he wants is nourishment by degrees, – and above all, warmth, warmth, – not fire warmth, but a little personal trouble – a little *real* charity – a bed'. Beadles, surgeons and overseers of the poor had done 'nothing to the purpose'. The stall-keeper left him. The shopkeeper left him. The night-watchman left him. The 'possessors of income, high and low, *left* him'. He was 'found "quite dead and cold", – *cold as charity*'.[22] Another dark dreadful death.

'Surely all this demands great explanation,' Hunt resumed in the next week's *Examiner*, 'above all, it demands *reflection* on the part of all of us, – a little thinking on the nature of our being, – a little grave and humble thought on the wretched mistakes we are in with regard to our duties, in consequence of the bad translation which selfishness makes from the language of Nature.'[23] Hunt thought of Shelley. He thought of his mother. He thought of Shakespeare's imagining of Albion in *King Lear*, and a king 'who had ta'en too little care of this'. The parish authorities eventually got around to announcing an inquiry, eleven days after the death. Hunt's disgust echoed Lear: 'Pshaw! – "An ounce of civet" . . . to sweeten the thoughts of it.'

It was 19 October again, his birthday. He was thirty-three. During nine years' editing the *Examiner* he had moved a long way from the independent principles of the paper's early days. To get rid of selfishness and right the 'bad translation' from nature required 'a change from theoretical humanity to practical'. Readers objected. Hunt's views were '*revolutionary*'. Impostors would take advantage of the charitable. Surely this was a matter for govern-ment?[24] Even John Hunt quailed. He told his brother that his 'system of charity' had 'gone too far'. It was '*Ultra Sentimental*'. What was needed instead was 'a good system of Police'.[25] The contrast with Shelley and the woman on icy Hampstead Heath could not be starker. It had been *sentimental* to accommodate her.

'Jackals of despotism' lurked in the literary world too. One such was 'Z', the author of essays 'On the Cockney School of Poetry' that began to appear in *Blackwood's Magazine* in October. The 'Cockney School' maligned Hunt, Hazlitt and Keats as a disreputable literary-political coterie: 'LEIGH HUNT . . . is a man of little education. He knows absolutely nothing of Greek, almost nothing of Latin, and his knowledge of Italian literature is confined to a few of Petrarch's sonnets, and an imperfect acquaintance with Ariosto.' The 'Z' essays were the work of two Edinburgh lawyers, John Lockhart and John Wilson. They understood that the *Examiner*'s influence was in proportion to its 'numerous' readership, and were contemptuous of both. The pair knew little of Hunt's poetry beyond *The Story of Rimini:* political bias, misogyny, snobbery and racism made up the rest. Attacks on Hunt's deism, 'jacobinism' and 'moral depravity' were stock-in-trade among his political opponents, and 'Z' rallied to defend the honour of poetry too. Poetry was 'dignified'; it was the preserve of an educated élite that included the Cambridge-educated William Wordsworth. The 'Cockney School' essays set up Wordsworth – the author of 'Simon Lee'! – as a model of 'classic' correctness, but their effusive praise of Wordsworth's 'noble compositions', 'purity of thought' and 'patriarchal' virtues in fact heralded his demise as a poet. 'Z' was unable to see that Hunt's 'vulgar' poetry and 'plebeian' readership were vitally aligned with the *Lyrical Ballads* of 1798. The idea that poetry might be 'vulgarly accessible' was shocking. While 'Z' was fixed in the past, Hunt was about making the future – a modern poetry that is a colourful, cockneyfied assembly of 'Young Poets', demotic 'New Voices', and everything that 'Z' deemed 'rancid' and 'obscene'. John called for 'Z' to identify himself and threatened legal action, but Hunt cheerfully dismissed the *Blackwood's* essays as 'atrocious nonsense'.[26]

On Thursday, 6 November Princess Charlotte, the Regent's only child and heir, died in childbirth. Unlike her father, she was a popular figure and public mourning was declared. The *Examiner* carried a black border, and commiserated with 'real sorrow and sympathy' on this reminder of 'the naked humanity of us all'. Even royalty shared our common nature, as King Lear discovered. The same issue of the *Examiner* reported that, the day after Charlotte's death, three leaders of the Pentrich rising had been convicted of treason and executed at Derby. Jeremiah Brandreth, William Turner and Isaac Ludlam were dragged on a hurdle to the scaffold. Among their last words were 'OLIVER HAS BROUGHT ME TO THIS', 'THIS IS ALL OLIVER AND THE GOVERNMENT'. Then they were hanged, cut down and beheaded. Seizing each head by the hair the executioner held them up, one by one, and exclaimed: 'Behold the head of the traitor.' A *'tremendous shriek'* rose from the crowd as if they were gripped with *'sudden phrenzy'*. Dragoons with drawn swords moved in, and 'all became immediately calm'. The heads and bodies were thrown into shells, and the spectators dispersed. Vigorous policing ensured that these public deaths would not excite displays of public grief.[27]

In the next week Hunt and the Shelleys met on every day but one. Shelley began a pamphlet *Address to the People on the Death of the Princess Charlotte* and by Wednesday the 15th it was finished.[28] Next Sunday the *Examiner* carried Hunt's article 'Death of the Princess Charlotte – Lamentable Punishments at Derby'. Hunt and Shelley present identical juxtapositions between sympathy for the Princess and the miseries of the 'thousands' of poor people. Both detail the awful executions in Derby. Hunt reflects on the 'elements of our nature', Shelley on 'domestic affections' and 'private virtues'. For Hunt as for Shelley it was the 'circumstances' of distress that provoked the 'calamity'/'catastrophe' of the Pentrich rising. Both were convinced that the spy 'Oliver' was involved (Shelley's pamphlet repeated details of 'Oliver' from pre-publication copy for the *Examiner*). To Hunt the events had 'shaken every sense of justice and decency between man and man'; for Shelley, Pentrich was 'a calamity such as the English nation ought to mourn with an unassuageable grief'.[29]

The interweaving of their work continued when the *Examiner* published an extract from *Laon and Cythna* – newly published by Ollier – in which the 'domestic relations' prized by Hunt and Shelley were given a passionate intensity to inspire 'Hymns . . . woven to Freedom'.[30] Hunt's end-of-year article, 'Christmas and other Old National Merry-Makings Considered', drew upon the paganism of Albion House, Shelley as the 'green man', and *King Lear*. England is described as bustling, talkative, 'very successful in the world', but 'not happy'. Commercialism, money-getting, 'utility', avarice and bigotry have stifled the pleasures and freedoms of 'long-lost "Merry Old England"'. The time has come to act, to sow a future 'blossoming with plenty and joy again'. Hunt envisages a revolution of cheer, a 'new and kind sociality' recalling folk traditions and attuned to the natural rhythms of the year: 'the sports, the pastimes, the Christmas greens and gambols, the archeries, the May-mornings, the May-poles, the country-dances, the masks, the harvest-homes, the new-year's-gifts, the gallantries, the golden means, the poetries, the pleasures, the leisures, the real treasures'.[31]

All this, after Pentrich? Surely Hunt's vision is as ultra-sentimental as John Major's prediction that England in 2050 would 'still be the country of long shadows on county grounds, warm beer, [and] invincible green suburbs'? Ideas of an eternal England, like memories of a 'green and pleasant land', are always symptoms of lost content and stress.[32] It was Pentrich that urged Hunt's 'melancholy recollections', and his 'system' (as he called it) was by no means naïve. At a time of rapid industrialisation, urban growth, poverty and unrest, Hunt set out 'to improve mankind through the medium of the pleasureable parts of their nature'. Little, individual acts of pleasure could start the gradual process of ameliorating society at large. Hunt's idea of recuperative leisure sounds strikingly modern; so does his warning that society 'cannot go on as it did', and that 'however slow may be the changes which must result, those changes . . . will infallibly be connected *with* the soil, – with subsistence, with internal government, with the cultivation of home tastes, and consequently with manners and customs, and the choice of good'. Ancient manners and customs are the patterns for what we might now describe as a 'green' way of life, a revival of the *Religio loci* and 'the great God Pan'.[33] Hunt continued his articles on 'National Merry-Making' into the New Year, and would return to the theme in a piece on 'Old May Day' and, towards the end of 1818, in his preparations for a *Literary Pocket-Book*.

The *Examiner*, 7 December 1817: 'BIRTH. On the 4th instant, in Lisson Grove, Mrs. Leigh Hunt of her fifth child, – a boy.' They called him Percy Bysshe Shelley Leigh Hunt. By the New Year the whole family was 'quite hearty', and the children dancing and singing 'from morning to night'.[34] Further afield, however, there wasn't much merrymaking among Hunt's London friends, who were all 'dreadfully irritated against each other'. Lisson Grove was one such war zone: Hunt and Haydon had quarrelled over Marianne's failure to return some silver tableware she had borrowed. They 'got to words & parted for ever'. Keats called several times, and was dissatisfied at Hunt's response to the first book of *Endymion*.[35] Then, on 21 January, Hunt showed Keats a 'real authenticated Lock of *Milton's hair*', the first in the collection of locks of hair he would gather throughout his life (it would include Keats, the Shelleys, Lamb, Hazlitt, Dr Johnson, Swift, Napoleon, Carlyle, and the two Brownings). For Hunt these locks of hair touched the imagination, and he endeavoured to steer Keats back into short intense lyrics by suggesting that he should try a poem 'On Seeing a Lock of Milton's Hair'. It isn't one of Keats's best poems, but it shows him rising to the challenge set by Hunt.

Next day Keats sat down to re-read *King Lear* and, before he did so, he wrote a sonnet on the occasion. Why? 'On Sitting Down to Read *King Lear* Once Again' has often been said to express Keats's dissatisfaction with 'golden-tongued Romance' and the mythical world of *Endymion*. But it has not been noticed that Keats's 'prologue' to reading echoes Hunt's view of *Endymion*, and that it was Hunt who had alerted Keats to a more urgent, Shakespearean poetry:

> Chief Poet! and ye clouds of Albion,
> Begetters of our deep eternal theme!

When through the old oak forest I am gone,
   Let me not wander in a barren dream:
But, when I am consumed in the fire,
Give me new phœnix wings to fly at my desire.[36]

Shakespeare and the clouds of Albion had been key themes in Hunt's articles on English liberty, and it was Hunt who put the poets of Albion at the
centre of his political-poetic agenda. Keats knew of Hunt's months at Albion
House, perhaps also of Shelley's altar to Pan in Bisham Woods. His sonnet
appears a brilliant refraction of the *Examiner* and the Marlow summer, calculated to wrest Hunt's attention back from Shelley. The final line bursts the
sonnet form with its final word 'desire' – an exuberant endorsement of Hunt's
ethic of pleasure.

   Competing for Hunt's attention was Shelley's *Revolt of Islam*. Hunt's
substantial and admiring review of this 'extraordinary production' extended
through three issues of the *Examiner*, and concluded with a résumé of Shelley's
opinions: 'in short, make the best and utmost of this world, as well as hope
for another'. All the reasons which made the poem the work of one of the
'leading spirits of the age' meant, however, that it 'cannot possibly become
popular'. This was hardly an encouraging note on which to conclude his
review, so Hunt added an upbeat paragraph about the power of the press to
crush tyranny 'as a steam-engine would a great serpent'.[37]

Keats and Shelley met Hunt at Lisson Grove, on Wednesday, 4 February, and
joined in a last sonnet-writing contest. Displays of Egyptian sculpture at the
British Museum had already inspired Shelley's 'Ozymandias', and Hunt
suggested the 'River Nile' in fifteen minutes. They fell to, and Hunt used the
hush as a start for his poem:

   It flows through old hushed Ægypt and it's sands,
   Like some grave mighty thought threading a dream,
   And times and things, as in that vision, seem
   Keeping along it their eternal stands, –
   Caves, pillars, pyramids, the shepherd bands
   That roamed through the young world, the glory extreme
   Of high Sesostris, and that southern beam,
   The laughing queen that caught the world's great hands.
   Then comes a mightier silence, stern and strong,
   As of a world left empty of its throng,
   And the void weighs on us; and then we wake,
   And hear the fruitful stream lapsing along
   Twixt villages, and think how we shall take
   Our own calm journey on for human sake.[38]

The relics of ancient cultures in the British Museum had given many of Hunt's contemporaries pause for thought about the passing of civilisations. Hunt's sonnet ventures the idea that 'old hushed Ægypt' might foretell the 'mightier silence' of a world 'empty of its throng'. But loss of love (Cleopatra) and community ('shepherd bands') is more troubling to Hunt than the ruins of empire, and he characteristically turns from the sublimity of the Nile to a village stream and thoughts of human life imperfectly 'lapsing along'. Keats's sonnet on the Nile was less successful; but Hunt's dream of a world 'empty of its throng' had registered, and the image would re-emerge in the lines about a little town 'emptied of . . . folk' in Keats's 'Ode on a Grecian Urn':

> thy streets for evermore
> Will silent be; and not a soul to tell
> Why thou art desolate, can e'er return.[39]

Early in February the Shelleys quit Albion House for London, where they lodged in Great Russell Street. Over the next month the Hunts and Shelleys saw each other nearly every day for operas, plays and dinners. Hunt and Marianne passed Tuesday, 10 March with them. Together they went to the first London performance of Rossini's *Barber of Seville*, returned for supper, and when the time came for 'adieus' Shelley had already fallen asleep. Hunt could not bear to part from his heart's companion, and they left quietly without waking him or bidding farewell. At five the next morning the Shelleys left for Dover, and Italy.

As a gift for the journey Hunt had given Shelley an inscribed copy of *Foliage*, just published. Many of the poems were already familiar: 'The Nymphs'; poems and sonnets to Hunt's children, friends and Hampstead; verse epistles and translations. The 'Preface' set out Hunt's ideas of 'poetry and cheerfulness', and the whole book was a manifesto for the new society both men wanted to see. Hunt speaks up for 'sensativity', 'unsophisticated impulses', 'beauty', 'cheerful tendencies', 'nature's goodness', 'health and sociality' and 'cheerful leisure' to counteract the 'vicious', 'melancholy', 'blasphemous' and 'desponding' effects of what he called 'partial systems'. *Partial* meant the partisan – 'bigoted' – interests of church and state, and the 'coterie of town gentlemen' who presumed to control notions of poetry.

In the wake of Z's campaign in *Blackwood's*, *Foliage* was 'roughly handled' in the reviews.[40] Hunt's language was nothing like the 'sublime', 'immense' and 'supernatural' characteristics of 'true poetry'. Only the *Eclectic* was hospitable to *Foliage*, in the one review to notice how 'The Nymphs' presented the 'demonology of Paganism' as 'an imaginable possibility'.[41] Damned and faintly praised, *Foliage* was a critical failure, but in it Hunt succeeded in making public his ideals of poetry, cheerfulness and justice. Unlike *Laon and*

Cythna, 'The Nymphs' escaped Charles Ollier's censorship and it delighted Shelley: 'It is truly *poetical*, in the intense and emphatic sense of the word.'[42] But Shelley wrote those words from Lyons in France, six hundred miles away.

With the Shelleys gone, life at Lisson Grove changed. Hunt set up 'a nook to write in' with his books, busts, prints and flowers, and began a comedy set in Venice. He bought a blue frock coat, a new hat and orange gloves, and 'walked out quite a buck again'. In the evenings they went to plays and operas, sometimes to 'a sort of conversazione' at the Lambs'. Hazlitt was busy lecturing on English poetry at the Surrey Institution, and Hunt had resumed 'Theatricals' for the *Examiner*. He went in to the office on Saturdays. Life became more orderly.[43]

This was Hunt's way of coping with Shelleys' departure, and it was made possible by his friend's overwhelmingly generous gift of £1,400 and a loan of £200 from Charles Ollier. The summer of 1818 was the best in living memory – 'real, uninterrupted southern continuance' – and Hunt's health gradually improved.

Domestic politics were quieter than they had been in 1817, although riots at the general election in June and July indicated that the country was still in a 'combustible state'.[44] The reformers Samuel Romilly and Francis Burdett were returned as MPs for Westminster, and Hunt had high hopes for Brougham in the Westmorland election despite Wordsworth's support for Brougham's reactionary opponent, the Earl of Lonsdale (who won). Lord Liverpool's Tory administration continued in power. Hazlitt carried the literary war to the enemy, avenging the *Quarterly*'s attacks on Hunt, Shelley and Keats with a 'character' of the editor William Gifford as one of the 'jackals', 'the *Government Critic*' who forms 'an invisible link that connects literature with the police'.[45] In the *Examiner* Hunt dismissed the *Quarterly*'s insinuations about Shelley's private life, described Shelley's philosophic retreat at Marlow, and concluded with a panegyric on his 'noblest heart' and Christ-like eminence as the 'height of humanity'.[46] He also started to draft the satirical poem on Gifford that would eventually be published as 'Ultra-Crepidarius' in 1823.

Early July saw the Hunts move the short distance to 8, York Buildings on the New Road (now the Marylebone Road) between Gloucester Place and Baker Street. With large windows and folding doors across the drawing-room, this was a roomier house than Lisson Grove and had recently been refurbished. The windows looked out on other houses, but for the first time there would be space for the children. Hunt established his study behind the folding doors, laid aside his Venetian comedy, and started to write a tragedy about the legendary Spanish patriot El Cid. Carpets and curtains were ordered, indicating that Marianne now aspired to graceful as well as comfortable living.

The artist John Wildman was hired as a drawing-master for Thornton, and he was commissioned for ten guineas to sketch a portrait of Hunt for the Shelleys. Marianne thought the likeness 'astonishing'. It was packed into a box with some books Ollier was sending to the Shelleys, and would take a whole year to reach them.

The letter post between England and Italy usually took around two weeks, and at first the Shelleys wrote frequently. The Hunts' three letters of April, August and November were packed with details about family life, the weather, houses, mutual friends such as the Lambs, Hogg, Peacock, Horace Smith and Hazlitt, recommendations about Italian authors, and questions about Italian art. Government 'jackals' sometimes opened letters in the post, and Hunt was careful not to discuss politics. On 5 June Shelley wrote to Peacock asking him to post the *Examiner* each week, 'clipped' so that it would weigh as little as possible.[47]

At Lisson Grove Marianne had started to run a school for two hours every morning, though this turned out to be a short-lived venture. With the move to York Buildings, Bess had gone to live with her younger brother Thomas, who was beginning a medical career: Marianne had long looked forward to this moment when she had her 'nice roomy house' to herself. Better times had apparently arrived, but Bess's departure did not solve all her unhappiness. To the Shelleys she wrote lively letters full of gossip and family news – but emphasised that they were 'mere letters of chit, chat: more I cannot even aim at'. Thornton's progress delighted her – 'he promises to be a most eminent artist' – yet even this stirred despondent reflections: 'How bitterly do I regret the same care was not bestowed upon me! I might have been worth something by this time, if it had.'[48] After nine years of marriage, hardship, temporary homes and five children, the thirty-year-old Marianne felt worthless.

Marianne and Bess had been on good terms at Lisson Grove. They had even ventured to the theatre together. This was bold, exciting and dangerous – usually the only unchaperoned women at the theatre were prostitutes. Hunt noted that the pair came back full of talk and were the best company in the world.[49] Marianne's impulse had been to break out and live the liberated life she had heard Hunt and Shelley talk about, and this was one way of asserting herself and gaining self-esteem; it was a revival of the gregarious Mary Anne Kent who years before had enjoyed dancing with soldiers at military balls. But there was another side to Marianne's gaiety. Crabb Robinson met the Hunts at Lamb's house and found Hunt in sparkling form, imitating Hazlitt and Wordsworth. He thought Marianne 'a very disgusting woman'. This may not carry much weight: Robinson, a curmudgeonly misogynist, also judged Wordsworth's sister-in-law Mary Hutchinson to be 'rather repulsive', though he conceded that with acquaintance she blossomed into a 'sensible little woman'.[50] Drink always flowed copiously at Lamb's and this may have been the time when Marianne started drinking heavily to bolster her spirits and courage. A few years more would bring attacks of rheumatism and signs of consumption, and she would increasingly turn to alcohol to try to alleviate depression and numb feelings of regret. Towards the end of her life she was consuming a bottle of brandy a day, and was described by her physician as 'sodden with drink'.[51] Hunt does not seem to have noticed – perhaps, after his father, he did not want to see what was happening. He established a life of writing routines, and continued to believe Marianne was capable of dealing with domestic matters and the household accounts. They lived together, and remained affectionately bound to each other, but 1818 initiated a separation of lives that would continue up to Marianne's death in 1857. Thornton eventually came to see that his parents were 'strangers to each other'.[52]

'I have been writing a Pocket-Book,' Hunt announced to the Shelleys in his letter of 12 November. It promised to be a commercial success, and he had been careful to retain the copyright.[53] The first 'Pocket-Book' contained poems by Hunt, Shelley, Keats, and Bryan Waller Procter (another 'young poet', who wrote under the pseudonym 'Barry Cornwall'). Hunt's 'Calendar of Nature' was reprinted from a monthly article in the *Examiner* begun in January 1819. Headed by a quotation from Spenser, the 'Calendar' listed the month's classical and literary associations, the festivities of 'merry England', observations of nature (birds, fruits, flowers) and the weather. Hunt drew on Gilbert White's *Natural History and Antiquities of Selborne* and cast back to memories of Marlow. The 'Pocket-Book' proved popular with the public. It introduced Shelley and Keats to new readers, and was a model for the annual souvenir albums of poetry enjoyed by the Victorians. Bess Kent took note of Hunt's mingling of natural description with passages of poetry and used it in her *Flora Domestica*, published in 1823.

As 1818 drew to a close Hunt was settling into a new life, but Shelley's letters longed for their old companionship. He wrote in December urging Hunt to come to Italy. Byron would lend money for the journey, and sums of four and five hundred pounds were mentioned. Hunt could sail from London, and it would be an 'inexpressible pleasure' to be reunited in Italy. Byron would be pleased too, and Hunt's company would 'do him great service'. 'Now pray write directly,' Shelley added, 'because I shall be in a fever till I know whether you are coming or not.' Peacock was enlisted to ask Hunt 'what he means to answer to Lord Byron's invitation'.[54]

By the end of the year difficulties were gathering at 8, York Buildings. No one thought about outgoings. Debts had not been cleared. Shelley's gift had been spent.[55] Hunt doubted that a visit to Italy would be practicable, and told the Shelleys so. Peacock said Hunt would be 'utterly ruined' if he went, 'for what in the interval would become of his paper?'[56] John Hunt was talking of a move to Somerset as a better environment for his family, and his absence would add to Hunt's responsibilities. Still, the 'Pocket-Book' promised much; the tragedy of the Cid was almost finished, and he was close to completing the 'Hero and Leander' volume. Without doubt, Hunt entered 1819 with 'prospects'.[57]

TWENTY-FOUR

ENGLAND IN 1819

The day had arrived. Samuel Sibley, his wife Maria, and six others put on white cockades and stars of yellow ribbon, then set off along Fleet Street, up Ludgate Hill, and across St Paul's Churchyard. Sibley led the procession carrying aloft a golden trumpet. At Budge Row, in the heart of the City and close to the Bank of England, they paused. Sibley sounded the trumpet, and proclaimed the second coming of Shiloh, Prince of Peace on earth. It was Wednesday morning, 13 January. 'Woe! woe! to the inhabitants of the earth,' Maria exclaimed in a loud voice, 'because of the coming of Shiloh!' They all joined in loudly: 'Woe! woe! to the inhabitants of the earth!' The crowd then pelted them with anything that could be found in the gutter, and a tremendous fight ensued.

Sibley and Co. were followers of Joanna Southcott, the prophetess who died in 1814 believing she was pregnant with the 'spiritual man' Shiloh, 'the man-child that was to rule the nations with a rod of iron'. Southcott had been thoroughly at home in the excited, millenarian atmosphere of the 1790s, and to find her sect parading through London on a winter day early in 1819 was also a sign of the times. Sibley said he had '*vestigated* the business thoroughly', and was convinced.[1]

This was the year Britain came close to revolution – a year when Despard's '*completest plan in the world*' might well have succeeded. Shelley's sonnet, 'England in 1819', gives us a snapshot of a nation drained by parasitic rulers:

> An old, mad, blind, despised, and dying king, –
> Princes, the dregs of their dull race, who flow
> Through public scorn – mud from a muddy spring;
> Rulers, who neither see, nor feel, nor know,
> But leech-like to their fainting country cling,
> Till they drop, blind in blood, without a blow;
> A people starved and stabbed in the untilled field, –
> An army, which liberticide and prey
> Makes as a two-edged sword to all who wield –
> Golden and sanguine laws which tempt and slay, –

> Religion Christless, Godless – a book sealed;
> A Senate – Time's worst statute unrepealed, –
> Are graves, from which a glorious Phantom may
> Burst, to illumine our tempestuous day.[2]

England had not begun the year with tempestuous days, although, like Shelley and Sam Sibley, Hunt was alert to the mood of unease. 'This is the commencement, if we are not much mistaken, of one of the most important years that have been seen for a long while. It is quiet; it seems peaceable,' he observed, 'but a spirit is abroad, stronger than kings, or armies, or all the most predominant shapes of prejudice and force.' Hunt's 'spirit' was knowledge. Knowledge of 'the general good'; knowledge spread by the 'diffusion of the press'; knowledge that 'something must be done'. The world was looking eagerly for change, democracy and 'equal rights': if rulers and privileged orders were 'slow to follow', Hunt felt sure that the nations were now ready to 'quit them, and go on'.[3]

But nothing happened, and Hunt directed his energies into reviewing. On Saturday, 3 April he went to see Charles Brucke's tragedy *The Italians* at Drury Lane. It was known that Kean had retitled the play 'The Deranged Intellect' and warned the management that it would fail. London's streets may have been more or less quiet, but the audience at Drury Lane was in rebellious mood. The curtain rose to a barrage of 'hisses, yells, groans, coughings, beatings of sticks, and slapping of benches'. A young American tourist, George Ticknor, was sitting two boxes away from Hunt and saw him stand up and try to address the crowd 'in a furious manner' – but no one could hear a word.[4] Back in his peaceful study, Hunt reviewed Moore's *Irish Melodies* ('the natural poetry of sympathy and enjoyment'), Hazlitt's pamphlet *Letter to William Gifford* ('Oh, how true is this!'), *The Works of Charles Lamb* ('deeply seated in our common humanity'), *Peter Bell, a Lyrical Ballad* ('another didactic little horror of Mr. Wordsworth's'), and Shelley's *Rosalind and Helen* ('another poem in behalf of liberality of sentiment and the deification of love'). Readers who glanced across the page from the article on Shelley would have seen how the 'Calendar of Nature' for May formed a seasonal commentary on the state of the nation: spring and the revival of poetry were helping 'to restore England', and in the *Examiner* office at Catherine Street changes were also under way.[5]

John had determined to quit London for Somerset. He had been working non-stop on the *News* and *Examiner* since 1805, and had recently launched a short-lived radical miscellany, the *Yellow Dwarf*, to which Hazlitt and Keats had contributed. All this and two years at Coldbath Fields prison had wrecked his health. He needed a break – as Hunt had needed his months at Marlow – and Cheddon Fitzpaine on the Quantock Hills would be a healthier environment for his children. Still, at forty-four years old John had not reached retirement. Was there another reason for his decision to leave? For Hunt,

Hazlitt and others, John had always been the man of steel who stuck to his principles and his post. To find him leaving London just as Hunt was predicting 'one of the most important years' is puzzling – unless the public mood of smouldering discontent was itself the reason. The battle of Budge Row showed that the city was a tinderbox, ready to flare at even the slightest provocation. Did John like many others believe that an uprising was about to begin, and decide to take his family to safety? If so, he would be following in the footsteps of the 1790s radicals who had all sought refuge in Somerset from oppression and the threat of civil violence.

John would continue as publisher and proprietor of the *Examiner* but his place in the office would be taken by his eldest son Henry – and it was an article by Henry that revealed 'on what a slight foundation our present calm is built'. Accounts of unemployment, wretchedness and poverty were arriving from the manufacturing towns of the north. Parish rates for relief of the poor were 'every where enormously high'. Wages were low, and trade 'much depressed'. The 'long injured . . . feelings of Ireland' were aired once more in two petitions presented by Sir Francis Burdett to the Commons. Shortly afterwards, the journalist Richard Carlile was charged with blasphemy and seditious libel for publishing Paine's *Age of Reason* and 'other argumentative works against the Christian faith'. Hunt highlighted this outrage against liberty of conscience: from now on the *Examiner* would follow Carlile's fortunes closely, and Carlile reciprocated by pledging support for Hunt's struggle for liberty of the press. June brought new taxes on spirits, malt, pepper, coffee, cocoa and tobacco – and an upsurge of protest meetings. At the beginning of what turned into a swelteringly hot month, a comet appeared in the skies over England. Anyone walking out in the evening would have noticed it, very bright and apparently 'directing its motion northward'. Calls for change continued to ring out across the country. Mass meetings at Leeds and Nottingham demanded 'Universal Suffrage', and then, on 21 July, a gigantic gathering of 70,000 people at Smithfield, London resolved that the present House of Commons had not been 'justly elected' and the people were not bound by a government that did not represent them. 'Reformers are becoming every day more numerous,' Hunt noted, 'more intelligent, more earnest.'[6] With no prospect of relief, a catastrophe must be expected.

Hunt soon heard that his tragedy of the Cid had been rejected by Edmund Kean and Covent Garden, but his poems 'Hero and Leander', 'Bacchus and Ariadne' and 'The Panther' were now ready for publication. Published together in early July, the three poems reworked classical stories into celebrations of love and 'natural impulses'. In 'Hero and Leander' love triumphs over the world's 'poisoning' of joy and, for a while, over the ocean: the Greek youth Leander swims the Hellespont to meet his lover Hero, 'fighting towards the cordial joy'. Hunt's couplets can create sudden surges of energy –

> . . . when he saw the torch, oh, how he sprung
> And thrust his feet against the waves, and flung
> The foam behind, as though he scorned the sea
> (112–15)[7]

– and, elsewhere in the poem, they prolong the moment when dawn slowly reveals Leander's drowned body:

> But when he came not, – when from hour to hour
> He came not, – though the storm had spent its power,
> And when the casement, at the dawn of light,
> Began to show a square of ghastly white,
> She went up to the tower, and straining out
> To search the seas, downwards, and round about,
> She saw, at last, – she saw her lord indeed
> Floating, and washed about, like a vile weed . . .
> (282–9)

Perilous seas, and a faery land forlorn. Hunt's tale of 'drowned love' and a starkly unenchanted casement may have helped Philip Larkin to the 'soundless dark' and 'curtain-edges [growing] light' in his own poem of death's unresting routines, 'Aubade'.[8] In Hunt's sequence of poems, 'Bacchus and Ariadne' follows as a tale of consolation: having been abandoned by Theseus, Ariadne is saved from Hero's fate by Bacchus's love, proving that love 'out-relishes' betrayal and sorrow (as it had done in *The Story of Rimini*). In 'The Panther', Hunt's third poem in this group, the arrival of spring impels the captured animal to 'burst his chains' and leap into liberty. Like William Blake's Tyger, Hunt's Panther embodied the pent-up energies of a nation on the verge of revolution.

News of little William Shelley's death reached Hunt at the end of June. He sensed his friends reaching out for sympathy and responded with a letter that deliberately avoided 'ordinary topics of consolation'. 'I cannot conceive, that the young intellectual spirit which sat thinking out of his eye, & seemed to comprehend so much in his smile, can perish like the house it inhabited. I do not know that a soul is born with us; but we seem, to me, to *attain* to a soul, some later, some earlier.' 'This is poetry, you will see, & not argument,' Hunt goes on, and his idea of attaining a soul recalls his notion of soul-making – that life itself 'is necessary to make us'.[9]

Over the next six months Hunt would send a series of letters to the Shelleys in which he develops a conversational style as if they were 'almost actually chatting together'. Hunt ranges energetically over all kinds of topics – opera, painting, weather, 'Hero and Leander', the failure of his tragedy, the *Literary Pocket-Book*, Smollett, Fielding, surgery, old friends like Hogg and Peacock, new ones like Charles Lloyd ('one of the earliest Lake poets'), and his former garden at Horsemonger Lane 'dressed up with trellises & a handful of turf, & some flowers'. Hunt writes in late July: 'I wish in truth I knew how to amuse you just now, & that I were in Italy to try . . . I would walk about with Shelley, wherever he pleased . . . & I would be merry or quiet, chat, read, or impudently play & sing you Italian airs.'[10]

Hunt's letters to the Shelleys are diverting, and his breezy 'chat' overlies a sophisticated aesthetic of intimacy. Each letter is a fascinating experiment in talking to his friends as if 'transported to [their] presence': 'Imagine that in this sheet of paper, which your eyes are now engaged upon, you are perusing my petitioning face: – (don't take your hand from my chin: –) I am sure there is enough sincerity in it to obtain my pardon.' Hunt's friendly efforts were assisted by the arrival, a year late, of the portrait he had sent to Italy. This was 'a pleasure in a time of need', Shelley responded, 'How we wish that it were *you*.'[11]

On one occasion the thought of poets visiting Italy prompted Hunt to digress about 'a fine ghastly image' in John Donne's 'Elegy XVI: On his Mistris'. 'He is dissuading his wife from going with him,' Hunt explains, '& hopes that she will not start in her sleep at night, & fancy him slain; –

> Crying out 'Oh! Oh!
> Nurse, O my love is slain!' *I saw him go*
> *O'er the white Alps alone* I saw him, I,
> Assailed, taken, fight, stabbed, bled, fall, & die.'[12]

Hunt's familiarity with Donne is unusual for the time. But why these four lines? The idea of going to Italy had been growing on him throughout the year, and his letters to the Shelleys show him already there in imagination. Associated with the idea of Italy, however, were thoughts of English writers dying abroad – Fielding in Lisbon, Smollett in Leghorn (today, Livorno) – but, so far, 'no poet out of our green earth'. Hunt's darker reflections belong with a cluster of references to water and fire that mirror the apocalyptic mood of England in 1819, including the drowning of Leander; Hunt's idea of London in summer like 'vallies of burning bricks'; and his promise to 'go through a dozen fires' for Shelley. Were these combinations of drowned hopes and transforming fires merely matters of the moment, or had Hunt glimpsed the future? This is a risky conjecture, to be sure, but it is in keeping with various spectral intimations experienced by Shelley himself and by the Hunts. After Shelley's death Hunt would insist that he remained spiritually present to him, and Marianne claimed her thoughts were 'haunted by their daily and nightly visitor'.[13]

Shelley's response to the arrival of Hunt's portrait was to dedicate his new drama, *The Cenci*, to him. 'I asked your picture last night,' Shelley wrote, '& it smiled assent.'[14] Hunt wrote back immediately of his feelings of honour and pleasure. When *The Cenci* was published, Hunt read that Shelley never knew

One more gentle, honourable, innocent, and brave; one of more exalted toleration for all who do and think evil, and yet himself more free from evil; one who knows better how to receive, and how to confer a benefit, though he must ever confer far more than he can receive; one of simpler, and, in the highest sense of the word, of purer life and manner . . .

Shelley saluted 'that patient and irreconcilable enmity with domestic and political tyranny and imposture which the tenor of your life has illustrated', and concluded, 'let us, comforting each other in our task, live and die'.[15] The message to the rest of the English public was grimmer. 'Hitherto,' Shelley wrote, 'I have written of things as they might be'; *The Cenci*, a blood-soaked tragedy of patriarchal oppression and blighted youth, was a portrait of things as they are.

Over the summer of 1819 prospects did not improve in the ways Hunt had hoped. The *Examiner*'s circulation revived, but there were setbacks too. The paper was sued for claiming that the Honourable Charles Spencer Churchill's 'furious and negligent driving' had killed a woman. Churchill won, and although he was awarded only £50 the *Examiner* had to pay the legal costs too.[16] Then the *Examiner*'s paper supplier was bankrupted, and arrears were called in. To save money the Hunts gave no dinners at York Buildings, and passed whole days out in the fields with books and sandwiches. The first *Literary Pocket-Book* had proved so successful that Hunt agreed to sell the rights to Charles Ollier for £200, even though this did no more than offset the loan Ollier had advanced back in 1818. After John's departure for Somerset Hunt was busier than ever, yet money was always tight and it was clear that they would have to leave their elegant rooms at York Terrace for cheaper accommodation. Kentish Town appealed as 'a sort of compromise between London & our beloved Hampstead'.[17] Then came the catastrophe the *Examiner* had long predicted.

On Monday, 16 August the citizens of Manchester – perhaps as many as 80,000 – gathered at St Peter's Fields to hear Henry 'Bristol' Hunt, Richard Carlile and others speak on reform. They carried banners proclaiming 'Annual Parliaments', 'Universal Suffrage', 'No Corn Laws', 'Vote by Ballot', 'Taxation without Representation is Unjust and Tyrannical'. Some flags depicted the figure of Justice holding her scales. The meeting proceeded peacefully until, 'according to all accounts', the horse soldiers of the Manchester and Salford Yeomanry 'dashed through them sword in hand, trampled down opposition, bruised and wounded many, and bore off the flags and speakers to the county jail'. Lives were lost and some five hundred people were wounded. No one was sure if the Riot Act had been read. Great waves of grief, outrage and bitterness flooded over the north of England and beyond. Soon each detail of the 'Peterloo Massacre' was being discussed and analysed in every corner

of England. 'Bristol' Hunt and the other speakers were charged with 'treasonable conspiracy'. The country was gripped by 'universal anxiety', and in
the *Examiner* Hunt warned that 'thousands and thousands of Englishmen'
were ready to rise in 'irresistible might'.[18] As August came to an end and
summer turned to autumn, the country was poised for revolution. Which way
would the balance tip?

On 5 September Hunt's 'Calendar of Nature' drew attention to the 'exuberance of harvest and the sign of the Zodiac in this month' as a 'lesson on
justice'. For Hunt autumn was the English season of commonwealth, a time
of plenty and 'a certain festive abundance for the supply of all creation'.
Readers were reminded that September lies under the constellation Libra,
and that the image of the scales was traditionally the symbol of justice. In
the *Examiner* the 'Calendar' was carefully placed between an article about the
dead and wounded at Peterloo (the 'carnage . . . baffles description'), and the
report of a prosecution for 'Seditious Placards'. Surrounded by accounts of
oppression, Hunt's 'Calendar' emphasised that to avoid bloodshed and revive
liberty the nation must attune itself to the rhythms of nature and the long,
liberal traditions of the past.

The charges against 'Bristol' Hunt were quickly dropped, and on Monday,
13 September an enormous crowd gathered in the Strand to welcome his
triumphal return to London. John Keats, up from Winchester where he had
been lodging for the past month, described the scene: 'It would take me a
whole day and a quire of paper to give you any thing like detail – . . . 30, 000
people were in the streets waiting for him – The whole distance from the
Angel Islington to the Crown and Anchor was lined with Multitudes.'[19] Later
that week Keats returned to Winchester, where on Saturday the 19th he
composed his ode 'To Autumn':

> Season of mists and mellow fruitfulness,
>   Close bosom-friend of the maturing sun;
> Conspiring with him how to load and bless
>   With fruit the vines that round the thatch-eves run . . .[20]

Keats's poem has often been regarded as serenely detached from the turmoil
of current events, and indeed its third line folds anxieties of 'conspiracy' into
the natural cycle of the year at its golden autumnal mean of 'mists and mellow
fruitfulness' – poised between summer and winter, warmth and chill. Hunt
was autumn's child, and that mingled season had always attracted him in
'doubled pleasures' that kept opposing sensations and impulses in play. His
early Spenserian poem, *The Palace of Pleasure*, had depicted a knight battling
with fiery temptations and 'imps from hell' to win a land of temperate
'Content'; now, against a backdrop of real bloodshed at Peterloo, Keats had
been drawn to scenes of autumnal harmony and the equable rhythms of natural

life that Hunt associated in the *Examiner* with 'long-lost "Merry Old England"'. Far from seeing 'To Autumn' and the poems in Keats's *Lamia* volume as insulated from history, Hunt detected in them 'the modern philosophy of sympathy and natural justice' and 'a high feeling of humanity'. In the aftermath of Peterloo, Keats had taken his place among the English poets – and Hunt was the first to say so.[21]

Having shown Keats the way to the lyrical justice of 'To Autumn' with September's 'Calendar of Nature', Hunt revived the satirical spirit of his father's 'Scurrility Hall'. The speaker of 'The Manchester Yeoman' is a lethally drunk cartoon soldier:

> With CASTLEREAGH and Co., man,
> And things *in statu quo*, man;
> I make the goblet flow, man,
> And beef and port I stow, man,
> Within my bow-window, man;
> And then like any Roman,
> I take on me, I trow, man,
> Power *ex-officio*, man,
> And ride to meet the foe, man,
> And prove that there is no man
> Such 'more than man' can show, man,
> By cutting down – a woman.[22]

If the Peterloo killings made soldiers 'so much more the man', in the court scenes that followed, 'The Chary Manchester Chairman' was keen for a cover-up. Hunt's poem refers to magistrates who prevented the prosecution witness, Matthew Cowper, from responding to 'Bristol' Hunt's questions:

> Says HUNT to MAT COWPER – Pray where do you live?
> Says COWPER – In Manchester here.
> Says HUNT – Have you more addresses to give?
> Says the Bench – Don't you answer him, dear.
>   *Chorus of Magistrates.* Shocking suggestion! Don't answer the
>   question.
> Don't answer – don't answer – oh dear![23]

'Truth's a dog must to kennel'; Like the Fool's songs in *King Lear*, Hunt's post-Peterloo ballads, squibs and jingles in the *Examiner* needle and ridicule rulers who neither see, feel, or know.

In October Richard Carlile was brought to trial for blasphemy and seditious libel, found guilty, and sentenced to three years in Dorchester Prison and a fine of £1,500 (the *Examiner* began its transcript of the trial on page 666, the number of the beast in Revelation). Writing from Florence, Shelley predicted 'awful times' and 'a military & judicial despotism'; he drafted an article for the *Examiner* declaring Carlile's jury 'illegal & partial' and demanding a new trial.[24]

As 1819 drew to a close, risks of prosecution for sedition intensified dramatically when the draconian 'Six Acts' became law. In framing them the Tory government assumed that a conspiracy to subvert the Constitution did in fact exist, and that the effective way to stop it was to tighten the laws on sedition and seditious libel; limit public meetings; outlaw paramilitary training; and increase the taxes on newspapers, periodicals and pamphlets. These measures recalled the notorious 'Gagging Acts' of 1795, and their effects were similar. Radicals went underground, gave up the fight or, like Hunt, took careful stock of the crisis and adopted more oblique modes of expression. Hunt and Shelley saw that the Six Acts put England on the road to a 'government of military tyranny': anyone who had been convicted for blasphemous or seditious libel would now be liable on a second conviction to fourteen years' transportation.[25] Botany Bay, not Kentish Town, might be the Hunts' next home – and they now had six children to care for when, on 28 September, Marianne gave birth to Henry Sylvan.

'Ollier gets more timid & pale every day,' Hunt confided to Shelley, 'I hope I shall not have to add time serving; but they say he is getting intimate with strange people.'[26] Was this a warning for Shelley that publisher Ollier had received unwelcome visitors from the Home Office? During this autumn of arrests and prosecutions, John urged Hunt to relinquish proprietorship of the *Examiner* so that, in the event of a further prosecution for libel or sedition, the government would be unable to imprison or banish both of them at once.[27]

Hunt was also cautious about another important matter. When he received Shelley's furious response to 'the bloody murderous oppression' at Peterloo, *The Masque of Anarchy*, he decided not to publish the poem in the *Examiner*.[28] Instead, he kept the manuscript for thirteen years before issuing it as a pamphlet, with a Preface that looked back on the situation in 1819. In his Preface, Hunt recalls thinking that the suffering masses 'would believe a hundred-fold in [Shelley's] anger, to what they would in his good intention; and this made me fear that the common enemy would take advantage of the mistake to do them both a disservice'. The danger was not that the poem incited violence – Shelley explicitly warned 'DO NOT DO THUS' – but that the 'Tory-kind' would deliberately misconstrue Shelley's words. Rephrase Hunt's sentences slightly, and one hears a prosecution lawyer setting out the government's case: 'This poem has a wicked and malicious tendency to inflame opinion against the lawful government of this country.'[29]

In 1832, the year of the Great Reform Act, *The Masque of Anarchy* could be seen as a triumphant example of '*political anticipation*', but in 1819 to write

'Blood is on the grass like dew' was a ticket to Botany Bay. There is some evidence that shortly after he received Shelley's poem, Hunt may also have had a run-in with 'strange people'. A tantalising reference in one of Keats's letters dated 12 November tells us: 'Hunt was arrested the other day. He soon however dated from his own house again.'[30] Keats says no more, and Hunt's letters and the *Examiner* are silent on the matter too. As in 1794, when Isaac was arrested, spies were everywhere and the post was routinely intercepted: had word about *The Masque of Anarchy* somehow reached Whitehall, prompting the 'common enemy' to call on Hunt and threaten him with arrest if he published Shelley's poem?

Hunt was no time-server, but his problem was how to stay in print and evade prosecution. When he could snatch a 'holiday hour' he worked on a translation of Tasso's *Amyntas* and, looking positively to the future, he projected an entirely new periodical that would adopt the cheerful, chatty manner of his letters to the Shelleys, as if writing in his own 'private room'.[31] The *Examiner* would continue to be his public 'tavern-room' for politics and, as in the taverns of London, there would be the risk of spies, informers, prosecutions. Hunt's new journal would resemble the privacy of his own fireside, a private space for 'chit-chat' and sociality carefully insulated from the dangerous England of the Six Acts.[32]

The title of his new journal, the *Indicator*, was suggested by a friend, Mary Novello, and there were opportunities for friends to contribute. It was printed at the *Examiner* office, and from May 1820 was sold by Hunt's new acquaintances, Arthur and Alistatia Gliddon, at their tobacco shop and coffee-house in nearby Tavistock Street. The contents would be an 'agreeable miscellany' of short pieces, including biography and autobiography, stories of old times, essays, fictional prose, natural description, translations, original poetry and literary criticism. First published on Wednesday, 13 October at twopence, Hunt's new weekly was an immediate hit with readers. By the end of the year he reported to the Shelleys, 'they tell me I am at my best in this work, which succeeds beyond all expectation'.[33]

Hunt was at his best because at liberty to write about whatever caught his interest – London shops, sticks, hats, 'Names', 'Dolphins', 'Coaches', 'Rousseau's Pygmalion', 'Gray's Bard', 'Play-House Memoranda', 'May-Day', 'A Rainy Day', 'Songs of Robin Hood'. The *Indicator* also contained extracts from Hunt's ill-fated tragedy, criticisms of Shelley's *Cenci* and Keats's *Lamia* volume, Coleridge's *Ancient Mariner* and the *Christabel* collection. Shelley contributed a lyric, 'Love's Philosophy'. Keats's 'La Belle Dame sans Merci' and his sonnet on Paolo and Francesca first appeared in the *Indicator*. 'A Now, Descriptive of a Hot Day' was a collaboration between Hunt and Keats. Hunt's breadth of reading appeared in his astonishing gallery of literary references, reflections, quotations and allusions that ranged through classics like Catullus and Virgil to Ariosto, Dante and Tasso, and the English poets including Chaucer, Gower, Spenser, Sidney, Donne, Shakespeare, Jonson, Drayton, Marvell, Milton, Beaumont and Fletcher, Dryden, Gay, Thomson, Johnson, Burns, Ossian, and contemporary writers. The list could be doubled in length.

The *Indicator* succeeded in welcoming readers as if to a delectable meal, and Hunt announced that the title was taken from 'a bird of that name who shews people where to find wild honey'. It sounds hopelessly quaint, but that reference to 'wild honey' was a coded allusion to hard times in England when, as Keats wrote, 'honey / Can't be got without hard money!'[34] Wild honey and 'Twopenny Trash' – as Hunt described the *Indicator* – knowingly signalled a source of sweet sustenance beyond the world of money-getting, unemployment and unrest.

But it was hard work. Fridays and Saturdays were devoted to the *Examiner*, and now Mondays and Tuesdays were given over to writing for the *Indicator*. Hunt told the Shelleys he was 'now in fact emerging', by which he meant he was paying his way 'to a farthing'.[35] Still, the ceaseless round of deadlines told on his health and towards the end of 1820 a recurrence of nervous illness obliged him to make up *Indicator* copy from material previously published in the *Reflector*, *Examiner* and *Literary Pocket-Book*. Shelley was worried by what he heard of Hunt's 'incredible exertions' and the collapse of his health.[36] On 21 March 1821 the *Indicator* bade farewell to its readers, after a run of seventy-six issues over seventeen months.

In the *Indicator*, Hunt's sociable fireside was a setting for personal conversations behind the more confrontational platform of the *Examiner*. He had written in this manner before – in the *Reflector*, for example – and his return to it now meant that the *Indicator* created links between his earlier radical years and his later literary career. Here we see essays growing from memories of his childhood, schooldays and youthful travels. The article on 'Dolphins' remembers boyhood sightings of the porpoise; 'Hats, New and Ancient' touches the texture of the 'old friar's dress' he wore at Christ's Hospital; 'Translation from Milton into Welsh' revives his meetings with the Welsh Bards; 'Coaches' relives his cramped, cold journey to Cambridge in 1811. Benjamin West's death prompts tender recollections of visiting Newman Street with his mother. Hunt was increasingly being drawn to autobiography, and his technique of adapting and reusing material, often when under pressure for copy, established his compositional habits in later life. Many of his personal recollections in the magazine would be incorporated into *Lord Byron and some of his Contemporaries* and his *Autobiography*. Future directions are signalled in other articles too. Hunt's criticisms of Shelley and Keats, interspersed with extensive quotations, look forward to *Imagination and Fancy* (1844); his choice selections from various authors open the way for *A Jar of Honey from Mount Hybla* (1848), *A Book for a Corner* and *Readings for Railways*

(1849); an article on 'Pleasant Recollections Connected with various Parts of the Metropolis' anticipates both *The Town* (1848) and his articles for the *Atlas* magazine (1847) later gathered in *A Saunter through the West End* (1861). *The Companion* (1828), *Chat of the Week* (1830), *Tatler* (1830), *Seer* (1840–1), and *Men, Women, and Books* (1847) would all attempt to revive the manner of the *Indicator*. In short, Hunt's *Indicator* set up his later career.

It was also a milestone in British journalism. Moving away from the waspy tone of *Blackwood's* and the patrician posturing of the *Edinburgh* and *Quarterly*, Hunt perfected a playful, mobile editorial style that ranged over miscellaneous materials, wearing its learning lightly. In some ways he anticipated nineteenth-century periodicals like Dickens's *Household Words*, the *Cornhill Magazine*, *Punch* and the *Illustrated London News*. As the 'Indicator' Hunt also cultivated authorial personality (unlike 'Z') and invented the byline of modern journalism. His 'chit-chat' was not frivolous, but written in a style designed to take the Hunt–Shelley ideals to a new audience of men and women who, like Bess Kent and John Keats, had received no university education but were avid readers receptive to new ideas.

1819 had begun with Hunt sensing imminent change and predicting 'one of the most important years that have been seen for a long while'. The year 1820 opened with the Hunts leaving York Place for 13, Mortimer Terrace, Kentish Town, another development on the frontier between London's northern suburbs and the open countryside. The new house was chaotic after the move, but 'convenient & cheerful', and Hunt considered it 'quite a bargain'. Outside the terrace was busy with street vendors, ballad singers and musicians, but the view across the fields to Hampstead – 'hill, trees, church & all' – more than made up for the noise.[37] This was a fresh start of a kind: 1820 would see Hunt's most intensive exertions for the *Examiner* and *Indicator*, but also the faltering of his energies as he succumbed once again to ill health and the depressing realisation that readers and subscribers had started to drift away. From now on there would be a retrospective slant to many of Hunt's writings.

George III died on 29 January 1820. A month later the Cato Street Conspiracy to assassinate the cabinet was uncovered, and the perpetrators, Arthur Thistlewood and nine others, arrested. Hunt saw them as 'paupers driven to desperation in unconstitutional times'; the spring would bring more treason trials, and five grisly executions in the street outside Newgate Prison. On Wednesday, 29 March, Hunt was in the congregation at St Paul's for West's grand public funeral. Two months later, on 15 May, 'Bristol' Hunt was convicted of 'exciting and attending an unlawful meeting' at York, and sentenced to two and a half years in prison.[38] All through the summer the unedifying spectacle of the 'Caroline Affair' unfolded, as the Prince of Wales tried to rid himself of his estranged wife before his coronation as George IV.

For Hunt these events stirred memories of the old King's reign: his own childhood and schooldays, insurrections and conspiracies, and his efforts to bring greater freedom and honesty to relations between men and women. What had been gained over all those years? The execution of the Cato Street conspirators demonstrated that nothing had been learned since Despard's day: 'These things never were, and never can be settled, by such measures.' The 'bulky Beau of fifty-eight' was about to become King. Much might be said, but Hunt had said it all already: 'What a pity that royalty – but we have done.' He would not abandon the cause just yet, but what difference could another broadside at courtly corruption make?[39]

On 5 June Caroline arrived back in England determined to claim her rights as Queen. She was a popular figure, and it was not easy to see how the 'delicate emergency' of Caroline, now effectively Queen Consort, could be resolved without revealing her husband's numerous mistresses to public gaze. In August the investigation into Caroline's alleged adulteries was under way in the House of Lords – in Hunt's view 'one of the greatest pushes given to declining royalty that the age has seen'. He told Shelley that the British public was 'constantly occupied in reading trials for adultery'.[40] The stained bedlinen and below-stairs gossip displayed in the Caroline investigations were tokens of the double standard that plagued sexual relations in England. *The Story of Rimini* had balanced the claims of human feeling and justice against legally sanctioned 'forms' of sexual morality, and demonstrated the hypocrisy of judging 'damnable offences' in others. Now the Caroline affair was bringing the 'selfishness and barbarism' of laws relating to women into full public gaze. Caroline had long since been rejected by her husband, who was a flagrant adulterer like many of the peers sitting in the Lords,

> men, who at the very moment they practise 'adultery and fornication' as peccadilloes not worth mention, insist upon our believing them damnable offences . . . They assume all sorts of imaginary distinctions, and beg the question, with infinite hypocrisy; about the worse consequences of the offence in women; when the injuriousness, real or imaginary, of those very consequences is nothing but the result of their own previous and false system of society.

Either adultery is a crime in everybody, or it is not. 'If it is not,' Hunt argues, 'then why all this cant against a supposed adulteress? If it is, then why is there no recrimination against an adulterer notorious?'[41]

Hunt's questions crystallise his lifelong effort to bring about equality of the sexes. Men and women are equally flesh and blood, his argument ran: 'The love of two loving people I love & reverence, & wish & believe they may remain together to all eternity, whether they think as I do on the subject of

Marriage or not.'[42] In November 1820, he had announced in the *Indicator* that he was 'not a friend to marriage', and the next generation would put Hunt's ideals of communal living and free love into practice at the Phalanstery commune in Bayswater and Hammersmith.[43]

'"Write me as one that loves his fellow-men"': this famous line from Hunt's enduringly popular poem of 1838, 'Abou Ben Adhem', captures the spirit of the Phalanstery experiment, as well as the passionate idealism of Hunt's male intimacies since his schooldays. If Hunt's friendship with Shelley had an unworldly aspect – he literally thought him 'a kind of angel'[44] – his practical affection for Keats finally won through against any lingering hostility from the young poet.

By now Keats's symptoms of tuberculosis were unmistakable. On 22 June 1820 he had suffered a serious haemorrhage, and Hunt – who was ill himself – immediately took him into the family home at Mortimer Terrace where he received medical attention. Keats was overwrought, resentful, easily agitated, but his time at the Hunts' brought him genuine respite from his suffering. 'Hunt amuses me very kindly,' he reported to Fanny Brawne, and a little later he told his sister: 'Mr Hunt does every thing in his power to make the time pass as agreeably with me as possible.'[45] Keats was kept occupied with reading, walking, and marking passages in a copy of Spenser for Fanny Brawne. Marianne cut a silhouette of him resting on two chairs. On one occasion, perhaps Monday, 26 June when the weather was extremely hot, Keats helped Hunt with copy for the *Indicator* by contributing to his prose-poem, 'A Now, Descriptive of a Hot Day': 'Now rooms with the sun upon them become intolerable; and the apothecary's apprentice, with a bitterness beyond aloes, thinks of the pond he used to bathe in at school.'[46] Advance copies of *Lamia, Isabella, The Eve of St. Agnes, and Other Poems* arrived from Taylor and Hessey, and Keats presented Hunt with an inscribed copy that immediately became one of his most treasured books.

Others were concerned about Keats's health too. Shelley's friends John and Maria Gisborne, visiting London from Italy, had seen how ill Keats looked. Word of this reached Shelley, and he immediately wrote to Keats, care of the *Examiner* office, inviting him to 'take up residence' with him at Pisa.[47] Shelley's letter arrived on Saturday, 12 August, shortly before an 'unpleasant accident' came to light. Two days earlier, a note for Keats had been delivered from Fanny Brawne, and Marianne, who was busy with the children, asked the maid to take it up to his room. The note did not reach Keats. When Thornton handed it over on the Saturday with the seal broken, Keats could not bear the thought that her words had been read by another, and broke down and wept for several hours. Despite Hunt's entreaties he left Mortimer Terrace and staggered through the lanes to the Brawnes' house at Hampstead. The rift was brief, and Keats was soon thanking Hunt for his 'many sympathies with me'. Hunt responded immediately: 'I need not say how you gratify me by the impulse which led you to write a particular sentence in your letter, for you must have seen by this time how much I am attached to yourself'.[48] His translation of *Amyntas*, published this summer, opened with these words: 'To John Keats, Esq. this translation of the early work of a celebrated poet, whose fate it was to be equally pestered by the critical, and admired by the poetical, is inscribed, by his affectionate friend, Leigh Hunt.'[49]

Keats's fate was not to return to Mortimer Terrace. He also declined Shelley's invitation at first, although the comparatively benign winter climate of Italy offered his only possibility of recovery. A month after the exchange of heartfelt letters with Hunt, Keats boarded the brig *Maria Crowther* with Joseph Severn, and set sail for Naples. Hunt's poignant farewell appeared in the *Indicator*: 'dear friend, as valued a one as thou art a poet, – John Keats, – we cannot, after all, find it in our hearts to be glad, now thou art gone away with the swallows to seek a kindlier clime'.[50] On 8 March 1821 he wrote to Joseph Severn, evidently expecting the worst: 'tell him – tell that great poet & noble-hearted man, that we shall . . . never cease to remember & love him . . . all who are of one accord in mind or heart are journeying to one & the same place, and shall unite somehow or other again, face to face, mutually conscious, mutually delighted.'[51] After nursing Keats for seven weeks, Hunt knew that any attempt to console might cause further anguish. It was another seven days before he heard that Keats had died in a house on the Piazza di Spagna, Rome, on 23 February 1821.

TWENTY-FIVE

THE GATHERING STORM

MPs who were in the House of Commons on Tuesday, 25 July 1820 heard themselves described as a set of 'venal boroughmongers, grasping placemen, greedy adventurers and aspiring title-hunters . . . a body, in short, containing a far greater portion of Public Criminals than Public Guardians'. Castlereagh was quoting a letter from one 'Ch. Fitzpaine' in the *Examiner*, as a particularly torrid example of the 'licentious' press. Four months passed before its author, John Hunt – 'Ch. Fitzpaine' – received an information for libel. His letter was 'a foul and infamous calumny'. In the New Year John returned from Somerset to stand trial in London. Hunt fondly hoped that the 'vindictive malignity of government' would not succeed, but on 21 February 1821 a special jury brought in a verdict of guilty. Three months later John was sentenced to another year in Coldbath Fields, and required to find sureties of £1,000.[1]

Hunt had already withdrawn from the *Examiner* because of ill health. Anxiety, nerves, and sheer mental exhaustion had taken their toll. His brain was 'bruised' with writing. Dosing himself with wine and laudanum, he felt as if he was 'going to break up at once, body and mind'. Preparing the last issues of the *Indicator* almost killed him.[2]

By the beginning of March 1821 warmer weather and vigorous walks on Hampstead Heath – Hunt's favourite cure – had restored a 'more *promising* state of health'.[3] The family had moved from Mortimer Terrace out to the Vale of Health, where they returned to the same 'little packing-case' of a house they had shared with the Shelleys in 1817.[4] Right on cue, the fractiousness of that earlier time revived. The first volume of Hazlitt's *Table Talk* had been published on 6 April with an essay 'On Paradox and Commonplace', in which to Hunt's fury Shelley was described as a 'philosophic fanatic' with 'a fire in his eye, a fever in his blood, a maggot in his brain, a hectic flutter in his speech'. Shelley, said Hazlitt, was merely a child who loved to 'shock'. Hunt himself was set down as a 'vivacious mannerist', an egotist insatiably eager 'to be the hero of the piece'.[5]

Both a friend and a good cause were at stake, and Hunt went on the offensive. 'I think, Mr Hazlitt, you might have found a better time, and place too, for assaulting me and my friends in this bitter manner.' Hunt did not know whether Hazlitt's spleen, vanity, intolerance or resentment of Shelley had prompted this outburst, but to attack a fellow-reformer was 'no advancement to the cause of liberal opinion'. And if Hazlitt insisted on making Hunt's foibles stand for his whole character, then he should quarrel in private, not 'draw and quarter' him in public.[6]

Hazlitt replied: 'I have no quarrel with you, nor can I have. You are one of those people that I like, do what they will.' Then followed a long list of Hazlitt's grudges against Reynolds, Godwin, Lamb, Coulson, Bentham and Basil Montagu. Hunt had 'shirked out' of the *Blackwood's* 'business', leaving Hazlitt to do solitary battle with 'Z'. Only John Hunt had never played him any 'tricks'. The postscript summed up Hazlitt's feelings of wounded innocence: 'I want to know why every body has such a dislike to me.'[7]

Hunt cleared that up in a trice: Hazlitt should understand his repellent nature. His friends never know whether he is well-disposed or sarcastic, pleased or displeased, cordial or uncordial. No wonder he complains of not having a soul to stand by him. Hunt later recalled someone telling him that Shelley had 'cut up' Hazlitt at Godwin's – and Hazlitt was known to '*pocket up*' slights until they stank. Still, the attack on Shelley was unnecessary, impolitic – *and* Hunt had taken all the pains he could to make the 'raff and coward, Z, come forward'.[8] Their friendship somehow survived, and both went into mourning when news of Napoleon's death reached London in early July. The *Examiner's* tribute – 'The age has lost its greatest name' – was framed by a thick border of black print.[9]

Hunt had resumed writing politics for the *Examiner* in March, excited by reports that Italy was rebelling against the Austrians and its liberation was 'almost certain'. Then came news that the Greeks had risen against the Turks. But these advances in the cause of liberty were short lived, and inevitably overshadowed by England's failure to reform – George IV was crowned on 19 July in a 'shewey Coronation' described in the *Examiner* as 'an involuntary mock-heroic'. Once again *King Lear* came to mind: 'Robes and furred gowns hide nothing. Faith is dead; and works are your only wear.' The nation looked on with 'sorry eyes' at the sumptuous ceremony and threadbare sovereign.[10]

Ever since the move back to the Vale the Hunt children had been ill: measles, scarlet fever (caught from Horace Smith), 'inflammatory fever and rheumatism' and, for young John, pleurisy. Nine-month-old baby Henry had an attack of fits. Hunt's thoughts were increasingly drawn to the idea of a new home in Italy. 'I long to come over the sea to you,' he wrote to the Shelleys on 10 July, 'but it cannot be.' And, again: 'I would come to you instantly, and do not say that I shall not come to you before long.'[11] The *Examiner's* precarious fortunes, family illnesses, and the awful prospect of another English

winter were preying on Hunt's mind. His return to the paper with a short
series of 'Sketches of the Living Poets'. – Bowles, Byron, Campbell and
Coleridge – had brought back readers; if these could be kept, there was some
prospect of maintaining his income. At present it seemed necessary for him
to be on the spot but if the paper went on 'swimmingly', he told Shelley on
28 August, it might be possible for him to 'write from Italy on general subjects,
and even furnish a letter every week upon my journey there, the state of the
country, & c.'[12]

While Hunt's idea of writing from Italy was taking shape, Shelley was visiting
Lord Byron at Ravenna. They had last met at Venice, when Byron had appeared
debauched, debilitated, and about to succumb to serious illness. At Ravenna
His Lordship was transformed, recovered in health and, Shelley reported,
enjoying a 'permanent sort of liaison' with Contessa Teresa Guiccioli. Shelley's
days began at noon, Lord Byron's at two in the afternoon. They breakfasted,
talked until six, rode out though the pine forests in the cool evening air, and
then returned to dine and while away the night chatting about 'poetry & such
matters' until the sky lightened. A move to Switzerland had been mooted,
but Byron now fell in eagerly with the suggestion that he should move across
country to Tuscany. Mary Shelley was instructed to 'inquire for the best
unfurnished palace in Pisa', and by the end of the month she had secured
for Byron the gigantic Casa Lanfranchi on the Lung'Arno.[13] At the beginning of November Byron was installed at Pisa with Teresa and her father and
brother, the Counts Ruggero and Pietro Gamba.

One of the matters Shelley and Byron touched upon at Ravenna was the
idea for a periodical to be edited from Italy and published in England. Byron
had already tried to interest Tom Moore in a similar project, and was keen
to pursue this new direction. In this first rush of enthusiasm Shelley
mentioned Hunt's name, and Byron apparently responded with the proposal
that Shelley forwarded to Hunt on 26 August.

'My dearest friend,' Shelley wrote:

> Since I last wrote to you, I have been on a visit to Lord Byron at Ravenna
> . . . the material part of my visit consists in a message which he desires me
> to give you, and which I think ought to add to your determination – for
> such a one I hope you have formed – of restoring your shattered health
> and spirits by a migration to these 'regions mild of calm and serene air'.
>
> He proposes that you should come and go shares with him and me, in a
> periodical work, to be conducted here; in which each of the contracting
> parties should publish all their original compositions, and share the profits.
> He proposed it to Moore, but for some reason it was never brought to bear.
> There can be no doubt that the *profits* of any scheme in which you and Lord
> Byron engage, must, from various yet co-operating reasons, be very great.

As to myself, I am, for the present, only a sort of link between you and him, until you can know each other and effectuate the arrangement . . .[14]

Shelley's letter communicated a business proposal from Lord Byron. Hunt was invited to Italy to collaborate on a periodical, and the business terminology was unequivocal: 'go shares', 'contracting parties', *profits*'. Hunt responded immediately and emphatically: 'I agree to his proposal.'[15] Byron's genius and Hunt's experience in periodical publishing would make a formidable combination. Hunt's income from the *Examiner* had dwindled from £443 in 1820 to £275 in 1821: now he could retain his connection with the *Examiner*, and the Italian venture would be a rewarding 'set up'.[16] Hunt's understanding was that he would travel to Pisa to begin a new 'literary speculation', and he immediately assumed that John would be involved as the publisher. The move was a breakthrough in another way too, in that it demonstrated Hunt's mobility as a man of letters prepared to earn his living by his pen where opportunities arose. 'We are coming,' he announced to the Shelleys, 'what with your kind persuasions, the proposal of Lord Byron, and last, be sure not least, the hope of seeing you again and trying to get my health back in your society, my brother as well as myself think I had better go.'[17]

Shelley recommended a voyage direct from London to Leghorn. By the end of September Hunt had booked the passage, but the captain delayed, and then Marianne was seized with an alarming recurrence of the illness that had afflicted her fifteen years earlier. She was 'throwing-up blood'.[18] Hunt understood that her condition was 'decidedly affected by the greater or less *alarms* which she goes through' – in other words, by stress.[19] It would probably be diagnosed now as an ulcer, and there may have been a secondary infection as well: at least one physician believed she was mortally ill, most likely with consumption. At Mortimer Terrace Keats had spent nearly two months in close proximity to the Hunts, when his tuberculosis was advanced and contagious. It is possible that Marianne had caught tuberculosis from Keats, and certain that Hunt feared this was the case. The doctor recommended a sea voyage as the best possible cure.

After weeks of waiting, word came from Captain Francis Whitney, master of the brig *Jane*, to come aboard. And so the Hunts cleared their little house in the Vale of Health for the second time, and on Wednesday, 14 November the family climbed into a hackney coach and set off for the docks. Next day Hunt, Marianne, the six children, Elizabeth the servant and a goat to provide breakfast milk, boarded the *Jane* at Blackwall. The Novellos came to bid them farewell. Early on Friday morning Hunt was wakened by the motion of the *Jane* as she moved off down the Thames. In his cell at Coldbath Prison, John Hunt sat down to write to Shelley, letting him know that his brother was on his way. Because John's means were very much reduced, 'all care' for Hunt's wants in Italy would necessarily fall upon Shelley. At Pisa Shelley was already expecting them '*here* every day'.[20]

The *Jane* was a two-masted brig of 120 tons, with a crew of nine. Below deck the Hunts' cabin was at the stern. In the middle was a table fastened to the floor, and on each side were three narrow bunks or cribs, one above the other. The six children had a bunk each, and Hunt and Marianne made their bed on the floor. Elizabeth the servant slept in a cupboard. A wide sloping window extended across the stern with a bench and locker beneath, and on the inner bulkhead was a little fireplace. They dried the baby's nappies and clothes on pegs above it. The *Jane*'s cargo was sugar from the West Indies and a 'surreptitious stock' of fifty barrels of gunpowder bound for Greece, some of which were stowed right underneath the Hunts' cabin. From time to time the ship's cook, a West Indian who was 'constantly drunk' on rum, would descend unsteadily through a hatch in the cabin floor, candle in hand, in quest of provisions.

After four days and a collision with another ship, the *Jane* rounded the Nore on 19 November and entered the English Channel. Here they met such rough weather that the captain was forced to put in at Ramsgate. The harbour was shallow, and as the *Jane* edged towards a mooring she ran aground and damaged her rudder. Repairs would take three weeks, so the Hunts went ashore and took lodgings in the town. Hunt had been here twenty years before, on the walking tour that led to his meeting with Marianne and Bess. The Novellos came down from London, and Hunt visited CCC who was staying at his mother's house nearby. Then, on Tuesday, 11 December, Marianne was carried to the harbour in a sedan chair and Vincent Novello bade them farewell a second time.

With all the Hunts and the goat aboard, the *Jane* set sail and headed into another gale in what would prove one of the worst winters in living memory. For ten days the *Jane* was beaten up and down the Channel – as far west as the Scilly Isles and the edge of the Atlantic, then back toward the French coast. None of the crew had been tested by a storm of such length and ferocity before. The ship laboured through tremendous waves with the sea crashing over the deck and the pump constantly in action.

Down below the Hunts kept to their cabin. The fire would not light in the high wind, so they were cold and, except for Hunt, dreadfully seasick. The children slept fitfully in their bunks while Marianne, who was exhausted by fear, dozed uneasily on the floor and woke repeatedly with 'starts & sudden terrors'.[21] Hunt stayed awake at nights expecting the worst. He tried to read. He stared at the grotesque shapes of the baby's clothes swaying in the dim light. He thought of friends chatting, laughing, playing music, and retiring to their dry, restful beds. Then he fed morsels of biscuit to the goat he had brought into the cabin, and tried to gather up pellets of dung. Through the storm he glimpsed the fiery eye of the lighthouse on the Lizard. On 21

December the *Jane* narrowly escaped being run down in the night by a much bigger ship, an Indiaman that was wrecked a few hours afterwards. On the following day the *Jane* made Dartmouth harbour.

Hunt knew that Chaucer's 'Schippmann' had been born in Dartmouth, but it was a dreary, muddy place – 'a sort of sublime Wapping'.[22] Christmas and the New Year passed, and on Friday, 5 January the *Jane* put to sea again. This time the Hunts were not aboard. Marianne was so shaken by the frights and dangers of their voyage that her illness – 'weakness and light-headedness, throwing up more blood' – made it impossible to move her.[23] By the end of the month they had made the short journey overland to Plymouth, where Hunt quickly located another ship, the *Placidia*, bound for Genoa. The name was reassuring. He paid the captain £30 for berths, and the Hunts passed two nights on board waiting to sail – even though it was clear that Marianne was far too ill to continue the journey. Hunt now saw that he would have to put his family before his desire to see Shelley again. They went back ashore, and settled in a house at Devil's Point, Stonehouse, owned by a Mrs L'Amoureux. Here they would wait for the spring and fair weather, before resuming their voyage.

Devil's Point projects into Plymouth Sound, and across the water Hunt was able to see the elegant house at Mount Edgcumbe surrounded with land-scaped gardens and trees. It looked like Hampstead-on-Sea. Closer to the Hunts' lodging was the Marine Barracks, with a band that played morning and evening – including Mozart 'pretty well'.[24] Hunt's first task was to write to Byron and the Shelleys with news of 'the disasters of our first voyage'. His letter to Byron – the first since Byron's departure from England in 1816 – was understandably awkward to write, not least because Hunt wished to borrow 'as much as £250'. He ballasted that request by detailing his expectations for 'a monthly or two-monthly publication' of essays, stories, poetry and translations – a publication not unlike the *Indicator*. Hunt's letter to Shelley revisited the storms and setbacks of the voyage, including Marianne's sickness and the gunpowder, and in a postscript confessed his need for a loan.[25]

Hunt's letter annoyed Shelley – and for more than one reason: he was cautious of dealing with Byron on financial matters, and he had already responded to an earlier letter Hunt had mailed at Dartmouth by sending £150. With Shelley guaranteeing repayment, however, Byron advanced, with '*tolerable willingness*', £250 in Italian bills. From this Hunt eventually received £220 from Shelley's London bankers; the remaining £30 Shelley reserved at Pisa to await the Hunts' arrival.[26] Hunt claimed to have left London leaving 'no ordinary debt unsatisfied', but as usual it was the extraordinary debts he chose to overlook.[27] John had hinted at further debts in his letter to Shelley, and the disastrous voyage had proved unavoidably expensive. Hunt had already booked and paid passage twice, and would have to do so a third time. There was accommodation at Ramsgate, Dartmouth and Plymouth to pay for, plus doctors' fees for Marianne. From Hunt's point of view they were enduring these difficulties at the invitation of Shelley and, above all, Byron. The publication scheme stood a real chance of success – John had said so, and had urged him to go. The loan Hunt had requested was offset by that prospect and, Hunt reflected, it had always been Byron who had sought him out – in prison, after his release, and during the separation scandal – not the other way round. So £250 was a trifling sum to bring Hunt and his family to Pisa.

Byron agreed. On 23 February he informed his business executor Douglas Kinnaird of the £250 loan to Hunt, and added: 'With regard to L. Hunt – he stuck by me through thick & thin – when all shook, and some shuffled in 1816. – He never asked me for a loan till now. – I am very willing to accommodate a man to whom I have obligations. – He is now at Plymouth – waiting for a ship to sail to Italy.'[28] Byron wrote at once to Hunt, urging him 'to make all . . . haste'. Reports of Byron in Shelley's letters were unvarying: 'He expresses himself again *warmly* about this literary scheme' (17 February); 'He expresses again the greatest eagerness to undertake it & proceed with it, as well as the greatest confidence in you as his associate' (2 March); 'Lord Byron has the greatest anxiety for your arrival' (10 April).[29]

Unknown to Hunt, another narrative was now unfolding at Pisa. Hunt's arrival had long been expected, and Byron had furnished the lower apartments at Casa Lanfranchi in readiness for him. A cook had been hired. By the end of January Hunt's non-appearance was producing a 'chaos of perplexities', and as time passed Shelley began to dread that Byron's commitment to the journal would waver: 'he is so mentally capricious that the least impulse drives him from his anchorage'.[30] Byron's proximity in Pisa had exposed deep differences between them: there were tensions of personality, social standing, money and poetic fame.[31] Before Hunt left England, the Pisan circle had broken up. At the end of April the Shelleys had moved some forty miles along the coast to a new home at Casa Magni, between San Terenzo and Lerici. Shortly afterwards Byron transferred his household, including Teresa Guiccioli and the Gambas, to a villa at Montenero a few miles south of Leghorn. On the 30th Shelley wrote of the 'great gulph' between himself and Byron, 'which by the nature of things must daily become wider'.[32]

At Devil's Point the Hunts passed the winter quietly. Marianne was bled '46 ounces of blood' in one day to prevent 'inflammatory fever on the lungs'. Leeches were applied to her eyes, and Hunt remained 'very uneasy about her'. He found time to write for the *Examiner* some short 'Fables for Grown Children', and in May began a series of letters to the paper 'trusting to a more than ordinary intimacy between the author and his readers'. 'I am of a tropical race,' Hunt confided, 'and shall probably get better and better, as I slip from under the clouds of my beloved but somewhat rainy country, and emerge into the blue æther of Italy.' He visited Plymouth Public Library and several 'landscapes in the neighbourhood', including the grounds at Mount Edgcumbe where he was pleased by the Italian garden with its statue of Mercury and bust of Ariosto. He met the painter Philip Rogers, a fellow pupil of Haydon's at Plymouth Grammar School, and also the schoolmaster Joseph Hine who would later try to teach Hunt's wayward second son, John. Local 'Examinerians' – 'liberal to an extreme and esoterical degree' – presented him with a silver cup as a tribute to his exertions for 'FREEDOM, TRUTH and HUMANITY' (see illustrations). He hired a piano for a month and invited the Novellos to stay, but even assurances about the new patent safety-coach on the London–Plymouth route did not lure them.[33]

By the end of March 1822 Hunt had secured berths on another ship, the *David Walter*. Elizabeth had been afraid to travel any further, and a 'jolly Plymouth damsel' came as servant in her place. They went aboard on Monday, 13 May, the goat too, and sailed that day with a fine wind from the north-east. Next day they cleared the English Channel and by the 15th they were in the Bay of Biscay, becalmed in a sea that heaved and swelled like oily-looking fields. A small shark played about the boat all day, while the ship's crew busied themselves painting the hull black and yellow. Hunt learned that the ship would call first at Genoa, then proceed to Leghorn. With an eye to the forthcoming periodical, he was keeping a journal in which he noted the weather, wind and various sights – porpoises, grampuses, dolphins, waves, wavelets, billows and 'fluctuosities'.[34] He was also drafting passages that would help Bess with *Flora Domestica*, her encyclopaedia of plants for suburban gardens. With a fresh breeze from the north-east, the voyage resumed. Hunt sat on the deck, enjoyed the motion of the boat and the healthy air, gazed up at the sails, looked out for new sights, read and chatted. At night, when the children and Marianne were below in their bunks, Hunt went up to look at the phosphorescent wake streaming away into the dark.

Throughout the voyage Hunt was confronted with sights, sounds and sensations that sent him to poetry, gemstones, paintings, puddings, and even shop-counters as he searched for images and textures to describe his experiences. Coleridge's *Ancient Mariner* was constantly in his mind, although Hunt was as frequently drawn to more domestic comparisons: the sun reflected on to water like 'shot silk'; a shoal of little fish leapt from the water 'like a sprinkle of shillings'; the sea's phosphorescence was an 'ethereal syllabub'.

They passed Cape Finisterre in a heavy Atlantic swell on 21 May, and over the next few days fair weather and a brisk northeasterly breeze accompanied them down the coast of Portugal. Just when they needed it, the wind veered to the north-west, speeding them around Cape St Vincent and on towards the Strait of Gibraltar. Now they passed sites of modern interest like Cadiz and Cape Trafalgar; looking south, the coast of Africa came into view with its walled towns and unknown animals. The clear air made the Strait of Gibraltar look narrower than thirteen miles across.

Monday, 27 May was two weeks into the voyage. The *David Walter* was creeping along the coast of Málaga in almost calm weather, with Hunt on deck repeating the word 'Mediterranean' as a word in verse. That evening the sky over the Sierra Nevada blazed in a spectacular sunset: 'Clouds like great wings of gold & yellow, & rose colour, with a smaller minute set in one spot like a shower of glowing stones from a volcano'. Hunt had never seen a volcanic eruption, but he felt free to imagine one: the voyage was having a restorative effect on his mind and his sense of well-being. He jotted in his journal: 'If alone in a wreck my feeling would be that I should escape & this confidence would give me a good chance of doing so.' Lights on the coast might be smugglers; flickering red streaks on the hills were from heath burning – Hunt had seen that on the Quantocks. Repeatedly his thoughts turned to Coleridge and *The Ancient Mariner*. Moonlight on water moved like silver snakes. On the 29th a gull flew across the ship at ten minutes past ten, and hung in the air above the trysail at the stern.

By 11 June they were off Toulon. Hunt found the blueness of the water most remarkable in the shadow of the ship, where the 'gloss of the sunshine' was 'taken off, and the colour was exactly that of the bottles sold in the shops with gold stoppers'. It struck him that at some time during the night of the 12th they must have crossed the path Bonaparte had taken in 1815, as he slipped away from Elba. Next morning Hunt had his first glimpse of the Alps – 'cold, lofty, and distant'. One more day of calm was passed watching dolphins, then the breeze freshened and at two o'clock in the afternoon of Saturday the 15th the *David Walter* entered Genoa harbour, 'a glorious amphitheatre' of white houses, palaces, churches, shipping, busy small boats with coloured awnings, men and women bathing, and as a sublime backdrop the dark slopes of the Apennines and, beyond them, the Alps.[35]

'Cheapness of provisions,' Hunt noted in his journal. After a month at sea, fresh food was their first need, and they were not disappointed. Baskets of fruit were ferried across the harbour to them: figs, apricots, fresh almonds, oranges, pears, cherries. Milk came in bottles stopped with vine leaves, and there was fresh grass for the goat. Hunt wrote Bess a brisk, happy letter to tell her of their arrival, and enclosed the passages he had written at sea about Juniper, Heath, Amaranth, Roses, Oranges, Poppy and Laurel. He signed it: 'Mille baci, & as many hopes to see you in Italy.'[36] Next he fired off a note to the Shelleys letting them know that the children were all marvellously well and Marianne already in better spirits. In four or five days, perhaps a week, they would set sail again for their home: 'I embrace you both a hundred times, each one warmer than the last.' Letters to John and to Lord Byron went by

the same post, snatched out of his hands by the boatman who had been kept
waiting. That night they ate lean kid's meat, and toasted their arrival in
tumblers of red wine.

The *David Walter* had tied up alongside a boat that looked hardly seaworthy,
although the captain could be heard saying that it had weathered the last
winter and would come through any 'gal o'wind'. Hunt knew that voice. This
was the brig *Jane*, and her master Captain Whitney. Now Hunt heard how
the *Jane* had left Dartmouth in January and almost foundered in a violent
storm in the Gulf of Lyons. Laid on her side with the sea washing over the
deck, the only shelter for the crew had been the Hunts' former cabin. Hunt
was in no doubt that if they had stayed with the *Jane*, Marianne would be
dead.[37]

Next day, 16 June, Captain Whitney accompanied Hunt when he first set
foot in Italy. Hunt wrote excitedly to the Novellos: 'My sensations on first
touching the shore I cannot describe to you. Genoa is truly *la superba*. Imagine
a dozen Hampsteads one over the other, intermingled with trees, rock, and
white streets, houses, and palaces.' The whitewashed houses and the blueness
of the sky radiated lightness and, Hunt thought, cleanliness (most English
travel writers of the day winced at the filthiness of Italian towns). The quay
and narrow streets were bustling with the noise and activity of the warm
south, but the men and boys looked ugly – 'no foreheads' – and most of the
women 'disappointed'. There were exceptions, however, like the handsome
boy with ear-rings, a girlish haircut and 'no modesty in his aspect', going out
to bathe with a flabby customs officer 'like a man made of dough'.[38]

Everywhere Hunt went he absorbed impressions with his painter's eye:
faces, the colours of houses, great dusty artificial flowers in the churches,
huge gold ear-rings, 'a merry old brown gardener, with a great straw-hat and
bare legs'. A boatman 'with his brown hue, his white shirt, and his red cap,
made a complete picture', and the intensity of Mediterranean light made the
cap 'like a scarlet bud in the blue atmosphere'. Here were gardens like
Benjamin West's, with statues and orange trees, and windows with vines trailed
sinuously over them 'like great luxuriant green hair'. He strolled out to the
suburbs, threading his way among olive, cherry, orange and almond trees, and
picked fresh lemons to take back to the boat. His next letter to Bess recalled
how they had once liked to pore over the 'little vignettes in the *Parnaso
Italiano*, and fancy Italy'. Here he was in those very scenes, and everything
was exactly as they had imagined, although 'greatly heightened in beauty'.
The dream was coming true. 'I dare not dwell upon the wish I have that you
were with us . . . I shall begin looking out for your Pisa lodging almost as
soon as I get there. *Mille baci, mille et mille volte.* – Your ever friend of friends.
L.H.'[39]

After years of reading, singing and writing Italian, Hunt was fluent in the

language. He went into every church he came to, pausing in one to hear a
sermon on tears – 'the tears of joy, and the tears of sorrow, of penitent tears,
tears of anger, spite, ill-temper, worldly regret, love, patience'. The delivery
seemed more florid and luxurious than 'northern sermons', closer to his
father's style. At each turn there were scenes that reminded him of the poets
– Chaucer was said to have been at Genoa. A man in a back street was singing
and playing a pipe exactly like the 'ancient shepherds'. As he wandered down
another street he heard distant music, a 'bustling sound of feet', and was
caught up in a religious procession: he noted a four-year-old girl with silver
crown and sceptre, a little St John dressed in lambskin, clergymen with lighted
candles, hordes of ragged boys collecting drips of wax to sell, a young friar
with a head from a Raphael painting, and another friar trying to look saintly
while eyeing the girls; St Antonio in wax, large as life, kneeling before a waxen
Virgin; and yet more friars, their heads cowled like executioners. The paganism
of it all fascinated him – there was no doubt that, just as Jupiter now sat
under his new name of St Peter, 'the ancients, under other names, had these
identical processions'. The Italian music Hunt had enjoyed in his soirées with
the Novellos could now be enjoyed in its home. On one evening he went to
the Opera and heard Rossini. The performance was 'indifferent enough', and
Hunt was astonished to see that men in the pit were cooling themselves with
fans.[40]

The vivid details Hunt harvested from the streets and alleys of Genoa
would later bring 'life's flash' to the painterly impressions of Italian life in
Robert Browning's 'Fra Lippo Lippi' – 'a hurry of feet' and 'whifts of song',
the urchin watching

> Which gentleman processional and fine,
> Holding a candle to the Sacrament,
> Will wink and let him lift a plate and catch
> The dropping of the wax to sell again . . .[41]

Brother Lippo's gathering of 'old gossips', 'candle-ends', 'earrings and a
bunch of flowers' would revisit the territory that Hunt had discovered in 1822
and written about in his 'Letters from Abroad'. Hunt's sense of lurking danger
– the friars cowled like executioners – would later be at the heart of Dickens's
and E. M. Forster's visions in which Italian vivaciousness can quickly turn
to violence.

A letter arrived from Shelley on Friday the 21st: 'A thousand welcomes my
best friend to this divine country – many mountains & seas no longer divide
those whose affections are united.' Shelley says he will set off for Leghorn
the moment he hears Hunt has sailed from Genoa. 'We now inhabit a white
house with arches near the town of Lerici in the gulph of Spezia', and Hunt

will pass by as he sails south – 'think of us', or, better still, 'stop at Lerici – imagine the delightful surprize'.[42]

To approach Lerici and Casa Magni from the sea would have been delightful. The setting was exquisite, and the house was so close to the sea that in bad weather breakers crashed into the ground floor. Shelley adored it. His friends Edward and Jane Williams were staying, and the two men had passed the beginning of June happily sailing Shelley's new twin-masted boat, the *Don Juan*, 'in the evening wind, under the summer moon, until earth appears another world'.[43] But Shelley had not mentioned to Hunt how desperately his presence was needed to defuse tensions that had become unbearable for both Shelley and Mary.

Shelley had continued his flirtation with Jane Williams, embittering Mary who was pregnant and in fragile health. After a week of illness Mary suffered a near-fatal miscarriage on 16 June. She had long thought herself blighted by Harriet's suicide, and the deaths of two (now three) children intensified her sense of living under a curse. Having acted decisively to stop Mary's bleeding and save her life, Shelley was close to collapse himself, afflicted with nervous pains and tormented by frightening dreams and visions. He tried to acquire prussic acid in order to commit suicide if his suffering became too severe. One of Shelley's visions so terrified him that his screams alarmed the whole house. 'What had frightened him was this,' Mary recollected. 'He dreamt that lying as he did in bed Edward & Jane came into him, they were in the most horrible condition, their bodies lacerated – their bones starting through their skin, the faces pale yet stained with blood, they could hardly walk, but Edward was the weakest & Jane was supporting him – Edward said – Get up, Shelley, the sea is flooding the house & it is all coming down.'[44]

Shelley's letter had invited Hunt to imagine the pleasure of calling at Casa Magni. Eleven days later a bitter note from Mary gave Hunt an entirely different insight. She entreated him not to be persuaded by Shelley to come to Casa Magni: 'it w^d be complete madness to come . . . I wish I c^d break my chains and leave this dungeon.'[45]

TWENTY-SIX

ON THE BEACH

The *David Walter* put to sea again on Friday, 28 June, and after a day baffled by contrary winds, a fair breeze sprang up which proved the strongest of the whole voyage. On the second night Hunt watched a tremendous thunderstorm thrust pillars of lightning into the waves. Confident in his new-found sense of optimism, he knew that the ship would not be struck. It was impossible, he thought, that the sunny, lucid Gulf of Spezia would play him any 'serious trick' – and the *David Walter* was not carrying any gunpowder.[1] On the 30th they arrived off Leghorn and put into the harbour at two o'clock that afternoon.

Next morning Hunt went ashore where he encountered Edward Trelawny, self-styled Corsair, adventurer, and master of Lord Byron's schooner the *Bolivar*. He took a battered 'country carriage' through the hot suburbs, along lanes with dusty hedges full of vines and garden walls topped with olive and fig trees, then up a winding track to Byron's Casa Rossi – a flaring, salmon-pink villa on the hills at Montenero.

Hunt was welcomed with marked cordiality, and immediately plunged into 'a singular adventure'. In an inner room he was introduced to a tearful Teresa Guiccioli: there had been a fracas among the servants. Teresa's brother, Count Pietro Gamba, had intervened and been stabbed, and the would-be assassin was now lurking outside the villa. Byron's household was in a state of blockade. Suddenly Hunt found everything new, foreign and violent, as if he had been pitched into a scene from the *Mysteries of Udolpho*. There was nothing for it but to confront the ruffian, whereupon the servant collapsed at Byron's feet weeping and asking for pardon. Byron dismissed the man from his service, but otherwise made light of the matter.[2]

And there things might have rested, except that the Tuscan authorities heard of the affray. The Gambas were already suspected of involvement with the revolutionary Carbonari, and this provided an excuse to get rid of potential trouble-makers. An order was issued banishing Count Ruggero and Count Pietro, giving them just three days to leave. Teresa would go with them, and Byron – who took the Gambas' banishment as a personal affront – would follow.

* * *

Back in Leghorn, the Hunts had disembarked and installed themselves at an hotel. 'Everything is going on *promisingly*,' Hunt assured Bess, 'I am expecting Shelley's arrival every instant.' When they met, Hunt and Shelley rushed into each other's arms. Shelley cried out in his shrill voice that he was 'so *inexpressibly* delighted! – you cannot think how *inexpressibly* happy it makes me!' Eleven-year-old Thornton was looking on wide-eyed at the impetuousness and fervour of their greeting. Talk, reminiscences and plans cascaded out of them both. Hunt found his friend 'the same as ever', except that he detected 'less hope' – 'He could not be otherwise.' Thornton, who remembered this meeting to the end of his life, was convinced that his old playmate had grown taller.[3]

By now Hunt had received Mary's unhappy note warning him away from Casa Magni, and he revealed to Shelley that he had no money at all. The £400 was completely spent, he owed sixty crowns, and was in 'the worst possible situation'.[4] The children were thriving in the hot weather, but Marianne obviously needed more comfortable lodgings. They must move immediately to Pisa and, with Shelley as their guide, the Hunts journeyed on twelve miles through fields of corn and vine-clad trees. After their months at sea the Tuscan air was dry and soft. In the evening of Wednesday, 3 July they arrived at Pisa, 'a small white city', Hunt called it, 'with a tower also white, leaning very distinctly in the distance at one end of it'. As they rattled over the Ponte della Fortezza, Hunt saw the sandy-coloured River Arno winding away through the city under two other bridges. High above each bank were wide streets, pavements, elegant houses and, in the far distance, way beyond the city walls, the dark blue Apuane Alps. The carriage stopped outside the grandest of the mansions fronting the river.[5]

Casa Lanfranchi was and is a cavernous feudal *palazzo*. Byron reported dungeons below, cells in the walls, a wide marble staircase said to have been built by Michelangelo, and ghosts that frightened the servants.[6] After the glaring light of the open road, the Hunts found the interior dim, cool and full of echoes. Byron had furnished the ground floor rooms for them, and he was expected to arrive shortly from Montenero. Shelley set about helping the Hunts settle in. The children scattered in games, dashing along the hall, up the marble staircase, and out into Byron's garden. Marianne went straight to bed.

There was 'plenty of room and distance for the children', as Hunt recalled, although they were curious about Byron's upper floors and the exotic animals kept there. Hunt's study looked out on a garden with orange trees, a weeping willow, and Byron's bathing-room.[7] Visiting the Hunts' rooms today it is still possible to see that the walls and ceilings were once covered with frescos of classical temples, trees and ruins. Painted foliage framed the doors. The vaulted ceiling in one room may have suggested Byron's idea of a 'dungeon', and in another room the ceiling was painted sky-blue with billowing clouds. 'The look is at first very gloomy and prison-like,' Hunt remembered, 'but you get used to it.'[8] He longed for Bess to join him.

Hunt had anticipated that the warm south would embrace him as a haven of sunburnt mirth and happy love. Byron's arrangement with Teresa showed 'how lightly the Italians think of certain heavy English matters', he told Bess, and wrote encouragingly of his hopes for her arrival in Italy.[9] But just as Hunt's seven-month journey came to an end, his dream of a cordial community started to unravel. On their first evening at Casa Lanfranchi, Shelley brought in the eminent physician Andrea Vaccà, who examined Marianne and concluded she was in a consumptive decline. Her case was 'hopeless', according to Shelley, and 'must inevitably end fatally'.[10] Throughout the long voyage Hunt had cared for Marianne, assured that the warmth of Italy would restore her health. Shelley could see that Vaccà's diagnosis had dashed Hunt's spirits. And then a letter arrived from John, reminding his brother of unpaid debts and explaining that this time it would be impossible for him to help out. Hunt was now entirely dependent on Shelley and Byron.[11]

He flung himself into work on the new periodical. Byron had offered his satire on Southey and the late George III, *The Vision of Judgment*, and had written directing John Murray to send the corrected proof copy to John Hunt. In a few days he would instruct Murray to forward to John his translation of Pulci's *Il Morgante Maggiore* and 'any *prose* tracts'. For someone as conscious of public image as Byron, this was a huge shift of loyalties from the fashionable, establishment publisher Murray to the imprint of the convicted 'cockney' John Hunt. Byron had delivered, and was supporting the new venture with 'great ardour'. Hunt resolved to make a start on writing up his impressions of Pisa for a series of 'Letters from Abroad'. Shelley assisted 'in any, & every way', Marianne recalled, 'almost anticipating our wishes before we had formed them, with an instinct that nothing but an entire abandonment of self, & deep regard for others can give'.[12]

Shelley's selflessness covered anxieties. He and Byron had been at odds for months: *The Vision of Judgment* was 'more than enough to set up the journal', he told Mary, but only if Byron's offer was sincere. He feared that the alliance would not succeed, and later confessed to Edward Williams that Byron's behaviour to Marianne had been 'shameful' – when they met, he had 'scarcely deigned to notice her'.[13] Byron was well disposed towards Hunt, and knew that he had dependants – so why did he behave like this to Marianne?

Mary Shelley once told Hunt that he was lucky never to have lost a child. An obvious source of tension in the Hunt/Byron/Shelley circle at Pisa was the presence of Hunt's six offspring. Byron notoriously loathed Hunt's children, and described them as 'dirtier and more mischievous than Yahoos'; but he was an intensely fond if negligent father himself, and enjoyed childish glee as much as Shelley.[14] Byron's natural daughter, Allegra, had died in April 1822 aged five. He had not seen Ada, his daughter by Lady Byron, since her birth and she was now six years old. The arrival of the Hunt children in all their dishevelled vigour would have exacerbated guilty pangs that had already been stirred by Shelley's presence. Against the wishes of Claire Clairmont and the Shelleys, it had been Byron's decision to place Allegra in the convent where she died. Now Casa Lanfranchi was ringing with children's voices and laughter. Little Mary Florimel in particular was a painful reminder of his own dark-eyed Allegra, and the cries of baby Henry brought unwelcome memories of Piccadilly Terrace. The dog that Byron chained outside the doors of his apartment was to keep his own demons at bay, as much as Thornton and John, Mary, Swinburne and Percy.

With the Gambas about to be exiled, Byron's loyalties were divided and he was under pressure on several fronts. He could see at a glance that Marianne was seriously ill, and the last thing he needed was a further responsibility. Marianne also brought out the worst of Byron's misogyny. Edward Williams, who had just met Marianne at Leghorn, described her to Jane as 'like no one you know – not handsome – not pretty – not passable even – I speak of person'.[15] As an example of the 'dumpy' matronly physique Byron hated, Marianne held no attraction or interest whatsoever – and the dislike was mutual. Marianne had been sceptical about Byron ever since he first entered Hunt's life at Surrey Gaol; now he was the reason she had endured months of sickness in three boats and various other makeshift lodgings.

While Hunt was enjoying his reunion with Shelley, what were Marianne's feelings at Casa Lanfranchi? Despite the benefits of the Italian climate for her health, she must have dreaded the prospect of becoming an outsider all over again. She had always felt excluded from the close intellectual bonds between Hunt and his literary friends. We know that she was conscious of her own lack of education and now, after protracted illness and a gruelling journey, she would have been all too aware of her wrecked physical appearance. The tubercular symptoms preyed on her mind, and she had no physical stamina left to look after the children. Miserably aware that she would be condemned as a bad mother as well as an inferior wife and woman, Marianne felt isolated, insecure and unhappy. Her irritation at Byron –

Can anything be more absurd than a peer of the realm – and a *poet* making such a fuss about three or four children disfiguring the walls of a few rooms

– was one expression of Marianne's regret that they had come to Italy.[16]

At Leghorn, Edward Williams was waiting impatiently to sail back to Lerici. He had heard from Shelley how Byron's conduct to Marianne had 'cut H.

to the soul', although there was no mention of this wound from Hunt himself. He told Bess he was longing for her companionship and her 'mind to interchange with', and was otherwise absorbed with Byron, Shelley, and his first impressions of Pisa.[17] When he settled down to write about the Casa Lanfranchi, he was immediately in touch with centuries of gaiety and violence:

> It is curious to feel oneself sitting quietly in one of the old Italian houses, and think of all the interests and passions that have agitated the hearts of so many generations of its tenants; all the revels and the quarrels that have echoed along its walls; all the guitars that have tinkled under its windows; all the scuffles that have disputed its doors. Along the great halls, how many feet have hurried in alarm! how many stately beauties have drawn their quiet trains! how many huge torches have ushered magnificence up the staircases! how much blood perhaps has been shed![18]

Byron dropped in to Hunt's study to chat and borrow books, and Hunt was welcomed into the luxurious rooms upstairs where, on the first day, he witnessed a heartening specimen of Italian manners. A smiling young servant came in followed by his sister, a beautiful girl who 'advanced to his Lordship to welcome him back to Pisa, and presented him with a basket of flowers. In doing this she took his hand and kissed it; then turned to the stranger, and kissed his hand also. I thought it a very becoming, unbecoming action; and that at least it should have been acknowledged by a kiss of another description; and the girl appeared to be of the same opinion.' 'We ought to have struck up a quartett,' Hunt thought, 'but there might have ensued a quintett, not so harmonious; and the scene was hastily concluded.'[19]

On Sunday, 7 July the *Examiner* was published in London as usual, with Hunt's review of *Adonais*, Shelley's elegy for Keats. At Pisa, Hunt and Shelley set off arm in arm to explore the city. Their journal was already under way, and a title had been fixed upon – it would be called the *Hesperides*. It seemed as if the happy months at Marlow might be recaptured after all: they wandered through every quarter of the city; walked out into the fields to look at the mountains; and visited the Leaning Tower (to Hunt's eyes, 'never sufficiently praised'), the round Baptistry, the Cathedral, and the burial ground at the Campo Santo. While the organ was playing in the Cathedral, Hunt and Shelley mused on how a truly divine religion might be established on the principle of charity, not faith.[20]

That evening Shelley borrowed Hunt's copy of Keats's last poems, saying he would not part with the book until he returned it to his friend. Then he took the post-chaise to Leghorn. On Monday afternoon he set sail in the *Don Juan* with Edward Williams and the boat boy, Charles Vivian. Trelawny watched them clear the harbour and hoist full sail to catch what little wind there was. A sea-fog enveloped Shelley's boat, and it disappeared.[21]

Pisa, 9th July, 1822

Shelley mio,

Pray let us know how you got home the other day with Williams, for I fear you must have been out in the bad weather, and we are anxious. Things go on remarkably well. Lord B. has given power to my brother John to get all his magazinable MSS. out of the hands of Murray. I am writing every morning; and the sooner we have your own MS. to send off, the better. Loves from Marianne and myself, which you must divide as becomes such precious commodity. When shall we see Marina and all of you? Marianne often wants you for the sublime purpose of facilitating her dialogues on shorts and neckcloths.

Yours affectionately, L. H.[22]

There was no reply to Hunt's letter. Mary and Jane Williams were already uneasy when it was delivered at Casa Magni on Friday, 12 July, and set off immediately for Pisa. 'I settled that we should drive to Casa Lanfranchi that I should get out & ask the fearful question of Hunt, "do you know any thing of Shelley?"' But Mary found the prospect of seeing Hunt for the first time in four years, and asking him such a question, too terrible to contemplate. When they arrived at Casa Lanfranchi that night Hunt was already in bed, so they saw Byron and Teresa instead: 'They knew nothing – he had left Pisa on sunday – on Monday he had sailed – there had been bad weather monday afternoon – more they knew not.'[23]

Next morning Hunt heard of Mary's visit and, like Byron, clung to the hope that the storm had blown Shelley's boat off course. From hour to hour no tidings came. 'Beg that it may be not so,' he scribbled at the back of his journal.[24] On 17 July Hunt went with Byron to make enquiries at the mouth of the River Serchio 'about a body lately buried'.[25] Both of them now knew it was all over. Before Friday the 19th Hunt learned that Shelley's drowned body had been washed ashore at Viareggio, and identified by the volume of Keats's poems in his pocket. Williams had also been found. Both corpses had been buried in the sand with quicklime.

Hunt's first thought was to comfort Marianne and the children, especially Thornton, and to make contact with Mary at that 'dismal place' Casa Magni: 'God bless you,' he wrote, 'and enable us all to be a support for one another . . . I belong to those whom Shelley loves, and . . . all which it is possible for me to do for them, now and ever, is theirs.' To write 'Shelley loves' was a kind of solace, although Hunt's grief was inconsolable: 'My beloved friend Shelley, – my dear, my divine friend, the best of friends & of men – he is no more' – so Hunt broke the news to Bess: 'I know not how to proceed for anguish.'[26]

He felt abandoned, suspended in double anguish between a life that was gone and the need to rally for Shelley's sake, and begin afresh. Yet how on earth was he to go forward? In short fragmentary notes at the back of his journal, Hunt confronted his loss:

> One has been taken, & the other left. Instead of the health which I looked for in his society to restore the springs of life, I waste them with the perpetual pall of sorrow.

And again:

> Wilt thou, whatever summer clime I gain,
> Be taken from me still, thou winged heart?
> At every summit which I earn with pain,
> Shall we but clasp each other but to part?

> Is it thy virtue summons thee, giving thee a fresh wing & a supernatural call every time, which thou art obliged to consent to, leaving me who am inferior to &c. &c.[27]

Alongside these harrowing confessions are notes that show Hunt gathering up his memories of Shelley. 'All things were one betwixt us, which our wills could render such – one pulse, one pain, one pleasure'; 'his books – The pleasure of seeing them mingled together like our thoughts & love.' The mingling of books had been one of the raptures of friendship since Hunt's schooldays. And, again: 'The Cathedral at Pisa, when we heard the music together'; 'To shew & ~~vindicate~~ his real possession of religion – of the purest & devoutest kind.' Hunt struck through 'vindicate', but the impulse to fight for his friend was there.

On 16 August Shelley's body was exhumed and cremated on the beach. Hunt and Byron arrived by carriage from Pisa to watch as Trelawny and his assistants prepared and ignited the pyre. The day was unbearably hot and eventually Byron walked down to the sea to swim. Hunt remained inside the carriage, 'now looking on, now drawing back with feelings that were not to be witnessed'.[28] When Trelawny retrieved a piece of charred flesh not consumed in the fire, Hunt begged to have it and received Shelley's heart as a sacred token of their love.

So began Hunt's cult of Shelley, 'my divine-minded friend, your friend, the friend of the universe'. 'I cannot help thinking of him as if he were alive as much as ever,' he told Horace Smith, 'so unearthly he appeared to me, and so seraphical a thing of the elements; and this is what all his friends say. But, what we all feel, your own heart will tell you.'[29] Years earlier Hunt had written to Marianne: 'When the heart is not in action, happiness is not in being.' Now his own happiness depended on Shelley's after-life as a spiritual partner: 'Cor Cordium', heart of hearts, was the epitaph Hunt devised for his friend, as he faced up to the wreck of his hopes and embarked on the rest of his life.

After Life

Dearest friend of all, it is but a night till I see you again . . .

Leigh Hunt, *Christianism* (1832)

In September 1822 the Hunts, Byron and Mary Shelley left Pisa for Albaro, near Genoa, where the Hunt family and Mary shared a large villa, the Casa Negroto. Relations between them were uneasy. Immediately after the cremation there had been a row between Hunt and Mary over the right to keep Shelley's heart. At Byron's insistence Hunt relinquished it to Mary, but he continued to suspect that she had not made Shelley happy in his last days. Mary found sharing the Hunts' noisy accommodation intolerable.

The periodical plan went ahead, with the title changed at Byron's suggestion to the *Liberal*. Just four issues were published in 1822–23, with the majority of contributions coming from Hunt. The first issue was published by John Hunt in October 1822; it sold over 4,000 copies, and could be counted a success. But Byron was getting cold feet: in October he saw the journal as 'a bad business', and by February he claimed to have '*opposed* it from the beginning'.[1]

Money problems hastened the parting of ways. Byron described Hunt's circumstances at Albaro succinctly: 'I have done all I can for Leigh Hunt – since he came here – but it is almost useless – his wife is ill – his six children not very tractable and in the affairs of this world he himself is a child. The death of Shelley left them totally aground – and I could not see them in such a state without using the common feelings of humanity – & what means were in my power to set them afloat again.'[2] Byron had been as good as his word. He had stood in Shelley's place, and kept Hunt in funds. Meanwhile, Byron's exasperated complaints about Hunt in a letter to John Murray were assiduously circulated in London, and the gist of them swiftly got back to Genoa. Hunt was, Byron admitted, 'violently hurt'. They were scarcely on speaking terms in 1823, although Byron continued to 'dole out' money.[3]

A physician had recommended pregnancy as the only way to save Marianne 'from utter ruin', and Vincent Leigh Hunt was born at Albaro on 9 June 1823, with Mary Shelley assisting at the birth.[4] Next month Byron left Genoa for Greece, and Mary Shelley set off for England with her sole surviving child,

Percy. Hunt and Thornton accompanied them for the first twenty miles of
their journey.

The Hunts remained at Albaro over the summer and then, in September,
journeyed across country to Florence. They took lodgings in the Via delle
Belle Donne and Piazza Santa Croce, then moved several miles north of the
city to an old farmhouse at the village of Maiano. When Hunt was there
Maiano was a Tuscan Hampstead, perched amid 'worlds of olives and vines'
between Florence and Fiesole with a view of Boccaccio's house and his setting
for the *Decameron*. An idyllic setting for Hunt, one might imagine, though it
proved otherwise. The Hunts had no money and lived in 'a primitive manner',
enduring a harsh winter in rooms that were dreary, uncomfortable and cold.
Hunt looked forward to spring when he would establish his study in a 'cheerful
little summer-house at the very top of the house in a turret', but he was far
from happy and longed for Bess to come to him. 'I shall have green blinds,'
he wrote, in a pointed allusion to the rooms they had shared in prison: '*When*,
WHEN, WHEN do you come?'[5] He made it clear to Bess that if Marianne
died, he would wish to marry her: 'you understand all my feelings on this
subject, and know them all to the *core*'.[6] The echo of Shelley's epitaph revealed
both the passion and the misery behind what he said.

At the same time, he was fearful that if Bess did come to live at Maiano,
her demands on his affection and attention would precipitate a relapse in
Marianne's health:

> A family of love may be a heaven in itself, and defy the world. It may retain
> all the cheerfulness to say the most entertaining things, and all the spirit
> to do the best and kindest for society; but when I think any more of the
> smallest discord, and other sad contradictions to good and comfort, a thou-
> sand reflections pour upon me, that force me to go through any other pain
> and wretchedness, rather than hazard an evil so overwhelming.[7]

Hunt had changed. Formerly he had been prepared to face down 'all hazards',
'bold as a lion when defending a friend or a principle'.[8] Shelley's death and
Marianne's illnesses had chastened his idealism. The family of love he had
projected with Shelley was now inconceivable, although his passion for Bess
continued.

Regretting that he had surrendered his interest in the *Examiner*, Hunt quarrelled with John about payment for articles.[9] Hunt's relinquishing of the
proprietorship in 1819 had been a prudent step, but it had not been formally
arranged and when John proposed an annuity of £100, with payment of two
guineas for each article, Hunt was incensed. Angry letters crossed in the post
between London and Maiano. Keats's friend Charles Armitage Brown, who
was living in Florence, tried valiantly to disentangle their differences and

eventually decided in favour of Hunt's claims. The two brothers were estranged for years before they discovered that the quarrel had arisen from 'misconstruction on both sides'.[10] While at Maiano Hunt met the poet Walter Savage Landor, and in 1824 he was visited by his Taunton friend John Marriott, and by William Hazlitt who was touring Italy with his second wife.

Towards the end of 1824 Hunt contemplated a return to England. Mary Novello wrote to warn him 'against expecting London . . . to be what it was'. The city had been utterly changed by new industries, with 'clouds of dust' from macadamised roads and 'endless projections' so that 'everything is to be improved, but no time for enjoying those improvements'. A new steam coach was projected for the London–York route, and 'good Mr. Brunell' was 'burrowing under the Thames'.[11]

Their journey back overland with seven children took less than a month in the autumn of 1825.[12] A second daughter, Julia, was born in December 1826, and Jacyntha in May 1828. Another child, Arabella, died in infancy. Three years after his return, Hunt gained fresh notoriety with the publication of *Lord Byron and some of his Contemporaries* (1828). Agitated by 'grief and anger' at what had happened to him in Italy, he presented an embittered portrait of his former friend.[13] After the disaster of Hunt's Italian years those feelings were understandable, although there were other causes that lay deep in his own past. Hunt's initial impression of Byron in 1813 had been coiled around memories of his father, Isaac, and this explains the bitterness of his recollections:

> talents, poetry, similarity of political opinion, the flattery of early sympathy with my boyish writings, more flattering offers of friendship, and the last climax of flattery, an earnest waiving of his rank, were too much for me in the person of Lord Byron; and I took out, with my new friend as I thought him, hearty payment for my philosophical abstinence. Now was the time, I thought, to show, that friendship, and talents, and poetry, were reckoned superior to rank, even by rank itself; my friend appeared not only to allow me to think so, but to encourage me to do it. I took him at his word . . .[14]

This accords with what Hunt had written about Byron in his prison letters of 1813, and it accurately represents the partnership of 'talents' on which business arrangements for the *Liberal* would, in Hunt's view, have rested. *Lord Byron and some of his Contemporaries* has often been dismissed as a scandalous, ungrateful book, hurried into print for money. The author's own turmoil has been ignored.

Hunt had been careful not to dine with Lord Holland when invited to do so, lest he compromised his independence. Lord Byron had seduced him with a 'flattering self-reflection', and played upon susceptibilities of which Hunt himself was hardly aware: 'he could see very well, that I had more value for lords than I supposed'.[15] Hunt's independence as a critic and editor had long been the guarantee of his journalistic integrity and, more crucially, it had also been a security against repeating his father's mistakes and humiliations. His relationship with Byron proved that all of this had been no more than a bright-eyed pretence; while reckoning friendship, talents and poetry superior to rank, Hunt had been treading in Isaac's footsteps all along. His resentment of Byron reflected how bitterly Hunt was disappointed in himself.

By 1828, at the age of forty-four, Hunt had long outlived his younger contemporaries Keats, Shelley and Byron. Looking back in his *Autobiography*, he remembered how he had revisited places associated with them: Hampstead Heath, Millfield Lane, the Vale of Health, and 'the ponds in which Shelley used to sail his boats, and very little brooks unknown to all but the eyes of their lovers'.[16] If Hunt felt that something within him had died with those friends, he would discover new resources, and fresh generations of protégés and admirers in the decades ahead.

With Hunt's return from Italy, it is in many ways a second life that is beginning.

ACKNOWLEDGEMENTS

This book has grown from the work of Leigh Hunt's editors and biographers Edmund Blunden, Luther Brewer, Eleanor Gates, Thornton Hunt, Louis Landré and George Dumas Stout. Stephen F. Fogle's *Leigh Hunt's Autobiography: The Earliest Sketches* reproduces Hunt's draft reminiscences from 1827 with a helpful commentary. Focusing on Hunt's later life, Timothy Webb's essay, 'Religion of the Heart: Leigh Hunt's Tribute to Shelley' in the *Keats–Shelley Review* (Autumn 1992) gives an intricate account of Hunt's need to 'dematerialise' his friend.

Hunt's great-great-great-grandson Richard Russell took an interest in this book from its early stages and provided invaluable information about Hunt family history and Hunt's presentation cup from Plymouth. David Cheney generously arranged for me to see the typescript of his collected edition of Hunt's correspondence, the magnificent outcome of a lifetime's scholarly dedication. Sid Huttner and Robert A. McCown at the Special Collections Department, University of Iowa Libraries, Iowa City doubled the pleasure of researching in the Luther Brewer Leigh Hunt Collection. David Fairer read the manuscript of this book and suggested numerous improvements. Jane Stabler's insights appear on every page.

I am grateful to the staff of the following institutions for assistance with my research. The American Philosophical Society, Philadelphia; Beinecke Rare Book and Manuscript Library, Yale University; Berg Collection of English and American Literature, New York Public Library, Astor, Lenox and Tilden Foundations; The Bodleian Library; The British Library; The Brotherton Collection, Leeds University Library: Novello-Clarke Collection; Buckinghamshire County Museum Resource Centre; City of Westminster Archives Centre; The Clark Library; The Courtauld Institute of Art; Department of Archives, Barbados; Dover Museum; Edinburgh University Library; Exeter Cathedral Library; Exeter Central Library; Friends Historical Library of Swarthmore College, Pennsylvania; Guildhall Library Manuscripts Section; The Hampstead Museum, Burgh House; The Harry Ransom Research Center, University of Texas at Austin; The Historical Society of

Pennsylvania, Philadelphia; The Huntington Library; John Murray Archive; Keats House, Hampstead; Keats–Shelley House, Rome; Lambeth Palace Library; The Library Company of Philadelphia; Lilly Library, University of Indiana, Bloomington; Lincolnshire Archive; London Metropolitan Archives; The Luther Brewer Leigh Hunt Collection, Special Collections Department, The University of Iowa Libraries, Iowa City, Iowa; Manchester Public Libraries; M. I. King Library, University of Kentucky; National Library of Scotland; National Portrait Gallery, London; Northamptonshire Record Office; Parker Library, Corpus Christi College, Cambridge; Public Record Office, Kew; Sabin Galleries Ltd.; Sheffield Archives; Somerset Record Office, Taunton; St Andrews University Library; St Andrews University Photographic and Reprographic Units; Stirling University Library; Toledo Museum of Art; Ward M. Canaday Center for Special Collections, University of Toledo; Worcestershire Record Office. Permissions to reproduce material are cited elsewhere in the book.

I am grateful to the following friends and colleagues for points of information, advice and encouragement: Jonathan Allison, John Barnard, Jonathan Bate, Betty T. Bennett, James D. Birchfield, Anna Bosch, John Bushby, James Butler, Allan Clayson, Jeffrey Cox, Rob Cox, Robert Crawford, Damian Walford Davies, Roberta Davis, Christopher Densmore, Douglas Dunn, Angus Easson, Michael Eberle-Sinatra, Rodney Stenning Edgecombe, Robert Essick, Francesco Fiori, Barbara Floyd, Reg Foakes, Michael Foot, Stephen Freeth, Peter Funnell, Jill Gamble, Christine Gascoigne, Avery Gaskins, Marilyn Gaull, Christina Gee, Isaac Gewirtz, Harry Hine, John Hinks, Clare Hopkins, Brian Hunt, Sid Huttner, Jon Iveson, Cilla Jackson, Lawrence and Mary James, Tom Jones, Ian Kidd, Greg Kucich, Phil Lapsansky, David Leigh-Hunt, Alexandra MacCulloch, Hugh Macpherson, Susan Manly, Ian Maxted, Tom Mayberry, Vincenzo Mazzaccaro, Robert A. McCown, Michael McMahon, Hugh Morris, Frances Mullan, Andrew Murphy, Virginia Murray, Vincent Newey, Pat O'Donnell, Michael O'Neill, Michele Ostrow, Catherine Payling, Seamus Perry, Mark Philp, Oliver Pickering, N. M. Plumley, Karla Pollmann, Cecilia Powell, Sarah Price, Sandra M. Rayser, Tony Reeve, Neil Rhodes, Andrew Roberts, Jeffrey Robinson, Susan Rowe, Sidney F. Sabin, Malabika Sarkar, Paul Schlicke, Philip Shaw, Christopher Sheppard, Karl Smith, Jane Sommerville, Allen Staley, Eric Stevens, Jack Stillinger, Helen Sunderland, Jane and Simon Taylor, Peter Thomas, Barbara Thompson, Nicola Trott, Michael Lawrence Turner, Stephen Wagner, Giles Walkley, Reggie and Shirley Watters, Timothy Webb, Robin Whittaker, Sarah Wickham, David Williams, Elizabeth Wood, Duncan Wu.

I thank David Godwin for believing in *Fiery Heart*, and my editor at Pimlico, Will Sulkin, for his patience and excellent advice at all stages of the book's production. The typescript was fortunate to find Beth Humphries, most vigilant of copy editors. Ros Porter at Pimlico cheerfully coped with numerous versions of 'The Hunt Family from the Sixteenth to the Nineteenth Century'. I am indebted to the School of English, University of St Andrews, the British Academy and the Arts and Humanities Research Board for periods of leave during which I researched and wrote this book.

The index was compiled by Jim Stewart and the family tree was designed by Duncan Stewart.

A NOTE ON MONEY AND THE WEATHER

In Hunt's lifetime British currency used the old units of pounds, shillings and pence. One pound (£1) = 20 shillings (20s.); 1 shilling (1s.) = 12 pennies (12d.).

Hunt was never 'very thoughtful on money matters' and seldom out of debt. Shelley's generous gift of £1,400 in 1818 was the largest of many contributions from friends and well-wishers. When the *Examiner* was at its peak circulation of 7,000–8,000 copies a week in 1812–13, Hunt could expect an income of over £500 a year; even in less successful years like 1820 he earned more than £400. But his expenditure always outstripped these large sums. Legal costs defending the four libel charges between 1808 and 1812 strained his resources, and the £500 fine imposed after the 1812 trial left him in difficulties for years. Throughout Hunt's first life the war with France, heavy taxes and the Corn Laws contributed to price inflation, particularly in the years 1812–14.

Two hundred years later, it is difficult to ascertain how much the early nineteenth-century pound was worth in terms of today's currency and values. A more helpful guide is to see what the figures above meant in the contemporary economy. For example, in Hunt's childhood Elizabeth West's household accounts for the whole of January 1786 amounted to £13 16s. 11½d. Her cook was paid £5 5s. for six months' employment. In 1801 Hunt's *Juvenilia* volume sold for six shillings. In 1810 an agricultural labourer might earn £42 a year, a clergyman £300, and a solicitor or barrister £450–£500. In 1812 a copy of the *Examiner* cost 8½d. and a large loaf of bread 1s. 6½d. In 1822 Hunt made a payment of £30 for the voyage to Italy (Plymouth–Leghorn). These figures provide only an approximate indicator of the cost of living during Hunt's first life, but they are sufficient to indicate that Hunt and Marianne would have been comparatively wealthy but for their inability to keep accounts and manage debts.

Throughout this book I have drawn on the records of London's weather published in the *Philosophical Transactions of the Royal Society* and the *Gentleman's Magazine*.

ABBREVIATIONS

A	*The Autobiography of Leigh Hunt* (3 vols, London, 1850).
A (1860)	*The Autobiography of Leigh Hunt. A New Edition, Revised by the Author* (London, 1860).
AES	*Leigh Hunt's Autobiography: The Earliest Sketches,* ed. Stephen F. Fogle, University of Florida Monographs: Humanities, 2 (Gainesville, Florida, 1959).
Berg	The Berg Collection of English and American Literature, The New York Public Library, Astor, Lennox and Tilden Foundations. All mss quotations with permission.
BFE	Luther A. Brewer, *My Leigh Hunt Library. The First Editions* (1970; Iowa, 1930).
BL	Luther A. Brewer, *My Leigh Hunt Library. The Holograph Letters* (Iowa, 1938).
BLJ	*Byron's Letters and Journals,* ed. Leslie A. Marchand (13 vols, London, 1973–94).
Blunden	Edmund Blunden, *Leigh Hunt. A Biography* (London, 1930).
Brewer Collection	Luther Brewer Leigh Hunt Collection, Special Collections Department, The University of Iowa Libraries, Iowa City, Iowa. All mss quotations with permission.
BrL	The British Library. All mss quotations with permission.

Captain Sword	Leigh Hunt, *Captain Sword and Captain Pen. A Poem* (London, 1835).
Cheney	David R. Cheney Papers, MSS–157, Boxes 1, 16, 17, Ward M. Canaday Center for Special Collections, The University of Toledo.
Corr.	*The Correspondence of Leigh Hunt, Edited by his Eldest Son* (2 vols, London, 1862).
Critical Essays	Leigh Hunt, *Critical Essays on the Performers of the London Theatres* (London, 1807).
Descent	Leigh Hunt, *The Descent of Liberty, A Mask* (London, 1815).
E	The *Examiner*.
EE	Edmund Blunden, *Leigh Hunt's 'Examiner' Examined* (London, 1928).
Feast (1814)	Leigh Hunt, *The Feast of the Poets* (London, 1814).
Feast (1815)	Leigh Hunt, *The Feast of the Poets* (2nd edn, London, 1815).
Foliage	Leigh Hunt, *Foliage; or, Poems Original and Translated* (London, 1818).
FP	The Fulham Papers at Lambeth Palace Library (42 vols, London, n.d.). Microfilm of the papers of the Bishops of London.
Gates	*Leigh Hunt: A Life in Letters. Together with some Correspondence of William Hazlitt*, ed. Eleanor M. Gates (Essex, Conn., 1998).
HC	*Benjamin Robert Haydon: Correspondence and Table-Talk* (2 vols, London, 1876).
HCR	*The Diary, Reminiscences, and Correspondence of Henry Crabb Robinson*, ed. Thomas Sadler (3 vols, London, 1869).

HCRB	*Henry Crabb Robinson on Books and their Writers*, ed. Edith J. Morley (3 vols, London, 1938).
HD	*The Diary of Benjamin Robert Haydon*, ed. W. B. Pope (5 vols, Cambridge, Mass., 1960).
HL	*Life of Benjamin Robert Haydon*, ed. Tom Taylor (3 vols, London, 1853).
Howe	*The Complete Works of William Hazlitt*, ed. P. P. Howe (21 vols, London and Toronto, 1930–34).
I	Leigh Hunt, The *Indicator* (London, 1820).
JMS	*The Journals of Mary Shelley, 1814–1844*, ed. P. R. Feldman and D. Scott-Kilvert (Baltimore and London, 1995).
Juvenilia	Leigh Hunt, *Juvenilia; or, a Collection of Poems* (3rd edn, London, 1801).
Landré	Louis Landré, *Leigh Hunt (1784–1859). Contribution à l'histoire du Romantisme Anglais* (2 vols, Paris, 1936).
LBsC	Leigh Hunt, *Lord Byron and some of his Contemporaries* (2nd edn, 2 vols, London, 1828).
LH	Leigh Hunt
LJK	*The Letters of John Keats, 1814–21*, ed. Hyder E. Rollins (2 vols, Cambridge, Mass., 1958).
LL	*Letters of Charles and Mary Anne Lamb*, ed. Edwin Marrs Jnr. (3 vols, Ithaca and London, 1978).
LMWS	*The Letters of Mary Wollstonecraft Shelley*, ed. Betty T. Bennett (3 vols, Baltimore and London, 1980–88).
LPBS	*The Letters of Percy Bysshe Shelley*, ed. F. L. Jones (2 vols, Oxford: Clarendon Press, 1964).
NRO	Northamptonshire Record Office.

PBSMW   *Percy Bysshe Shelley. The Major Works*, ed. Zachary
                   Leader and Michael O'Neill (Oxford, 2003).

PJK   *Poems of John Keats*, ed. Jack Stillinger (Cambridge,
                   Mass., 1978).

Poetical Works   *The Poetical Works of Leigh Hunt* (London, 1832).
(1832)

PWLH   *The Poetical Works of Leigh Hunt*, ed. H. S. Milford
                   (Oxford, 1923).

R   *The Reflector, A Quarterly Magazine, on Subjects of
                   Philosophy, Politics, and the Liberal Arts. Conducted by
                   the Editor of the Examiner* (2 vols, London, 1811–12).

Recollections   Charles and Mary Cowden Clarke, *Recollections of Writers*
                   (1878; London, 1969).

Rimini   Leigh Hunt, *The Story of Rimini: A Poem* (London,
                   1816).

SC   *Shelley and his Circle 1773–1822*, vols 1–4 ed. K. N.
                   Cameron (Cambridge, Mass., 1961–70); vols 5–10 ed. D.
                   Reiman et al (Cambridge, Mass., 1973–2002).

WPBS   *The Works of Percy Bysshe Shelley*, ed. R. Ingpen and
                   W. E. Peck (10 vols, London, 1926–30; 1965).

Quotations from Shakespeare are from *Complete Works*, ed. Peter Alexander
(London and Glasgow, 1975). Quotations from Wordsworth's *Prelude* are from
William Wordsworth. The Prelude 1799, 1805, 1850, ed. J. Wordsworth et al.
(New York and London, 1979), 1805 version. Unless indicated otherwise,
Byron's poems are quoted from *Complete Poetical Works*, ed. Jerome
J. McGann (7 vols, Oxford, 1980–93). 3 lines from 'Summoned by Bells' by
John Betjeman on p. 39 from *Summoned by Bells* (London: John Murray,
1960); 7 words from 'An Arundel Tomb' on p. 249 and 5 words from 'Aubade'
on p. 318 by Philip Larkin from *Collected Poems* ed. Anthony Thwaite (London
and Boston: Faber & Faber, 1988).

NOTES

Preface

1. For 'last survivor', BrL Add. MS 38524. George Thornbury to Hunt, 1853; for Byron, *BLJ*, ix. 190.
2. Blunden, xi.

Prologue: The Wit in the Dungeon

1. *BLJ*, iii. 49.
2. Ellenborough's summing-up of the prosecution case, *The Trial of Edward Marcus Despard, Esquire, for High Treason* (London, 1803), 264.
3. Ibid., 133; E. P. Thompson, *The Making of the English Working Class* (1963), 521–8.
4. *The Life of Colonel Despard* (1803), in V.A.C. Gatrell, *The Hanging Tree. Execution and the English People 1770–1868* (Oxford, 1994), 50–1, 88; Thompson, 521–8.

1 First Lives

1. 'An Attempt of the Author to estimate his own Character & Writings', Brewer Collection MS H94; Commonplace Book of Leigh Hunt, presented to him by Vincent Novello, 14 Aug. 1828. Brewer Collection MS H94.
2. 'A Now, Descriptive of a Hot Day', *I* (28 June 1820), 302.
3. For Byron, *BLJ*, ix. 113–14; for Keats, *LJK*, i. 110.
4. *HD*, ii. 81.
5. Gates, 42; Thornton Hunt, 'A Man of Letters of the Last Generation', *Cornhill Magazine* (Jan.–June 1860), 85–95.
6. Cosmo Monkhouse, *Life of Leigh Hunt* (London, 1893), 118; *A* (1860), vii; *Illustrated London News* (10 Sept. 1859), 249; *Literary Recollections of Barry Cornwall* (Boston, 1936), 84.
7. *LBsC*, i. 247.
8. *Blackwood's Magazine* (May 1818), 201.

9. *Blackwood's Magazine* (Aug. 1818), 520.

10. *Poetical Works* (1832), xvi; *LBsC*, i. 247, 409–10.

11. 'Wordsworth in the Tropics', in Aldous Huxley, *Do What You Will. Essays* (London, 1929), 113–29.

12. *A*, i. 3.

13. Richard S. Dunn, *Sugar and Slaves. The Rise of the Planter Class in the English West Indies, 1624–1713* (New York and London, 1972), 76, 77, 85; Vincent T. Harlow, *A History of Barbados, 1625–1685* (Oxford, 1926), 46.

14. FP, ix. 206.

15. John Walker, *An Attempt towards Recovering an Account of the Sufferings of the Clergy of the Church of England . . . in the Late Times of the Great Rebellion* (London, 1714), Part II, 'A List', 26; Allan Brockett, *Nonconformity in Exeter, 1650–1875* (Manchester, 1962), 23, 36.

16. Richard Russell, *The Wider Family of Leigh Hunt* (1989), 11, 13; J. and J. A. Venn, *Alumni Cantabrigiensis, Part I to 1751* (4 vols, Cambridge, 1922–7), ii. 433; will of Edward Hunt, 1694, courtesy Richard Russell; Gerald Fothergill, *A List of Emigrant Ministers to America, 1690–1811* (London, 1904), 35.

17. FP, ix. 124, 126, 136, 166; FP, x. 238–9.

18. FP, ix. 192, 199.

19. Ibid., 199, 202.

20. *Foliage*, 17.

21. FP, ix. 206–13.

22. Ibid., 214, 231, 233–8.

23. *A*, i. 6; Edward MacLysaght, *Irish Families: their Names, Arms and Origins* (Dublin, 1957), 62–3.

24. Barbados Archives, Baptisms Vol. RL1/30, 22.

25. *A*, i. 5, 6.

26. Vere Langford Oliver, *The Monumental Inscriptions in the Churches and Churchyards of the Island of Barbados, British West Indies* (1915; San Bernadino, 1989), 178–9; Joanne McRee Sanders, *Barbados Records: Baptisms 1637–1800* (Baltimore, 1984), 468.

27. Griffith Hughes, *The Natural History of Barbados* (London, 1750), 127. Hunt's copy is in the Brewer Collection.

28. Ibid., 10.

29. Thomas Clarkson, *Memoirs of the Public and Private Life of William Penn* (2 vols, London, 1813), ii. 417.

30. *Papers of William Penn*, ed. M. M. and R. S. Dunn et al. (5 vols, Philadelphia, 1981–7), ii. 121.

31. Edwin Wolf, *Philadelphia: Portrait of an American City* (Philadelphia, 1975), 71.

32. Carl and Jessica Bridenbaugh, *Rebels and Gentlemen: Philadelphia in the Age of Franklin* (Oxford, 1962), 10; Wolf, 44.

33. Wolf, 43.

34. Bridenbaugh, 42; Horace Wemyss Smith, *Life and Correspondence of the Rev. William Smith D.D.* (2 vols, Philadelphia, 1880), i. 54.

35. William Smith, *Discourses on Several Public Occasions during the War in America* (London, 1759), 217–20.

36. *AES*, 4; T. H. Montgomery, *A History of the University of Pennsylvania* (Philadelphia, 1900), 541.

37. *A*, i. 7.

38. Wemyss Smith, i. 57–9.

39. Montgomery, 362, 364.

40. *A*, i. 7–8.

41. *AES*, 1. The Shewells were descended from Nonconformists at Painswick, Gloucestershire; in 1722 they arrived in Philadelphia as 'republicans & quakers'. Elizabeth was related on her mother's side to the Bickley family, whose Quaker ancestors emigrated to America in 1682.

42. *A*, i. 8; MS 'Memorial of Revd. Isaac Hunt Clk', Brewer Collection MS LH 94; *The Case of Isaac Hunt. Esq., of Philadelphia* (London, 1776), 1.

43. Montgomery, 460.

44. Alison Olson, 'The Pamphlet War over the Paxton Boys', *Pennsylvania Magazine*, 123 (1999), 31–55.

45. *The Quaker Unmask'd; or, the Plain Truth: Humbly Address'd to the Consideration of all the Freemen of Pennsylvania* (Philadelphia, 1764).

46. *A Looking-Glass for Presbyterians. Or A brief Examination of their Loyalty, Merit, and other Qualifications for Government. With some Animadversions on the Quaker Unmask'd. Humbly Address'd to the Consideration of the Loyal FREEMEN of PENNSYLVANIA* (Philadelphia, 1764), 17–18.

47. *A Letter from a Gentleman in Transilvania* (New York, 1764), 4; *A Humble Attempt at Scurrility* (Quillsylvania, 1765), 28–9.

48. *A Continuation of the Exercises in Scurrility Hall. No III* (1765), 6–7.

49. Martin Snyder, *City of Independence. Views of Philadelphia before 1800* (New York, 1975), 74–80.

50. Montgomery, 460.

51. The Historical Society of Pennsylvania (HSP), Society Collection (under Franklin).

52. *A*, i. 26.

53. *The Political Family* (Philadelphia, 1775), 5, 18, 29.

54. *Pennsylvania Gazette* (6 Sept. 1775).

55. *Passages from the Diary of Christopher Marshall*, ed. W. Duane (Philadelphia, 1839–49), i. 46–7.

56. *A*, i. 26–7.

57. Lydia Lorain to John Hunt, 24 Oct. 1839, Berg.

58. *A*, i. 11–12.

59. See Chapter 10, pp. 123–4.

60. *A*, i. 30–31.

61. Ibid., 41.

62. Ibid., 16.

63. *Jane Austen's Letters. A New Edition*, ed. Deirdre Le Faye (3rd edn, Oxford, 1995), 548–9.

64. *A*, i. 4, 5.

2 The Political Family

1. *A*, i. 74–80, and prefaces to *Rimini* (1816) and *Foliage* (1818).

2. *A*, i. 32–3.

3. *AES*, 17; *A*, i. 32, 59, 69; BL, 5, 6.

4. *A*, i. 54–5.

5. Ibid., 60–1; *I* (2 Aug. 1820), 338, 311.

6. *Corr.*, i. 1–2; *A*, i. 60, 62; *AES*, 16; BL, 2; *E* (1 June 1817), 245; (13 July 1817), 443.

7. *A*, i. 34.

8. BL, 6. Letter of 21 March 1804.

9. *A*, i. 16, 17.

10. *A* (1860), 13–14.

11. *Political Magazine and Parliamentary, Naval, Military and Literary Journal, for the Year MDCCLXXX*, 740, and John Trumbull to Edmund Burke, 10 May 1781, NRO Fitzwilliam (Burke) A ii 9. I am grateful to Sir Philip Naylor-Leyland Bt. for permission to quote from these letters.

12. *The Autobiography of Colonel John Trumbull, Patriot Artist, 1756–1843* (New Haven, 1953), 1–44, 69–72. John Trumbull to Edmund Burke, 10 May 1781, NRO Fitzwilliam (Burke) A ii 9; John Trumbull to Mr Chamberlayne, Solicitor to the Treasury, NRO Fitzwilliam (Burke) A xxi 8.

13. *Autobiography, Reminiscences and Letters of John Trumbull, from 1756 to 1841* (New York and London, 1841), 319–20.

14. *A* (1860), 14.

15. *AES*, 10.

16. 'Household Account Book of Mrs Benjamin West 1785–1789', Friends Historical Library of Swarthmore College.

17. *The Farington Diary*, ed. J. Greig (8 vols, London, 1922–8), viii. 97.

18. Gates, 87; BL, 162.

19. *A*, i. 19.

20. Thomas De Quincey, *Confessions of an English Opium-Eater and Other Writings*, ed. G. Lindop (Oxford, 1985), 85.

21. *A*, i. 305.

22. *E* (17 May 1812), 314.

23. *A*, i. 20, 85; *A* (1860) 17, 19.

24. *A*, i. 16–17.

25. *E* (3 Oct. 1813), 626.

26. BL, 3.

27. *Stationers' Company Apprentices*, ed. D. F. McKenzie (Oxford, 1978), 287.

28. *Rights of Englishmen. An Antidote to the Poison now Vending by the Transatlantic Republican Thomas Paine* (London, 1791), 6, 8, 11.

29. *A*, i. 80–81.

30. Ibid., 22, 34.

31. Elhanan Winchester, *The Universal Restoration Exhibited in Four Dialogues* (London, 1792), xii.

32. *The Process and Empire of Christ* (London, 1793), XI. ll. 466–9.

33. *A*, i. 13.

34. Ibid., 71.

35. Ibid., 22–3; *The Universalist's Miscellany; or Philanthropist's Museum*, ed. W. Vidler (2nd edn, London, 1797), 18–19, 307.

36. *AES*, 17.

3 At School

1. *The Christ's Hospital Book* (London, 1953), 6.

2. *A*, i. 97.

3. *The Fortunes and Misfortunes of the Famous Moll Flanders*, ed. Juliet Mitchell (London, 1985), 258; Peter Ackroyd, *London, The Biography* (London, 2000), 247–57.

4. 'Christ's Hospital', *Juvenilia*, 20.

5. *A*, i. 96, 101.

6. Ibid., 102.

7. *AES*, 27.

8. See *A*, i. 105–6; *Collected Letters of Samuel Taylor Coleridge*, ed. E. L. Griggs (6 vols, Oxford, 1956–71), i. 389; 'Christ's Hospital Five and Thirty Years Ago', *The Works of Charles and Mary Lamb*, ed. E. V. Lucas (7 vols, London, 1903–5), ii. 12–13, 15.

9. *A*, i. 107–9.

10. Ibid., 141; Charles Lamb, 'The Convalescent', *Works*, ii. 184.

11. *A*, i. 111–15.

12. Ibid., 116, 128–9; S. T. Coleridge, *Biographia Literaria*, ed. J. Engell and W. Jackson Bate, Bollingen Collected Coleridge Series, 7 (2 vols, Princeton and London, 1983), i. 11.

13. *A*, i. 116–18, 120–25, 143; James Gillman, *The Life of Samuel Taylor Coleridge* (London, 1838), 20.

14. *AES*, 23–4; *A*, i. 92, 113–14.

15. *A*, i. 147–54; *I* (7 June 1820), 278; *I* (14 June 1820), 285–6.

16. *A*, i. 93–4; *E* (17 May 1818), 306; *E* (31 May 1818), 338. Ian Gilmour, *The Making of the Poets: Byron and Shelley in their Time* (London, 2002), 88.

17. *A*, i. 143; *AES*, 27.

18. *A*, i. 146.
19. Ibid.
20. Ibid., 144.
21. John Betjeman, *Summoned by Bells* (London, 1960), 72.
22. *A*, i. 144–5; *AES*, 31.
23. Church of Jesus Christ of Latter-day Saints 'Family Search' website at http://www.familysearch.org/Eng/default.asp; *A*, i. 57–8, 158–9.
24. *A*, i. 158–9.
25. Ibid., 165.
26. Ibid., 168–70.
27. Ibid., 160–2.
28. *E* (10 Jan. 1808).
29. *E* (17 May 1818), 305; *A*, i. 172–4.
30. *AES*, 29.
31. Leigh Hunt, *The Town; its Memorable Characters and Events* (2 vols, London, 1848), i. 69–70, 74.
32. *E* (17 May 1818), 306; *E* (24 May 1818), 322; *E* (7 June 1818), 353.
33. 'The Nymphs', *Foliage*, xxvii.
34. *A*, i. 131; Andrew Tooke, *The Pantheon* (London, 1783), iii–iv.
35. *A*, i. 135.
36. Ibid., 133.
37. Ibid., 260.
38. *AES*, 21–2.
39. *Feast* (1814), 85 n.
40. *S.T. Coleridge. Poems*, ed. John Beer (London, 1999).
41. 'Remembered Friendship', *Juvenilia*, 25–30.
42. *Lamia, Isabella, The Eve of St. Agnes, and Other Poems* (London, 1820), 121.

4 *Juvenilia*

1. *A*, i. 183; BL, 5.
2. BL, 4.
3. *Stationers' Company Apprentices*, ed. D. F. McKenzie (Oxford, 1978), 287; Boyd's Marriage Index, on line database at www.englishorigins.com; W. Carew Hazlitt, *Four Generations of a Literary Family* (2 vols, London, 1897), i. 268–9.
4. BL, 4–5.
5. *AES*, 37.
6. *A*, i. 183–5; *AES*, 32–4, 38.
7. Michael Mason, *The Making of Modern Sexuality* (Oxford, 1994); Thomas De Quincey, *Confessions of an English Opium-Eater and Other Writings*, ed. G. Lindop (Oxford, 1985), 20–22; *AES*, 40–41.
8. Mason, 75.
9. *AES*, 38–9.

10. *Times* (11 Dec. 1799).

11. *Times* (12 March 1800).

12. Ibid.

13. *A*, i. 237–8.

14. *Critical Essays*, v, vii.

15. *The Juvenile Library* (3 vols, London, 1800–1801), i. 60.

16. Alexander Knox, *Essays on the Political Circumstances of Ireland* (London, 1799), xi, 64–5, 240.

17. Ibid., 18.

18. William Sandby, *The History of the Royal Academy of Arts* (2 vols, London, 1862).

19. Ibid., i. 224.

20. *A*, i. 193.

21. Ibid., 195.

5 Native Scenes

1. *A*, i. 200–5.

2. Ibid., 205–7; Gates, 6.

3. 'Translation of Milton into Welsh', *I* (10, 17 Jan. 1821); *A*, i. 206–7.

4. *AES*, 45.

5. *A Description of Brighthelmstone, and the Adjacent Country* (London, 1792), 66–7.

6. *Adam and Eve: A Margate Story* (London, 1824), 3.

7. *The Margate Guide* (London, 1775), 22–3.

8. *A*, i. 207–10. Hunt told this story again in the *Companion*, 16 (23 April, 1828), 223.

9. *The Margate Guide*, 14–16; *Picturesque Pocket Companion to Margate* (London, 1831), 78; *Excursions in the County of Kent* (London, 1822), 116.

10. *Excursions in Kent*, 119.

11. *E* (7 June 1812), 355.

12. 'Composed in the Valley, near Dover on the Day of Landing'; 'September, 1802', *William Wordsworth*, ed. S. Gill (Oxford, 1984), 284.

13. Baptism register for St Andrew's Church, Pershore; Worcestershire Record Office, BA 9185/1(iii).

14. *AES*, 46–7; Thornton Hunt, *Proserpina*, in Blunden, 358–60.

15. See Keith Thomas, *Man and the Natural World: Changing Attitudes in England, 1500–1800* (London, 1983), 50, 184–5.

16. *Corr.*, i. 6.

17. *AES*, 46–7; Gates, 42.

18. For Hunter: *SC*, i. 415, and G. P. Tyson, *Joseph Johnson. A Liberal Publisher* (Iowa City, 1979), 180, 212–14.

19. *AES*, 47.

20. Letter of Friday 22 April 1803, extracted in *Corr.*, i. 4 and BL, 9–10; additional material from MS in Brewer Collection.

21. *A*, i. 187–93; Ian Gilmour, *The Making of the Poets: Byron and Shelley in their Time* (London 2002), 119–21; Kenneth Johnston, *The Hidden Wordsworth: Poet, Lover, Rebel, Spy* (New York and London, 1998), 118–34; Andrew Motion, *Keats* (London, 1997), 196–7. Clare Hopkins, archivist of Trinity College, Oxford, kindly supplied details of Papendieck's bill.

22. *A*, i. 188.

23. Ibid., 185.

24. BL, 9; *Corr.*, i. 3–5.

25. BL, 32.

26. Ibid., 19–20; *Corr.*, i. 5.

6 Theatres of War

1. J. Steven Watson, *The Reign of George III, 1760–1815* (Oxford, 1960), 401.

2. *The Farington Diary*, ed. J. Greig (8 vols, London, 1922–8), ii. 33–6; iv. 48–9; Robert C. Alberts, *Benjamin West. A Biography* (Boston, 1978), 258–73.

3. *James Gillray. The Art of Caricature* (London, 2001), 124–5.

4. *Times* (19 Sept. 1803), 2.

5. BL, 8.

6. *A*, i. 219.

7. *Times* (26 March 1803), 3; (23 June 1803), 3.

8. Leigh Hunt, *A Saunter Through the West End* (1847; London, 1861), 26.

9. *Times* (3 Oct. 1803), 2.

10. *Times* (7 Oct. 1803), 3.

11. *A*, i. 224.

12. BL, 20–21.

13. *Times* (27 Oct. 1803), 2.

14. *Times* (16 Feb. 1804), 3; *A*, i. 220–25; *A Saunter*, 26–7.

15. *A*, i. 146.

16. *A*, iii. 237; *Captain Sword*, 1, 8, 9, 10, 38, 39.

17. *Captain Sword*, 9.

18. Blunden, 266, quoting Hunt's note in *PWLH*, 704; *Times* (27 Oct. 1803), 2; *Captain Sword*, 46.

19. BL, 12.

20. Ibid.

21. Leigh Hunt, *Juvenilia; or, a Collection of Poems* (2nd edn, London, 1801), ix.

22. Philip Ziegler, *Addington. A Life of Henry Addington, First Viscount Sidmouth* (London, 1965), 59; *A*, i. 83.

23. *A*, ii. 13; 'Memoir of Mr James Henry Leigh Hunt. Written by Himself', *Monthly Mirror* (April 1810), 245; *The London Kalendar; or, Court and City Register* (London, 1808), 232.

24. *A*, ii. 13.
25. See Blunden, 40.
26. *Captain Sword*, 74–5.
27. *A*, ii. 14.
28. BL, 15; *A*, i. 227.
29. BL, 18–20.
30. Hunt's MS notes in his copy of *The Life and Works of Robert Burns*, ed. Robert Chambers (4 vols, Edinburgh, 1851), ii. 133. Brewer Collection.
31. *A*, i. 72, 74.
32. Ibid., 227–8.
33. Ibid., 229–35.
34. *E* (1 June 1817), 345.
35. *Recollections*, 39; Thornton Hunt, *Proserpina*, in Blunden, 361. For Hunt and music, Percy M. Young, 'Leigh Hunt – Music Critic', *Music and Letters. A Quarterly Publication*, 25 (1944), 86–94.
36. *Corr.*, i. 11.
37. *A*, i. 280.
38. 'The Critic's Farewell to his Readers', *News* (13 Dec. 1807), 399; Barron Field to Hunt, 11 Aug. 1807, BrL Add. MS 38108.
39. J. Steven Watson, 438.
40. *News* (22 Feb.; 8 March; 17 May 1807).
41. 'Condition of Ireland', *News* (4 Oct. 1807).
42. John Hunt to Leigh Hunt, *c*. 1805–1807, Berg.
43. BL, 13.
44. *London Kalendar*, 137.
45. Hunt to Marian Kent, 24, 29 July, 1806, BL, 13–14, 46.
46. 'Military Affairs', *News* (20 Sept. 1807); 'Christ's Hospital', *News* (25 Oct. 1807).
47. 'Prospectus of the New Daily Evening Paper, Called The Statesman'.
48. *Corr.*, i. 25; John Hunt to Leigh Hunt, *c*. 1805–7, Berg.
49. *Classic Tales, Serious and Lively: With Critical Essays on the Merits and Reputation of the Authors* (5 vols, London, 1807), i. 43, 55, 62, 63.
50. Ibid., i. 52; iii. 10, 13.
51. *News* (6 Sept. 1807); *E* (3 Jan. 1808).
52. *News* (9 Aug. 1807); (23 Aug. 1807); *A*, i. 282.
53. *Traveller* (29 Jan. 1806).
54. *Critical Essays*, x, xi, xiii.
55. Ibid., vii.
56. Ibid., 10.
57. *A*, i. 292.
58. *Critical Essays*, 2, 16, 47.
59. But see Jonathan Bate, *Shakespearean Constitutions: Politics, Theatre, Criticism 1730–1830* (Oxford, 1989), 136 n.

60. *Antijacobin Review* (June 1809), 191; *Lady's Monthly Museum* (July 1808), 42; *Monthly Review* (Dec. 1808), 423–4.

61. *Satirist* (March 1808), 77.

62. *HC*, i. 33; *HL*, i. 171–2.

7 Heart and Hypochondria

1. *A* (1860), xii.

2. *A*, i. 312.

3. Thornton Hunt, *Proserpina*, Blunden, 358.

4. Gates, 42.

5. BL, 9.

6. *Corr.*, i. 14.

7. BL, 10.

8. Ibid., 11; Gates, 8.

9. BL, 45.

10. Letter of 16 Dec. 1805, Brewer Collection; Cheney.

11. BL, 14, 15, 31, 48.

12. BrL Ashley MS 3393.

13. Blunden, 358–9.

14. Ibid., 39.

15. BL, 14–15.

16. Ibid., 28.

17. Ibid., 16, 26.

18. Ibid., 28, 29.

19. Ibid., 36–7.

20. *Gentleman's Magazine* (Nov. 1805), 1085.

21. 'Hampstead Parish Register for Burials Beginning in the Year 1802', London Metropolitan Archives microfilm XO94/004; *A*, i. 36–7; Landré, i. 21.

22. *A*, i. 294, 297, 306.

23. Ibid., 296.

24. William Buchan, *Domestic Medicine; or, The Family Physician* (Edinburgh, 1802), 240, 422, 423.

25. Ibid., 242, 425; *A*, i. 295, 300; BL, 25.

26. *A*, i. 294, 299.

27. Ibid., 305.

28. Ibid., 294.

29. *HD*, ii. 68, 81.

30. *A*, i. 296–8.

31. *HD*, ii. 81.

32. Ibid.

33. *A*, i. 296.

34. BL, 21.

35. Ibid., 14.
36. Ibid., 15.
37. Leigh Hunt, *Christianism; or Belief and Unbelief Reconciled* (1832), xi, xv, 11.
38. Gates, 10.
39. BL, 31.

8 The *Examiner*

1. *The Autobiography of Leigh Hunt*, ed. R. Ingpen (2 vols, Westminster, 1903), ii. 262–6.
2. Ibid., 264–5.
3. BL, 17.
4. *E* (3 Jan. 1808), 1–2.
5. Ibid., 7–8.
6. Ibid., 1.
7. *E* (22 May 1808), 331–3.
8. *E* (25 Sept. 1808), 621–2; (26 Feb. 1809), 143.
9. *E* (17 Jan. 1808), 45; (12 July 1812), 444.
10. *E* (19 May 1811), 316; (16 June 1811), 379; (12 July 1812), 444.
11. *E* (19 May 1811), 316; (6 March 1808), 158; *A*, i. 229.
12. *E* (6 Nov. 1808), 711; (18 Dec. 1808), 811; (25 Dec. 1808), 829.
13. *E* (14 Aug. 1808), 524.
14. *E* (5 June 1808), 354.
15. *E* (17 April 1808), 241; (18 Dec. 1808), 801; (25 Dec. 1808), 847.
16. *E* (6 Nov. 1808), 706; (5 June 1808), 362; (10 April 1808), 226; (21 Aug. 1808), 541; (10 April 1808), 226.
17. *E* (27 March 1808), 193.
18. *E* (10 April 1808), 225.
19. Ibid., 226, 227.
20. *E* (2 Oct. 1808), 625.
21. *E* (23 Oct. 1808), 673–5.
22. *E* (30 Oct. 1808), 690.
23. *E* (25 Dec. 1808), 824.
24. *Corr.*, i. 44.
25. *E* (1 Jan. 1809), 1, 3.
26. *E* (8 Jan. 1809), 17, 29.
27. *LL*, iii. 4; *E* (5 Feb. 1809), 96; (19 Nov. 1809), 772; (10 March 1811), 147.
28. *A*, ii. 4.
29. *E* (12 March 1809), 173.
30. *Slavery: A Poem* (1788).
31. See Gates, 11–13; *Corr.*, i. 33–8; BrL Ashley MS 3393.
32. BL, 33–4.

33. *Corr.*, i. 39; BFE, 28; BL, 35–6.

34. BL, 38; letter to Marian, 17 Oct. 1808, BrL Ashley MS 3393.

35. BL, 37–8. The letters Hunt gave to Marian were those to her 'lost' son Isaac and her sister Frances; see BL, 6–8.

36. BL, 17.

37. 'Hunt, L. 75 manuscript letters', Berg.

38. John Lorain to Stephen Hunt, 11 Nov. 1808, '75 manuscript letters', Berg.

39. *E* (22 Oct. 1809), 676; *Corr.*, i. 40; BrL Add. MS 38523; BL, 17; Landré, i. 57.

40. BrL Add. MS 38523; *EE*, 4; *HC*, i. 260; BrL Add. MS 38523; Samuel Smiles, *A Publisher and his Friends: Memoir and Correspondence of the Late John Murray* (2 vols, London, 1891), i. 154.

41. BL, 42.

42. Ibid.; *Inferno*, V. 106.

43. *E* (18 June 1809), 399.

44. BrL MS Ashley 3393.

45. Ibid.

46. BL, 39–40.

47. *Corr.*, i. 46.

48. *SC*, ii. 553.

49. *A*, ii. 309.

50. *Corr.*, i. 46.

51. BL, 43; *SC*, ii. 554.

52. St Clement Danes Marriage Register for 1809, entry 62. City of Westminster Archives Centre.

9 Pluto's Dog

1. *E* (9 July 1809), 434; (16 July 1809), 449; (23 July 1809); (30 July 1809).

2. *E* (29 Jan. 1809), 78.

3. *E* (20 Aug. 1809), 538–9.

4. BrL Add. MS 38108.

5. *Corr.*, i, 51.

6. *E* (24 Sept. 1814), 618–20; (15 Oct. 1814), 665–7; (22 Oct. 1814), 681–3; (17 Dec. 1814), 808–10.

7. BL, 49–51.

8. Gates, 20, 52.

9. Phyllis G. Mann, 'Death of a London Bookseller', *Keats–Shelley Memorial Bulletin*, 15 (1964), 8–12.

10. *A*, i. 21.

11. *AES*, 4–5.

12. Brewer Collection, MS LH 94; 'Hunt, L. 75 manuscript letters', Berg; Landré, i. 16.

13. *A*, i. 23.

14. 'St Botolph Bishopsgate, Burials 1803–1812', Guildhall Library, London, MS 4518/2; Lydia Lorain to John Hunt, 24 Oct. 1839, 'Hunt, L. 75 manuscript letters', Berg.

15. *Critical Review* (Jan. 1810), 88; *Monthly Mirror* (Apr. 1810), 275.

16. *E* (17 Sept. 1809), 605.

17. Ibid.

18. William Blake, *Jerusalem*, Plate 70, in *The Poems of William Blake*, ed. W. H. Stevenson, text by David Erdman (Harlow, 1971, 1985), 778; David Erdman, *Blake: Prophet against Empire* (3rd edn, Princeton, NJ, 1977), 455–60.

19. *Blake: Prophet against Empire*, 457.

20. *E* (26 Nov. 1809), 758; (19 Nov. 1809), 772.

21. *E* (31 Dec. 1809), 835.

22. *E* (7 Jan. 1810), 7.

23. *E* (31 Dec. 1809), 835; (5 Nov. 1809), 720.

24. *E* (1 Oct. 1809), 625–6. Hunt also used the sentence about the King's successor in his pamphlet *An Attempt to Shew the Folly and Danger of Methodism* (London, 1809), vi, where he says the successor will become 'popular by reform' and by 'ceasing to insist on subscription' to the Church of England.

25. Quoted in *E* (8 Oct. 1809), 641.

26. Ibid., 642.

27. *E* (4 March 1810), 140.

28. *E* (19 Nov. 1809), 772.

29. See George Dumas Stout, *The Political History of Leigh Hunt's Examiner* (St Louis, 1949), 6–7.

30. *A*, ii. 68.

31. *E* (4 March 1810), 144.

32. Ibid., 129; *E* (11 March 1811), 145, 147.

33. *E* (11 March 1810), 146.

34. *E* (18 March 1811), 162.

35. See *E* (18 and 25 March; 1 April 1810).

36. John Bald, 91st Highlanders, quoted in Lawrence James, *The Iron Duke: A Military Biography of Wellington* (London, 1992), 144.

37. James, *Iron Duke*, 144–5.

38. E. (21 Jan. 1810), 33–4.

10 Gathering Fame, Losing Fortune

1. *SC*, i. 69.

2. Bodleian Library, Abinger–Shelley Papers, e. 196–227, The Diary of William Godwin.

3. *A*, ii. 36–44; G. P. Tyson, *Joseph Johnson: A Liberal Publisher* (Iowa City, 1979), 66.

4. *E* (8 April 1810), 220, 223; (15 April 1810), 226; (5 Aug. 1810), 481–2.
5. *A*, ii. 17; Cyrus Redding, *Fifty Years' Recollections* (3 vols, London, 1858), ii. 212.
6. *A*, ii. 17–27.
7. BL, 49.
8. Kenneth E. Kendall, *Leigh Hunt's 'Reflector'* (The Hague and Paris, 1971), 11.
9. *Monthly Mirror* (April 1810), 243–8; 'sister' was corrected to 'aunt' in *LBsC*, ii. 67.
10. BrL Add. MS 38108.
11. Blunden, 57–8.
12. Gates, 15; BrL Add. MS 38108.
13. *E* (21 May 1809), 331.
14. *HD*, i. 60–61.
15. *E* (2 Feb. 1812), 76–7.
16. *HC*, i. 53.
17. BL, 50; *E* (4 Nov. 1810), 692.
18. BrL Add. MS 38108.
19. *E* (2 Sept. 1810), 557–8.
20. Ibid., (4 Nov. 1810), 693.
21. Ibid., (11 Nov. 1810), 710.
22. BL, 51; Gates, 16.
23. *Corr.*, i. 51.
24. 'Hunt, L. 75 manuscript letters', Berg. Unless noted otherwise, the following account of Stephen Shewell's estate is drawn from these papers.
25. *A*, i. 25, 195; *AES*, 7.
26. BL, 89.
27. 'Hunt, L. 75 manuscript letters', letter of 20 June 1851.

11 Politics and Poetics

1. *Corr.*, i. 47–8.
2. Ibid., 47, 49–51; *E* (6 Jan. 1811), 14.
3. *R*, i. iii–ix.
4. Ibid., 218, 220, 231.
5. Ibid., 232–6, 236–42, 242.
6. Ibid., 381–8, 424–9, 429–35.
7. *A*, ii. 84; *R*, ii. 313–23; Blunden, 67.
8. *E* (21 Aug. 1808), 541.
9. Ibid.
10. 'George IV', *Works of Henry Lord Brougham* (4 vols, Edinburgh, 1872), iv. 49.
11. *E* (21 Aug. 1808), 529–31.
12. Ibid., (10 Feb. 1811), 86; (27 Jan. 1811), 50; (10 Feb. 1811), 82.
13. *R*, 144–56.

14. Ibid., 400–419.
15. Ibid., 400.
16. Ibid., 410–11.
17. *A*, i. 298.
18. *R*, ii. 416, 419.
19. Ibid., 5.
20. *E* (13 Jan. 1811), 17.
21. *E* (20 Sept. 1812), 601.
22. *E* (13 Sept. 1812), 589; (4 Oct. 1812), 635; (27 Sept. 1812), 619; (1 Nov. 1812), 697.

12 The Fearless Enlightener

1. *E* (24 Feb. 1811), 119.
2. *E* (10 Feb. 1811), 82.
3. Ibid., 92–3.
4. Ibid., 86.
5. *E* (17 Feb. 1811), 97.
6. *The Life and Times of Lord Brougham. Written by Himself* (3 vols, Edinburgh and London, 1871), i. 501.
7. *E* (17 Feb. 1811), 112.
8. William Cobbett, *Complete Collection of State Trials . . . from the Earliest Period to the Present Time* (33 vols, London, 1809–28), xxi. col. 369.
9. *E* (24 Feb. 1811), 119.
10. *State Trials*, xxi. col. 383; *E* (24 Feb. 1811), 125.
11. *E* (24 Feb. 1811), 126–7.
12. Ibid., 128; *State Trials*, xxi. col. 401.
13. *E* (24 Feb. 1811), 128.
14. *E* (3 March 1811), 129, 131.
15. *E* (17 March 1811), 168; (12 May 1811), 301–3; (26 May 1811), 320–1; (30 June 1811), 413; (28 July 1811), 483.
16. Cyrus Redding, *Fifty Years' Recollections* (3 vols, London, 1858), i. 166.
17. *Times* (23 Feb. 1811), 2.
18. *E* (10 March 1811), 145–7.
19. Ibid., 149; *E* (31 March 1811), 199.
20. *A*, ii. 106–8.
21. Leslie Mitchell, *Holland House* (London, 1980), 11–38.
22. *A*, ii. 106–8.
23. *LPBS*, i. 54–5.
24. *A*, ii. 187.
25. Hazlitt on Godwin, *Spirit of the Age* (1825) in Howe, xi. 16.
26. *E* (10 March 1811), 145.
27. *LPBS*, i. 28.

28. *LBsC*, i. 305.

29. Thomas Jefferson Hogg, *The Life of Percy Bysshe Shelley* (2 vols only published, London, 1858), i. 69–70.

30. *LPBS*, i. 44.

31. Ibid., 51.

32. Ibid., 42n.

33. *WPBS*, v. 209.

34. *LPBS*, i. 52.

35. Edward Dowden, *The Life of Percy Bysshe Shelley* (2 vols, London, 1886), i. 124; *LPBS*, i. 56.

36. *E* (24 March 1811), 177–8; *LPBS*, i. 56.

37. *LPBS*, i. 56.

38. *A* (1860), 255.

39. *A*, ii. 179.

40. Hogg, i. 55.

41. *LPBS*, i. 77.

42. *A*, ii. 179.

13 Eighteen Hundred and Eleven

1. BrL Add. MS 38108; *E* (16 and 23 June 1811).

2. Gates, 16–17; *HD*, i. 64–5, 202, 207–8.

3. 'The Harp that Once Through Tara's Halls', from *Irish Melodies* (1808).

4. *A*, i. 6.

5. *The Letters of Thomas Moore*, ed. W. S. Dowden (2 vols, Oxford, 1964), i. 158–9.

6. *E* (15 Sept. 1811), 593–6.

7. *Letters of Thomas Moore*, i. 207–8.

8. *E* (28 April 1811), 257; (19 May 1811), 304; (2 June 1811), 336–40.

9. *A*, ii. 114–15.

10. 'George IV', *Works of Henry Lord Brougham* (4 vols, Edinburgh, 1872), iv. 24.

11. *Letters of Richard Brinsley Sheridan*, ed. Cecil Price (3 vols, Oxford, 1966), iii. 150. Fintan O'Toole, *A Traitor's Kiss. The Life of Richard Brinsley Sheridan* (London, 1997), 440–1.

12. *E* (15 Sept. 1811), 587–8.

13. *E* (23 June 1811), 394.

14. Ibid., 397, rpt. from the *Morning Herald*.

15. *E* (30 June 1811), 415–16.

16. Ibid., 411.

17. *E* (10 Nov. 1811), 723.

18. *E* (24 Nov. 1811), 747.

19. Ibid., 748.

20. *The Poems of William Blake*, ed. W. H. Stevenson, text by David V. Erdman (Harlow, 1971, 1985), 489.
21. *E* (17 Nov. 1811), 731–2; (19 July 1812), 449.
22. BrL Add. MS 38108; Gates, 18–19.
23. *LJK*, ii. 11; *A*, ii. 169.
24. 'Eighteen Hundred and Eleven', *The Poems of Anna Letitia Barbauld*, ed. W. McCarthy and E. Kraft (Athens, Georgia, 1994), 154.
25. BrL Add. MS 38108.
26. Leigh Hunt, *Men, Women, and Books* (2 vols, London, 1847), ii. 146–50.
27. 'To a Great Nation', and 'To Dr Priestley. Dec. 29, 1792', *Poems of Anna Letitia Barbauld*, 124–5.
28. *Poems of Anna Letitia Barbauld*, 310.
29. *E* (29 Dec. 1811), 827.
30. *E* (4 Aug. 1811), 492.
31. *E* (8 Sept. 1811), 579–80.
32. *E* (15 Sept. 1811), 597.
33. *E* (8 Sept. 1811), 580.
34. Gates, 18.
35. *E* (8 Oct. 1809), 652.
36. *E* (13 Oct. 1811), 662.
37. Johann Winckelmann, *Reflections Concerning the Imitation of the Grecian Artist in Painting and Sculpture* (1755) and Richard Payne Knight, *An Analytic Inquiry into the Principles of Taste* (1805), 4, quoted in William St Clair, *Lord Elgin and the Marbles* (Oxford, 1998), 266, 168.
38. St Clair, 290.
39. *HD*, i. 208, 18 Aug. 1811; *E* (15 Sept. 1811), 597.
40. *HD*, i. 210 n.
41. *E* (17 March 1816), 163.
42. *E* (9 March 1817), 155.
43. 'On Seeing the Elgin Marbles', *E* (9 March 1817), 155.
44. *A*, ii. 170.
45. BrL MS Ashley 4855.

14 Leviathan

1. Gates, 20–1.
2. *E* (16 Feb. 1812), 98.
3. E.V. Lucas, *The Life of Charles Lamb* (2nd edn, 2 vols, London, 1905), i. 318; *HCR*, i. 368–70.
4. *E* (15 March 1812), 173.
5. *Paradise Lost*, ed. Alastair Fowler (London, 1971).
6. *HCR*, i. 375–6.
7. *E* (23 June 1811), 397.

8. *E* (23 Feb. 1812), 113.
9. Ibid., 115.
10. *E* (22 March 1812), 177–80.
11. Ibid., 178.
12. Ibid., 179.
13. *A*, ii. 115; *E* (26 April 1812), 257.
14. *E* (26 April 1812), 257–9.
15. *E* (29 March 1811), 204; (5 April 1811), 217–18.
16. *E* (17 May, 1812), 304, 314–15; *HCR*, i. 383; *Collected Letters of Samuel Taylor Coleridge*, ed. E. L. Griggs (6 vols, Oxford, 1956–71), iii. 410.
17. *E* (12 Jan. 1812), 24; J. Steven Watson, *The Reign of George III, 1760–1815* (Oxford, 1960), 493–4; Lawrence James, *The Iron Duke: A Military Biography of Wellington* (London, 1992), 204–8; *E* (27 Dec. 1812), 825.
18. *E* (7 June 1812), 353, 356.
19. Ibid., 356. 'Recollections and Memorandums Written during my Imprisonment in Surrey Jail', f. 5, Berg.
20. *E* (28 July 1812), 401–3.
21. Gates, 24.
22. Ibid., 21.
23. Ibid., 15; BL, 89.
24. Gates, 21, 22.
25. Ibid., 24.
26. *Corr.*, i. 58; *E* (16 Aug. 1812), 513; *SC*, iii. 105–8; *Correspondence of Jeremy Bentham*, ed. T. L. S. Sprigge et al. (11 vols publ., London and Oxford, 1968—), viii. 256–8.
27. BrL Add. MS 38108; *The Letters of Thomas Moore*, ed. W. S. Dowden (2 vols, Oxford, 1964), i. 156; *Corr.*, i. 60.
28. BL, 53, 54.
29. 'Prospectus', *Taunton Courier* (22 Sept. 1808), 2.
30. Edward Jeboult, *A General Account of West Somerset* (Taunton, 1873), 7.
31. *Rimini*, 3–4.
32. BL, 54–7; *E* (6 Sept. 1812), 561.
33. *Corr.*, i. 61, 57.
34. *E* (4 Oct. 1812), 625.
35. *E* (1 Nov. 1812), 697.

15 In the Heart of the Place

1. *Memoirs, Journal, and Correspondence of Thomas Moore*, ed. Lord John Russell (8 vols, London, 1853–6), viii. 120–23.
2. BL, 90; *Corr.*, i. 61; D. Weindling and M. Colloms, *Kilburn and West Hampstead Past* (London, 1999), 44.
3. BL, 90; *Corr.*, i. 61; Gates, 27; *HC*, i. 267.

4. 'A Letter to Lord Ellenborough', *WPBS*, v. 277–94.

5. *The Life and Times of Lord Brougham. Written by Himself* (3 vols, Edinburgh and London, 1871), ii. 72; *A*, ii. 132.

6. *A*, ii. 133.

7. *E* (13 Dec. 1812), 787.

8. *Times* (10 Dec. 1812).

9. *E* (13 Dec. 1812), 790.

10. *LPBS*, i. 346.

11. *E* (13 Dec. 1812), 787–96.

12. *E* (20 Dec. 1812), 804.

13. Ibid., 807.

14. *Life and Times of Lord Brougham*, ii. 72–3.

15. *E* (13 Dec. 1812), 785–7.

16. Ibid., 791.

17. Gates, 27.

18. *HD*, i. 288.

19. *E* (3 Jan. 1813), 1–3.

20. *E* (10 Jan. 1812), 17–20.

21. Lilly Library, University of Indiana, Bloomington. English Literature MSS.

22. *A* (1860), 230.

23. 'Macbeth; or The Ill Effects of Ambition', *Juvenilia*, 1–2.

24. *E* (7 Feb. 1813), 95.

25. *Rimini*, 18.

26. *A* (1860), 230.

27. *E* (7 Feb. 1813), 82.

28. *Taunton Courier* (11 Feb. 1813), 2–3.

29. *A*, ii. 136.

30. Ibid., 137.

31. Ibid., 141; BL, 153.

32. *LPBS*, i. 353.

33. *HC*, i. 268.

34. Acts, 12. 7–10.

35. BL, 92; *E* (21 Feb. 1813), 113; BrL Add. MS 38108.

36. *LPBS*, i. 353–4; *A*, ii. 154.

37. *Taunton Courier* (11 Feb. 1813), 2–3.

38. BL, 97.

39. *Correspondence of Jeremy Bentham*, ed. T.L.S. Sprigge et al. (11 vols publ. London and Oxford, 1968–2), viii. 252.

40. *E* (31 Jan. 1813), 73–4.

41. *E* (14 Feb. 1813), 104.

42. BrL Add. MS 38108.

43. *A*, ii. 146; BrL Add. MS 38108.

44. BrL Add. MS 38108.

45. 'Recollections and Memorandums Written during my Imprisonment in Surrey Jail', f. 2, Berg.

46. Ibid. f. 3.

47. Ibid. f. 5.

48. BL, 152–4; *E* (21 Feb. 1813), 113; Blunden, 75.

49. *E* (28 Feb. 1813), 129.

50. For Hunt's rooms, *Corr.*, ii. 85; *A*, ii. 148; *Recollections*, 17.

51. *A*, ii. 155; Cyrus Redding, *Fifty Years' Recollections* (3 vols, London, 1858), i. 274.

52. *E* (12 June 1814), 378.

16 The Place of the Heart

1. Gates, 42; BL, 59, 62, 65, 69.

2. BL, 63, 64, 69, 72, 78; Gates, 36.

3. BL, 60; *A*, iii. 185; Gates, 37, 44.

4. For Hunt's visitors: BL, 58; *A*, ii. 140, 152; P. G. Patmore, *My Friends and Acquaintance: Being Memorials, Mind Portraits, and Personal Recollections of Deceased Celebrities of the Nineteenth Century* (3 vols, London, 1854), ii. 342; 'Recollections and Memorandums Written during my Imprisonment in Surrey Jail', f. 10, Berg; Landré, i. 76; Blunden, 76–7.

5. *Recollections*, 4, 16, 191; John Barnard, 'Leigh Hunt and Charles Cowden Clarke, 1812–18', *Leigh Hunt: Life, Poetics, Politics*, ed. Nicholas Roe (London, 2003), 32–57.

6. *LJK*, ii. 107–8.

7. Gates, 30.

8. Ibid., 51.

9. BL, 67.

10. Ibid., 75.

11. Ibid., 57; Gates, 38, 44, 30.

12. BL, 62.

13. *HD*, ii. 83.

14. Bodleian Library MS Shelley Adds d.5, ff. 47–8. Quoted with permission.

15. Gates, 144–5.

16. Ibid., 169, 172.

17. *New Monthly Magazine*, 12 (May 1826), 425.

18. BL, 73–4.

19. Gates, 40.

20. *E* (2 May 1813), 280.

21. *E* (18 Oct. 1812), 664.

22. *BLJ*, iii. 50.

23. Gates, 41.

24. *LBsC*, i. 4.

25. *BLJ*, iii. 228.

26. For the birth, *A*, ii. 151 and *I* (16 Feb. 1820), 152; *A* (1860), 239, Thornton Hunt's note.

27. *E* (21 March 1813), 178–9.

28. *E* (17 Jan. 1813), 32.

29. *Poems by William Wordsworth* (2 vols, London, 1815), ii. 258.

30. *E* (4 July 1813).

31. *E* (17 Jan. 1813), 34–5.

32. *E* (26 Sept. 1813), 609.

33. *E* (29 Aug. 1813), 545–7.

34. *E* (25 April 1813), 265.

35. *E* (26 Sept. 1813), 609–11.

36. *E* (9 March 1817), 157–8; *Parliamentary Debates, from the Year 1803, to the Present Time* (41 vols, London, 1804–20), xxxv. 1088–92.

37. *A*, iii. 283.

38. Ibid., 277.

39. *E* (29 Aug. 1813), 556.

40. Gates, 44; *BLJ*, iii. 189, 228.

41. BL, 80, 77.

42. *Feast* (1814), 18.

43. Ibid., 126–33.

44. Ibid., 56–7; *Memoirs, Journal, and Correspondence of Thomas Moore*, ed. Lord John Russell (8 vols, London, 1853–6), viii. 172.

45. *Feast* (1814), 90, 93, 95.

46. Ibid., 93–7, 107.

47. Ibid., 94.

48. Ibid., 93, 96, 97–9.

49. Ibid., 107–8.

50. BrL Add. MS 38523; *Champion* (28 May 1814), 174–5; BrL Add. MS 38108; *BLJ*, iv. 50.

51. *British Critic* (May 1814), 550; *Champion* (20 Feb. 1814), 62; *Critical Review* (March 1814), 303; *Monthly Review* (Sept. 1814), 100.

17 Ice and Fire

1. *A*, ii. 151.

2. *E* (23 Jan. 1814), 60; (6 Feb. 1814), 87; *BLJ*, iv. 49; *Gentleman's Magazine* (Feb. 1814), 144, 192; *Annual Register for the Year 1814* (London, 1815), 8–9.

3. *Memoirs, Journal, and Correspondence of Thomas Moore*, ed. Lord John Russell (8 vols, London, 1853–6), viii, 173; *E* (9 Jan. 1814), 24; (10 April 1814), 225.

4. *E* (17 April 1814), 255–6.

5. *LL*, iii. 96–7.

6. *HCRB*, i. 142; *HCR*, i. 429.

7. *LBsC*, i. 50; LH to Byron, 2 April 1814, *Works of Lord Byron: Letters and Journals*, ed. R. E. Prothero (6 vols, London, 1904), iii. 416.

8. *E* (10 April 1814), 236; (24 April 1814), 257.

9. *E* (29 May 1814), 337; (5 June 1814), 360.

10. *E* (10 April 1814), 228, 236.

11. *E* (17 April 1814), 225, 251.

12. *E* (24 April 1814), 257.

13. *Rimini*, 5–6.

14. *E* (24 April 1814), 257–8.

15. *Jane Austen's Letters. A New Edition*, ed. Deirdre Le Faye (3rd edn, Oxford, 1995), 256; *E* (13 Feb. 1814), 108–9.

16. *E* (27 Feb. 1814), 138; (5 June 1814), 364–5; *Drury Lane Journal*, ed. A. L. Nelson and G. B. Cross (London 1974), 4.

17. *HCR*, i. 426

18. *E* (5 June 1814), 364.

19. *E* (24 July 1814), 478–9.

20. *E* (7 Aug. 1814), 505–7.

21. *E* (14 Aug. 1814), 525–6.

22. *LPBS*, i. 390.

23. *E* (22 May 1814), 335–6.

24. *E* (21 Aug. 1814), 541–2.

25. To Richard Woodhouse, 27 Oct. 1818, *LJK*, i. 387.

26. *E* (2 Oct. 1814), 637–8.

27. S. T. Coleridge, *Biographia Literaria*, ed. J. Engell and W. Jackson Bate, Bollingen Collected Coleridge Series, 7 (2 vols, Princeton and London, 1983), ii. 119, 136.

28. *PJK*, 28; *E* (1 May 1814), 273; *Recollections*, 124.

29. *The Eden of the Imagination* (London, 1814), 25 n.

30. Leonidas M. Jones, *The Life of John Hamilton Reynolds* (Hanover and London, 1984), 51, 61; *Letters from Lambeth. The Correspondence of the Reynolds Family with John Freeman Milward Dovaston, 1808–1815*, ed. Joanna Richardson (Woodbridge, 1981), 118, 130–1.

31. *Eden of the Imagination*, 27 n.

32. *E* (1 May 1814), 287–8.

33. Gates, 56–7.

34. BL, 92–6; *E* (21 Aug. 1814), 530–33; (28 Aug. 1814), 547–8; (4 Sept. 1814), 562–4.

35. *Descent*, v; John Barnard, 'Leigh Hunt and Charles Cowden Clarke, 1812–18', *Leigh Hunt: Life, Poetics, Politics*, ed. Nicholas Roe (London, 2003), 39; *E* (22 May 1814), 322–3.

36. *Descent*, xix.

37. Ibid., 8, 14, 18, 20–1, 40.

38. Ibid., viii, xvi.
39. Ibid., 26, 28–9.
40. *A*, ii. 151.
41. *Descent*, 9, 11, 18, 38.
42. *E* (31 July 1814), 480–3; (16 Oct. 1814), 657–8; (23 Oct. 1814), 674.
43. *E* (12 June 1814), 337.
44. *E* (20 Nov. 1814), 747; (18 Dec. 1814), 804; (25 Dec. 1814), 818.
45. *E* (19 June 1814), 386; (25 Sept. 1814), 617; (2 Oct. 1814), 625.
46. *Corr.*, i. 96; *BLJ*, iv. 209.
47. *HC*, i. 282–3.
48. Gates, 60.
49. *George Bullock, Cabinet-Maker* (London, 1988), 141–2.
50. For Hunt's recommendations, see Barnard, 'Leigh Hunt and Charles Cowden Clarke', 55 n. 18.
51. Theodore Fenner, *Leigh Hunt and Opera Criticism: The 'Examiner' Years, 1808–21* (Lawrence KS., 1972), 33–4, 274.
52. Barnard, 'Leigh Hunt and Charles Cowden Clarke', 41.
53. *E* (4 Dec. 1814), 769.
54. *E* (25 Dec. 1814), 819–20.

18 Life Masks

1. *E* (1 Jan. 1815), 11.
2. Ibid., 12; (8 Jan. 1815), 26; BL, 54.
3. *Letters from Lambeth. The Correspondence of the Reynolds Family with John Freeman Milward Dovaston, 1808–1815*, ed. Joanna Richardson (Woodbridge, 1981), 131.
4. *Augustan Review* (March 1816), 291; *Critical Review* (March 1815), 285, 287; *Champion* (26 March 1815), 102.
5. *Champion* (26 March 1815), 102.
6. *Descent*, 23.
7. *British Critic* (Aug. 1815), 205–6.
8. *E* (1 Jan. 1815), 11; BrL Add. MS 38108.
9. 'To J**H** Four Years Old', *Foliage*, li–lvii.
10. *Corr.*, ii. 89.
11. *E* (5 Feb. 1815), 81.
12. *A*, ii. 158, 167.
13. Gates, 66.
14. *A*, i. 54–5.
15. Ibid., 159.
16. *Recollections*, 127.
17. *PJK*, 32.
18. *Recollections*, 4, 16.

19. John Barnard, 'Leigh Hunt and Charles Cowden Clarke, 1812–18', *Leigh Hunt: Life, Poetics, Politics*, ed. Nicholas Roe (London, 2003), 53.

20. *A*, ii. 160–3.

21. *E* (19 Feb. 1815), 113, 121–4.

22. *E* (26 Feb. 1815), 140.

23. *E* (4 June 1815), 364.

24. *A*, ii. 170.

25. *E* (12 March 1815), 162–3.

26. *HL*, i. 299–300.

27. *E* (26 March 1815), 193.

28. *The Letters of Thomas Moore*, ed. W. S. Dowden (2 vols, Oxford, 1964), i. 357; *BLJ*, iv. 295.

29. *E* (26 March 1815), 203.

30. *E* (2 April 1815), 209–11; (9 April 1815), 225.

31. *E* (28 May 1815), 338.

32. *E* (7 May 1815), 300.

33. Edmund Burke, *A Philosophical Enquiry into the Origin of our Ideas of the Sublime and Beautiful*, ed. Adam Phillips (1757; Oxford, 1990), 103, 105.

34. Nicholas Roe, 'Leigh Hunt and Wordsworth's *Poems* 1815', *The Wordsworth Circle* (Winter 1981), 89–91.

35. *BLJ*, iv. 294.

36. *E* (21 May 1815), 321.

37. *BLJ*, iv. 294–5; *E* (21 May 1815), 321.

38. *A*, ii. 162–3.

39. *E* (20 Aug. 1815), 542; 'Sleep and Poetry', in *PJK*, 73, ll. 185–6.

40. *BLJ*, vi. 10.

41. *Feast* (1814), 90; *HD*, i. 450–1.

42. *HCR*, i. 487.

43. *E* (11 June 1815), 361–2.

44. *HCRB*, i. 169.

45. *E* (28 May 1815), 348.

46. *E* (25 June 1815), 413; (2 July 1815), 417.

47. *HL*, i. 299.

48. *HD*, i. 456–7, 458.

49. 'Feelings of a Republican on the fall of Bonaparte', *WPBS*, i. 206, ll. 13–14.

50. Advertisements from *The Times*, Aug.–Sept. 1815.

51. *HL*, i. 303.

19 Elaborate Snares

1. *E* (2 July 1815), 417.

2. Ibid.

3. *LJK*, i. 281; ii. 102.

4. *LJK*, ii. 102.

5. *E* (6 Aug. 1815), 500.

6. *E* (30 July 1815), 491; *Don Juan*, XI. 55.

7. *E* (6 Aug. 1815), 508–9.

8. *E* (19 Nov. 1815), 745.

9. *E* (14 July 1816), 432–6.

10. *E* (18 Feb. 1816), 105; (30 June 1816), 401; (9 June 1816), 355–6.

11. Gates, 77–8, Hunt's letter to Constable 19 Aug. 1816.

12. Gates, 77.

13. Hunt to Byron, 30 Oct. 1815, *Works of Lord Byron: Letters and Journals*, ed. R. E. Prothero (6 vols, London, 1904), iii. 420.

14. Gates, 67, 82.

15. BrL Add. MS 38108.

16. Alan Farmer, *Hampstead Heath* (London, 1996), 148–9; *A History of the County of Middlesex*, ed. J. S. Cockburn et al., Victoria History of the Counties of England (11 vols, Oxford 1969–98), ix. 71.

17. *LBsC*, i. 413.

18. *BLJ*, iv. 319–20.

19. BrL MS Ashley 906.

20. *BLJ*, iv. 320.

21. BrL MS Ashley 906.

22. *BLJ*, iv. 320.

23. *A*, ii. 171.

24. *Works of Lord Byron: Letters and Journals*, iii. 419.

25. *Poems, Written Chiefly in the Scottish Dialect, By Robert Burns* (Kilmarnock, 1786), iii–iv.

26. *Edinburgh Magazine* (Oct. 1786); *Monthly Review* (Dec. 1786); *London Chronicle* (July 1796); *Dumfries Journal* (Aug. 1796); *Monthly Magazine* (June 1797).

27. *BLJ*, iii. 239; iv. 326.

28. *Works of Lord Byron: Letters and Journals*, iii. 420.

29. *BLJ*, iv. 331.

30. Samuel Smiles, *A Publisher and his Friends: Memoir and Correspondence of the Late John Murray* (2 vols, London, 1891), i. 307–12.

31. *Works of Lord Byron: Letters and Journals*, iii. 422.

32. *Rimini*, 1–22.

33. Ibid., 26.

34. Ibid., 26–8.

35. Ibid., 30.

36. Ibid., 39.

37. Ibid., 44.

38. Ibid.

39. Ibid., 77.

40. Ibid., 77–8.
41. Ibid., 111; Philip Larkin, *Collected Poems*, ed. Anthony Thwaite (London and Boston, 1988), 110–11.
42. 'Preface', *Rimini*, xv–xvi.
43. *Foliage*, 17.
44. *A*, ii. 170.
45. *Memoirs, Journal, and Correspondence of Thomas Moore*, ed. Lord John Russell (8 vols, London, 1853–6), viii. 215.
46. Blunden, 39; for 'family-partners', *E* (23 Dec. 1820), 63.
47. BL, 101.
48. John Murray Archive, Ledger BB 1; BrL Add. MS 38108; *LL*, ii. 209–10; *BLJ*, v. 35.
49. *Dublin Examiner* (June 1816), 131; *Monthly Review* (June 1816), 138, 146; *Eclectic Review* (April 1816), 380; *Quarterly Review* (Jan. / May 1816), 481.
50. *Memoirs, Journal, and Correspondence of Thomas Moore*, viii. 215; *A*, ii. 173.
51. *Address to that Quarterly Reviewer who Touched upon Mr Leigh Hunt's 'Story of Rimini'* (London, 1816), 3.
52. *Blackwood's Magazine* (Oct. 1817), 40, 41; (July 1818), 453–7; *Quarterly Review* (Jan./May 1816), 481.
53. *BLJ*, v. 32.
54. Fiona MacCarthy, *Byron: Life and Legend* (London, 2002), 268, 273.
55. *BLJ*, v. 54.
56. *E* (28 Jan. 1816), 49–51.
57. *A*, ii. 176.
58. Ibid., 228; *BLJ*, v. 50; v. 59.
59. *LBsC*, i. 7, 10.
60. *E* (21 April 1816), 248–9.
61. *LPBS*, i. 518.

20 Seas of Trouble

1. Fiona MacCarthy, *Byron: Life and Legend* (London, 2002), 284.
2. *E* (28 April, 1816), 266–7.
3. *E* (18 Feb. 1816), 97–8; *LBsC*, i. 221.
4. *E* (31 March 1816), 203; *HD*, ii. 4; *E* (20 Oct. 1816), 663; Brewer Collection, MS LH 94 and Cheney.
5. *WPBS*, i. 178, l. 60.
6. *The Excursion* (London, 1814), 184.
7. Ibid., 179, 182.
8. *HD*, ii. 68.
9. *LJK*, i. 114.
10. *PJK*, 63–4, ll. 7–8.
11. *E* (5 May 1816), 282.

12. *EE*, 62.

13. 'The Poetry of Hardy', *Required Writing* (London, 1983), 174.

14. *E* (30 June 1816), 409–10; *E* (7 July 1816), 424.

15. *E* (14 July 1816), 440.

16. *HD*, ii. 62–3.

17. BrL Add. MS 38523; Samuel Smiles, *A Publisher and his Friends: Memoir and Correspondence of the Late John Murray* (2 vols, London, 1891), i. 310–12.

18. *Memoirs, Journal, and Correspondence of Thomas Moore*, ed. Lord John Russell (8 vols, London, 1853–6), viii. 214–16; Cheney.

19. National Library of Scotland, MS 789, 'Constable Letter Book', 622.

20. Gates, 77.

21. Ibid., 82. John Hunt's letter is undated, but was addressed to the Vale of Health.

22. Letter to Moore, 3 July 1816, Cheney.

23. Tim Chilcott, *A Publisher and his Circle* (London, 1972), 59.

24. *E* (24 March 1816), 179.

25. *E* (2 June 1816), 348.

26. *E* (17 March 1816), 162.

21 Young Poets

1. *LJK*, i. 110.

2. *E* (20 Oct. 1816), 664.

3. *Recollections*, 132–3.

4. *LJK*, i. 113.

5. John Barnard, 'Leigh Hunt and Charles Cowden Clarke, 1812–18', *Leigh Hunt: Life, Poetics, Politics*, ed. Nicholas Roe (London, 2003), 45–6.

6. *Feast* (1814), 125–6.

7. *LBsC*, i. 410.

8. *HL*, i. 359.

9. *The Keats Circle: Letters and Papers 1816–1878 and More Letters and Papers 1814–1879*, ed. H. E. Rollins (2nd edn, 2 vols, Cambridge, Mass., 1965), i. 4–6.

10. *LJK*, i. 114–15.

11. *E* (3 Nov. 1816), 694.

12. *E* (25 Aug. 1816), 537.

13. *PJK*, 370, ll. 15–16.

14. Ibid., 77–8, ll. 350–403.

15. Ian Jack, *Keats and the Mirror of Art* (Oxford, 1967), 132–3.

16. *Foliage*, cxvix; *PJK*, 88–9.

17. *Recollections*, 133.

18. *HD*, ii. 75.

19. *PJK*, 67, ll. 11–12.

20. *HD*, ii. 62.
21. *Classic Tales, Serious and Lively: With Critical Essays on the Merits and Reputation of the Authors* (5 vols, London, 1807), ii. 17; *HD*, ii. 54–60.
22. *E* (12 March 1815), 170.
23. *E* (29 Sept. 1816), 610.
24. *E* (17 Nov. 1816), 730.
25. *E* (24 Nov. 1816), 737–8; *A*, ii. 5.
26. *E* (8 Dec. 1816), 772, 778.
27. *E* (15 Dec. 1816), 803.
28. *E* (1 Dec. 1816), 760.
29. Ibid., 761–2.
30. Ibid., 762.

22 Et in Arcadia

1. *LPBS*, i. 517–18.
2. Ibid., 517.
3. 'On Launching Some Bottles Filled with Knowledge into the Bristol Channel', *PBSMW*, 8–9.
4. *LMWS*, i. 22.
5. Arthur H. Beavan, *James and Horace Smith* (London, 1899), 136–9; *A*, ii. 201–2; *JMS*, 150.
6. *Times* (12 Dec. 1816), 2.
7. *SC*, iv. 769–810.
8. *HCRB*, i. 211. Crabb Robinson recorded in his diary: 'It is singular that it was not suggested to Basil Montagu by Shelley that he was not the father of his wife's child. Mrs Godwin had stated this to me as a fact. Basil Montagu thinks it improbable.' Mrs Godwin had reason to cast Harriet in a bad light, and her statement of 'fact' should be treated cautiously.
9. *SC*, iv. 776–7.
10. *Shelley: The Pursuit* (London, 1976), 353.
11. *LPBS*, i. 521.
12. Ibid., 520–1.
13. *PJK*, 88, ll. 6, 11–13.
14. *LPBS*, i. 522–3.
15. *E* (8 Dec. 1816), 775; (22 Dec. 1816), 809.
16. Alan Farmer, *Hampstead Heath* (London, 1996), 53–4.
17. For Hunt's account and the gossips of the Vale, *LBsC*, i. 316–18 n.
18. *Philosophical Transactions of the Royal Society of London for the Year MDCCCXVII* (London, 1817), 'Meteorological Journal', 25, afternoon of 19 Dec. 1816: '37°' and 'Snow'.
19. *LBsC*, i. 316–18 n.
20. 'Shelley. By One Who Knew Him', *Atlantic Monthly*, 11 (1863), 186.

21. *WPBS*, iii. 118–19.

22. Ibid., 163, ll. 1–7.

23. 'Memoirs of Percy Bysshe Shelley', *Works of Thomas Love Peacock* (10 vols, London and New York, 1924–34), viii. 110–11.

24. *A*, i. 32–3.

25. Blunden, 176.

26. BL, 107–8.

27. *A*, ii. 34.

28. *E* (5 Jan. 1817), 7.

29. *LPBS*, i. 528–9.

30. *A*, ii. 196; 'Shelley. By One Who Knew Him', 186.

31. *E* (19 Jan. 1817), 41–2.

32. *HD*, ii. 80–87, 372.

33. *A*, ii. 202.

34. *HD*, ii. 84.

35. Ibid., 76, 78–9.

36. Ibid., 81.

37. *E* (26 Jan. 1817), 53–4, 60.

38. *JMS*, 163.

39. *HD*, ii. 83.

40. *HC*, ii. 112.

41. *JMS*, 164, 626.

42. *Philosophical Transactions of the Royal Society of London for the Year MDCCCXVIII* (London, 1818), 'Meteorological Journal', 4–5, entries for 13–15 February 1817; BL, 101.

43. *JMS*, 165.

44. *LMWS*, i. 29, 33, 34.

45. *SC*, v. 221.

46. Cheney.

47. *E* (2 Feb. 1817), 65; (9 Feb. 1817), 81.

48. *E* (23 Feb. 1817), 122–3.

49. Ibid., 122.

50. *E* (9 March 1817), 145–6.

51. *E* (23 Feb. 1817), 124.

52. *E* (2 March 1817), 138.

53. Quoted from *Poems, by John Keats* (London, 1817), v.

54. *LJK*, i. 170.

55. Ibid., 135.

56. Ibid., 136–40.

57. Ibid., 143.

58. *E* (1 June 1817), 345; (6 July 1817), 428–9; (13 July 1817), 443–4.

59. John Barnard, 'Leigh Hunt and Charles Cowden Clarke, 1812–18', *Leigh Hunt: Life, Poetics, Politics*, ed. Nicholas Roe (London, 2003), 49.

23 Marlow and London

1. *Recollections*, 195; *JMS*, 166.
2. 'Shelley. By One Who Knew Him', *Atlantic Monthly*, 11 (1863), 187.
3. *Recollections*, 197–8.
4. *Foliage*, vii, xvii.
5. Ibid., xxvii.
6. *E* (27 April 1817), 257–9.
7. Elizabeth Kent, *Flora Domestica* (New edn., London, 1831), xix.
8. *Collected Poems* (London, 1979).
9. *E* (20 April 1817), 250; (15 June 1817), 372.
10. BrL Add. MS 38523.
11. *E* (15 June 1817), 370.
12. *E* (29 June 1817), 409.
13. *E* (13 April 1817), 233.
14. *E* (10 Aug. 1817), 498.
15. *SC*, v. 256.
16. *LMWS*, i. 338–40; *SC*, v. 256–7; *Flora Domestica*, 394.
17. *LPBS*, i. 546 n.
18. *E* (31 Aug. 1817), 552.
19. *LPBS*, i. 553–5; *E* (21 Sept. 1817), 597.
20. *LPBS*, i. 560.
21. *LJK*, i. 169–70.
22. *E* (12 Oct. 1817), 641–3.
23. *E* (19 Oct. 1817), 661.
24. *E* (2 Nov. 1817), 689.
25. Gates, 86–7.
26. *Blackwood's Magazine* (Oct. 1817), 33–41; *Corr.*, i. 103.
27. *E* (9 Nov. 1817), 505, 715–17.
28. *JMS*, 183–4.
29. *E* (9 Nov. 1817), 705, 715–18; (16 Nov. 1817), 721–3.
30. *E* (30 Nov. 1817), 761.
31. *E* (21 Dec. 1817), 801.
32. Jeremy Paxman, *The English: A Portrait of a People* (London, 1998), 142, 145.
33. *E* (21 Dec. 1817); Cheney, Hunt to T. J. Hogg, 22 Jan. 1818.
34. *E* (7 Dec. 1817), 784; Cheney, Hunt to T. J. Hogg, 22 Jan. 1818.
35. *LJK*, i. 205, 206.
36. *PJK*, 225, ll. 9–14.
37. *E* (1 Feb. 1818), 75–6; (22 Feb. 1818), 121–2; (1 March 1818), 139–41.
38. *Foliage*, cxxxiv.
39. *PJK*, 373, ll. 38–9.
40. *The Letters of Thomas Love Peacock*, ed. N. A. Joukovsky (2 vols, Oxford, 2001), i. 126.
41. *Literary Gazette* (April 1818), 210; *Eclectic Review* (Nov. 1818), 488.

42. *LPBS*, ii. 2.

43. *SC*, vi. 553–6.

44. *Letters of Thomas Love Peacock*, i. 130–1.

45. *SC*, vi. 611–12; *E* (14 June 1818), 378–9.

46. *E* (10 Oct. 1819), 652–3.

47. *LPBS*, ii. 18; *Letters of Thomas Love Peacock*, i. 128–9.

48. *SC*, vi. 605–12; 696–8.

49. Ibid., 554.

50. *HCRB*, i. 167, 221.

51. Blunden, 328.

52. Ibid., 359.

53. *SC*, vi. 739–40.

54. *LPBS*, ii. 64, 67.

55. *SC*, vi. 790.

56. *Letters of Thomas Love Peacock*, i. 163.

57. *SC*, vi. 790.

24 England in 1819

1. *E* (17 Jan. 1819), 47.

2. *WPBS*, iii. 293.

3. *E* (3 Jan. 1819), 1–2.

4. *E* (11 April 1819), 238; *Life, Letters, and Journals of George Ticknor* (2 vols, London, 1876), i. 291–2.

5. *E* (17 Jan. 1819), 43–4; (21 March 1819), 187–9; (2 May 1819), 282–3; (9 May 1819), 302–3.

6. *E* (2 May 1819), 274; (23 May 1819), 321–2, 322–3; (11 July 1819), 441; (25 July 1819), 466, 477–8. For Carlile's letter to Hunt, BrL Add. MS 38523.

7. 'Hero and Leander', *PWLH*, 37–44.

8. Philip Larkin, *Collected Poems*, ed. Anthony Thwaite (London and Boston, 1988), 208–9.

9. 8 July 1819, *SC*, vi. 839.

10. 25–27 July 1819, *SC*, vi. 880, 846.

11. 23 Aug. 1819, *SC*, vi. 879; 25–27 July 1819, *SC*, vi. 846; *LPBS*, ii. 111.

12. *SC*, vi. 911–12.

13. 'Unpublished Diary of Mrs Leigh Hunt, (Pisa, September 18, 1822 – Genoa, October 24, 1822)', *Bulletin and Review of the Keats–Shelley Memorial Rome*, 2 (1913), 76.

14. *LPBS*, ii. 112.

15. *The Poems of Shelley, Volume Two, 1817–1819*, ed. K. Everest and G. Matthews (Harlow, 2000), 726.

16. *E* (6 June 1819), 364–7.

17. BrL Add. MS 38108; *SC*, vi. 907.
18. *E* (22 Aug. 1819), 529.
19. *LJK*, ii. 194.
20. *PJK*, 476, ll. 1–4.
21. *I* (9 Aug. 1820), 352.
22. *E* (5 Sept. 1819), 567.
23. Ibid.
24. *LPBS*, ii. 148; *E* (17 Oct. 1819), 666–72; (24 Oct. 1819), 673–7; *LPBS*, ii. 137.
25. *E* (5 Dec. 1819), 770.
26. *SC*, vi. 1090.
27. *Corr.*, i. 162; Cheney.
28. *LPBS*, ii. 117.
29. *The Masque of Anarchy. A Poem. By Percy Bysshe Shelley* (London, 1832), vi, x.
30. *LJK*, ii. 230.
31. *Corr.*, i. 149.
32. *SC*, vi. 912–13, 935; 'The Indicator and Examiner', *I* (20 Oct. 1819), 9.
33. *SC*, vi. 1090.
34. Ibid., 912; 'Robin Hood. To A Friend', *Lamia, Isabella, The Eve of St. Agnes, and Other Poems* (London, 1820), 135.
35. *SC*, vi. 1091.
36. *LPBS*, ii. 239.
37. *LJK*, ii. 309; *Recollections*, 202–3.
38. *E* (5 March 1820), 144; (21 May 1820), 333–5.
39. *E* (7 May 1820), 289; (23 July 1820), 467; (13 Feb. 1820), 98.
40. *SC*, x. 692.
41. *E* (11 June 1820), 370; (20 Aug. 1820), 531–2.
42. Gates, 233.
43. *I* (29 Nov. 1820), 57.
44. *A*, i. 144.
45. *LJK*, ii. 301, 309.
46. *I* (28 June 1820), 300–303; *Maria Gisborne and Edward E. Williams, Shelley's Friends: Their Journals and Letters*, ed. F. L. Jones (Norman, Oklahoma, 1951), 37.
47. *LJK*, ii. 310.
48. *Maria Gisborne and Edward E. Williams*, 44–5; *LJK*, ii. 313, 316, 317.
49. *Amyntas, A Tale of the Woods* (London, 1820), [v].
50. *I* (20 Sept. 1820), 399.
51. *Corr.*, i. 107–8.

25 The Gathering Storm

1. See *E* (23 July 1820), 466–8; (30 July, 1820), 486; BL, 121; *E* (25 Feb. 1821), 113–22; (3 June 1821), 350.

2. *Corr.*, i. 163.

3. Ibid., 161–3.

4. Helen Bentwich, *The Vale of Health on Hampstead Heath, 1777–1877* (London, 1968; 1977), 35–6; *Corr.*, i. 164.

5. 'On People with One Idea', Howe, viii. 69; 'On Paradox and Commonplace', Howe, viii. 148–50.

6. P. P. Howe, *The Life of William Hazlitt* (London, 1928), 318–20.

7. *The Letters of William Hazlitt*, ed. H. M. Sikes (New York, 1978), 204–6.

8. *Life of William Hazlitt*, 323–5; Corr., i. 163–7.

9. *E* (8 July 1821), 417.

10. *E* (18 March 1821), 167; (15 April 1821), 231; *Corr.*, i. 163–7; *E* (8 July 1821), 417–21; (22 July 1821), 449–50; *King Lear* (IV. vi. 165).

11. *Corr.*, i. 163–7.

12. Ibid., 167–9.

13. *LPBS*, ii. 316–17, 322, 333, 343.

14. Ibid., 343–4.

15. *Corr.*, i. 172–3.

16. BrL Add. MS 38108; *Letters of Charles Armitage Brown*, ed. Jack Stillinger (Cambridge, Mass., 1966), 168.

17. *Corr.*, i. 172.

18. Ibid., 174.

19. Ibid., 187.

20. Ibid., 172–4; Hunt to Brougham, 19 Nov. 1821, Cheney; *LPBS*, ii. 355–6, 367, 382–3 n.

21. Hunt to Shelley, 27 Jan. 1822, Cheney.

22. *Recollections*, 211.

23. *Corr.*, i. 176.

24. *Recollections*, 212–13.

25. Hunt to Byron, 27 Jan. 1822; Hunt to Shelley, 27 Jan. 1822. Both in Cheney.

26. *LPBS*, ii. 379, 389–90, 394, 404–5, 413.

27. Hunt to Brougham, 19 Nov. 1821, Cheney.

28. *BLJ*, ix. 113–14.

29. Hunt to John Gisborne, 26 March 1822, in Cheney; *LPBS*, ii. 390, 393, 405.

30. *LPBS*, ii. 379, 380, 435.

31. Ibid., 423.

32. Ibid., 429.

33. *Recollections*, 208–12; *E* (26 May 1822), 329; *A*, ii. 268–9; *Corr.*, i. 179, 274; *Recollections*, 213.

34. 'Autograph Manuscript Notes of Hunt's Sea Voyage to Italy', Beinecke Rare Book and Manuscript Library, Yale University, Leigh Hunt Collection Gen. MSS 65, Box 1, Folder 18. Quoted with permission.

35. 'Letters from Abroad. Letter II. – Genoa', *The Liberal. Volume the First* (London, 1822), 270.

36. BL, 124–5, and Cheney.

37. *A*, ii. 305–6.

38. *Recollections*, 215; 'Genoa', 273.

39. 'Genoa', 282–4; *Corr.*, i. 187.

40. 'Genoa', 277–8.

41. *Browning. Poetical Works, 1833–1864*, ed. Ian Jack (Oxford, 1970), 568–78.

42. *LPBS*, ii. 437–8; *Corr.*, i. 182–3.

43. *LPBS*, ii. 435.

44. *LMWS*, i. 244–5; *Maria Gisborne and Edward E. Williams, Shelley's Friends: Their Journals and Letters*, ed. F. L. Jones (Norman, Oklahoma, 1951), 155.

45. *LMWS*, i. 238.

26 On the Beach

1. *A*, ii. 307.

2. *LBsC*, i. 14–22.

3. *Corr.*, i. 187; 'Shelley. By One Who Knew Him', *Atlantic Monthly*, 11 (1863), 189–90; *LBsC*, i. 22; *LPBS*, ii. 444.

4. *LPBS*, ii. 444.

5. 'Letters from Abroad. Letter I. – Pisa', *The Liberal. Volume the First* (London, 1822), 99–100.

6. *BLJ*, ix. 74.

7. *Corr.*, i. 192.

8. 'Pisa', 101.

9. *Corr.*, i. 188.

10. *LPBS*, ii. 444.

11. BrL Add. MS 38523, Hunt to Byron, 8 April 1823.

12. *BLJ*, ix. 179, 182; *Corr.*, i. 189; 'Unpublished Diary of Mrs Leigh Hunt' (Pisa, September 18, 1822 – Genoa, October 24, 1822)', *Bulletin and Review of the Keats-Shelley Memorial Rome*, 2 (1913), 71–2.

13. *LPBS*, ii. 442, 444; *Maria Gisborne and Edward E. Williams, Shelley's Friends: Their Journals and Letters*, ed. F. L. Jones (Norman, Oklahoma, 1951), 163.

14. *LMWS*, i. 170; *BLJ*, x. 11.

15. *Maria Gisborne and Edward E. Williams*, 162.

16. 'Unpublished Diary of Mrs Leigh Hunt', 73.

17. *Corr.*, i. 188.

18. 'Pisa', 101.

19. *LBsC*, i. 28.

20. *A*, iii. 20.

21. *Records of Shelley, Byron, and the Author*, ed. David Wright (Harmondsworth, 1973), 158; *Corr.*, i. 190.

22. Richard Garnett, *Relics of Shelley* (London, 1862), 113; Cheney.

23. *LMWS*, i. 246–7.

24. Notes about Shelley in 'Autograph Manuscript Notes of Hunt's Sea Voyage to Italy', Beinecke Rare Book and Manuscript Library, Yale University, Leigh Hunt Collection Gen. MSS 65, Box 1, Folder 18.

25. *Corr.*, i. 184.

26. Ibid., 185, 190.

27. Notes about Shelley in 'Autograph Manuscript Notes of Hunt's Sea Voyage to Italy'.

28. *A*, iii. 16.

29. *Corr.*, i. 194–5.

After Life

1. *BLJ*, x. 13, 110.

2. Ibid., 13.

3. Ibid., 68; *LBsC*, i. 31.

4. *Corr.*, i. 196.

5. BL, 129, 130; *Corr.*, i. 221.

6. BL, 127.

7. *Corr.*, i. 230.

8. 'An Attempt of the Author to estimate his own Character & Writings', Brewer Collection MS H 94.

9. *Corr.*, ii. 167–8; Gates, 151–2.

10. See BrL Add. MS 38108; *Corr.*, i. 245.

11. Letter of 19 Dec. 1824, BrL Add. MS 38108.

12. *A*, iii. 162–9.

13. Ibid., 3.

14. *LBsC*, i. 55.

15. Ibid., 4, 108.

16. *A*, iii. 181–2.

INDEX